ANDERS NYGREN

Meaning and Method

Prolegomena to
a Scientific Philosophy of Religion
and a Scientific Theology

Authorized Translation by
PHILIP S. WATSON

FORTRESS PRESS *Philadelphia*

*This book is a translation of a
Swedish manuscript prepared originally
for English publication and
never before published in any language.*

© *Anders Nygren 1972
First published 1972 by
Epworth Press, London
First American Edition 1972 by
Fortress Press*
*Library of Congress Catalog
Card Number 72-157541*
ISBN *0-8006-0038-X
1-38*

*Made and printed in Great Britain
by W & J Mackay Limited, Chatham*

Contents

Preface   ix

Translator's Note   xi

Acknowledgements   xiii

Abbreviations   xv

Chapter I

Introduction   1
1. The Problem   1
2. The Treatment of the Problem   6

Chapter II

What is Philosophy of Religion?   15
1. A Problematical Science   15
2. The Inevitability of the Religio-philosophical Problem   20
3. The Philosophy of Religion as a Philosophical Discipline   23

Chapter III

Metaphysical and Scientific Philosophy   29
1. 'Under a Double Star': Two Tendencies in Philosophy   29
2. The Separation of the Two Tendencies   31
3. Metaphysical Philosophy   33
4. Scientific Philosophy   57

Chapter IV

Different Forms of Scientific Argumentation   65
1. The Concept of Science   65
2. 'Eternal and Contingent Truths'   78
3. Axiomatic and Empirical Argumentation   102
4. Philosophical Argumentation?   119
5. The Limits of Science   123

Chapter V

Philosophy as Analysis of Meaning   127
1. A Philosophical Change of Scene   127
2. Analysis of Existence   131
3. Logical Analysis   138
4. Language Analysis   153
5. Analysis of Presuppositions   160

CONTENTS

Chapter VI

Meaning and Validity   167
1. Meaning and Validity as Interchangeable Terms   167
2. The Material for Philosophical Analysis   170
3. The History of Philosophy and the Problems of Philosophy   173
4. Problems, Statements of Problems and Solutions of Problems   175
5. Verification, Justification, Validation   179

Chapter VII

The Concept of Presupposition   187
1. Presupposition and Prejudice   187
2. Presupposition, Axiom, Hypothesis   191
3. 'Absolute Presuppositions'   194
4. Presupposition and Preunderstanding   199
5. Presupposition and Prescription   201
6. Logically Necessary Fundamental Presuppositions   205

Chapter VIII

Logical Analysis of Presuppositions   209
1. The Analysis of Presuppositions as a Critical Method   209
2. Conceptual Analysis and the Logical Analysis of Presuppositions   215
3. The Possibility of Objective Argumentation in Philosophy   219
4. The Logical Structure of Presuppositional Analysis   220
5. Presuppositional Analysis, a Logical Circle?   223

Chapter IX

Meaning and Context   227
1. Meaning and Method   227
2. 'Sinn und Bedeutung'   229
3. Logical Atomism. Verification as a Criterion of Meaning   237
4. From Atomism to Context of Meaning   243
5. Importance of the Context for Meaning and Argumentation   254

Chapter X

Contexts of Meaning   265
1. Terminology   265
2. Philosophy and the Different Contexts of Meaning   270
3. The Autonomy of the Contexts of Meaning   273
4. The Absolutization of the Contexts of Meaning   278
5. Category Mixing and Meaninglessness   282

6. Philosophy as a Clearing House for the Contexts of Meaning 287
7. Integrity and Integration 292

Chapter XI

The Religious Context of Meaning 299

1. The Task of the Philosophy of Religion 299
2. Demythologization 303
3. The Method of Correlation 316
4. The Problem of Hermeneutics 325
5. Metaphor, Symbol and Paradox as Expressions of
   Religious Meaning 334
6. The Category Problem 341
7. Religion, Philosophy of Religion, and Theology 345

Chapter XII

Motif Contexts 351

1. Necessary and Self-Evident Presuppositions 351
2. The Fundamental Motif as a Historical Problem 359
3. The Hermeneutical Significance of the Fundamental Motif 365
4. Systematic Theology and Motif Research 371
5. Objective Argumentation in Theology 376

Additional Notes 379

I The Concept of Experience 379
II On the Use of the Terms 'Metaphysics' and 'Truth' 380
III Subjectivity and Objectivity 382
IV Marburg Hermeneutics 384
V Motif Research in a Variety of Fields 384

Bibliography 387

Index 403

(1) Proper Names 403
(2) Subjects 406

Preface

THE circumstances in which the work on this book began have already been described in an article I wrote for *The Christian Century* in 1958. In connection with its golden jubilee that journal addressed to me and a number of other theologians who had been at work during the previous decades, a question worded as follows: 'Would you write an article in which you describe the topics and methods, attitudes and expectations that might be yours if you were today beginning your writing and teaching career? Beginning where you are now, what problems would you turn your attention to, what subject would you centre on if you were just now getting ready to write your first book?'

This question was exactly suited to my situation. It came to me, not as an artificial or merely hypothetical question, to which only a theoretical answer could be given, but as a very practical proposition. It was in effect a description of the situation in which I found myself, and my answer to it had already been given before it came. After ten years during which other duties had prevented me from giving more than a limited attention to theological and philosophical problems, I was now in a position to devote my whole time to them. It was just like beginning all over again. And in answer to the question I could say without hesitation: 'The problem which more than any other demands treatment at present is that of the philosophy of religion.' My earliest research and writing had been done in this area, and now I could return to the same subject, though in a greatly altered situation.

The investigation I then had in mind is now presented in this book. The basic viewpoint is the same as in my earlier work, but here it has had to be brought into relation to new ways of stating theological and philosophical problems. In many respects the more recent developments in these fields have opened up new possibilities for the philosophical approach to religion. But we are still only at the beginning, and the time is obviously not yet ripe for a fully developed philosophy of religion. For the present and for a long time to come we must work to lay a solid foundation. It is with foundation-laying rather than architectonic construction that this investigation is concerned. All too often scientific work is undertaken without sufficient attention to the kinds of tools that are needed for dealing with its very diverse problems. Things are not all alike, and it is wrong to treat them as if they were. Hammer and tongs are excellent instruments for their purpose, but they are of no use for solving philosophical or theological problems. It is indispensable that we should sharpen and refine our instruments, and still more that we should see just what instruments are appropriate for different purposes. This is where the emphasis lies in the present investigation, and the need for it should be plain from what has been said.

Just when I was on the point of starting work on these problems, I received an invitation from the University of Minnesota to spend a term there lecturing on the philosophy of religion, and another from the Ecumenical Institute then at Evanston, Illinois, to pursue my work there as a Resident Scholar. Both of these invitations I was enabled to accept by a grant from the Danforth Foundation, for which I wish to express my gratitude here. I was thus given the opportunity to become closely acquainted with American philosophy. I have grateful memories of the discussions that took place in connection with my lectures in Minneapolis, in which a number of professors representing different disciplines participated and contributed very much to a most fruitful exchange of ideas. I think gratefully also of the seminar on the philosophy of religion that I was privileged to conduct at the Ecumenical Institute in Evanston, and of the excellent collaboration of the then Director of the Institute, Dr. Walter Leibrecht. Then there was the opportunity subsequently given me as Visiting Professor at the Divinity School of the University of Chicago, of discussing with a select group of younger scholars the problems of meaning and method in theology and philosophy. It is my hope that the enrichment of the present work through these many contacts has not interrupted the continuity of its argument or obscured the unity of its thought.

Finally, I wish to express my deep appreciation and thanks to *Statens Humanistiska Forskningsråd*, Stockholm, and to *Kungliga Humanistiska Vetenskapssamfundet i Lund*, for their generous grants towards the production of this book in English. And above all, I must acknowledge my immense indebtedness to Professor Philip S. Watson of Evanston, both for valuable discussions of the subject matter and for his meticulous care in translating my manuscript. He more than anyone has helped by his excellent translations to make my work available to the English speaking world. He showed his outstanding ability first in the translation of *Agape and Eros*, and now he has undertaken the even more exacting task of turning the present work into English. It is with the profoundest gratitude that I think of what he has done.

ANDERS NYGREN

Translator's Note

DURING the making of this translation I have been in constant communication with the author, who has examined the proofs and also compiled the index.

In translating Chapters IX § 4 and XII §§ 1–5, where the author has incorporated some of his earlier essays, I have made use—with considerable modifications—of English versions supplied by him along with his own manuscript. For these I understand that thanks are due chiefly to my friends Professor Bernhard Erling and the Reverend Peter W. Russell, who made them for the author some years ago. I wish also to thank Professor Erling for assistance in compiling the Bibliography, particularly with regard to the tracking down of English editions of foreign works quoted.

With few exceptions (noted by an asterisk thus: ET*) the renderings of quotations from foreign language sources are my own, and should not be cited as from published English translations, although references to these are given as far as possible for the convenience of readers. This applies also to the passages from Ludwig Wittengstein's *Tractatus*, of which I have either translated the author's German excerpts or freely adapted the English of his earlier translator in the essay included in Chapter IX § 4.

Acknowledgements for permission to quote copyrighted material appear below. I am grateful for prompt and affirmative replies to my requests for such permission, but perplexed (to say no more) by the lack of uniformity among them as to the terms and conditions on which the permission is granted, particularly with regard to the form in which acknowledgement should be made. I trust that the form employed below will be regarded as sufficient in cases where it fulfils the spirit rather than the strict letter of the law. Any errors or omissions that may have inadvertently occurred will be corrected in any future printing on notification to the publishers.

PHILIP S. WATSON

Acknowledgements

The author, translator and publishers are grateful to the following for permission to reproduce copyright material:

George Allen and Unwin Ltd and the Macmillan Company of New York for extracts from
> Bertrand Russell, *Logic and Knowledge* (1956)

Appleton-Century-Crofts Inc for extracts from
> H. Feigl and W. Sellars (eds), *Readings in Philosophical Analysis* (1949)

Basil Blackwell for extracts from
> L. Wittgenstein, *Philosophical Investigations* (1958)
> L. Wittgenstein, *The Blue and Brown Books* (1958)

Clarendon Press, Oxford, for
> R. G. Collingwood, *An Essay on Metaphysics* (1940)
> R. G. Collingwood, *An Essay on Philosophical Method* (1953)
> J. Griffin, *Wittgenstein's Logical Atomism* (1964)

Harper and Row, New York, for extracts from
> C. W. Kegley, *The Theology of Rudolf Bultmann* (1966)

The Macmillan Company of New York for
> M. Bunge, *The Critical Approach to Science and Philosophy* (1964)
> C. W. Kegley (ed), *The Theology of Paul Tillich* (1959)
> C. A. Mace (ed), *British Philosophy in the Mid-Century* (1957)

J. C. B. Mohr (Paul Siebeck), Tübingen, for the extract from
> Professor E. Fuchs, *Marburger Hermeneutik* (1968)

The Ronald Press Company, New York, for
> T. E. Hill, *Contemporary Theories of Knowledge* (1961)

Routledge and Kegan Paul for the quotation from
> Bertrand Russell's *Introduction to L. Wittgenstein's Tractatus Logico-Philosophicus*

Springer Publishing Company, New York, for
> M. Bunge, *Scientific Research I* (Studies in the Foundations, Methodology and Philosophy of Science, vol. 3/1) (1967)

University of Chicago Press for
> Paul Tillich, *The Protestant Era* (1948)
> and *Systematic Theology*, vol I (1951)

Yale University Press for
> Charles L. Stevenson, *Facts and Values* (1963)

Abbreviations

BGBW	Britannica Great Books of the Western World, vol. 42, Chicago, 1952
DVG	Dogmatikens vetenskapliga grundläggning (Nygren)
ET	English Translation
FAH	Festskrift tillägnad Axel Hägerström, Uppsala, 1928
FAK	Festskrift till Anders Karitz, Uppsala, 1946
FHL	Festskrift tillägnad Hans Larsson, Stockholm, 1927
FKE	Filosofisk och kristen etik (Nygren)
FOM	Filosofi och motivforskning (Nygren)
GRE	Die Gültigkeit der religiösen Erfahrung (Nygren)
GT	German Translation
LAK	Logic and Knowledge (Russell)
NEB	New English Bible
NTT	Norsk teologisk tidsskrift
PEGA	Philosophical Essays dedicated to Gunnar Aspelin, Lund, 1963
RAP	Religiöst Apriori (Nygren)
RGG	Die Religion in Geschichte und Gegenwart (3rd edn)
RGP	Det religionsfilosofiska grundproblemet (Nygren)
RSV	Revised Standard Version
ST	Summa Theologica (Aquinas)
STK	Svensk Teologisk Kvartalskrift
SuB	Über Sinn und Bedeutung (Frege)
SwT	Swedish Translation
TCPS	Transactions of the Cambridge Philosophical Society
TWNT	Theologisches Wörterbuch zum Neuen Testament (Kittel)
WA	Weimarer Ausgabe

CHAPTER I

Introduction

1. The Problem

THE problem proposed for discussion here is of an extremely far-reaching kind. It covers the immense fields of two sciences—philosophy and theology—and is concerned in both cases with the most fundamental issues. What it involves can be put most simply and directly in terms of the two questions: 'How is philosophy as a science possible?' and 'How is theology as a science possible?' It thus has to do with the clarification of the scientific status of philosophy and theology respectively.

But is not a subject like this much too vast and too general to constitute a genuine problem? Can a question of such universal scope possibly have a meaning clear and concrete enough for it to be capable of being answered? For 'science' is such a variegated phenomenon that we can hardly hope to start with it and derive from it certain general requirements which philosophy or theology must fulfil in order to be recognized as a science. Moreover theology and philosophy are likewise such variegated phenomena that in this regard also the question of their scientific status may appear meaningless. Hence although we are accustomed to seeing great, sweeping titles used to introduce dissertations which are actually quite limited in scope, it may nevertheless seem rather presumptuous to propose an investigation of the scientific foundations of both theology and philosophy.

Yet although these difficulties are not entirely imaginary, the problem cannot be wholly ignored. For it is, despite all, a real problem and an important one. To evade it on the plea that it is too comprehensive and 'sweeping', and that there would be something presumptuous about attempting to tackle it, is completely unrealistic. It is not those who insist on clarity that can be charged with 'sweeping notions', but those who make the extent of the problem an excuse for sweeping it aside—thus evading the light that discussion might shed on it, and the consequent challenge to their own unexamined and possibly baseless opinions. It is not those who insist on an investigation that can be charged with presumption, but those who insist on asserting their own preconceptions, not to say prejudices, without accounting for them.

The problem we are speaking of here is formulated in our title as that of 'Meaning and Method'. This formulation is intended to express a certain limitation of an otherwise much too comprehensive problem. The singling out of the questions of meaning and method brings the problem into a quite definite focus.

There is nothing haphazard about the juxtaposition of theology and philosophy. It arises from the actual state of affairs in these two sciences, which show a striking parallel to one another as regards the matter that chiefly interests us here. Other sciences generally have less difficulty in defining their tasks and devising methodologies that satisfy the requirements of science. In the case of philosophy and theology, however, the question of their meaning and method is often extremely obscure and uncertain. To the question 'What is philosophy?' almost every philosopher, or at least every philosophical school, has a different answer to give; and the position is much the same with regard to the question 'What is theology?' If, moreover, we ask about their scientific character, we frequently find among both philosophers and theologians a remarkable indifference to the question. A number of outstanding representatives of these two disciplines have frankly expressed doubt as to whether we ought to call them 'sciences' at all. It is enough in their view to say that we have here a certain 'activity', which can in a measure be described, and which in one way or another performs a useful function—whether or not it is 'science' is of little or no importance.

In reply to this, however, it must be said that indifference to the scientific status of philosophy or theology easily entails a lack of clarity that can have serious consequences. Sometimes philosophy or theology represents itself as a science, and yet when it is charged with arbitrariness in its proceedings, it evades the issue on the plea that it is not a case of science in the strict sense, but of theology or philosophy, and hence that it is wrong to make such demands on it. But this sort of vacillation between responsible and irresponsible talk is inexcusable. An investigation aimed at getting a clear answer to the question 'What is theology?' and 'What is philosophy?' and clarifying their scientific status is very greatly needed.

A substantial reason for the difficulty we thus encounter both in theology and philosophy is that both of them, not only in the past, but down to our own time, have been mixed up with what goes by the name of 'metaphysics'. The quandary in which the latter finds itself, with its claim to scientific validity on the one hand and its fundamental inability to live up to that claim on the other, is thus communicated to philosophy and theology, and it is this that causes the uncertainty as to their scientific status. An inquiry into this subject will therefore have to make a special point of clarifying their relation to metaphysics.

But now our problem can be challenged with a line of argument which appears to run in the opposite direction to that with which we have so far been dealing. Whereas it was held by the latter to be too comprehensive to constitute a genuine problem, it can be held from another point of view to be too small and trivial. The formulation 'Meaning and Method' indicates that it has to do with certain very general questions of principle, and there is a widespread notion that the discussion of such 'formal' questions is nothing but a fussing over tautologies, things which at bottom are self-evident, self-evidently trivial, and not worth discussing. The word 'method' has contributed not least to the impression of triviality. In many quarters it is held that interest in questions of method is due to a lack of interest in questions of content: when concrete problems do not give a man enough to do, he turns to the abstract problems of method. This objection, however, is even less cogent than the one we have already considered. It rests on a complete misunderstanding of the meaning and purpose of 'method'.

We must linger a little here over the question of the relation between material and method, because it is precisely a lack of clarity on this point that gives rise to the very common misconceptions of the meaning and importance of method. It is frequently assumed that there is an opposition between method and material, as if methodology were something external and peripheral, from which we need to move on to what is central and of substantive significance—the material. Naturally there can be an element of truth underlying this idea, inasmuch as the focus of attention in an investigation is usually certain matters of fact which it is intended to elucidate, and in this methodology plays an auxiliary role. Nevertheless this idea as a whole must be said to be completely wrong.

Far from being merely peripheral, methodology has to do precisely with what is central. There is no tension between material and method, but rightly understood they belong inseparably together, in a reciprocal relation to one another. What would be the use of a method without material? It is after all in order to handle the material that one develops the method. Apart from this the method would not exist. Conversely, what sense will any material make if we have no questions to put to it and no method for handling it? There can as little be any meaningful 'material by itself' as there can a 'method by itself'. To parody a well-known saying of Kant, we might say: material without method is blind, method without material is empty. It is beyond question that a method without any material to work on will accomplish nothing at all, while material simply as material, unrelated to any method, will be nothing but a chaotic, meaningless agglomerate. 'Dead data tell many tales'—too many to make sense.

A variant of the misunderstanding just mentioned appears in the idea that a method is something imported from outside, something that is forced on the material and does injury to it. The situation is conceived more or less as follows: first, one performs the independent, self-contained task of developing a method; then, with the method in hand, one goes to the material, and if the material does not fit the method—so much the worse for the material. The reply to this idea has really been given already. For the recognition that material and method are inseparable and interdependent shows it to be nothing but a caricature. A method is not and cannot be simply a free-hand construction. It is in the course of intensive work on the material that the method is developed and refined. This can be illustrated by the story of the famous huntsman who, when asked about the best way of trapping a fox, replied: 'Start trapping—the fox will teach you!' Which for our purpose means: Start working on the material, try to master it and discover its meaning; you'll hit on the method, you'll get the necessary holds and learn the better to use them, as you wrestle with it—the material will teach you!

We must completely revise our time-honoured ideas about the dualism of material and method. Nothing can be more meaningless either than an arbitrary, haphazard assemblage of material, or than a method floating in the void, unattached to any given subject matter. Here we see the interconnection of meaning, method and material: it is the meaning that furnishes the link between material and method, and only the linking of material and method that yields any meaning.

Our chief concern thus far has been to correct certain common misunderstandings with regard to the problem of 'meaning and method', and it is now time to draw attention—though briefly, for we shall have occasion later to return to this as well as the previous questions—to the very great practical importance of the subject.

From one point of view, of course, the things we are going to discuss in the following chapters are among the most elementary and self-evident, since they have to do with ideas and concepts that are in constant use both in ordinary language and in science, where they are for the most part correctly used. As Ludwig Wittgenstein aptly remarks: 'In philosophy it is always a matter of applying a number of extremely simple principles which every child knows, and the only difficulty—which is enormous—is that of applying them amid the confusion which our language creates. . . . The difficulty of applying the simple principles, however, perplexes one about the principles themselves.'[1] Plainly, then, we cannot conclude from the elementary and apparently self-evident nature of the subject that it is trivial and not worth further investigation. On the contrary, the elementary and self-evident is what is most often overlooked, and it is there that the big and serious mistakes are made and the common confusions have their roots. Elementary and self-evident therefore though it may be, it is by no means trivial. Indeed, discussion of the most general and elementary questions is among the most exciting and significant things in the intellectual history of mankind.

How far these questions are from being trivial is shown by the disastrous consequences that follow from neglecting them; for this has led on the one hand to the setting up of sciences that are really nothing but

[1] *Philosophische Bemerkungen*, pp. 153f. (For particulars of works cited, see Bibliography. In the footnotes titles will frequently be abbreviated or indicated simply by a key word or phrase.—Tr.)

pseudo-sciences, and on the other to the elimination of large and complex areas of human life, which has thereby been much impoverished. A mistake made at the centre leads to grotesque errors at the circumference. We can therefore never spend too great pains on questions of ultimate principle. The precision which is elsewhere demanded in science must be more than usually evident here. In this regard the philosophy of recent decades, with its insistence on more precision in philosophical thought, has done important work, although in its zeal for the cause it has often fallen into the very error it sought to combat—of which more anon.

In connection with the problem which particularly concerns us here, the philosophy of religion is of special interest, since in it theology and philosophy converge. It shares its subject matter, religion, in common with theology, while standing with philosophy as regards its aim and method. Hence the difficulties encountered in these two sciences are redoubled in the philosophy of religion. It is also clear that the philosophy of religion is more exposed than theology and philosophy to the danger of slipping over into metaphysics and thereby losing its scientific character.

Far too little has yet been done to clarify the function of the philosophy of religion and distinguish it from metaphysics. The subtitle of the present work, 'Prolegomena to a Scientific Philosophy of Religion', is meant to suggest something of a programme for this purpose. If the philosophy of religion is to attain scientific status, it must resolutely break its traditional connection with metaphysics and assume the character of a scientific discipline. We must, however, emphasize the word 'Prolegomena'. Although many laudable efforts have been made in recent years towards a scientific philosophy of religion, the time is still far from ripe for the full attainment of this goal. There must first be an extensive clearing of the ground in order to lay bare the foundations. As a rule the religio-philosophical problem has been approached with far too little sense of the difficulties it involves. The tradition of recent centuries has borne heavily on the philosophy of religion, with the result that even those who have sought to place it in a new, analytical or semantic context have all too easily slipped back into metaphysical ways of thinking. As long as we lack essential clarity regarding the task and possibilities of philosophy, we have no prospect of achieving at any point a clear-cut treatment of the philosophical problems presented by religion.

In any philosophical investigation it is important to state clearly at the outset from what point of view it is undertaken. The universality of outlook and interest that characterizes philosophy precludes our viewing it from every possible angle, and we are therefore bound to select a particular point of departure—which of course will involve a certain modification of perspective. For us the point of departure is the philosophy of religion; and in this there are many advantages, of which three deserve special mention. 1. As a science the philosophy of religion occupies a place among the ranks of the sciences, and thus comes under the surveillance of the 'philosophy of science'. 2. Thanks to its subject matter, religion—which is something quite other than science—, it runs no risk of landing in a narrow 'scientism'. Its subject matter and its own character as philosophy of religion help it to preserve the more comprehensive philosophical outlook. 3. Owing to the constant risk of slipping in a metaphysical direction, it is obliged to make a sharp demarcation with regard to metaphysics, and can therefore be of considerable assistance to philosophy in maintaining its scientific status. Hence although these 'Prolegomena' may take us no further than to the threshold of the philosophy of religion, they are none the less important enough and have a big enough task to fulfil.

2. The Treatment of the Problem

Thus far we have given a preliminary—and very sketchy—presentation of our problem. Its nature will appear more concretely if we now give a relatively detailed survey of the way in which we propose to treat it. Before we set out on our travels it may well be useful to map out the route, so that the reader may be apprised in advance of the stages of the journey. As a rule the giving of advance information of this sort is avoided on the ground that the investigation should develop as the work proceeds. If the road is too well signposted, the reader's interest can easily flag, for he knows the answers already. There is furthermore the danger that he may be unduly bound by the preview thus given him.

Such ideas, however, have little cogency. It can rather be said that the omission of such orientation can be a great disservice to the reader. It is an illusion that the investigation should develop as the work proceeds. After all, the author (who has already done the work) knows the plan, and he owes the reader a clear account of it. He has an obligation to let him know from the start where the road lies and to what it leads. As for the idea that this might bind the reader, the opposite is the case: it liberates the reader. Being oriented from the outset and prepared for what is coming, he is in a position to follow every step of the way with critical attention. Thus the advantages of such a preview are enough to outweigh by far its possible disadvantages.

The starting point in Chapter II is, as has already been said, the philosophy of religion. 'What is philosophy of religion?' With this we are plunged at once into a tangled mass of problems. It is by no means clear what the function of the philosophy of religion is. Sometimes it is conceived as a theological, sometimes as a philosophical discipline. Nor is there clarity about its scientific status. Is the philosophy of religion a science at all? It is burdened with a centuries-old liability, and in short must be described as a problematical not to say suspect science. On the other hand, it is not difficult to show that there is an inescapable problem which

6

can be called the religio-philosophical problem, and this without regard to the question whether the traditional philosophy of religion has contributed anything to its solution or not. But if the philosophy of religion is to have any legitimate function, we must at all costs maintain that it is a philosophical discipline and that its problem is a purely philosophical problem. This, however, only pushes the question a stage further back. In order to answer the question 'What is philosophy of religion?' we must first find the answer to the question 'What is philosophy?'

That is the subject of Chapter III. And here we are immediately faced with new complications, inasmuch as philosophy appears in two widely different forms, on the one hand that of metaphysics, and on the other that of scientific philosophy. This dualism has dogged philosophy ever since it first began. In the course of its subsequent development it has devoted itself in large measure to airy metaphysical speculations, while at the same time it has at least claimed to be a science and perhaps the chief of all the sciences. But there have always been opposing forces that have sought to secure for philosophy not only the appearance but the reality of scientific status.

If we are to speak of philosophy as a science, we must examine the specifically philosophical form of argumentation, showing both its connection with other forms of scientific argumentation and also how it differs from these. This is done in Chapter IV, where we start, as we must, with the concept of science. Here we find that Leibniz, with his theory of different kinds of 'truths', has had a disastrous effect on the tradition, and that it is therefore essential to take issue with his view. We have to show that, besides the customary forms of scientific argumentation, the axiomatic and the empirical, there is both room and need for a philosophical argumentation which is other than they and yet is just as strictly scientific in character. There is here, however, no question of different kinds of 'truths', but only of different ways of arguing. With these three forms of argumentation we reach the limit of anything that can be called science, a limit which is, however, often heedlessly transgressed.

This brings us to contemporary philosophy, in which, despite all the variety of views, there is exhibited a certain common concern inasmuch as almost all schools—though naturally each with its own particular interpretation—insist on analysis and are able to define philosophy as 'analysis of meaning'. If we compare contemporary with earlier philosophy, we can speak of a genuine philosophical change of scene. Under the heading of 'Philosophy as Analysis of Meaning' (Chapter V) we come to deal with such disparate views as those of existentialism, logical empiricism and semantic or linguistic philosophy. Through discussion with these different schools we arrive at a closer definition of the task of philosophy as 'analysis of presuppositions'. This gives us also a preliminary indication of the method which philosophy as distinct from other sciences must use. It is

7

possible here to preserve the gains of contemporary philosophy without having to let go the achievements of the older scientifically oriented philosophy. Indeed, it helps us to a deeper grasp of the idea of 'meaning' if we notice its affinity to that of 'validity' which was favoured in an earlier period. With this we have the subject for Chapter VI.

There is actually in the history of philosophy abundant material for philosophical analysis. For it is only natural that even in earlier times men should have come upon genuine philosophical problems; and although the history of philosophy is not alone in providing material for philosophy to analyze, yet the work that has already been done in the history of thought is extraordinarily important. We must not, however, concentrate on the purely historical question of how this or that thinker thought on the basis of his own historical presuppositions, but must pay chief attention to the contribution which some of his ideas may possibly make towards the handling of a problem with which we still have to wrestle. From this it follows that we cannot here be content simply to consider the solution he propounded. We are more interested in his way of stating the problem, and the extent to which it can serve as a paradigm for us. Yet even this is not the decisive thing. We must work our way through both solutions and statements of problems to the problem itself which gave rise to philosophical reflection at that time, and which gives occasion for it still today. This is particularly the case with the philosophical concept of 'validity', with which earlier philosophical thinkers can help us a good deal, if not directly by their solutions of the problem, yet in some degree by their statements of it, and above all by making us aware that it really is a problem, and indeed the basic problem of philosophy. Here important work has already been done, of which contemporary philosophy should not neglect to take advantage.

Meaning and validity are interchangeable terms. Both of them equally point back to 'The Concept of Presupposition', which is the subject of Chapter VII. When it is used in philosophy the term 'presupposition' must be clearly distinguished from a number of other concepts with which it is commonly and disastrously confused. The presuppositions which are the object of philosophical analysis are something quite other than 'prejudices', and also other than the 'hypotheses' which various sciences employ in explanation of observed phenomena. Philosophy is concerned with the most general, necessary and inescapable 'presuppositions', which have to be accepted as valid in all scientific work and in all experience whatsoever.[2] Yet while this may be maintained, new divergences from the philosophical concept of presuppositions continually occur. One example is the equation of the latter with those 'absolute presuppositions' which set their mark on different historical periods, but which may be quite arbi-

---

[2] On the meaning and importance of the concept of 'experience' in the author's thought, see Additional Note 1.—Tr.

trary and must not in any case be confused with logically necessary pre-suppositions. Another example is the equation of 'presupposition' with '*Vorverständnis*' or 'preunderstanding'. Finally we should note that the philosophical presuppositions must on no account be conceived as authoriz-ing the consciousness to 'prescribe laws for nature'. In contrast to all these, it is the business of philosophy to show what have to be recognized as 'logically necessary basic presuppositions'.

As analysis of meaning and validity, therefore, philosophy will take the form of a 'Logical Analysis of Presuppositions'. This is the subject of Chapter VIII, which deals with the question of philosophical method. This requires us to show in some detail the nature of the philosophical analysis of presuppositions, and how it opens up the possibility of objec-tive argumentation in philosophy. Above all, we have to clarify the logical structure of such analysis and the part played in it by the idea of implica-tion. A matter that calls for special attention here is the frequent assertion that philosophy, or at least epistemology, rests on a logical circle. If that were so, it would apply equally to philosophy understood as analysis of presuppositions. But when the logical structure of presuppositional analysis is clearly seen, it is at once apparent that no charge of circularity can be sustained. The analysis of presuppositions is from a logical point of view unimpeachable, and it is only misunderstanding that has given rise to the objection just mentioned.

Now that we have focussed the task of philosophy on the question of meaning, shown how meaning is dependent on presuppositions, and indi-cated finally the method philosophy must use, it might appear as if we had already attained our goal. 'Meaning and Method'—what more is there to be said? Have we not now the answer to our problem? Unfortunately we have not. What we have reached is a turning point rather than a terminal point. We need in particular a closer definition of the concept of meaning. If we have thus far been able to say 'without presuppositions, no meaning', we must now add something no less important, namely, 'without context no meaning' or 'without context no argumentation'. The idea of 'context' must therefore play a key part in our further investigation. For what is ultimately decisive for the meaning of a judgment or proposition is the context in which it occurs. If I know nothing of the context, then neither do I understand the judgment.

In Chapter IX these two concepts, meaning and context, are brought together. As a starting point we take Gottlob Frege's well-known distinc-tion between '*Sinn*' and '*Bedeutung*' ('meaning' and 'reference'). In spite of certain ambiguities Frege has undoubtedly seen where the problem lies, and his definition of the term '*Sinn*' can therefore serve as a basis for the further discussion of the concept of meaning. Frege's achievement was, however, dissipated, and that by one of his immediate successors, Bertrand Russell, who was chiefly interested in the concept of *Bedeutung*, and who—

in contrast to Frege, who strictly maintained the distinction between *Sinn* and *Bedeutung*—mixes up these two concepts in the most confusing manner. This prepares the way for Russell's 'logical atomism' and in general for an atomistic theory of meaning in which the significance of the context is largely eliminated. The way is then also open for logical positivism (empiricism) to propound its theory of verification as a criterion of meaning, and its theory of 'sense-data'. The first to break out of this circle of ideas and reach a more adequate conception of the meaning of meaning was Ludwig Wittgenstein, who to begin with was in some measure dependent on Russell's logical atomism. Wittgenstein's philosophical development is an extraordinary illustration of 'the way from atomism to contexts of meaning', a tendency which is very characteristic of a good deal of contemporary philosophy. One of our main tasks, therefore, is to make clear the significance of the context for both meaning and argumentation.

Chapter X under the heading of 'Contexts of Meaning' marks the preliminary conclusion of the purely philosophical discussion. The expression 'contexts of meaning' may sound a little strange, but the thing it stands for can be found almost everywhere in contemporary philosophy. It is therefore important to begin by identifying and characterizing a number of frequently used parallel expressions, and to give our reasons for sticking to 'context of meaning'. This faces us with the problem of the relation of philosophy to the different contexts of meaning. Philosophy is essentially one, while the contexts of meaning are essentially many (although for the purpose of distinguishing them from other things we can use the term 'context of meaning' in the singular). What then does this mean for philosophy? It is this problem that lurks at times in philosophical literature behind the twin expressions 'philosophy proper' and 'philosophy of'. What is meant here cannot be that there are two kinds of philosophy, one of them philosophy in itself or as such, and the other philosophy in relation to something else. The nature of philosophy is always the same, although it has to take account of diverse contexts of meaning.

From this there immediately follows the thought of philosophy as a doctrine of categories. The importance of carefully observing the distinction between the contexts of meaning lies in the fact that an individual judgment or proposition can preserve its meaning if, and only if, it is viewed in its own context of meaning. If it is torn out of its natural context and thrust into another, it either at best acquires a quite different meaning, or else becomes quite meaningless. In the philosophy of recent decades things have often been declared meaningless because no meaning could be got out of them when they were placed under false categories or presuppositions. But in such a case the meaninglessness is not in the subject under consideration, but in the arbitrary procedure of the person considering it. It will not do to make one context of meaning normative for the rest, and take its presuppositions as a law for things that depend on quite different presuppositions. In this sense every context of meaning is autonomous, governed by its own laws, dependent on its own categories or presuppositions.

From this it follows also that there must be no absolutizing of any one context of meaning as the only legitimate one. Such absolutization leads inevitably to category mixing and so to meaninglessness. By contrast, it is the business of philosophy to see to it that every judgment is judged by its own presuppositions. In other words, philosophy has to act as a 'clearing house' for the different contexts and to ensure their integrity. This does not mean, however, that we are left with a series of contexts of meaning that stand side by side unrelated to one another. Philosophy has a second task, namely to ensure their integration, though this can only be done by reference to their presuppositions and the way these are related to one another.

Now that we have the answer to the question 'What is philosophy?' Chapter XI returns to the question 'What is philosophy of religion?' Confused though the situation was to begin with, the foregoing clarification of it has made it easy to find the answer to this question. The task of the philosophy of religion is analytical, and what it has to analyze is the religious context of meaning. The fundamental problem of the philosophy of religion cannot be anything else but to explain the nature of the religious context of meaning, or in other words to show what is characteristic of religious language. This means that the central task of the philosophy of religion is to get back to the basic presuppositions or categories of religion. Where this primary task is neglected, the result is disastrous not only for the philosophy of religion but also for theology. The consequences can be studied in many quarters in contemporary theology, as for example in the theology of demythologization, in the quest for 'the secular meaning of the gospel', in the theory of a 'correlation' between philosophical questions and theological (religious) answers, and in much of contemporary hermeneutics. Everywhere it is the same lack of clarity regarding fundamental questions of principle that underlies the prevailing confusion.

When once we have become clear about the nature of the religious context of meaning, we understand also the part played in religious language by parables, symbols, and paradoxes. If we wish to express something given in one context of meaning in terms borrowed from the language of another, this can only be done by means of parables and symbols; and often that which in its own context is in no way paradoxical will appear paradoxical to one who sees it in the light of a different context. What has been called 'the religious paradox' has the important function of alerting us to the fact that in religion we are in a quite different context of meaning from the theoretical. Whether there is a real contradiction can only be determined by paying attention to the part the expression plays in the context to which it actually belongs.

Finally, the religio-philosophical problem culminates in the question of the categories (presuppositions) or the fundamental category, by which the religious context of meaning is governed. This faces us with an extraordinarily complicated problem, which does not, however, belong to the prolegomena, but is a subject for the philosophy of religion itself to handle. For our present purpose it is enough to mention quite briefly the formal 'category of eternity' as the category which ensures both the integrity and the integration of the religious context of meaning.

As it is the task of the philosophy of religion to clarify the presuppositional concepts of religion, so it is the task of theology to clarify the content of an individual religion, and to do this in terms of the central idea of the religion itself. It is this central idea that we call its 'fundamental motif'. When, for example, we are dealing with an affirmation of Christian faith, we have not understood its meaning until we have related it to its centre, its fundamental motif. This takes us into our concluding Chapter XII, with the title of 'Motif Contexts'. 'Meaning and Method' overarches the distinction between philosophy of religion and theology. As the philosophy of religion has its method of 'logical analysis of presuppositions' and knows that a statement from any religion can only retain its meaning if it is understood and judged in the light of its own (i.e. the religious) category, so theology (in so far as it works systematically) has its own basic method of motif research or motif analysis, and knows that a statement from a particular religion can only retain its proper meaning if it is understood and judged in the light of its own fundamental motif. It is possible for exactly the same formulation to mean extremely different things according as it is placed in the context of one fundamental motif or another. The fundamental motif is the 'self-evident presupposition' that gives a statement its specific meaning and content. If we neglect to pay attention to the motif context we misunderstand the meaning of what is said.

When we speak, however, of 'self-evident presuppositions', these must not be confused with the 'logically necessary presuppositions' of which we spoke earlier. The latter can be obtained by a simple logical analysis, whereas the fundamental motif must be derived from what is historically given. The logical analysis of presuppositions and motif analysis are located on quite different levels and are subject to quite different conditions. The former are of an entirely logical nature, while the latter are subject to historical conditions. Yet it is only when they are taken together that we obtain a clear insight into the real meaning of an expression. By continually testing the fundamental motif in relation to the factual material, theology has the possibility of strictly objective argumentation, and it is this above all that gives to a theology that works systematically 'the sure progress of a science'.

In an investigation of the problems of 'contexts of meaning' and 'motif contexts' it cannot but be a matter of primary importance that the connection of thought should be clearly apparent from start to finish. We have therefore adopted the somewhat unusual procedure of giving already in the Introduction a rather detailed outline of the course the inquiry is to take. A comparison of this with the Table of Contents should make the main line of the argument clear enough to enable the reader to see every point in relation to the whole, and so to make possible a critical appraisal. If this aim is achieved, the Introduction has fulfilled its purpose.

CHAPTER II

What is Philosophy of Religion?

1. A Problematical Science

FROM one point of view it could be said that the purpose of our entire investigation is to answer the question 'What is philosophy of religion?' Although it is limited to mere 'prolegomena' to the philosophy of religion, it cannot but have a special responsibility for defining the nature and function of the latter.

When therefore the question 'What is philosophy of religion?' is raised at this introductory stage, there can be no thought of giving a conclusive answer to it as yet. That must be reserved for the investigation as a whole. At this early stage all that can be done is to point out the kind of factors that make this question a real problem and necessitate a thorough investigation of it. For the fact is that as regards its scientific status the philosophy of religion is in a much more complicated position than most of the other sciences. It is not as a rule difficult to characterize and define a science, at least in general terms, by referring to the subject matter it has to investigate and the questions it has to raise about it; but in the case of the philosophy of religion this proves to be a matter of extreme difficulty. Admittedly this is a predicament which the philosophy of religion shares with philosophy in general, but for the former it is more particularly acute. A glance at the introductory paragraphs of works by different authors on the philosophy of religion is enough to illustrate this difficulty and to show how uncertain everything in that discipline is. It is plainly still at an imperfect stage of development.

In order to explain this lack of clarity it is not enough simply to point out that the philosophy of religion, as its name indicates, moves on the borderline between philosophy and religion with all the complications which that entails. Nor is it enough to point out that the subject matter of the philosophy of religion, namely religion itself, is one of the most incomprehensible things in human life. The real reason is to be found elsewhere, and in purely historical terms it is not difficult to locate it. Before we go into that question, however, it will be appropriate to illustrate the above-mentioned uncertainty with some concrete examples.

What is the philosophy of religion about, and what kind of an investigation is it engaged in? Even to questions as central and basic as these it is impossible to get a reasonably uniform answer. Proposals there are in plenty, of which the following questions may give some idea. Is the philosophy of religion a theological or a philosophical discipline? Both views have their partisans. Is it the business of the philosophy of religion to be a 'religious philosophy',[1] that is, more or less a philosophy with a religious background and religious colouring? There has also of course been talk at times of a 'Christian philosophy', that is, a philosophy on a Christian basis and with a Christian colouring. But then we have to ask ourselves what becomes of the 'philosophical' element when it gets mixed up in this way with the religious or the Christian? Is it really the business of the philosophy of religion, as has sometimes been suggested, to propound a 'philosophical faith'?

Again, what is the relation of the philosophy of religion by and large to freely developing, historically given religion? Is it its business simply to try to understand the latter—understand it philosophically, whatever that may mean—or has it the duty of intervening formatively in this area and thus in a measure fulfilling a religious function? What is the relation of the philosophy of religion to systematic theology? With what justification has it recently become fashionable to speak of 'philosophical theology'?[2] Is the philosophy of religion, as has sometimes been asserted, a superior because more objective investigation of religion, and one that in the last resort makes theology superfluous?

In this way one could go on at great length, piling up questions which it seems must be answered before we can reach an answer to the question 'What is philosophy of religion?'—Or is it perhaps the other way round, so that we must first have an answer at least in principle to the question 'What is philosophy of religion?' before we can sort out this mass of confused questions and get rid of some of them while giving others a correct content and a soundly based answer?

This brings us back to the question of the reason for the problematical position of the philosophy of religion. The answer is not difficult to find if we consider the history of the subject, and it can be summarized very briefly thus: *the philosophy of religion suffers from a twofold inherited liability.*

A recent work on the philosophy of religion begins by sainyg: 'Religio-philosophical thinking is as old as human intellectual history, but philosophy of religion as a science is no older than the Enlightenment.'[3] It is easy to agree with this judgment in both its parts, but it is unlikely that most people are aware of what the two facts stated mean in terms of inherited liability for the philosophy of religion. In this connection we may distinguish between a general liability arising from the entire preceding history of the subject, and a particular liability arising from the thought

---

[1] *Cf.* such titles as W. G. De Burgh's *Towards a Religious Philosophy* and G. MacGregor's *Introduction to Religious Philosophy.*

[2] *Cf.*, e.g., P. Tillich, *The Protestant Era*, p. 83: 'The term "philosophical theology" points to a theology that has a philosophical character.' *Cf.* also Flew and MacIntyre, *New Essays in Philosophical Theology.*

[3] K. Feierls, *Die Umprägung der natürlichen Theologie*, p. 1.

pattern of the Enlightenment. Although no sharp line of demarcation can be drawn between these, inasmuch as the Enlightenment was heir to all the religio-philosophical ambiguity of earlier times, it will nevertheless be an advantage to discuss them separately.

(1) As regards the *general liability*, the reason for it lies in the fact that philosophy originally sprang from the soil of religion. There is a direct connection between the mythological cosmogonies of ancient religion and the cosmological speculations of the early Greek philosophers. Moreover, just as it is impossible to understand the latter without taking account of their mythological background, so it is impossible to understand Plato's doctrine of Ideas without taking into account how much of it has its roots in the religion of the ancient Mysteries, particularly Orphism. Something similar is the case with Aristotle and Stoicism and still more with Neo-platonism.

Now it would be natural to assume that this original connection between religious and philosophical thinking would provide a favourable seedbed for the philosophy of religion, so that it ought really to be regarded as an asset. Ought it not to facilitate the philosophical understanding of religion? It may therefore seem strange to speak of a liability in this connection. Yet the fact undoubtedly is that the common rootage of religion and philosophy has had an inhibiting effect on philosophy, and this in two directions: 1. it has prevented philosophy from becoming clear about its own task, and 2. it has prevented it from stating the religious or religio-philosophical problem correctly.

The first of these statements, that the dependence of philosophy on religion has prevented philosophy from coming to itself and discovering its own independent task, seems immediately evident. The second, that the original affinity between religion and philosophy has prevented a proper grasp of the problem presented by religion to philosophy, appears harder to understand. Yet in fact the two statements are only different aspects of the same thing. When philosophy and religion get mixed up with one another, it is inevitably to the detriment of both. A philosophy which takes it upon itself to be more or less a substitute for religion ceases to be philosophy, and a religion which wraps itself in the philosopher's cloak ceases to be real religion. And if on this confusion we try to base a 'philosophy of religion' which is meant to be both, it will be neither; the result will be an unhappy hybrid. Yet it is just this—the mixing up of religion and philosophy—that has gone on in religio-philosophical thinking down the ages.

An unbroken line runs from the ancient mystery religions through Platonism and Neoplatonism, through Gnosticism, Alexandrian theology and pseudo-Dionysius the Areopagite, through mediaeval scholasticism and mysticism, and through various forms of more modern philosophical thought, on to German Idealism and its culmination in Hegel's philosophy of religion. It is a tradition which—although in somewhat different forms—still survives in our own time, even in philosophical outlooks which are otherwise quite alien from those just mentioned. A symptom of the stubborn persistence of this tradition is the tendency on the part of philosophers to identify religion with 'mysticism'. This is in line with the dominant trend of the religio-philosophical tradition through the centuries, namely the Neoplatonic, metaphysical philosophy of religion. The characteristic thing about the latter is precisely the intermingling of philosophy and religion—that is, a particular conception of religion—which it has promoted.[4]

This last is a point specially worth noting. The intermingling of philosophy and religion which has gone on from the beginning, has not only meant that philosophy has acquired a general religious tinge, but also that one quite specific religious tradition has been 'philosophically sanctioned'. That the result of combining such disparate elements is neither scientifically, philosophically nor religiously acceptable is only too evident. Enough has been said to show what a liability it constitutes for religio-philosophical thought to have to look back on such a past.

(2) Besides this general liability there is now the *particular liability* that arises from the original close connection of the philosophy of religion with the thought of the Enlightenment. Here too it can be said that there is a quite special conception of religion underlying the interest of the Enlightenment in the philosophy of religion. It is not so much religion as it actually exists that draws this interest, but an idea, a preconceived notion, which is believed to be discernible behind all the different forms of religion. When a man of the Enlightenment talks about 'religion' it is not religion in its concrete actuality that he has in mind, but a sort of 'religion in general' or 'universal religion'. There is for him only one true religion. But this one true religion is neither Christianity nor any other historically given religion, but a religion grounded in human reason, a 'rational religion'. Any element of truth that there is in the various historical religions, including Christianity, goes back to and is adequately represented by the religion of reason. In this the essence of religion and its inner core of truth finds expression. It represents 'religion' in its purity, religion as such, and this—it is believed—is what awaits discovery beneath all the contingent historical trappings.

When the thought of the Enlightenment is faced with the question of the relation between the different historical religions and 'rational religion'

---

[4] I have dealt more fully with this tradition and its fusion of philosophy and religion in my RGP, pp. 14ff. Speaking of the metaphysical philosophy of religion I say there: 'Its attempt to be both philosophical and religious thinking at once has misfired: it intellectualizes religion and mysticizes philosophy, and thus produces an unhappy religious and philosophical hybrid, which neither of its parents is really willing to acknowledge.'

or 'natural religion', there are various courses it can take. Basically, the historical or positive religions exist to be superseded. Whatever they contain beyond 'natural religion' must be regarded merely as time-conditioned accretions, which can only obscure the pure rational truth of religion. They are externals, which should disappear when an adequate conception of religion is reached. If only we can extract from the positive religions the rational kernel concealed in them, we shall find that there are a certain few simple ideas which are characteristic of all religion: the ideas of the existence and providence of God, and of virtue and immortality. Such is the religion that arises out of the rational nature of man, and that can therefore rightly be called 'natural religion'. It can also be called a 'moral religion of reason', since ultimately the essence of religion proves to be identical with the moral reason. The ideas of God, virtue and immortality belong very closely together, and they all point in the same moral direction.

It is here that the philosophy of religion has its important work to do. It has to deduce these rational truths of religion from human reason, and to demonstrate their necessity. As to the criterion it employs in doing this, there is only one possibility, which may be called either 'reason' or 'philosophy'. Reason is the only recognized court of appeal in matters of faith, philosophy the only standard by which the truth of religion must be judged. It is thus the task of the philosophy of religion to distinguish between the kernel and the husk of religion, or between its inner essence and its unessential externals.

Although many of the representatives of the Enlightenment took a purely negative attitude towards Christianity, and indeed towards every historical form of religion, there was no necessity for them to do so. For there were some who found it possible to conceive of and even value the historical religions as pedagogical stages on the way to the pure religion of reason. It was, however, essentially the task of the philosophy of religion to purge and purify religion by freeing it from its contingent, historically conditioned traits. For the historical elements in a religion must never be confused with the essential kernel and rational truth of religion. Hence the philosophy of religion has a double task: 1. to set forth the true essence of religion and 2. to show how the differences between the positive forms of religion can be overcome by reducing the latter to the universally identical essence of religion. The goal towards which the philosophy of religion must work is thus the elimination of the historical religions by their absorption into natural religion. But this means that the philosophy of religion has also a constructive role and a positive contribution to make to the development of religion. It has to represent religion as it ought rationally to be, and it thus becomes itself a version of religion, a version resting on 'the foundations of sound reason', '*die Gründe der sunden Vernunft*'—to use Reimarus's characteristic phrase.

But to look in this way for 'religion' in the religions, and so to use the

very concept of religion itself for an attack on the concretely given historical religions, is obviously to pursue a phantom, a thing that does not exist.
The fundamental error of this whole theory is unmistakable: it involves a
disastrous conceptual realism. And that being so, the roles of the philosophy
of religion and theology are reversed. For although the former looks down
its philosophical nose at theology, since it has to do only with contingent
historical truths while the philosophy of religion deals with the necessary
'rational truth' of religion, it now appears that from a scientific point of
view theology has the great advantage of dealing with a real object instead
of a merely imaginary one.

It was not long before a reaction set in, and the decisive word came to
be spoken by Schleiermacher. Like Hamann and Herder before him, he
attacked the whole approach of the Enlightenment to religion. Against it
he propounded his own thesis, that there is no natural religion. What goes
by the name of natural religion is nothing but an empty fiction. All real
religion is positive and historical.[5]

To sum up. When the philosophy of religion first emerged as an independent discipline, it did so on the basis of belief in a particular idea, the
idea specially cherished by the Enlightenment of a universal, rational,
natural religion. The philosophy of religion was from the start a means for
the realization of this idea. That it has had difficulty in freeing itself from
the circumstances of its origin as an independent scientific discipline is
not surprising, but it is this that has made and still makes it a problematical
discipline. At least it is clear that so long as it remains on this questionable
footing, the philosophy of religion is neither scientifically, philosophically
nor religiously acceptable. The same point that was made above with regard
to its general liability thus reappears here with regard to its particular
liability. It is impossible to overestimate the handicap imposed on the
philosophy of religion by the fact that it came into existence as an independent discipline precisely as a means to the end described above. It should,
however, be added that at present many forces are at work to rescue it from
its dependence on its origin and to provide a new basis for it. What
prospect of success there is in this matter, only the further course of the
investigation can show.

2. The Inevitability of the Religio-philosophical Problem

If the philosophy of religion is as severely handicapped and problematical
a science as the foregoing argument suggests, and if the very nature of its
starting point makes it so liable to go wrong, the question very naturally

---

[5] On this whole subject see my DVG, esp. pp. 117–40, where I deal with the
question of 'natural religion and history'. The Catholic scholar Konrad Feierls, in the
book cited above, illustrates with a wealth of material the process that led from scholastic
natural theology to the philosophy of religion as an independent discipline, and shows
the difference this made to the intellectual temper of the Enlightenment.

arises: Why bother with it at all, why not simply leave it alone? The attempt has been made to follow this advice, and from the 1920s onwards interest in the philosophy of religion fell very much into the background. There were other matters occupying men's minds.

Although theology since Schleiermacher had come to see what was wrong with the conception of religion characteristic of the Enlightenment, it had by no means been able to free itself from the dominating influence of the latter. In this regard Schleiermacher's own position is instructive. Although he saw in principle quite clearly that the 'natural religion' of the Enlightenment was merely an empty fiction, and that all real religion is positive and historical, yet he proved unable consistently to maintain this insight throughout his work. Both in his *Addresses on Religion* and in *The Christian Faith* he allows the general concept of religion (*'Anschauung des Universums'*, *'das schlechthinnige Abhängigkeitsgefühl'*)[6] to become, quite contrary to his avowed intention, the standard of value by which all religion, including Christianity, is measured; and what is more, this general concept is the fixed point from which the whole content of the Christian faith is to be derived. Now what else is this but a new edition of the concept of religion inherited from the Enlightenment? It may be possible to say that the theory of religion produced by the Enlightenment was in principle overcome by Schleiermacher, yet there is more justification for saying that it has *never* in principle been overcome.[7]

From one point of view what happened in the 1920s in the shape of 'dialectical theology' and related movements of thought, was a revolt of theology against the philosophy of religion. It was perhaps not so much a revolt against the philosophy of religion as such, as against the presuppositions on which it then rested—its 'inherited liabilities'—and the quasi-theological conclusions drawn from them. This marked a new phase in the conflict between 'natural religion' and Christianity. Whereas for the Enlightenment it was 'religion' that was of chief concern, so that in extreme cases 'religion' could be set in opposition to Christianity, the position was now reversed, so that Christianity became the centre of interest and was not infrequently set in direct opposition to religion. Christianity versus

6 'Intuition of the Universe', 'the feeling of absolute dependence'.

7 How deeply both philosophy and theology at the turn of the present century were under the influence of the Enlightenment can be illustrated from R. Eucken's *Die Wahrheitsgehalt der Religion* (3rd edn) which is based on the twin concepts of 'Universal Religion' and 'Characteristic Religion', and which treats the historical religions as 'embodiments' of the 'absolute religion' (p. 362, ET p. 539) and maintains that 'above all individual religions there must stand the religion of all mankind' (p. 333). 'As surely as there is only one truth, so there can be only one absolute religion, and this religion by no means coincides with any one of the historical religions' (p. 359, ET p. 535). A further example is furnished by E. Troeltsch's *Psychologie und Erkenntnistheorie*, in which the philosophy of religion is given among other things the task of showing how far the historical religions give expression to the universally valid truth-content of religion.

religion became in many quarters the new slogan—Christianity as a message from God, religion as an invention of man. Christianity, it was held, expresses the true relationship with God, religion a false relationship. Christianity can therefore never, on this view, be rightly described as a religion, since all religion whatsoever is false and worthless.

In other words, what we have here is a direct inversion of the outlook of the Enlightenment—which as a reaction against the persistent influence of that outlook on theology is both understandable and to a large extent justified. But the same thing happened here as usually happens when people are preoccupied with refuting an opponent: they become negatively bound by his position. They are so anxious to negate his answer that they pay too little attention to his question. They let his way of putting the question stand, and merely give the opposite answer. If the Enlightenment misconstrued the concept of religion and used it for an attack on Christianity, that is no reason for theology to use Christianity for an attack on religion. There is a legitimate way of speaking about Christianity as a religion, and nothing is gained but a good deal lost by committing oneself to such an unnatural use of language as to deny that Christianity is a religion. Furthermore, granted that the philosophy of religion was misconceived by the Enlightenment and used as a means to an illegitimate end, that is no reason for ceasing to use it altogether. We ought rather to inquire whether it has a legitimate function, and if it has, to define it. If the religio-philosophical problem is inescapable—and that it is so we can already affirm in advance—then it cannot be simply dismissed without more ado.

That, however, is what was done for several decades, and the consequences were inevitable. Both theologically and in the general cultural debate the price paid for the neglect of the religio-philosophical problem was that the Christian faith seemed to stand in complete isolation. As a result there soon developed an urgent need to demonstrate its relevance in the contemporary situation. It was this that led to the discussions about a 'point of contact'—the contact of the Christian message with 'modern man', his world of thought and his total situation. It led also to the debates of more recent decades about 'demythologizing' and to the special form taken under their influence by the perennially important 'problem of hermeneutics', not to mention other ill-conceived programmes of a similar kind. In this connection we may also recall Paul Tillich's attempt to combine philosophy and religion in his 'philosophical theology', his 'apologetics' and his 'method of correlation'—all of which we shall have occasion to look into later. These various trends have been cited here only as examples of the lack of clarity that has resulted from the extreme neglect of the religio-philosophical problem. Profound study of it could have saved theology from many a wild venture and spared the cultural debate a great deal of confusion.

The inevitability of a problem can be demonstrated in different ways.

It can be done positively by explaining what it involves and showing that discussion of it is necessary both because of its intrinsic importance and because of its connection with other inescapable problems. This is the course we shall take as we continue our exposition. But the inevitability of the problem can be attested also by pointing out the consequences which have in fact followed from neglecting the discussion of it. Thus far we have had to confine ourselves to this latter, negative course, since it is only through further investigation that the conceptual material required for the positive demonstration can be made available.

In conclusion it should be observed that the negative procedure cannot yield more than symptoms of the inevitability of the problem. But that for the moment is enough, for it shows the need for a serious investigation of the subject. The problem is not solved either by a theological fiat or theological neglect. The problem of the philosophy of religion is a philosophical problem, and it can only be solved by philosophical means.

3. The Philosophy of Religion as a Philosophical Discipline

In any attempt to define the meaning of the term 'philosophy of religion' attention should first of all be paid to the genitive construction. Genitives are often deceptive and can be extremely ambiguous, and that is so in the present instance. What is the nature of the genitive here? Is it subjective or objective, or perhaps qualitative? There have certainly been attempts to interpret it as if it meant a philosophy possessing a religious quality. But this inevitably arouses the suspicion that it involves a contradiction in terms. It was no doubt possible in the childhood of humanity to mix up religion and philosophy without a qualm, but this no longer seems possible when once their relative independence of one another has been perceived. Neither philosophy nor religion has anything to gain from the blurring of distinctions between them. It is always risky to be careless about distinctions. The old saying, *Qui bene distinguit bene docet* ('He teaches well who distinguishes well'), is extremely pertinent in the present instance. Although the term 'philosophy of religion' brings together the two concepts, philosophy and religion, it must not be allowed to blur the distinction between them. The philosophy of religion is not a religion which is at the same time philosophy, nor yet a philosophy which is at the same time religion. It is neither a philosophical religion nor a religious philosophy. How then are we to define it so as to show due regard for the distinction between religion and philosophy?

The only way to avoid confusion here is to distinguish clearly between the science and its subject matter, and observe the nature of each. The philosophy of religion is a science which as to its nature is purely philosophical, and which has for its subject matter religion. In both respects it differs characteristically from theology, although the latter also is a science and also deals with a subject matter of a religious nature. From this point of

23

view it is not difficult to see where the difference lies. The philosophy of religion serves a different purpose from theology both as regards the nature of its investigation and the subject matter it investigates. It is unlike theology in that its investigation is directed towards philosophical understanding, and its subject matter has a wider range. For while theology occupies itself with a particular concrete religion, seeking to elucidate its content and meaning, if possible in terms of its own central concern, the philosophy of religion has the task of understanding the phenomenon of 'religion' as it is found not only in a particular religion but in anything and everything we call by that name. It is thus concerned with defining a universal concept and answering the question: What do we really mean when we describe something as 'religion' or 'religious'?

If we are to speak of a universal concept of religion, however, we must explain more precisely what is intended by it and how we arrive at it. This requires us to continue making distinctions, for there are at least five different possible ways of speaking about the concept of religion. These may be described respectively as: statistical, logical, normative or ideal, structural, and presuppositional. On closer examination, however, most of them prove untenable and useless for the purpose of the philosophy of religion.

(1) The question what is meant by 'religion' could very easily be taken as referring to what men in general mean when they describe something as 'religion' or 'religious'. In that case the only way to answer it would seem to be by means of a statistical inquiry as to what men in general understand by these terms and what ideas they associate with them. Such an inquiry, however, would certainly be inconclusive, since men in general do not associate any clear idea with the words 'religion' and 'religious'. All it could do would be to give us a more diffuse picture than we had to begin with. The statistical concept of religion is therefore useless as a starting point for the philosophy of religion.

(2) It looks more promising to concentrate on the 'logical universal' of religion, and this is what the philosophy of religion has to a large extent done. If we want to know what religion really is, or in more traditional terms, what the 'essence of religion' is, it seems obvious that we should start with the actually given religions and work back by means of logical abstraction to what they have in common, while ignoring the differences between them. What all religions have in common would then be the 'essence of religion'. But aside from the disturbing similarity between this procedure and that of the Enlightenment, whose idea of religion we have seen to be untenable, and aside from the risk it entails of 'conceptual realism', this programme is unworkable. The relation between the different religions is not such that they have in common a substantial core of religious truths on which a generic definition of 'religion' can be based, while their differences have to do with less essential things. The fact is rather

that it is often precisely the particularities of a religion that are the essential thing. In abstraction from everything distinctive the remainder—if there is any remainder—becomes so insignificant and unmeaning that it cannot possibly be described as 'the essence of religion' or the universal concept of religion. Logical abstraction here leads nowhere, and it is therefore ruled out as far as the philosophy of religion is concerned.

(3) The impossibility of getting at the universal concept of religion by means of abstraction has sometimes led to the abandonment of any attempt to determine objectively what religion is. The concept of religion is then regarded, not as being the result of an inquiry that starts with the existing religions, but rather as the norm or ideal with which we must start as something postulated by us. The concept of religion, it is said, is not in any sense a universal concept, but a normative or ideal concept. This, however, is no real solution of the problem. A science that takes a normative concept for its starting point puts itself in an impossible position. For what gives me the right to set up this or that as a norm? Simply to say that I have postulated it gives it no scientific legitimation. The thought of the concept of religion as a norm or ideal thus entails an inevitable subjectivism and an obvious arbitrariness in the very starting point. Consequently, this theory also is unacceptable for the philosophy of religion.

(4) Things look better if we take the concept of religion to be a structural concept. For is it not essentially the aim of religio-philosophical inquiry to determine in one way or another the structure of those phenomena to which we give the name of religion? This view has the great advantage over the three preceding that it directs the question to the proper quarter. The difficulty with it, however, is that the concept of structure seems more applicable to a particular religion than to religion in general. It is easy to see that a particular religion may possess a definite structure and this can often be empirically demonstrated; but it is more difficult to show that everything we call religion has a definite structure. That is why the use of the traditional phrase 'the essence of religion' is so highly questionable, although it undoubtedly makes good sense to speak (for example) of 'the essence of Christianity' with reference to what is characteristic of Christianity, peculiar to it and structurally distinctive of it. Furthermore, speaking of the 'structure' of religion easily leads to thinking on ontological lines and conjures up visions of an entity whose structure is to be defined. Although therefore the idea of taking the concept of religion as a structural concept points in the right direction, the philosophy of religion cannot be content with it but must proceed a step further.

(5) This brings us to the definition of the concept of religion as a pre-suppositional concept. What is it that is presupposed when anything is described as 'religion' or 'religious'? Here we are finally rid of ontological speculation as to what religion 'is' or what its 'essence' is, and the religio-

25

philosophical inquiry is brought into line with that analysis of presuppositions which is characteristic of philosophy in general. In saying this we are
of course anticipating a great deal that remains to be explained and justified in the following chapters, but it has been necessary to pursue the
matter thus far in order to clarify the position of the philosophy of religion
as a purely philosophical discipline.

We began with the question of the meaning of the term 'philosophy of
religion' and the confusion arising from the genitive connection between
religion and philosophy. It is now clear that 'philosophy of religion' has
nothing to do with 'religious philosophy' or 'philosophical theology' or
'religious ontology', but must be classed as a purely philosophical investigation, of which the subject matter is religion. An important question still
remains, however, in connection with the sharp distinction that is sometimes drawn between 'philosophy' and 'philosophy of'—whether it be 'of'
religion or science or whatever. The idea here is that 'philosophy proper',
'philosophy pure and simple', or whatever else it may be called, is not
restricted by attachment to any particular subject matter, whereas a 'philosophy of' is shaped and coloured by its subject matter. 'Philosophy proper'
is then supposed to be concerned with 'being as such' and to issue in some
sort of ontology or metaphysics, while 'philosophy of' deals with some
particular aspect or form of being which it takes as the subject matter of
its philosophical reflection. Hence 'philosophy of religion' is a philosophy
which has religion for its subject matter and is accordingly restricted. This,
however, is another instance of the need to be careful about distinctions.
    The distinction just mentioned can easily give the impression that
there are a number of different philosophies, of which one is genuine,
'pure' philosophy, while the rest are more or less 'applied philosophy'.
There is, however, something spurious about this distinction. To put it
paradoxically we might say: there is no 'philosophy proper', and no
philosophy that is not 'philosophy proper'. In other words, we cannot
philosophize in a vacuum, and a philosophy without any sort of subject
matter is no more possible than a consciousness which is not conscious of
anything. Yet it is equally true that 'philosophy pure and simple' is the
only sort of philosophy there is, since the naming of the subject matter in
the phrase 'philosophy of . . .' merely designates the area to which the
philosophical question (which is always essentially the same) is being
addressed. It can thus be said that 'philosophy proper' *is* 'philosophy of',
because it is never without some subject matter, and that 'philosophy of'
is 'philosophy proper' because the philosophical question remains purely
and unalterably philosophical no matter to what subject matter it is
addressed.
    It is now at last clear what we mean by saying that the philosophy of
religion is a purely philosophical discipline. We mean that it puts the

characteristically philosophical question to its subject matter, religion. There is one thing, however, that we must add. As a philosophical discipline the philosophy of religion has an important contribution to make to philosophy in general. By putting the philosophical question in this particular area it helps to clarify its meaning for all areas. What gives the religio-philosophical problem this wider significance is the fact that the special difficulties and weaknesses with which the philosophy of religion has to contend, are merely symptoms of a general philosophical weakness which it is equally important to overcome wherever it is found. At a particularly sensitive spot the philosophy of religion brings to light a problem of universal range which otherwise might pass unnoticed. The chief example of this is the problem of metaphysics, which makes itself felt in the context of the philosophy of religion more than anywhere else, although it is certainly not only a religio-philosophical problem but one that affects all philosophy whatsoever. Just because of its sensitivity in this matter the philosophy of religion can become the starting point for an exposition of the problem of philosophy as a whole and for an elucidation of its scientific status.

It is to this general problem that we must now turn our attention. Only when we have dealt with it shall we be able to return with the resources we need to the special problem of the philosophy of religion.

CHAPTER III

Metaphysical and Scientific Philosophy

1. 'Under a Double Star': Two Tendencies in Philosophy

PHILOSOPHY appears in two forms, one metaphysical and the other scientific. It is often difficult to say just which is which, for metaphysics has long claimed to be a science, and scientific philosophy has often slipped unawares into metaphysical ways of thinking; yet there is a clear distinction between the scientific and metaphysical tendencies. If we seek the reason for this state of affairs, we must go back to the beginnings of philosophy, where the conditions for it were already present. Philosophy was born 'under a double star', and this has influenced not only its beginnings but the whole of its subsequent history. This observation sheds light on far-reaching relationships and furnishes the key to an understanding of essential features of philosophy which are otherwise difficult to grasp; and it explains the duality, not to say ambiguity, which has made and still makes the position of philosophy so problematical. We must therefore begin by giving a little attention to this thesis—that philosophy was 'born under a double star'—and showing precisely what it means.

(1) The first thing to be said is that philosophy was born under the star of religion. We have already had occasion to say something like this in connection with the philosophy of religion (p. 17 above), and the same is true of philosophy in general. When we take this broader view of the subject, however, the perspective is somewhat altered. In our earlier discussion the main thing was to show what a disadvantage it was for the philosophy of religion to have been so closely connected with a particular kind of religion, and how this had prevented it from becoming a purely philosophical discipline. Something similar can of course also be said of philosophy in general, for it is undeniable that its original connection with religious and mythological ideas has been disadvantageous to it. This is one of the main reasons why philosophy has found it so easy to take to metaphysical speculation—a subject to which we must return in more detail later. For the moment, however, another and more positive aspect draws our attention, namely the universalizing tendency of philosophy.

There is good reason to describe this tendency as a legacy from the more or less religiously coloured cosmogonies of antiquity. Just as the latter sought to explain the origin of the universe, so the first philosophers sought to explain all existence, everything that is: 'All is water' (Thales), 'All is air' (Anaximenes), 'All is number' (the Pythagoreans), 'All is one' (the Eleatics). This tendency to universality which philosophy has in common with religion, is no merely external and accidental feature unnecessarily borrowed from religion, but is integral to it and of its very essence.

Since religion was the first on the scene, we are justified in saying that philosophy was born under the star of religion, or perhaps more precisely of mythology. In view of the original connection between philosophy and religion, and the universalizing tendency of both, it is hardly surprising that in the course of history so many philosophical outlooks, which have otherwise had little to do with religion, have none the less allowed their systems to culminate in the concept of God as that towards which all lines converge and in which they find their central point of unity. This is only a further proof of our thesis that philosophy was born under the star of religion. It is an ultimate testimony to the strength of the universalizing tendency and to the way in which philosophy has sought to do justice to it with the help of concepts borrowed from religion.

(2) At first the boundaries between philosophy and poetic myth-making are quite fluid; the two can mingle without difficulty. Yet there is in philosophy a clear tendency in another direction, to which we can give expression in a second thesis, namely that philosophy was born under the star of science. Naturally this must be taken with a grain of salt. There was at that time no science in our sense of the term, and philosophy itself was the first shoot of the scientific tree. In this respect philosophy had nothing to fall back upon in the way it had in its relation to religion or mythology. There was, however, a tendency in the direction of science, otherwise philosophy would never have come to exist. Even the earliest natural philosophy distinguishes itself from the old cosmogonies by seeking to reduce all existence to something naturally or rationally given. In this we can undoubtedly detect a beginning of scientific reflection.

It is to this double origin that philosophy owes the persistent duality of its character with its universalizing and its scientific tendencies. Neither of these tendencies should be overlooked or ignored. If philosophy abandons either its universal or its scientific aim it ceases to be philosophy. Both aims are legitimate and necessary, and neither can be given up. Indeed, the combination of them is an important criterion of the genuineness of philosophy, and their separation is a sign that philosophy has gone astray and failed in its purpose. Yet it is plain that there is a tension between them, and that they cannot be held together without difficulty. The history of philosophy is in large part the story of how these two tendencies have fallen apart and one has been cultivated at the expense of the other.

Putting it in a rather too neat formula we might say that metaphysics has taken charge of the universal tendency, and scientific philosophy of the scientific. But that is an oversimplification. For both tendencies are necessary, and it is in their togetherness and tension that they constitute philosophy whether scientific or metaphysical. There is no scientific philosophy that can be totally unconcerned about universality, and no metaphysical philosophy that does not at least claim some kind of scientific basis. Although there is sometimes hesitancy about the latter, yet no metaphysics will admit to resting on a purely arbitrary foundation. Both tendencies are constitutive of scientific philosophy, and both are constitutive of metaphysical philosophy. How then are we to distinguish between these two kinds of philosophy?

2. The Separation of the Two Tendencies

Opinions differ as to the point in history at which metaphysics in the strict sense of the term can be said to have arisen. The general view has been that metaphysics is as old as philosophy itself, and that it can in fact be regarded as the original form of philosophy. Although the actual term 'metaphysics' is of later date, and first occurs in connection with the philosophy of Aristotle, yet the metaphysical tendency seems to have been present from the beginning. This view has been strongly denied by Werner Jaeger, who says: 'From the historical point of view it is an abuse of language, not in the least excused by its frequency, to call these [pre-Socratic] philosophies metaphysical systems because they contain elements that are metaphysical in our sense.'[1] That is undoubtedly true for one who is seeking to exhibit the specifically Aristotelian idea of metaphysics and distinguish it from other ideas, but for our more comprehensive purpose it is irrelevant. Where metaphysics as a generic term is concerned, we cannot be bound by the historical question of its specific meaning in Aristotle.

No matter where we think of placing Aristotle in the history of metaphysics—whether as the actual originator of metaphysics or as the one who gave it its classical form—in either case he holds the key position in it. The two chief ingredients of metaphysics, which appear in Plato as *logos* and *mythos*, are found again in Aristotle. He is clearly aware of the original connection of philosophy with mythology, and aware of it not merely as a historical fact but as something that affects his own understanding of what philosophy is about. It is odd to find a sober thinker like Aristotle prepared, at the beginning of his *Metaphysics* (or *The First Philosophy*—I, 2), to recognize 'the lover of myth' as a philosopher, the φιλόμυθος as a φιλόσοφος, and to discover that his metaphysics is at the same time 'theology'. What makes him interesting in the history of philosophy, however, is not so much his thinking on those lines. More important is the fact that in him more than anywhere else we can study the beginning of the process which was eventually to lead to the dissolution of metaphysics. For while on the one hand he can be said to be the founder of metaphysics in the strict sense, or 'metaphysics as a science', he is on the other hand the very man who by his contribution to the history of scien-

[1] W. Jaeger, *Aristoteles*, p. 403, ET* p. 377.

tific thought prepared the way for the collapse of metaphysics. Not of course directly, for there is nothing to suggest that he was conscious of any tension between scientific and metaphysical thinking. For him, both of them were genuinely scientific, and they could be combined in the most harmonious way, since one took over where the other left off.

Like the polymath he was, Aristotle could find room in his philosophy for everything that was known to his time as science. Mathematics, physics, astronomy, kinematics, and the whole series of empirical sciences, all had their place. As for metaphysics, what he did was to give it scientific form, to make it formally a science, and to place it as the coping-stone on the scientific edifice. It might no doubt be thought that if the individual sciences each had its own aspect of the world of being to investigate, there would be no room for a special metaphysical science; but that is an anachronistic idea, belonging to a later time. Aristotle knew that there was still a problem waiting to be solved: the problem of a universal science, the question of the nature of existence and of the ultimate principles of all being, or in other words, the ontological problem.

So far all seemed well and good. But there was another aspect of the matter. Although it was not yet plainly visible, there was a serious crack in the imposing edifice, or to use perhaps a more apt metaphor, there was an explosive built into it, which when the time came would wreck the whole building. Oddly enough, this explosive had been introduced by the builder himself, though not as a result of any carelessness on his part, but rather owing to his scientific conscientiousness; for it was part and parcel of the sciences which Aristotle had associated with metaphysics. The more strictly he insisted on the requirements of scientific thought, the more inevitable it became that metaphysics should stand in a questionable light. In this respect both his logical-analytical work (which was no less important for the development of the special sciences than for philosophy) and the general rigour of his methodology contributed not a little towards heightening the tension. The situation had not yet reached the critical stage, however, and what prevented its doing so was partly the fact that the 'sciences' had not attained the requisite independence over against metaphysics, and partly that their methods were still not fully developed. It is true that Aristotle had already been able to speak of induction, but it was only with the empirically oriented sciences of modern times that the methodological presuppositions were given for an attack from a scientific standpoint on metaphysics—and why not on philosophy as a whole?

In due time the two tendencies of philosophy parted company as they were bound to do. It should not be forgotten, however, that the explosive was present from the beginning, and that Aristotle himself provided a considerable part of it. Without his epoch-making contribution to scientific methodology it could not have happened, at least not in the form in which it did.

In the first two sections of this chapter we have seen how philosophy was marked from the beginning by two distinct tendencies, and how these already at an early stage began to fall apart. It would take too long here to describe the progress of their separation historically, and to show how under the influence of the gradual development of the special sciences the traditional metaphysics moved towards its dissolution and a new 'scientific philosophy' began to emerge. For that we should have to trace on the one hand the great metaphysical mainstream in the history of thought, from Aristotle[2] through High Scholasticism[3] to the Enlightenment (Chr. Wolff) and Kant, and thence through 'transcendental philosophy' to the existential philosophy and ontological trends of our own time, including such theological derivatives as, for example, Paul Tillich's onto-theology— an extraordinarily consistent tradition, in which, despite all variations on the theme, no really significant changes have taken place in the state of the problem since ancient times. On the other hand we should have to trace the mutual claims and counter-claims of the special sciences and philo- sophy during modern times. In other words, we should have to give a com- plete account of the history of philosophy, which would naturally take us far beyond the limits of our present inquiry. Fortunately we have no need to do any such thing. For although in the preceding sections it has been necessary to introduce historical viewpoints, the dominant interest all along has been systematic. Our intention has been simply to show what lies behind the divergent tendencies in philosophy as we find it practised today; and for this purpose enough has already been said to make the breach between these tendencies entirely understandable.

It would however be an oversimplification of the position to interpret it as involving a conflict and trial of strength between the universalizing and the scientific tendency, such as can only end in the elimination of one or the other of them. On the contrary, as we have emphasized above, both tendencies are legitimate and it is only as they are held together that they constitute philosophy. This makes it clear what is really at stake here. When we compare and contrast metaphysical and scientific philosophy, the question is to what extent either of them can do justice to both tendencies. Since metaphysics has made the universal interest its special concern, what we chiefly have to ask about it is how far it can do justice to the scientific interest; and conversely, since scientific philosophy has mainly stressed the scientific interest, we must ask how far it has done justice to the universal. These questions are the subject of our discussion in the next two sections.

3. Metaphysical Philosophy

What is metaphysics? That is a question which there is very good reason

---

[2] *Cf.* W. Jaeger, *Aristoteles*, and J. Owens, *The Doctrine of Being*.
[3] *Cf.* A. Zimmermann, *Ontologie oder Metaphysik?*

to ask; for few words are as vague and ambiguous as 'metaphysics', and everyone gives it the meaning he pleases.[4] This is in large measure connected with the fact that the word has come to be used perhaps oftener in an evaluative sense—positive or negative—than a descriptive. The vaguer the term is and the less of definite content it represents to the general consciousness, the greater are the possibilities of using it for evaluative purposes, that is, for the expression of approval or disapproval. Sometimes we find it used as a compliment, sometimes as a mark of disparagement. The former is the case when 'metaphysics' (often with 'mysticism' as an alternative) is used without further explanation to indicate that something is 'obscurely profound'—the obscurity giving no reason to doubt the profundity. Naturally such a compliment can turn into its opposite if the obscurity gets the upper hand and one begins to doubt whether there really is anything behind it.

During recent decades the word 'metaphysics' has also been widely used in a pejorative sense. Its very fuzziness makes it specially useful for saying something negative about an idea or conception which one has not fully grasped but does not want to reject out of hand. Hence the word 'metaphysics' has become in contemporary debate something of a negative catchword. In this connection we may recall Axel Hägerström's famous device, *Praeterea censeo metaphysicam esse delendam*,[5] which he set as a motto over his 'Self-Portrait',[6] and thus over his whole philosophical career. It is true that when he came to elaborate his critique of metaphysics Hägerström himself was not quite so extreme, but that did not prevent his dictum from being commonly understood to mean much the same as '*écrasez l'infâme!*'[7] We may also recall logical positivism with its often completely unqualified talk of metaphysics as 'nonsense'. Although our further discussion will lead to the conclusion that the metaphysical way of looking at things is indefensible from a scientific standpoint, this must not be understood simply as a negative value-judgment. To begin with, all evaluation must be abjured and we must concern ourselves solely with description, that is, with answering the question:

(1) *What is metaphysics?*
Not that we shall attempt to define metaphysics in the strict sense of

---

[4] There have rightly been complaints about the vagueness and ambiguity of the term 'metaphysics', which in different authors means such different things that there is almost no common ground for discussion of it. J. Hemberg, for instance, in his *Religion och metafysik*, gives a detailed analysis of its use by a number of Swedish writers, which well illustrates what he calls 'the chequered history of the concept of metaphysics'. (See further additional note II.1.—Tr.)

[5] 'Moreover I propose that metaphysics be destroyed'—a parody of Cato the Elder's proposal regarding Carthage.

[6] Hägerström, '*Selbstdarstellung*' (in *Die Philosophie der Gegenwart*, VII).

[7] 'Crush the infamous thing!'—an echo of Voltaire.

definition. For our purpose it will suffice to pick out a few characteristic features from its varied history, which may shed light on its meaning and its relation to the 'scientific tendency' in philosophy. The natural starting point for this is the position in which philosophy found itself as a result of the emergence of the special sciences. The latter have had important consequences for philosophy in two ways: 1. as apparently depriving it of its subject matter and 2. as furnishing a criterion by which its scientific status can be tested. For the moment we will let the first of these points serve as an introduction to our characterization of metaphysics.

Originally philosophy included everything that could be called knowledge or science, and was in that sense a universal science. It was therefore a revolutionary event when alongside of philosophy there arose a series of special sciences, which had broken away from it to pursue in their several fields their own special inquiries. What was there now left over for philosophy to do? This made it necessary for philosophy to legitimate itself as a science by showing that it had a province of its own to investigate, or at least that it had a function of its own and a special job to do, distinct from the rest of the sciences. But the difficulty was that philosophy seemed to be gradually being left without any subject matter or any function at all. As the special sciences were dividing all the different aspects of existence among themselves, philosophy was being disinherited, or so it seemed. In this situation the obvious thing was to fall back on the age-old problem of philosophy, the question of the ἀρχή or *principium* of existence.[8] No matter how completely the world may be divided up among the various special disciplines, there still remains one question with which none of them deals: the question of being as such, or the ultimate nature of being. Here metaphysics had its own domain, and here it could make good its claim to universality. As distinct from the special sciences, each of which dealt with its own special part or aspect of the realm of being, metaphysics had for its subject matter 'being in general', 'being itself'.

Although the idea of being as such (*ens qua ens*), like the old question of the ἀρχή of existence, proves exceedingly obscure, there is none the less one thing that it makes perfectly clear, namely the desire for a universal principle. The principle in question here, however, is of a peculiar kind, not a logical but an ontological principle, from which the totality of existence can be derived. Already in this starting point there are implicit a number of characteristic features which continually recur with more or less clarity in the history of metaphysics. Some of these should be noted here.

1) *Metaphysics as ontology.* Metaphysics is the science of being as such (*ens qua ens*); its task is to explain the nature and ultimate ground of all being. This of course we have already said in showing where metaphysics starts, but in view of its fundamental importance it is desirable to empha-

[8] On this *cf.* A. Lumpe, 'Der Terminus *APXH*', and K. von Fritz, 'Die *APXAI*'.

35

size it and treat it as a special feature. Throughout the entire history of metaphysics we find something of the same idea, from Aristotle to our own time.[9] It is there in what Aristotle says about τὸ ὄν, and there again today in (for example) Gustav Bergmann's ontology[10] and Martin Heidegger's formulation of the fundamental metaphysical question as: '*Warum ist überhaupt Seiendes und nicht vielmehr Nichts?*'[11] If in recent years there has been a growing interest in metaphysics, it has been brought about largely through an interest in ontology. Metaphysics and ontology belong so inseparably together that it is difficult to imagine what a metaphysics without ontology would be. It would not at any rate be metaphysics in the usually accepted sense of the term.

2) *Metaphysics as the unity of being and value.* A further characteristic feature of metaphysics is its tendency to equate being and value. This is very closely connected with its ontological orientation, which makes the idea that being and value coincide seem so obvious that it hardly needs to be explained.[12] There are, however, plenty of explanations, of which the commonest is the one that starts from man's intermediate position between 'being' and 'nothing'.

If a place is to be found for man—value-conscious man—in the scheme of 'being and nothing', it will naturally be in an intermediate position. Man's existence cannot be described either simply as being or simply as nothing; it is something in between. It is a relative being, and one that can be increased by man's seeking security in absolute being, or diminished by his clinging to inferior things. This idea found classical expression in Augustine, with his doctrine of God as both the Absolute Being (*summum ens*) and the Absolute Value (*summum bonum*). God is the fullness of all reality, and there is therefore in him all that man, threatened by nothing-

---

[9] For a survey of the nature and history of the ontological problem see S. Holm, *Ontologi.*

[10] Bergmann, *Logic and Reality*, p. 108: 'There is *philosophy proper*, also called first philosophy or metaphysics. . . . The heart of philosophy proper is ontology. . . . Ontology asks what exists'; and p. 195: 'To have some ontological status is to be an entity.'

[11] 'Why is there any being at all—why not a rather nothing?'—Heidegger, *Was ist Metaphysik?* p. 38, ET p. 380. Heidegger agrees with Hegel that pure Being and pure Nothing are one and the same. The dialectic of 'Being and Nothing' is in fact a constantly recurring theme in the history of metaphysics. When Being as the ultimate abstraction has been emptied of all concrete content, it comes to coincide with Nothing. By no means every occurrence of this idea involves a genuine dialectic, however; for often it is rather in the nature of an uncritically accepted tradition or a passive habit of thought. We shall have occasion to return to this question (below, pp. 131f.).

[12] This idea has been so firmly rooted in the metaphysical tradition ever since Plato and Aristotle, and is regarded as so self-evident, that the question of the reason for it is hardly ever raised. 'Aristotle believed as much as Plato that being and value in the absolute sense coincide in the conception of God. In that respect he remained a Platonist to the day of his death. The highest being is also the highest good' (W. Jaeger, *Aristoteles*, p. 85, ET* p. 84).

ness as he is, needs or can desire. Unlike God, who is his own being and his own *bonum*, man as a creature must seek these things outside himself. He is created by God and created 'out of nothing'—hence his intermediate position and his divided state. As created by God he possesses a certain being, though it is only relative; and as created out of nothing he is in constant danger of falling back into the nothingness out of which he came. The lack of being which is inherent in his creatureliness and finitude, can be remedied only as he cleaves to God, the Absolute Being, and finds in Him his *summum et incommutabile bonum*, his supreme and unchangeable good. Echoes of this theme can be heard down to our own time, for example in certain existentialists.

That will suffice to illustrate how the ontological scheme of 'being and nothing' results by a certain necessity in the equation of 'being and value'. This does not strictly speaking add anything new to ontological metaphysics, but only emphasizes a certain aspect of it. The unity of being and value is an idea that underlies nearly all metaphysics, and it explains a good deal about it, particularly with regard to metaphysics as 'world-view'.

3) *Metaphysics as 'world-view'*. One of the most important undertakings of metaphysics is to furnish us with a scientifically based world-view. Here we have both of the two tendencies of philosophy, the universal and the scientific. The universal expresses itself in the concern with the world and the viewing of the world as a wholeness and unity, while the scientific finds expression in the insistence that this view must not be arbitrarily chosen but scientifically established. Here too we are not far from ontology, nor from the idea of 'being = value'. For it is only too evident that a 'world-view' includes a 'value-view', and that the latter often takes priority.

It is no doubt as presenting a 'world-view' that metaphysics has made its greatest appeal down the ages. Here we find the great world-view philosophies—particularly those of idealism and materialism—in ceaseless conflict with one another as to which of them gives the right interpretation of existence as a whole. Is the world ultimately of a spiritual or a material nature? Is its true meaning to be found in ideas or in matter? It is of course generally recognized that there is some truth in the old saying that the kind of philosophy a man has depends on the kind of man he is; that is to say, the attitude he takes to the various 'philosophies' is evaluative. But this, as metaphysics sees it, need not imply any abandonment of the scientific attitude, because value itself is something objectively given and can be objectively discussed. Here the idea of the unity of 'being' and 'value' proves useful. For whether being or value is regarded as the primary and decisive thing, we are in either case on the firm ground of scientific objectivity. The difference between the special sciences and metaphysics lies simply in the fact that the former, as being attached each

37

to its own aspect of reality, can only present particular and partial views of it, whereas metaphysics as a world-view presents it as a whole.

4) *Metaphysics as conceptual realism.* The expression 'conceptual realism' no doubt suggests first and foremost Platonic realism and kindred views, which start with general concepts and values and transpose them into the realm of reified and substantialized Ideas, where as self-subsistent entities they represent the true reality of which sensible things are only shadow-images. However, conceptual realism belongs not only to a particular kind of metaphysics, but is characteristic of all metaphysics whatsoever. Even materialism operates with certain general concepts—chiefly that of matter itself—which it substantializes and treats as true reality and the ground of being. There is a common element that binds all the different forms of metaphysics together, and this in turn goes back to the 'ontological' way of thinking about 'being', although they conceive of 'being' in very different ways. Whether they speak of eternal ideas and eternal objective values, or of an eternal matter and eternal laws of nature, the basic structure is in both cases the same, namely metaphysical and conceptually realist. It is ultimately the same ontological conception of 'being' that underlies the different outlooks, and that justifies our describing all of them as 'metaphysics' despite all differences between them in other respects.

5) *Deductive and inductive metaphysics.* At first the obvious method for metaphysics to use was that of deduction. Since its aim was to present a unified view of the world, it had to find a unitary starting point for the contemplation of existence, a point from which everything could in some measure be derived and deduced. This was also in excellent accord with its claim to be a universal science. The deductive method seemed to furnish the possibility of arriving both more easily and more surely than the special sciences at an indisputable knowledge of the nature of being. More easily, because the laborious researches of the special sciences could at best lead only to a fragmentary knowledge, whereas metaphysics in virtue of its deductive procedure seemed very well able to reach an all-embracing view. It would do this also more surely, because deduction appeared capable, as induction in its permanent imperfection and incompleteness was not, of providing it with firm ground on which to stand. Whereas the empirical sciences could furnish information about the factual but always contingent situation, metaphysics as a rational science could determine how things *must* be—and that not only in our empirical world, but 'in all possible worlds'.

A change was bound to come, however, as the departmental sciences progressed and learnt really to master their improved methods. It could not in the long run be overlooked that the special sciences, just because of their specialization, were able to obtain results that far surpassed those of metaphysics in their incisiveness and dependability. Deduction, which was the accepted method of the rational sciences such as formal logic, geometry and so forth, appeared increasingly questionable when it was employed in other areas; yet metaphysics still claimed the ability to handle the ontological problem with its objective implications. In this situation it found itself obliged at least to some extent to switch to the inductive line. Only so did it seem able to maintain its claim to be a science. It thus came to be seen as the task of metaphysics, not so much to compete with the departmental sciences in answering the same questions by a different method, but rather to take their results and fit them together in a unified world-view.

6) *The idea of a metaphysical system.* By way of summary and conclusion we may refer briefly to the idea of a system in metaphysics. Inasmuch as metaphysics conceives being as a unity, maintains the unity of being and value, aims at producing a unified world-view, and presupposes (in its conceptual realism) the unity of the logical and the ontological, it follows that it can finally come to rest only in a completed system of thought which is all-inclusive in the sense that all being and all value find their place in it. This is so not only for aesthetic reasons but by a certain positive necessity. It is only in an all-embracing system that the inherent tendency of metaphysics to universality comes to rest. At the same time justice is apparently done also to the scientific tendency. The individual sciences are not, after all, content simply to observe and record the phenomena they find in their several spheres, but they seek also to *explain* them. To this end they put forward certain general theories and hypotheses which alone make it possible to view the different phenomena together and so to understand and explain them. This urge to interpret and unify which is inherent in all science, metaphysics as a universal science seeks to carry through to completion. The doctrines of metaphysics, whether they are arrived at deductively or inductively, are conceived as scientific theories or hypotheses, which differ from those of the other sciences only in that they are of higher rank and of such comprehensiveness that they can serve to interpret existence as a whole.

(2) *The scientific status of metaphysics?*

In the preceding paragraphs we have given a short account of the nature of metaphysics and the factors that have produced it. In doing so we have been able to confine ourselves to pointing out a number of its specially important features. We have now to face the all-important question of the scientific status of metaphysics. That the philosophical interest in universality has been preserved, has been clear at every point, but we have been left in uncertainty as to how far the requirements of science have been met. It is, of course, plain enough that metaphysics in general believes it can do justice to the demands of science as well. The question that now arises therefore is this: Does metaphysics merely claim to be a science, or is it able also in practice to satisfy the demands of science? Might it perhaps be described as 'holding the form of science but denying the power of it'?[13] Before we try to answer this question, however, a preliminary observation is necessary concerning the claim of metaphysics to be a science, since even about this claim there is some ambiguity.

If metaphysics is a science, it cannot in the nature of the case be so in quite the same sense as the special sciences. Yet it is from the latter that we learn what real science is, and it is inevitable that we should take our cue from them in deciding what the criterion of science is. Now when this criterion is applied to metaphysics, there is a double reaction to it as regards the claim of the latter to be a science. On the one hand there is a readiness to *scale down* the scientific requirements almost to vanishing point, and on the other a directly opposite tendency to *inflate* the claim to scientific status far beyond the bursting point.

The *scaling down* occurs not only as a defensive measure on the part of metaphysics when it has difficulty in sustaining the more exacting requirements of science. The idea has also infected scientific philosophy itself, which ought to have no difficulty in satisfying those requirements. Hence we often find, quite outside the realm of metaphysics, a remarkable reserve and caution in speaking of the scientific status of philosophy. There is a marked tendency to avoid describing philosophy as a science, and to speak of it instead as a special sort of 'activity', different in kind from science. In itself such caution may be laudable, even from the standpoint of scientific philosophy; for although philosophy definitely belongs in the scientific camp, it is not science in the same sense as the special sciences, and it has a different structure from theirs. To this extent the idea of philosophy as an activity different—though not in kind—from science (= the special sciences) is entirely correct. Yet the effect of it is unfortunate as regards the question we are concerned with here. For it encourages the blurring of the distinction between metaphysical and scientific philosophy, and makes it easier for metaphysics to evade the careful inquiry into its scientific status which ought to be made. It enables metaphysics both to maintain its claim to be scientific and yet to suit its own convenience by scaling down the scientific requirements and so to continue unperturbed on its traditional, methodologically ambiguous way.

At the same time there is on the contemporary scene a metaphysics that puts itself forward with the most *inflated* scientific claims. The plainest example of this is in Heinrich Scholz—and that, surprisingly enough, in his later, logicistic period. Whereas the representatives of logicism, especially those of a logical positivist or empiricist type, have generally had no use at all for metaphysics, Scholz has retained his interest in it from his earlier period, and since his encounter with logicism he has made still more exalted scientific claims for it. The titles of two of

[13] *Cf.* 2 Tim. 3:5 (RSV).

the most important works of his later period clearly attest his double concern: *Metaphysik als strenge Wissenschaft* (1941) and *Mathesis Universalis* (1961).

What Scholz is after, as the first of these titles shows, is a metaphysics which is not only in a general way scientific, but which deserves to be called an 'exact science'. He wants 'a new, dependable metaphysics, a metaphysics whose metaphysical character is as evident as its dependability'.[14] The double claim could not be more clearly formulated: strictly metaphysical and at the same time strictly scientific. Indeed, Scholz anticipates a metaphysics that will surpass even mathematics in the precision with which it defines its terms. It is of course obvious that this is an idea for which there is no support whatever. We have here two 'sciences' that are subject to totally different conditions: mathematics, which is directly intended for 'precise mathematical' definition, and metaphysics which is no such thing; mathematics, which can build its intellectual house with such simple and easily defined things as numbers and their relations, and metaphysics which operates with the most elusive and basically indefinable concepts.

Scholz's position has been quoted here, however, not in order to present a critique of it, but simply to illustrate how far a man can go in stepping up the claim of metaphysics to scientific status. It should moreover be said that to all appearances Scholz does not mean by 'metaphysics' quite the same as is generally understood by that term, though he never makes himself really clear on this point. He vacillates between logical clarification in a more modern vein, and metaphysics in the traditional, ontological sense.[15] But this uncertain veering between scientific philosophy and metaphysical speculation has serious consequences. It surrounds metaphysics with a spurious aura of science, and it compromises philosophy as a whole, including scientific philosophy.

The second title, *Mathesis Universalis*, is equally illuminating. It reveals very plainly the source from which the inspiration for this whole conception has come. The spirit of Leibniz broods over it all. Here is Leibniz's idea of a '*characteristica universalis*' (somewhat modified under the influence of Frege); here is the idea of a language formalized on the mathematical model, which is supposed to make exact mathematical calculation possible in metaphysics and thus to give metaphysics the status of an 'exact science'. There is in Scholz as in Leibniz the same combination of strictly mathematical method with free metaphysical speculation, all gathered up in a common *Mathesis Universalis*. This is what explains the vacillation mentioned above between scientific philosophy on the one hand and metaphysical speculation on the other.

As we have already said, Scholz has been cited here chiefly in order to

14 Scholz, *Metaphysik*, p. 5; *cf.* p. 11: 'A metaphysics of the order of an exact science.'
15 *Ibid.*, pp. 172ff.

41

provide an example of a modern metaphysics which lays claim to be an 'exact science'.[16] We thus have before us a contemporary metaphysical outlook which, while preserving the characteristic features of metaphysics that we sketched briefly above, claims at the same time to do full and complete justice to the requirements of science. This claim must now be examined.

As soon as we turn to this task it is clear that the entire series of characteristics which we attributed to metaphysics, constitutes as many gravamina against its scientific character.

1) Take to begin with the *ontological* question, or the question of 'being'. This could undoubtedly be put in an entirely legitimate way if it were simply a matter of asking what we *mean* when we say that something is or exists. Nor would there be any reason to object, if by 'ontology' no more were meant than a discussion of the copula 'is' and what it implies. Such questions are clear and unequivocal; it makes good sense to ask them, and they can be scientifically analyzed and answered. It is entirely different with the questions metaphysics raises when it speaks of 'ontology'. These have to do with 'being in general', 'being itself', 'true reality', 'the ultimate nature of existence', or however it may be phrased. Here we must ask: Have these questions any meaning? Are they capable of being answered? This is not to suggest that such questions are too vast or profound for us with our limited intellectual resources to be capable of answering them. There are, of course, questions of that kind, but the deficiency of our intellectual equipment is no reason for denying the scientific validity of questions. A much more serious issue is at stake here, namely whether such ontological questions as metaphysics poses are in any way meaningful. What makes it impossible to answer them is not that the right answer is too difficult to find; it is rather that there is no right answer, because there is simply no answer at all. An answer presupposes a genuine question, and what makes things impossible here is that the question has no recognizable meaning.

If we start with the 'ontological' questions we described above as legitimate, and ask what we mean when we say that something is or exists, we can easily see how metaphysics has gone off on the wrong track. It happens in several stages. To begin with there is the concrete meaning of the words 'is' and 'exists' and so forth. The first mistake is made when the verb is replaced by a substantive, and that which 'is' becomes a 'being'. With this there is already an incipient obscuration of thought; for what, after all, really is this 'being'? The next step is to substantialize it, so that the being becomes a substance. But that is not all: the substance is further hypo-

---

[16] We might also have cited in this connection Bertrand Russell, who displays a similar combination of strict mathematical precision and loose metaphysical speculations, and who is likewise influenced by Leibniz. We have preferred, however, to stick to Scholz as a better and more extreme example of the type.

statized and projected on to a higher plane, a higher level of existence, which can be called 'the world of true being'. The simple 'is' has been turned into an 'entity', and a question is raised as to its 'nature'. Then there is a further question as to which phenomena can be described as 'entities'. Can only things be so described, or can their properties also be regarded as 'entities'? Does this apply to relations as well as to universals? At this final stage there is no end of questions—though they are pseudo-questions, sham questions, without any clear meaning. One cannot help recalling the old formula: *Entia non sunt multiplicanda praeter necessitatem.*[17] Metaphysics has 'entities' far beyond what is necessary. They are necessitated only by the habit metaphysics has of asking unnecessary and meaningless questions.

2) The equation of *'being'* and *'value'* has accompanied metaphysics throughout its history, and can be reckoned as one of its most important characteristics. At the same time this theory constitutes a serious threat to everything scientific. Here the contrast between metaphysics and science is unusually clear. For unless the distinction between being and value is preserved, the idea of the objectivity of science becomes illusory. The way in which reality is conceived will then depend in the last resort not so much on what can be objectively read out of it, as on what the evaluating subject wishes to find in it. This may be illustrated by two or three examples drawn from widely different times and places.

That value has the primacy in *Platonic thought* is beyond question. It could almost be said that because Plato values the world of Ideas, therefore it becomes for him the true reality, and because he has a low opinion of the sense-world, it becomes for him a world of shadows. Plato himself makes no secret of the fact that for him the way leads from value to being. How indeed could it be otherwise at that early stage, when science was still undeveloped and the preconditions were therefore lacking for a clear distinction between being and value, or between ascertaining and evaluating? It could in fact be argued that in comparison with other metaphysicians Plato comes off best, because for him it was possible to regard the flight into the world of ideas as precisely the way to ensure objectivity. Yet even when the preconditions for a distinction between being and value were present as a result of the subsequent development of science, metaphysics still persisted in ignoring the distinction and letting the two run together.

Our second example comes from a later time and from *Marxism*. Although its exponents are in the habit of describing 'dialectical materialism' as the 'scientifically' established view, it has in fact nothing whatever to do with science. Here again we have a theory in which being is value and value is being. The centre of interest lies in the economic and social aspect of life, and this represents the value; hence it is this that is con-

[17] 'Entities must not be multiplied beyond necessity'—Ockham's Razor.

ceived as the really real, while anything else that appears to exist can at most be accorded a secondary status as an 'ideological superstructure'.

Our third example comes from the contemporary situation. The most widespread and deeply rooted metaphysics in our time is that which is called '*scientism*'. This is specially interesting because, although its conscious intent is to stand for science and nothing but science, yet in fact it is nothing else but a crude form of metaphysics. Sometimes described as 'scientific superstition' it is rarely met with among genuine scientists, who know from their own experience what science is, but it is all the more frequent among those who admire science from a distance. As a result of the value attached to it, no account is taken of anything but science and 'what Science says'. Everything else vanishes out of sight. There is a blind faith in 'Science', although science itself does not want anyone to 'believe' in it in that way. This sort of 'scientific metaphysics' or 'scientific superstition' is completely foreign to all genuine science. If it is asked why such a 'believer in Science' takes no account of anything in the world but 'Science', the answer is wholly tautological: it is because he takes no account of it. There is an arbitrary, unwarrantable judgment of value behind all this, together with the equation of being and value. With this, however, we come to the question of a 'scientific world-view'.

3) Metaphysics as *world-view*. That metaphysics cannot claim to mediate any scientific knowledge of reality is implied already in the term 'world-view'. The point is that what it involves is a unified *view* of the world. But a view by its very nature is subjective. Just as the world around us presents a different appearance according to the point of view from which we look at it, so existence as a whole looks very different according as we choose one or another starting point for our reflection on it. If we choose an idealistic starting point, the whole will quite naturally reveal itself in an idealistic light. If we choose a materialistic starting point, everything will be coloured by that, and so forth. There is of course nothing to prevent people from choosing different starting points for their view. But when metaphysics sets itself up as a doctrine, it naturally cannot take account of all the available possibilities, for that would never lead to a unified world-view, which is what metaphysics wants. It has to make a choice, and for this choice it can give no really objective grounds. If metaphysics would simply and forthrightly admit that it has selected one of the many possible aspects and made this its starting point, it would be less open to objection.

Although the term 'world-view' is rather pretentious, all of us presumably have some sort of conception of the world we live in, and in that vague, general sense a sort of 'world-view'—and no harm in that. If we were content with this, we could if we wished assign a reasonable function to metaphysics at this simple level, by saying that each of its different varieties has the task of developing its own particular one of the many fundamentally possible outlooks on life and thereby ministering to the individual's need for orientation. But metaphysics has never been willing to be content with this, and to be simply one among many possible views. Instead, it regards its own point of view as the right one, and others that differ from it as wrong. It claims to have adopted the only legitimate standpoint. This is the cardinal error of metaphysics, that it puts forward its own more or less subjective and often quite arbitrarily chosen starting point as alone objectively valid and scientifically based. By doing so it involves itself in a great self-contradiction. For any idea of a 'scientific world-view' is a monstrosity, a contradiction in terms. Science is not a world-view, and a world-view is not science. The fact that metaphysics is based on a confusion between these two, robs it of every trace of scientific legitimacy.[18]

What has been said here about 'world-view' applies also in a measure to the closely related concept of 'world-picture'. During the later part of the nineteenth century and around the turn of the century, it was believed in many quarters that science had progressed to a point where it could gather up its findings in a 'scientific world-picture' or, as it was often called, 'the modern world-picture'—by which was meant the mechanistic conception of the world. This was at a time when men believed they had solved 'the riddles of the universe', or at least were well on the way to doing so. That time is now past. Subsequent research has clearly shown the mechanistic picture to be untenable.[19] It would however be wrong to interpret this—though it has often been done—as meaning that the mechanistic has given place in modern natural science to another picture—one of a more living and organic character, for example. No, what has happened in more recent research is of a far more revolutionary nature. We have reached a point where not only one particular picture but all such pictures have proved unwarrantable. It has become essentially meaningless to speak of a picture of the world. We stand at a parting of the ways which is of far more decisive significance than is generally realized.

Intoxicated by the natural sciences and the unprecedented triumphs of technology based on them, mankind had for several centuries been persuaded that the world was essentially a vast machine governed by the laws

[18] On metaphysics as 'world-view' see my more detailed discussions in 'Den metafysiska filosofiens betydelse' in FKE (pp. 116ff.). 'World-view' here represents the Sw. *världsåskådning*, Ger. *Weltanschauung*. It has become familiar enough to be used instead of 'outlook on life' or 'philosophy of life' which would often be the more natural English phrase, but which would complicate the translation and obscure important points in the argument.—Tr.)

[19] G. Ludwig, *Das naturwissenschaftliche Weltbild*, p. 65: 'The mechanistic world is not a scientific but a philosophical hypothesis.' ('Picture of the world' and 'world-picture' represent the Sw. *världsbild*, Ger. *Weltbild*. 'World-picture' is less familiar in English than 'world-view', but there is good precedent for it in E. J. Dijksterhuis's *The Mechanisation of the World-Picture*.—Tr.)

of nature as its 'efficient causes'—a fundamentally primitive notion which no modern scientist shares. The modern scientist knows only too well that the laws of nature are our attempt to formularize the order which we find in nature, and to which we must pay heed if we wish to deal with it successfully. But this is a long way from the promulgation of any sort of metaphysics. Modern science and technology have certainly far greater conquests to show today than in the past, but at the same time they have become more clearly aware of the nature and scope of their own methods, and of the fact that the strict application of these can never lead to any scientific metaphysics or scientific world-view or world-picture. Contemporary natural science has thus come to a clear realization of those 'limits of scientific conceptualization' of which Heinrich Rickert spoke prophetically at the turn of the century.

The more that modern natural science reduces its investigations to basic mathematical formulae, the further it becomes removed from any kind of visual perception, and for that reason alone it is impossible to go on talking about a picture of the world. Certainly the scientist can work with visual models in order to make his theory plain to himself and others; but he knows that what he is speaking about is essentially invisible and can therefore never give rise to any picture of the world. This is the new situation in which we find ourselves, and it reveals in a new way how indefensible metaphysics is from a scientific point of view. Both its world-views and world-pictures merit the trenchant verdict that they are 'views of something that cannot be viewed'.

4) *Conceptual realism*. This point calls for no lengthy discussion. It is true that conceptual realism is at the very heart of metaphysics, and is closely connected with all its other main features. At the same time, the error of this kind of thinking is so obvious that a detailed analysis of it would be superfluous. The nature of the error may be indicated by reference to Axel Hägerström's well-known description of metaphysics as the view 'which makes of reality as such—reality itself—something real'. Modifying this a little we could say that it involves a confusion between the concept of reality (or what we *mean* when we describe something as real) and that to which the concept is applied when we describe something as real. What this means can be simply illustrated by a glaring example from another sphere. In a class of little children the teacher is trying to explain the meaning of the number 'four', the concept of 'four', and for this purpose places four real objects, say four apples, on the desk. Then, when the children are asked what 'four' is, they answer that it is the apples. They confuse the four real objects with the concept of four.

Metaphysics is guilty of an analogous confusion. It seizes on one or other of the many things we call real, and says this is 'reality'. It identifies certain real objects with the concept of reality, and then proceeds to the idea (or rather the delusion) that this is 'reality itself'. It is not only with the concept of reality that this happens, however, although metaphysics has always had a special leaning to the latter. The same mistake is made when the concept of validity is taken to imply that there is a 'validity itself' which is supposed to be the principle underlying whatever is judged to be valid, and from which all other forms of validity can be derived. The same happens again when the concept of truth, or the simple fact that we describe one statement as 'true' and another as 'false', is taken to imply that there is a 'truth itself' which is the principle of all truth—another leading idea of metaphysics.

The confusion here spoken of is obvious; and it might well tempt us to go a step further and say with positivism that metaphysics is just plain 'nonsense', a congeries of words without meaning. But a word of caution is necessary here. Even if metaphysics is meaningless and therefore 'nonsense' in so far as it is regarded as a scientific theory, is it not possible that from other points of view it might have some meaning? We shall discuss this possibility in the section on 'Conceptual Poetry' below—though it cannot acquit metaphysics of the charge that it is from a scientific point of view completely indefensible.

5) *Deductive and inductive metaphysics.* In an inquiry into the scientific status of metaphysics, the question of its methodology cannot but be of particular interest. As we have already observed, metaphysics has made use of both the deductive and the inductive method. The question therefore is, what the use of these methods implies with regard to its standing as a science.

The fact that metaphysics has traditionally worked with the *deductive* method, has often been taken as an objection to it and as evidence of its scientific defectiveness. That in itself is not an argument that necessarily carries much weight, for there is nothing compromising in the deductive method as such. Not even the fact that metaphysics starts with certain primary axioms, which in the nature of the case are indemonstrable, need be taken in itself as a decisive objection to it. It is a procedure with which we are familiar from all axiomatic theorizing. Its weakness becomes apparent, however, when in order to bring itself fully into line with other axiomatic sciences metaphysics describes its axioms as 'self-evident'. For it is just here that the decisive difference between the axiomatic sciences and metaphysics lies. The primary axioms of metaphysics are anything but 'self-evident'. It is rather these that all the controversy is about.

What one metaphysical theory regards as axiomatic is precisely what others attack as a prime delusion. On many particular points the various theories may be in agreement, but about the principles, or the starting point and the primary axioms, there is heated debate. To describe these axioms as 'self-evident' when they are so thoroughly controversial, cannot be said to be anything but an abuse of words. 'Disputed', 'uncertain', 'doubtful', 'arbitrarily assumed'—these are the only adequate descriptions

47

of them. The only justification that can be offered for them is that this or that school of thought has elected to regard them as axioms and is determined to stick to them. In short, their only justification is a *'sic volo, sic jubeo'*.[20] To establish metaphysics as a science on such a basis is obviously impossible. As a deductive science metaphysics is indefensible, though not because there is anything wrong with deduction as such, but because of the complete arbitrariness of the primary axioms which are the starting point for the deduction—an arbitrariness which it seems impossible to avoid within the framework of deductive metaphysics.

It was in order to overcome this difficulty that the change was made in metaphysics from the deductive to the *inductive* method. What it could not accomplish by deduction it might perhaps accomplish by induction. This seemed to bring it into line with the trend that was characteristic of so much of the science of recent centuries: the empirical trend. If its earlier, speculative bent had led it into a cul-de-sac, it might have better success if it were remodelled in conformity with the empirical sciences. Such a remodelling must, of course, have its limits; it must still be the main business of metaphysics to deal with first principles. But it would unquestionably be an immense gain if with the aid of the inductive method the arbitrariness of the primary axioms could be overcome.

Whereas the deductive method generally speaking starts with a proposition of which the validity is assumed, and proceeds from that to the particulars, it is characteristic of the inductive method that it starts with particular ascertained facts and works its way back from these to the general laws and principles underlying them. Now is not the latter just what metaphysics needs? Here it stands, completely unable to give any reason for its primary axioms, when along comes induction to the rescue and by linking the axioms with empirical observations gives it the possibility of an inductive legitimation of them. Induction thus seems to give metaphysics firm ground under its feet and put it on a par with the other, empirical sciences, which also have to anchor their general laws ('the laws of nature') inductively in empirical reality. Granted that metaphysics cannot now, as it once did, claim supremacy over the rest of the sciences; that it cannot lay claim to any superior cognitive faculty which opens the way to 'the nature of existence'; and that it cannot solve all problems by the royal road of deduction; yet thanks to induction it does not need to stand in isolation from the rest of the sciences, alone suspected of lacking scientific legitimacy and of busying itself with 'pseudo-problems'. It can, by the same means and with the same cogency as the rest, legitimate its initial affirmations and axioms.

They are no slight advantages which the inductive method holds in prospect for metaphysics. They can be summed up in three points as

[20] *Cf.* Juvenal, *Satires* iii. 223: 'I will it, I insist on it! Let my will stand instead of reason.'

follows. 1. The chief of them is the one already mentioned, that induction points the way to overcome the arbitrariness which otherwise seems unavoidable when metaphysics enunciates its first principles. For deductive metaphysics these principles were given in advance, they were the starting point of the demonstration, and consequently they had about them and imparted to the whole an air of prejudice and arbitrariness. Inductive metaphysics takes a precisely opposite course. For it, the principles are not the first thing, which it knows in advance, but the last, which its investigation is intended to discover, and which emerges as a result of the induction. From this two other advantages follow. 2. Metaphysics appears by this means to gain a firm foothold in given experience. It is thus delivered from the appearance of being nothing but 'empty speculation'. For it is from experience, not speculation, that induction draws its material. 3. Lastly, metaphysics appears by this means to be put in very close touch with the special sciences, and that in two ways.

First of all there is their community of method. For while metaphysics still sticks to its universal task, it nonetheless has its place among the ranks of the sciences and works essentially with the same method as they. Just as they put forward their general hypotheses and test them as to their agreement with what is empirically given, so does inductive metaphysics. It sets up hypotheses, which are admittedly of so general a kind that they can be called axioms or principles, but which—and this is the essential thing—are not simply enunciated but are also subjected by means of induction to verificational testing. Metaphysics thus finds a place in the ordinary context of the sciences. Its axioms can be described as 'scientific hypotheses'—though of a higher order—which are capable of being tested like any other scientific hypothesis. There is, however, also another respect in which induction establishes a close working relationship between inductive metaphysics and the special sciences, inasmuch as metaphysics is founded on them and seeks to be a compendium of them. There is still something incomplete about the results at which the special sciences have arrived. These results serve as the basis of induction for metaphysics; they are the material out of which it seeks to construct a unified worldview.

The program looks promising; but can it be carried out? To this question the answer can only be a decided No. The advantage promised by inductive metaphysics is more apparent than real. On the face of it, the new metaphysics is the diametrical opposite of the old, but in reality it is nothing else but the old in a new dress. It makes its propositions look as if they are founded on experience and arrived at by induction; yet in fact these propositions are themselves the basis of the induction. This is connected with the difficulties which are involved in all induction, and which are commonly summed up in the phrase 'the problem of induction'. But these difficulties are intensified when induction comes to be employed in metaphysics. When inductive metaphysics seeks to furnish empirical proof of the principles of experience—in itself an impossible task—its procedure is a typical *circulus in demonstrando*. Its attitude to the principles is just as dogmatic as that of deductive metaphysics, only it knows how to conceal this with the help of a specious proof. The arbitrariness remains, the relation to experience is only apparent, and the connection with the special sciences is fictitious. What is more, when inductive metaphysics has thus arbitrarily obtained its principles or axioms, it conceives them as ontological realities in the metaphysical sense, and so lays itself open to the same objections that have had to be brought against deductive metaphysics.[21]

When in its desire to draw as close a parallel as possible between metaphysics and science, inductive metaphysics compares its 'axioms' with the 'hypotheses' of the sciences, it both suggests a correspondence that does not exist and diverts attention from fundamental differences that do. It is true that in scientific work 'hypotheses' play a decisive part; but there is one thing about them we must never forget. Hypotheses exist in order to be tested and verified. It is only through confrontation with the empirical material, and only after they have survived this test, that they are recognized as genuine scientific hypotheses. It is thus a basic requirement for a hypothesis that it should be amenable to such critical examination and thus capable of being confirmed or possibly refuted by experience. There is nothing corresponding to all this on the metaphysical level.

What decisively distinguishes metaphysical doctrines from scientific hypotheses is the fact that they are essentially incapable of being tested, criticized, refuted. No negative instance can be brought to bear against them. By their very construction metaphysical ideas are protected against all attack. They are completely sovereign in their own sphere. They have thus nothing in common with the hypotheses of science. Consequently not even as 'inductive metaphysics' can metaphysics attain scientific status. Whether deductive or inductive, metaphysics is equally far from meeting the requirements of science.

6) *The idea of a metaphysical system.* Everything said in the preceding paragraphs amounts in effect to a single sustained attack on the idea of a metaphysical system. For in that idea everything is gathered up—ontology and the unity of being and value, world-view and conceptual realism, deduction and induction. To refute it therefore would be to repeat bit by bit the criticism already presented. We are in the odd position here of having to refute an idea that has already been refuted. Instead of engaging in that unprofitable task, we prefer simply to let the idea itself—without formal refutation—provide the final flourish of this section, which has had the purpose of showing how untenable the claim of metaphysics to be a science is.

[21] For a more detailed treatment of the position outlined here, see my essay, 'Hur är filosofi som vetenskap möjlig?'

(3) Metaphysics as a 'natural disposition' and as 'conceptual poetry'

So far our investigation has led to a purely negative result. It has shown that the claim of metaphysics to rank as a science is completely unjustified and must be rejected. Its slippery use of terms, its baseless identifications, and its continual confusion of things that ought to be kept distinct, make it impossible not to question its meaningfulness. Measured by the standards of science it falls short on every count. Whatever else metaphysics may be, science it is not.

In reaching this negative conclusion, however, we are far from having done with metaphysics. For whatever may be said of it from a scientific point of view, and no matter how abstruse its ideas often seem to be, there is nevertheless something very natural about the metaphysical way of thinking. The transition from everyday thinking to metaphysics is almost automatic. There is accurate and significant observation behind Kant's often quoted words about metaphysics as a *'natural disposition'*. There is a bent towards metaphysical thinking. In attacking metaphysics we have nature against us. Even when we see it to be scientifically indefensible, we find it anything but easy to avoid. This is very clear from the fact that many of its bitterest opponents themselves fall victims to an open or concealed metaphysics. The more vigorously they try to overcome it, the more it lurks in the background. It recalls Horace's famous line, *'Naturam expellas furca, tamen usque recurret'*[22] and its amusing Danish parody: *Naturam furca pellas ex Hun kommer dog igen, den Heks.*[23] Nature returns; metaphysics returns. It presents us therefore with the never-ending task— not of destroying it, but of rendering it innocuous by continually exposing it, exposing the falsity of its claim to rank as a science.

The metaphysical way of looking at things can be compared to an optical illusion. Even when we see and know it is an illusion, we cannot without more ado free ourselves from it. Nor is it necessary to do so. There is no need to be constantly combating optical illusions, no need to be continually reminding ourselves that things are not in reality the same as they quite naturally seem to be to us. We can go on calmly speaking of the sun as rising and setting. Why? Because we do not make a scientific theory of it. With metaphysics the position is different. Metaphysics does claim to be a scientific theory. If only it did not, we should not be obliged to be continually combating it. But as it does we must, because it involves a falsification of existence. Its fundamental error, the illusion on which it lives and which must be combated, consists in its imagining that it sees reality as it really is. It is the ontological mistake.

Even if at some point metaphysics happened to be right—and why should it not?—about a particular matter under discussion, it would still

[22] Horace, *Epistles*, I. x. 24: 'You may expel nature with a pitchfork, but she will soon find a way back.'
[23] 'Back she'll come again, the witch!'

be wrong as a whole. For its error lies not so much in the outlook or theory it propounds, as in the confusion of which it is guilty in its presentation. This confusion is twofold: it involves a failure to distinguish 1. between reality and given reality, so that a certain particular reality is wrongly identified with the concept of reality—which is the big, fundamental mistake of all metaphysics; and 2. between metaphysics and science, which is a disastrous case of category mixing—and the most compromising thing of all for metaphysics. For nothing makes metaphysics more suspect than its insistence on forcing itself into the category of science, where it does not belong. By doing so it also forces its critics to measure it by the standards of science. When they do this they are not applying an extraneous criterion, but one which is demanded by the subject matter itself. Even when metaphysics very substantially moderates its scientific claims, as we have seen that it sometimes does, it does not thereby become exempt from this scientific testing. For in practice it still keeps up the pretensions which in theory it may have found itself obliged to tone down.

Metaphysics has in reality no claim whatever to scientific objectivity. Yet even when on occasion it admits this itself, the admission rarely goes further than a theoretical statement. In practice and in expounding its views, it likes to preserve the appearance of science. The argument proceeds *as if* metaphysics were a science, and this is misleading: scientific pretentions are both renounced and retained. The requirements of science are set aside—as they must be in order to produce a theory about things which by nature are inaccessible to science—and at the same time they are insisted on because otherwise the argument would not be taken as seriously as is desired. This ambiguity, quite as much as the clearly expressed claim, makes it necessary to test metaphysics by scientific standards.

When the problem of metaphysics is approached from this angle, it has to be admitted that Hume was right in his total rejection of it, and that logical positivism (or empiricism) is amply justified in characterizing it as 'nonsense'. For from a scientific point of view it is impossible to find any concrete meaning in an outlook which is so largely based on factual and linguistic confusion. Yet without in any way denying this, we must at the same time observe that the Humean and positivist criticism rests to a large extent on false premises. Hume is an excellent example, and logical positivism not less so, of the way in which it is possible to combat metaphysics from a metaphysical starting point and in a metaphysical manner. This explains, incidentally, the ruthless will to destroy which in both cases accompanies the objective criticism. It is a case of one metaphysic taking the field against another.

In this connection the words with which Hume concludes his *Enquiry concerning Human Understanding* are revealing. He ponders there the devastating effect it would have on libraries if his principles were put into practice. With regard to every book we take from the shelves we ought to ask two questions: 1. '*Does it contain any abstract reasoning concerning quantity or number?*' and 2. '*Does it contain any experimental reasoning concerning matter of fact and existence?*' If the answer to both these questions is 'No', Hume's recommendation is: 'Commit it then to the flames: for it can contain nothing but sophistry and illusion.'[24] Naturally this advice of Hume's is not intended to be taken literally, but it sufficiently reveals his own metaphysical commitment. The fundamental error of metaphysics is not, after all, that it is not a science—for it might well be something else—but that it unjustifiably claims to be a science. Hence the shift of emphasis in Hume from what metaphysics claims to the simple fact that it is not a science, points in the direction of a 'scientistic metaphysics', as if the fact that something is not a science constituted a decisive argument against it. There may after all be other things than science that are worth noticing; and to deny that there are, is to betray a metaphysical identification of 'being and value'.

How much poorer our libraries and our entire cultural life would be, if everything that did not 'contain any abstract reasoning concerning quantity or number' or any 'experimental reasoning concerning matter of fact and existence' were committed to the flames! Hume presents himself here as an iconoclast, launching an assault on everything that cannot be reduced to the formulae of mathematics or 'experience'; and it is the iconoclasm that reveals the metaphysician. The fact that Hume in spite of his 'empiricism', or rather just because of it, is most decidedly a metaphysician, is of course nowadays generally acknowledged. His verdict, 'Commit it to the flames', would apply not only to the whole world of Platonic thought (for example), but to the greater part of the priceless treasures of mankind, and also—alas!—to the work of Hume himself.

What has just been said of Hume and his attack on metaphysics is true, moreover, also of logical positivism, which has in substantial measure drawn its inspiration from him. Its exclusive concentration on the tautologies of logic and the sense-data of experience as the only guarantee against the 'nonsense' of metaphysics, bears all the marks of Hume's metaphysical position.

We cannot, however, be content simply to establish the negative fact that the claim of metaphysics to be a science is illegitimate; we must go further and inquire into its genuine status—if it has one. The most apt characterization of it is that introduced by F. A. Lange, who calls it '*Begriffsdichtung*', 'conceptual poetry'. That is exactly what metaphysics is. It is not science, but poetry, though a poetry which works with concepts as its material. The term 'conceptual poetry' sums up all there is to be said, both positively and negatively, about metaphysics. Perhaps it is natural to seize first on the negative aspect—if it is poetry, then it is *not* science. That is no doubt why the term 'conceptual poetry' has often been taken as

[24] Hume, *Enquiries*, p. 165.

simply one more derogatory epithet, and as implying that there is no need to pay much attention to metaphysics, since it is only a matter of poetry, not reality. This negative aspect, however, we have had ample opportunity to illustrate in the preceding pages, and our primary concern now is with the positive. For the idea of 'conceptual poetry' carries with it a certain liberation for metaphysics. It takes it out of the category of 'science', where it is so little at home, and places it in another category, that of 'poetry'. It transfers it from one context to another, where it can perhaps do itself more justice.

Naturally the comment may be made here that this is a peculiar and more than questionable way of employing concepts. Is it not contrary to the very nature of a concept to be used in the work of a poet? Are not concepts cut and polished for quite other purposes? There is undoubtedly much truth in this observation. What is more, it is precisely the use of concepts as material for poetry that has led to the habit of regarding what by nature belongs to the category of poetry as if it belonged instead to that of science. On the other hand, it is unwise to prescribe rules for poetry as to what material it may or may not use. Here we have to face facts. Poetry does not call a halt either at the everyday meaning of words, or at images and metaphors, concepts, paradoxes and much more besides.

The characterization of metaphysics as 'conceptual poetry' greatly alters its status. Much of the objection made to it when it appears as having scientific aspirations, loses its point when it appears in its true colours as 'conceptual poetry'. Why should we 'commit it to the flames' just because it is not science? In its new status we can no longer judge it in terms of logical tautologies or empirical sense-data, nor can we speak of it without qualification as 'nonsense'. The term 'conceptual poetry' underlines the need for us to recognize the fact that there can be *meaning* even where words are not put together in the way they are in scientific language. Poetry has a different meaning. Anyone who reads a poem and thinks of it as if it were a scientific theory will of course find it to be 'nonsense'. Nevertheless it has its own meaning. What is 'different' is not necessarily meaningless. Terms like 'nonsense' and 'meaninglessness' must be used in a more qualified—and therefore more meaningful—way.

It has been necessary to find room for this section on 'Metaphysics as a "natural tendency" and as "conceptual poetry"', although it seems essentially irrelevant to our main argument, which is concerned with showing how indefensible metaphysics is from a scientific point of view. For if we did no more than demonstrate this negative thesis, there would always remain an impression that we had not after all done justice to the deepest intention of metaphysics. Is it really correct, for example, to describe the philosophy of Plato quite simply as 'nonsense'? No one who is familiar with it can help but find it profoundly meaningful, even though he finds it at the same time unacceptable when regarded as a scientific theory about 'the ultimate nature of existence'. Like all great art it has something suggestive and persuasive about it, to which no justice is done by calling it 'meaningless'. It just happens not to be science in our sense of the term, but poetry. Plato is poetizing—and he knows what he is doing; this is clear not least from the way in which he blends 'logos' and 'mythos' together. Later poet-philosophers have often not known what they were doing; they have thought it was science, not poetry, they were busy with.

Plato was able to take a relatively free and independent attitude toward the science of his time, since it was not so far developed as to confront him with our present problem. For thinkers of later times, who in spite of the more stringent demands of science both engage in poetic composition and claim to be practising science, the position becomes untenable. As for ourselves, it is imperative that—without falling into the trap of anachronism in our judgment of earlier forms of metaphysics—we should here draw a very sharp line of demarcation. As long as we are content simply to dismiss metaphysics as meaningless talk and 'nonsense', we have not yet drawn any such line. We have not explained how it is that, in spite of its being scientifically indefensible, metaphysics can give the impression of being entirely meaningful. This fact is explained when the two categories of 'science' and 'poetry' are clearly distinguished from one another, and metaphysics is assigned to the latter. In this way metaphysics has its meaning restored to it without entitling it to make any kind of claim to scientific status. To that extent the discussion of 'conceptual poetry' is not irrelevant to our main argument, but necessary to round it off.

With this we have also returned to the point we started from, namely the duality which has been characteristic of philosophy from the beginning. The word 'philosophy' is used to signify two very different things. It denotes on the one hand an endeavour to give a comprehensive world-view, an interpretation of 'the nature of existence'. Since a world-view is always personally and subjectively conditioned, however, such a 'philosophy' will at least in part stand on the same level as religion and certain types of art. It is a kind of poetry. The philosopher becomes something of a prophet and poet. He seeks to point humanity to an ideal, or to rally it round a symbol. On the other hand, philosophy represents itself as having a claim to objectivity. It is not content to be simply a persuasive inspiriting message, but it must also be an inquiry in line with other scientific inquiries, doing objective research; it states 'problems' and seeks to solve 'problems'. The philosopher becomes an objective scientist.

It is obvious that the relation between these two tendencies in philosophy is one of inverse proportion. The more stringent the scientific demands anyone makes on himself, the less confident he is of being able to give any philosophical answer to the question of 'the nature of existence'; and conversely, anyone who seeks to propound a comprehensive world-view must in all honesty admit that what he is doing is not objective science. There is a qualitative difference between a scientist and a seer. Yet both are called 'philosophers'. If we are to avoid confusion here, we must obviously distinguish between two fundamentally different kinds of philosophy, one being 'world-view philosophy' or 'metaphysical philosophy' and the other 'scientific philosophy'.

By characterizing metaphysical philosophy as 'conceptual poetry' and thus depriving it of any claim to scientific status, we have also opened the way to a more unprejudiced treatment of it. Provided it is clear from the start that metaphysics is not science and cannot in any circumstances be science, there is nothing to prevent our seeing and acknowledging that in certain circumstances it can actually make a fruitful contribution to science. Many a scientist whose background has included a very one-sided metaphysical vision, can be seen to have gained leverage from this in his scientific work. Not in spite of his metaphysical one-sidedness but just because of it, he has been in a position to detect significant scientific clues which he might otherwise have missed. His 'speculative' background has helped him to discover even important empirical relations.[25] This fact, however, in no way alters the non-scientific character of such metaphysical contributions.

Naturally it is an advantage if the scientist himself is clearly aware that these metaphysical presuppositions have no proper place in science. It is also of course a fact that 'metaphysical visions' can just as often hinder as help a man's perception of crucial scientific questions, so that he never asks them where otherwise he might have done.

But whether the metaphysical elements in a scientist's work have helped or hindered it, whether they have tended to widen his horizon or to limit and obscure it, they remain non-scientific factors. They may play a part in the work, but just because of this it is vitally important that there should be no blurring of the distinction between what is metaphysical and what is scientific. In this matter we cannot be too strict. What we must avoid above all is any suggestion of a parallel between metaphysical axioms and the hypotheses of science. As was shown above, the decisive difference between them is that the hypothesis is precisely and essentially 'hypothetical', so that it is necessarily subject to testing and open to possible refutation, whereas the metaphysical axiom is not so subject but is essentially inaccessible to testing and refutation. It is all the more important to notice this inasmuch as even thinkers who have insisted more strongly than most on the falsifiability of every hypothesis, have allowed the distinction be-

[25] For the importance metaphysics can have in a scientific context (e.g. in the scientific study of religion) just because of its one-sided cultivation of certain leading ideas, see my essay on 'Den metafysiska filosofiens betydelse'. 'The general advantage of every metaphysics is that the crystallization of a special form of consciousness is derived from it which can be grasped only through the one-sided accent that metaphysics lends to it' (*ibid.*, pp. 156f., ET* p. 289). It should be noted that metaphysics is only subject matter for the scientist's work, and that that work is not of a metaphysical nature.

56

tween scientific hypotheses and metaphysical axioms to remain rather vague. In this connection names like Karl R. Popper[26] and Joseph Agassi[27] come to mind. The danger here is that the demarcation between science and what is not science becomes blurred and in the end obliterated, and with it the distinction between metaphysical and scientific philosophy.

4. Scientific Philosophy

(1) *Philosophy as a special science*

We are not judging philosophy by an alien and inappropriate standard when we raise the question of its scientific tenability. Philosophy began as science; but alongside of it or directly out of it there gradually emerged various special sciences. As these developed, their methods were refined and awareness of what science demanded was heightened. Then, when its scientific status was examined in the light of this more exacting demand, philosophy inevitably failed to pass the test. This development we traced in the preceding pages with respect to metaphysical philosophy.

Compared with the sciences, which could each point to relatively assured results of their work, and in which a later generation could base its researches on what an earlier had achieved, philosophy with its succession of competing metaphysical systems, each of which had to start from scratch, could not but seem highly precarious and uncertain. Although we ought not to overestimate either the continuity of scientific work or the permanence of its results—for it too is very much subject to the law of change, as new insights or points of view overturn what were previously regarded as incontestable ideas—there is nevertheless a palpable difference between the genuine sciences and philosophy. The tackings and veerings of the latter are of a quite different kind. It is impossible to speak of any assured methodical progress here; everything seems haphazard and unstable, the arbitrariness is obvious and extreme.

---

[26] See particularly his discussion of 'The Demarcation between Science and Metaphysics' in *Conjectures*, pp. 253–92.

[27] J. Agassi, 'The nature of Scientific Problems' (in M. Bunge, *The Critical Approach*, pp. 190ff.). Agassi is aware that the doctrines of metaphysics are not open to criticism in the same way as scientific theories, and that metaphysics can therefore not be described as a science in the strict sense. 'There is usually no refutation, and hence no crucial experiment in metaphysics.' He nevertheless places it in an extremely close relation to science. He describes it as the 'framework of science', its 'regulative idea', and as 'a coordinating agent in the field of scientific research' (p. 190). 'Metaphysics is a framework for science' (p. 191). 'Metaphysical theories are views about the nature of things. Scientific theories and facts can be interpreted from different metaphysical viewpoints' (*ibid.*). 'Metaphysical ideas belong to scientific research as crucially important regulative ideas' (p. 193), and 'as a research program' (p. 204). The main thing for both Popper and Agassi is the stimulus that metaphysics can give to science, and in this they are very close to our position as stated above; but the danger of confusion between science and metaphysics remains.

No wonder that in this situation philosophy cast envious eyes on the sciences and wished it had some of the stability they possessed. It wanted, as Kant put it, to secure for itself '*den sicheren Gang einer Wissenschaft*', 'the sure progress of a science'.[28] What was it that gave the sciences their advantage over philosophy? Quite simply, their status as *special* sciences. This is very clear if we compare them with metaphysics. The latter with its universal interest speaks in sweeping terms of the nature of the universe and the ultimate nature of existence. How can such general and ill-defined questions be answered? The special sciences go to work in a directly opposite way. They confine themselves to special problems. That is the secret of their success. They ask only such questions as are capable of being answered, such as can be subjected to serious investigation. It is precisely this self-limitation, this specialization, that has given them their 'sure progress'. How would it be if philosophy took a similar line, and itself took the form of a special science? How if it sought out an area of its own, where it could pursue its investigations with the same precision as the natural sciences?

There are in fact many instances in which philosophy has sought to become one among the other special sciences, or to adopt the methods of particular special sciences, and so to ensure its scientific status. It will be enough to cite only two or three of these.

1) When metaphysics proved unviable, philosophy was glad to take refuge in *psychology*. This was a more or less obvious thing to do, inasmuch as empirical philosophy had always tended in a psychologistic direction. In this connection we need only recall Hume's association psychology and psychological atomism. It has, however, become increasingly evident that this experiment is doomed to failure. Psychology in its old form, based primarily on introspection and general psychological considerations, undoubtedly had a certain affinity with philosophy; but it was an affinity, we must note, with metaphysical philosophy, and it was precisely the arbitrariness of metaphysics that the recourse to psychology was intended to overcome. What is more, the later development of psychology in an experimental direction, while putting it more clearly in line with the special sciences, also removed it further from philosophy and made its methods less usable for philosophical purposes.

2) Ever since the Pythagoreans and Plato, philosophy has been very closely connected with *mathematics*, from which it has always drawn ins-

---

[28] It is astonishing how large a part this idea played for Kant. In the Preface to the 2nd edition of the *Critique of Pure Reason* the expression occurs no less than three times on the first page, and then repeatedly on the following pages. That alone is enough to suggest that for Kant it was a primary aim of the *Critique* to secure for philosophy 'the sure progress of a science'. (The expression '*sicheren Gang*' is variously rendered in ETT as 'secure method', 'sure path', 'certain course' and 'certain progress'.—Tr.)

piration for its methodology. In the rationalist tradition the desire has been to develop philosophical propositions *more geometrico*. Leibniz saw in mathematical calculation the possibility of overcoming the prevailing arbitrariness in philosophy, which he believed could and should be developed into a '*Mathesis universalis*'. In our time there has been a revival of this kind of thinking in logicism, which displays a curious combination of rationalism and empiricism. In logicism we have an attempt to turn philosophy in the direction of a special science by the application of mathematical methods.

That there is a close connection between mathematics and logic, and thus between mathematics and philosophy, cannot be denied—especially after the advances in mathematics during the past century and the gains these have brought to logic and the mathematicizing of logic in logicism. But it is a far cry from this to the demand that philosophy should conform to the methods of mathematics as the only means by which it can secure for itself 'the sure progress of a science'. What makes this idea so attractive is the precision of mathematical thinking, which has gained it the reputation of being the very paragon of a genuine science. What would not philosophy gain if it followed the example of mathematics? To this we may reply that philosophy like other sciences has undoubtedly much to learn from mathematical thinking as regards precision and clarity, and in this matter logicism has already made an important contribution. But that is by no means to say that philosophy ought to derive its methodology from mathematics. The problems of philosophy are of much too different a kind to allow of that possibility. To this subject we shall have occasion to return later.

3) As a further example of the attempt to turn philosophy into a special science we may take the 'philosophy of *language*'—semantic or linguistic philosophy. In certain of its forms this school of thought has connections with logicism, in so far as it calls for the formalizing of philosophical language in order to avoid the ambiguity which gives rise to metaphysical pseudo-problems. Yet even where the impossibility of such formalization is recognized, and the task of philosophy is seen instead as the clarification of the meaning of 'ordinary language' by means of a thorough analysis, there is still the question how such a specialized investigation differs from other linguistic investigations, and what makes it philosophically relevant.

This last point, simple and obvious though its seems, constitutes a fundamental and far-reaching objection to the idea of philosophy as a special science. It shows how that idea leads into a cul-de-sac, owing in particular to two difficulties to which it gives rise. First, if philosophy like other special sciences were to look for an area of subject matter to make its own, it would have the same experience wherever it turned: it would find all areas already occupied. Yet even if that were not so, and philosophy

59

could find some area still unoccupied by any special science, this would only mean that there was room for yet another special science—but not for philosophy. In so far as it claims to be a science in the same sense as the special sciences, philosophy is destined to be 'a science without a country'. Secondly, the very purpose for which the attempt is made to develop philosophy as a special science, itself involves a contradiction. It was in order to avoid metaphysics, with its arbitrary enunciation of principles, that philosophy first turned towards the special sciences. But this has resulted in its adopting a particular scientific point of view and treating it as a general philosophical standpoint, and thus we are landed in the very metaphysics we wanted to avoid. For it is the hallmark of metaphysics that it selects a part of what is given in experience and treats it as if it were the whole. Hence it does not matter to what special area we assign philosophy —whether psychology, mathematics and logic, sociology, linguistic analysis, or any other—the result is the same: we land in metaphysics, we involve ourselves in the confusion that is typical of metaphysics. We fall into the very trap which by thinking in terms of a special science we were trying to avoid.

The reason for this is indicated also by the question raised above, namely how philosophical investigation differs from that of a special science in the same area, and what makes it philosophically relevant. Here once more we are confronted by the two tendencies of philosophy—the scientific and the universal—which we observed at the outset. Philosophy cannot renounce either of these without negating itself. Hence its attempt to take refuge among the special sciences is like trying to escape from its own shadow. Here its inveterate tendency to universality has its revenge when philosophy in its eagerness to become a special science finds itself driven straight into the arms of metaphysics.

Philosophy as a special science—it won't work. How then are we to get off the horns of the dilemma and out of this cul-de-sac? We can do it only by taking quite seriously the thought of philosophy as a *universal science* and giving equal weight to both its scientific and its universal character.

(2) *Philosophy as a universal science*

The result so far has been entirely negative. Metaphysical philosophy cannot do justice to the scientific requirement, nor philosophy as a special science to the universal. In demonstrating this it has been necessary to go into considerable detail. We have had to try on the one hand to clarify, at least in main outline, the meaning of the very ambiguous and ill-defined term 'metaphysics', and on the other to show it to be scientifically indefensible. Then with regard to the question of philosophy as a special science, we have had similarly to outline what it involves and to show that it too is unworkable.

When we now turn to the positive aspect of the matter, we must expect it to require just as extensive treatment. Indeed it demands a much more thorough investigation; for in arguing for rather than against a position, we can less afford to neglect anything that might add to the coherence and cogency of the argument. Nevertheless, in this concluding section we can be exceptionally brief, and that for a relatively superficial reason. For although it would be possible under the heading of 'Philosophy as a universal science' to deal with the whole problem of scientific philosophy it would require such detailed and extensive treatment as to make the presentation quite unwieldy. It has therefore seemed best to give here only a brief indication of the kind of problems with which we are now faced. It will then be the task of subsequent chapters to carry out the investigation in detail.

For the moment, therefore, all we need do is to describe in broad outline the task of scientific philosophy as a universal science. Just by defining it as a universal science we have prescribed a number of requirements for it, several of which it will be appropriate to mention here.

1) Philosophy must not be allowed to minimize the *scientific* requirement. Philosophy has something in common with other sciences, something which entitles it as well as them to the name of science. Yet there is something in its whole attitude and point of view, purpose and procedure, which makes it quite different from them. Its relation to the special sciences must be clearly defined. It is no answer to this question, and no solution of the problem that faces us here, to explain—as is often done today—that philosophy is not really a science at all, but an 'activity' of another kind than science. To say that it is 'of another kind' than science, gives us no positive information whatever as to what philosophy is. It merely negates the idea that it is of the same kind as the rest of the sciences—that is, the special sciences—and thus leaves us where we started, namely with the fact that philosophy is quite different from these. The next step should surely be to explain in what the difference consists. But this question is not raised, and in consequence philosophy is robbed—quite unnecessarily—of its scientific character. At the same time the demarcation between philosophy and metaphysics is obliterated. Where the alternative of 'scientific philosophy' is lacking, it becomes difficult to see why one form of philosophy should not be as good as another. It is, however, quite arbitrary to limit the concept of science to such work as can be done only in special fields and by methods like those, for example, of the natural sciences. Why should it be impossible to adopt the position of an objective observer in relation to the ways in which general questions are put? This is one of the problems we must examine in the next chapter, where we shall be dealing with different forms of scientific argumentation.

2) To describe philosophy as a *universal* science is to imply not only that it cannot be confined to any special area, but also that it cannot be excluded from any special area. This is what makes the question of the centre and

circumference of philosophy so important.[29] To say that philosophy is not a special science is to say that it has strictly speaking no area of subject matter to call its own. But has philosophy then no centre? No, not in the sense that it can point to any particular segment of existence and claim it as specifically philosophical material. Instead it has its own central questions which are specifically philosophical, and which it raises in all the different areas. It thus takes its centre along with it, so to speak, as it pursues its inquiries in different fields. Philosophy is at home everywhere and has questions to raise everywhere. That is why we can never precisely say when it is at the centre and when at the circumference. If philosophical problems were not latently present all around us, both in the sciences and in everyday experience, philosophy would simply have no problems. It has to go to these areas in order to find them. But it is only as it finds them and handles them in its own particular way that they become genuine philosophical problems.

This, then, is the state of affairs as regards the centre and circumference of philosophy, and its relation to the special sciences and everyday experience. Just when it is occupied with its central task, it is driven to what might well look to an outsider like the circumference; and when it is occupied with the ultimate presuppositions of the sciences, or with similar questions underlying everyday experience, it is pursuing its own central task in different areas. For it is not with respect to the area in which it works that it differs from the other sciences, but with respect to the question it raises in their areas and the method it employs in answering it. All these are matters that will occupy us at length in the following chapters.

3) In its capacity as a *universal science* philosophy must not go beyond the formal presuppositions which are included in the sciences and everyday experience. The basic mistake of metaphysics was that it believed it could gather up all science and all experience into a unified metaphysical system. Scientific philosophy has no such confidence. Instead, it conceives its task as being to carry out a strictly scientific analysis of the fundamental presuppositions that are implicitly given in science and in experience generally. There is no question of its constructing anything of its own and imposing it as it were from the outside on science and experience. It simply clarifies the presuppositions on which these in fact rest. It thus becomes an 'analysis of meaning' (Chap. V), an investigation of the relation between 'meaning and validity' (Chap. VI) and an 'analysis of presuppositions' (Chap. VII and VIII). In daily life and in science we employ certain general presuppositions but give no account of them. They are there, but only implicitly. Philosophy makes them explicit and gives an account of them, and it does this by means of scientific analysis. Scientific philosophy is, in short, analysis of meaning, of presuppositions, of categories. With this, however,

[29] *Cf.* my essay on 'Filosofiens centrum och periferi'.

we have anticipated much that will only become clear in the course of our further discussion.

In order to gain a deeper insight into the questions facing us here, however, we must first consider the nature of philosophical argumentation and its relation to argumentation of a distinctively scientific kind. This will be the subject of the next chapter.

CHAPTER IV

Different Forms of Scientific Argumentation

1. The Concept of Science

(1) *The need for more precise definition*

THUS far in our inquiry we have had to be content with preliminary and not too well defined concepts. This is particularly the case with regard to the concept of 'science', which is so fundamental to this investigation. We have used it as a well-known term, and as if there were no risk of misunderstanding in working with it. To get any further, however, we must have a more precise definition of it. Now that we have come to the point of seeking to demonstrate the possibility of a 'scientific philosophy', it will clearly no longer do to use the terms 'science' and 'scientific' in a vague, indefinite way that can all too easily reduce them to mere clichés and empty words.

How then are we to define the term 'science'? It functioned above as the criterion by which metaphysics was disqualified and 'scientific philosophy' was to be justified; but it is a defective criterion in that it is imprecise. A yardstick which is not itself clearly measured off, will at least in some situations be useless for measuring anything else; and we are in just such a situation when we are considering the possibility of 'scientific philosophy'. As long as we were concerned only with the negative business of ruling out metaphysics, it was possible to work with such an imperfect criterion. No special subtlety was needed to show that metaphysics is sub-standard from a scientific point of view. Here we could proceed largely by rule of thumb.

It is different, however, when we turn to the positive side and want to show that and how scientific philosophy comes up to standard from a scientific point of view. Here we need to be much more precise, and there must be no ambiguity about the criterion. Putting it metaphorically, we could say that for such an obviously unscientific fish as metaphysics the net did not need to have too fine a mesh; a quite coarse mesh was sufficient to catch it. But for the positive purpose of assessing the claims of 'scientific philosophy' and judging its scientific status, the coarser mesh is no longer enough. Even if scientific philosophy passed unscathed through it, that would tell us literally nothing about its scientific tenability. Here the net must be so finely meshed that it lets nothing through which is not clearly up to standard from a scientific point of view. The first thing that has to be done, therefore, is to determine exactly the criterion we are going to use, or in other words, to define clearly what is meant by 'science'.

Only one further point need be made here. Have we not, by what we have just said, quite arbitrarily introduced a bit of the 'philosophy of science' into the discussion? That may well be true in so far as the questions raised here belong in the context of what is commonly called 'philosophy of science', but it is not true that they have been arbitrarily introduced. It is rather the case that this bit of scientific theory has a definite and necessary part to play in our investigation. It is necessary that philosophy should for its own sake find its place and its method among the sciences. In this connection there are three questions that have to be answered: 1. What is it that is characteristic of a scientific procedure? 2. How far does philosophy possess the requisite qualifications for this? 3. What is the difference between philosophy and other sciences?

(2) *The indefinability of science?*
To give a complete and adequate definition of 'science' is naturally not our intention. It is in fact questionable whether by all the rules of the art there is any possibility of such a definition. Science is an extremely variable phenomenon, in a state of continual growth and development, and what at one period seems most characteristic of it often falls quite into the background for the next generation. There is therefore little inducement to try to establish a definition which is likely to be out of date as soon as it is propounded.

In the past there was more optimism about the possibility of defining science in the traditional way. The very fact that the sciences had historically sprung from a common root, and then, as new objects came into view and new methods were devised, had differentiated themselves from this original unity, favoured the idea that it should be possible without difficulty to define 'science' and 'the sciences' by means of the traditional logical scheme of *genus proximum—differentia specifica*. 'Science' here represents the genus, and the 'special sciences' the different species within it. It was then possible to go further and set up an encyclopaedic 'system of science', a scheme in which every particular science had its place, subsumed under the general concept of science and integrated into the great 'organon' of the sciences. This idea of science and the sciences belongs to the past; and from this point of view at least, the concept of science must be said to be indefinable.

We seem to be in a dilemma. The continuation of our inquiry demands a more precise definition of 'science' and 'scientific', yet these terms appear to be indefinable. There is, however, a simple way out. For our present purpose we by no means need a complete and adequate definition such as would be necessary for the systematization of science. All we need is a clear indicator of what can be reckoned as science and what can not. Although the term 'science' is difficult to define and perhaps indefinable, it is not merely an empty word. There is something that must be present and something else that must not, if we are to talk about science. Our immediate task, therefore, is to try to point out such a feature as must be present—and its opposite absent—before we can rightly call anything science. It is not difficult to do so.

(3) 'The possibility of objective argumentation'

There is a fundamental distinction between scientific activity and other kinds of activity, and our present concern is to discover what constitutes this distinction. We are asking, in other words, what is the *conditio sine qua non* for describing anything as science. Put in that way the question is not difficult to answer, and the answer is remarkably simple. We can speak of science where, and only where, there is a 'possibility of objective argumentation' concerning a stated idea or opinion. To speak of science where there is no such possibility, is a misuse of words.[1]

What then precisely are the implications of this important formula, 'the possibility of objective argumentation'?

To begin with, it implies a number of simple, elementary facts. To *argue* is to give reasons for and against a proposition or idea put forward by oneself or somebody else. Where reason cannot be weighed against reason, we are at all events not dealing with science. What is more, this weighing of reasons must be able to be done in an *objective* manner. This too is of decisive importance. For it is of course possible to speak of argumentation in a very subjective context. When a politician or propagandist produces his 'arguments', he is not really seeking to have them carefully examined and weighed against other arguments that might point in another direction. He is clear about his position from the start, and his 'argumentation' is aimed at getting his hearers to join him. It is a form of persuasion. Scientific argumentation differs fundamentally from this, in that its purpose is objective examination and inquiry.

[1] In STK, 1928, pp. 68ff., I reviewed a work on the philosophy of religion which, in partial dependence on H. Scholz's *Religionsphilosophie*, sought to provide philosophical legitimation for the claim of religion to truth and reality by using the idea of a 'philosophical confession', an idea which the author claimed could 'stand the test of reputable thought'. I sharply attacked this idea as a disreputable mixture of objective science (philosophy) and subjective stance (confession of faith), essentially a contradiction in terms, and at best deliberately ambiguous, at worst meaningless. This gave rise to a considerable debate, which came to centre mainly on the question of the conditions on which it is possible to speak of a scientific problem. In this connection I formulated the minimal requirement as 'the possibility of objective argumentation'. In the forty years since then I have had many opportunities of testing the reliability and effectiveness of this formula. Where the possibility of objective argumentation is present, the condition prerequisite to the scientific treatment of a problem is fulfilled. Where that possibility is absent, if we still press for a scientific answer, then plainly we are putting a question which science with its concern for objectivity cannot put and consequently cannot answer. More recently the question of argumentation has attained some prominence in philosophy, as works like those of Toulmin, Naess, Simonsson, and Linnér, listed in the Bibliography show. (On the meaning of 'objectivity' see Additional Note, III.—Tr.)

When we speak of 'the *possibility* of objective argumentation' our intention is to distinguish what is scientific from other forms of life and activity. There are matters concerning which no such possibility exists—and to say this is in no way to belittle them. They can be just as significant as the most important scientific problems. The difference in question here is not one of importance but of kind. A question that is not open to objective argumentation and testing, may be as vitally important as you please, but it is not science. Here we are exposed to two different risks. On the one hand, because of the importance of the question we may wrongly attribute a scientific quality to it, or on the other hand, when we realize that it cannot be settled by objectively scientific arguments we may dismiss it as unimportant or even as a wrong question to ask. Against both of these errors it must be strongly emphasized that our sole intention in speaking of 'the possibility of objective argumentation' is to distinguish scientific activity from what is not scientific. It is to draw the line of demarcation between science and other kinds of activity, without implying any judgment whatever as to the value of the other kinds.

In all its elementary simplicity this formula, 'the possibility of objective argumentation', provides an effective means of distinguishing between what is and what is not science. Without claiming to be a definition it indicates just that requisite *minimum*, the absence of which disqualifies anything from being called science—though without in any way disqualifying it from the point of view of value, as we have said. Here then we have the finely-meshed net which lets nothing slip through as science which is not science; and with this we have the criterion we need for the continuation of our inquiry.

On closer inspection, however, this formula proves to be by no means as simple as it might seem. On the contrary, it includes a whole complex of presuppositions, without which it is quite impossible to speak of objective argumentation. To argue is to put something to the test, a test which can have a positive or negative result, a test which the thing tested either passes or fails or there has to be a suspension of judgment pending more decisive arguments. Such testing presupposes not only a clearly stated criterion but also some sort of testability, and this in turn presupposes intersubjectivity and at least in some instances reproducibility. For a test that can only be carried out by the subject who has put forward the proposition, and is incapable of being checked by others, cannot be acknowledged as a genuine test, and an experiment that cannot be reproduced cannot be described as a genuine experiment. In this way we could go on adding point after point to the simple formula 'the possibility of objective argumentation', which would both qualify and in a measure complicate it, while at the same time enhancing its capacity to express what is common to and characteristic of all science.

The fruitfulness of the idea of 'objective argumentation' is evident from the fact that it enables us to clear away a whole series of ambiguities and misconceptions that commonly attach to the popular idea of science.

1) First of all we can get rid of the widespread but mistaken notion that science comprises a deposit of 'truths'. A glance at the actual state of affairs in science shows that this idea must be false. Science is not in command of 'truth' as a kind of capital sum which can be gradually increased and improved. The thought of absolute truth as an actual possession has no place in science. Paradoxical as it may seem to the popular mind, science includes both true and false judgments, and it is no simple matter to draw the line between them. Only too often it happens that what today is regarded as utterly improbable or even demonstrably false, turns out later to be the right solution.

To think of science as a deposit of 'truths' and to speak of 'the present standpoint of science' as if it represented a complete unanimity of view, is an extremely questionable proceeding. Science does not consist of a consensus of views and opinions. In reality it presents a quite different picture. It often appears in the form of a number of different and competing ideas which cannot all be true. Yet—and this is the decisive thing—science is not a gratuitous jumble of notions and fancies, but is comprised of ideas supported by arguments that can be examined and tested. It is in this way that errors of fact or thought which a theory may contain are corrected; they are exposed when argument meets argument and one is methodically weighed against the other. That is how science progresses—by means of objective argumentation. It is this that makes science scientific, both when it is wide of the mark and when it reaches its goal.

So long as we have no real alternative to the idea of science as a deposit of truth, it is difficult not to fall victim to that idea. There is, however, an alternative available in 'the possibility of objective argumentation'.

2) From this it becomes clear, furthermore, what is the real reason for the 'sure progress' of science. It is not that science contains only true judgments—for we have already seen that the opposite is the case, and that it contains both tenable and untenable theories. The 'sure progress' of science does not depend on its ever achieving definitive results or its never needing to take a step backwards. In other words, it is not the tenability of the theories that gives science its 'sure progress', but the possibility of a critical examination and methodical testing of them, no matter whether this procedure eventually confirms or refutes them. It is in this methodically critical way that science goes steadily forward; it is this that puts firm ground under its feet. Again we come back to 'the possibility of objective argumentation'.

3) If it is through continual testing that science makes its 'sure progress', we may well be tempted to transfer our interest from the object to the method, from 'truth' to the way in which theories are tested. But then we can easily get involved in the question of what characterizes 'the scien-

tific method'—which again puts us on the wrong track. Just as science does not consist of a consensus of views and opinions, so neither does it consist of an established scientific method accepted and employed by all. There are sciences of many different kinds, and in all of them we find there is method, methodical procedure. But there is no universal scientific method. If objective testing is to be done, it must be done according to some method; but this does not mean that all testing must be done according to the same method. To speak of '*the* scientific method' is nonsense. It is also nonsense to expect a science to become 'more scientific' by taking over from another science a method found effective in the other's field. We shall have occasion to return to this subject in the next section, on 'science and the humanities'. It is meaningless to speak of *the* scientific method, for there are many scientific methods. What makes them 'scientific', however, is the fact that each of them in its own way provides for 'the possibility of objective argumentation'. Here it is just as important to pay attention to the differences between them as to what they have in common. The common element is the objective argumentation, but in different scientific fields the argumentation can take different forms without being any the less objective.

4) When we were speaking above about the special sciences, we described the difference between them as one of subject matter. This could give rise to misunderstanding. The fact is that a number of different sciences have the same subject matter but are concerned with different aspects of it. A special science is not a science that is so attached to a special material as to derive its character from it, but what gives it its own distinctive stamp is the point of view it adopts and the method it employs in dealing with the material. It consciously specializes in a particular point of view and a particular aspect of the material, without denying—indeed it rather presupposes—that the latter can be regarded from other points of view. Thus the same object, the same given reality, can be regarded from a chemical, biological, psychological, historical point of view, and so forth. If a science insisted on its own point of view as alone decisive, and sought to force everything into its own category, it would thereby cease not only to be a special science, but to be any sort of science at all. It is not the material but the unique type of argumentation that distinguishes one special science from another. Every science provides its own frame of reference and places its material in a context which is governed by the special category of the science in question.

5) There is a great advantage in approaching the problem of 'the concept of science' from the standpoint of 'the possibility of objective argumentation'. If we were obliged instead to start by constructing an idea or ideal of science, and then to use this as a criterion for judging the existing sciences, we could hardly escape metaphysics. Such a 'concept of science', more or less freely constructed, would involve a form of conceptual realism.

This is avoided entirely, however, if we start at the other end, with the question of the nature of scientific argumentation. For here we turn first to the concretely given sciences and direct our inquiry to them as they actually are and actually work. When we wish to investigate the scientific status of a discipline, the question to be asked is this: How does one argue in this discipline? How, for example, does the mathematician argue, or the archaeologist, or the historian, the literary historian, the theologian, the art historian, the natural scientist? The question of argumentation covers everything, for even an experiment is a kind of argumentation. Wherever we find work that is capable of being methodically checked being done in the treatment of a given material, that is, material which admits of objective argumentation, we can recognize the presence of science.

6) If we start with the idea of 'the possibility of objective argumentation' as decisive for science, we open up the possibility of overcoming the schizophrenia which has come to characterize so much of contemporary science and cultural life. We are often told today that our culture is divided,[2] that we are living in fact on the frontier between two different cultures, where a person who finds himself in the one no longer understands the language of the other. Here the idea of 'objective argumentation' offers a basis for mutual understanding. This brings us, however, to the important subject of 'science and the humanities'.

(4) *Science and the humanities*

The view presented above with regard to the nature of science and the importance of 'the possibility of objective argumentation' as a criterion for distinguishing between what is and what is not science, can best be illustrated and put to the test by being confronted with the intricate question of 'science and the humanities'. In this question we have in a nutshell the fundamental difficulty that besets the traditional concept of science and discloses its divided state. Are only the natural sciences 'science' in the strict sense of the term, or can the humanities also be described as science? Are the latter merely the lower orders of science, or are they perhaps not science at all? The extent to which the idea of 'the possibility of objective argumentation' can contribute to the clarification of these problems, is the best proof of its rightness and fruitfulness.

Before we go into this question, however, it is necessary to make a preliminary observation with regard to terminology. This is the more important inasmuch as the question in the last resort is by no means merely terminological, but has practical implications of the most far-reaching kind, and as long as it remains unclarified it can effectively bar the way to correct understanding. What we have in mind here are the different uses of the term 'science' in different languages.

[2] *Cf.* C. P. Snow, *The Two Cultures,* and F. S. C. Northrop, *The Logic of the Sciences and the Humanities.*

In English, 'science' is generally synonymous with 'natural science'. In German and the Scandinavian languages, on the other hand, the nearest equivalents to 'science'—*Wissenschaft*, *vetenskap*, etc.—have a much wider reference and are used as including both 'science' and the 'humanities'. We have therefore to distinguish between two concepts of 'science': 1. a *narrower* concept in which the prototype and norm of all science is found in the mathematical procedures of the natural sciences, and real science is held to exist only where their methods can be used; and 2. a *wider* concept which includes both the natural sciences and the humanities. Unless this terminological diversity is clearly recognized, it can give rise to much confusion. In our preceding discussion we have been using the wider concept of science. To those accustomed to English usage, with its narrower concept, it may therefore have seemed strange that we have so monotonously insisted on a 'scientific philosophy', and perhaps even stranger that we have been able to speak of a 'scientific theology'. Naturally it makes little or no sense to interpret these expressions as referring to a philosophy or theology based on the natural sciences. But in the light of the wider concept of science the idea of 'scientific philosophy' and 'scientific theology' makes clear and important sense. Here a qualitative requirement is laid down for philosophy and theology, though without any preconceived notion as to the method these sciences must employ.

Rightly to understand these two concepts of science, we must notice what lies behind them historically; and this takes us back to the Renaissance. For the dividedness from which at present we are suffering in both our science and our culture is a legacy from that period. On the one hand Renaissance humanism represented an attempt to revive the cultural ideal of antiquity, particularly in its Ciceronian form. Its interests were one-sidedly humanistic. On the other hand there were at the same time, but quite independently of the humanistic trend, developments in the area of the natural sciences which would soon contend for pride of place with humanism. There was no overarching unity that could combine or contain these divergent tendencies. It is a proof of the impotence of the Renaissance that it could not give natural science the place it deserved, but allowed the two tendencies to fall apart, retaining for itself the 'humanistic' in the limited sense of the term.

At two main points Renaissance humanism failed to achieve its aims. One of these was to bring about a renaissance of the Latin language. Over against the 'barbaric' Latin of the Middle Ages, the language of the Ciceronian golden age was set up as the ideal and norm; but the consequence was that Latin, which had hitherto been a living language, became a dead one and incapable in the long run of holding its own. A further aim was to bring about a renaissance of humanism; but when this proved unable to absorb the new vigour of the natural sciences, the consequence was that the latter went their own way and gradually became the most dangerous rival of humanism. From that time onwards there developed a continual trial of strength between the two, in which the natural sciences with their more tangible technological consequences forced humanistic concerns to give ground step by step until the natural sciences and their methods came gradually to be regarded as normative for all science whatsoever.

In this situation there were two ways in particular that humanistic scholarship took to defend itself. One way was to accommodate itself as much as possible to the natural sciences, imitating their methods and becoming as it were one of them, in order to attain 'the sure progress of a science'. The other was the directly opposite way of reflecting on its own distinctive character and independent task in contrast to the natural sciences. This was in its way a necessary and wholesome reaction, which set in during the later decades of the nineteenth century and around the turn of the century. It led in effect to a declaration of independence on the part of humanistic scholarship over against the natural sciences. The grounds for this were found by some in the uniqueness of the subject matter of humanistic research—which led to the contrast of '*Naturwissenschaft—Geisteswissenschaft*' (W. Dilthey, E. Spranger)—while by others they were seen rather in the difference of method—which led to the contrast of '*nomothetisch—idiographisch*' (W. Windelband) or '*Naturwissenschaft—Kulturwissenschaft*' (H. Rickert). By the very concepts they use and methods they employ the natural sciences are debarred from certain crucial scientific problems, and therefore to point out 'the limits of conceptualization in the natural sciences' is at the same time to proclaim the independence of the humanistic or cultural sciences.[3]

Neither of these ways, however, could lead to the overcoming of the division in the concept of science and the cultural consciousness. The first way led to the self-immolation of 'the humanities', and the resultant dismissal of important scientific problems as being outside the realm of science was bound to provoke a reaction. The second way certainly emphasized the independence of the tasks and methods of natural science and the humanities, but this tended to increase the tension and division. The schizophrenia was not overcome. The breach between 'science and the humanities' rather became wider, and the breakdown into two separate cultures which did not understand each other's language, was lurking in the background.

From this division in the concept of science we are delivered the moment we let the idea of 'the possibility of objective argumentation' be our guiding principle. Then we find that the opposition which is supposed to exist between science and the humanities is more imaginary than real.

When the natural scientist makes his experiments and by induction or

[3] H. Rickert, *Die Grenzen der naturwissenschaftlichen Begriffsbildung* and *Kulturwissenschaft und Naturwissenschaft*.

some other means arrives at certain general laws or hypotheses, and when he proceeds to test these hypotheses by means of new experiments, then what he is doing is science, because it is open to inspection and objective verification. Even if his theory is the result of a happy inspiration, he is not content simply to announce it, but he subjects it to rigorous testing and submits it also to the critical examination of other scientists. This is by no means to say that the theory is true, and it is certainly not the truth of a theory that determines whether we are dealing with science. Even if a theory is false and can be shown to be false, it is none the less a scientific theory inasmuch as its truth or falsity is capable of objective testing. Against the arguments of one scientist can be set those of another, which may possibly show his theory to be untenable; or else—in a positive instance—by checking his arguments other scientists may confirm his theory, and by adding new arguments may further support and strengthen it and possibly improve it.

But something similar is true also of the student of the humanities. When a historian, for example, is faced with a document of which he must seek to give a correct interpretation, he is certainly not thrown back merely on his own subjective fancy, but there are usually enough objective facts to block his interpretation if it is on the wrong lines. A host of conditions must be fulfilled if his interpretation is to be accepted—questions relating to the character of the source material, its place in its natural historical context, and so forth. This means that he must produce objective arguments for his interpretation, that is, arguments which make it accessible for examination and possible refutation by other scholars. His interpretation may be erroneous and his arguments insubstantial—for the possibility that a theory may be wrong must always be reckoned with in science, and it applies to the hypotheses of the historian and the natural scientist alike. Science is therefore always open to the future, and it refuses to absolutize the results it has so far obtained. The rightness or wrongness of the historian's interpretation, therefore, is a matter for further examination and testing by which it may possibly be refuted. Yet even if it is refuted, it is still a scientific interpretation, inasmuch as its truth or falsity is capable of objective testing. We can say of the historian the same as we said above about the natural scientist. Against his argumentation another scholar can set other arguments, which may possibly show that the interpretation he has proposed cannot stand; or other arguments than those so far employed may be produced, which give support to his interpretation.

It is this methodical progression, this objective argumentation, that is the hallmark of all science, whether in the natural sciences or the humanities. This shows the wrongness of the idea that the humanistic sciences would improve their scientific calibre by adopting methods from the natural sciences. That is simply an example of the common fallacy which is usually called 'the expansion of method'. When a method has been employed successfully in one area, it is taken to be applicable everywhere. The mistake is made of confusing 'objective argumentation' with 'quantification of the object'—as if there were no other way of arguing objectively than to transform the argumentation into a mathematical equation, and as if objectivity were to be guaranteed by reducing the question to quantitatively measurable terms. This often means instead, however, that objectivity is sacrificed and a false picture given of the phenomenon we are trying to explain. We fasten on one aspect of it, an aspect which undoubtedly exists, but which is not the essential thing.

The reason why we treat this one aspect as if it were the only one, is that it puts us in control of the phenomenon mathematically. But the result in many cases is that the phenomenon we were going to investigate never gets investigated, is never given serious and thorough examination, so that what is characteristic and essential to it goes unperceived. This may be illustrated by an example. Ever since the time of the Pythagoreans it has been known that there is an intimate connection between music and mathematics. From that point of view it is undoubtedly possible to turn the entire phenomenon of music into mathematical formulae and reduce it to the numerical frequencies of sound waves. But to say that when we speak of musical experience we *mean* merely sound waves and frequencies, would be the very opposite of an objective description of the phenomenon. It is at this point that 'phenomenology', despite all that is questionable about it, can make an important contribution to 'objective argumentation'. There is an ill-concealed remnant of arbitrary metaphysics in the notion that the quantitatively measurable is the same as the really real, 'reality itself'. It is the antithesis of everything that can be called science, the reverse of objective argumentation.

There is something artificial about the whole discussion of 'science and the humanities'.

On the one hand it is held that they are separated from one another as by watertight compartments. Each of them has its own methods, which must be kept strictly separate and not allowed to encroach on one another. Yet if we take the sciences as they actually operate, we find that they make very large use of one another's methods. The 'transscientific' plays an important part. When for example a historian can turn to chemical analysis for help in determining the date of a document, he does not hesitate to do so. He does not say that because chemical analysis is a method of natural science and not of historical research it cannot be used by a historian, but he thankfully accepts the help it can give him. But this does not mean that history is turned into chemistry, or that chemistry is turned into history. Each discipline preserves its own identity and its concern with its own problems. It is simply a question of transscientific collaboration, without which no science can carry out the task that is uniquely its own. There is thus in fact a continual coming and going between one science and another. Specialization is necessary in science, but it must never be allowed to mean isolation and alienation from other sciences. From this point of view it is impossible to exaggerate the unity that in the last resort prevails in all scientific thinking.

On the other hand it must be just as strongly emphasized that the thought of the unity of science must not be allowed to give rise to any sort of monism of science or scientific method. The chief example in our time of such an interpretation of the unity of science is furnished by logical positivism with its plea for a 'unified science'.[4] Here we have a case of just the kind of monistic thinking based on the natural sciences to which we took exception above. When it is regarded as the task of philosophy to produce a 'Unified Science', then obviously the positivistic legacy of Comte is making its influence felt. This is something that crops up again and again—as for instance in the conception of philosophy as an encyclopedic compendium of all the results obtained by the sciences. Behind the positivistic idea of a unified science lies the narrower concept of science and the metaphysical notion of a universal scientific method; and what this implies emerges in the demand for a unifying 'physicalistic' language common to all, with the eventual aim of achieving a 'unity of laws' and with prediction as the ultimate goal of science. Hence, if the humanities are to be reckoned as science, they must be shown to be reducible to physical terms. One of the leading ideas of logical positivism is that of 'reducibility', for it is only by the reduction of everything else to the unified language of physical objects that the unity of science is made possible.

All this is an illustration of the way in which we must *not* talk about the unity of science. This unity is not exhibited in an encyclopedic metaphysical summation of the results of the different sciences under the hegemony of natural science, nor in a physicalistic reduction. As we have already seen, the unity of the sciences rests on a quite different basis, namely the 'possibility of objective argumentation' which exists in all the various sciences. This opens up quite other possibilities of respecting the individuality of the different sciences. We can let each of them be what it is, without requiring it to conform to other sciences as regards its aims and methods. There is no central science on which the other sciences depend like satellites that shine by borrowed light. There is no universal scientific method, but the methods must be adapted to the nature of the different objects of scientific investigation. Yet the sciences do not go off at a tangent. There is something that holds them together and makes a unity of them. This unity, however, does not consist in any sort of 'unified science', but rather in the fact that all sciences—in spite of all the differ-

---

[4] As prime evidence of this we have the ambitious positivistic project of the *International Encyclopedia of Unified Science* (ed. O. Neurath). *Cf.* also R. Carnap, *The Unity of Science*.

ences between them—bear one and the same signature: their common concern with objective argumentation.

In sum, we may say that the idea of 'the possibility of objective argumentation' as the hallmark of science has convincingly passed the tests to which it has been put. It has demonstrated its correctness and fruitfulness not least in that it has been able to clarify the stubborn and tangled problem of 'science and the humanities'. It thus enables us to overcome the false dichotomy, the schizophrenia, in science and culture without resorting to the equally false notion of a unified science, in which the procedure of the natural sciences engulfs everything in an identical 'physicalism' and singleness of method. It gives us the possibility of seeing the sciences as they really are, both as to their essential differences from one another and as to their basic affinity and practical transscientific collaboration with one another. The individual branches of science belong together, and they have this in common, that each in its own way—and one no less than another—provides for 'the possibility of objective argumentation'.

(5) *The problem of scientific philosophy*
Step by step we have been approaching what for the present is the central focus of our inquiry, namely the question of the possibility of 'scientific philosophy'. If we are to speak of philosophy as a science in the strict sense, then all we have so far said about the distinctive character of science and its *conditio sine qua non* must be fully applicable also to philosophy. In short, what we have now to do is to examine the philosophical type of argumentation and show that it is open to objective testing. In this our discussion of 'science and the humanities' has given us a significant lead. It was shown there in a preliminary way that 'science' is not an undifferentiated uniformity, but that there are different kinds of objective argumentation. There are modes of argumentation that are proper to the natural sciences, and modes that are distinctive of humanistic studies, and both are rightly included in science inasmuch as in both cases the argumentation is objective. The question that must now be raised with regard to philosophy is whether there can be shown to be a form of argumentation peculiar to it, which puts it in the same class as the 'sciences'—in the wider but no less strict sense of that term.

This indicates the direction in which our further inquiry must proceed. We must take a closer look at the different sorts of argument which the sciences employ in order to get to grips with their material. It is true that we have already to some extent dealt with this question in the foregoing pages, particularly in the section on 'science and the humanities', but the discussion there was much too sporadic to serve as a basis on which to establish the scientific status of philosophy. It is therefore necessary here to present a broader picture, exhibiting more systematically the chief

77

varieties of argumentation that are found in the special sciences, and showing the place of philosophical argumentation in this context. What is it, from a methodological point of view and as regards its type of argumentation, that makes philosophy a science?

Our task therefore is to give a more precise account of the specifically philosophical mode of argumentation and show that it is capable of being objectively tested. That philosophy works with a specific form of argumentation is plain from the fact that it is not a special but a universal science, and its needs cannot be met by the kind of argumentation proper to the special sciences. The big problem now is to see what sort of argumentation a universal science can employ, and how it can be objective. From this point of view it is easy to perceive the impossibility of metaphysics, which purports to be a universal science but lacks the possibility of objective argumentation. It bases its thinking on unfounded assumptions; it cannot argue, at least not objectively, but can only assert, postulate, proclaim. By contrast 'scientific philosophy', while claiming to be something other than the special sciences and refusing to resign its task as a universal science, claims also to possess just as strictly scientific a status as the special sciences and to be just as open to testing by objective argumentation. How is this possible?—That is the problem of scientific philosophy, to which we must devote the rest of this chapter and the chapters immediately following.

2. 'Eternal and Contingent Truths'

It is odd how the forms of argumentation employed in the present-day sciences, despite all the innovations there have been, go back in the main to old models. Yet this is not really surprising if we reflect on the fact that there are not an unlimited number of ways of arguing *appropriately* about a given material. We cannot argue just as we please: the material sets limits, and thinking sets limits. It would be more surprising, therefore, if there had not already at an early stage developed certain procedures and modes of argumentation which would gradually come to constitute a tradition.

For the sake of clarity it should be expressly stated that we are not here concerned with the special methods which different sciences have developed and are continually developing in order to master their material and solve their special problems. In that regard we can speak to a far greater extent of something new, something neither governed nor guided by tradition. Here the scientist is often faced with situations so novel that they demand quite novel treatment, often of a very tentative kind. New, hitherto unknown domains compel him to devise new special methods, and these lead in turn to the discovery of new domains, on and on in a continual progression. Yet behind all the endless variety of such innovations in method there lie a small number of typical modes of argumentation, and it is these that we have in view here.

These different basic modes of argumentation—they could very well be called structures of argumentation—display a curious combination of positive necessity and historically conditioned form. That we should employ just these modes of argumentation is a matter of positive necessity, but that we reason about them as we do, and distinguish them from one another terminologically as we do, is in the highest degree conditioned by the historical tradition underlying them. It is therefore necessary to pay attention to both of these facts. It might no doubt be thought that in the present context, where our concern is to exhibit the positively determined modes of scientific argumentation and confront them with the philosophical mode, it would be enough to concentrate on the positively necessary aspect and ignore the historical background. That, however, is something that cannot be done, because the two questions have such bearing on one another and are so completely interlocked that the meaning of the positive question cannot be analyzed without knowledge of the historical tradition behind it and the preconceptions and sources of error this entails.

We are faced here with the familiar situation that when an outstanding thinker has put a question in a certain way, other men readily adopt that way of putting it and base their work on it as if it were the only possible way. They discuss and refine their views and follow them out in all their ramifications—views, it should be noted, which arise from that way of putting the question, which thus functions as a limiting horizon—but the way the question is put is not itself discussed, it is taken as self-evident and inevitable. Hence the sources of error that are built into it, historically conditioned as it is, are never seriously discussed and exposed. It is in just this situation that we find ourselves with regard to the modes of scientific argumentation. These exist as facts in the actually existing sciences, and their content can be analyzed; but the analysis is coloured by habits of thought inherited from the historical tradition, which shape the general understanding of the various types of argumentation. That is why a look back into history is indispensable.

Naturally we cannot undertake here an exhaustive inquiry into what lies historically behind the discussion of the nature of scientific work and the kind of argumentation it involves. That would present us with an incredibly vast and complex problem. The only thing we can do is to look for a historically critical juncture at which the lines leading to the modern outlook were more definitively laid down. When we do this it is quite obvious that we must give attention first of all to the work of Leibniz; and it is so not least because of what Leibniz has come to mean in our own time. In this connection we need only recall the succession: Leibniz-Frege-Russell-logicism-Scholz.[5] But even where his name is not directly

---

[5] Gottlob Frege's *Begriffsschrift* is an original development of certain ideas taken from Leibniz—the formalization of language to make mathematically exact reasoning

mentioned, it is the spirit of Leibniz that broods over much of contemporary thought, his ideas that are reproduced, his explanations that men largely live by, and also his ambiguities that men suffer from.

What we shall chiefly discuss here is Leibniz's famous theory of 'eternal and contingent truths' or 'truths of reason and truths of fact' (*vérités de raison et vérités de fait*), 'necessary and contingent truths', and whatever else he calls them.

(1) '*Truths of reason and truths of fact*'

This distinction is characteristic of Leibnizian thought. Not that it was Leibniz's own invention; for it was in the air, so to speak, and in various forms and guises it has been present throughout almost the whole history of thought. It is found already in Plato, for whom the contrast between the world of ideas as the world of true being and the world of the senses as the world of shadow-images has its counterpart in the realm of knowledge, where the knowledge of ideas (mathematics, philosophy) with its absolute truth stands over against the altogether inferior and deceptive semblance of knowledge acquired through the senses. The same distinction occurs in medieval scholasticism, with its contrast between the 'necessary' and the 'contingent', and it can be traced further both in Descartes and other philosophers of modern times prior to Leibniz.[6] There were rich resources on which Leibniz could draw. Yet the fact that he could thus base his work on both the Platonic-Aristotelian and the Medieval tradition as well as the insights of later thinkers, in no way diminishes the significance of his own contribution, which has indeed been overwhelming.[7] It was he who blazed the trail for future developments down to our own time, and it was he who produced the winning formula—for good or ill. For it was not only a highly significant but also a highly disastrous step that was taken when Leibniz propounded his theory of eternal and contingent truths, or *vérités de raison et vérités de fait*.

---

possible, the *calculus philosophicus* or *ratiocinator*, etc. As for Bertrand Russell, it should be noted that his earliest work was a study of Leibniz, and that his *Principia Mathematica* would be unthinkable without the influence of the latter. Finally, as regards Heinrich Scholz, the title of his *Mathesis Universalis* speaks plainly enough. He follows Leibniz, not only in seeking to formalize language and mathematicize philosophy, but also in adopting his metaphysics, particularly his 'theological metaphysics'; *cf.* Scholz, *Metaphysik*, pp. 142ff.—Note that for Leibniz the idea of the calculus is also of theological significance. '*Cum Deus calculat et cogitationem exercet, fit mundus*' ('When God calculates and exercises thought, the world is created'). And on Leibniz's importance for modern logicism, see Lewis and Langford, *Symbolic Logic*, pp. 5ff.

[6] F. H. Heinemann, in his essay on 'Truths of Reason and Truths of Fact' has traced the line in an instructive way from Descartes to Leibniz and beyond.

[7] On Leibniz see works with titles naming him by B. Russell, G. Martin and G. H. R. Parkinson, listed in the Bibliography.

1) It was significant because it provided a simple, easily manageable and apparently clear formula for an important distinction which had not until then been really successfully grasped.

When we say that something is true, this can mean two widely different things. On the one hand it can mean that it is true in all circumstances and can never—never in all eternity—be anything else. Such are the eternal truths, the necessary truths, the rational truths. They are called eternal and necessary because they hold good not only in our world but in 'all possible worlds'. They are called rational because they are founded solely on reason, and because their truth can be discerned by reason alone without any assistance from experience and observation. They can also be described as logical truths or logically necessary truths. The best example of such necessary truths of reason is afforded by the law of identity or the law of contradiction. We cannot conceive of a world in which such laws would not hold good, a world in which it would not be true that A=A or false that A= not-A. It is thus a logical necessity that is asserted here.

On the other hand, it is possible for the statement that something is true to have a quite different meaning, namely that that is simply how things are, though there would be no absurdity in their being otherwise. For example, if I say 'It's raining now', my statement may be true—it will if it is in fact raining at the time. But on what do I base my assertion that this statement is true? Obviously I can never discern its truth by means of reason alone. There is no logical necessity that it must be so. That it is so is a matter of fact which only experience can show me. What we have here is thus a contingent truth, a factual but not necessary truth, a 'truth of fact'. The importance of this Leibnizian distinction is seen not least in its capacity to function as a unifying formula on which the most diverse schools of thought have been able to agree, whether rationalist or empiricist. Everyone here seems to be given his due: the rationalist in the reference to rationally necessary truths, *vérités de raison*, and the empiricist in the reference to empirical truths, truths founded on experience, *vérités de fait*. It is usually Kant who is credited with the feat of combining rationalism and empiricism, but this combination exists already in Leibniz, though in more embryonic form, in his theory of 'truths of reason and truths of fact'.

The different traditions had thus apparently joined forces. To one coming from the rationalist tradition, as Leibniz did, the idea seems quite natural. But Hume also, who came from the empiricist tradition, makes use of a very similar distinction—which he obviously owes to the direct influence of Leibniz. This is the distinction which for him is so fundamental, between '*Relations of Ideas*' and '*Matters of Fact*'.[8] When he speaks of Relations of Ideas, Hume has in mind propositions which, like Leibniz' 'truths of reason', bear the stamp of necessity, so that their nega-

[8] 'All the objects of human reason or enquiry may naturally be divided into two kinds, to wit, *Relations of Ideas* and *Matters of Fact*' (Hume, *Enquiries*, p. 25).

tion involves a contradiction. Hence in order to demonstrate their truth there is no need to fall back on the facts of experience, but a simple reference to rational necessity is sufficient. With regard to Matters of Fact, however, the position is that all propositions based on them are only contingent; their negation involves no contradiction, and in order to see and demonstrate their truth we have to turn to experience and its facts. 'The contrary of every matter of fact is still possible.'[9]

It is interesting to see how closely Hume here follows Leibniz's distinction between the two kinds of 'truths'. Admittedly he formulates it in other terms and even draws other conclusions from it, yet his pattern of thought is none the less borrowed from Leibniz. The idea of different sorts of 'truths', necessary and contingent, rational and empirical, has become the common property of the most diverse schools of thought, and as it were the self-evident background for the continuing philosophical debate. From Leibniz the line runs directly to philosophy of a rationalistic type, while through Hume, and as reformulated by him, the Leibnizian idea is carried into the empiricist camp. On every hand we find such concepts as 'necessary truths', 'logical truths', 'analytic truths', 'truths of reason', etc., set over against such concepts as 'contingent truths', 'empirical truths', 'truths of fact', etc. All the way from Leibniz to contemporary 'logical empiricism' we encounter the doctrine of different sorts of 'truths' which he inaugurated. It underlies, for example, the common idea that a meaningful statement must be either a tautology or an empirical proposition, and that the stipulation of truth is the decisive criterion of meaning. Leibniz, indeed, with his *vérités de raison et vérités de fait* and his 'eternal and contingent truths', can be said to have succeeded in founding a school, though in a way that cuts across the party-lines of all schools.

All of this goes to show how extremely important Leibniz's theory of different kinds of 'truths' has been for the development of philosophy since his time. With it the lines were laid down along which that development would largely proceed. It is, however, another and a very important question, whether these lines were rightly laid, or whether they have led us in the wrong direction. That is the question we have to answer as we now go on to discuss the disastrous aspect of Leibniz's theory.

2) It was in fact a disastrous step that was taken when Leibniz enunciated his twin concepts of *vérités de raison* and *vérités de fait* and the theory of different sorts of truths gained acceptance in philosophy. A simple analysis is enough to show that it put philosophy on the wrong track. To begin with, the idea of different kinds of 'truths'—'truths' in the plural, be it noted—is itself very much open to question. It is an instance of the fuzzy thinking, not uncommon in philosophy, which obscures the real issue, and which develops according to a fairly constant pattern. The trouble starts—quite innocently, it seems—with substantivization, goes on through the

[9] *Ibid.*

addition of the definite article and the use of the plural form to substantialization, and ends in a metaphysical fog. We touched on this problem above
when we were dealing with the way in which metaphysics runs off into
ontology and conceptual realism;[10] and now we have a new concrete
example of this metaphysical deviation.

The reality underlying the crazy notion of different 'truths' is the simple
fact that in science as in everyday life we distinguish, and must distinguish,
between some things that are true and some that are false. Here, at the
starting point, everything is simple and clear; everyone understands immediately what it is all about. It is when we leave this immediate level and
proceed to substantivization, describing what is true as 'truth', that complications begin to arise. By itself, of course, substantivization need not be
a sign of anything wrong, and it would not if it were only a different way of
saying the same thing, so that 'this is the truth' = 'this is true'. However, it
does not generally stop at that, but what is true is given the status of 'a
truth'. With this the way is open for the deviation into conceptual realism:
'truth' becomes a sort of spiritual 'entity', it acquires something of the
character of a 'substance', and the process is completed with talk about
different 'truths', each with its own distinctive character. From the simple
statement 'this is true' (= 'this is how things are') and 'this is false' (= 'this
is not how things are'), or in other words, from the simple affirmation or
negation of a proposition, we move on to a whole system of different
degrees and kinds of truth—and all the conditions are set for a metaphysical fog.

If we start with the idea that there are two different kinds of 'truths',
necessary and contingent, we are inevitably exposed to a double temptation: that of *reducing* one kind of truth to the other, and that of *judging* one
kind of truth by the standard of the other. Both in Leibniz and his successors there are plain instances of yielding to both these temptations, with
—we may add—ruinous consequences for the concept of truth.

(2) *The reduction of one kind of 'truth' to the other*
By reducing one kind of truth to the other, or conceiving it as a modification of the other, it becomes possible for everybody to find in the two–part
formula the one thing that is most in accord with his own standpoint. For
one who comes from the rationalist tradition it is entirely natural to trace
vérités de fait back to *vérités de raison*. Even those truths which belong
essentially to the sphere of experience, he will seek if possible to trace back
to the truths of reason or logical truths. Only when he has succeeded in
deducing the former from the latter, and has thus in the last analysis transformed contingent truths into necessary truths, does he feel that he has
reached his goal. For one who comes from the empiricist tradition, on the
other hand, it is just as natural to take the opposite course and seek to

[10] Above, pp. 42f. and 46f. (See also Additional Note II.2.—Tr.)

83

trace all truth back to truths of experience. That is to say, he tries to reduce *vérités de raison* to *vérités de fait*, and regards all knowledge as having its source in sensations. Only when he has succeeded in showing how even that which most seems to possess a necessity independent of experience, is merely a modification of what through repeated sense-perception we have become accustomed to regard as inevitable—only then does he feel he has reached his goal.

1) The most outstanding example of the attempt to reduce *vérités de fait* to *vérités de raison* is Leibniz himself. He comes from the rationalist tradition, and he is never unfaithful to it. Admittedly he speaks of different kinds of truths, but if these are to be for him truths in the strict sense of the term, they must be rational truths, *vérités de raison*. Strictly speaking we ought according to Leibniz to be able to *deduce everything*, and until we are we cannot speak of truth and knowledge in the deepest sense. This is in harmony with the Aristotelian ideal of science and the rationalistic outlook he espouses. Mathematics, geometry, is the prototype of a science which *demonstrates* its 'truths'. In mathematics and geometry we have access to 'the true source of the eternal truths',[11] and even the logical syllogism can be described by Leibniz as a kind of 'universal mathematics' and 'an art of infallibility'.[12] It is the absolute certainty which mathematics, like logic, affords, that makes it the science par excellence. A science which cannot show such precision cannot strictly be called science. Not even physics, judged by this exacting standard, can vindicate its position as a genuine science.[13] The words often quoted from the preface to Kant's *Meta-physische Anfangsgründe der Naturwissenschaft*: 'I affirm, however, that in any particular doctrine of nature only so much real science can be found as there is mathematics', while they only partly cover Kant's own view,[14] can be applied without qualification to Leibniz. For science consists for him essentially in mathematical calculation, and the goal that beckons him is always the thought of a *Mathesis Universalis*.

Yes, it ought to be so: everything ought to be deducible. Only deduction leads to genuine knowledge and to necessary truths. It ought to be so—but alas it is not, for there are things we call contingent and empirical. With these we have to remain on a lower level, since in this area no deduction is feasible. Here we must be content simply to state that it *is* so, without being able to say why it is so or that it must necessarily be so. Yet even on this lower level we can of course say that something is true. Hence the question arises, how we are to define the relation between these inferior, contingent truths and the eternal, necessary truths. The contingent truths

[11] Leibniz, *Philosophische Werke*, III, p. 543.
[12] *Op. cit.*, p. 580.
[13] 'I therefore believe that physics is not capable in our hands of becoming a science' —at all events 'never . . . a complete science' (*op. cit.*, p. 545).
[14] *Cf.* F. Delekat, *Immanuel Kant*, pp. 238f., 249.

are of a peculiar kind, for the direct opposite of them could be the case. They are truths that are not really truths, not really in accord with the idea of truth as Leibniz understands it. On the other hand, they cannot be said to be completely devoid of any truth-value whatever.

From this dilemma Leibniz escapes by means of a leap into metaphysics. The idea of God, as we know it from his *Théodicé*, is brought in to provide the solution. On the human level there is a difference between necessary and contingent, but on God's level this duality disappears. For God every-thing is necessary. The contingency of the contingent truths is simply an effect of our human finitude. We call them contingent because we cannot see their necessity. But this does not alter the fact that in the last resort and from God's point of view they too are necessary.

When Leibniz sets the two kinds of truth *sub specie Dei*, their relation-ship to one another is vastly changed. This has little effect on the 'eternal truths'; they are and remain in one sense unchanged, whether on the human level or the divine, for they are already by definition such as to be incapable of change. They hold good equally for us and the world we live in, as for all other possible worlds; indeed they hold good for God himself. The laws of logic (the law of identity and the law of contradiction) as well as the truths of mathematics are valid for every conceivable world, and not even God has it in his power to invalidate them. They can very well be identified with the nature of God. God, the Eternal, is the source of the eternal truths, the logically and mathematically necessary truths. It is therefore out of the question that he should ever change them or declare them invalid. Here God and man are so to speak on common ground, and thanks to the eternal truths man is able to think the thoughts of God him-self.

Far more striking is the effect on the 'contingent truths' when these are set *sub specie Dei*. In this area, with regard to things contingent, there is no possibility of our thinking God's thoughts. We cannot see how they hang together, we cannot derive them from general principles. Our human existence bears the stamp of contingency, but with God nothing is con-tingent, everything is necessary. From our point of view we can certainly say that not even God could alter the eternal truths—they are not subject to his will—whereas the world, the world of facts, is as it is because God's creative will has given it this form. That is why the world and its affairs bear the stamp of contingency. It means, moreover, that the world and its affairs could have been quite different. Or could they—really? It certainly seems so to our limited human understanding. But the situation is greatly changed when the question is transferred to the divine level.

Everything God does is rational, has its rational ground, for the very nature of God is *ratio*. His creation of our world was an act of divine reason. He had the choice between an infinite number of possible worlds. Why did he choose just ours? His choice could not be completely arbitrary and for no reason. He chose it because he calculated it to be 'the best of worlds'. This idea of Leibniz's has often been interpreted as simply an expression of groundless 'optimism'. But it has nothing to do with optimism in either greater or lesser degree. Its meaning is quite other than that. It is a simple corollary of Leibniz's conception of God and of reason. When God as *ratio* considers the different possible worlds and the advantages of one over another, it would be *irrational* if he did not choose 'the best of worlds' rather than any other world. God's *ratio* guarantees that he could not make any other choice. All thought of contingency and arbitrariness is eliminated here. This means, however, that necessity moves in to take its place. Even the contingent is—*sub specie Dei*—pure necessity. The result of holding together these two ideas (*a*) of the unconditional validity of logical truths in every possible world and (*b*) of our world as 'the best of worlds' is a complete alteration of the relationship between the eternal and the contingent truths. *Sub specie Dei* they are both equally necessary, equally rationally necessary.

Naturally there is something disingenuous about this metaphysical excursion of Leibniz and his attempt to get rid of the difficulties that beset our 'finite' human thinking by resorting to the divine way of thinking—what does Leibniz know about that? It is not this, however, that primarily interests us here, but rather what Leibniz is getting at with these odd ideas. The chief thing is that he is seeking by hook or by crook to get the contingent truths over to the side of the eternal truths. Like Descartes before him, Leibniz brings in God as the guarantor of 'truth'. God as the Eternal is in the first place the guarantor of the 'eternal truths', and then as the Creator of the world, which is 'the best of worlds', he guarantees that the 'contingency' of the world is governed in the last resort by rational necessity. The factual situation has thus its rationally necessary ground, and the *vérités de fait* are reduced to *vérités de raison*. The divine reason rules over all, both the contingent and the rationally necessary.

Leibniz has attained his goal. He has succeeded in reducing the contingent truths to the eternal. At the same time he has demolished his key conception of the two kinds of 'truths'. Is there really anything of it left? All that remains seems to be the assertion of the 'finitude' of human thought, and of our inability because of it to reach a true understanding of what to us looks contingent but in reality is not. No reason can be given for the distinction between 'necessary and contingent truths' other than that of human finitude. Yet Leibniz allows the distinction to stand, since from a rationalistic standpoint it is rendered innocuous by the assertion that even the contingent is from a higher point of view necessary. We can now see at once what is wrong with Leibniz's dichotomy of truth: he both does and does not distinguish between *vérités de raison* and *vérités de fait*. In fact everything is swallowed up, including the empirical, by the truths of reason, because God has *a priori* knowledge of the contingent; he can tell in advance what is going to happen and why it is necessary. The final result is that the empirical truths, which by definition are contingent, are nevertheless *a priori* for God. The contingent is in fact also the necessary, although we because of our finitude cannot grasp it as such. Only God as infinite intelligence can see how things really are.

We stated above that the significance of Leibniz's theory of 'eternal and contingent truths' lay in the fact that it provided a simple, easily manageable and apparently clear formula for an important distinction which had not until then been successfully grasped. But now, to the extent that the distinction between the two kinds of 'truths' is blurred, the significance of the formula is lost; for with the loss of its clarity it loses also the possibility of serving its intended purpose. Only its questionable features remain, particularly the erroneous use of the concept of truth in and with the notion of different 'truths'—a subject we have already discussed.[15]

2) As Leibniz furnishes an example of the attempt to reduce everything to '*vérités de raison*', so Hume furnishes an example of the opposite procedure, that is, of the attempt to reduce everything to 'matters of fact'. This is not however immediately obvious when Hume discusses the relation between 'relations of ideas' and 'matters of fact'. It is on the contrary amazing how far he can go in this matter with Leibniz. There are long passages of his in which it could very well be Leibniz who was speaking; and if these were all we had, we might easily think that Hume represented the rationalist rather than the empiricist tradition. This is a result of the fact already mentioned that he accepted the Leibnizian pattern of thought. Logic and mathematics have to do with 'relations of ideas', and here it is possible without any reference to experience to show in a purely demonstrative and deductive way the necessity or impossibility of an idea. With regard to 'matters of fact', however, we are wholly dependent on experience, and here we can never attain complete certainty but at most a certain probability. Yet it is none the less the empiricist tradition that is ultimately determinative for Hume, and this is in evidence almost everywhere—in the fact, for example, that his view of the nature of knowledge is in the usual empiricist way genetically oriented, or in his association-psychology and the tracing back of all our ideas to simple, atomistically conceived sense-impressions.

In order to understand Hume's thinking, it is necessary to observe the continual oscillation between the rationalistic scheme taken over from Leibniz, and the preoccupation with sense-data as the ultimately decisive thing, which he took over from the empiricist tradition. A good example of this oscillation is his famous criticism of the idea of causality. His objections to causality arise in part from his desire to find in it a 'necessity' of a logical kind. Since he does not find this, and since causality is not given as a simple impression, he has to reject it. Yet how little he himself was able to

15 Above, pp. 82f.

dispense with the idea of causation is plain, not only from his attempt to give a causal explanation of the idea of causality in psychological terms by referring it to custom, but also from his uninhibited use of the causal scheme in its popular form despite his own criticism of it. Even the idea that the cause produces the effect, which in this context is most extraordinary, is actually asserted by him: 'The same cause always produces the same effect.'[16] The weakness of his argument, however, is concealed by the oscillation mentioned above. Yet it is very plain where the centre of gravity lies in this oscillation: it is undoubtedly in sense experience. This is the only source of all genuine knowledge, and to it all knowledge and truth whatsoever must be traced back.

While this tendency is clear in Hume, in the subsequent development it becomes more and more powerful. It culminates in John Stuart Mill, who forthrightly declares that what have traditionally been called necessary truths—logic and mathematical axioms—are all ultimately based on 'experimental truths' and are nothing else but 'generalizations from observation'.[17] All our knowledge and all truth is thus derived from induction. For Mill's definition of induction is precisely 'Generalization from Experience'.[18] We have no need to look beyond experience for proof of the validity of the axioms. Our entire experience swarms with proofs of it.[19] Experiential proofs of the axioms crowd in upon us in such profusion that we cannot but believe them. This is what gives us the impression that there is an obviousness about the axioms which is other, greater and more incontrovertible than anything experience can supply.[20] But that idea conceals the true, empirical nature of the axioms, which in fact are nothing else but general empirical propositions or 'generalizations from observation'. Endless repetition with no exception to the rule gives rise to the impression that it is necessarily so and cannot be otherwise. When as a result we feel justified in making the generalization, we are entirely within our rights,

---

[16] Hume, *A Treatise of Human Nature*, pp. 173ff.

[17] Mill, *System of Logic*, I, p. 266: 'It remains to inquire, what is the ground of our belief in axioms—what is the evidence on which they rest? I answer, *they are experimental truths; generalizations from observation.* The proposition, Two straight lines cannot inclose a space—or in other words, two straight lines which have once met do not meet again, but continue to diverge—is an induction from the evidence of our senses.' Italics ours.

[18] *Op. cit.*, p. 354: 'Induction, properly so called . . . may, then, be summarily defined as Generalization from Experience. It consists in inferring from some individual instances in which a phenomenon is observed to occur, that it occurs in all instances of a certain class.'

[19] *Op. cit.*, p. 267: 'It receives confirmation in almost every instant of our lives.'

[20] *Ibid.*: 'Experimental proof crowds in upon us in such endless profusion, and without one instance in which there can be even a suspicion of an exception to the rule, that we should soon have stronger ground for believing the axiom, even as an experimental truth, than we have for almost any of the general truths which we confessedly learn from the evidence of our senses.'

provided we do not misinterpret it as if it were a more than experiential necessity.

For there is only one source of truth and knowledge, namely experience. From this everything derives, not only 'truths of fact' but also the supposedly 'necessary' truths, the axiomatic truths. This source is quite sufficient also to ensure the validity of the axioms. 'Where then is the necessity for assuming that our recognition of these truths has a different origin from the rest of our knowledge, when its existence is perfectly accounted for by supposing its origin to be the same? . . . The burden of proof lies on the advocates of the contrary opinion: it is for them to point out some fact inconsistent with the supposition that this part of our knowledge of nature is derived from the same sources as every other part.'[21]

3) Here we have touched on a well-known problem, to which thinkers have devoted a vast amount of effort, and which is usually called 'the problem of induction'.[22] What it involves in brief, is the question how we can show justification for the inductive method. For whereas the deductive method proceeds by drawing conclusions from the universal to the particular, the inductive method takes the opposite course, from the particular to the universal; and whereas the deductive method is logically unimpeachable and leads to correct and inescapable conclusions, there is something dubious about the inductive procedure.

From a purely logical point of view, of course, it is impossible to draw any valid conclusion from the particular to the universal. Not even if I know a very large number of particular cases in which a certain fact obtains, have I any right to draw the conclusion that it therefore obtains in all cases. Even if I have inspected and tested all the relevant cases accessible to me and found them in accord with my assumption, it is none the less a fallacy to proceed from this to a universal judgment. I have after all no guarantee that I have taken into account all the cases at present in existence. There may be within the bounds of present experience certain instances to the contrary which happen to have been overlooked—and a single negative instance is enough to overturn the general proposition. What is more, it is possible that future experience may confound the most careful and complete inductive statistics. We can never draw safe conclusions from the known present to the unknown future. Yet we make use of induction. What right have we to do so? What can be said in justification of the inductive procedure? Obviously there can be no deductive justification for induction—that would involve a logical fallacy. Nor can there be any inductive justification for induction—that would be a typical circular

---

[21] *Ibid.*

[22] See Bibliography for works on *Induction* and/or *Probability* by H. Feigl, J. J. Katz, W. Kneale, H. Reichenbach, G. H. von Wright. Note also M. Black, *Problems*, pp. 157–208, K. Popper, 'Philosophy of Science', H. Reichenbach, *Die philosophishe Bedeutung der neueren Physik.*

argument. Induction thus seems to hang in the air, with no visible means of support. Every method of justifying it seems to have been exhausted. Which makes it all the more absurd to think with J. S. Mill that by means of the unjustifiable inductive method we can provide a justification for deduction and its primary axioms.

As long as we hold to the theory of two kinds of truths, and try to reduce the contingent truths to the eternal and logically necessary (Leibniz) or the logical truths to the empirical (Hume, Mill), it seems quite natural to seek also to reduce induction to deduction or deduction to induction; for at bottom they are completely parallel problems, not to say one and the same problem. But when we have realized how untenable the theory of 'eternal and contingent truths' is, we can see at once how meaningless it is to want to give a deductive justification for induction or an inductive justification for deduction. It is simply impossible to reduce them consistently one to the other. Conversely, we could say that once we have perceived the absurdity of the 'problem of induction' we can infer from it the untenability of its presupposition, namely the distinction between 'eternal (or necessary) and contingent truths'.[23] The 'problem of induction' is an excellent illustration of the way to get into a vicious circle: reduce deduction to induction and induction to deduction, derive laws from particular observations and particular observations from laws—and all because of the different kinds of 'truths' which are supposed to give one another mutual confirmation and support. Behind it all, both in the attempt to reduce one kind of truth to the other and the attempt to reduce induction to deduction and vice versa, there lies the 'quest for certainty'—to use John Dewey's well-known phrase.[24]

'The quest for certainty'—this idea, which has characterized modern thought ever since Descartes raised his plea for an absolutely certain knowledge that cannot be doubted, with the extravagant and essentially absurd demand that it must be an absolutely necessary knowledge if we are to accept it, has made our knowledge more uncertain than it really is. The demand that every proposition must be logically proved and thus ineluctably certain before it can be accepted, is a demand which is quite out of place in the context of science. Its roots are elsewhere, and primarily in metaphysical theories like that of Leibniz concerning different sorts of 'truths' and their differing degrees of certainty. Can we really prove— logically prove—the existence of the external world as a mathematical theorem is proved? We cannot. It is therefore entirely consistent that thinkers who refuse to accept anything but what is logically proved, should

[23] There are different aspects to the problem of induction. Here we are dealing only with the one that relates to the question of 'eternal and contingent truths'. We shall have occasion later, however, to consider the significance of induction for scientific argumentation.
[24] J. Dewey, *The Quest for Certainty.*

deny the existence of the sense-world—despite the fact that in any case we know it is there, and these thinkers themselves in all other respects reckon with its being there. If reality does not agree with our theory, then it is, as we all know, so much the worse for reality; and what we are discussing here is evidence of this.

From this there arise the *meaningless* debates for and against. Both standpoints are meaningless. We cannot 'prove', but that is no reason for doubting. We have 'empirical knowledge', which although as empirical it cannot be logically proved, is not therefore defective. On the contrary, it does not have to be proved and it ought not to be proved, for that would involve us in very serious confusion. The empirical is something we verify, not something we prove. There is a fundamental difference between *proof* and *verification*. Verification belongs in the empirical, proof in the logical realm. Just as it is meaningless to wish to 'verify' a logical statement, so it is meaningless to wish to 'prove' an empirical statement. Wittgenstein has rightly called attention to the essentially self-evident fact that nothing can possibly be at once empirical and capable of proof.[25] The whole difficulty arises because we put the question wrongly and demand a 'necessary' knowledge where there can be no such thing, and starting with this basically perverse notion we depreciate the knowledge we in fact possess, because it is 'only' factual—as if it were not enough to know that it is 'in fact' true—or in other words, because it is 'only' true and not something else.

The original intention of Leibniz's distinction between necessary and factual truths, or at all events what could have made it of positive significance, was that it should provide a means of obviating confusion between the logical and the factual, and so preclude the kind of blundering we have just observed. Its significance lay in its potential for keeping the demarcation clear between the necessity and inevitability of the logical on the one hand, and on the other the character of the factual as something simply given, something which simply is so, and which thus has its own kind of inevitability. Yet this very distinction itself turns out to be a source of confusion and muddle. The two-way traffic we noticed above, where the factual was reduced to the logically necessary and the logical to the factual, induction to deduction and deduction to induction, arose from the fact that the two disparate ideas which were to have been kept apart, came to be subsumed under a common concept of 'truths', which seemed to make it right to bring them together and reduce them to one another. But presumably the purpose of distinguishing between the two kinds of truths and showing how different they are—one of them completely independent of experience and the other completely dependent on it—was to use the distinction and maintain the difference, not to obliterate it. Otherwise it would have been better to make no distinction at all, rather than one which

[25] Wittgenstein, *Philosophische Bemerkungen*, p. 145.

holds out the promise of a certain lucidity but which its author himself does everything to render ambiguous. The latter is what happened with Leibniz, owing to the inherent ambiguity of the concept of truth, by which disparate things were wrongly held together and allowed to get mixed up with one another.

(3) *The judging of one kind of 'truth' by the other*

The disastrous consequences of the theory of two kinds of 'truths' become still more evident when one kind of 'truth' is used as a standard by which to measure the truth-status of the other, the contingent being measured by the necessary and vice versa. When a distinction is made between two different sorts of 'truths' it seems legitimate, or at least very natural, to make a comparison between them in order to see what each of them is and is not capable of doing. All the preconditions for such an evaluative comparison are present. The fact that both can be described as 'truths' suggests that they have at least enough in common to furnish a fruitful basis for it. Yet they are different sorts of 'truths', and one sort does not give us the same as the other. What then does each give us of 'truth' when compared with the other and measured by the other? The question is, however, what the consequences of this are for the concept of truth itself.

We have already seen how the line of demarcation is obliterated and the distinction rendered useless by the inclusive notion of 'truths', and we are now faced with consequences of a still more serious nature, which go far deeper and compel us to ask whether with this as a starting point it is possible any longer to maintain the concept of truth, or whether scepticism is not the inevitable result. This issue emerges very plainly in the oscillation between the rationalist and empiricist trends in the history of thought ever since Leibniz and Hume. Each of these traditions, of course, claims to take care of truth and certainty ('the quest for certainty'), the rationalist by seeking to anchor all knowledge and truth in the logically necessary, and the empiricist by seeking to anchor them in what is immediately presented to the senses. Now it might well be thought that because of their one-sided approaches neither of them could do full justice to the question of truth in its entirety, but that taken together they could complement one another and jointly satisfy the requirements of knowledge and truth. For presumably when each tradition takes its own special view and develops it one-sidedly, it must at least do justice to that aspect of the matter. But the position is not so simple. It is one of the ironies of history that neither tradition has succeeded in doing justice to the aspect it has made specially its own.

1) The rationalist tradition puts its emphasis on the 'necessary truths', and in doing so it doubtless gives the empirical less than its due. What is more interesting, however, is to see how it handles its own speciality, the 'necessary truths'. For the idea of 'necessary truths' is bound to break

down, because it involves something that is merely hypothetical. This fact did not of course escape the notice of Leibniz. There are several statements of his which show him to be aware that logical and mathematical 'truths' are only hypothetical, and that we cannot strictly speak of 'truth' in connection with things of such a kind. Thus we find him saying: 'As far as the *eternal truths* are concerned, we must observe that they are all basically conditional statements, which mean in fact that if this or that is posited, this or that other follows.'[26] It is astonishing how lightly Leibniz takes this matter, speaking quite calmly of 'eternal truths' at the same time as he completely undermines them with admissions like the one just cited. For if it is a fact that the eternal truths are 'all basically conditional statements'— as they undeniably are—then the question arises whether they can be said to be 'truths' at all. There is something of a contradiction in speaking of 'hypothetical truths'. The word 'true' is a sensitive term, which we cannot juggle with as we please. Either a thing is true or it is not; either this is the way things are or it is not the way things are. A hypothetical statement says nothing about the truth, but only about the consequence. What it involves is expressed in the formula 'if . . . then'. *If* I have made a certain assumption, logical consistency requires me to accept also what is implicit in it. As to how far the assumption is true, logic has nothing to say; that is a question entirely outside its province. What logic is interested in and insists on is simply consistency in drawing conclusions. To introduce the idea of 'truth' or 'truths' here only confuses the issue, and Leibniz ought to have been more careful at this point.

Leibniz had borrowed a good deal from Hobbes, and he was under the influence of Hobbes while developing his theory of two kinds of truths; but one could wish he had been a more apt pupil. For although much of what Hobbes has to offer in this connection is very questionable, yet on the point that concerns us here he shows himself more perceptive than Leibniz. Just when he introduces the dichotomy which has obviously been of some significance for Leibniz's theory of 'truths of reason and truths of fact', Hobbes does not speak of 'truth' but uses instead the quite adequate term 'consequence'. He says: 'There are of knowledge two kinds, whereof one is *knowledge of fact*: the other *knowledge of the consequence of one affirmation to another*.'[27] In logic and mathematics what is at issue is not 'truth' but 'consequence', 'the consequence of one affirmation to another' as Hobbes puts it—and it could not be better put. In this connection he underlines also the conditional (hypothetical) nature of the reasoning with its 'if . . . then'. The position had thus been clarified and a good deal of preliminary work done, from which Leibniz might have learnt something that would have prevented his going wrong and spared us the disastrous results of his error. It was the empiricist mentality that saved Hobbes, while the

26 Leibniz, *Neue Abhandlungen*, pp. 536f., ET pp. 515f. Italics ours.
27 Hobbes, *English Works*, III, p. 71.

rationalist misled Leibniz. Leibniz was so preoccupied with his quest for 'pure rational truths', 'eternal truths', 'necessary truths', that he neglected to analyze the meaning of the 'necessity' involved in this context and failed to realize that it belongs to another category than that of 'truth'. This is a good example of the fact we noted above, that it is precisely rationalism with its special concern for logical necessity that has most difficulty in doing justice to it. What is simply a matter of 'consequence' is transformed by Leibniz into a particular sort of 'truth'.

In other words, Leibniz has taken logical necessity, which is a necessity and inevitability of consequence, and put a false label on it, representing it as a necessary logical 'truth'. But the false labelling of goods is always a serious matter, for the customer is deceived and the goods are compromised; and this is just what has happened as a result of using the false label of 'necessary truths'. Under this heading a host of 'truths' are introduced that have nothing to do with 'truth'. Leibniz was enough of a logician to see that the syllogism is not a 'truth', not even a 'logical truth', but a hypothetical statement of consequence, and that a tautology as lacking any content cannot be true (or false) but has a necessity and inevitability of a quite different kind. He was enough of a mathematician to see that the description of mathematical propositions as 'eternal truths' is a misuse of words, since such propositions are not 'truths' of any kind at all. 'That one plus one equals two *is not properly a truth*.'[28] Why then does he use such improper and fundamentally wrong expressions as 'eternal truths' and 'necessary truths'? He does so because he is metaphysician enough not to lose an opportunity of letting the necessity of logical consequence serve as a basis for the rationalistic demand for a special 'rational truth'.

With this, however, Leibniz has reached the point where the meaning of the word 'true' is compromised by the inclusion in the concept of truth of things that have nothing to do with truth but only with consequence. The so-called logical truths contain no affirmation which could be said to be true or false. The concept of truth is simply not applicable here. But if the 'eternal truths' which are supposed to be the foundation of all truth are themselves 'not properly truths', then the concept of truth is in fact abandoned and the way is wide open for scepticism. The result of insisting on 'eternal truths' is thus the dissolution of the concept of truth itself. There are no eternal truths, no intrinsically necessary truths; and therefore, in so far as all truth and certainty is held to be derivable from such 'truths', everything is now uncertain and there is nothing that deserves the name of truth.

2) We find things hardly better when we turn to the empirical truths and the way empiricism handles them. Here also the idea of 'necessary truths' has cast its shadow. The empirical truths have been depreciated and branded 'contingent'. In according them this status rationalists and em-

[28] Leibniz, *Neue Abhandlungen*, p. 484, ET p. 467. Italics ours.

piricists are surprisingly united. The question that interests us here, however, is whether empiricism has succeeded in doing real justice to that aspect for which it has assumed special responsibility. If the rationalist says that empirical knowledge is not logically necessary, no one can object; for it is of course a fact. The error of the rationalist is not that he denies the logical demonstrability of empirical knowledge (for in this he is quite right), nor is it that he has misunderstood the nature and logical status of such knowledge. His error lies rather, as we saw above, in his misunderstanding precisely of the *rational*. He seeks to measure all truth and knowledge by the standard of the 'necessary truths' and so becomes a metaphysician—not to repeat here what we have already said about the 'necessary truths' being no truths at all. But from a rationalist nothing else could be expected.

It is more serious, however, if the empiricist now says the same, and grants that empirical knowledge is only a 'contingent' affair. For if anyone should be concerned to see justice done to *empeiria* it is he. If he says we cannot *prove* the empirical, or that all empirical observation is liable to error—of perception, memory, etc.—he is right, for that is in fact the case. But if from this he draws a conclusion in the direction of scepticism, then he has betrayed the empirical which it was his business to defend. It is of course true that as regards anything based on empirical observation it can never strictly be proved that such is the case and must be the case. But to draw from this simple and basically self-evident fact any generally sceptical conclusions means the abandonment of all empirical knowledge whatever. Surely this cannot be what empiricism was intended to do? It is really astonishing how its representatives outdo one another in pointing out how unreliable empirical knowledge is, and how in this area we can never arrive at any truth but must always be content with a greater or less degree of probability. If we take a closer look at this question, however, we discover that what lies behind this depreciation of empirical knowledge is not so much empirical observation as a shadowy reminiscence of the rationalistic ideal of truth and knowledge, according to which all truth must be measured by the standard of the 'necessary truths' and only what can be proved by strict logic deserves the name of 'truth'.

Can the empirical be logically proved? No. Hence the conclusion is drawn that in this area we cannot have 'truth' but only probability. But the proper reply to the question whether the empirical can be logically proved is: Clearly it cannot, and neither ought it to be. It would not only be wrong, but meaningless, to try to give a logical proof or justification of the empirical. Again it is the quest for certainty that darkens the scene and causes confusion. The idea is that if we are to be really certain, we cannot rely on 'contingent' facts but must try to obtain a genuinely binding and inescapable proof, that is, a logical proof. Thus we are back at the contrast between necessary and contingent truths. It is no wonder that on this basis,

95

where empirical statements are measured by the standard of logical necessity, the notion can arise that there is something 'contingent' and suspect about a mere empirical fact. That is how things look from this point of view. Otherwise the idea of 'contingent truths' seems rather artificial. Why does anyone ever speak of such things? The only real reason for introducing this odd idea is that the factually given is being measured by the standard of logical necessity. But that is something there is no need to do.

To describe anything as 'true' is to say that it is *in fact* so; and to state this is in no way to depreciate it, but quite the reverse. The factual does not need to be measured by any non-factual standard in order to be recognized as fully accredited truth; it exists in its own right. We are, however, accustomed to thinking in terms of the scheme: possible—actual—necessary, so that the actual or matter of fact appears to occupy a sort of middle ground between possibility and necessity. What is actual is naturally possible; but is it also necessary—or is it 'merely' actual? What is actual is more than merely possible, but less than what is necessary as well, so it seems. Has then the actual or factual, as being in this intermediate position, sufficient status to be described as 'true'? Can a proposition which deals with a mere matter of fact ever be more than probable, seeing that it is not necessarily true?

It is a serious mistake to assert that we can never on the empirical level speak of truth in the strict sense of the term, but only of a higher or lower degree of probability. Empirical statements can be of many different sorts as far as their probability or truth is concerned. There are propositions that are extremely improbable, others that are highly probable, and yet others that are indubitably true. If for instance today as I write I say: 'There is a country called England, and that country is surrounded by the sea on three sides; and there is another country called France, and that is situated on the Continent', these empirical statements cannot be rightly rephrased and their meaning expressed by saying: 'There is in all probability a country called England and another called France.' Nor is it any better to say: 'There is a probability bordering on certainty that these countries exist.' For there is no question of probability here at all, either more or less, but it is simply a matter of fact that these things are so. What I say about the two countries is not probable, but quite simply true. Any attempt to transpose the truth of these propositions into some form of probability is a falsification. Only the acceptance of a preconceived opinion, a falsely based theory of the relation between probability and truth, can lead anyone to such a misinterpretation. That there is a country called England cannot be logically or mathematically proved; but this does not justify the proposition that it is only very highly probable that there is a country called England. Such a proposition is false, because what is involved is not probability at all, but a state of affairs which quite simply is so, factually so. It is a question of something that is true, factually and there-fore inescapably true. Nor is there any reasonable ground for labelling this a 'contingent truth'. If there were, it would be to guard against the mis-taken idea that we have here a logically or mathematically demonstrable proposition—surely a superfluous precaution, since no one would in any case entertain such an absurd notion.

(4) *The falsity of both kinds of 'truth'*
The conclusion to which we are led is this: 1. *There are no 'eternal truths' or 'necessary truths'*. What have wrongly been classed as such are quite out of place in the context of truth. Logical consequences and the necessity characteristic of them have been mistakenly interpreted as 'necessary truths'. Then, when once this mistake has been made, the next follows naturally: the empirical is misinterpreted as representing 'contingent truths'. The latter, however, are nothing but a mirage resulting from the previous error. 2. *There are no 'contingent truths'*. The words 'contingent' and 'truths' are an ill-assorted pair, and might well be regarded as a con-tradiction in terms. For although the empirical situation to which attention is directed may be 'contingent' enough, its contingency does not affect the truth about it. The 'truth' about a situation is what it is and cannot in any circumstances be otherwise (i.e. it is true and cannot possibly be false), so that even if the situation is contingent, the truth is not. The terms 'neces-sary' and 'contingent' are wholly inappropriate where truth is concerned.

The position, then, is this: if what is meant by the formula 'necessary and contingent truths' were the whole truth about 'truth', it would mean that there was no truth at all. It would be the ruination of the very idea of truth, and the inevitable result would be scepticism.

Something of this is reflected in the philosophical thinking of the last few centuries, especially in the oscillation between rationalism and em-piricism mentioned above. It is customary to speak of rationalism and empiricism as two great, independent streams of thought, and in doing so to concentrate—very naturally—on their antithetical features. What one affirms the other denies. Rationalism denies what cannot ultimately be traced back to *ratio*, empiricism what cannot ultimately be traced back to *sensus*, sense-experience. What is easily overlooked, however, is that this is a thoroughly superficial contrast, since both start with the same basic assumption, namely the theory of two kinds of 'truths', *vérités de raison et vérités de fait*. As each of them stresses its own kind of 'truths' they are opposed to one another, but as they both start with the same basic idea they are variants of one another. We therefore get a somewhat inaccurate picture if we think of them as two distinct and separate streams, each consistently following its own prescribed course. They present rather the picture of a surging sea, in which waves from one current break against waves from another, or just as often imperceptibly merge with one another.

97

At almost every point rationalism and empiricism can be seen to be variations on a common theme.

(i) Both have a common *intention*. They are impelled by the desire for absolute certainty. The quest for certainty underlies them both alike, although they seek anchorage for their certainty in different directions. While Leibniz seeks it in 'the eternal truths of reason', Hobbes and the whole empiricist tradition with him seeks it in what is given in sense-experience. For him it is in 'the knowledge of fact' that absolute certainty resides. When he draws the distinction we noted above between 'the knowledge of fact' and 'the knowledge of the consequence' he characteristically adds: 'The former is nothing else, but sense and memory, and is *absolute knowledge*.'[29]

(ii) Both have *parallel initial difficulties*. Rationalism has no difficulty of course in deriving theorems and conclusions from its ultimate axioms; for it has at its disposal such well-tried and unfailing methods as deduction and the syllogism, where each link in the chain is securely attached to the next, so that there is no room for uncertainty. There need be no gap in the argument. But if certainty is thus guaranteed for the derivative propositions, the difficulties presented by the axioms themselves, which are the starting points for the demonstration, are all the more formidable. The certainty of the derivative propositions is ensured by the axioms to which the chain of argument is anchored. But what ensures the certainty of the axioms? For as axioms they cannot be derived from anything else, and are thus incapable of rational proof. Yet if the starting point becomes dubious or proves indefensible, the whole closely knit structure threatens to collapse. This difficulty rationalism tries to gloss over by the flimsy expedient of affirming that the axioms are self-evident and need no corroboration. In this connection the idea of 'intuitive certainty' is also introduced. But suppose this intuitive certainty proves deceptive, suppose the self-evident nature of the axioms—like so much else that strikes us as self-evident—rests on an illusion? Clearly the whole building collapses when the foundation gives way. The weakness of rationalism lies in its very starting point, the axioms and their validity or certainty. This is its initial difficulty, that it cannot give a credible answer to the question, what there really is to support the whole affair.

Things are not much different for empiricism, which seeks its anchorage, not in the axioms but in what is given in experience. As long as it sticks to the concrete material, it encounters no real difficulties; for we can all agree that it is what is given in experience that constitutes the content of our knowledge. The real difficulty arises when it comes to defining what it really is that is given in experience. On what do we ultimately base our certainty when we appeal to experience? It cannot very well be the objects, for to them we have no direct access according to empiricism. All we can

---

[29] Hobbes, *English Works*, III, p. 71; *cf.* above, p. 93. Although few empiricists would follow Hobbes in this terminology, the tendency is the same.

be absolutely certain of is that we have certain concrete sense-impressions. Hence we are driven to the psychologistic and phenomenalistic line of thought which is so characteristic of empiricism.

The dilemma of empiricism is that in order to achieve complete certainty it must base itself on what is immediately given, but it cannot say what this is. Is it the momentary sensations, is it the perceptions, more or less atomistically conceived, or is it the sense-data? With the idea of obtaining an absolutely unimpeachable basis for certainty, we are driven to increasingly momentary, increasingly intra-psychic, increasingly phenomenalistic interpretations of what ultimately constitutes experience. If I am to stick to what I really know, I must express myself with the greatest caution. I cannot say that anything objectively *is* so, but only that it *appears* so. With this, phenomenalism is upon us. But I cannot even assert without qualification that it appears so. For *to whom* does it appear so? Perhaps to me but not to someone else. Perhaps to me at this moment but not at an earlier or later time. To give a completely accurate account of what is immediately given, I must present it in the form of a 'protocol-sentence', a 'minute', which records that a certain person P experienced something at a certain point of time T. But on that basis it is scarcely possible to build any coherent knowledge. The immediately given experience is emptied of its content in order that I may have a fixed point to which I can attach certainty. For it is not after all atoms and momentary sense-data that I really experience. These are abstractions designed to explain the immediately given experience, yet in the process of abstraction the immediately given gets lost.

This is from an empirical point of view a strange conclusion, to which empiricism is none the less bound to lead just because it is determined to reach complete certainty and to have a fixed point on which to base that certainty. Here is the initial difficulty of empiricism—exactly parallel to that of rationalism. In both cases it is at the starting point, where the basis for the whole way of thinking must be shown, that the difficulties make themselves felt. Rationalism sought to obtain certainty by basing everything on the axioms, but could give no convincing reason for them. Empiricism sought to obtain certainty by going back to the '*Bathos der Erfahrung*', the 'bed-rock of experience', but could give no credible explanation of what that might be. The parallel—*mutatis mutandis* of course—is complete. For if there is to be any meaning in the quest for an ultimate point of appui for certainty, that point must not itself be open to question. It is the quest for certainty that drives empiricism into further and further reduction. The desire is to be on the safe side and take no risks, hence the reduction. With regard, however, both to the rationalist and the empiricist attempts to ensure certainty, we can entirely concur with M. Bunge's comment: 'But what is the use of security if it involves ignorance?'[30]

[30] M. Bunge, *The Myth of Simplicity*, p. 87.

(iii) Both *betray their special trust*. Rationalism betrays logical necessity by misinterpreting it in terms of 'necessary truths'. Empiricism betrays experience by misinterpreting it in terms of more or less arbitrary abstractions, which have no claim to represent any real experience. We need not elaborate this point, as it has already been dealt with above.

(iv) Both result in the *destruction of the concept of truth*, and hence in *scepticism*. This point also has been sufficiently discussed. Here we will only point out how odd it is that both of these 'variants', starting with the theory of 'eternal and contingent truths' and seeking each in its own way to uphold the truth, should result in the destruction of the concept of truth, and that both of them, while desiring each in its own way to ensure 'certainty', should lead in the end to scepticism if not solipsism. Just as they have a common starting point in the quest for certainty, so they run on parallel lines all the way to the end, where both tend to develop symptoms of solipsism. Rationalism gives one answer to the question of certainty, and moves through phenomenalism into *idealistic solipsism*. Empiricism gives another answer to the question of certainty, and moves, also through phenomenalism, to *sensualistic solipsism*, the solipsism of private sensations. Hence in both cases the thought of intersubjectivity, which is the presupposition of all objective knowledge, disappears. In both cases scepticism has the last word.

It should be emphasized here that in objecting as we have done above to expressions like 'eternal truths', 'necessary truths', 'logical truths' on the ground that they are simply not 'truths' at all, we are not concerned merely with the question of appropriate or inappropriate terminology, but with a matter of very great material significance. So long as we allow logical consistency or logical consequences and their 'necessity' to sail under false colours and appear as some sort of 'truths', it is totally impossible for any light to be shed on the problems that occupy us here. With Leibniz's formula, 'eternal and contingent truths', we are given perhaps better than anywhere else an opportunity to study the pernicious effects of ambiguous language.

One cannot help asking whether our language is really so poverty-stricken that we have no choice but to use one and the same word for such widely different things, and to use it in as misleading a way as the word 'truth' is used in the formula 'eternal and contingent truths'. For it is otherwise a sound semantic rule that we should as far as possible let a word consistently represent the same thing and not use it for completely different things. Even if it is impossible to apply this rule without exception, we ought still to be able to demand that terms of the most central importance, like 'true' and 'truth', shall not be used now in one way and now in another, now to signify what we ordinarily mean when we say something is true, and now to signify something of a kind that has nothing whatever to do with truth. Ought we not in a case of this sort to avoid using the same word and thereby suggesting a likeness in things between which no such likeness exists?

Take a couple of examples. Once I have defined a term, logic demands that according to the law of identity I should stick to the meaning given in the definition throughout my entire argument. For if I begin to use the term—feeling perhaps that the definition is not quite right—now in one sense, now in another, the result can only be confusion. Consistency demands that I stick to the definition until it has been duly corrected. But what has this to do with truth? My sticking to the definition will, of course, if the definition is wrong, result in no truth whatever. It is therefore misleading to speak of anything being 'true by virtue of definition'. Is a definition *true*? And can anything be *true* simply because I stick consistently to the definition I have given? Is a tautology *true*? Is a syllogism *true*? The answer to all these questions is No, because what is involved is logical consistency, not truth. Or take another example. From a purely logical point of view there is no reason to object to the statement: Either things are so, or things are not so. But is this a 'truth'? The question of 'truth' arises only when I have to decide which of these two alternatives is the case; and about that logic has nothing to say.

It is certainly not the poverty of language in the matter of words and phrases that has brought about the confusion we are speaking of here. On the contrary, it is the confusion that has led us to be content to use one and the same word for such different things. For there is an abundance of words and phrases that could be used in order to avoid this confusion. We can speak of a logically correct or incorrect syllogism, a valid or invalid conclusion, a consistent or inconsistent procedure. Right or wrong, adequate or inadequate, proper or improper—to cite only a few out of many—are terms which are at our disposal for this purpose. It is not our intention here, however, to make any proposal with regard to an adequate terminology for what have been falsely described as 'necessary truths'. It is enough to have pointed out the error of speaking of 'truth' in this connection, and to have shown it to be one of the most urgent tasks of contemporary philosophy to recover for the concept of truth the clear, simple meaning which it has lost through misleading talk about 'necessary and contingent truths'.

In concluding this discussion of 'eternal and contingent truths' the author finds himself in the paradoxical position of having to apologize both for its length and its brevity. For its brevity, because anything like an exhaustive treatment of the problem would have required far more space, indeed it would have required a dissertation to itself. But also for its length—for was it really necessary to introduce all that complicated historical material in the context of our present inquiry? The answer to that question must be an unqualified Yes. For we are here faced with a 'Gordian knot', and it is one that must not be cut, but untied. In what follows we shall be much concerned with rational and empirical argumentation, and this could not but give rise to misunderstandings apart from the historical background we have given. A centuries-old tradition—which still lives on in the present—has so polluted the whole atmosphere that it is impossible to use the traditional terms without first thoroughly clearing the air. It is therefore not as a matter of historical, but of purely systematic interest, that we have had to insert this section. In order to understand its purpose we should remind ourselves of the aim of our present discussion.

What we are trying to do is to discover the nature and significance of philosophical argumentation. It is on the one hand a species of objective argumentation, and so belongs together with the special sciences. On the other hand philosophy is different from the special sciences, and we therefore have to ask in what respect its mode of argumentation differs from theirs. Now the rest of the sciences are characterized by the fact that they work with two distinct kinds of argumentation, the rational and the empirical. In these the traditional concepts are actualized, and so also is the need to rid them of their traditional distortions, which are concentrated above all in the formula 'eternal and contingent truths'. Behind this formula lies a metaphysical conception which has acquired something of a self-evident character and acts with the compulsiveness of an *idée fixe*.[31] That is what has made it necessary to devote a rather large amount of space to this subject.

3. Axiomatic and Empirical Argumentation

With the discussion of 'eternal (or necessary) and contingent truths' behind us, the way is now open for our main question concerning the different forms of scientific argumentation. The common stumbling blocks have been removed, and the matter can be presented in a relatively simple form without giving cause for misunderstanding.

By taking *argumentation* as the key word we are saying in effect that it is no longer a question of different sorts of 'truths'. Nor is there any need to consider various alternatives to the latter idea, such as that of different

---

[31] It would be possible to cite a great many instances in the philosophical literature of recent decades where this duality of the concept of truth is assumed. One example will suffice. In the Preface to his *Mind and the World Order*, C. I. Lewis writes (p. ix): 'At least it appears we must accept a kind of double-truth: there are certainties, such as those of mathematics, which concern directly only what is abstract; and there are the presentations of our sense-experience to which we seek to apply them, but of which a resultant empirical truth may be no more than probable. The nature and validity of such empirical knowledge becomes the crucial issue.' What is here said about mathematics and sense-experience is right enough, but to make two different sorts of 'truths' out of it is an error resulting from the weight and force of a tradition which we have shown to be indefensible. For Lewis the duality of truth is the self-evident starting point for his inquiry.

sorts of 'judgments'—analytic and synthetic, rational and empirical, *a priori* and *a posteriori*, etc.—or that of different sorts of 'concepts' and 'conceptualization' as employed in different sciences. All these, unlike the notion of different sorts of 'truths', can make good sense, but for the moment we are not concerned with these dichotomies either. Our main question is asked from another point of view. We need not even resort to the neutral suggestion of different sorts of 'sentences'. Our concern is not with an analysis of the content and structure of the different judgments by which the different sciences may be distinguished from one another, but with the modes of argumentation they employ. Which is also to say that it is no more our business now than it was before to attempt any systematization of science. Our purpose is simply to ascertain how the different sciences work, with what forms of argumentation they operate, and in some measure to exhibit the structure of objective argumentation.

Science knows and makes use of *two structurally different kinds of argumentation*. Only two? Yes, if we neglect for the moment philosophical argumentation, which may possibly be a third kind of scientific argumentation. What occasions surprise at the suggestion of two kinds of argumentation is the obvious fact that science has at its disposal a multitude of different procedures and methods. Every special science employs not only one but a number of methods in order to master its material. There is however no contradiction in thinking of two kinds of argumentation and many methods. The former also can be described as scientific methods, but then we must remember that 'method' can signify different things. It can signify something that has to do with technique, or something that has to do with meaning and structure. Only the latter signification has relevance for us here. The many technical devices and procedures that are needed in the special sciences are produced by the sciences themselves in the course of their work. This is something in which philosophy had better not interfere, for philosophers generally have too little first-hand knowledge of the concrete tasks of the special sciences to be able to take a fruitful part in the discussion of their methodologies. What is more, in so far as anyone has such knowledge he expresses himself not as a philosopher but as a special scientist. For the present, however, our business is exclusively with the question of meaning and structure.

The two differently structured modes of argumentation here in question can be fittingly described as *axiomatic* and *empirical* respectively. In a curious way there recurs in them that duality to which we gave considerable attention earlier, though we then described it as *rational* and empirical. Its reappearance here shows that there is a positive reason for making the latter distinction, and that the duality is not merely imaginary. What was wrong with the rational/empirical dichotomy as we saw it above, was that it led to the erroneous idea of two different kinds of 'truths', neither of which had really any right to be called 'truth', and the inevitable result of this was scepticism. If we drop the idea of different kinds of 'truths', it becomes entirely proper to draw a distinction between the rational and the empirical—though now as representing two different modes of argumentation, both of them necessary to science.

Axiomatic and empirical argumentation do not lead to special sorts of truth, but they are different ways of arguing which science needs in order to come to a sound judgment. In other words, there are no logical or rational truths, but there is correct rational and logical argumentation. Logical consequence does not represent any special truth-content, though it is indispensably necessary in scientific argumentation. Moreover, what we are saying about rational and empirical argumentation applies also to the two chief scientific methods, deduction and induction. There are no deductive truths, but there is correct deductive argumentation. There are no inductive truths—induction does not lead to any 'truth', nor even to probability in the logical sense—but there is correct inductive argumentation, of which science makes assiduous use and which it cannot do without. It is therefore of the greatest importance that the different types of argumentation should not be confused or equated with different sorts of 'truths'. Such a confusion would rob the whole of the following presentation of its meaning.

If instead of the traditional distinction between 'rational and empirical'[32] we have preferred to use the terms 'axiomatic and empirical', there are two reasons for this. First, to speak of 'rational argumentation' could be confusing and might be taken as a pleonasm. Is not *all* genuine argumentation essentially rational? To argue is to give reasons—*rationes*—for and against. A person is reasonable who is responsive to reasoning, open to argument and counter-argument, whether of a rational or empirical kind. To reason and to argue can thus be said to be interchangeable terms. It would therefore be inappropriate to use a terminology which itself suggested that one kind of argumentation was more rational, more in accord with reason, than the other. Secondly, the concept of 'reason' is such that it almost inevitably carries with it misleading associations. Reason has been traditionally conceived as a psychical or spiritual faculty, which as a part of man's natural endowment gives him a higher principle of knowledge, enabling him to discern and comprehend the true nature of things and the

[32] In my FKE, pp. 144–51, I compared and contrasted the philosophical mode of argumentation with the two modes employed by the special sciences, under the heading of '*Empiriskt, rationellt eller transcendentalt bevis?*' That section contains in embryo the position developed here regarding 'Different Forms of Scientific Argumentation'. The point made in both cases is essentially the same, though there is a certain difference in terminology. Thus the word 'rational' which was used in the earlier work is replaced here, for the reasons given above, by 'axiomatic'. The expression 'transcendental deduction' is replaced by 'presuppositional analysis', a term with which it was already stated to be synonymous in the earlier work, and which will be used for preference in what follows as descriptive of the distinctive character of philosophical argumentation.

essential structure of the world. All such ideas must be rigorously ex-cluded here, and it is therefore better to avoid the word that might suggest them.

(1) *How axiomatic argumentation functions*

To get an idea of how axiomatic argumentation functions, we must turn to logic, the logical syllogism, or still better to geometry. Euclid's geometry has always, and rightly, been regarded as a model of axiomatic argumen-tation, and it is easy to discover from it what is characteristic of the latter. It begins with a number of definitions, to which are appended axioms of such certainty that they are regarded as virtually self-evident. With this the starting point for the argumentation is given. From the axioms the whole series of geometrical propositions or theorems can be derived by purely logical deduction. They are already implicit in the axioms, and can be made explicit without the addition of anything new. It is thus on the axioms that the whole argument ultimately rests—whence the name 'axio-matic argumentation'. If the axioms are uncertain, what is derived from them is also uncertain. Yet while everything else can be proved from the axioms, the axioms themselves in the nature of the case cannot be proved. It was known already to Aristotle that not everything can be proved, and that in order to set about proving anything it is necessary to begin with certain assumptions, which as being the starting point lie outside the proof. But if the axioms cannot be proved, how can we be certain of their validity? How are we to decide which axioms should be accepted?[33] Merely to say that they are self-evident, or to appeal to 'intuition', is nothing but an evasion of the issue.

The fact that the axioms cannot be proved has the most far-reaching consequences for axiomatic argumentation. Because of it the latter is in its entirety of a purely hypothetical nature. The basic form of all axiomatic argumentation is the conditional sentence, the hypothetical statement with its 'if . . . then'. *If* we assume the axiom to be valid, *then* a multi-tude of consequences follow from it. Further than such a hypothetical statement it is impossible for geometry or mathematics to go. Its task is not to establish anything as true or real, but to exhibit a consequential relationship between a system of axioms and the propositions derived from it. *If* a certain system of axioms is valid, *then* the propositions which

[33] This is a difficulty which has always accompanied and is bound to accompany mathematics, though it is considerably eased by the realization that mathematics is not concerned with truth but with consequence or implication, which is a matter of consistency between the axiomatic system and what is deduced from it. In that regard there are basically no difficulties, since in the relation between an axiom and a theorem simple logic applies. The difficulties begin when we are faced with the question which axioms we are to accept. 'It is one of the most difficult tasks for a mathematician, to decide whether he has to accept or reject a new axiom' (A. Mostowski, *Thirty Years*, p. 83).

can be derived from it are also valid. With this hypothetical situation mathematics can afford to be content, because it is not concerned with truth but with consequence, and this is what finds expression in the hypothetical sentence construction.

Men have not, however, been generally willing to content themselves with this state of affairs, but have wanted to transform the hypothetical into a categorical statement. In place of 'if . . . then' they have sought to put ' since . . . therefore'. *Since* the axioms are valid, *therefore* the theorems are valid also. But this involves a radical distortion of the basic conditions of axiomatic argumentation. If we are to have axiomatic argumentation we must let an axiom be an axiom and nothing else. We must let it preserve its character as a basic assumption or presupposition which, *if* it is accepted, carries with it all the rest as a consequence. In order to affirm this consequential relationship there is no need to rob the axiom of its hypothetical character or deny its presuppositional nature. To deal rightly with axiomatic argumentation, we must reject every attempt to transform the axiom into a more or less platonically conceived reality.

Both logic and mathematics have often yielded to the temptation to platonize and transform the 'if' of axiomatic argumentation into a metaphysical 'since'. Both of them have been helped, however, to preserve the hypothetical character of the axiom when it has been realized that our generally accepted systems of axioms are by no means either self-evident or the only possible ones, but that there is room for other such systems, from which also theorems can be derived. Logical consistency, which is the main thing, can be maintained even if we change the system of axioms which we take as our starting point. In this connection the demonstration of the possibility of non-Euclidean geometries of various kinds has contributed largely to the clarification of the hypothetical nature of axiomatic argumentation. *If* we presuppose the Euclidean axioms, *then* certain theorems follow. *If* we start with other axioms, *then* certain other theorems follow. The one is just as logically possible and consistent as the other. In axiomatic argumentation nothing matters but logical connection, logical consistency. Everything therefore is cast in a hypothetical mould, and *deduction* is the natural method to use,[34] inasmuch as deduction means making explicit what is already implicit in the axioms.

It has often been demanded of science that it should be 'presuppositionless'. This may in one sense be right, but it can also be radically wrong. Which it is, depends on what is meant by 'presupposition'. We shall have occasion later to analyze that concept in some detail. For the moment we need do no more than point out certain misconceptions which are easily associated with the thought of science as presuppositionless. The prototype of a presuppositionless science is commonly taken to be mathematics.

[34] *Cf.* A. Tarsky, *Introduction*, esp. ch. VI 'On the Deductive Method': see also *ibid.*, pp. 23–32.

Nothing could be more false. It would be truer to say that mathematics is the science which more clearly than any other renders account of the presuppositions on which it rests. In no other science do presuppositions play so large a part as in mathematics. This is apparent in the very way it is built up, inasmuch as the presuppositions and what is derived from them are set out under distinct and separate heads. The axioms are the presuppositions, and without these mathematics would simply not exist. They are the foundation of its whole axiomatic argumentation. Putting it paradoxically we might say that just because it renders such a clear account of the presuppositions on which it rests, mathematics becomes in a deeper sense presuppositionless.

If axiomatic argumentation depends exclusively on logical connection and logical consistency between premisses and conclusion, axioms and inferences, then it is at once clear that it is a kind of *objective argumentation*. The demonstrative argumentation of logic and mathematics has no place for arbitrariness. Here there is no need for opinion to stand against opinion, for in this area we are not dealing with subjective notions but with objective necessity. Logical and mathematical propositions are open to proof, and the proof is open to inspection and testing. The criterion employed in this testing, moreover, is precisely that of *consistency*. It is simply impossible for a fallacious logical or mathematical theory to be consistently followed out; contradictions inevitably arise and there is an end to consistency—that is the objective argument which disposes of a wrong theory. It is therefore no difficult matter, if anyone makes a mistake in these areas, to point it out and get him to correct it. We thus have here not only testability but also 'intersubjectivity'. It is, furthermore, just because the argumentation remains on the level of logical consistency that everything is so transparent, and we can so easily follow the reasoning and perceive its inescapable necessity.

(2) *The nature of empirical argumentation*
With axiomatic argumentation alone, however, science would not get very far. Consistency in thinking is a necessary presupposition of all scientific work, but if consistency were the only thing science would be a purely formal affair without any content. Both logic and mathematics, which are themselves purely formal and axiomatic sciences, nonetheless presuppose that there is a world in which the principle of logical consistency and the quantitative measurements of mathematics are valid. These sciences themselves concentrate on logical and mathematical relations in abstraction from any factual content. Logic can disregard the content of a proposition and study only its logical structure or form. But naturally this implies neither a denial that the proposition has a content, nor an assertion that it is a matter of indifference whether it has a content or not. It is simply that the question of content is outside the range of problems with which logic deals. It

is the same with mathematics, which disregards empirically given content and concentrates on quantitative relations which are formally the same no matter to what concrete objects they may be applied. But naturally this does not mean that it is a matter of complete indifference whether or not there is anything that can be mathematically defined. There is a connection between the different sciences, and it is only because other sciences take care of the content aspect that sciences like logic and mathematics can ignore it. Otherwise, if logic and mathematics were regarded as constituting all there is of science, we should be landed in the crudest form of metaphysics.

This is where empirical argumentation comes in. What is commonly held to be characteristic of this form of argumentation is the *inductive method*. Just as we have seen that deduction is the method directly connected with axiomatic argumentation, so there is a generally accepted view that induction is the special method of empirical argumentation and thus of the empirical sciences. There seems, moreover, to be a good deal to be said for this view. In the natural sciences the aim of at least a substantial part of the work that is done is to exhibit the regularity of phenomena, the regular connections between them, and so ultimately to arrive at general and universally valid laws, the so-called 'laws of nature'. If this can be said to be the goal, then the starting point seems to be what is given and actually observed in experience. Between these two, the starting point and the goal, lies empirical argumentation, and apparently its purpose is to draw from the material furnished by experience and observation *conclusions* regarding the regularity that underlies them. This is the context in which the idea of 'inductive logic' has arisen.[35]

This whole train of thought suffers, however, from a fundamental defect: it ignores the fact that from singular or particular judgments it is logically impossible to draw universal conclusions and obtain a general law. Even if all cases hitherto observed point to the assumption of a general law, everything can be upset by a single negative instance. That is a matter of principle—though in practice we should naturally proceed with caution if we came across a negative instance only once or twice. We should then ask ourselves whether it was completely certain that the instance was negative. A theory that has proved its worth in a multitude of cases is not abandoned the first time we encounter a snag.[36] We are more likely to suspect faulty observation or some hidden source of error. But from a logical point of view one indisputable negative instance is sufficient, and that is enough to show that induction can never do what is demanded of it as regards proving a general law. This is where the problem arises which has come to be called 'the problem of induction'. We have already gone sufficiently into that subject,[37] however, and have no need to take it

[35] A work of prime importance on this subject is J. S. Mill's *System of Logic*.
[36] *Cf.* C. F. von Weizsäcker, *The Relevance of Science*, p. 100, *Die Tragweite*, p. 102.
[37] *Cf.* above, pp. 89f.

up again here. The question that concerns us now is a different one, namely that of the significance of induction for scientific, and especially for empirical, argumentation.

Here, however, we are at once faced with a considerable difficulty. For not only is 'the problem of induction' fundamentally insoluble—indeed it is impossible, strictly speaking, even to state clearly in what it consists[38]— but what is more, it is questionable whether there is any possibility of attaching a univocal meaning to the term 'induction' itself. It has had a chequered career and in consequence has acquired a highly fluid content, which seems to mock every attempt to arrive at a univocal definition.[39]

Although the thought of induction alongside deduction can be traced back as far as Aristotle, the heyday of induction dawned with the rise of empiricism (Bacon-Kepler-Galileo-Newton). It should be noted, however, that 'induction' had a different shade of meaning then from what it has come to have since. It has been rightly said that when Bacon and Newton 'speak of induction they seem to mean a method for making scientific discoveries rather than a mode of inference capable of justifying conclusions.'[40] It is important to observe this distinction, because it is the first of these meanings that we must have in mind if we wish to get at the significance of empirical argumentation in the context of science.

It was through John Stuart Mill that the wrong turn was taken. According to him there are two kinds of inference: 1. Deduction ('ratiocination'), which implies 'the inferring of a proposition from propositions equally or more general'; and 2. Induction, which implies 'the inferring of a proposition from other propositions less general'. There are thus according to Mill two things that are characteristic of induction: one that it is a 'generalization from observation' or a 'generalization from experience',[41] and the other that this generalization implies a scientific inference or proof. This

---

[38] We may recall here Max Black's remark about attempts to provide a 'justification for induction'. In his *Problems*, p. 190, he concludes a discussion of the subject thus: 'Professor Broad, in a famous phrase, once referred to inductive reasoning as "the glory of Science" but the "scandal of Philosophy". Perhaps it is on the verge of becoming scandalous that this ancient tangle of confusion should still be regarded as a "problem" that needs a solution.' Both Broad and Black may well be said to be right. For 'induction' as it is actually practised in science is of extraordinary importance, but 'the problem of induction' as we find it in philosophy is nothing else but a 'tangle of confusion' and not in any sense a problem that either needs to be or can be solved.

[39] *Cf.* on this, Blake, Ducasse, Madden, *Theories*.

[40] S. F. Baker in Black, *Philosophy in America*, p. 63. Baker has seen the difference between the various meanings of the term 'induction', but he still speaks of induction as a form of inference alongside of deduction.

[41] *Cf.* above, p. 88.—It can be said quite generally that the path of induction is strewn with inconsistencies. This is true not least of Mill's inductive logic. On this see Blake, Ducasse, Madden, *Theories*, pp. 218ff., and R. Jackson, *An Examination*. There is a similar inconsistency underlying Mill's 'naturalistic fallacy', however we may seek to interpret it; *cf.* M. Blegvad, 'Mill, Moore and the Naturalistic Fallacy'.

idea of Mill's has had immense influence, not least with regard to the meaning attached to 'induction' and the way in which 'the problem of induction' is discussed. For what makes the latter a problem is the two-fold assumption that induction is meant to furnish *proof* in the strict sense of the word, and that it proceeds by the logically dubious method of generalizing from particular cases in order to *prove* universal laws.

Now it is not difficult to see how this wrong road has come to be taken. Men have long been familiar with the idea of deduction as a means of con-clusive proof, and have known that it provides just what is needed to ensure the certainty of axiomatic argumentation. When therefore they turn to empirical argumentation they look for a method that is charac-teristic of it, and they find it in induction. This they assume to be both parallel to deduction and yet different from it—in a sense its opposite. Deduction is inference, so induction must also be inference, but of an-other kind, proceeding in the opposite direction. As deduction in elaborat-ing its proof starts with general axioms and descends from the universal to the particular—the individual propositions which are proved by being derived from the axioms—so it is regarded as characteristic of induction that in elaborating its proof it takes the opposite course and ascends by means of generalization from the particular to the universal—from the individual case or many such cases to the general law, the law of nature. As deduction proves the individual propositions by deriving them from the axioms, so induction is supposed to prove the general laws by basing them on empirical observations.

It is obvious that induction has suffered considerably by being treated as parallel to deduction. Deduction was the method established by long tradition, and when the need arose to explain induction there were con-tinual sidelong glances at the older method, with a view to co-ordinating the two while keeping them distinct. This requires us to face the question: is induction merely a mirror-image of deduction? At one point above all, the parallel with deduction has been misleading, in that it has fostered the idea that because deduction is a means of proof, induction also must be a means of proof, though of another sort. This, however, is precisely where the error lies, namely in taking induction to be a special form of inference. Induction is fruitful and necessary for science—but not as inference. To treat it as inference is to rob it of its real significance.

We have still not answered the question, what is induction? Nor are we really interested in this question for its own sake. Our concern is rather with what is characteristic of empirical argumentation. The reason why we have had to raise the question of induction is that it has been a traditional practice to combine or even identify induction with empirical method and to describe the procedure of the empirical sciences as induction. The name of course is not important; it can have both advantages and disadvantages. It can be an advantage to have a compendious term to denote the empirical procedure and distinguish it from the axiomatic. For obviously there are different kinds of argumentation involved here, and obviously there is something common to all empirical science which distinguishes it from the axiomatic and gives us reason to seek a common term to describe it. It is, however, a decided disadvantage that 'induction' is such a loaded term and so easily evokes the false associations we tried to get rid of above. Still, as we have said, the name is not important. We can therefore safely go on speaking of induction with reference to the procedure of the empirical sciences, provided we keep in mind that there is no question here of a new means of proof to set alongside the deductive. On the other hand it is obvious that we cannot discover the type of argumentation that is characteristic of the empirical sciences by analyzing the concept of induction. The only way to find that out is to go to these sciences themselves and observe them as they really are and as they show themselves to be when they are at work.

If we do this, and watch the sciences actually at work, we find no support whatever for the traditional view of what induction is and what it is supposed to do. We can rather say that this is just what is *not* done in empirical argumentation, which has never undertaken to *prove* anything. Proving belongs to axiomatic argumentation, and we misconceive empirical argumentation if we regard it as a less reliable and logically questionable method of proof on the lines of axiomatic argumentation. It is quite other than that, and in a class of its own. When we are dealing with empirical matters we have no call to try our hand at a quasi-proof. Nor does the scientist do this, but he has developed a method of his own, suited to his empirical material. Natural science does not, for example, prove the laws of nature, for they cannot strictly be proved. The empirical sciences do not prove, though they produce arguments for or against a formulated hypothesis. 'Hypothesis' is a particularly important and central concept for them.

What happens, then, in the actual empirical sciences—in natural science for example? Not at any rate what is often thought to happen. There is a common idea that the natural scientist proceeds more or less as follows. His first task is to collect a mass of particular empirical data. Then, when he has a sufficient and sufficiently representative quantity of these, gathered either from general observation or experiments conducted for the purpose, his next task is to try to grasp them as a unity, to construct a uniform theory about them and if possible arrive at a general law. This is a picture of empirical procedure that needs to be totally revised. For while not only observation and experiment but also induction (or what is now preferably called a confrontation between a general hypothesis and particular empirical data) certainly play a leading part in natural science, they do so in a quite other way than is popularly imagined. And while the natural scientist naturally has to take observation and/or experiment as the basis of his work—though he often does not start with that, but with a given theory which he wishes to test by means of his observations and experiments—yet he does so not merely for the purpose of collecting data of various kinds, but he works to a definite plan with a definite hypothesis in mind. An experiment is not an unplanned affair, in which one haphazardly does this or that to see what comes of it, but it is a carefully thought out strategy.

We could almost go so far as to say that the order should be reversed as between observation and theory or hypothesis. A theory is not built up out of a multitude of atomistic empirical data by means of observations and experiments—but it is tried and tested by these means. We observe all kinds of things in everyday life, but serious scientific work begins only when our observations are confronted by an idea, which is at least the embryo of a hypothesis or theory; for it is only then that there is anything to test. It is the idea that holds the material together and makes it something more than a mere collection of data. It is the idea or theory, vague and indefinite though it may be to begin with, that gives meaning and coherence to the work on the material and makes planned experimentation possible. For only then is there anything to test by means of experiment. The 'laws of nature', even the highest and most universal of them, are nothing but hypotheses and can never rise above that status. We misconceive them if we seek to raise them to the level of proven 'truths'. They are and remain hypotheses, which can never be finally 'proved'. They can, however, be tried and tested—though not of course directly, but by their implications or consequences. Every law or hypothesis has its implicit consequences, and hence the question arises: are these consequences in accord with the data present in experience? This is what makes experiment of decisive importance—primarily *negative* importance. For if an experiment happens to show that the consequence required by a law or hypothesis does not in fact occur, then we have indubitable proof that the hypothesis is wrong, or at least that it cannot be upheld in the form in which it has been propounded.

In the philosophy of science there has often been rather naïve talk about the possibility of proving the truth of natural laws and scientific hypotheses. In the nature of the case this can never be done, since we are moving here in the empirical realm. The truth of a general empirical law can never be proved either deductively or inductively. It may on the other hand be possible to prove that it is untenable. For that purpose all that is needed is to show that an inescapable consequence of the law does *not* occur in empirical fact. We have here a curious combination of the axiomatic and the empirical, and it is this that makes possible the negative—though not, be it noted, the positive—testing of the validity of a hypothesis.

Since we are dealing with a hypothesis, the inferential procedure of axiomatic argumentation comes into play, the hypothesis serving as the axiom. If the hypothesis is valid, then certain empirical states of affairs must of necessity occur. The test question therefore is, whether these states of affairs really do occur. That is what an experiment is designed to show. If the answer is affirmative, it tells us nothing about the validity of the hypothesis. For the claim that something follows as a *consequence* implies that it must follow always and in all circumstances, past, present and future; and this is something which no empirical experiment can show. If on the other hand the answer is negative, then it gives us decisive information as to how things stand with the law or hypothesis, namely the negative information that it is *not* valid. For if the experiment shows us a case in which the consequence required by the law or hypothesis does *not* occur, this is proof that the law does not hold good without exception and hence is not a universal law. It is a proof that the hypothesis cannot be sustained. Admittedly the latter is of such a general nature that it cannot be directly refuted by observation or experiment, but it can indirectly, by the refutation of its implicit empirical consequences. In this way the hypothesis is open to indirect testing.

The most important contribution in this area has been made by Karl Popper with his well-known theory of 'falsification'[42] and his refusal, closely connected with it, to ascribe to verification and induction the decisive importance in scientific procedure which has often been attributed to them. Popper's theory has no doubt often been understood rather as a modification of detail in the generally accepted position, a modification suggested by the logical observation of the asymmetry existing between verification and falsification, so that it should primarily be regarded as a limited counter-stroke against the 'verification' theory of logical empiricism. As the latter made 'verification' the key-word of empirical procedure, Popper's contribution would then consist simply in the replacing of 'verification' by 'falsification'. But this in no way does justice to his theory. What he proposes is anything but a mere parallel to logical empiricism at a single though vital point. It involves in fact a wholly new start—admittedly prepared for by earlier research[43]—which not only completely revolutionizes our understanding of the nature of empirical knowledge but opens up a more realistic view of the conditions on which it can be had.

Popper's insistence on the 'falsifiability' and empirical refutability of every scientific theory, which he regards as the hallmark of an empirical hypothesis, is only another way of expressing its 'testability', though a way

[42] In *Die Logik der Forschung* and *Conjectures*. *Cf.* also J. O. Wisdom, *Foundations of Inference*, and Hintikka and Suppes *Aspects of Inductive Logic*.
[43] *Cf.* on this C. J. Ducasse, 'William Whewell's Philosophy'. 'Whewell is the first to formulate a comprehensive and systematic theory of induction throughout in terms of the so-called Newtonian method of Hypothesis-Deduction-Verification' (*ibid.*, p. 217).

which takes note of the fact that the testing can be done only on negative lines. For the confrontation between a law or hypothesis on the one hand and empirical observation or experiment on the other can take place, as we have said, only via the empirical consequences that are implied in the hypothesis and are deducible from it. Only a hypothesis which implies such empirically testable, i.e. falsifiable, consequences has any real empirical meaning at all. In other words, it is only as a theory is open to 'falsification' that it possesses an empirical character. For the asymmetry mentioned above lies in the fact that no empirical observations, however numerous, can verify a hypothesis by confrontation with its empirical implications, whereas such a confrontation may possibly falsify it, and a single negative instance is sufficient to do so. When a law or hypothesis is said to have been confirmed by experience and experiment, all that this really means is that in spite of all attempts to refute it no decisive negative instances have been found—which in no way excludes the possibility that one may turn up later and show the hypothesis to be false. An empirical-scientific hypothesis thus has validity, not because it has been 'verified', but because and for so long as no one has succeeded in 'falsifying' it. This is the only test that counts with regard to a general hypothesis or law.

This sheds light also on the nature and conditions of empirical science, showing it as a matter of principle to be open to perpetual revision. Not as if that were a limitation, to which we must unhappily resign ourselves while wishing it were not so. That can appear to be the case only as long as we hold to the theory of 'eternal and contingent truths' and measure the latter by the standard of the former.[44] Once we have seen this theory to be untenable and have let it go, the way is clear for the genuine empirical sciences and for an independent empirical argumentation with a character of its own.

We have now reached the point where we can sum up our findings with regard to what is distinctive of empirical argumentation. It is characterized by the three steps: hypothesis—deduction—verification (via attempts at falsification). From this it can be seen that deduction, which is the characteristic method of axiomatic argumentation, plays a major part also in empirical argumentation. It is thanks to deduction that a connection is established between the general law or hypothesis on the one hand and empirical observation or experiment on the other. It is thanks to the deductive explication of the implicit consequences of the hypothesis that the latter is transposed, so to speak, down to the empirical level, where it can be tested as to its agreement or disagreement with the empirical observations.

Both in axiomatic and empirical argumentation logical implication is thus of decisive importance—though in different ways. In axiomatic

[44] *Cf.* above, pp. 92ff.

argumentation it is all that matters. Nothing more is needed than to establish that there is a logically necessary connection between the axiom and what has been derived from it. This completes the process of axiomatic proof, for here to prove has no other meaning than to point out the connection. That, however, is the reason why axiomatic argumentation can never get beyond the hypothetical statement: *if* the axiom is valid, then its implied consequences are also valid. In empirical argumentation the position is different. Here we can and must get beyond the hypothetical 'if . . . then' to a genuine (non-metaphysical!) 'since . . . therefore'. For logical implication is here the means of bringing out the empirical relevance of the hypothesis and thus putting it in touch with empirical, observed reality. Empirical argumentation can therefore never remain simply on the hypothetical level, but must step out into empirical reality, the realm of what is actually observed, where the fate of the hypothesis is ultimately determined. Hence, just as the axiom is what ultimately bears the whole weight of axiomatic argumentation and gives it its name,[45] so it is the empirical observations that bear the whole weight of empirical argumentation and give it its name. Moreover, just as everything derived by deduction from the axioms is shaken if the axioms are shaken, so there is a parallel situation in the empirical realm: if the empirical consequences derived by deduction from a hypothesis are shaken, then the hypothesis also is shaken and cannot consistently be maintained.

From this it is clear that despite the importance of logical implication for them both, the two forms of argumentation are significantly asymmetrical. For while the axiomatic sciences not only can but must be kept free from any admixture of empirical argumentation, the empirical sciences cannot carry out their tasks without the assistance of axiomatic argumentation. Here we have concrete evidence of the importance of making a sharp distinction, as we did above, between a 'systematization of science' and a mode of argumentation. We cannot make a systematic distinction between axiomatic and empirical sciences in terms simply of argumentation, as if the former used exclusively axiomatic and the latter exclusively empirical argumentation. Admittedly we can do it up to a point, thanks to the above-mentioned asymmetry. Thus logic and pure mathematics represent an axiomatic argumentation completely untouched by anything empirical—although geometry already occupies a middle ground, as the distinction between 'pure and physical geometry' indicates.[46] When we turn to the empirical sciences, however, we discover that there the two forms of argumentation continually interact with one another. While logic and mathematics may be purely axiomatic, we cannot say of any empirical science that it is purely empirical. In this connection we can point to the importance of logic and mathematics in the empirical sciences;

[45] Above, p. 105.
[46] *Cf.* C. G. Hempel, 'Geometry and Empirical Science'.

or we can approach the matter from the opposite end and view it empirically. Even the simplest empirical procedure always includes an element of axiomatic argumentation. This is true even of the most completely down-to-earth experiment; for in order to be a genuine experiment it must be logically constructed, and this means that axiomatic argumentation finds its way into the empirical realm. An experiment is not a merely casual observation, but logically organized observation in accordance with a prearranged plan. It presupposes a plan of operations which is open to inspection and provides the possibility of objective argumentation, of testing and possible refutation.

We have thus far exemplified empirical argumentation mainly by reference to the procedure of the natural sciences, but what we have said or something very like it applies also in the fullest measure to the humanities. Their mode of argumentation is the empirical, and it is if possible even more completely empirical than that of the natural sciences; for the latter in their concern with general laws can become very remote from what is given in immediate experience, whereas the humanities and the historical sciences by reason of their interest in what is unique in events stick much more closely to the immediately given. In spite of their different focus of interest, however, there is a surprising resemblance between the sciences and the humanities in the broad features of their argumentation, inasmuch as the basic elements of empirical argumentation (hypothesis—deduction—empirical testing) recur in the same form.[47]

When for example a historian is working on his material, whether it be texts, remains, oral traditions, documents, memoirs, or whatever, he forms a preliminary idea of its drift or of the pattern that runs through it all; and this gives rise to a hypothesis. The hypothesis, however, is only the starting point of historical work, which consists in an intensive confrontation between the implications of the hypothesis and the actually available material. Is the material such as to support the hypothesis? Are there objectively tenable grounds for the picture it presents of what historically happened? It is not enough for the historian to say: 'I have an impression that such is the case, in my opinion this is the correct interpretation.' That sort of information is quite unimportant. The important question is *what arguments* he can bring to support his view—arguments that can be objectively examined and checked, reason being weighed against reason. At every step he is faced with problems which call for objective argumentation: questions as to the source-value of the material, questions of genuineness, dating, literary criticism, the question how far the material

---

[47] In the section on 'Science and the Humanities' (above, pp. 71-7) we have already anticipated the main substance of what there is to say about the unity of the empirical sciences in the matter of argumentation, and can therefore content ourselves here with simply amplifying this in order to show how these sciences fit the pattern of 'hypothesis-deduction-empirical testing'.

is complete enough to permit a tolerably certain reconstruction, the question of possible tendentious insertions,[48] and so forth.

In the confrontation between the hypothesis (including its implications) and the empirical material we have what is characteristic of empirical argumentation in all its various forms. There is an intensive interplay between hypotheses and facts. The hypothesis helps us to see facts which were previously concealed from us. The facts support the hypothesis in so far as it provides a satisfactory explanation of them, or they call it in question if they cannot be naturally harmonized with it. Facts may indeed result in the refutation and overthrow of a hypothesis, and they thus give occasion for the emergence of new hypotheses by which earlier difficulties are resolved. But for every problem solved a number of new problems arise which have not been noticed before. That is the way in which genuine science progresses. It is not the case that the answer to problem after problem is found and that problems are thus removed, so that gradually all 'the riddles of the universe' will be solved and science will then have nothing to do but hand on all the 'truths' it has discovered to a problemless world. This naïve idea has nothing to do with what science is really about. The fact is rather that the problems change, new insights bring awareness of new problems, and these in turn open the way to further new insights, and so forth.

From what has been said it is evident that 'the empirical' is of enormous range. By 'empirical' we can mean things as diverse as a particular individual observation and the most comprehensive 'law of nature', inasmuch as the latter despite its universality possesses not axiomatic but empirical validity. Naturally the empirical argumentation takes a different form in the two cases. The immediately given is something that can be directly ascertained. Thanks to the intersubjectivity, testability and to a large extent the reproducibility of the empirical, an empirical proposition of this order can be checked without difficulty. This is the place for simple 'verification'. But the validity of a 'natural law' cannot be so established. Instead, the more complicated procedure must be followed which we sketched above, in which the 'law' (the hypothesis) is tested via its implied consequences in relation to given experience. This also is a form of empirical argumentation. Here is the place for 'falsification' or—if present circumstances do not permit this—the acceptance of the law (the hypothesis) as valid 'until further notice'.

(3) The place of 'intuition'. 'Correspondence and coherence'

1) In most sciences both types of argumentation occur, the axiomatic and

---

[48] Cf. on this R. Torstendahl, *Historia som vetenskap.*—It is not only with regard to chronicles and memoirs that one must be on guard against tendentious elements. The same applies to official documents, which can also have an interest in presenting a one-sided picture. Cf. on this Arthur Thomson, 'Fakta eller frihandsteckning?'

the empirical, in intimate reciprocity. They gear into one another, as is shown especially by the deductive element in empirical argumentation. But the question arises whether with these two forms of argumentation our description of scientific work is complete. Ought we not to add a third? This is a natural question if we compare the two types of argumentation with one another. Axiomatic argumentation can start with the axioms as self-evident or at all events as postulated. It can be content to do so because it is only concerned with their implications. It has no need to explain how the axioms have come to be there. It is enough that in one way or another they exist and are conceived and acknowledged as axioms. But the position is not so simple with regard to the empirical laws or laws of nature. They are not just simply there. They cannot be regarded as self-evident. They are not axioms, but hypotheses. No doubt as hypotheses they can be tested by confrontation with the empirical material, but this presupposes that they exist as hypotheses. Where then do they come from, and how do they ever come to be propounded? It was to this question that the answer used to be sought by reference to induction, which was conceived as a special form of argumentation involving generalization from certain particular facts of experience. But as 'the principle of induction' has now been shown to be untenable, the question how these laws or hypotheses ever arise remains unanswered. In order to fill this gap it is sometimes maintained that alongside axiomatic and empirical argumentation we should set a third, co-ordinate factor: 'intuition'.[49]

Now it must of course be admitted that scientific intuition or scientific imagination plays a vital part in the setting up of new hypotheses. Without a rich measure of imagination a scientist does not get very far. When he is faced with a complicated problem, he sees in imagination a multitude of different possible explanations of it, and often it is a lucky 'intuition' that leads him to select the right one and reach a fruitful solution. If we were dealing with the psychology of science we should have to pay attention to these facts. But in our present context this point of view is entirely out of place. It cannot be too strongly emphasized that intuition or scientific imagination is *not* a third type of argumentation alongside the axiomatic and empirical. There are accurate and less accurate 'intuitions', fruitful and not so fruitful imaginings, lucky and unlucky hunches. These may well serve as incentives to investigation, but never as arguments. What would it sound like if a scientist were to state as an argument for a particular view: 'I have a hunch that it is so; I feel it in my bones; it suits my fancy'? He may have a fruitful intuition, but it may also be a mere caprice. What has to be investigated and tested is precisely whether it is or is not a lucky hunch, a fruitful imagination, an accurate intuition. To take such an intuition or imagination as an argument—a typical *petitio principii*—and accept it as satisfactory, is to put oneself outside the province of science.

[49] *Cf.* G. Holton, 'Über die Hypothesen', pp. 66ff.

It has no scientific relevance unless and until it is objectively tested.

It thus remains that science works with the two forms of argumentation we have named, the axiomatic and the empirical, both of them objectively testable. Axiomatic argumentation involves testing with respect to logical consistency, and empirical with respect to correspondence or agreement with the empirically given. Simple questions of observation can be settled by means of 'verification', and general hypotheses or natural laws by the confrontation of their implied empirical consequences with what is empirically given—the absence of 'falsification' after rigorous testing being allowed to deputize for the unattainable verification.

2) It may be of interest to point out that our now completed investigation of the basic forms of scientific argumentation has yielded as a by-product a substantial contribution to the clarification of the old contrast between the correspondence and coherence theories of truth.[50] As the correspondence theory finds the truth of a judgment in its correspondence or accordance with facts, so the coherence theory finds it in its logical agreement with other judgments. From what has been said above it becomes clear why the quarrel between these two schools can never produce any decisive result. It is partly because their rivalry is connected with the idea of 'truths of reason and truths of fact', and partly because there are underlying it the two modes of scientific argumentation, which have been transformed, however, into two competing philosophical views. Behind the coherence theory there is axiomatic argumentation, with consistency and coherence as its prime concern, and behind the correspondence theory there is just as obviously empirical argumentation, with its anchorage in the empirically given. The ranging of these against one another as opposing views is due to the failure to observe that what we have here are two distinct but equally necessary modes of argumentation, two different points of view, which only when taken together give a complete picture of scientific procedure. Two complementary viewpoints have been turned into two rival standpoints. In the last resort this is nothing but a hangover of the old muddled thinking according to which the empirical must be judged by the standard of the rational and the rational by the empirical—an inevitable consequence of the theory of 'eternal and contingent truths'[51]—which has led to the transformation of the forms of argumentation into opposing views such as we find in the theories of correspondence and coherence. Now that the latter have been traced back to the forms of argumentation, this absurd 'problem' ceases to exist.

4. Philosophical Argumentation?

The foregoing exposition has shown the uniformity that characterizes all scientific argumentation, whether it is axiomatic or empirical, and whether

[50] *Cf.* S. E. Rodhe, 'Correspondence and Coherence'.
[51] *Cf.* above, pp. 92ff.

—in the latter case—it is used in the natural sciences or the humanities. Everywhere there is the same requirement of objective argumentation, although this takes different forms in different areas of science.[52] So far we have found two differently structured types of objective argumentation, the axiomatic and the empirical; and we have seen that the attempt sometimes made to augment these by introducing intuition as a third type is unworkable. From this it might seem natural to conclude that there are two, and only two, scientifically objective types of argumentation. Yet we are still very far from having disposed of this issue. Indeed it is now necessary for the question to be seriously raised, whether these two types really exhaust the possibilities of objective argumentation. Is there not room for something more besides these, which can meet the demand for objectivity in argumentation? For on the answer to this question everything depends with regard to our right to speak of 'scientific philosophy'.

This is still an open question, although we have taken a considerable step towards the answer. Our exposition of the different forms of scientific argumentation has provided us with the standard by which scientific philosophy must be measured. Not that philosophy is obliged to use any of these forms—rather the contrary—but they indicate the standard below which philosophy must not fall. The term 'scientific philosophy' must not be merely a manner of speaking, but must be seen as implying a demand laid upon philosophy, a demand for objectivity in argumentation, for intersubjectivity and openness to inspection, for the possibility of critically testing it and its results, and for whatever else belongs to a scientific procedure.

The heading of this section 'Philosophical Argumentation?' is followed by a question mark. This is meant to indicate that we are not yet in a position to give the final answer, nor able to do more than elucidate the question by showing what the problem is and what the prerequisites of a positive answer are. In the previous section, where we were dealing with 'Axiomatic and Empirical Argumentation', there was no need for a question mark because both these forms of argumentation are so clearly attested by the actual procedure of the sciences, which is seldom seriously questioned, that hesitation is quite unnecessary. With philosophy it is

---

[52] Awareness of the fundamental unity of science in the matter of argumentation has been increasing in recent years. Note in this regard the conclusion of T. T. Segerstedt's essay in PEGA, p. 229: 'I think an intensive analysis of the different fields of human knowledge should uncover the common denominator of all human knowledge. The true scientific revolution is to discover the common basis of all science.' Note also M. Bunge, *The Myth of Simplicity*, p. 11: 'The unity of science lies in its method rather than in a handful of all-purpose concepts;' and F. Delekat, *Immanuel Kant*, p. 17: 'The splitting up of scientific knowledge into different disciplines with different methods and terminologies makes it difficult to see how in spite of all specialization the essential questions of every branch of science hang together with those of the rest.' *Cf.* also above, pp. 75ff.

different. For philosophy has certainly not distinguished itself by clarity in defining its task. There has been no 'sure progress of a science' here. It has oscillated between unverifiable metaphysical assertions on the one hand and attempts on the other to get solid ground under its feet by attaching itself as far as possible to the methods and 'results' of the special sciences. But neither of these ways leads to a 'scientific philosophy' in any real sense. Metaphysics sacrifices objectivity and testability, and thereby excludes itself from the company of the sciences, while the attempt to turn philosophy into a special science robs it of its philosophical character.

From this we can obtain the following guidance for our further investigation. 1. If we are to speak of 'scientific philosophy' in any real sense, philosophy must be able to produce a type of objective argumentation which is the equal of the types employed by the other sciences, equally predictable, equally strict. Every step taken by philosophy must be capable of being as minutely scrutinized as a scientific proposition—axiomatically with respect to its logical consistency, or empirically with respect to its agreement with experience. 2. Philosophy must be able to produce a specific type of argumentation, clearly distinct from the other forms of scientific argumentation. This second point is as important as the first. It is connected with the philosophical urge to universality of which we spoke earlier.[53] Because of this, philosophy can never be forced into the argumentational mould of the other sciences. The question now is, whether these two conditions can both be fulfilled. The special sciences are of course in no difficulty, since their concentration on well-defined special problems itself ensures that the demand for objectivity, for scientific rigour and precision, can be met. It is a different matter when we are thinking in terms of a universal science. How can a science be universal? How is it possible to deal with such wide-ranging and universal problems with the same degree of scientific objectivity?

In his *Axiomatische Philosophie* Franz Austeda, starting with a clearly drawn distinction between the axiomatic and the empirical, has proposed that philosophy should accept the role of an axiomatic discipline. Superficially this idea may seem akin to the one presented above; but it is not really so. We have here in fact two vastly different conceptions, and it will not be out of place briefly to point out the difference. For while Austeda ranks philosophy with the axiomatic sciences, thus placing it in one particular group of the special sciences as far as its mode of argumentation is concerned, he is none the less anxious to emphasize the universality of its task, and the result is that he vacillates with regard to the question of its purely scientific character. Thus he sharply distinguishes between the task of the scientist and that of the philosopher, in a way which shows that the latter is not engaged in a strictly scientific pursuit. 'The *scientist* seeks to

[53] Above, pp. 29ff.

perceive reality, the *philosopher* to *understand* the world perceived by science, to comprehend the experiences of life and of science as consistently and completely as possible.'[54] Out of the piecemeal knowledge ('*Wissenschaftsfragmente*') to which the special sciences have led, the philosopher constructs a *Weltbild*, a picture of the world, in which every phenomenon is given its due place in the context of the whole. Whereas the scientist seeks to explore a particular *section* of reality as minutely as possible, the philosopher reflects on '*die Gesamtwirklichkeit*', the whole of reality, and seeks to give a consistent philosophical explanation of the world.

We recognize at once the age-old claims of metaphysics. But the interesting thing about Austeda's position is that he wishes to support these claims by pointing out that science too is familiar with a procedure in which axioms are quite simply *posited*. Like every axiomatic science philosophy must thus be content to postulate its starting point, its axioms. There is, however, an unfortunate difference between the axiomatic sciences and 'axiomatic philosophy'; for while the former, working with genuine axioms, never gets beyond the 'if . . . then' of logical consistency, the latter works with insecure hypotheses which it dignifies as axioms and declares that they represent '*reality*'. A 'universal science' of this kind, which explains reality as a whole, is nothing else but our old friend metaphysics, which for lack of argumentation has to postulate its starting point and then rest its entire system on this fictitious basis. Austeda himself is conscious that on these terms there can be no question of science in the proper sense, and it is not surprising when we find him explaining that 'in this connection "science" must naturally be taken with a grain of salt.'[55] Obviously it must, since there is no place here for objective argumentation, but only for arbitrary postulation. What we are trying to do, however, is to discover just how philosophy argues, what is characteristic of its scientifically objective argutation (without any 'grain of salt') in contradistinction to the modes of argumentation of other sciences.

It is clear that the question of the distinctive character of philosophical argumentation is too big and complicated to be answered in a moment, nor can it be done in a subsection of this chapter on 'Different Forms of Scientific Argumentation'. It demands separate treatment, which it will receive in the following chapters. All we have tried to do so far has been to show its exact location in its wider context and provide the background and criterion for the discussion of it that follows. Time and again we have been obliged to postpone the answer to this question in order first to obtain precision in matters on which the answer depends. It may seem a trifle pedantic to take one short step after another like this in order to make sure that nothing essential is overlooked. But one can never be 'pedantic' enough when dealing with questions of where to start and on

[54] Austeda, *Axiomatische Philosophie*, p. 101.
[55] Austeda, *op. cit.*, p. 104.

what principles to work. Lack of precision in these matters has been responsible for a great deal of confusion.

5. The Limits of Science

We can speak of the limits of science in several different ways. We have touched on one of these a number of times already. As long as men were under the spell of the idea of 'eternal and contingent truths' the thought of the limits of science was coupled with certain difficulties, unless it could be supposed that science was making rapid strides towards its limit, which was absolute truth and complete knowledge of the universe. It was the prevailing optimistic belief that science was well on the way to resolving all mysteries and revealing all truths. Although this view still lingers on in the popular mind, contemporary science displays a quite different spirit of 'humility in the presence of reality.'[56] Scientists are now genuinely aware of the limitations of science and that it has not by any manner of means reached its goal—if indeed there is now any sense in speaking of a goal which science might one day attain. This changed attitude is connected with the realization that in science for every problem solved a new set of problems arises.

If we conclude our chapter on 'Different Forms of Scientific Argumentation' with the question of 'The Limits of Science', we do so because this issue is a simple consequence of the scientific style of argumentation. There is an often-quoted saying of Kant to the effect that he set limits to knowledge in order to make room for faith, and it might perhaps be thought that we are here speaking of 'the limits of science' with a similar end in view. For often when lines of demarcation are drawn and it is shown that something is valid only within certain limits, this is done for the purpose of making room for something else. Hence it is natural to ask: For whose benefit are such lines drawn, whose interests are served by them? Nevertheless it cannot be too strongly stressed that our speaking here of 'the limits of science' has no such implication. Our intention is not at all to secure for faith or any other vital concern a 'sheltered haven' where it will be safe from the prying eyes of irreverent scientific curiosity. There is in that sense nothing in the world with which science may not have anything to do. There are no limits to science in the sense that certain areas of life are outside its province and completely 'out of bounds' for it. Thus

---

[56] The phrase comes from a natural scientist, being borrowed from an address by Professor Erik Ohlsson at a graduation ceremony at the University of Lund in 1967, where with reference to Niels Bohr and Werner Heisenberg he said: 'There is another change that has had a good effect. It began about the turn of the century with new winds blowing in the natural sciences, and gradually the unbridled hybris that characterized science at the end of the nineteenth century gave way to a humility in the presence of reality, which is characteristic of natural science in our time when it is at its best.' Cf. also E. Ohlsson 'Människan i den moderna naturvetenskapens världsbild'.

both faith and ethical conduct are within its range, as witness the scientific study of religion, theology and ethics, which are expected to be strictly scientific disciplines in these areas.

In what sense, then, and in whose interests do we speak of 'the limits of science'? We do it *in the interests of scientific argumentation itself*. Even in science discussions are often carried on in which there is no possibility of objectively scientific argumentation. Under an appearance of science, science is compromised and turned into something other than it is. What is at issue, then, to state it correctly, is 'the limits of scientific argumentation', the limits set by the nature of scientific argumentation itself. In what follows we shall have occasion again and again to return to the question of these limits, sometimes from a quite other point of departure than we have here.

For the moment we need only note that what we have said about scientific argumentation has been of a restrictive nature—restrictive of science itself. It has not, however, been such as to imply any restriction or reduction of anything else. There is nothing derogatory in saying of something that it is 'not science' or 'not scientific'. We are therefore delivered from any temptation to rescue it by forcing it into the scientific camp. Life does not consist of scientific argumentation. Nor ought we to encourage the illusion that there can be anything scientific where there is no 'possibility of objective argumentation'. For there are indeed other forms of human activity besides the scientific—things which are valid in their own right and do not depend on science to justify their existence. If we seek to support and explain such things by quasi-scientific arguments, they themselves acquire no additional validity or force—but science is compromised.

The prime example of failure to respect the limits of science and of the resultant compromising of science is 'metaphysics'. Its basic error is not that it concerns itself with transcendental matters. If it did this merely in the sense of 'conceptual poetry' we should not need to object. But its basic error is that under the guise of science it transgresses the limits of scientific argumentation. Moreover, metaphysics thrives in many forms and turns up where it is least expected. One of its commonest and most insidious forms at the present time is what has been called 'scientism', a scientific superstition which is a sheer mockery of science in its failure to respect the limits of scientific argumentation. It is rarely found today among genuine scientists, but all too often in popular circles, and occasionally among philosophers when for some reason they have failed to outgrow an antiquated conception of science.

In short, by means of its 'objective argumentation' science itself determines the limits as to what may or may not be regarded as science. That is to say, the limits of science are determined from within, by science itself in its own interest, in order that it may continue to be science and avoid contamination by alien interests that would rob it of its distinctive feature, objective argumentation.

The idea of the limits of science is extraordinarily important in connection with the question of the possibility of 'scientific philosophy'. If there is to be any such thing, it must be kept strictly within the limits which science has set for itself by its commitment to objective argumentation. It is even more important for philosophy than for other sciences to remember this, because in the form of metaphysics philosophy has for centuries been unaccustomed to reckoning with any such limits, and because even in the form of scientific philosophy it has to function as a universal science, so that it is in a measure its very nature to 'overstep the bounds'. But 'overstepping the bounds' can mean widely different things. For although philosophy as a universal science can never be confined to one particular science, but must continually be crossing the frontiers of all the special sciences, yet its overstepping of the boundaries *between* the different sciences can never mean that it has the right to disregard the limits of science and step beyond the bounds of science itself. The limits of science are also the limits of philosophy, and philosophy has no more right than any other science to ignore the demand for 'objective argumentation'. Where no such argumentation is possible, philosophy like science in general has nothing to say.

CHAPTER V

Philosophy as Analysis of Meaning

1. A Philosophical Change of Scene

THE still unanswered question is that of philosophical *argumentation*, its possibility and its distinctive character. In the preceding chapter we analyzed different forms of scientific argumentation and discovered in a preliminary way the place that philosophical argumentation must occupy in this wider context if it is to be in any way recognized as scientific philosophy. This is still an open question, and it presents itself in a double form: 1. Does philosophy represent an objective argumentation? and 2. Does philosophy have an argumentation of its own? We are brought a step nearer the answer if we now direct our attention to the profound change which has come over philosophy during the last half-century. For it can be said without hesitation that this change opens up new possibilities of answering our question—and that quite independently of whether that question itself has been a focus of attention or has been deliberately avoided or outright rejected. If our purpose hitherto has been to establish the 'systematic locus' of the question, it is now to establish its 'historical locus', and to do so with particular reference to the most recent developments in philosophy, since it is in the context of these that the answer must be given.

Anyone who was familiar with the older tradition of philosophy but not with the developments of the last half-century would find himself very much at a loss if he were suddenly confronted with the contemporary philosophical situation. He would probably agree with those who talk of a 'revolution in philosophy',[1] for nothing but a real revolution could have brought about such an altered state of affairs as he now faced. He would wonder if there was any continuity between what has traditionally been called philosophy and that which bears the name today. It is not only that the great philosophical systems are conspicuous by their absence—for the idea that the day of such systems was past was already familiar—but it now appears that what used to be considered the chief problems of philosophy have also been set aside, and the concern of philosophy today seems to be with questions of a different sort, such as logical and linguistic analysis. Moreover it is difficult to discern any clear connections and lines of development between the main trends of contemporary philosophy.

It must, however, be said that this first impression is somewhat mis-

---

[1] *Cf.* G. Ryle (ed), *The Revolution in Philosophy*.

leading. Clear lines of connection are by no means lacking here, either between contemporary and traditional philosophy or between at least some of the most important contemporary trends. There is always a temptation to exaggerate the significance of what has happened in one's own time, and it is questionable whether we are really justified in speaking of a 'revolution' in philosophy. It is however at least certain that there has been a very considerable philosophical 'change of scene'. We shall confine ourselves to using this more guarded expression, and we must therefore begin by explaining in what the 'change of scene' consists, and pointing out certain characteristic ways in which philosophy today differs from the philosophy of the past.

Already in the title of this chapter, 'Philosophy as Analysis of Meaning', two of the characteristic features of contemporary philosophy are suggested. The concepts of 'analysis' and 'meaning' are found almost everywhere, and most schools of philosophy today would agree that the philosopher's task is essentially 'analysis of meaning' even though they interpret that phrase very variously. Each of the words in it says something essential about the new direction of philosophy. Whereas the old metaphysical philosophy was decidedly synthetic in its structure, contemporary philosophy is almost entirely devoted to analysis. 'Analysis' is not only a key word in 'analytical philosophy' explicitly so called, but it cuts across the party lines between all varieties of opinion. On every hand there is comparative unanimity that what is required of philosophy is less a philosophical 'doctrine' than philosophical 'clarification'. Analysis and clarification belong closely together; clarification is the end, and analysis the means to the end. Just as doctrine belongs together with synthesis and is constructed on synthetic lines, so clarification and analysis are inseparably bound up with one another.

Something similar can also be said of the other leading concept, that of 'meaning'. Almost all schools of philosophical thought take it as a matter of course that philosophy has to do with 'meaning'. The clarification which is effected by analysis consists precisely in making clear the 'meaning' or 'meaninglessness' of a statement.

A third characteristic feature of contemporary philosophy can be said to be its concern with the 'analysis of language'. Whether this ought to be described as a distinct third feature may be doubted, since it is so intimately bound up with the other two and is already implicit in them. For it goes without saying that where there is analysis of meaning there must be 'statements' and 'language', since it is in linguistic form that meaning finds expression. But the important thing is that this has resulted in a shifting of interest from ontological to linguistic questions. For although ontology has recently experienced something of a renaissance, it is no longer naively taken for granted as it once was, and it is most likely to be approached via a linguistic analysis of meaning. The old Socratic question,

'What do you mean?' with particular reference to the formulation of meaning in propositions, has become more or less the stock question of philosophy.

Although the features just mentioned are variously emphasized and to some extent variously understood by different schools of philosophical thought, yet when taken together they represent something that is characteristic of contemporary philosophy, and by starting with them it is possible to get a general orientation in the present philosophical situation. We shall illustrate this by reference to three main trends in contemporary philosophy: existentialism, logical empiricism and linguistic philosophy. We shall not of course attempt to give a complete account of them, as if we were studying them for their own sake, but our use of them will be purely illustrative and for the purpose of helping us on our way towards answering our main question. We have quite specific, critically probing questions to put to them, which arise out of our previous discussion, as for instance: What is the relation of these trends to metaphysics? How far do they represent 'scientific philosophy'? Do they achieve any real clarification? How far do they succeed in distinguishing the function of philosophy from that of the special sciences, and so in discovering a specifically philosophical form of argumentation?

In order to explain the difference between existentialism and logical empiricism, reference has often been made to the centuries-old contrast between Continental rationalism and British empiricism. As existentialism goes back to the former, so logical empiricism goes back to the latter tradition. Sometimes these have been represented as geographically distinct schools of thought, and a line has been drawn between Continental and Anglo-American philosophy. To some extent this may be justified, but the situation is really far more complicated than it suggests. The strands of thought are much too closely intertwined to permit such a schematic simplification. Logical empiricism is by no means merely an offshoot of the old British empiricism. Its ancestry includes not only Locke, Berkeley and Hume, but also Continental philosophers like Leibniz, Frege, Wittgenstein (in the *Tractatus*) and in a measure Kant. And while it is easier to trace existentialism back to the old Continental philosophy, even it displays many features which do not fit into that context. If to this we add modern linguistic philosophy, for which we can draw the line Schleiermacher—Dilthey—Husserl, and to which also certain aspects of Schlink and Carnap, and still more the later Wittgenstein belong, then it is obvious there can be no sharp demarcation between the different traditions. Where, for example, should Husserl be placed, among the existentialists or among the linguistic philosophers? And as for the attempt to divide modern philosophy geographically into a Continental and an Anglo-American bloc, there has been traffic across that frontier from the start. The rise of contemporary Anglo-American philosophy was strongly influenced by Continental philosophy, especially through Wittgenstein, and the Continental influence increased when the Vienna Circle of the 1930s was broken by political events and scattered around the world—not least in America. All this must be borne in mind when distinctions are drawn between the various philosophical movements of our time. Unless we pay attention to the way in which the lines continually cross and recross one another, we can easily get a misleading picture of the situation.

With these reservations we can now proceed to examine the three philosophical trends named above—the existentialist, the logical empiricist or logicist, and the linguistic—in order to see what contribution they can make to our quest for a 'scientific philosophy'. The latter term already contains the criterion or criteria with which we must approach these different schools of thought.

To describe philosophy as 'scientific' means 1. *positively*, that it must satisfy the requirements of 'objective argumentation'; and hence our question is whether these schools can help us to discover a mode of philosophical argumentation which is objectively scientific in the strict sense. It means also 2. *negatively*, that philosophy must be something other than metaphysics, since metaphysics is characterized precisely by a lack of objective argumentation; hence our question is further, whether these trends in contemporary philosophy have really succeeded in overcoming metaphysics, or whether perhaps they themselves represent to a greater or less extent a hidden metaphysics. Lastly, 'scientific philosophy' must 3. *as philosophy* ensure that the universality of interest is maintained which makes philosophy something other than a special science; hence our question is finally, to what extent these different schools have succeeded in demonstrating a specifically philosophical mode of argumentation which can properly be called 'objective', while at the same time clearly distinguishing philosophy from the special sciences. We shall thus all along be applying the lessons learnt in our preceding investigation. For our question has to do with the contrast between metaphysical and scientific philosophy. It has to do with 'the possibility of objective argumentation' and its opposite, arbitrary metaphysical construction. It has to do with the scientific and the universal interests of philosophy and how the two can be united in a single philosophical argumentation.

It should be pointed out lastly that the application of these criteria to the main trends in contemporary philosophy does not mean judging the latter by alien standards arbitrarily imposed from outside. The various schools cannot therefore evade our critical examination by withholding recognition of it on the grounds that the criteria employed involve an unjustifiable transcendent critique. The fact is rather that what is involved is a thoroughly immanent critique employing exclusively internal and inescapable criteria.

2. Analysis of Existence

Of the several positions we propose to discuss, the philosophy of existence or existentialism, as it is often called, is the one that stands closest to the older philosophical tradition. For our present purpose there is no need to distinguish between the two names given to it (though in other contexts it might be important to do so) and we shall ordinarily refer to it as existentialism. Perhaps the first thing to be said of it is that in existentialism the Hegelian-Kierkegaardian issue has come to life again—the question of the contrast between 'essence' and 'existence'. To say this, however, is to place existentialism in a vast context of the history of ideas extending through centuries and millennia.

Existentialism is not a type of thought that is immediately transparent to the reader. One needs to know a good deal of its background in order even to begin to understand what is being said. Furthermore, it does not represent a clearly defined, homogeneous school, but is found in a host of different variations. When it has in its ancestry men like Pascal and Kierkegaard—to name only two from recent centuries—it is easy to understand that existentialism is apt to move on the boundary between metaphysics and religion. But that very fact only underscores the more heavily its unstable and polymorphous character. It embraces conceptions as diverse as those of Heidegger's rather neutral and religiously ambivalent outlook and Sartre's avowedly atheistic existentialism along with Karl Jaspers' 'philosophical faith', Paul Tillich's philosophico-religious doctrine of correlation and Gabriel Marcel's Christian philosophy. At first sight we might well be tempted to ask whether there really is any common bond between these very discordant views. Yet in spite of all their differences they do in fact have certain basic features in common, which make it possible to include them all under the common name of existentialism. This common element, moreover, is connected precisely with what has been taken over from the metaphysical tradition.

The best way to get a grasp of existentialism is to set it against the background of the basic religio-metaphysical outlook of Augustine. For in Augustine we find quite a number of the key words of existentialism, such as 'being' and 'nothing', estrangement and alienation, restlessness, anxiety and dread. Familiarity with these terms in the early and immediately meaningful form in which they appear in Augustine, makes it easier to grasp them in the less precise though more sophisticated form in which they occur in existentialism. What makes them so extremely imprecise and elusive is the fact that they are frequently used in detachment from the original context that gave them their meaning.

The train of thought here in question is found at its simplest in Augustine's *Confessions*, of which the basic theme is expressed in the famous formula: 'Thou hast made us for Thyself and our heart is restless [*inquietum*] till it finds rest [finds its *quies*] in Thee.' This short sentence sums up a whole religious metaphysic. Here is the thought of God as 'being'—though not as *a* being, one among others, but 'being as such', 'being itself', something which does not *have* being, but *is* being or is identical with being. This can only be said about God, and not about the world or man, although these do have some measure of being. God alone *is* his own being. What then is the world, and what is man? They are creatures of God, and the being that pertains to them has its ground exclusively in the fact that they have been created by God. There is an absolute demarcation between the being of God and the being of the creature, inasmuch as the latter is something intermediate between 'being' and 'nothing'. As created by God the creatures, including man, possess a measure of being, a certain reality, but as created out of 'nothing' they suffer from a lack of being, an absence of reality, and they are in constant danger of sinking back into the 'nothing' out of which by God's creative activity they were raised up.

Among the creatures man occupies a special place inasmuch as he stands highest in the scale, not much below God, and he has the possibility of compensating for his lack of being by seeking his good, his *bonum* in God. Here on earth, as a stranger in an alien land, he is constantly exposed to the temptation of seeking his *bonum* in the temporal things that surround him. Hence he is forever in pursuit of new things to satisfy his need of being. But all such striving is doomed to failure, because the things in which he thus seeks satisfaction stand lower in the scale than himself. To attempt to find what he lacks in things that suffer from a greater lack than he does himself is obviously senseless. The only result of this pursuit of temporal advantages is that man sinks still deeper down towards that 'nothing' against which he seeks to secure himself; and it is because he senses this, that he can never find 'enough' (*satis*) to satisfy him and let him rest in anything temporal. He is hounded by a perpetual restlessness, which can be genuinely overcome only when he binds himself to God (*adhaerere Deo*) who is 'being itself', or in other words, when God has become his *summum bonum*, his supreme good. As long as man is estranged and alienated from God, his existence is threatened by the peril of nothingness. When he has found his way back to the One who is the ground and goal of his being, and his existence in time has become anchored in God's eternal being, that peril is eliminated; for God is not only the highest but also the unchangeable good, the *summum et incommutabile bonum*. God is eternal being, eternally at rest, while man exists in time with its transience, change and decay; but when man's alienation from God is overcome, he becomes participant in the eternal being of God.[2]

[2] For the importance of this line of thought in Augustine see my *Agape and Eros*, 1st edn, II, 2, pp. 258–75, 2nd edn, pp. 478–93, and *Die Konfessionen Augustins*, pp. 14ff. See also above, pp. 36f.—A survey of the history of the problem of alienation, which is so important for existentialism, is given by Pierre Courcelle in his *Les Confessions de Saint Augustin*, esp. *Appendice* V. ('*Répertoire des textes relatifs à la "région de dissemblance" de Platon à Gide*'), pp. 623–40.

After this brief glance at a dominant theme in the thought of Augustine, we return to existentialism. Against this background we at once understand what has made the question of 'Being and Time' (*Sein und Zeit*) a major problem for Heidegger, and why the problem of 'Being and Nothingness' (*L'être et le néant*) is Sartre's problem. We understand what is meant by the idea that human existence has become detached and alienated from 'authentic being'; and we understand Paul Tillich's identification of God with 'being itself', and so forth.[3] In fact these ideas are much clearer and more meaningful at their source in Augustine (and even down to Kierkegaard) than in the emaciated form in which they now appear when they have been cut off from a good part of their presuppositions. We have no need, however, to go any further into the different varieties of existentialism,[4] for enough has been said to furnish an insight into the philosophical structure of that way of thinking. The only question is, why existentialism should be brought into consideration at all in connection with the 'philosophical change of scene'. For it does not appear to have moved beyond the old status of metaphysics. Closer inspection, however, reveals that it has certain features in common with the new philosophical orientation of the last half-century. In particular, it claims to be a kind of 'analysis of meaning', it takes a critical attitude towards certain forms of metaphysics, and it holds rigidly to its 'phenomenological' stance.

The way in which existentialism seeks to keep its distance from the old metaphysics can be stated very simply thus: whereas metaphysics as a rule in dealing with the relation between essence and existence has taken being or objective essence as its starting point and then made its way to existence (as Augustine does when he proceeds from God, the Eternal, to man's creaturely existence in time), existentialism takes the opposite course. On the principle that 'existence precedes essence' it starts from human existence—hence its name, existentialism or the philosophy of existence. Human existence is made the subject of analysis, and it is held that such an analysis of existence is the only way to get at the essence or essential nature of being.

What then is meant by existence? It could of course be said that everything there is, everything that in any sense exists, has existence. Existentialism, however, takes the word 'existence' in a special sense and means by it *man's* existence. Only man can be said to 'exist' in the strict sense. To speak of man's existence is to give expression to his intermediate position.

[3] It is only with decided reserve that Tillich can be reckoned among the existentialists. He is really from first to last a philosopher of essence, not of existence. We shall see further on, however, that existentialism in general has a tendency to slip over from existence to essence. *Cf.* J. B. Lotz, *Sein und Existenz*, and W. Bretschneider, *Sein und Wahrheit*.

[4] For an excellent survey of these, see T. Stenström, *Existentialismen*. *Cf.* also P. Roubiczek, *Existentialism*.

It is to say that man is neither pure being nor pure nothing, but something in between, having in him an element both of 'being' and of 'nothing'. The insecurity of human existence between being and nothing is the reason for man's 'estrangement' and 'alienation'; it is the reason for the constitutional 'restlessness' of his existence; it is the reason for the 'anxiety' and everything akin to it that existentialism is in the habit of citing as the hallmark of human existence. This then is the starting point for philosophical reflection, and the analysis of human existence thus prepares the way for an insight into the *Sinn des Seins*, the 'meaning of being'. Anthropology is the point of departure, ontology the destination, the goal.

But that being so, the question arises: what has become of the revolutionary impulse which was to have made existentialism something other than the old metaphysics? For what begins as analysis of existence ends as a metaphysic of essence. The 'analysis of meaning' practised by existentialism is plainly something very different from what other modern schools have in mind when they speak of 'analysis of meaning'. Both 'meaning' and 'analysis' are given here a quite other than their usual sense. The 'meaning' in question is the 'meaning of life' (or its possible meaninglessness); that is to say, it has to do in the first instance with the meaning of human existence and in the last resort with the meaning of existence as a whole (or with what may prove to be the lack of meaning in either).

From what has been said it is very clear to what type of philosophy existentialism belongs. It is not the 'scientific' type, but the 'metaphysical'. The new contribution of existentialism is more apparent than real. The philosopher is not so much a man of science, but rather something of a prophet or seer, a man who has had a deeper insight than others and believes he has something essential to say to his contemporaries about the meaning of life and of existence. In the nature of the case, no science can furnish answers to such questions. By asking and trying to answer them existentialism shows that it has gone beyond the limits of science and landed itself in metaphysics. All the features that we listed above (pp. 35ff.) as characteristic of metaphysics and as revealing its non-scientific status are accordingly to be found here. Existentialism is ontology; it represents a confused amalgam of being and value; it is a world-view philosophy and an outlook on life; it builds on conceptual realism ('being' and 'nothing'); its phenomenological analysis is at bottom nothing but a feint, which barely conceals the fact that it is really a matter of metaphysical dogmatism.

It is no accident that existentialism displays the kind of obscurity and abstruseness for which it has often been reproached. It is connected with the inherent ambiguity of its conception of the nature and function of philosophy. On the one hand philosophy is assigned the task of carrying out an analysis of existence that is at least in some measure objective, while on the other hand it is expected to provide us with an interpretation of life and a world-view. This ambiguity has always been a distinguishing feature of metaphysics, and hence what we have here is nothing even remotely akin to 'scientific philosophy' but rather a typical piece of 'conceptual poetry'. The affinity with poetry is, moreover, very evident in the foremost representatives of existentialism. In the case of Heidegger it manifests itself in his inclination during his later period to connect his philosophical analyses with various poets and poet-philosophers of the past, and in the case of Sartre it appears in his choice of the play, the novel or the short story as the medium for the presentation of his philosophical ideas.

We now know the answer to the questions we have to put to existentialism in our present context. It is very plain that we can expect no help from it in our quest for a form of 'objective argumentation' for philosophy—not least because it is precisely in argumentation that existentialism is weakest. Either it does not argue at all, but contents itself with asserting and metaphysical dogmatizing—in keeping with its character as representing a certain 'view of life', a certain conception of the nature of man and the world—or else, since complete abstention from all argumentation is in any case impossible, it takes refuge in etymological arguments that prove nothing. Nor is it only Heidegger who indulges in such flights of fancy; they are also found elsewhere from time to time, and are in no way uncharacteristic of existentialist thinking. Often these etymological derivations are quite precarious and arbitrary, being mostly of an associative kind. Yet even when they are etymologically correct, they are of no significance in the philosophical context, since the etymological origin of a term has become with the passage of time irrelevant to its *meaning*, and it is of course the meaning that is ultimately decisive for philosophy.

The reason why existentialism has nothing to offer from a methodological point of view is that there is nothing either verifiable or arguable about it. When we ask on what grounds it takes the view it does, we are referred to some sort of '*Wesensschau*', a sort of intuitive perception of how things are. It is assumed that if we see things in an existentialist light we have rightly understood them, while anyone who sees them differently is afflicted with 'value-blindness' (Scheler). Now it might have been expected that such ideas, which were characteristic of the early days of existentialism in a Husserl or a Scheler, would be shed as existentialism became more fully developed; but the contrary has been the case. It can in fact be said that Husserl, even in his later, phenomenological period, shows far more methodological sensitivity than does later existentialism. An illuminating example of its fundamentally assertive, dogmatic attitude, which precludes any genuine argumentation, is provided by a statement of Heidegger's quoted by Heinrich Ott. The statement was made in connection with a discussion in which the position maintained by Heidegger had been found '*schwer nachvollziehbar*', hard for the others to grasp. Ott tells us: 'I asked him afterwards: "I believe I see things in this matter exactly as you do, but how is one to prove it or make it under-standable to those present?" Heidegger's reply was brief: "You can't prove it. It has to be *seen*!" '[5] Just so; and that is precisely where the weakness is hidden—or perhaps rather fully exposed.

There are certainly things one cannot prove; but then one can at least produce arguments in their favour. To put off a puzzled questioner with the explanation that something 'has to be seen', instead of arguing the case for it, is to give him no answer at all. There is nothing here beyond the tautology: If you don't see, you don't see!—unless it is the arbitrary, un-warranted assumption: Anyone who doesn't see things as I do, doesn't see at all, he is blind. A person could hardly make it plainer that he was dispensing with argument and contenting himself with arbitrary insistence on his own point of view. This is what so clearly shows that existentialism has no connection with science or 'scientific philosophy'. It can of course happen even in science that someone does not *see* a particular fact; but it is then never enough simply to declare that he is blind to that fact, as if nothing could be done about it. Instead, the attempt is made by intensive argumentation to show him what is at stake and enable him to check and find out for himself how the matter stands.

The reason why existentialism is unable to make any contribution to 'scientific philosophy' is above all its impreciseness, which makes im-possible any checking, testing and weighing, and consequently any 'objective argumentation'. How then can it possibly have any methodo-logical relevance for scientific philosophy, which argues objectively? Here we must agree with Marc-Wogau, who says: 'What is offered is not an argument for the thesis, but a dogmatic assertion that such and such is the case, cloaked in irrelevant etymological considerations. The dearth of argument cannot be glossed over by playing with the etymology of words.'[6] We can also agree with his concluding remark: 'The interpre-tation of man's existence as *Sorge* rests on a fable! That sort of thing is not science nor is it scientific philosophy.'[7]

The result of our examination has been extremely negative and may seem to imply a total condemnation of existentialism. To prevent such a misunderstanding it should be pointed out that we have been putting very particular questions to existentialism, and not at all passing a total judgment on it. What we wanted to know was whether existentialism represents a form of 'objective argumentation' and to what extent it can contribute towards the establishing of a 'scientific philosophy'. To these questions we have found that the answer must be plainly and unreservedly negative. Where objective argumentation is concerned, no one has the right

[5] H. Ott, 'Martin Heidegger' in H. J. Schultz, *Tendenzen*, p. 349.
[6] K. Marc-Wogau, *Att studera filosofi*, p. 22.
[7] *Op. cit.*, p. 23.

to claim exemption from the rules. Yet although from that point of view the answer must clearly be negative, it does not follow that existentialism can have no positive significance from other points of view. By referring to it as 'conceptual poetry' (p. 135) we have called to mind what was said above[8] about the demarcation between the categories of 'science' and 'poetry', and about the possibility of letting poetry have a meaning of its own, though not one that has anything to do with science. This enables us to understand the characteristic ambiguity and frequent contradictions of existentialism.[9] For whereas obscurity and uncertainty or multiplicity of meaning are extremely disturbing in science, it is plain that they can be of real value in poetry. How often it is just the imprecise, ambiguous features of a poem—where one cannot be certain what is intended, and where incompatible ideas and tendencies are mingled without explanation—that give it its charm and its power. But obscurity, ambiguity and contradiction cannot therefore become the aim of science.

In science there must be an uncompromising demand for clarity, precision and freedom from contradiction, since without these there can be no scientific argumentation. Arguments based on obscurity and ambiguity inevitably lead to all kinds of false conclusions, and particularly to the fallacy of equivocation. That is why science must always strive after the greatest possible clarity and cannot tolerate contradictions. When a philosophical movement like existentialism so ostentatiously embarks on the path of 'conceptual poetry', it is obvious that *as regards methodology* it can make no contribution to objective argumentation in philosophy.

There is, however, nothing to prevent existentialism from being of significance in other respects for a scientifically oriented philosophy. To take only two examples: it can be significant on the one hand from a heuristic point of view, and on the other as underlining the importance of the universal perspective in philosophy.

First, as regards its *heuristic* significance, it is perhaps not least owing to its scientifically undisciplined behaviour that it is able to draw attention to things which might otherwise easily be overlooked if there were stricter observance of scientific canons. What we said above about scientific intuition[10] is applicable here. In an intuitive and imaginative way it is possible

[8] Above, pp. 53ff.

[9] An example of this is the quite violent contradiction in Sartre's conception of absolute freedom, which on the one hand presupposes that there cannot be any binding norms, yet on the other hand allows my action, by the mere fact of its being chosen and carried out, to become 'exemplary' and a binding norm for everyone else, since the choice I make in absolute freedom is a choice made on behalf of all mankind and thus acquires a universally normative character. At the same time as all normative thinking is rejected, it returns in an even more pointed form. It often looks very like Kant's idea of the ethical norm that is advancing in full array—though admittedly turned upside down.

[10] Above, pp. 117ff.

to form an idea of how matters stand with regard to a particular problem. This can often serve as a heuristic starting point for a scientific investigation, although it is certainly not science as long as it remains simply on the level of imagination and intuition. It becomes science only when it is subjected to examination and testing which involves objective argumentation. That is the only means of deciding whether what we have is a fruitful intuition or merely an idle fancy. Applied to existentialism this means that even if the latter does happen to hit upon a philosophically significant problem, it has found no more than the starting point for a scientifically philosophical inquiry—an inquiry which it is not itself capable of carrying out.

What is more important, though it is often overlooked, is the contribution existentialism has made by emphasizing the *universal perspective* of philosophy. There are after all in human life other problems than the scientific, and by making these others also the subject of philosophical reflection existentialism has sought to counteract the narrowing of perspective which is so typical of many schools of thought at the present time. What is not science is regarded in many quarters as non-existent. Existentialism has rightly reacted against this, and has not been afraid to look into the most intricate human problems, with all the risks entailed in doing so. It has thus acquired the function of a remembrancer, keeping us in mind of the range and extent of the problems. It is, of course, another matter that the way in which it has sought to provide for the universal perspective is in quite a number of ways extremely questionable. We have already given various examples of this—its arbitrariness, lack of precision, dogmatic assertiveness, appeal to a *Wesensschau*, and so forth. This is the price it has paid for its laudable intention of ensuring the breadth and comprehensiveness of its view: in order to gain universality it has surrendered its claim to be scientific. Philosophy is no longer a science but an activity of another sort; or else, in so far as it still wishes to count as a science, there is a diminution of scientific rigour and arbitrariness finds a place in science and philosophy. There comes to be something unpredictable about its way of working. The result is the old familar story of metaphysics once more: the universal interest displaces the scientific. It is therefore not surprising that little can be gained from existentialism with regard to the methodological question of objective argumentation in scientific philosophy.

3. Logical Analysis

If it is only with very definite reservations that we have been able to use existentialism as an example of the 'philosophical change of scene' and to give it a place in a chapter on 'analysis of meaning', we have much more justification for citing as examples of the change those developments of thought which are usually grouped together under the common name of 'analytical philosophy'. It should be said at once, however, that what we have here is not a homogeneous philosophical school, as the common name might suggest, but a number of different trends, relatively independent of one another, which developed spontaneously in various parts of the world[11] during the first decades of this century, but which in spite of all the differences between them have enough of a common concern to justify their being given a common name. There are two features in particular which they all share: 1. a markedly *anti-metaphysical* attitude, which makes the combating of metaphysics a fundamental part of the task of philosophy; and 2. the concentration of philosophy on '*logical analysis*', 'analysis of concepts', 'analysis of meaning', or whatever else it may be called, which means that the task of philosophy is not so much a matter of system building and expounding philosophical dogmas as of *clarification*.

It is debatable which of these elements is primary. They are in fact so interdependent as to be inseparable. The way in which a man defines his own analysis of meaning or of concepts becomes, as we shall see, determinative of the arguments he uses to attack metaphysics. On the other hand, the way in which he attacks metaphysics becomes determinative of the pattern on which he develops his own outlook. Since the anti-metaphysical interest is the most striking and constitutes the strongest bond between the various trends, it is most natural to begin with it. As we do so, however, we should observe that the type of metaphysics against which the attack is directed in different quarters, and which thus forms the background, also colours the different anti-metaphysical positions.[12]

[11] Three main lines of development can be distinguished: 1. in the Anglo-Saxon world, that associated primarily with G. E. Moore, but represented also by Bertrand Russell and Ludwig Wittgenstein; 2. in Scandinavia, that known as the Uppsala philosophy and associated with such names as Axel Hägerström and Adolph Phalén; 3. on the Continent, that called logical positivism (and later logical empiricism), which is chiefly associated with the Vienna Circle.

[12] In the Anglo-Saxon world the background was furnished by Hegelianism, which —in spite of British empiricism—had come to power and managed to remain in power for a surprisingly long time. It was against this form of idealistic metaphysics that the attack was launched, beginning with G. E. Moore's famous 'Refutation of Idealism' in *Mind*, 1903,—a title which recalls Kant's 'Refutation of Idealism' in the *Critique of Pure Reason* (Reclam, pp. 208-17, Kemp Smith, pp. 244-52), where Kant takes issue with Descartes and Berkeley. It was this essay of Moore's that gave the impetus for the tremendous volte-face in English philosophy.

In Sweden a similar breakthrough occurred about the same time. Here the background was furnished by the 'Swedish personalism' of Chr. Boström, who was sharply critical of Hegelianism although he remained within the idealistic tradition and his own thought could be described as a kind of subjective Platonism. It was in the first instance Boströmian metaphysics that drew the criticism of the 'Uppsala philosophy', although this was subsequently extended to all metaphysics whatsoever. It is significant that the first work of Phalén was a refutation of subjectivism (*Kritik av subjektivism i olika former*)—a counterpart of Moore's 'Refutation of Idealism'—and that his first major work concerned Hegel's philosophy and its epistemological roots (*Das Erkenntnis-*

What then are the charges levelled against metaphysics in the different quarters? By what arguments is the opposition to metaphysics supported? It is here that the theory of 'meaning' which a person holds becomes of decisive importance. Each of the groups we have named has its own particular view; and as if that were not enough, there are also within each group marked divisions of opinion. We therefore have to do with a whole spectrum of different understandings of logical analysis and with correspondingly different forms of anti-metaphysics.

If we take first the positions of Moore and Russell, we find here an anti-metaphysics on a metaphysical basis—a fact which very much cramps its style. Their attack is directed against a particular form of metaphysics, namely idealism (Berkeley-Hegel), and it is launched from another metaphysical base, namely realism. Moore, however, is much less of a metaphysician than Russell. As time goes on he concentrates increasingly on the defence of a commonsense view,[13] which is considerably different from traditional metaphysics both realistic and idealistic. His point of departure for the analysis of meaning is 'common sense' and 'ordinary language'. It is his conviction that ordinary language, if only it is allowed to be itself, is in perfectly good order and free from contradiction. It is philosophy that causes trouble by its frequently artificial use of words. When philosophy uses ordinary words in another than their ordinary sense, so that it seems to be still talking about the same thing though it is not, then it is itself responsible for the obscurity, ambiguity and contradictions from which common sense and ordinary language are free. Only by painstaking analysis coupled with a return to the meaning of ordinary language can the difficulty be overcome. Moore appeals constantly to the language that everyone understands and the understanding that everyone knows to be correct—which at heart the philosopher also knows, in spite of his confused misuse of the language. Such is the gist of Moore's commonsense philosophy and his analysis of meaning, and such are the means by which he seeks to solve the vexed questions and puzzles of philosophy.

Russell takes the opposite course. For him it is just the impreciseness of ordinary language, its rough and ready nature, that is the root of ambiguity, of contradictions and paradoxes. In order to remedy this, analysis

---

problem in Hegels Philosophie). In the latter he shows that 'the epistemological problem' as traditionally understood is merely a modification of the metaphysical problem of ontology.

Finally, the background for the attack of the Vienna Circle on metaphysics was the old hostility between metaphysics and positivism, which received fresh nourishment partly through influences from English philosophy and partly through the interest of the Circle itself in the philosophy of science. All this conspired to produce the extremely violent nature of the attack launched during the twenties and thirties by the Vienna Circle on everything that could be called metaphysics.

[13] See G. E. Moore, 'A Defence of Common Sense'.

must lead to the construction of an artificial, technical language, which avoids the obscurities of ordinary language. It must be a language so devised that the meaning of every word is clearly and unequivocally fixed and the words are combined with one another according to clearly stated rules, a language of such precision as to make logico-mathematical calculation possible. This is Leibniz's dream of a *calculus ratiocinator* and *characteristica universalis* and the gathering up of everything into a *mathesis universalis*. It is this Leibnizian idea, mediated through Frege, that has been the inspiration of modern logicism,[14] seeming as it does to provide an infallible means of overcoming the confusions of philosophy (metaphysics). Interest in logistic method as well as in artificial language passes through Wittgenstein's (admittedly often misunderstood) *Tractatus* to Vienna positivism, where it forms one of the bases of the latter's characteristic combination of the logical and empirical, and hence also of its anti-metaphysical bias. Before we pursue that subject, however, we must take note of the contribution made in these areas more than a decade earlier by the Uppsala philosophy.

In the Uppsala philosophy we find an anti-metaphysical attitude going far beyond that of Moore and Russell. How far the campaign against metaphysics is there regarded as a primary function of philosophy can be seen in the motto placed by Hägerström in his 'Self-Portrait' over his life's work: '*Praeterea censeo metaphysicam esse delendam*'.[15] Formally more temperate but actually more devastating for metaphysics is Adolf Phalén's critique of 'epistemological subjectivism'—a critique even more firmly grounded in conceptual analysis as the chief task of philosophy. Logical analysis or conceptual analysis thus becomes for the Uppsala philosophers also an analysis of meaning, though primarily with a negative thrust inasmuch as conceptual analysis is the principal means of exposing the meaningless of metaphysics. Whereas for Moore the impossibility of metaphysics was due to the factual impossibility of forming any idea or conception of what it is about, for the Uppsala philosophers it is a question of a still more serious impossibility, namely that of logical contradiction. The criterion by which metaphysics is judged and its meaninglessness exposed is the *law of contradiction*. Where that law is broken, nothing is really said; for the same thing being at the same time both affirmed and denied, the result is pure 'meaninglessness'. That is the status of metaphysics.

For the Uppsala philosophers there is no solution to be found by turning to common sense. What is wrong with metaphysics is not that it departs

[14] See, e.g., Whitehead and Russell, *Principia Mathematica*, and Lewis and Langford, *Symbolic Logic*.

[15] See above, p. 34, nn. 5 and 6.—Works dealing with Hägerström's philosophy are listed under the following authors in the Bibliography: Lindroth, Cassirer, Fries, Logren, Sandin, Hemberg, Nygren (G.). Note particularly Sandin's translation of Hägerström's own work under the title of *Philosophy and Religion*.

from the commonsense view, or as they like to say, from 'the general consciousness', so that all would be well if only there were a return to the latter. Metaphysical 'problems' are not unreal in the sense that the contradictions of metaphysics arise merely from its own artificial use of concepts. Those contradictions are rooted rather in contradictions which are present already in the general consciousness. Metaphysics only draws out the mutually nullifying implications of vague and self-contradictory ideas latent in the general consciousness. Conceptual analysis has thus a double task: it has to show that the metaphysical concepts are self-contradictory or 'dialectical', and it has to trace the contradictions back to their roots in the general consciousness.

A similarly critical attitude to everything metaphysical is taken by the 'Vienna Circle', which can be said to represent a fusion of traditional positivism in the spirit of Ernst Mach with logicism as it is found above all in Wittgenstein's *Tractatus*.[16] This fusion finds apt expression in the description of this school of thought as 'logical positivism' (later 'logical empiricism'). As 'positivism' it is bound to demand the total elimination of metaphysics. There is complete agreement with John Stuart Mill and Auguste Comte as to the meaninglessness of metaphysics. Metaphysics represents an inferior, antiquated stage of development, which has now been replaced by the positive stage of science. The influence of logicism and Wittgenstein, who supplies the school with its decisive theoretical argument against metaphysics, tends in the same direction. Special reliance is placed on Wittgenstein's theory of truth-function and his understanding of analytical judgments as tautologies, together with his view of the importance of empirical judgments for knowledge of any content. Since metaphysical statements are neither empirical nor tautological, the conclusion is that they are no kind of propositions at all. It is not simply that metaphysics is false, but that it is completely meaningless.

But what is involved in speaking of meaning and meaninglessness in this context? Is there any criterion by which we can decide what has meaning and what has not? At this point the well-known 'verification principle' of logical positivism comes in. This principle has been very simply stated thus: 'the meaning of a statement is the method of its verification.'[17] If we cannot show any way in which a given proposition can be verified, then that proposition has no meaning. Hence a sentence which as far as its

[16] In his programmatic essay, 'Die Wende der Philosophie', the original leader of the Circle, Moritz Schlick, notes its dependence on logicism: 'The roads start out from logic. The beginning of them was obscurely seen by Leibniz, important stretches have been opened up during recent decades by Gottlob Frege and Bertrand Russell, but the first to make his way to the decisive turning point has been Ludwig Wittgenstein (in his *Tractatus logico-philosophicus*, 1922)'—Schlick, *Ges. Aufs.*, pp. 33f. For the succession, Leibniz-Frege-Russell, see above, pp. 79f.

[17] *Cf.* Schlick, *Ges. Aufs.*, p. 90: 'To explain the circumstances under which a statement is true is the *same* as to explain its meaning, and nothing else.'

outward, linguistic structure is concerned seems to be entirely in order, may in reality be nothing but empty words without assignable meaning, or quite simply nonsense. This then is the standard, the criterion, by which metaphysics is to be judged, and the result cannot but be completely negative. Since there are only two legitimate kinds of statement, the empirical and the tautological, and since metaphysics is neither based on empirical observation nor is by nature tautological, it must be wholly without content and meaning.[18]

Having surveyed the arguments advanced against metaphysics by the three main schools, we now turn to a critical examination of them, and in doing so we must give attention to the theories of 'meaning' that underlie them. The questions we have to ask about the different theories are those we raised above (p. 120f.). We shall inquire first, how far these arguments really touch metaphysics, and how far the different schools have themselves succeeded in eluding the metaphysical snare. Then we shall ask what contribution they can each make towards establishing 'philosophy as analysis of meaning'—how far they meet the demand for objective argumentation, and how far they can help towards a genuine philosophical clarification. Then finally the question will be whether they manage to produce a form of argumentation which is peculiar to philosophy.

From what has already been said it is evident that the arguments brought against metaphysics vary a greal deal in their content and cogency.

To begin with *logical empiricism*, it is quite obvious that its criticism of metaphysics, although prosecuted with the greatest vigour, only partly strikes home. The reason for this is that the 'verification principle' which has been proposed as the criterion of meaning is simply not capable of serving that purpose. Today, after a couple of decades, this is clear to everyone and is generally acknowledged. Yet even in the early stages it was noticed by logical empiricists themselves, and there was in consequence a constant succession of reformulations and modifications of the principle in the hope of making it more serviceable. The result, however, was rather the reverse, for in its watered-down form the principle became even less suitable for its intended purpose.[19] What is it then that makes the verifica-

---

[18] A. J. Ayer sums the matter up as follows: 'We may accordingly define a metaphysical sentence as a sentence which purports to express a genuine proposition, but does, in fact, express neither a tautology nor an empirical hypothesis. And as tautologies and empirical hypotheses form the entire class of significant propositions, we are justified in concluding that all metaphysical assertions are nonsensical' (*Language, Truth and Logic*, 2nd edn, p. 41).

[19] This process of gradual dissolution, which was brought about largely within the ranks of logical empiricism itself, can be observed in A. J. Ayer's Introduction to the 2nd edition of his *Language, Truth and Logic*. In the 1st edition he had accepted the original, strict formulation of the 'verification principle'. In the 2nd edition he has discovered in how many ways it is indefensible, and he explains his modification of it in the Introduction. *Cf.* also C. G. Hempel, 'Problems and Changes in the Empiricist

tion principle unusable as a criterion of meaning? It is the fact that its net has a mesh at once too coarse and—paradoxically enough—too fine for it to serve as a criterion at all. It is too coarse because it lets much slip through which it was intended to catch, and too fine because it catches much that is obviously meaningful and ought to be let through.[20]

The trouble is not that it so decidedly focuses attention on the question of meaning. On the contrary, that is its strength, and logical empiricism deserves unhesitating recognition as having done perhaps more than any other school towards reorienting modern philosophy to the 'analysis of meaning'. Schlick's description of the task of philosophy is worth recalling here. He says: 'In the past, philosophy asked about the ground of being . . . the meaning of the world and the guiding principle of conduct; but we ask nothing more than "What exactly do you mean?", "What is the meaning of the things you say?" '[21] The task of philosophy is not to investigate 'the ground of being', nor is it to make pronouncements about 'the meaning of the world'. It does not help matters that the question of 'meaning' has been smuggled into the latter formulation, for what we have in both cases are questions to which no objective answer can be given; they are meaningless metaphysical questions. By contrast it is the task of 'scientific philosophy' simply and straightforwardly to investigate 'the meaning of the things we say', and this should not be an impossible question to answer. Such was the programme, and in itself it was highly admirable. How then did it come about that it could not be fulfilled? The reason is to be found, as we have suggested, in the unfortunate 'verification principle'. If only what is empirically verifiable is to be recognized as meaningful, then there will be a good many things that are meaningless besides metaphysics.

Consistently applied, this method of verification would have a devastating effect on nearly everything we call science. For it is not only true of the 'laws of nature' but also of all general scientific hypotheses, that they are neither empirically verifiable facts nor tautologies—hence they would one and all be meaningless! But if the criterion of meaning is such as to render meaningless the major part of what the sciences as they actually

---

Criterion of Meaning'. No one has done more, however, to expose the unsoundness of the principle than K. R. Popper, particularly in his *The Logic of Scientific Discovery* and *Conjectures*.

[20] *Cf.* H. Feigl: '. . . . that *that* criterion [the original verification criterion] not only eliminated metaphysics but, alas, science as well' (in M. Bunge, *The Critical Approach*, p. 50). Cf. also J. R. Weinberg, *An Examination*, p. 199: 'It is now clear that Logical Positivism cannot eliminate metaphysics without destroying itself, and that it cannot establish the logical foundations of science without alteration of the principles absolutely essential to its teaching.'—For criticism of the verification principle see P. Marhenke, 'The Criterion of Significance', in Linsky, *Semantics*, pp. 139–59.

[21] M. Schlick, *Ges. Aufs.*, p. XXIII, where the editor, F. Waismann, in his Preface gives the above quotation from Schlick's literary remains.

operate regard as their main business, why should metaphysics worry if it too is declared to be meaningless? At least it is in good company! This illustrates how the verification principle is a net that has both too coarse and too fine a mesh to be used as a criterion. The web is so closely woven that the ordinary and obviously legitimate work of science cannot get through, which is an absurd state of affairs. The error has therefore to be corrected by arbitrarily letting first one thing then another slip through, until for lack of a clear criterion the meshes become so slack that almost anything can get through, including metaphysics. And by the way, how is it with the verification principle itself? Can it be empirically verified? No. Is it a tautology? No. Then it is itself meaningless. So it is by a meaningless standard that metaphysics is judged and found to be meaningless! This shows better than anything else that some factor or factors extraneous to the question of meaning must be involved, and it is these that make the attack on metaphysics so ineffectual. The nature of the extraneous element can easily be seen. It is the continual slipping over from logic and analysis of meaning to metaphysics and ontology. Logic provides the starting point, but the aim is to move on from there to the ontological structure of existence. It is held that there is a structural resemblance between logic and reality. The ontological interest forms a bridge that leads from the analysis of meaning to metaphysics.

It is no accident that one of the chief works of Vienna positivism bears the title 'The Logical Structure of the World'.[22] This is both programmatic and symptomatic. In terms of the programme it is a logical inquiry; yet it is also a symptom of the underlying metaphysic. For while metaphysics is to be overcome by means of logical analysis, this analysis itself is based on a definite metaphysical position, namely that of positivism. That a philosophy on such a foundation is not 'scientific philosophy' is indisputably clear. For it not only claims to be *the* scientific world-view'[23]—which is a contradiction in terms, seeing that science can never lead to any particular world-view, and metaphysics shows itself to be non-scientific just by proclaiming a world-view—but it also expects philosophy to be ultimately able to set up a positivistic 'unified science' on an inductive basis.[24] The

---

[22] R. Carnap, *Der logische Aufbau der Welt*. In this connection we should recall G. Bergmann's three works: *The Metaphysics of Logical Positivism*, *Meaning and Existence*, and *Logic and Reality*. He himself describes these as the steps that led him from an original phenomenalism to a clear realism, and thus from a more hidden, implicit ontology to a fully developed ontology. 'Logic without ontology is merely a calculus' (*Logic and Reality*, p. 151). 'Logic is but a reflection of the world's form. Hence, one cannot fully articulate one's realism without ontologizing logic' (*ibid.*, p. vii).

[23] On 'metaphysics as world-view' see above, pp. 37 and 44ff.

[24] A survey of this and related problems in logical empiricism can be found in J. Ruytinx, *La problematique philosophique*, pp. 187–349. J. W. N. Watkins is right when he says: 'Verificationism, positivism, inductionism hang together—and they fall together too' (in M. Bunge, *The Critical Approach*, p. 115).

attack of logical empiricism on metaphysics cannot therefore be described as conspicuously successful. Admittedly it has helped to keep alive the thought that there is something suspect about the claim of metaphysics to rank as a science, and that the question simply has to be faced whether metaphysics has any meaning at all—which is no small achievement. But the arguments by which the meaninglessness of metaphysics was to have been exposed, are not suited to the task. Metaphysics cannot be driven out by metaphysics. When, moreover, the arguments intended to strike down metaphysics strike so much else which they were never meant to touch, then clearly the logical empiricist has failed in his laudable purpose of demonstrating the indefensible nature of metaphysics.

We shall now take leave of logical empiricism with its problematical criterion of meaning and its attempt to combat metaphysics on that basis. We can do so the more easily as we shall have occasion at a later stage to return to the question of 'verification as a criterion of meaning' (Chap. X.3). Our discussion of it here, however, has been particularly useful in that it has, among other things, reminded us of that movement back and forth between logic and ontology which is so typical of much of contemporary philosophy. This delivers us from the necessity of a similar discussion in relation to the remaining schools of analytical philosophy. A more detailed inquiry of that kind would take too long, and it would not produce any new factors with decisive bearing on our question. What has been said of logical empiricism can be taken as a paradigm for the rest, at least as regards the all-important matter of slipping over from the logical to the ontological.

Although the *Uppsala philosophy*, as we have already suggested, thanks to its concentration on the 'law of contradiction' as decisive for meaning or meaninglessness, goes considerably deeper in its conceptual analysis and is far more effective in its criticism of metaphysics, yet even it does not escape the confusion between logic and ontology which is so characteristic of metaphysics. This is evident above all in the fact that for Hägerström everything centres ultimately in the 'concept of reality' as the focal point of philosophy. His identification of 'self-identity'—'definiteness'—'reality' —'spatio-temporal reality' is what turns his philosophy, despite all his intentions to the contrary, into metaphysics.[25] With this the situation

[25] Already in 1923 I criticized Hägerström's concept of reality with reference to its implied metaphysics. Since what I wrote then is exactly in line with our discussion here, a passage from it may be quoted: '. . . that this initial mistake takes its revenge in that the philosophical theory based on it turns out despite contrary intentions to be of a metaphysical—albeit negatively metaphysical—stamp. For if the concept of reality is made central in philosophy, the question necessarily arises how reality in general is related to spatio-temporal reality; and no matter in what direction the answer is given, it inevitably lands us in metaphysics, and it does so because the question itself is of a metaphysical character. If the answer given is that spatio-temporal reality is not the whole of reality, but that there is also a "higher" reality, then clearly, no matter how we

becomes very much like what we saw in logical empiricism. In both cases there is a duality—on the one hand a frenetic struggle against metaphysics, a struggle with something of '*écrasez l'infâme*' about it, and on the other hand a disguised metaphysics which is integral to the outlook of the anti-metaphysician himself. Owing to this family likeness, and because Hägerström too makes spatio-temporal reality the whole of reality, it has been taken for granted that he holds a positivistic view. That is not, however, the case. His philosophical position rests on a quite different basis, and is rather on the side of rationalism than of positivism or empiricism. It is this that explains his sharp criticism both of the sensualism of positivism and of Bertrand Russell's views.

In this connection a further comment is necessary. When we speak of the metaphysics of Uppsala philosophy, it should be observed that there is no simple uniformity about that philosophy, and our objection to Hägerström's metaphysics does not apply to it as a whole—particularly in the form in which it has been developed by Adolf Phalén. With his both keener and more cautious mind Phalén has known how to avoid slipping off into metaphysics[26] and instead has steadily concentrated on 'conceptual analysis' with the sole object of furthering philosophical clarification. In this way he can be said to have prepared the way both for the

---

define this higher reality, we are involved in metaphysics. The same is true, moreover, if we simply equate spatio-temporal reality with reality as such, and assert that there cannot be any reality of another than the spatio-temporal kind. If this assertion is meant to be anything more than a more or less arbitrary limitation of the concept of reality, then it is a metaphysical assertion. In other words, a theory which denies the possibility of any other sort of reality than the spatio-temporal, is not a negation of metaphysics, but is itself metaphysics of a negative kind. Thus whether we affirm or deny a reality beyond the spatio-temporal, we are moving in the realm of metaphysics. The only way to avoid metaphysics altogether, therefore, is to relieve philosophy of responsibility for the question of reality, and let it concentrate on that of validity' (*Bibelforskaren*, 40 årg., 1923, pp. 274f.).—*Cf.* on this R. Sandin, 'Axel Hägerström's Philosophy of Religion', pp. 118f. (quoted here from J. Hemberg, *Religion och metafysik*, pp. 84f.): 'Hence for Hägerström it is *reality*—the world *an sich*—that is spatial and temporal. Such a view is required by his rejection of subjectivism. . . . The question now arises whether such a claim is not metaphysical. . . . We must inquire, therefore, whether Hägerström, who vociferously denounces metaphysics in all forms, has not himself lapsed back into metaphysics.'

[26] Symptomatic of the difference between the two founders of the Uppsala philosophy is Phalén's decided repudiation of Hägerström's peculiar theory, obviously of a metaphysical type, that all judgments are in themselves true. *Cf.* Hägerström's *Selbstdarstellung*, p. 127: ET* p. 50: 'In itself every judgment is true', and his autobiographical article in Ahlberg's *Filosofiskt lexikon*, p. 84: 'Hence the truth of a judgment is the same as the definiteness of its content or its non-contradictoriness. Since in a contradictory "judgment" something is in fact only apparently conceived as real, the judgment as such is true.'—For Phalén's view, see his essay 'Om omdömet' in FHL, esp. p. 175.

'analysis of meaning' in general and for philosophy as 'analysis of pre-suppositions' in particular.

Turning now finally to *logicism* we find that one of its chief aims is *clarification*. It is in order to overcome the obscurities which are characteristic of ordinary language that logicism engages in logical analysis, and for the same purpose it constructs its artificial, symbolic language. As to how far it has succeeded in effecting such a clarification, however, it is difficult to arrive at a definite answer. There are indications both for and against.

The concern for clarity and precision which finds expression in logicism is of course of the utmost positive significance for both philosophy and science. Anyone who is familiar with the history of philosophy knows what a disastrous part has been played in it by vague and ill-defined concepts; hence any means of increasing precision must obviously be welcomed. If we wish to have a 'scientific philosophy' in the proper sense of that term, we cannot but attach prime importance to clarification and precision; and in this connection logicism has put its finger on a weak spot in philosophy and offers us a new means of dealing with it. 'The formal interpretation by means of the symbolic apparatus is also in line with the scientific endeavour to express oneself in a way that cannot be misunderstood. For when the interpretation of a statement is formal, and thus independent of context and milieu, the statement can be freely transported, so to speak, from context to context and milieu to milieu without affecting its content.'[27] This, however, brings us to a point where we have to begin to put question marks.

If there is much to enter on the credit side of logicism with regard to clarification, there is also much, and perhaps more, to enter on the debit side. A number of factors have conspired to prevent it from fulfilling the hopes of those who looked to it for precision. Here we shall mention only a few of the main objections to it.

1) Logicism offers a technique which is easy to learn and can be applied more or less mechanically and without any very profound thought. The formally technical method devised to ensure deeper penetration and objective treatment can easily have exactly the opposite effect by encouraging all too soon the feeling that a question has been disposed of when its real significance has not in fact been fathomed.

2) The logistic method produces an impression of inevitability, an impression which form and formalism are very apt to give, when in reality the question at issue is about something quite conventional. Logicists therefore often regard this particular way of tackling philosophical problems as the only legitimate one. There is a wholesome reminder of its relativity, however, in Wedberg's remark: 'There are things that people simply take a fancy to, and just now the formalized languages are among the things that many philosophers (especially in the Anglo-Saxon countries

[27] A. Wedberg, *Filosofiens historia*, p. 285.

and Scandinavia) and still more mathematicians all over the world have simply taken a fancy to.'[28]

3) Logicism is no guarantee of greater precision in the handling of philosophical problems. It has been no barrier, for example, to Bertrand Russell's metaphysical excesses. On this subject we need not go into detail here, as we shall have occasion to return to it later in connection with Russell's 'philosophy of logical atomism' (Chap. IX.§3) and the metaphysic it involves—one of the many metaphysical theories which Russell has espoused at different times. It is interesting to note, however, that logicism has not found it intolerable to be associated with such unclear and unpredictable views. Leibniz' dream of being able to do mathematical calculation with philosophical problems is and remains a dream. It is a serious encumbrance for logicism that owing to its connection with Leibniz it has to take along that whole set of problems which we analyzed above under the heading of 'Eternal and Contingent Truths'.[29]

4) The symbolic language of logicism, rightly used and applied to material that is suited to it, is an excellent means of directing our aim when we are seeking the greatest possible clarity and precision. But an apparent clarification can easily be transformed into its direct opposite. There is only too much evidence, not least in philosophical contexts, that an attempt to make the contents of a sentence logically precise can result instead in completely obscuring its real meaning. The strange thing is that it is often just the desire for logical precision that leads to the most imprecise results. To put it metaphorically, there is precision-shooting and marksmanship of the highest order, but often aimed at the wrong target. This is what happens when precision in detail is accompanied by a limitation of the field of vision—and the two often do go together. There need be nothing wrong with the 'telescopic sight', which may afford extraordinary precision, but if the field of vision is limited the precision can only too easily be demonstrated by hitting a target quite other than that offered in the sentence that is being analyzed.

What therefore was supposed to be the strength of logicism—its use of formalized language to enable a statement to be 'freely transported, to speak, from context to context and milieu to milieu without affecting its content'—becomes its weakness. For in general a statement cannot be 'freely transported' in this way without losing something if not all of its original meaning. The context is the wider field of vision, and when logicism thinks it can neglect this, we get the situation described above, where the aim is taken with great precision and the shot very accurately fired—but at the wrong target. Minute attention is paid to the parts while the whole, the context, is neglected. In other words, we get an 'analysis of meaning' which ignores the very thing that gives a statement its meaning.

[28] *Op. cit.*, p. 284.
[29] *Cf.* above, pp. 78–102.

Such an analysis is apt to do grave injury to statements, which cannot stand being 'transported from context to context', so that when they are torn from their natural context they not only acquire another than their originally intended meaning but are in many cases rendered quite meaningless by such treatment. The 'analysis of meaning' does not show them to be meaningless, for in their proper place they are entirely meaningful, but by its fallacious procedure it robs them of the meaning which in their own context they possessed. What such an 'analysis of meaning' reveals is its own meaninglessness.—In order to pursue this line of thought to its conclusion it has been necessary to anticipate a good deal that will be fully discussed and explained in what follows.

This brings us to the important question of *clarification* and *reduction*. It is a question that concerns not only logicism but all the analytical schools we have mentioned. They all strive after clarification, and they all have a tendency to reduction. It is undoubtedly the business of philosophy to effect clarification, but not, most certainly not, by means of arbitrary reduction. There is a kind of clarification that can be obtained in that way, but it is no real clarification. When the material to be mastered is too complicated, it may be a relief to go in for reduction and get rid of the most troublesome material. The simplicity of the material that remains may be felt to be a genuine clarification. But it is not a clarification of the kind that is the business of philosophy.

Reductionism is in fact one of the greatest perils of contemporary philosophy, and the very opposite of philosophical clarification. At first sight it looks as if reductionism is bound up with metaphysical philosophy. For inasmuch as the latter has a tendency to let a particular reality stand for reality as a whole,[30] it follows as a simple consequence that it has to let reduction take care of everything else. Thus idealism reduces everything to ideas, phenomenalistic metaphysics reduces everything to 'mere' phenomena, sensualistic metaphysics to 'mere' sensations, while for materialism the psychical is 'merely' an epiphenomenon, 'nothing but' another form of material reality, and so on. Every form of metaphysics selects its own point of view from which to contemplate existence, and everything else is reduced and traced back to this, which it designates as the 'nature' or 'essence' of existence. What appears to be the whole scene is thus surveyed, and when everything has been reduced and traced back to what is regarded as central it is held to have been 'explained'. In other words, reduction is taken to be a form of 'clarification'.

It is not only in metaphysics, however, that we find such reduction. It occurs also in those forms of philosophy which are consciously moving in the direction of 'scientific philosophy', and in analytical philosophy it is to be found almost everywhere. It is there in the logicists' reduction of

[30] *Cf.* above, p. 46f.

everything to logico-mathematical formulae, not to mention Bertrand Russell's attempt to reduce everything to its atom-like 'constituents'; it is there in Hägerström's reduction of all reality to 'spatio-temporal reality', and in the logical empiricists' reduction of everything to 'sense-data', and so forth. On every hand reduction is employed as a means of clarification. At the same time it is a symptom of the inherent metaphysics of the outlook in question. For 'scientific philosophy', however, it is supremely important not to fall victim to such reductionism, but to keep the field of vision universally open. Its task is not to 'reduce' but to 'penetrate', while maintaining the breadth of view which allows each thing to be what it is. It does not help towards clarifying the function of philosophy if we try to reduce it simply to logic or mathematics. Behind all attempts to make philosophy a 'department of logic' or a 'department of mathematics' there is reductionism, which robs philosophy of its distinctive character and proper task.

Reduction can never lead to genuine clarification. This has been seen and said by the more perceptive of contemporary philosophers, regardless of the school of thought to which they belong. It is enough to recall here the indefatigable campaign which Herbert Feigl, one of the most outstanding logical empiricists, has waged against 'the reductive fallacy' with examples both historical (Comte, Hume) and contemporary.[31] Reductionism is just as inimical to science as to philosophy; it explains away what are for both of them fundamental problems by representing them as pseudo-problems. 'It is only too tempting to push a very difficult problem aside and by stigmatizing it as meaningless to discourage further investigation. . . . They cut with Ockham's razor far into the flesh of knowledge instead of merely shaving away the metaphysical whiskers.'[32] To which we may add as one more testimony to the danger that clarification may turn into its opposite if it relies on reductionism: 'We are likely in our eagerness for clarity that avoids pseudo-problems to attain only a pseudo-clarity that avoids problems.'[33]

Philosophy is *analysis of meaning*—that and nothing else. Its business is *clarification*, the making clear of concepts—that and nothing else. It is important to be rigorous here and not admit other tendencies which can ruin everything by luring philosophy into bypaths. What these seductive tendencies are, we have seen: ontology and reductionism. These two are closely related and spring from the same source. Philosophy has a proud tradition of sailing under this double flag, and it therefore likes to think it

[31] H. Feigl, 'Logical Empiricism', in Feigl and Sellars, *Readings*, pp. 10, 15. *Cf.* also W. V. Quine, 'The Verification Theory and Reductionism' in his *From a Logical Point of View*, pp. 37–42.
[32] Feigl, *op. cit.*, p. 13.
[33] C. L. Stevenson, *Facts and Values*, p. 184.

can solve 'problems' that are entirely beyond its scope. While it busies itself with these other matters, however, its own business, the analysis of meaning, gets neglected. Reductionism explains away the real problems, ontology transfers them to another area. There is literally a *metabasis eis allo genos.*—All of which sheds light on the forms of philosophy we have been dealing with under the heading of 'logical analysis'. We have seen above both where their strength lies and where they meet their difficulties.

Their strength is in their concentration on analysis of meaning and clarification. It is concern for clarification that drives logicism to its formal, symbolic language, by which it hopes to avoid ambiguity and secure complete univocality in its concepts. It is the desire for clarity and univocality that drives the Uppsala philosophy to conceptual analysis; and the same desire for clarity drives logical empiricism to raise its question about meaning—'What do you mean?' So long as they confine themselves to this task of clarification, all is well. What they are doing is very much in line with 'scientific philosophy', as it opens the way to objective argumentation.

But they all come to grief when the analysis of meaning is allowed to slip over into ontology and hence also into reductionism. Logicism then tries to proceed from logic to 'the logical structure of the world', and Uppsala philosophy moves from conceptual analysis to the ontological-metaphysical idea of spatio-temporal reality as the whole of reality, while logical empiricism imagines it can derive from the idea of meaning and the analysis of meaning a single, uniform criterion of meaning—the verification principle with its ontological implications. The result is that clarification is turned into its opposite, and all we have is obscurity and confusion.

The present situation is thus by and large clear. Philosophy is 'analysis of meaning'; but it has a persistent tendency to jump from this to ontological conclusions. This simply will not do. No ontological consequences follow from the analysis of meaning, nor is there any logical way of getting from the analysis of meaning to ontology. If we nevertheless try to link the two, we distort the analysis of meaning and transform it into metaphysical dogma. The reason for this is very simple, namely that it is always the metaphysical stance that in the last resort dictates what is to be regarded as meaningful. We have seen a number of examples of this already. It was this that happened, for instance, when logical empiricism introduced its verification principle as the criterion of meaning. Positivistic ontology, a positivistic metaphysics, was made the measure of what could be considered meaningful. That is only one example of what always happens when ontology is smuggled into the analysis of meaning. What can be accommodated to the preconceived ontological scheme is meaningful, what cannot is meaningless. This observation can be turned into a general principle which will always be found to hold good: when ontology gets mixed up with the analysis of meaning, it transforms the latter also into metaphysics. Little is then gained by the concentration of philosophy on the question of meaning.

It is necessary to make the status and function of philosophy entirely clear. We have come here to a great parting of the ways, and are faced with an inescapable choice. Philosophy is:

either ontology—and then also metaphysics,
or analysis of meaning—and then not ontology.

Our earlier discussion of 'eternal and contingent truths' has filled in the background, showing us what happened when the trail was blazed from which philosophy has since found it so difficult to break away, and exposing the conceptual muddle which in consequence has dominated philosophy for centuries. We now have before us a concrete example of what this conceptual muddle leads to, and how it prevents philosophy from fulfilling its proper function. The Leibnizian legacy is still being taken as the self-evident starting point for philosophy, although so far from being an asset it is a liability. The source of the trouble is the will to master life by logic and turn everything ultimately into 'eternal truths', 'necessary truths', 'logical truths'. But there is no 'logically necessary' knowledge of the world. Things are as they are and cannot be logically constructed. Logic says: You must be consistent in all your reasoning. But from mere logical consistency no real knowledge, no empirical knowledge, can be derived.

In view of this we are bound to ask whether it is not high time to dissolve the traditional partnership between logic and ontology, analysis of meaning and ontology. The Leibnizian tradition with its illicit union of *disjecta membra* has held philosophy captive long enough. Must not the attempt be made to liberate it from this oppressive heritage and give it the opportunity to think in different terms, on another and more adequate basis? The way to do this which presents itself here is to let philosophy be 'analysis of meaning' and nothing else—analysis of meaning pure and simple, without any ontological aspirations.

The most recent phase of contemporary philosophy points in the same direction with its concentration on 'language analysis' as the proper business of philosophy. Our next task therefore will be to see how this project has turned out and how far it takes us.

4. Language Analysis

It has been aptly said with reference to the contemporary philosophical scene that 'the philosophy of language is the fashionable branch of philosophy today'.[34] It can also be said that the philosophy of language is often not content to be only a 'branch' of philosophy, but claims to represent the whole of philosophy.

Why this interest of philosophy in linguistic questions? We might easily

[34] H. Wein, *Philosophie als Erfahrungswissenschaft*, p. 184.

take the description of it as the 'fashionable branch' of philosophy in much the same sense as the statement about logicism, that it is something which people 'have simply taken a fancy to.'[35] But that would be to misread the situation. The statement may be true of logicism, but it is certainly not true of linguistic analysis. Here a much deeper issue is involved. The analysis of language has an essential relation to the problems of philosophy such as logistic method has not. There is no compelling reason for applying the symbolic resources of mathematical logic to philosophy—unless perhaps indirectly in connection with language analysis. Philosophical thinking is not mathematical calculation, although the latter may at certain points assist towards clarification in philosophy as elsewhere. With language analysis the position is quite different. It is not something we can take or leave at our pleasure, according as it strikes our fancy. The philosopher is involved willy nilly in language analysis, because it is an essential part of his business as a philosopher. Language analysis is not merely ancillary to philosophy, but integral to it, so that it is a bit—and perhaps the most vital bit—of philosophy itself.

It is not difficult to find arguments to support this thesis. Language is after all the clothing of thought; hence by analyzing the language we can hope to get at the thought and its meaning. Language is the most important means of communication; hence by analyzing language we can hope to bring out the social aspect of all thinking. And perhaps most important of all, by analyzing language we can hope to clear up the linguistic ambiguities which have played so large and disastrous a part, not only in other areas, but above all in philosophy. As we have suggested, language analysis may be said to be an essential feature of *all* contemporary philosophy. The philosophy of existence (existentialism) is to a large extent language analysis, though of a very undisciplined sort. Moore's common sense philosophy can in large measure be regarded as a contribution to language analysis, Moore having been one of the pioneers of the philosophy that concerns itself with 'ordinary language'.[36] Logicism also in its way is a philosophy of language, inasmuch as it criticizes ordinary language and seeks to remedy its defects by means of an artificial, formalized language. This is true both of Russell and of his followers in Vienna positivism (Carnap and others). Finally, with regard to the Uppsala philosophy, it too in its conceptual analysis deals very extensively with the linguistic aspect of concepts.

When, however, we use 'language analysis' as a technical term, we think first and foremost of the philosophical movement which has drawn its inspiration from Ludwig Wittgenstein and seeks in various ways to complete his pioneering work. For he more than anyone else is responsible for having led philosophy into the path of language analysis and turned it into linguistic philosophy or ordinary language philosophy. Already in the

[35] A. Wedberg, *op. cit.*, p. 284; *cf.* above, p. 149.
[36] *Cf.* N. Malcolm, 'Moore and Ordinary Language'.

Tractatus he defines the task of philosophy as a 'critique of language', although there he is still pretty much tied to the Frege-Russellian idea of a formalized, artificial language, and also in some measure to Russell's ontology and atomistic metaphysics. At this stage Wittgenstein sees it as the task of philosophy to overcome the general lack of clarity and the logical defects of ordinary language by replacing it with a 'logically perfect language'. In his later period, which is represented above all by his *Philosophical Investigations* (posthumous, 1953), he plainly dissociates himself from the position taken in the *Tractatus*, though he still retains the idea of philosophy as essentially a 'critique of language' and as language analysis. He now starts, however, from the opposite point of view, namely that 'Ordinary language is all right'. It is philosophy itself that by its abuse and mishandling of ordinary language gives rise to all the philosophical pseudo-problems and perplexities. The task of philosophy is accordingly to show by means of analysis where things have gone wrong, and so to resolve false problems by showing them to be no problems at all. These arbitrary 'problems' thus disappear, their 'solution' being found when we return to ordinary language and inquire how it works and how things look in the light of it.

We need not here detain ourselves with the question of the strength or weakness of 'language analysis' philosophy, although it has occasioned a great deal of discussion, much of which has been very unclear—in part owing to the abstruse and aphoristic terms in which the nature and purpose of language analysis has been presented. Its proponents are rightly afraid of philosophical dogmatism, and they seek to avoid it by keeping their exposition in some measure fluid. As far as Wittgenstein himself is concerned, the problems emerging at this point need not be gone into here since we shall devote considerable space later to his position and its significance in connection with the analysis of meaning (Chap. IX. § 4). Aside from Wittgenstein himself, two men who would merit more extensive consideration are Gilbert Ryle and John L. Austin.[37]

We must, however, confine ourselves here to the question which is decisive for our present purpose, namely what help we can get towards defining the task of philosophy. From one point of view it can be said that language analysis philosophy is the purest example of 'philosophy as analysis of meaning', for it opens up the possibility of an analysis of meaning without any of the traditional ontological-metaphysical implications. In that respect it has contributed a great deal towards clarification of the

---

[37] For Ryle see his *Philosophical Arguments, The Concept of Mind* and *Dilemmas*; note also his essay on 'Ordinary Language'. For Austin see his *Philosophical Papers* and *How to Do Things with Words*. (An interesting development of the leading idea of the latter work is to be found in Bejerholm and Hornig, *Wort und Handlung*.) Note also Austin's essay, 'A Plea for Excuses'. On the relation between Wittgenstein and Austin, see D. F. Pears's essay, 'Wittgenstein and Austin'.

task of philosophy. But now another problem arises, which is basically the old question of how philosophy is related to the special sciences. Have we not here simply a new version of the old story of how philosophy, for lack of a clearly defined task of its own, seeks a place among the special sciences in the hope of finding work to do there and getting besides the firm ground under its feet which the methods of the special sciences provide? It used to be a question of philosophy as logic, philosophy as psychology, sociology, and so forth. Is it not perhaps now, after all, merely a fresh manoeuvre in the retreat from philosophical problems to an area of special science, this time the science of language or linguistics?

The answer to that question must be a decided No. It is a purely objective necessity that has driven philosophy in this direction. The difference can be seen at once if we compare the two ideas of 'philosophy as psychology' and 'philosophy as language analysis'. Admittedly there is a close connection between philosophical and psychological problems, but here the important thing is to keep them distinct and not let them get mixed up with one another. For whereas psychology is concerned with the *act* of consciousness, philosophy is concerned with its *content*. The consequences of failure to distinguish these two are amply and alarmingly illustrated in the history of philosophy, as for instance by psychologism, phenomenalism, solipsism, to name only a few. If philosophy is analysis of meaning, then it is *not* a question of psychological analysis; and although the analysis of meaning has to do with the 'intention' of a statement or proposition, yet it is not a question of 'intention' in the sense of a psychological act. When philosophy lets itself become psychology, there is a real *metabasis eis allo genos* and a confusion which can only lead to chaos.

It is quite otherwise with the equation of philosophy and language analysis. If philosophy is analysis of meaning, then it is also by implication language analysis. There is thus no question of a retreat on the part of philosophy from its own problems to something else. There is no *metabasis* here, but when philosophy engages in language analysis it is occupied precisely with its own philosophical problem, the question of meaning. As 'language analysis' philosophy remains within its own province and is engaged in answering its own question. In view of the part which language actually plays in the business of thinking it is simply not possible to bypass language analysis. Ambiguity of language carries with it ambiguity of thought, false linguistic formulations give rise to pseudo-problems. A verbal fog descends, which prevents us from seeing where the real problems lie. If clarity and precision are necessary in all scientific work, they are doubly important in philosophy, which unlike the empirical sciences does not have the advantage, when it has taken a wrong turn, of being overtaken by the facts and being set right by them. The most important means philosophy has at its disposal for attaining comparable precision is no other than the critique of language.

Now if philosophy is thus tied up with language analysis and the critique of language, the problem boils down to this: What is there from a purely methodological point of view that makes such an essentially linguistic investigation *philosophically relevant*? For language analysis occurs in all the linguistically oriented sciences, and the question is whether there is anything specially characteristic of such an investigation in the area of philosophy. This is a question to which the answer is generally lacking. If philosophy is defined simply as 'language analysis' without qualification, the effect can easily be that it is robbed of any distinctively 'philosophical' character. Language analysis is, after all, needed in many different areas, and there is no difficulty about using it in connection with a special science, which has a definite 'area' to cultivate and thus definite material for analysis. But this situation is embarrassing for philosophy, which cannot point to any such special area as its own. If philosophy is defined as 'language analysis' with the qualification that the analyzing must of course be done in the area of philosophy and with reference to philosophical problems, the result is the virtual annihilation of philosophy. For it makes little sense to speak of language analysis in the area of philosophy when philosophy itself has been defined as 'language analysis'. There must clearly be in the background here another concept of philosophy, another set of problems, which is meant to be the subject matter of 'language analysis'—otherwise it would be in effect an act of philosophical suicide.

That this is no merely imaginary difficulty is confirmed by a glance at the various attempts which have been made to explain exactly what 'language analysis' is. Here we can distinguish two tendencies, one represented by Wittgenstein and Ryle, the other by Austin. For Wittgenstein and Ryle the important thing is the application of language analysis to philosophical problems—the assumption being that there are such problems, even though the result of the analysis may be that these are shown to be pseudo-problems and thus dissolved—while for Austin the emphasis is on 'language analysis' qua language analysis and less on the connection with 'philosophical' problems. In the last resort, however, the two views come very close to one another, and in both cases it is evident that philosophy, at least in the sense of 'scientific philosophy', is put in jeopardy. When Wittgenstein in the *Tractatus* defines the task of philosophy as 'critique of language', this idea goes hand in hand with a denial that philosophy is a science. For the scientific problems are divided without remainder between the various special sciences, so that there is nothing left over for philosophy. Philosophy is an 'activity' of another kind than science.

Wittgenstein comes to this conclusion partly because he understands by 'science' only the natural sciences, among which there is of course no place for philosophy, and partly because when he speaks of 'philosophy' it is primarily metaphysical philosophy he has in mind. The philosophy he himself practises in the form of a 'critique of language' is at this early stage of such an indefinite sort that it cannot exhibit any clear scientific profile of its own. It is metaphysics, yet not metaphysics but the abolition of metaphysics; it is some sort of 'activity', perhaps in some ways akin to science but more akin to art. Hence the final result is that just as metaphysics is 'nonsense' so also the 'activity' that abolishes metaphysics must be described as 'senseless' or 'nonsensical' and got rid of along with the propositions of metaphysics. This is the purport of his well-known saying: 'He must so to speak throw away the ladder, after he has climbed up on it.'[38]

Although in his later period Wittgenstein becomes very critical of the position taken in the *Tractatus*, and assigns a very different and much wider function to philosophy, the logical status of philosophy remains nonetheless obscure. It is still a 'critique of language', its business is to effect a 'clarification' of the language we use, it has to put a stop to the philosophical (metaphysical) abuse of language, it has to analyze language as it actually functions when in use, it has to exhibit the different 'language games', and so on—but what is it itself? What is the nature of the activity represented by philosophy? Is it scientific, or is it an activity of another sort? Even in his later period Wittgenstein gives no clear answer to these questions. Yet it is observable that there are certain definite groups of problems which are the object of his language analysis. He does not practise this for its own sake, as if it were a matter of indifference to what object it was applied, but there are certain particular problems which he regards as calling for it, and they are the very problems which are usually called 'philosophical problems'. Although his interest in these is very negative and his aim their total dissolution, it nonetheless remains that his interest in language analysis is connected just with these 'philosophical' problems. Without them language analysis would have no ground to stand on. Admitted that these problems can be compared to a disease, and language analysis to the remedy for it, yet the fact is that the remedy would lose its meaning if there were no disease to be cured.

At this point Austin's view is essentially different from that of Wittgenstein and Ryle. He holds as they do that it is the misuse of ordinary language and the arbitrary departures from it that are the reason for many of the controversies in philosophy, and it is certainly this insight that has driven him into the 'language analysis' camp. But the clarification of language has become for him so much of an end in itself that he sometimes actually toys with the idea of incorporating philosophy into language analysis and letting the linguistic interest completely absorb the philosophical. Which faces us with the question: Has philosophy, then, no problems whatever that are peculiarly its own? Can philosophy with its universal aim really be contained within a special science, the science of language or

[38] Wittgenstein, *Tractatus*, 6.54.

linguistics? Here Wittgenstein shows a very different concern for the interests of philosophy itself and for its universal range, although with him too the question of the scientific status of philosophy, and hence also that of the possibility of objective argumentation in philosophy, is left without an answer.

One of the most significant things about 'language analysis' philosophy is that it opens up the possibility of a philosophy which is not ontology. If the confusion of philosophy with ontology has had such disastrous consequences as we have seen above, we cannot value too highly the possibility afforded by 'language analysis' of a purely analytical philosophy without any admixture of ontology. It should however be noted in this connection that there have been attempts not only to connect linguistic philosophy in general with ontology,[39] but also to interpret the language analysis of the later Wittgenstein ontologically[40]—something which can hardly be done without contradicting Wittgenstein's plainly expressed intention.[41]

If the issue is thus at this point relatively clear, there remain none the less a number of other questions to which no unequivocal answer is provided by the definition of philosophy as language analysis. We have no answer yet to the central question, what it is that makes 'language analysis' *philosophically relevant*. It may well be that philosophy is linguistic clarification, yet not any and every clarification of a linguistic expression can be described as philosophical. The task of philosophy may be the analysis of meaning, but not any and every explanation of the meaning of a word or phrase can be said to be a philosophical analysis. True though it is that philosophy has to do with the question of meaning, yet the question of meaning is not as such and in all circumstances a specifically philosophical question. We naturally want there to be meaning in all aspects of life, and we intend there to be meaning in all that we say; and when the question is asked 'What do you mean?' or 'What exactly does that mean?' there is nothing necessarily philosophical about it. Not every linguistic analysis is a philosophical analysis. But what it is that makes a particular kind of 'language analysis' philosophical, has as yet by no means been made completely clear. Only when this has been done shall we be able to answer

[39] An example of this is G. Küng, *Ontologie und logistische Analyse*, though it should be observed that Küng deals only with the linguistic analysis of logicism and the earlier Wittgenstein, in which we noted above the strong tendency towards ontology.

[40] *Cf.* e.g., E. K. Specht, *Die sprachphilosophischen und ontologischen Grundlagen im Spätwerk L. Wittgensteins.*

[41] Specht himself is conscious of the problematical nature of his attempted interpretation. In his Preface he says: 'The aim of the interpretation is above all to bring the ontological aspect to the fore. This procedure is open to criticism.' It certainly is. Specht, however, is more concerned with 'thinking out afresh *the traditional problems of philosophy* in the light of Wittgenstein' (*op. cit.*, p. 8), than of thinking through the problems as they are found in Wittgenstein himself. We shall return to this question in the next section.

the other essential questions, which have to do with the kind of argumentation that is characteristic of philosophy, the extent to which this opens up the 'possibility of objective argumentation' and thus enables us to determine the scientific status of philosophy, the way or ways in which philosophy differs from the special sciences, and how it is able nonetheless to preserve its scientific character. To all these questions we shall find answers in the next section, where philosophy is defined as 'analysis of presuppositions'.

5. Analysis of Presuppositions

We have now reached a point in our investigation where the lines really converge, so that we can at last state the task of philosophy in a brief formula and answer all the questions which have so far either received only a partial answer or no answer at all.

(1) The formula is: *Philosophy is 'analysis of presuppositions'*; and it is not difficult to see that it truly sums up the entire result of our discussion so far.

1) Philosophy is *analysis*, not metaphysics. It has no business with synthesis and system building, but is entrusted with the apparently more modest but really far more important analytical task, namely that of the 'analysis of presuppositions'.

2) Philosophy is *analysis of meaning*, not ontology. It must respect the distinction between logic and ontology, and it may therefore not presume to derive any 'ontological' insights from 'meaning'. It is confined to the more meaningful task of giving a genuine 'analysis of meaning'—which it can only do if it carries its analysis back to the presuppositions which are ultimately determinative of what a statement means. It is in short 'analysis of presuppositions'.

3) Philosophy is *language analysis*, though not all language analysis is of a philosophical nature. Philosophy is concerned with the meaning of language, not as being interested in the meaning of arbitrarily selected words and phrases, but as seeking to discover the presuppositions that underlie every linguistic expression and determine its meaning and structure. Thus we find here too that philosophy even as language analysis is 'analysis of presuppositions'.

4) The task of philosophy is *clarification*, but not reduction. Clarification is an inescapable philosophical requirement, but it is not achieved by dismissing as meaningless anything that does not fit into one's own scheme of things. Nothing is gained by that but 'a pseudo–clarity that avoids problems'. The only way to get real clarification is to let the expression which is being philosophically analyzed be seen in the light of its own presuppositions. It then often turns out that something which has been viewed in the light of alien presuppositions and found meaningless, when it is viewed in the light of its own presuppositions becomes in the highest degree meaningful. If no meaning can be found in a thing when it is viewed in the

light of its own presuppositions, then and only then is it meaningful to declare it meaningless. Only by going back in this way to the presuppositions can full and complete clarity be obtained. Thus the idea of clarification as the task of philosophy also leads to the position that philosophy is 'analysis of presuppositions'.

5) Philosophy is *logical analysis*, though not in the form of a logical calculation. The concern of logicism with its logico-mathematical analysis was to get rid of obscurity, ambiguity and subjective arbitrariness, to reach a clear, unequivocal definition of the terms and expressions used, and so to achieve exactitude, precision and clarification in philosophy. Now undoubtedly exactitude and precision represent a value of first importance both for science in general and philosophy in particular. Without clarity and univocality there can be no objective argumentation. It is impossible to argue either for or against a position which is stated in obscure, uncertainly allusive terms. It must be made precise, so that something definite is said, something with definite implications which can be called in question and possibly proved wrong. A clearly arguable case is an indispensable requirement in all scientific work, and not least in philosophical discussion. An inexperienced student who is out of his depth will readily resort to such statements as: 'To my way of thinking this is how matters stand, I feel there is a good deal to be said for this view.' That may be a way of confessing uncertainty, but often it is only a way of evading the issue, inasmuch as it gives no clear indication of the degree of uncertainty. What matters is not what this or that person thinks or feels, but what reasons he can give for his view and whether his arguments can stand up to serious criticism. Whatever can be done to ensure that the argumentation is unambiguous, precise and open to critical appraisal must be done.

We have seen above, however, that the attempt of logicism to secure precision often has the opposite effect, leading to a lack of clarity and possibly meaninglessness owing to the fact that statements are torn out of their natural context and 'transported from context to context'.[42] The remedy for this lies simply in letting philosophy fulfil its function as 'analysis of presuppositions'. Only so can there be any meaning in the 'logical analysis', for only so do the terms and expressions involved in the analysis come to possess, so to speak, a common denominator. There is thus in the 'analysis of presuppositions' no question of lowering the logical standard or lessening the demand for precision—quite the reverse. But the logical procedure is meaningful only if we let statements remain within their own frame of reference, and it is just this that the analysis of presuppositions has to ensure. A purely technical-mechanical manipulating of terms as if they were immutable units of meaning which must necessarily mean the same thing no matter in what context they occur, ultimately robs

[42] *Cf.* above, pp. 148, 150.

them of their meaning and makes even logical analysis meaningless. By unearthing the presuppositions by which meaning is conditioned, the analysis of presuppositions makes a fruitful logical analysis possible. It is not feasible to isolate these two forms of analysis from one another, because they mutually condition one another. The analysis of presuppositions is by nature a '*logical* analysis of presuppositions', and the 'logical analysis' consistently carried through, and in order to preserve its meaningfulness, leads on to the 'analysis of presuppositions'.

(2) From the point we have now reached, light is shed on the large measure of interrelatedness and homogeneity which, in spite of all its apparently bewildering mutliplicity, is in fact to be found in contemporary philosophical discussion. The different schools and trends which at first sight seemed to be striking out on independent and mutually incompatible lines, are seen in the end as converging towards the 'logical analysis of presuppositions'. What is more, light is shed also from this point on the 'remaining questions', the questions which our discussion thus far has left open and unanswered. It will be enough here to look at only four of these.

1) What is it that distinguishes philosophy from the special sciences? We have hitherto been unable to go beyond the general statement that while the special sciences have each an objective area or province of their own to investigate, philosophy has no such area. Philosophy claims to be a 'universal science'—whatever that may mean—and it is the ambiguity of this concept that makes it so easy for philosophy to slip over into metaphysics and lose its scientific character. We are now, however, in a position to answer this question about philosophy and the special sciences, as follows.

The concentration of philosophy on the 'analysis of presuppositions' provides it with a set of problems which is both of a completely comprehensive nature and yet at the same time clearly enough delimited to admit of strictly scientific treatment. It is now the business of philosophy to exhibit and clarify by means of analysis the ultimate presuppositions which are present, though often concealed, in all the different areas—as for example those general presuppositions which the different sciences make use of, but which they do not themselves attempt to analyze, for the simple reason that they are not among the objects of their research but are precisely its 'presuppositions'.

The special sciences operate with the concepts of 'truth' and 'falsity', and without them they could not carry out their investigations; but no special science can take upon itself to analyze such extremely general presuppositional concepts. It is these seemingly self-evident and often unconscious presuppositions that philosophy has to draw out and elucidate. That is why philosophy can never be confined to any special objective area, but must be omnipresent; for its analysis has to do with the presuppositions that are common to all such areas. In this way the universal tendency of philosophy is safeguarded. Without having to claim any objective area as its own, it none the less has its own province or field of research in the universal presuppositions—a province which admittedly is no 'province' in the sense of an objective area, yet is a clearly defined 'field' with regard to the one unvarying problem.

2) Has philosophy any independent method of its own, a mode of argumentation peculiar to itself? This question also has been answered, at least in a preliminary way. Besides axiomatic and empirical argumentation there is the specifically philosophical mode of argumentation that is characteristic of the 'analysis of presuppositions'. So far this is of course only a proposal, the feasibility of which remains to be shown by our further discussion. But already as a proposal it suffices to distinguish philosophical argumentation from both of the main forms of argumentation mentioned. If philosophy is 'analysis of presuppositions', this analysis cannot be carried out by the axiomatic method, since these presuppositions are not of the same kind as scientific axioms, and still less can they be classed with propositions or theorems derived from the latter. Nor is empirical argumentation applicable here, for the presuppositions which philosophy has to analyze are neither empirically given nor are they comparable to scientific 'hypotheses' which can be verified or falsified. It is important that philosophical presuppositions should not be confused with axioms or hypotheses—just how they differ from these remains to be seen[43]—but should be allowed to retain their own distinctive character. We now have at least enough of an answer to the question about a specifically philosophical mode of argumentation to see clearly in what direction the complete answer must be sought.

3) With this we have also an indication of the 'possibility of objective argumentation'. Axiomatic and empirical argumentation are two main forms of objective argumentation in science, and to these there is now added a third, the analysis of presuppositions. This is a form of objective argumentation inasmuch as it is a logical analysis of the presuppositions implied in different judgments and propositions, an analysis which quite plainly lies wholly on the objective level and admits of factually based arguments for and against.

4) If what we have suggested is feasible, then it also answers for us the question of the kind of shape a purely 'scientific philosophy' must take.[44]

The foregoing presentation may possibly have given the impression that contemporary philosophy has been so busy with other things as to neglect the fundamental philosophical task of 'analysis of presuppositions', and that we have been able to maintain contact with it only by drawing out certain implications of what it has been doing. That, however, would be

[43] *Cf.* pp. 191–4 below, on 'Presupposition, Axiom, Hypothesis'.
[44] *Cf.* my essay, 'Hur är filosofi som vetenskap möjlig?'.

a most misleading impression. Contemporary philosophy has certainly not neglected the analysis of presuppositions. A very great deal of recent philosophical work has been directed towards just such an analysis, although it has often gone under another name and has not been explicitly regarded as the central issue. But the thing itself is there—of that there can be no doubt, as two or three examples may show.

The Uppsala philosophy appears in the form of *conceptual analysis*; but if we ask what its chief representative, Adolf Phalén, has really been doing, the answer is that it is precisely analysis of presuppositions. For it is not any and every concept that conceptual analysis takes as subject matter for its investigation. It occupies itself with a quite definite group of concepts. When Phalén seeks to show roughly the sort of concepts with which conceptual analysis is concerned, he gives such examples as true and false, real and unreal, conception and judgment, consciousness and knowledge, contingency and necessity, and so forth. On examination all these prove to be *presuppositional concepts*; a fact which gives us the right to say that conceptual analysis is at the same time analysis of presuppositions. This is also its quite deliberate intention. In a statement of aim Phalén describes the task of theoretical philosophy as being the analysis of concepts 'which are *the presupposition* of our theoretical judgments in general, and of the groups of theoretical judgments defined by the existing sciences or general research projects'.[45] It could not be more clearly stated that conceptual analysis is analysis of presuppositions.

To this only two further comments need be added. 1. The analysis of presuppositions often reveals that concepts which are prevalent in the general consciousness, in the sciences, and above all in philosophy (metaphysics), rest upon unclear, 'dialectical' presuppositions. In that case the analysis has the negative task of dissolving these pseudo-concepts. But the analysis of presuppositions is never limited to this negative function; it has also the positive task of defining the presuppositional concepts in a non-contradictory way. 2. It is true that Phalén's conceptual analysis is mainly confined to the presuppositions that occur in scientific research, so that his philosophical work becomes primarily a philosophy of science. But this by no means implies for him a denial of the meaningfulness of other than scientific judgments. He was accordingly himself quite open to the idea of an analysis of presuppositions in other areas as well as in that of science. Nothing was more foreign to him than a narrow 'scientism'. This very openness made him immune to every form of metaphysics, including that of science.

A second example is Ludwig Wittgenstein's work, a great part of which can be said to be analysis of presuppositions. This fact is to some extent

[45] Phalén in *Filosofiskt lexikon* (ed. Ahlberg), 3rd edn, p. 148.—The same idea is concisely expressed by K. Marc-Wogau in *Att studera filosofi*, where he says (p. 40): 'The discussion of presuppositions is the life of philosophy, as it is of science in general.'

obscured by the conclusions which have been more or less justifiably drawn from his thought by different philosophical schools. Thus he came through his *Tractatus* to play a decisive part in logical positivism, although he himself was anything but a positivist, and through his later work in the *Philosophical Investigations* he became the founder of that linguistic philosophy which could conceive of philosophy being to a certain extent replaced by simple language analysis. Throughout all Wittgenstein's philosophical work, from the *Tractatus* to the *Philosophical Investigations*, there runs in spite of all the differences between the two a continuous *philosophical* line, where language analysis is never merely that but is at the same time a 'critique of language', and this not in the sense of criticizing ordinary language in favour of an artificial language—Wittgenstein soon got beyond that—but precisely in the sense of an analysis of presuppositions. This can be most simply illustrated by reference to the idea of 'language games' which is so central to his thought. Here Wittgenstein has gone completely over to the analysis of presuppositions. What he means by talking of 'language games' is something that goes far beyond simple language analysis. Every language game is governed by its own 'rules of play', and only where these rules are presupposed do we have that particular language game. Hence it follows that language analysis is at the same time analysis of presuppositions.

A third, parallel example is furnished by Gilbert Ryle. When Ryle speaks of different linguistic 'categories' and warns against 'category mistakes' and 'category mixing', he is saying that every statement depends for its meaning on the linguistic category to which it belongs, and hence that it preserves its meaning only as that category is presupposed. Ryle's investigation also is thus clearly a form of the 'analysis of presuppositions'.

We can go further than this, however, and state that the analysis of presuppositions is by no means something that has first arisen in recent times. What it stands for has been present in philosophy during earlier periods—and it could hardly not have been. The real philosophical problems are not merely time-conditioned notions. Metaphysics and the various world-views change with changing circumstances, but the question of the presuppositional concepts of philosophy recurs time and again, often under other names but with closely related content. Thus the centrality of the concept of 'meaning' in current philosophical discussion is not a complete novelty. It largely corresponds to the concern of an earlier period with 'validity'—so much so indeed that the ideas of 'meaning' and 'validity' can often be used interchangeably.[46]

---

[46] The above examples have been taken from the work of logical and linguistic analysts. But presuppositional analysis occurs also among the phenomenologists and existentialists, as e.g. in Husserl's phenomenology, which is one of the starting points of existentialism. Despite the ontological-metaphysical tendency of his later work, it is presuppositional analysis that predominates in Husserl. In Heidegger, admittedly, the

The connection between these two ideas can be seen if we observe that both of them are *creative of structure*. They are the 'rules of the game' which must be *valid* (presupposed) if our thought and speech are to have any *meaning*. Without presuppositions we should have no clearly structured thought or clearly structured speech. When the question of meaning and the question of validity are thus brought together, the result is a fruitful co-operation. Many of the obscurities which used to beset the discussions of validity can be cleared away with the help of insights gained from investigations of the concept of meaning. Moreover, many of the difficulties attaching to the present discussion of meaning can be removed if it is considered in connection with the question of 'validity'. The latter is already well-tilled ground, on which much preparatory work towards the question of meaning has already been done. Before we go on to a direct discussion of the analysis of presuppositions, therefore, it will be appropriate to introduce a brief confrontation between the concept of 'meaning' and the concept of 'validity'.

---

ontological-metaphysical tendency takes control; yet the influence of the other tendency from Husserl is still apparent. Let it suffice here to refer to G. Funke, *Phenomenologie— Metaphysik oder Methode?* where the task of philosophy is 'to understand what is in one way or another given, in terms of its presuppositions' (p. 9) or 'to discover the basic contexts' (p. 168). Funke is aware of the 'either-or', the choice that must be made between the arbitrariness of metaphysics and the methodology of scientific philosophy —an awareness shown already in his title, 'Metaphysics *or* Method?'

CHAPTER VI

Meaning and Validity

1. Meaning and Validity as Interchangeable Terms

IN the preceding chapter we witnessed the great change of scene—the 'revolution in philosophy'—which has taken place since the turn of the present century. Talk about a revolution in philosophy has sometimes given the impression that everything belonging to the past has been liquidated and something quite new has taken its place. But nothing could be more false. Philosophers are wrestling today with problems which their predecessors also had to face. The only difference is that the emphasis has shifted, and that other questions have become for the time being the centre of interest, without the old problems having therefore disappeared. The problems are still there, but often apparently unrecognized because they do not appear in their traditional guise. The interesting thing, however, is to observe how the same problem can reappear in new forms. The question is put in a somewhat different way, but at bottom it is the old question in a new form. Both of these aspects must be stressed: it is really the old problem, and it is also really in a new form.

We can exemplify what has just been said by comparing and contrasting with one another the concepts of 'meaning' and 'validity'. The relation between these two reflects both the change which has taken place in the way of stating the problem, and also the permanence which despite all is a feature of the problem itself. For many people the terms 'meaning' and 'validity' have become something of a philosophical shibboleth, as if the mere use of one or the other were evidence of a certain philosophical bias. 'Meaning' is the term mostly used in contemporary philosophy to indicate what the main problem of philosophy is, whereas 'validity' was used for that purpose in earlier times. It is, however, a mistake to suppose that the two terms necessarily represent two different philosophical outlooks. Instead they belong most intimately together, and each in its own way points back to one and the same basic issue. The question that used to be asked about the 'validity' of a proposition, was very much the same as that which is now raised about its 'meaning', and vice versa. We are not faced here with two different philosophical outlooks, an earlier and a later, but with one and the same problem seen from two points of view between which there is a distinction with very little difference. We have indeed two *interchangeable terms*, two ways of saying the same thing,[1] and we do well

[1] A. Liebert, *Das Problem der Geltung*, p. 4, rightly states: 'Instead of the word "validity" (*Geltung*) we could just as well use "meaning" (*Sinn*), "value" (*Wert*),

not to play them off against each other. We need them both, and it is only by letting them illumine one another that we can properly grasp the problem with which they have to do. If the concept of 'meaning', with all that it stands for, can help to purge the term 'validity' of its traditional metaphysical associations, and if the concept of 'validity' can help in turn to clear away the ambiguity of the term 'meaning' and give it its plain philosophical sense, then a decisive step will have been taken towards a 'scientific philosophy'.

The chief disadvantage in speaking of 'validity' is that it is so easily associated with metaphysical ideas. We saw above that as a rule it is the ontological tendency that is chiefly responsible for metaphysical thinking, and that the remedy for this is to substitute the 'concept of validity' for the ontological 'concept of reality' as the central point of orientation in philosophy.[2] The concept of validity itself, however, is exposed to the risk of metaphysical contamination, and this occurs when 'validity' is conceived as an ultimate, self-evident principle, from which all validity whatever is supposed to be derived. What then is gained by the rejection of ontology in favour of the concept of validity? Here it may possibly be helpful—and 'possibly' should be stressed—to turn to the concept of meaning. The more we are aware of the connection between 'validity' and 'meaning' the less we shall be in danger of conceiving 'validity' in a metaphysical way. To ask about the validity of a proposition is in fact the same as to ask about its meaning, and the latter way of putting it makes it much easier to prevent unwarranted metaphysical intrusions. The reason why we stress the fact that this is only a possibility, lies in our earlier observation that the concept of meaning itself can so easily slip in a metaphysical direction, and even the analysis of meaning can become a form of 'disguised metaphysics'.

What must be specially emphasized in this context is that it is only in the light of the connection between meaning and validity that we can come to a clear understanding of what it is that in certain circumstances makes the concept of 'meaning' philosophically relevant. For the word 'meaning' can be used in many different senses, and only a few of them can be said to have any philosophical significance.[3] A preliminary suggestion as to the conditions under which the concept of meaning is philosophically relevant, might be that it is usually so when we are dealing with the alternative of 'meaning or meaninglessness'. When I ask what the word 'isotope' means,

---

"substance" (*Gehalt*), "significance" (*Bedeutung*), "justification" (*Rechtfertigung*), "ground" (*Begründung*), "basis" (*Grundlegung*). For all these are involved as soon as the question is put in a truly philosophical way.' What particularly interests us here is the equation of 'validity' and 'meaning'. That the rest of the terms listed are also closely connected with our theme is obvious, but they would need closer definition and fuller explanation if we were to use them.

[2] Above, p. 146, n. 25.
[3] *Cf.* above, p. 159.

I am not asking whether it has a meaning or is meaningless. I assume that it has a meaning, and am asking to have it explained. Even if the word has no meaning for me until it is explained, there is in this context no question of meaninglessness. The word has a meaning, though one which I do not know but am seeking to learn. This then is an example of a use of the term 'meaning' which does not involve any philosophical problem. It is only with the alternative of 'meaning or meaninglessness' that the philosophical problem arises.

From one point of view it is tempting to say that the concept of 'meaninglessness' is of even more philosophical significance than that of 'meaning', since the latter can be used in so many other ways. When we describe something as 'meaningless' we are generally getting close to philosophical issues. Yet even so, we must proceed with the greatest caution here, for the term 'meaningless' can also be used in a variety of ways, by no means all of which are philosophically relevant. For example, when we read in a newspaper that a completely 'meaningless' outrage has been committed, or when the evidence of an accused person's guilt is so overwhelming that a continued denial seems 'meaningless', or when in a debate on education it is asserted that without some form of discipline in schools teaching can become totally 'meaningless'—in none of these cases are we dealing with the philosophical idea of 'meaninglessness'.

The only way to get things clear at this point is to introduce the concept of 'validity' into the discussion. The idea of 'meaning' is far too open to diverse interpretations, and it needs to be given precision by being related to the idea of 'validity'. A single word can have meaning if it can be shown to symbolize a particular thing or idea,[4] although this does not even approximate to the philosophical concept of meaning. On the other hand, it is hardly possible to ascribe validity to a word as such. A conclusion, a principle, a law, can possess validity or be invalid. It is the task of philosophy to investigate such instances of validity and to show on what presuppositions they are valid.

We have here three concepts which in a most fortunate way complement one another and if need be counterbalance one another, and which taken together indicate the essential purport of philosophical investigation —the concepts of *meaning, validity* and *presuppositions.* Philosophy has to do with meaning, it is 'analysis of meaning'—but not all senses of the term 'meaning' are of philosophical importance. Here the concept of validity comes to our aid. When 'meaning' is used in the sense of 'validity', then there is a philosophical question. Philosophy has to do with validity, it is 'analysis of validity'. But here also we must add: not every proposition which is valid is therefore a philosophical proposition. Here the concept of 'presupposition' comes to our aid. Every valid proposition, whether mathe-

---

[4] It will be seen later that this statement is subject to definite qualifications; see below, Chap. IX.

matical, empirical, ethical, or of any other sort, certainly includes a philosophical problem, but it does so not by reason of its content but in virtue of the 'presuppositions' which can be analyzed out of it. Philosophy has to do with presuppositions, it is 'analysis of presuppositions'. But once more: not every presupposition is of philosophical importance. When one begins to analyze a proposition, one quickly discovers that there is a whole host of things presupposed. It is not with all of these that philosophy is concerned, but only with such presuppositions as are decisive for validity and determinative of meaning, so that the proposition owes to them whatever type of meaning it possesses.

It is only where these three—meaning, validity and presuppositions—mutually support and counterbalance one another, that we have philosophical problems on hand. From this it follows, however, that the propositions of philosophy are not of the same kind as other propositions. Scientific propositions, for example, lay claim to be meaningful and valid. But on what *presuppositions* are they so? That is the philosophical question. Wittgenstein is undoubtedly right when he insists that philosophy does not set up any ordinary scientific propositions. Yet we have no reason to follow him in asserting a dichotomy between science and philosophy as two mutually exclusive procedures. On the contrary, what we have in philosophy is a scientific argumentation, though of another sort than those of the special sciences, namely the axiomatic and the empirical. The philosophical mode of argumentation is neither of these, but an independent third, being precisely an analysis of presuppositions with regard to the question of the meaning and validity of propositions. Not that philosophy dispenses with 'propositions', for indeed it puts forward propositions of its own, which can be debated with objective argumentation for and against, and which can thus be tested and possibly refuted just like any other scientific proposition. But what distinguishes philosophy from the special sciences is the fact that its propositions are *propositions about presuppositions*.

2. The Material for Philosophical Analysis

Philosophy is analysis of concepts, analysis of meaning, analysis of validity, analysis of presuppositions—at all events it is analysis. But just what does it analyze? What material has it available as the starting point for its analysis? What is the datum which philosophy conceives itself called upon to analyze with respect to the presuppositions it contains?

There are three main sources on which philosophy draws: 1. the concepts of everyday life or what is usually called 'common sense', in which certain very general fundamental concepts are employed in a pre-scientific way; 2. the most fundamental principles and methodological concepts of the special sciences; and 3. the history of philosophy with its rich profusion of fundamental principles. Concerning the first two of these there is not a great deal that needs to be said.

1) In common sense and ordinary language we find a series of concepts which have philosophical relevance, such as 'true and false', 'reality', 'cause and effect', etc. They are all of an extremely vague and indefinite character in everyday usage, and if we ask anyone who uses them what exactly he means by them, we shall rarely receive a satisfactory answer. But at the level of everyday life this is not necessary; a vague, general idea is enough, and its indefiniteness seldom occasions serious misunderstandings. It is not, however, in order to enhance the usefulness of these concepts in everyday affairs that philosophy subjects them to analysis. Nor does it point out obscurities and contradictions in the everyday application of certain fundamental principles in order to make people aware how little they really understand of what they are talking about. For although contemporary philosophy has revived the Socratic question, 'What do you mean?' its interest in doing so has been other than that. It is for its own ends, and for the sake of its own analysis, that philosophy asks this question. For it seems in fact that most cases of obscurity and meaninglessness in philosophy can be traced back ultimately to ambiguities in the everyday application of fundamental principles.

2) The second source from which philosophy draws its material for analysis is science and the scientific definition of terms. Here it finds concepts which, in contrast to those of common sense, have at least in some degree been analyzed. Science aims at exactness and precision. It can therefore not be content with the vagueness of ordinary language. Although it is bound largely to use ordinary language as a means of expression and communication, it cannot but seek to define its terms and give them a clear, unambiguous meaning. That is why we find in every science a terminology that is characteristic of it and precisely adapted to its needs, often involving a whole system of technical terms, each of which gets its definitive meaning only from its place in the system. There are thus already in the ordinary work of the sciences the beginnings of an artificial language. It is therefore the more remarkable in the light of this scientific concern for precision, that diffuse and ill-defined concepts can be tolerated at the very starting point, as in fact they are in the case of the most general concepts presupposed by the sciences.

Even here, however, it should be observed that the purpose of philosophical analysis is not to assist the special sciences towards a clear view of their subject matter. The special sciences themselves deal best with that, without the aid of philosophy. Moreover, in this context also philosophical analysis has a purpose of its own. Philosophy exists as little for the purposes of the special sciences as for the practical purposes of everyday life. Even if philosophy succeeded in completely elucidating the presuppositions of a scientific experiment, that experiment would not be in any way better performed or more securely based. Nothing more would have happened than that the philosopher had reached a clear understanding of what the scientist had already in fact come upon but had not made directly explicit in his scientific procedure. In relation to the special sciences philosophical analysis involves no more than the conscious, deliberate statement of the presuppositions with which those sciences actually work and by means of which they obtain their results.

3) The third source from which philosophy draws its material for analysis is the structure of philosophical ideas which are plentifully available in the history of philosophy. At this point our inquiry calls for a rather fuller explanation, for it is here that the problem begins to take shape.

From one point of view the material available in the history of philosophy is even more valuable than that furnished by the two sources previously mentioned. The analysis of a concept with respect to the meaning it bears in common sense and ordinary language is of course beset with great difficulties. In the rough, unpolished state in which it is found, we are often obliged to ask whether it is a genuine concept at all, or whether it is not simply a collection of words and phrases that conveys no distinct meaning. This is a difficulty that confronts every semantic investigation of ordinary, everyday language. Admittedly something can be said to have been achieved, if the analysis only proves that certain common expressions are not associated with any clear meaning. But that is a rather meagre result, since from such an analysis we only learn what we knew before, namely that ordinary language employs vague and imprecise expressions which are by no means adequate for the formation of intelligible concepts.

But even by comparison with the material from the special sciences, that drawn from the history of philosophy takes precedence. What we have here is not simply material such as ordinary scientific work provides for scientific analysis with respect to the methods of science and their presuppositions, but it is material on which philosophical work has already been done. Admittedly the utilization of this material is attended by unusual difficulties, because the treatment it has received has often been based on different conceptions of what philosophy is. Philosophers in the past, working with another idea of philosophy than ours, did not carry out a preliminary stage of analysis which we can simply take over for ourselves. In this regard philosophy is in a less fortunate position than the special sciences, where there is a certain fund of accumulated experience to which new contributions can be added and on which further building can be based. In philosophy there is no such continuous progress. For there, not only have the different metaphysical systems superseded one another, but even if they had not, how could scientific philosophy with its analytical approach possibly base itself on what had been produced by metaphysical philosophy?

It is of course true that even a metaphysically minded philosopher cannot avoid facing the critical problems of philosophy. But the difficulty is that he gets them mixed up with considerations of a quite different sort.

Hence if this material is to be used, it must be extracted from the context in which it was originally placed, and then of course it will have quite another content than it had originally. That is how progress is made in philosophy: when material with which an earlier generation has worked is placed in a new context and thus acquires a new content. We should deprive ourselves of our best material if we felt bound either to abide by an earlier philosophical interpretation of it, or to put it aside as already dealt with and start again from scratch.

Incomparably the most important material for philosophical analysis, and the material that does most to stimulate philosophical thinking, is and remains the problems which the history of philosophy puts at our disposal. G. E. Moore describes not only an individual but a very general experience when he says: 'I do not think that the world or the sciences would ever have suggested to me any philosophical problems. What has suggested philosophical problems to me is the things which other philosophers have said about the world and the sciences.'[5]

3. The History of Philosophy and the Problems of Philosophy

This puts us in a double position with regard to the history of philosophy. On the one hand we study the history of philosophy out of a purely historical interest, in order to discover how a particular thinker or school of thought really looked at things. In that case, all the ingredients that have determined the thinking must be exhibited. It is illegitimate to select some material and ignore other elements which may have been more influential in the outlook in question. To do so would be to produce a historically false picture. On the other hand we study the history of philosophy also as the history of philosophical *problems* and as the foundation for contemporary philosophical work. Nor can any objection be raised if with a living contemporary issue in mind we go back into the history of thought and look for points where this problem has previously come to the fore, and for possible contributions of earlier thinkers to our discussion of it. But with this a selective principle is introduced. It is not the thinker's own ideas that are important here, but the *problem* and the extent to which *it* has been present in his work. If he has touched upon a problem which many others have unwittingly passed by, if by chance he has not only surmised it but seen it and contributed something to the discussion of it, we find in him a kindred spirit. How this problem came to be a constituent of his total outlook is not a question of primary importance here. We are not concerned, as we should be from a purely historical standpoint, to view this problem in its setting in the context of his system, for it has often been just this kind of setting that has proved an obstacle to progress, preventing a man from getting any further with the problem. Our concern is rather with the problem itself and the contribution towards its solution which we

[5] Moore in his 'Autobiography' in P. A. Schilpp, *The Philosophy of G.E.Moore*, p. 14.

173

may find in a philosopher quite independently of the use he himself has been able to make of it in his system.

Of the two approaches to the history of philosophy which we have just outlined, it is obvious that the first, the purely historical, needs no defence. No one disputes its legitimacy, even if many regard it as of very secondary importance—for why should we bother with these long outmoded and superseded views? If none the less we wish to do this, then of course we must do it with all possible historical precision. As for the second approach, the systematic, which concentrates on the problems, we affirmed that it too is entirely legitimate. But this is not undisputed. The objection has been raised that it treats the philosophical thought of the past as a quarry, out of which everyone selects what suits him for the construction of his own intellectual edifice, although this often has little in common with that of the philosopher from whom the material is taken. This objection rests, however, on a misunderstanding of the nature of the philosophical material. The history of philosophy is not simply an old curiosity shop. The history of philosophy is also the history of the problems of philosophy.

It is possible to have an entirely legitimate concern with the history of philosophy other than that of becoming acquainted with the often extremely odd, time-conditioned views and doctrines which thinkers of the past have advocated. All of these are of historical interest, of course, and must always be included in a presentation of the history of philosophy. Here we want to know how philosophers in times past really thought in the context of their own age and place. But as we have said, it is possible to have other business with thinkers of the past. For they did not merely propound curious doctrines, most of them perhaps abandoned since their time, but at a deeper level they were wrestling with problems which are still of importance today—quite apart from any solutions they proposed or doctrines they developed for that purpose. Their involvement with the problems, their wrestling with them, can itself be of assistance to us in our attempt to grapple with them. The attention we have given in the preceding chapters to certain lines of thought in Leibniz, Hume, Kant and others, has been intended throughout to serve this latter, systematic purpose.

Now it is of the utmost importance to keep these two aspects of the history of philosophy clearly distinct. Failure to do so inevitably causes confusion.[6] It must therefore be understood that when we now single out

[6] The importance of keeping the two aspects separate is illustrated by Hj. A. Lindroth's essay, 'Anders Nygrens kriticism' (1955) and his 'Anders Nygren und der Kritizismus' (1957), both of which try to show that the use I make of Kant and Schleiermacher is not always in accord with their own stated views. But this is pushing at an open door, since I myself have said quite plainly that all I have done is to pick out certain lines or incipient lines of thought in these men, which could serve as a springboard for the further development of problems they were interested in. As what is involved is *further development*, it is no argument to say that this is not carried out in the way Kant or Schleiermacher did it. Naturally it is not. In terms of the distinction we

the problem of validity from the history of thought, we are taking the second of the two courses described above. The concept of 'validity' has been a leading motif in the development of philosophy. At the moment it is overshadowed by other concepts, but it contains essential elements which are indispensable with regard to our immediate problems.

4. Problems, Statements of Problems and Solutions of Problems

When we turn to the history of thought for help in dealing with a philosophical problem, we must be careful to distinguish between three different aspects of the concept of 'problem': 1. the problem itself, 2. the statement of the problem, and 3. the solution of the problem.

1. There are certain fundamental philosophical problems which have persisted throughout the entire history of thought, problems which may at times have been concealed by other problems but which continually reappear and demand attention. Such a problem is that of validity. We distinguish between what is valid and what is invalid, and we cannot help doing so. What do we mean by this distinction? And with what right do we make it? This is one example of such an inescapable philosophical problem—and the one that most closely concerns us in our present context.

2. The statement of a problem is the way in which a thinker takes hold of it, his methodological device for getting to grips with it. The statement of the problem is not the same as the problem itself, although at first sight it might seem to be so. A problem is after all a problem for somebody, and without somebody's statement of it there would surely be no problem. The position is not, however, quite so simple. It would be so only if the problem were contrived and arbitrary. Real philosophical problems are of a kind that thrust themselves upon us whether we are interested in them or not. They do not go away because no one pays attention to them. Even if we do not state them we shall encounter them again and again. The statement

---

shall introduce in the next section between problems, statements of problems and solutions of problems, what we are interested in is not the solution offered by Kant or Schleiermacher, but their statement of the problem in so far—and only in so far—as it can help us to see the problem and its difficulties more clearly. The odd thing is that Lindroth himself at an earlier stage was aware of this distinction, though he must somehow later have forgotten the fact. In his *Schleiermachers religionsbegrepp* (1926), pp. 19ff., he wrote: 'With his logical concept of objectivity or validity Nygren is probably . . . *building further* on the basis of certain intentions of the Kantian theory rather than interpreting the latter as it historically exists . . . he picks out and develops a certain aspect of Schleiermacher's outlook for a *systematic* purpose, and as an original thinker he has every right to do this. But he is not primarily interested in Schleiermacher's conception of religion as that conception *historically* exists.' I thus find myself in the unusual position of being able to appeal from the ill-informed Lindroth of 1955 and 1957 to the better-informed Lindroth of 1926.

of a problem is the methodology we employ when we seek to grapple with these unavoidable issues.

3. The solution of a problem is something that either really or apparently does away with it, providing an answer to it that makes it no longer a problem. That a philosophical problem can really be solved in the sense of dissolved, and so done away with, seems of course highly improbable. It would only be possible if the problem could be shown to be merely a pseudo-problem. Yet in the construction of philosophical systems we find many attempts to solve these perpetually recurring problems by giving them a definite place and function in the system. What results from such an attempt is a philosophical doctrine or dogma. These obviously have their place in a presentation of the history of philosophy, which at least to some extent must be a history of philosophical doctrine and dogma. Accordingly, the history of philosophical problems must give an account, not only of the problems and statements of problems, but also of the solutions proposed for them.

What interests us, however, in the historical material thus made available to us, is not the solutions—which in present circumstances could hardly be real solutions—but the statements, the ways in which a problem has been formulated, though even these interest us, not for their own sake, but for the help they can give in getting us back to the problem itself.

From what has been said it should be clear that in taking up the 'Kantian' problem of 'validity' we are not intending to imply that Kant has 'solved' this problem and that we can make his solution our own. There is in general something questionable about the idea of 'solving' philosophical problems. If we are to speak of 'solutions' at all in this area, we must understand them to be very provisional and in need of constant revision. They represent rather a forward thrust in the direction of the problem than a position already secured on which we can fall back. They do not constitute a doctrine which we can take over, but are pointers to a problem on which we must work. There is, incidentally, no reason for calling the problem of validity 'Kantian' as if Kant had a monopoly of it. It had always been a problem, even though no one had paid as much attention to it as Kant, or made as important methodological contributions to the treatment of it. It is also a very pressing problem in our time, even though in many quarters it has been rather pushed into the background.

Genuine philosophical problems have a tendency to keep on cropping up again and again, which is a sign that they can never be regarded as finally solved and disposed of. Pseudo-problems can be disposed of by being exposed as wrongly stated 'problems' to which no answer can be given, but the genuine philosophical problems persist and keep on furnishing fresh material for philosophical analysis, which aims rather at clarification than solution. The idea of 'solving' philosophical problems is largely based on a false analogy between the problems of philosophy and those of the special sciences, some of which at least are of a kind that can be 'solved'. This applies both to the empirical and the axiomatic sciences. There are particular empirical phenomena which to start with may be very puzzling and present us with real problems, but when once the 'solution' is found lose all their puzzling features and cease to be problems any longer. They are then reclassified as demonstrated facts. Above all, there are problems in the area of mathematics for which definitive solutions have been found, or about which at all events little remains to be said. Mathematics is the natural place for 'problem-solving'.

Yet not even in these empirical and axiomatic sciences is the ordinary idea of 'solved problems' entirely appropriate. The problem of the ultimate foundation of mathematics, which has divided the mathematicians into such different camps as intuitionism, logicism (Whitehead, Russell) and formalism (Hilbert), and which has led to Gödel's 'incompleteness theorem', speaks only too clearly on this point. And the same is true with regard to the most universal of the 'laws of nature', which were long regarded as firmly established dogmas, but which in more recent research (Planck, Bohr, Heisenberg, Einstein) have recovered something of their problematical character.

It makes even less sense to talk of 'solved' problems in philosophy, where there are only great, universal problems, which defy all attempts at definitive solution. What gives the researches of the special sciences their scientific status is not their permanently established results or definitive solutions of problems, but the possibility of penetrating more deeply into a problem by means of objective argumentation. This applies even more to philosophical problems. Here we ought once for all to stop talking about 'solving' problems. The important thing here is not that we should solve problems, but that we should gain a profounder understanding of their nature by means of objective argumentation and thus bring about a much-needed clarification.

Unfortunately there is more interest in forming schools and propagating doctrines than in the problems themselves—which is plainly a hangover from metaphysical philosophy. It has happened more than once in the history of thought, that when a new idea has appeared on the scene men have been so completely taken up with it that they have lost sight of things already achieved. There has been a step forward in one respect and a step backward in another. An analysis of the present situation shows that we are in just such a position today. The present situation—at least from the point of view of scientific philosophy—is marked by a return to lines of thought which were originally associated with early English empiricism and Hume. As a result we have had to take along a good deal that was already superseded before our time, and have thus forfeited something of the gains our predecessors had made. This is particularly the case with the concept of 'validity', the logical-philosophical content of which was given a central place in critical philosophy (Kant) but has since been rather pushed into a corner by the development of more recent schools.

It is, however, being increasingly recognized that Kant and the critical philosophy have a decisive contribution to make in the present situation. Many recent testimonies to this effect could be cited, of which one example may suffice. Gilbert Ryle writes: 'Until fairly recently philosophers have not often stepped back from their easel to consider what philosophy is, or how doing philosophy differs from doing science, or doing theology, or doing mathematics. Kant was the first modern thinker to see or try to answer this question—and a very good beginning of an answer he gave.'[7] It was only a beginning. It was made by Kant and not by Hume. And it consisted in the actual discovery of the philosophical content of the concept of validity.

When Hume and Kant are brought into the discussion here, it is not with the intention of reviving their solutions or their philosophical doctrines—such things belong to the past—but simply in order to see what if any contribution each can make towards elucidating our present problem. It must then, however, be said that the problem of epistemology, in the strict sense of the philosophical problem of validity, did not yet exist for Hume, or in so far as it existed it was so permeated by the question of the psychology of knowledge that its philosophical significance was missed. Here Kant with his clear distinction between *quaestio facti* and *quaestio juris* made a demarcation of which philosophy ought never to lose sight. There is some awareness of this in contemporary philosophy, which particularly as influenced by the logico-mathematical investigations of the last century has set itself against psychologism in philosophy. But it is one thing to reject psychologism in theory, another to avoid it in one's own thinking.

Enough has been said to make it clear that the focusing of our inquiry on the concept of 'validity' has nothing in the least to do with any particular school of thought, but is wholly determined by the problem of the form of objective argumentation that is peculiar to philosophy. Here the circle is completed, the gap hitherto left open is closed: philosophy takes its place among the different forms of scientific argumentation.[8]

We may sum up as follows. The term 'validity' reminds us of something already achieved by earlier philosophical work, a contribution to our inquiry that is much too important to be overlooked. The term 'meaning' reminds us of the new gains which have been made in connection with the 'philosophical change of scene', and which are also a contribution much too important to be overlooked. These two must be held together. Indeed,

[7] G. Ryle, 'The Theory of Meaning' in C. A. Mace, *British Philosophy*, p. 257.
[8] *Cf.* above, Chap. IV, pp. 65–125, especially §4, headed 'Philosophical Argumentation', pp. 119–23.

if 'meaning' and 'validity' are, as we have said, essentially interchangeable terms, then we have no need to choose between them, for they belong inseparably together. Once this is realized, it becomes possible to take the step forward which the 'change of scene' requires, without having to take at the same time a step back from something already attained in philosophy. Whether we speak of 'validity' or of 'meaning' we are speaking essentially of one and the same thing. 'Validity' accentuates the depth in the philosophical use of 'meaning', while 'meaning' supplies the philosophical clarification of 'validity' and prevents it from slipping away into the obscurities of metaphysics. Fundamentally, I ascribe meaning to something when I speak of its validity, just as I ascribe validity to it when I speak of its meaning. To speak of these two as if they were quite independent of one another is to misrepresent them and misconstrue the task of philosophy. The philosophical analysis of meaning is in fact an analysis of validity, of structure, of presuppositions.

5. Verification, Justification, Validation

In Chapter IV we saw how scientific argumentation takes three different forms, empirical, axiomatic and philosophical. It is most important that these three should not be confused with one another. Each of them has its own character, each operates with its own criterion or criteria, and if we apply the criterion of one in the province of another, all kinds of complications arise. An *empirical judgment* must be tested with reference to its relation to given reality. Are things really as the judgment affirms them to be? If the answer is 'yes', the judgment is said to be true, if the answer is 'no' the judgment is false. In other words, an empirical judgment must be *verified*. The confirmation of an empirical judgment is called its *verification*.

It is different with an *axiomatic judgment*. Here it is useless to seek verification by comparison with anything given; for what an axiomatic proposition states is not anything given. It holds good independently of experience and can be neither confirmed nor refuted by experience, because it is simply not speaking about the empirical world. If we wish to show that a proposition belonging to an axiomatic system is correct, we must do it in a different way. We must *prove* it; that is to say, we must refer it to another, accepted proposition, which has already been proved, till we get back finally to a non-provable axiom which serves as the self-evident foundation of the axiomatic system. This is the place for inference in the proper sense of the term. The way in which the correctness of an axiomatic proposition is confirmed, is appropriately called its *justification*. Here everything depends on consistency and consequence. But consistency, be it noted, is not equivalent to truth. It tells us nothing whatever about the truth of the proposition in question, for even from false assumptions logically consistent conclusions can be drawn, which naturally in that case are themselves false. The inference is correct but the conclusion is false. We must not let ourselves be misled into describing an inference as true, for there is no question of truth here[9] but of something quite different, namely consistency. The description of an inference as right or correct does not depend on its being in agreement with truth or reality. It is called correct because of its consistency.

It is customary in philosophy to distinguish between the correspondence and the coherence theory. These are not, however, two rival theories but in fact two different methods of confirming different sorts of judgments. If it is an empirical judgment that has to be confirmed, what matters is its correspondence with the empirical fact it is intended to express. If it is an axiomatic judgment, what matters is its place in the axiomatic context, that is, its coherence with other propositions in the axiomatic system.[10]

It is not, however, possible in either of these ways to confirm a *philosophical judgment*. This cannot be done by comparison with anything given, nor yet by derivation from other, 'higher' propositions established in advance, for the philosophical judgment has no such propositions over it. It is itself the highest, the ultimate. If it is to be confirmed, a quite different procedure is necessary. It is of this problematical situation that Kant is speaking in his well-known saying: 'Now here we see philosophy placed in an awkward position, which is supposed to be secure although it neither depends on nor is supported by anything in heaven or earth.'[11] This is a good description of the situation of philosophy when the attempt is made to locate it among the other modes of argumentation. It has no foothold in the empirical ('on earth') nor yet in the axiomatic ('in heaven'), but must develop a third procedure of its own, suited to its subject matter and the concern it has with it, which is indicated by the word 'validity'. If we wish to give a name to this specifically philosophical procedure, it may appropriately be called '*validation*'.

We have thus to distinguish between three concepts: *verification, justification, validation*. The last-named is the one that particularly interests us, but we need to take account of the other two as well in order to differentiate between them and philosophical 'validation'. It might of course not seem to matter much which term is used, since there is always something conventional and in a measure arbitrary about the choice of terminology. On the other hand it is of the utmost importance to have a *fixed and clear terminology*. Without it we cannot hope to avoid confusing the different modes of argumentation, with all the serious consequences that such confusion entails. That is why we have introduced the three terms, verification, justification, validation. Only by this means can we become finally clear about the different modes of argumentation. The

[9] *Cf.* above, p. 93.
[10] *Cf.* above, p. 119f.
[11] Kant, *Grundlegung, Ges. Aufs.* IV, p.425; ETT Abbott p. 270, Manthey-Zorn p. 43.

distinction we drew earlier between empirical, axiomatic and philosophical argumentation was not designed to set up a system of science, dividing it up into different branches. That would be misleading, since in most sciences the different forms of argumentation are found in close association and co-operation with one another. If, for example, it has been shown experimentally that such and such is the case, then we have firm empirical ground on which to base further scientific inquiry. But this is no guarantee that the scientific theories developed on this basis will be correct. If there is inconsistency in our reasoning, the result will be erroneous in spite of its empirical foundation. Thus empirical and axiomatic argumentation continually interact with one another.

But co-operation is one thing, confusion quite another, and it is the latter that must at all costs be avoided. We have already seen the disastrous consequences of measuring the empirical by rational and the rational by empirical standards. But in philosophy this kind of confusion is even more disastrous. Philosophy is concerned with meaning and validity, and here neither verification nor justification is sufficient. Even a metaphysical system can find room for correct empirical data, and it can be a self-contained, self-consistent unity, yet it may nonetheless be meaningless. We have already seen what happens when philosophical validation is confused with verification, and we shall see more of it when we discuss the principle of verification as a philosophical criterion of meaning. But the result is just as bad when philosophical is confused with axiomatic argumentation, and philosophy is conceived as a science designed to furnish logico-mathematical proof of the existence and nature of reality. It is this that underlies a great deal of scepticism in philosophical thought. People ask: Can you *prove* this? Can you *prove* that the external world really exists and is not merely an illusion? Can you *prove* that there are other individuals who have perceptions and ideas like yours? Or is not solipsism the only consistent philosophical position? That all this is a mere pseudo-problem is at once apparent if we have seen the difference between verification, justification and validation.

Philosophy has to do with the question of meaning and validity, and is not concerned with that of either verification or justification. It is not its business to prove to some eccentric that the world is not a dream, still less to encourage such wild notions itself by mixing up the different modes of argumentation. Philosophy has more serious matters to attend to. The following may serve to illustrate this point. If someone is dunned time after time for payment of a bill he has already paid, and for which he has a receipt, he does not start speculating as to whether all this is not merely his own imagination. He refuses to pay and produces the receipt (which in some languages is actually called 'verification'), and he is not to be fooled by any quasi-philosophical demonstration that no one can logically *prove* the reality of the external world, including himself, his creditor, the bill and the receipt. Naturally all this cannot be logically proved; it is an empirical matter, which does not have to be proved but verified. But that is a very trivial and uninteresting discovery for anyone who has once understood the import of, and distinction between, verification, justification and validation. A philosopher must not be less clear and realistic than the man in our illustration. He has nothing to propose as an alternative to this man's verification, but he has a quite different problem to deal with, namely that of validity, meaning and presuppositions.

Philosophy has got into disrepute owing to the pseudo-problems that arise from the confusing of verification, justification and validation. That is why it is often regarded as a mere intellectual pastime. There are not likely to be many who take seriously the philosopher who stated recently that he did not know for certain that he like other men would one day die; at all events he could not *prove* it. Quite right—that question is not on the logical level and is not capable of logico-mathematical demonstration. But to say that it is therefore only with a certain degree of probability that he reckons he will one day die, makes the confusion complete. It is this kind of reasoning that has deservedly brought philosophy into contempt.

Under the heading of 'scientific argumentation' we dealt extensively with the axiomatic and empirical forms of argumentation, to which we added as a third possibility philosophical argumentation. In order to indicate that this was only a matter of possibility we put a question mark after the reference to philosophical argumentation. We can now drop the question mark. For there is no reason to reserve the term 'scientific' for only the two first-named modes of argumentation. Just as one can analyze a judgment and argue entirely objectively about the truth or falsity of what is said in it, and just as one can argue entirely objectively about the consistency of an axiomatic system, so also one can argue entirely objectively concerning the presuppositions involved in a judgment. Here there is no essential difference. In all these three areas the inquiry can be made with the same exactitude and stringency, the same intersubjectivity. Not even in the philosophical field is it necessary to take refuge in subjective opining and imagining. The question is quite clearly definable that is put when we ask what the presupposition (or presuppositions) of a particular judgment is (or are). Here we can argue for and against, with arguments that are purely objective. What is at issue is the question of meaning, of validity, of presuppositions, inseparably bound up with one another as these are. Even though we are not yet able to state definitively the method by which they must be answered, the questions are already so precisely defined that there need be no doubt about their scientific character.

If we now compare with one another the questions with which the three types of scientific argumentation are concerned, we find that the philosophical is in a measure primary and basic to the other two. This is apparent already in the fact that philosophy has to do with ultimate *pre*suppositions, the presuppositions that are determinative of the meaning of a proposition. Although philosophical problems are as a rule the last to be reached, they actually involve a *prius* and a *prae* to the others. *First meaning, then truth and logical consistency*—that is the actual, objective sequence. We can describe an empirical proposition as true, or an axiomatic train of thought as consistent, only on the presupposition that we are dealing with meaningful statements. A meaningless utterance cannot be true or false, nor can a meaningless concatenation of words be consistent. How could one express an opinion about the truth or consistency of something whose meaning one did not know? In this connection we may well recall Ludwig Wittgenstein's saying: 'Every proposition must *already* have a sense; assertion cannot give it a sense, for what is asserted is precisely the sense. And the same holds of denial.'[12]

We must go as it were 'behind' the individual proposition and by exhibiting its presuppositions clarify its meaning. If these presuppositions are absent, then the conditions prerequisite to making any judgment are absent. What is expressed in a judgment or a proposition is one thing, the presuppositions implied in it are another. The simplest illustration of this can be seen in connection with the philosophy of science. Here the position is that the individual sciences deal with what is *expressed* in a judgment, while philosophy deals with what is *presupposed* by it. Something of this is reflected in the distinctions which have been made in recent times between object-language and meta-language, theory and meta-theory, logic and meta-logic, mathematics and meta-mathematics, etc. Underlying expressions of this kind there is a correct and important observation and a distinction that is necessary for a proper understanding of the function of philosophy. Yet we cannot but question the choice of terminology. 'Metaphysics' has played so disastrous a part in the evolution of philosophy that we need to think very carefully before introducing words combined with 'meta' to describe its function. This can all too easily become a springboard for metaphysics. The prefix 'meta-' itself tells us little about the subject, but brings to it its own traditional bias and a mass of ambiguous associations. We shall therefore stick to the expression 'analysis of presuppositions' for which there are objective grounds and which does not invite misunderstanding, as a description of the characteristic function of philosophy.

To describe (as we have done) the philosophical mode of argumentation as 'validation' is essentially the same as to say that it takes the form of an analysis of presuppositions. For it is by laying bare the ultimate presuppositions that it answers its fundamental questions of meaning and validity in so far as they can be answered at all. This also sets philosophy free from a number of tasks which have been assigned to it in the past, and by which it has been led astray. Its task is not verification or justification.

[12] *Tractatus* 4.064.

To demand of philosophy that it shall decide *what* is true, *what* is real, *what* is meaningful, and so forth, is to drive it into the arms of metaphysics. Anything of that kind is beyond the scope of philosophy. Even when philosophy is described as 'analysis of meaning', this does not imply that it is its business to set up a universal 'criterion of meaning' which guarantees that whatever corresponds to it is meaningful and whatever does not is meaningless. Such a task would be impossible and itself meaningless. Nor when philosophy is described as 'analysis of validity' does this imply that it is its business to conjure up something 'valid in itself', an ultimate principle of validity, from which all validity whatsoever could be derived or axiomatically deduced; it simply means that by its analysis of presuppositions philosophy shows on what assumptions or under what conditions the judgments we make possess any meaning and validity whatsoever.

When validity and presuppositions are linked together in this way, new light is shed on an old problem which is formulated in the question: 'How are synthetic judgments *a priori* possible?' On this subject opinion has been very much divided during recent decades. In many quarters it has been dismissed, often rather cavalierly, on the grounds that it is not a genuine problem. Particularly where the influence of logical empiricism has been strong, this idea has become something of an established dogma. Underlying it there is a simple but questionable identification, namely that of the alternatives 'analytic—synthetic' with the alternatives 'apriori—empirical'. Analytic and apriori are thus conceived as interchangeable terms, as are also synthetic and empirical. Then there is an obvious contradition in speaking of a 'synthetic judgment *a priori*' since it is equivalent to a synthetic judgment which is not synthetic—an example of pure meaninglessness. The position is not, however, quite so simple. A significant advance was made when Wittgenstein and logical empiricism after him insisted that analytical judgments are essentially nothing but tautologies, and that empirical judgments require verification. Yet at the same time something of absolutely vital importance for philosophy was lost through the above-mentioned identification. Its consequences can be seen in the ambivalent attitude of Wittgenstein and logical empiricism to the scientific status of philosophy. There is strictly speaking no place for a 'scientific philosophy' if we reckon only with tautological and empirical propositions and regard whatever is not included among these as meaningless. It is there that the idea of 'synthetic judgments *a priori*' has an important part to play. For it serves to remind us that the disjunction 'tautological/empirical' is incomplete. It is only when the idea of 'synthetic judgments *a priori*' is introduced that the disjunction becomes complete. To dismiss or explain away this formula and what it stands for is to dismiss or explain away scientific philosophy.[13]

[13] It is therefore not surprising that the idea of 'synthetic judgments *a priori*', though

In general it can be said that Kant with his idea of 'synthetic judgments *a priori*' picked up a trail which is worth following out, and which can give us substantial help in getting to grips with the problem of presuppositions. If we make use of a formula borrowed from Kant, however, it must be emphasized once again that we have no intention of reviving Kant's ideas in their historically given form. There is much to object to in his thinking on this subject, and to that extent it belongs to the past. All we are saying here is that certain lines of thought which Kant began to follow, can help us with our present problem. The analysis of meaning and validity thus comes to be focused in the question of presuppositions. But this presents us with a new problem. For 'presupposition' is an ambiguous word, and its philosophical import must be distinguished from other senses which it can bear.

---

often dismissed as a contradiction in terms, keeps on cropping up in philosophical discussion. Everything depends, however, on the meaning ascribed to it. It is often understood differently from the way we have taken it here. See, e.g., H. Delius, *Untersuchungen*, and *cf.* the essays on the subject by C. H. A. Langford and N. R. Hanson.

CHAPTER VII

The Concept of Presupposition

1. Presupposition and Prejudice

A DIFFICULTY which has to be faced in any discussion of the philosophical idea of 'presupposition' is that it is continually confused with other ideas which either have nothing to do with it or are only very loosely connected with it. It is therefore necessary to begin by distinguishing the philosophical idea from at least some of these others.

The most serious instance of such confusion is that of 'presupposition' and 'prejudice'. These are two ideas so remote from one another that one would think it impossible for them to be confused. Yet this confusion is perpetually occurring, and in recent times has reached such proportions that it must really be regarded as a cultural menace. When the presuppositions on which all thought and cultural life rest, come increasingly to be described as 'prejudices' which we could well do without, this is no longer merely a harmless linguistic confusion but something with far-reaching consequences in every direction. Frightful disorder results from treating presupposition and prejudice as interchangeable terms, and this is just what is happening on a very large scale today. That subject would be worth investigating on its own, though naturally we cannot go into it here. We must confine ourselves to fencing off the philosophical concept of 'presupposition' and protecting it against that sort of meaning-destroying confusion.

In seeking to maintain a distinction between presupposition and prejudice, however, we have against us—besides the frequently tendentious confusions just mentioned—the very common practice in ordinary speech of using the two terms as if they were synonymous. There is, for example, the generally accepted habit of saying about science that it is and must be 'presuppositionless'. Any scientist knows of course that there is no such thing as 'presuppositionless science'. Every judgment he makes, every experiment he performs, includes a large number of presuppositions without which the judgment would be meaningless and the experiment impossible. Even with regard to the simplest experiment in natural science it is a fact that the design and entire apparatus for it is one great complex of presuppositions, which alone make the experiment possible and give it meaning. Or to take another example: parliament resolves that a certain matter shall be the subject of a 'thorough investigation without presuppositions'. Everyone understands that this is not meant to prohibit all presuppositions whatsoever. For it is of the very nature of an 'investigation' that it cannot be carried out without a great many presuppositions. Clearly, in this as in the previous example the word 'presupposition' is being used in a special sense, and what is meant is very much the same as if we spoke of an 'unprejudiced inquiry' or of examining something 'without prejudice'.

To say that in conducting any examination or inquiry one must be as far as possible free from prejudice, uninhibited by prejudice, is only another way of saying that the matter in question must be genuinely and seriously investigated. If the result is settled in advance, there cannot possibly be a genuine and seriously intended investigation. If the answer is clear from the start, the investigation will be merely a tactical manoeuvre, or at most a subsequent rationalization. In the case of a genuine investigation, only the investigation itself can show what the result will be. The result has to emerge from the investigation. When therefore in order to make this point the expression 'presuppositionless' is used, it by no means implies that there are to be no presuppositions at all—which would be absurd—but that the investigation is to be free from 'preconceived opinions' or 'prejudices'. And this word 'prejudice' means just what it literally says; it means that an opinion has been formed and a judgment passed *before* (*prae*) the case has been brought to trial (*judicium*). A judgment thus reached in advance, before the evidence is examined, is a 'prejudice'. It is a judgment given on no proper grounds, without regard to the pertinent facts. A child unfamiliar with a particular dish of food, and therefore refusing to taste it, has a prejudice against that food. How it tastes can only be decided by tasting it. First taste, then decide! First investigate, then judge!

So far it all seems simple enough. People have got into the way of saying 'presupposition' where they ought strictly to say 'prejudice'—a careless use of words, but we can get used to it, and it is harmless so long as it is seen in its proper context. But now the situation becomes more complicated, owing to the fact that 1. the term 'prejudice' is used in very different senses and is thus very *ambiguous*, and 2. this hazy, ambiguous concept is treated as *essentially* equivalent to 'presupposition'.

The word 'prejudice' is one of the most negatively charged emotional words in the language, and it is generally used in a pejorative sense. In this connection the *social prejudices* of class and race play an important part.[1] Not least in recent history we have had examples of the way in which social prejudice underlies much of the aggressiveness that has been displayed both on the domestic and the international scene. We can also observe how these prejudices are often combated by new prejudices. Prejudice has thus become one of the great world problems. As a rule, prejudice is connected with lack of understanding. But while ordinary lack of

[1] These have in recent times been made the subject of detailed research, as, e.g., by G. Saenger, W. Allport and P. Heintz—for titles see Bibliography.

understanding can be easily remedied by more information, it is considerably more difficult to find a cure for prejudice. Even a prejudice that has been intellectually recognized for what it is, has an astonishing ability to survive. Prejudices are 'contagious', and this makes it difficult to protect oneself intellectually against them. They are also extremely deep-seated so that it is hard to get at them by purely intellectual means.

Just as prejudice is expressive of a strongly negative attitude and is generally regarded as reprehensible, so freedom from prejudice is regarded as of the highest positive value. But to complete the confusion, we find the expressions 'unprejudiced' and 'without prejudice' also used in a pejorative sense. When for example it is said of an embezzler that he laid his plans in an extraordinary clever and unprejudiced way, the meaning is obviously not that he was free from prejudice in the ordinary sense. To describe a man as 'unprejudiced' in his choice of means to a fraudulent end, only means that he has put aside all such considerations as truth, honesty, decency, and so forth, which are basic presuppositions of life in human society. It does not mean, however, that these presuppositions and these considerations are of inferior worth and can properly be described as 'prejudices'. Yet the very fact that the word 'unprejudiced' can be used to dignify the putting aside of such necessary presuppositions, helps to obscure the distinction between presupposition and prejudice. For philosophy, however, it is of the greatest importance that the line of demarcation between them should be sharply and clearly drawn. Presupposition is not equivalent to prejudice, and unprejudiced is not equivalent to presuppositionless.

Presuppositions and prejudices are in many respects diametrically opposed to one another. Prejudices are something we must be on guard against and if possible destroy. Presuppositions we are bound to use, and it is highly desirable to be quite clear as to what presuppositions we are using. This is one of the best means of combating prejudices. If we are not aware of the presuppositions with which we do and must operate, we become an easy prey to prevailing prejudices. It is the business of philosophy to elucidate by means of analysis the most general presuppositions of all thought and judgment.

But the very nature of these ultimate, general presuppositions, that is, their very generality and ultimacy, makes it possible—so it seems—to treat them as assumptions we are not bound to make. It looks as if we have only to deny them or cast doubt on them in order to free ourselves entirely from them. For there is a distinct difference between facts, which command respect, and assumptions, which we can accept or reject as we please. It is difficult to get away from facts, but with regard to assumptions and presuppositions we can always ask: Why presuppose this, why make this assumption at all? Hence the dividing line between presupposition and prejudice still seems very indistinct, and presuppositions appear in an unfavourable light. Facts are, after all, objective and in the last resort beyond our manipulating; they remain facts, no matter what attitude we take to them. Presuppositions behave very differently and give by comparison the impression of being quite subjective and arbitrary. They seem to disappear when we doubt or deny them—which means that we no longer make use of them as presuppositions. Their entire meaning and function seems to depend on our taking them for granted and making use of them. But if that is so, must there not in the last resort be something subjective and arbitrary about presuppositions? For either we presuppose them and employ them in our argumentation, and then they are for us valid presuppositions, or else we reject them, and then they are by the same token invalidated.

The matter is not, however, quite so simple. The whole of this last argument rests on the false assumption that presuppositions and prejudices are to be regarded as on the same level. Prejudices, it is true, have more to do with what we imagine than with facts, and as such they are arbitrary. But the presuppositions which are the object of philosophical analysis stand in a quite different relation to facts. There are things which, whether we are aware of it or not, we do *in fact* presuppose, and what is more we *necessarily* presuppose them and cannot help doing so. It is only with presuppositions of this latter type that philosophy is concerned—ultimate, inescapable presuppositions, which it is the business of philosophical analysis to lay bare and in doing so to show the grounds of their validity.

To sum up, we may say that the worst prejudice of which one can be guilty is to imagine that all presuppositions whatsoever are to be equated with prejudices. One cannot make a single statement which does not imply a multitude of presuppositions. But this does not mean that every statement is based on a prejudice.[2] To pursue the question of presupposition and prejudice to a conclusion, however, one further point must be noted, namely the constant risk that by being wrongly used presuppositions may be transformed into prejudices. A presupposition which in its own sphere is perfectly correct can suffer this fate, and it does so when it is used for an attack on other presuppositions, each of which in its own sphere is equally

[2] Perhaps no one has done more to popularize the confused notion of 'prejudice' (*Vorurteil*) as a substitute for 'presupposition' than Nietzsche. With his customary confident exaggeration he says: 'Every word is a prejudice' (*Menschliches, Allzumenschliches*, II, 19, 55; ET, p. 225). If 'prejudice' can be here interpreted as referring to the fact that every word and every sentence rests on a number of presuppositions, it may be pointing in the right direction. But Nietzsche is no more clear than the many who echo him, as to the relation between prejudice and presupposition. *Cf.* his statement that 'Good and evil are the prejudices of God' (*Die fröhliche Wissenschaft* 63; ET, p. 207). The result of this lack of clarity is that Nietzsche repudiates morality on the one hand, yet is himself a pronounced 'moralist' on the other—pitting the morality of the superman against slave-morality, and the values of antiquity against Christian values as he understands them.

correct. From this point of view it is the task of philosophy to see to it that a presupposition is not transformed into a prejudice by false generalization and extension. Such transformation is what happens above all in metaphysics, which has the characteristic habit of seizing on a particular idea, which in its place may very well be correct, and making it the dominant presupposition of its system, with the result of transforming it into a prejudice. But this is to anticipate a subject which will be fully discussed at a later stage.

2. Presupposition, Axiom, Hypothesis

To distinguish between presupposition and prejudice is to disentangle from one another two concepts which have really nothing in common beyond their superficially identical prefix ('pre-'). It is otherwise when we come to distinguish presupposition from two other concepts, namely axiom and hypothesis.[3] These three have really a great deal in common, so much in fact that we might regard presupposition as an inclusive term covering axioms and hypotheses as well as philosophical presuppositions.

An *axiom* is a form of presupposition. If we examine axiomatic argumentation we find that it starts with an axiom and is determined by the axiom throughout. On the assumption that the axiom is valid, the theorems deduced or deducible from it are also valid. They are merely simple consequences of what is already implicit in the axiom. But while theorems can be proved by reference to their axioms, the axioms themselves cannot be proved. They are assumptions or presuppositions, which may appear to be self-evident, but which cannot be proved to be so. If I start with a different assumption and set up other axioms, I can just as consistently draw other conclusions from them. This is what makes it possible to set up different axiomatic systems without any possibility of deciding which of them is 'the right one', for rightness in axiomatic argumentation is decided solely by consistency, and consistency has to do exclusively with the relation that obtains between axioms and inferences. In other words, we remain within the system and have therefore no possibility of judging it as a whole with respect to its relation to others that are formally of equal standing. The axioms are thus the basic assumptions that serve as a starting point for axiomatic argumentation or proof. They are the presuppositions of the axiomatic system, its fundamental presuppositions.

Philosophical presuppositions, however, are quite another matter. They are not starting points or initial assumptions from which a system might be deductively derived. Admittedly that is what they are thought to be in one sort of 'philosophy', namely deductive metaphysics. The latter has been apt to regard itself as an axiomatic science, and has seen in mathematical thinking the model for its own procedure. This is what underlies the idea

---

[3] On axioms and hypotheses see above, pp. 105ff., 111ff., 116ff.

of a philosophy constructed *more geometrico*, with its starting point in self-dependent, undemonstrable axioms and inferences drawn from them, by which method it is also supposed to be possible to reach a consistent, tenable world-view. The only trouble is that the parallel breaks down at the decisive point. Mathematics does not profess to furnish a 'world-view'. It stays within the bounds of the axiomatic, and has therefore every right to start with unproved axioms. But metaphysics, which seeks to provide a world-view, has not the same right. If it posits unconfirmed axioms, it bases itself on *arbitrary* presuppositions. And it is just this arbitrariness that scientific philosophy regards it as its task to overcome. Hence it follows that a scientific philosophy can never be constructed *more geometrico*, and that its presuppositions must not be equated with axioms.

A *hypothesis* likewise is a form of presupposition. And there is all the more temptation to identify or confuse the hypothesis with the philosophical presupposition, in that the Greek word 'hypothesis' can actually be translated as 'presupposition'. It is of course above all in empirical argumentation that the hypothesis plays a decisive part. It could indeed be argued that the hypothesis comes first in empirical argumentation, just as the axiom comes first in axiomatic argumentation. Not of course formally in the same way; for as a rule empirical observation is regarded as the starting point, and rightly so. But what makes it possible to consider that the hypothesis may be primary, is the fact that science never consists merely in the gathering of unconnected empirical data. These are something that science has in common with experience in general. We can only speak of science when the empirical observations are conducted from generic points of view which serve to explain the phenomena observed, or in other words, on the basis of more or less general hypotheses. If we take the example of the natural sciences, it is always a major concern of science to work towards more and more general and comprehensive hypotheses, which enable it to include more and more observations under a common explanation. What then could be more obvious than to regard philosophical argumentation as a normal and natural extension of this scientific endeavour? The sciences set up hypotheses, each in its own province, and try to make them as general as possible, but they never get further than particular hypotheses, since each is confined to its own province. Here then philosophy must come in—so it might seem—and set up all-inclusive, universal hypotheses. This is the programme of inductive metaphysics, though not, be it noted, of scientific philosophy.

When scientific philosophy speaks of presuppositions, it means something quite different from hypotheses. The difference between it and metaphysics could be expressed thus: metaphysics *posits* presuppositions, scientific philosophy *analyzes* presuppositions. Scientific philosophy is 'analysis of presuppositions'. Metaphysics postulates and proclaims presuppositions itself, imposing them on its material; scientific philosophy starts from a given material and analyzes it with regard to the presuppositions included in it. From this it follows that philosophical presuppositions are of quite another order than scientific hypotheses. The latter can be tested, and may be refuted, by means of empirical observation. Although the general hypotheses ('laws of nature') cannot be directly verified,[4] they can be indirectly checked by confronting the propositions deduced from them with what is observed in experience. A hypothesis which does not pass this test is thereby refuted. There is nothing corresponding to this in the case of philosophical presuppositions. They cannot be refuted by any kind of experience, since they themselves constitute the basis of all experience.

The comparison thus made between axiomatic and empirical argumentation with their axioms and hypotheses on the one hand, and philosophical argumentation with its 'presuppositions' on the other, gives us a good insight into the distinctive character of philosophical argumentation. We have here three different kinds of presuppositions which are clearly distinguishable from one another.

An *axiom* is a presupposition (an initial assumption) which is conceived as self-evident, and from which certain consequences can be deduced and conclusions drawn by logical necessity. Hence the acceptance of an axiom involves the acceptance of what follows from it. *If* the axiom is accepted, *then* the conclusions in which its consequences are drawn out must also be accepted.

A *hypothesis* is a tentative presupposition, intended as an explanation of certain empirically observed phenomena. That it is correct can never be directly verified. It is never more than a hypothesis, an assumption, though perhaps a very probable one. It can, however, be indirectly tested by confronting the propositions deduced from it with empirical observations made independently of it.

A *philosophical presupposition* is one that finds its starting point in judgments and propositions which are intersubjectively accepted by us, and concerning which philosophy raises the question: What is here *presupposed*? Philosophy seeks by means of analysis to show what presuppositions we have actually and necessarily employed in the very act of making these judgments and stating these propositions, even though we ourselves are often unaware of having employed them. It is impossible to affirm these judgments and propositions and at the same time to deny the presuppositions on which in fact they rest. Here too, then, it is a question of consistency, in this case between propositions and presuppositions—the

---

[4] Wittgenstein, *Philosophische Bemerkungen*, p. 285: 'When I say that a hypothesis is not definitively verifiable, I do *not* mean that there is a verification of it to which one can keep getting closer without ever reaching it. That is nonsense, and of a kind into which people often lapse. But a hypothesis has a different formal relation to reality than that of verification.'

propositions stated by us and the presuppositions derived from them by analysis.

In all three cases it is a matter of logical consequence and consistency— very naturally where presuppositions are concerned. In *axiomatic* argumentation it is a question of logically consistent inference from the axiom to the conclusions derivable from it, that is, to the propositions which are already in some measure given in the axiom and can therefore be deductively drawn out of it. In *empirical* argumentation things are more complicated. Here there is a question of consistency in two directions: on the one hand between the hypothesis and the conclusions deductively derived from it, and on the other between these conclusions and observed empirical data. If these conclusions conflict with data given in experience, this has consequences for the hypothesis itself, which is thereby shown to be untenable and must be regarded as false. Finally, in *philosophical* argumentation it is a question of consistency in working back analytically from generally accepted propositions to their presuppositions, which must logically be credited with at least the same validity as the propositions on which the analysis is based. Conclusions are thus drawn here from propositions with regard to presuppositions. *If* these propositions are valid, *then* the presuppositions implied in them are also valid. Naturally there is no reason why we should not put it the other way round and say: only if these presuppositions are accepted can those propositions be maintained. But the difference this makes is merely superficial. The rejection of a presupposition necessarily leads to the rejection of the proposition which includes it. On the other hand, there can never in philosophical argumentation be any question of deriving propositions deductively from presuppositions.

3. 'Absolute Presuppositions'

No contemporary philosopher has done more than R. G. Collingwood to direct the attention of philosophy to the question of presuppositions. In this connection he deserves a chapter to himself. But here we must confine ourselves to differentiating our concept of presuppositions from his. For while our concept has certain points of contact with Collingwood's, it also has decisive differences from it. For both reasons a demarcation is necessary here.

The first objection we have to bring against Collingwood's view may seem to be mainly terminological. It has to do with his persistent equation of philosophy with 'metaphysics'. This equation is reflected even in the title of the work in which he most of all insists on 'presuppositions' as the central thing in philosophy. The title is: *An Essay on Metaphysics*. Now he is clearly aware that metaphysics is a problematical science, and that it cannot be maintained in the form it has traditionally had ever since the time of Aristotle. It contains disparate elements which cannot be held together, and part of it must be sacrificed in order that the other part may be saved. The traditional definition of metaphysics includes two propositions: 1. Metaphysics is the science of pure being (ontology); and 2. Metaphysics is the science which deals with the presuppositions underlying ordinary science. Collingwood is quite clear that the first of these propositions is untenable 'because a science of pure being is a contradiction in terms'.[5] Every science must have a clearly defined subject matter to deal with. But the alleged 'science of pure being' has nothing to 'differentiate it from anything else or from nothing at all'. 'There is not even a pseudo-science of pure being.'[6] This kind of thing must be jettisoned if metaphysics is to be saved. Collingwood therefore proposes a 'Metaphysics without Ontology',[7] that is to say, a science of presuppositions. But not every presupposition is philosophically significant. There are relative and absolute presuppositions. It is only the latter with which philosophy is concerned. Philosophy (metaphysics) is 'The Science of Absolute Presuppositions'.[8]

What must be questioned here is whether it is possible in this way to jettison one half of metaphysics and still call the other half 'metaphysics'. It will not do to describe ontology as 'a mistake which people have made . . . about metaphysics',[9] as if it were something we could get rid of and then metaphysics would be all right. On the contrary, as we have seen,[10] ontology is an integral part of metaphysics, without which metaphysics is no longer metaphysics in the established sense of the word. Metaphysics is characteristically a combination of diverse tendencies, among which the ontological plays a leading role. To break up this combination is to destroy metaphysics itself. That is what Collingwood does— yet he retains the name. Now this could of course be merely a matter of terminology or nomenclature, without material consequences—although the name would be misleading. But the opposite is the case with Collingwood. For despite the distinction he draws within metaphysics, and his attempt to get rid of ontology, he does not succeed in steering clear of ontology himself. The plainest evidence of this is his lengthy defence of the ontological proof of the existence of God,[11] in which he appeals to Anselm, Descartes, Spinoza and Hegel. With Hegel, he says: 'the Ontological Proof took its place once more among the accepted principles of modern philosophy, and it has never again been seriously criticized.'[12]

Collingwood thus accepts the idea of an *a priori* deduced *ens realis-*

[5] R. G. Collingwood, *Metaphysics*, p. 11.
[6] *Op. cit.*, pp. 14f.
[7] *Op. cit.*, pp. 17–20 (the title of Ch. III).
[8] *Op. cit.*, pp. 34–48 (the title of Ch. V).
[9] *Op. cit.*, p. 17.
[10] Above, pp. 35ff., 42ff.
[11] Collingwood, *Philosophical Method*, pp. 124–27.
[12] *Op. cit.*, p. 126.

simum. 'What it does prove is that essence involves existence, not always, but in one special case, the case of God in the metaphysical sense: the *Deus sive natura* of Spinoza, the Good of Plato, the Being of Aristotle: the object of metaphysical thought. But this means the object of philosophical thought in general.'[13] Here we have presuppositions and metaphysics and ontology all in one.[14] Collingwood has obviously not succeeded in rescuing metaphysics from ontology, nor could he possibly do so in view of the way in which they have been interwoven and interfused with one another throughout history. We are reminded here of the old adage: 'You can't unscramble a scrambled egg.' Obviously this has consequences also for the concept of 'absolute presuppositions', which otherwise might seem very close to our idea of 'presuppositions'. Enough has been said to show that Collingwood's idea of presuppositions, in spite of all outward similarity, is very far removed from the philosophical concept of 'presupposition' which we are in process of discovering by our analysis.

What then is meant by an 'absolute presupposition'? It is clear that there are different kinds of presuppositions, and that many of them are relative. With these philosophy has nothing to do. If therefore we wish to distinguish philosophical presuppositions from these others by calling them 'absolute', there can be no objection to this. Collingwood is undoubtedly on right lines when he identifies his absolute presuppositions with the ultimate presuppositions that underlie our very way of asking questions. These absolute presuppositions always have to do with the question, not with the answer. The relative presuppositions, on the other hand, have to do with both. For 'each of them stands now as the presupposition to a question, now as the answer to one. Each is both a presupposition and a proposition.'[15] It is a correct and important observation that there is a connection between our presuppositions and our way of asking questions. Between relative and absolute presuppositions there is the difference that the former both can and must be verified, whereas it is meaningless to seek to verify the absolute presuppositions. To seek to

[13] *Op. cit.*, p. 127.

[14] It should be observed that the last quotation is taken from a work several years earlier (1933) than *An Essay on Metaphysics* (1940), and that there has clearly been a development between these two writings. None the less we are justified in citing it as typical of Collingwood's outlook, not least because he reverts in the later work (pp. 189ff.) to the same line of thought, though with certain qualifications. One does not, however, get rid of ontology by substituting the term 'Anselm's proof' for 'the ontological proof of the existence of God' (p. 189). It is also significant that Collingwood finally has to appeal to the argument that the matter is clear and easily understandable 'for a man with a bent for metaphysics' (p. 190). From this it is evident that the question of 'absolute presuppositions' is not amenable to objective argumentation, and that Collingwood's philosophy, in spite of his attempts to get rid of ontology, really is what it professes to be, i.e. metaphysics, and not 'scientific philosophy'. *Cf.* also A. Donagan, *The Later Philosophy of R. G. Collingwood.*

[15] Collingwood, *Metaphysics*, p. 40.

verify or prove them would be to treat them as relative presuppositions, and would thus be self-contradictory. It would mean that we no longer had any absolute presuppositions, which are 'suppositions which in principle neither admit nor require verification.'[16]

The question now is, how these absolute presuppositions can be detected and demonstrated. The answer is: 'only by analysis.'[17] This sounds promising: philosophy is 'analysis of presuppositions'. It is ominous, however, when Collingwood explains: 'The analysis which detects absolute presuppositions I call metaphysical analysis.'[18] When we ask what is 'presupposed' in the philosophical sense, the answer can only be obtained by means of a *logical* analysis. Philosophy is a '*logical* analysis of presuppositions'. But it is not quite this for Collingwood. Underlying what he says about absolute presuppositions there is his whole philosophy of mind and theory of consciousness, which diverts his thinking from the logical to the psychological level. A presupposition is conceived as an 'act of thought', often an act of 'unconscious thought'.[19] Here, in the way in which he slips over from the logical to the psychological, lies one of the main difficulties in Collingwood's theory of presuppositions. Even from a logical point of view we can speak of 'tacit presuppositions' or 'unconscious presuppositions', in the sense of presuppositions which one is not aware of having in fact made, and which are only discovered as presuppositions by means of logical analysis. But that is quite different from saying that the presupposition itself is an act of thought, whether conscious or unconscious. Logical implication must not be confused with a psychological act of thought.

The matter is further complicated, however, by Collingwood's description of metaphysics as a 'historical science'. What he means by this he explains briefly thus: 'Metaphysics is the attempt to find out what absolute presuppositions have been made by this or that person or group of persons, on this or that occasion or group of occasions, in the course of this or that piece of thinking.'[20] With this he moves a step further away from the thought of the philosophical presupposition as a logically necessary presupposition. Indeed, he really no longer asks the genuinely philosophical question. When Collingwood speaks of philosophy (metaphysics) as an analysis of presuppositions, it is a wholly different sort of analysis from that which was shown above to be characteristic of philosophical argumentation. Instead it is a more or less psychological inquiry about unconscious presuppositions which affect the character even of

[16] *Op. cit.*, p. 42.
[17] *Op. cit.*, p. 43: 'It is only by analysis that anyone can ever come to know either that he is making any absolute presuppositions at all or what absolute presuppositions he is making.'
[18] *Op. cit.*, p. 40.
[19] *Op. cit.*, p. 48.
[20] *Op. cit.*, p. 47.

conscious thinking, and affect it the more successfully inasmuch as they cannot be brought under conscious scrutiny since they are regarded as self-evident. It is furthermore a historical quest for general and supposedly self-evident presuppositions of this kind which have been accepted without examination by individuals or by whole epochs and have helped to shape their entire outlook.

All this is interesting as a research project; but where is the philosophical problem in such an investigation? Here the term 'metaphysics' has done much to obscure the fact that the basic problem of philosophy has totally disappeared. One consequence of this is that the demarcation between presupposition and prejudice, between presuppositions and axioms-hypotheses, and sometimes between absolute presuppositions and even very relative hypotheses which show every sign of being relative presuppositions, has been obliterated. It can indeed be questioned whether under the cloak of absolute presuppositions 'suppositions' have not actually been able to slip over into 'superstitions'.

Collingwood has been criticized on the ground that he has not clarified the logic of presuppositions, and also that while he has no doubt postulated absolute presuppositions he has not shown them to exist. The first of these criticisms is undoubtedly justified.[21] It is also clear that with the kind of analysis he proposes, he has no possibility of getting at the kind of philosophical presuppositions which his term 'absolute presuppositions' would lead us to expect. At the same time it is obvious that there are such presuppositions as he has in mind—whether we call them 'absolute' or give them some other name—which do determine the outlooks both of individuals and of whole historical periods. What is important to bear in mind here, however, is that these do not represent the basic philosophical idea of 'presupposition', but are to be found on a quite different level, where objective argumentation is out of commission. At a later stage we shall have occasion to look more closely at this type of 'presupposition' under the heading of 'fundamental motif'.[22] Such a 'fundamental motif' is a 'self-evident presupposition', but of a totally different kind from the fundamental presuppositions of philosophy. It is something like the idea of a fundamental motif that Collingwood is after, but his failure to distinguish it from that of a philosophical presupposition results in his losing sight of the latter. Fundamental motifs are indemonstrable, not capable of being either proved or disproved by means of philosophical or any other kind of scientific argument.

We now have the requisite differentiation between our concept of philosophical presuppositions and Collingwood's 'absolute presuppositions'. In the latter concept, as Collingwood defines it, two distinct issues

[21] M. Bunge, *Scientific Research*, I, p. 419: 'Collingwood did not study the logic of presuppositions, nor did he show that there are absolute presuppositions.'
[22] See below, pp. 351–65ff.

are mixed up together, one of them logical, the other psychological. The logical task is to draw out by means of analysis what is implicit and make it explicit. This must not be confused with the psychological task of drawing up an 'act of unconscious thought' out of the darkness of the subconscious and making it conscious.

4. Presupposition and Preunderstanding

In seeking to differentiate the concept of presupposition from other concepts which are in some way similar and with which it might be confused, it is important to make a clear demarcation between 'presupposition' and '*Vorverständnis*' or 'preunderstanding'. Otherwise it may easily be thought that these two concepts are very closely related if not indeed identical with one another. For the purpose of the analysis of presuppositions is to show what the underlying presuppositions are which shape the meaning of the propositions we make, and on the basis of which alone we can understand the meaning and content of these propositions. And what else but this is intended by the idea of *Vorverständnis*? The aim is to grasp meaning and content, to arrive at understanding (*Verstehen*, *Verständnis*). But we cannot start from nowhere, we must have certain presuppositions; and the question is, what are the necessary presuppositions, the things that we must have so to speak in advance, in order even to begin to understand the meaning? It is this idea of *pre*-suppositions, of something given *in advance*, that finds expression in the prefix *Vor-* in *Vorverständnis* (*pre*-understanding). Hence it might well seem as if what we have here were the same as the presuppositions of philosophy. But that is by no means the case. The two ideas are very far removed from one another, and in certain circumstances can be diametrically opposed to one another.

'*Vorverständnis*' or 'preunderstanding' is a leading concept in contemporary 'hermeneutics', and rightly so. For when we seek to interpret a statement and determine its exact meaning, we are faced with the question whether we are approaching it with the same presuppositions as the one who made it. Unless we do so, we shall not correctly understand its meaning. Here two possible lines of interpretation are open to us. Either we must go back to the presuppositions on which the statement was originally made, or else, if we approach it with our own differently oriented presuppositions, we must translate it in such a way that without losing anything of its original meaning it fits in with our presuppositions. Hermeneutics has tried both of these ways. Ideally of course they should coincide if the interpretation is to be reliable. But they often do not, owing to the fact that they have different interests at heart. We may therefore distinguish between two different kinds of hermeneutics, two different ways of interpreting a given statement. One is the purely historical hermeneutics which seeks to establish as exactly as possible the original meaning of the statement. The other kind of hermeneutics seeks to determine what meaning it has for us here and now, that is, its contemporarily relevant meaning. The danger of purely historical hermeneutics is that it can make the statement irrelevant in the present situation. The danger of contemporary hermeneutics is that it can easily become anachronistic, so that the statement is given another than its original meaning and instead of interpretation there is misinterpretation and distortion.

Hermeneutics has always revolved around these questions. It would take far too long here to review the debate of the past several centuries about the problem of interpretation, which has led to the now current concept of 'Vorverständnis'. We must be content to note its results. Since existentialism (Heidegger) took up the problem and adopted the term 'Vorverständnis' for the purposes of its own theory, this concept has come to play a leading part in influential phases of contemporary theology. To name only a couple of examples: it is this concept of 'preunderstanding' that underlies Rudolf Bultmann's 'demythologization'; and the 'correlation' theory of Paul Tillich, with its pattern of 'question and answer' is on similar lines. In both cases there is first a philosophical analysis—an 'analysis of existence'—intended to provide the anthropological or ontological preunderstanding which is supposed to open the way for the gospel to modern man. Philosophy puts the question and theology gives the answer. Here, however, we cannot but ask: Are we really to believe that the meaning of the gospel will be made plain by making it furnish answers to modern philosophical questions? Is it not more probable that such a 'preunderstanding', such an approach to the gospel with questions framed in advance, will bar the way to a correct understanding of it? Was the gospel ever intended to provide answers to such questions? Here the risk of arbitrariness is only too evident, with a pattern laid down in advance, a question defined independently of the material, a 'preunderstanding' reached which is supposed to lead to an 'understanding' of the material but which may instead prove a barrier to the understanding of its real meaning. The idea that one must first familiarize oneself with the anthropological and ontological conceptions of the philosophy of existence in order to get at the real meaning of the gospel, is hardly calculated to inspire confidence even if we are given an assurance that it is only a matter of formal philosophical presuppositions.

The disastrous nature of a 'preunderstanding' thus established in advance can be illustrated by an analogy. Suppose I lock a telescope at a particular position in advance, without regard to the object I wish to observe. Suppose I then declare that only what I can observe clearly through it in that position is clear reality, while what appears blurred to me is blurred in reality, and what cannot be seen does not exist. Obviously I am wrong, and the fault lies in my own locked 'preunderstanding'. I fail to see what I otherwise could have seen if I had not bound myself to this limited and limiting view.

The most delusive thing about such a preunderstanding is that once a person has committed himself to it he imagines he can verify it by means of empirical observation. This too can be illustrated by an analogy. If I look at the world through coloured spectacles, then I can plainly *see* that the world is of this colour—until I take off the spectacles and give up my preunderstanding. My preunderstanding is such that it alters the material I wish to observe and understand. I do of course 'understand' the material, but in *my own* way, not in accord with *its own* meaning and con ent.

It is now clear how a preunderstanding differs from philosophical presuppositions, of which it is in many ways the very opposite. By working with a preunderstanding we do violence to the material, not letting it be what it is and mean what it means. The issue is decided in advance, before we even get to the material; it is decided by our preunderstanding. But what this means is that *Vorverständnis = Vorentscheidung = Vorurteil*, which means that preunderstanding = prejudice. The preunderstanding which was to have been a means for understanding becomes instead a hindrance to understanding. The preunderstanding which was to have enabled us to do justice to the material, leads us instead to do violence to it, since only such material as fits in with my preunderstanding is accepted.

It is an elementary consequence of the preunderstanding, that one falls victim—in Herbert Feigl's words—to 'the reductive fallacy'. We can see this exemplified in Bultmann and Tillich. When Bultmann takes his world-view (i.e. metaphysical) type of preunderstanding as the starting point for his demythologization, this means that an alien criterion is applied to the material, which results in an interpretation that severely reduces the latter and alters its character. And when Tillich poses his philosophical (i.e. metaphysical) question, he determines the direction of the answer and reshapes the material to suit the question. In both cases what we have is a metaphysically conditioned reduction. To this subject we shall return. For the moment we are only concerned to differentiate presuppositions from preunderstanding, and already we have drawn the line between them clearly enough. There is the same distinction between them as between scientific philosophy and metaphysics.

In short, scientific philosophy analyzes the presuppositions that are implied by the material, implicitly present in it. Metaphysics postulates a preunderstanding of its own. Philosophical presuppositions widen the range of vision, making it open and comprehensive. Metaphysical preunderstanding narrows the range of vision, making it exclusive, since only such things are reckoned with as fit in with its own particular point of view.

5. Presupposition and Prescription

There is a frequently quoted statement of Kant's to the effect that by means of its categories the understanding 'prescribes laws for nature'—

laws which nature must obey. Kant's intention with this is to show more precisely the character of the presuppositions which philosophy has to detect and analyze. These presuppositions, he would say, are not merely pre-conditions of thought, but something like natural laws. Here, however, we cannot help asking whether this is a correct description of what is meant by presuppositions. And the answer must be that it decidedly is not. Kant has made a disastrous mistake, and has interpreted the concept of presupposition in a way that robs it of its real meaning. To our earlier differentiations we must therefore add yet another, namely that between presupposition and prescription.

How did Kant come to take this line? That question brings us to an interesting juncture in his thought, where we not only see changes occurring, but also an idea that survives these changes. It is well known that there is a marked difference between the first and second editions of the *Critique of Pure Reason*, and that this has to do not only with particular conceptions or modes of expression, but with the central theme itself, the question of the transcendental deduction and its significance.[23] To put it in a neat though rather oversimplified formula, we might say that the first edition represents in the main an epistemological subjectivism, while in the second Kant is engaged in overcoming that subjectivism and working towards a critical, objective analysis of knowledge.

If we now return to the idea of the understanding as functioning in such a way as to 'prescribe laws for nature', it is evident that this idea is most closely connected with the epistemological subjectivism, of which indeed it can be regarded as a simple consequence, whereas there is really no room for it at all in the context of a critical, analytical epistemology. From the point of view of epistemological subjectivism, the problem of knowledge appears—still speaking in terms of our formula—to be conditioned by the tension between two poles, one subjective and the other objective. On the one side there stands the knowing subject with his sensory and intellectual equipment, his more or less psychologically conceived subjective 'faculties', and on the other side the object known with its given objective character. Accordingly the problem of knowledge takes the form of the following twofold question: 1. How can the subject go outside himself and become participant in the object? and 2. How can the object pass over into the subject and become his knowledge? The difficulty that has to be overcome is 'how *subjective conditions of thought* can

---

[23] See the chapter on 'The Deduction of the Pure Concepts of the Understanding', of which §§ 2 and 3 in the 1st edition have been replaced by a completely revised §2 in the 2nd. References to the former will be given here from the Reclam Ausgabe of the *Critique*, pp. 112–37, and ET by N. Kemp Smith, pp. 129–50; and to the latter from Reclam pp. 657–83, and Kemp Smith pp. 151–75. On the relation between the versions of the transcendental deduction in the two editions, see also F. Delekat, *Immanuel Kant*, pp. 80–107.

have *objective validity*.[24] This way of putting it reflects both the problem of epistemological subjectivism as to how subject and object can find one another and be united in knowledge, and also Kant's discovery of the logical problem of presuppositions and validity as the chief problem of philosophy—a discovery that drives him step by step away from epistemological subjectivism towards the critical analysis of knowledge, and leads him to give a quite different account of the transcendental deduction in the second edition of the *Critique of Pure Reason*.

Since the idea of the knowing subject as prescribing laws for nature is, as we have said, primarily a consequence of epistemological subjectivism, it might have been expected that the move towards a critical, analytical epistemology would have the effect of weakening and undermining that idea. Yet the idea of prescribing laws for nature is at least as prominent in the *Prolegomena* and the second edition of the *Critique of Pure Reason* as in the first edition. This is clearly connected with the fact that the thought of the activity and spontaneity of the subject is a favourite with Kant, and he will not give it up even though it has become clear to him that it must not be understood in psychological terms. Hence the idea of the 'faculties' and their creative role continues to maintain its hold on his thinking. It is symptomatic of this when in the theoretical sphere the 'prescription of laws for nature', and in the ethical sphere the 'autonomy' of the practical reason has the last word. It is a proof that Kant never finally overcame the metaphysics which he showed to be unfeasible, yet for which he sought to lay a firm foundation—the foundation for 'Any Future Metaphysic that will be able to present itself as a Science'. If we ask simply what Kant was aiming at, there can be no doubt that his goal was metaphysics. But on the way he stumbled upon 'scientific philosophy' in the form of the problem of a critical analysis of knowledge.[25] Here it is important to bear in mind the difference between 'problems, statements of problems, and solutions of problems'. The thought of the understanding as prescribing laws for nature belongs to Kant's solution of the problem. But the problem itself which Kant has detected, namely that of philosophical presuppositions, requires us to maintain as Kant did not a clear distinction between presuppositions and prescription.

The equation of presupposition and prescription is carried from the first edition of the *Critique of Pure Reason* (1781) through the *Prolegomena*

[24] Reclam, p. 107; Kemp Smith, p. 124.

[25] This subject is treated in more detail in my essay 'Söka och finna'. I say there: 'We cannot but diminish his importance if we only ask what he was seeking. What made him so extraordinarily significant was just what he and no one else found. This is the point to which above all attention must be paid. What Kant sought was undoubtedly a new foundation for metaphysics, but while seeking it he found . . . the critical problem, which is quite other than the metaphysical, and the transcendental method, which puts an end to metaphysical disputes, but does so by putting an end to metaphysics and transferring the problem to another area' (FHL, p. 222; FOM, p. 196).

(1783) to the second edition of the *Critique* (1787).[26] By means of its categories (presuppositions), Kant holds, the understanding prescribes laws for nature (prescriptions). The only problem is how it comes about 'that nature must adapt itself to them'.[27] The answer to this question, according to Kant, lies in the fact that nature is only an *Erscheinung*, an appearance, not a *Ding an sich*. In other words, 'phenomenalism' provides the explanation. But what is a metaphysical theory like this doing in a critical analysis of knowledge? It is a relic of Kant's earlier epistemology, which was both psychological and ontological. Kant is struggling to get away from metaphysical ontology. 'The proud name of Ontology, as a science that professes to supply in a systematic doctrine synthetic knowledge *a priori* of things as such, must give way to the more modest claims of an analytic of pure understanding.'[28] The critical analysis of knowledge offered a possibility of effectively escaping ontology. But Kant was unable to take advantage of this possibility, owing to his original commitment to the dichotomy of knowing subject and ontological reality. What he could do was to transfer the emphasis from the ontological object to the knowing subject, and treat existence as a 'world of phenomena', a 'nature' which has to obey the laws which the knowing subject 'prescribes'.[29] But this is only apparently an escape from ontology, since the very distinction between '*Ding an sich*' and 'phenomenon'[30] is an ontological distinction. Kant's idea of a critical analysis of knowledge and a quest for the logically necessary presuppositions of knowledge opens the way for us to overcome metaphysical ontology. But then we must not blur as Kant does the distinction between presupposition and prescription.

It is not *we* who prescribe laws for nature. It is not the understanding that prescribes how nature shall be, or how it shall appear to be. 'Nature' is not a world of phenomena behind which an unknown '*Ding an sich*' is

[26] In the *1st edition*: 'Exaggerated and absurd therefore though it may sound to say that the understanding is itself the source of the laws of nature, and thus of its formal unity, such a statement is nevertheless correct and in keeping with the object to which it refers, that is, experience' (Reclam, p. 135; Kemp Smith, p. 148). It is the understanding that 'imparts to phenomena their regularity. . . . The understanding is itself the lawgiver of nature' (Reclam, p. 135; Kemp Smith, p. 148). In the *Prolegomena*: It seems at first strange, but is not the less certain, to say: The understanding does not derive its laws (*a priori*) from, but prescribes them to, nature' (Reclam, p. 102; ET by L. W. Beck, p. 67). In the *2nd edition*: 'Categories are concepts which prescribe laws a priori to phenomena, and consequently to nature' (Reclam, p. 680; Kemp Smith, p. 172).

[27] Reclam, p. 680; Kemp Smith, p. 172.

[28] Reclam, p. 229; Kemp Smith, p. 264—original wording identical in both 1st and 2nd editions.

[29] Reclam, p. 126; Kemp Smith, p. 140.

[30] 'But if we consider that what we call nature is nothing but an aggregate of phenomena, and not a thing in itself', we need no longer be surprised at the idea 'that nature should conform to our subjective ground of apperception'. Thus the impression of something 'very strange and absurd' about this idea is dispelled. (*Ibid.*)

concealed. The categories of the understanding so conceived have less to do with the 'understanding' than with the postulate of a spontaneously creative 'reason' ('*Vernunft*'). These ideas are to be found in the *Analytic*, but they are most at home in the *Dialectic*. Rightly understood the categories 'prescribe' nothing, they are purely and simply presupposed. They are presuppositions, not prescriptions.

6. Logically Necessary Fundamental Presuppositions

The preceding part of this chapter has taken the form of a progressive differentiation of the concept of presupposition from other concepts which are akin or at least apparently akin to it. This negative differentiation has been undertaken for a positive purpose, namely in order to bring out the real significance of the distinctively philosophical concept of presupposition. We have proceeded by the method of exclusion or elimination. Step by step one after another of the concepts which commonly enter into the discussion of presuppositions has been dismissed. But important as this elimination is, it is only preparatory to a positive definition. Not that positive definition has been wholly lacking in what has been done so far; for through its progressive confrontation with divergent concepts the philosophical concept of presupposition has taken concrete shape. Each differentiation and each negation has been accompanied by a positive statement of what the term 'presupposition' means in a philosophical context. Its positive significance has perhaps been made all the more clear by being set at every point against the background of contrasting ideas. All that now remains to be done is to draw the scattered elements together and present them in their essential unity. To sum it up in a concise formula we might say that it is the task of philosophy to give an analysis of *logically necessary fundamental presuppositions*. This really says everything that is essential—provided we remember that everything it says is essential, every word of this formula is of decisive importance.

(1) The approach of scientific philosophy to presuppositions is *analytical*. It starts with the concrete material present in everyday life, the sciences and other activities, which it does not occur to anyone to doubt or deny. It works with the propositions in which this finds expression, and with which we reckon as a matter of course in all other contexts than the 'philosophical' (metaphysical). On this material it bases its analysis, the purpose of which is to lay bare the presuppositions which, whether we are conscious of them or not, are in fact implied in it, and which we cannot possibly avoid accepting if we are to maintain the propositions which we do not for a moment hesitate to state. Indeed we can go further and say that what philosophy has to do is to exhibit the presuppositions which, whether we affirm or deny their legitimacy, alone are able to give *meaning* to our statements. What these presuppositions are can be made clear only by painstaking analysis.

This attitude of scientific philosophy to presuppositions is the direct opposite of that of metaphysics, which is characterized by the fact that it does not really analyze but rather *posits* presuppositions of its own choosing, and lets these determine the meaning of the propositions derived from them.

(2) The presuppositions of scientific philosophy are *necessary* presuppositions—in contrast to every kind of prejudice and also to metaphysics, which arbitrarily selects its presuppositions. By its necessity the philosophical presupposition is distinguished also from both the axiom and the hypothesis. An axiom is a selected starting point; and it is not difficult to conceive of a different axiom or set of axioms, from which different conclusions logically follow. A hypothesis is a tentative theory put forward in order to explain given phenomena, and therefore capable also of being refuted by experience. In contrast to these, philosophical presuppositions are obtained by analysis of what is given in experience, and they are of such a nature that without them experience itself would not exist, would not be possible. It is on this fact that their necessity is based.

(3) The necessity that characterizes the presuppositions of scientific philosophy is a *logical* necessity. That is to say, it is not a question of psychological necessity or compulsion, as if it meant that, circumstances being as they are, I *cannot* think otherwise than I do. Such psychological limitations undoubtedly exist, but they have nothing to do with philosophical presuppositions. As we have already pointed out: 'Logical implication must not be confused with a psychological act of thought.'[31] But neither is it a question of ontological necessity. It has to do with a necessity of thought, but of the purely logical kind that finds expression in the idea of 'implication'. If I have affirmed a proposition, I cannot *logically* at the same time deny something which that proposition implies; I *must* affirm all its logical presuppositions. Psychologically there is no compulsion; I can after all contradict myself—and is not that often just what happens? But it is otherwise from a logical point of view. Here I must affirm the presuppositions, for I *have* already affirmed them by asserting the proposition. They are implicit in my own assertion. The task of philosophy is to draw out what is implicit and make it explicit.[32] Philosophical necessity is the necessity of logical implication.

(4) Scientific philosophy is concerned with *ultimate presuppositions, fundamental presuppositions*. Every proposition we state includes a host of presuppositions, many of them of an empirical nature. With these latter philosophy has nothing to do; they are not within its sphere of competence. What it is concerned with are the presuppositions which in the strictest sense are *ultimate*, since they underlie not only certain particular propositions but all our reasoning and argumentation. These propositions can be

[31] Above, p. 197.
[32] *Cf.* above, pp. 198f.

described as 'creative' (although this is an essentially questionable use of that term) in the sense that they contribute to the shaping of our whole way of arguing, our way of speaking and thinking. In this sense they are truly 'creative of meaning' or preferably 'determinative of meaning', since without them there would be no meaning at all in our propositions. Indeed without them there would be no propositions, for propositions claim to express something meaningful. Let that go and they go with it.

(5) All the points listed here lend support to one another. At the same time they can be said to counterbalance one another and prevent false or one-sided conclusions being drawn from any one of them. Taken together they furnish the philosophical analysis of presuppositions with a quite definite content, and this is the next thing we must discuss. From what has already been said, the ambiguous term 'presupposition' has acquired the preliminary definiteness and concretion that is necessary for our continued investigation.

One further comment. Fundamental presuppositions are such that they can be said to be 'self-evident'. But there are different kinds of 'self-evident presuppositions', located so to speak on different levels. There are the fundamental categorical presuppositions, and there are presuppositions which, being regarded as self-evident, set their mark on whole complexes of meaning and colour the outlook of entire epochs. Now inasmuch as it is the business of philosophy to analyze *meaning*, and to carry the analysis through to the very end, the question might be asked whether philosophy can wholly neglect this latter kind of self-evident presuppositions, seeing that they too—though in another way than the categories—are determinative of meaning. It is impossible to get to the bottom of the question of meaning without taking account of both sorts of self-evident presuppositions. In reply to this, however, it must be firmly maintained that the specific task of philosophy is to clarify the categorical presuppositions. At the same time philosophy needs to be aware that it cannot by itself give the final answer to the question of the meaning of propositions, but must be open to contributions from other sources which put the question of meaning more from the point of view of content. In order to clarify the distinction between these two sorts of 'self-evident presuppositions' and the different ways in which they appear as 'self-evident' we need to distinguish between 'categories' and 'fundamental motifs'. But that is another chapter, to which we shall come later. For the present the main thing is to get it quite clear that the specific and essential function of philosophy is and remains the analysis of the utimate presuppositions, or what we might call the categorical task.

CHAPTER VIII

Logical Analysis of Presuppositions

1. The Analysis of Presuppositions as a Critical Method

THE foregoing discussion has brought us several stages nearer an answer to the question of the possibility of scientific philosophy. But there are still a few essential questions that have not yet received definitive treatment. In particular there are the two questions concerning the method of scientific philosophy and how that method provides the possibility of strictly objective argumentation in philosophy. Although both of these questions have been touched upon again and again, they have not yet been finally answered. What we must do now, therefore, is to give first a definite, concrete picture of the way in which philosophy sets about analyzing presuppositions, and the methodological resources available to it for that purpose, and then secondly to show just as definitely and concretely that thanks to its methodology philosophy has a possibility of objective argumentation which in stringency is second to none among the sciences. Only when these two things are demonstrated have we the right to speak of philosophy as in the strict sense 'scientific'.

It can be seen at once how crucial the point we have now reached is. It is the point to which the whole of our preceding discussion was meant to lead. That is why we drew the sharp distinction between metaphysics and scientific philosophy. That is why we went into such detail regarding the different forms of scientific argumentation, in our search for a starting point and criterion by which to judge the scientific character of philosophy. That is why we examined the possibility of philosophy as analysis of meaning, and why we distinguished between verification and justification on the one hand and validation on the other, in an endeavour to demonstrate the independence and uniqueness of philosophical argumentation. And that is why, finally, we put the concept of 'presupposition' through a rather detailed analysis.[1]

[1] In other words, we start here with the conclusions thus far reached, particularly in Chap. IV, § 4, 'Philosophical Argumentation?'—note the question mark as a reminder that the discussion there was still hypothetical and provisional—and then in Chap. V, § 5, which was concerned precisely with 'Analysis of Presuppositions', and Chap. VI, § 5, where philosophical argumentation as 'validation' was distinguished from axiomatic and empirical argumentation. Although we were still unable to give a definitive account of the method of philosophy, its way of doing things had become clear enough for us to regard its scientific character as relatively assured, so that the question mark noted above could be dropped. It is this line of argument that must now be completed. By looking back we have seen what has been done and what remains to be done. What

We come now therefore to the question of the *method* of scientific philosophy. From our preceding discussion it is at least clear that this must be a specifically philosophical method. Neither of the otherwise available forms of scientific argumentation—the axiomatic and the empirical—can do what is necessary here. Neither of them can provide an answer to the philosophical question concerning ultimate presuppositions and their validity. There is need for a third way—the way the 'critical philosophy' (Kant) discovered. The latter was basically an attempt to procure a clear methodology for the 'logical analysis of presuppositions', and although it only very imperfectly fulfilled this aim, it can none the less rightly be regarded as a precursor of the analysis of presuppositions. A great deal remains of course to be done as regards mapping out this third way and making it generally serviceable, but just for that reason it is instructive to begin by lingering a little over some basic problems from this prehistory of presuppositional analysis There are three such problems in particular that draw our attention: 1. philosophy as *critical* philosophy versus dogmatism and scepticism; 2. the question of 'synthetic judgments *a priori*'; and 3. the question of the transcendental deduction.

(1) If there is any one thing that is in all circumstances characteristic of scientific philosophy, it is its *critical* attitude. This is something that all science has in common, but in the area of philosophy it assumes a quite special importance. Science is not a conglomeration of arbitrary opinions, but insight based on painstaking critical inquiry. Philosophy has to adopt a similar critical stance towards its object, the most general presuppositions. Its business is the critical examination of presuppositions. But this means that philosophy is closely and in a special way linked to the sciences, since among other things it has to examine the presuppositions which the sciences make but do not themselves examine because they are not within their objective province.

It was an entirely sound move when Kant called for a *critical* philosophy, and did so in opposition to both dogmatism and scepticism of any and every kind. As far as dogmatism is concerned, we have already considered it sufficiently in connection with metaphysics and we need not spend much time on it here; it is more important to distinguish critical philosophy from scepticism. It is through dogmatism that metaphysics comes to grief. Its error lies in its credulous acceptance and arbitrary promulgation of principles and maxims for which it has no grounds. It is against this that scepticism with some justice protests. It refuses to accept anything for which absolutely certain grounds cannot be given. And since

---

remains is above all to show concretely what *method* philosophy must employ in order to demonstrate the nature and inevitability of the presuppositions with which it is concerned. It further remains to show the importance of this for the stringency of objective argumentation. With this the task immediately facing us is exactly defined.

it is impossible to 'prove' the ultimate presuppositions which underlie all knowledge, it does not see that it has any alternative but to dispute all claims to knowledge.

Now to adopt a sceptical attitude towards knowledge in general may at first sight appear very prudent and indicative of a 'critical' temper. It means a refusal to take any step without first feeling solid ground under one's feet. But where in the realm of knowledge is one to find this solid ground? What judgment, what 'knowledge' is there that cannot be exposed to criticism and doubt? On closer inspection, however, it appears that scepticism as a philosophical theory suffers from an inner contradiction which shows it to be untenable. The starting point may be right enough: there is no single item of knowledge, no single judgment, which is beyond the possibility of doubt. But to conclude from this that all knowledge and all judgment whatsoever ought to be doubted and disputed is completely false. The sciences are constantly engaged in revising earlier views and weeding out such 'knowledge' as has shown itself untenable. But from this they do not draw the sceptical conclusion that there is no knowledge, or that all we call 'knowledge' is equally groundless and false. To do that would be to renounce all scientific work. Any form of inquiry would be meaningless. Scepticism has not grasped the problem of presuppositions, which can be expressed very briefly thus: There are ultimate presuppositions which can be neither 'proved' nor questioned, and they cannot be questioned for the simple reason that in the very questioning of them we make use of them; that is to say, we depend upon the very thing we call in question.

This is the dilemma of scepticism: it affirms what it denies, and affirms it precisely in denying it. Here the inner contradiction of scepticism can be seen, which has the effect of making it less radical than it imagines itself to be. Strictly speaking, scepticism is just as dogmatic as dogmatism, though in a negative way. To doubt or deny particular judgments or some particular 'knowledge' is entirely in order, but when scepticism concludes from this that no knowledge is possible at all, it involves itself in contradiction and meaninglessness. Absolute scepticism is a theory that cannot be put into practice, a theory that undermines its own presuppositions or is undermined by them. In general, however, the result is not as tragic as might be feared. The sciences go on their way, undisturbed by the idea that any kind of knowledge is impossible, and even the sceptic himself sits securely on the branch he imagines he is sawing off. In terms of this metaphor we could say that critical philosophy is interested in discovering what sort of branch it is on which a person can sit securely even while he thinks he is sawing it off. Or in plainer terms, critical philosophy wants to know what the presuppositions are of which we make use even while we deny them, and which by that very fact are most clearly shown to be necessary and inevitable.

In short, scepticism is no real antithesis to dogmatism, but a negative variant of it. It is therefore essentially wrong to set dogmatism, scepticism and critical philosophy side by side as three different schools of philosophical thought. What they represent is not at all different outlooks, schools and doctrines, but different attitudes of mind. And of these there are only two: the attitude of dogmatism, including its variant, scepticism, and the critical attitude which is the antithesis of both dogmatism and scepticism. What both of these variants lack is a spirit of critical examination. It should be noted that in every case the issue is that of presuppositions. Even dogmatism has to do with presuppositions—ultimate, basic presuppositions. But what it does with them is to postulate certain presuppositions on subjective, arbitrary grounds, and employ them as axioms from which it derives its structure of thought, which is consequently of the same arbitrary character as the presuppositions. It is against this that scientific philosophy with its critical attitude takes its stand, demanding a critical examination of presuppositions. Its concern with presuppositions is thus directly opposite to that of dogmatism, and also to that of scepticism, which rejects presuppositions without examining them.

To describe philosophy as 'critical' and thus give it a central place among the sciences, does not mean that it should intervene in the discussions going on in the individual sciences, and set itself up as a critical arbiter between differing scientific views. It is 'critical' in that it lays bare the presuppositions which are *in fact*—though more or less unconsciously —taken for granted in the various sciences and quite generally in different areas of human experience. Above all, its critical character means that it is self-critical and does not imagine itself capable of freely setting up presuppositions to which others must conform. It draws out and analyzes presuppositions which are in fact present in different areas, and so far is it from desiring to impose any presuppositions of its own that it is rather one of its chief aims to show what presuppositions are proper to each area, and how they impart to it its distinctive character.

(2) Philosophy cannot operate on either purely axiomatic or purely empirical lines, but must seek a third way of its own. An expressive description of this third way is contained in Kant's question: 'How are synthetic judgments *a priori* possible?' Rightly understood this expression says something essential about the task of scientific philosophy. There was a time when the formula 'synthetic judgments *a priori*' was the object of violent criticism, and it was quite generally held to be self-contradictory and to amount to nothing but empty verbiage. The question must be asked, however, whether the critics have not completely missed the point of the formula. Behind their criticism, as we have shown above,[2] there lies the dubious equation of the terms '*a priori*' and 'analytical'. Once this equation is accepted, there is no longer any meaning in asking about the possibility

[2] *Cf.* above, pp. 184f.

212

of 'synthetic judgments *a priori*'. A simple, arbitrary definition by equation is thus the means of dismissing a significant problem, namely, *whether all basic presuppositions are really mere tautologies*? A whole series of pre-suppositions relating to the philosophy of science and philosophy in general is by this means explained away.

The mistake made here is the common one of starting with an in-complete disjunction and regarding it as self-evidently complete. Kant was more perceptive at this point. Besides the axiomatic-tautological pre-suppositions there is also the philosophically more important and more basic group of presuppositions, the necessity of which is grounded in their nature as conditions of experience. In order therefore to demonstrate their validity and inevitability we must start with what is given in experience; not, however, treating it as a matter of induction based on empirical observations—which never yields any necessity—but simply as a matter of logical consistency, although in this case the logic moves in a direction precisely opposite to that of axiomatic argumentation. The term '*a priori*' intimates that what is involved is a *pre*supposition, while 'synthetic' inti-mates that it is not an analytic-axiomatic presupposition but one which is in a quite different way directly bound up with experience, and which cannot possibly retain its meaning and content if it is detached from this relation to experience.

The importance of Kant lies in the fact that he was the first to perceive this distinctive character of the philosophical presupposition, and that he understood it far more profoundly than later thinkers who have often handled the subject of 'synthetic judgments *a priori*' without ever per-ceiving what the problem is that underlies it. It must however be remem-bered that at a number of points Kant drew questionable conclusions from this formula, several of which we have already had occasion to point out and reject. It is sufficient here to recall his idea that the understanding by means of its presuppositions 'prescribes laws for nature'. There is need to beware of the misinterpretation of 'synthetic judgments *a priori*' which undoubtedly exists in Kant, both in an ontological and a psychological direction. But this cannot obscure the fact that the discovery was Kant's, and that a thorough study of the problem as it appears in him can best help us to get to grips with the philosophical problem of categorical presup-positions.

(3) If by asking 'how synthetic judgments *a priori* are possible' Kant can be said to have shown where the problem of scientific philosophy really lies, something similar is true also of his endeavour to develop a special method for the solution of this problem, namely *the transcendental deduc-tion*. The actual term 'transcendental deduction' no doubt sounds strange and perhaps impressively abstruse, but the thing it stands for is very simple and easily understandable. And so indeed it should be, like all the basic scientific methods and modes of argumentation. Behind axiomatic

argumentation is the simple idea that certain conclusions can be drawn by logical necessity from the axiom, and that these in turn derive their justification from the fact that they can be traced back to the axiom. Behind empirical argumentation is the simple idea that empirical statements are tested by the way in which they relate to observations made in experience, and that the more general of such statements can be tested by confronting conclusions drawn from them with observations made, the result of this testing being their verification or falsification.

In a similar way there is behind philosophical ('transcendental') argumentation the simple idea that if anything is to be regarded as a basic presupposition it must be possible to legitimate it as such by showing that some form of 'experience' which no one doubts implies it as its necessary presupposition. The starting point of philosophical analysis is thus 'experience'—and hence the 'synthetic' aspect of philosophical argumentation. And the aim of the analysis is to show that this experience would not be possible if the presuppositions implied in it were not accepted—hence the 'a priori' (and analytic) aspect of the argumentation. To demonstrate that the presuppositions in question are in that sense conditions of experience is at the same time to legitimate them as basic presuppositions. That is how they receive their 'validation'. It is this line of thought that we find in Kant in the classical formulation: 'The transcendental deduction of all a priori conceptions must therefore be guided by the principle, that these concepts must be the a priori conditions of the possibility of experience. Concepts which supply the objective ground of the possibility of experience are for that very reason necessary.'[3]

Objection has sometimes been taken to the description of this mode of argumentation as 'deduction', on the ground that there can be no room for deduction in philosophy as long as we are determined to steer clear of metaphysics. This objection arises, however, from a mistaken habit of thought in connection with the contraposition of deduction and induction. There is of course a deductive metaphysics, but it has nothing in common with the deductive procedure of critical philosophy beyond the name of 'deduction'. The deduction practised by metaphysics is a matter of regular axiomatic inference that starts from arbitrarily chosen presuppositions (axioms). The transcendental deduction, however, takes the opposite course and examines the presuppositions with regard to their significance for 'the possibility of experience'. Yet although 'experience' and 'the possibility of experience' are the starting point, and the aim is to work backwards from this to the necessary presuppositions contained in it, what we have here is still a deductive procedure despite the fact that it moves in the opposite direction to that of axiomatic inference. There the movement

[3] Kant, *Critique of Pure Reason*, Reclam, p. 110, Kemp Smith, p. 126 (same wording in both editions of the *Critique*). *Cf.* on this my analysis of Kant's idea of the transcendental deduction in RAP pp. 206–15, or (in shorter form) GRE pp. 53–8.

is from presuppositions to propositions, here from propositions back to their presuppositions.

So far from being an embarrassment to critical-philosophical argumentation, the term 'deduction' is the only correct description of its procedure.[4] The difficulty with the formula 'transcendental deduction' does not lie in the term 'deduction' but in the very ambiguous term 'transcendental', which is really extremely liable to conjure up false metaphysical associations. When post-Kantian philosophy strayed from the path of critical philosophy and reverted to metaphysics, it became known as 'transcendental philosophy'. That alone is reason enough for avoiding the expression 'transcendental deduction'. If we use it at all, it must in any event be made clear that nothing else is intended by it but the 'logical analysis of presuppositions'.

2. Conceptual Analysis and the Logical Analysis of Presuppositions

The task of scientific philosophy is to investigate and critically examine the basic presuppositions which we consciously or unconsciously make in the various sciences and indeed in all experience, testing them with regard to their legitimacy and validity; that is to say, it is what we have called 'validation'. But then the question arises: Is this a possible undertaking? What means has philosophy available for carrying it out? This question too has kept appearing in a variety of contexts in the preceding discussion, and a good deal of the material needed for a positive answer to it has been assembled. Nothing more is now required than a final summing up and formal clarification of the problem of philosophical method. For all the evidence supports the view that philosophy does in fact possess a method of its own, specially suited to its task and fully in accord with scientific standards. Our present purpose is to make it still more clear that this really is the case, and that philosophy is thus equipped with the methodological tools that enable it to test the most general fundamental concepts, the ultimate principles or basic presuppositions, with regard to their validity.

The method of philosophy is in this respect twofold: 1. *the analysis of concepts* and 2. *the logical analysis of presuppositions*.

(1) To the extent that all science can be said to aim at conceptualization, that is, at defining in clear, non-contradictory terms what is given more obscurely in immediate consciousness, the analysis of concepts is plainly present in every scientific inquiry. Yet it is only when the investigation

---

[4] It might seem tempting to describe the logical analysis of presuppositions (the 'transcendental deduction') as a combination of axiomatic and empirical argumentation. But that is not so much characteristic of it as of certain empirical sciences, in which such a combination of methods plays a big part; *cf.* above, pp. 114ff. Presuppositional analysis does not start from particular empirical observations, but from the concept of experience, 'the possibility of experience'. From this point of view it can be said that the analysis of presuppositions remains permanently within the conceptual sphere.

reaches back to the most general fundamental concepts that the need seriously arises to develop conceptual analysis as an independent method. With regard to the more empirical concepts this need is not so much felt, since owing to their intuitive character they are not as a rule in danger of metaphysical misinterpretation. When however we leave concrete ideas behind and mount up into the realm of abstraction, the capacity for critical judgment often vanishes in the rarified atmosphere. In the concreteness of life things press so hard against one another that the contradictions in which we involve ourselves are easily enough discovered. In abstract thinking on the other hand, contradictory ideas are able to lie quite peacefully side by side. It is astonishing what contradictions can pass unnoticed in a theory. But it is obviously necessary that fundamental concepts should be free from contradiction.

When philosophy approaches these fundamental concepts, a simple conceptual analysis is often sufficient to disclose that the usual metaphysical attempts to establish them as 'fundamental concepts' are abortive. They do not satisfy even the most elementary requirement of a concept—that it should not involve any contradiction. If we analyze such alleged concepts and exhibit their constituent elements separately, we shall generally find that these cancel each other out, so that there is really no concept at all. What looks like and claims to be a unitary concept is really nothing but an agglomeration of ideas, of which the various components taken together make no unified sense. That such confused and contradictory agglomerations of ideas cannot be recognized as inescapable presuppositions of experience or as fundamental principles of scientific knowledge, needs no special demonstration.

The method of conceptual analysis can thus assist us in the philosophical examination of alleged principles and fundamental concepts, at least as regards the negative task of exposing their claims as unjustified and showing that they represent nothing that is or can be conceived, in which case no real concept, much less any fundamental concept, exists. Naturally conceptual analysis can also lead to a positive result, namely that the ideas contained in the concept under examination do when taken together yield a unitary meaning. But even when that is so, it does not yet tell us that we are in the presence of a *fundamental* concept. Conceptual analysis can at most show that the concept is free from contradiction, not that it is a fundamental concept or a basic presupposition. At this point the second method, the logical analysis of presuppositions, comes in to complete the inquiry.

(2) The importance of the *logical analysis of presuppositions* and the difference between it and ordinary conceptual analysis can be most simply illustrated by an example. If we ask a natural scientist what causality means, we may perhaps receive an answer which on closer inspection is seen to contain a contradiction and therefore to be untenable. But the

question of causality is not answered by showing this to be so. All that is clear is that causality *conceived in this way* cannot be maintained. Nothing is even settled with regard to the way in which the said natural scientist himself employs the principle of causality. For even if the conscious *idea* he has formed of what causality means is vitiated by a contradiction, yet the *use* he makes of the principle of causality in his scientific work may be completely unobjectionable. Theories about the meaning of causality vary, but there is essential agreement as regards the application of the principle of causality.

Now the logical analysis of presuppositions is not concerned with the negative task of detecting and refuting false ideas about principles or ultimate presuppositions, but with the positive task of seeking to establish valid principles. It therefore takes for its starting point, not the existing ideas about these, which are questionable, but the application or *use* of them which is recognized as valid, and from this it seeks to work back to what is presupposed by it. Hence the question it asks—to continue with the category of causality—is not: what is causality actually conceived to be? For that as a rule is quite uncertain. Instead it asks: what logical presuppositions are involved in the use which the sciences actually make of the principle of causality?[5] What does one consciously or unconsciously presuppose every time one makes a causal judgment or undertakes an experiment?[6]

[5] The line of thought developed above—that what matters in philosophy is not so much the conscious ideas anyone has formed with regard to the meaning and content of the basic concepts or presuppositions, but rather the *use* that is made of them—is one of the most prevalent in contemporary philosophy. We recall Wittgenstein's emphatic insistence on 'the use', and the constantly reiterated slogan: 'Don't ask for the meaning, ask for the use.' On similar lines we have Einstein's dictum: 'If you want to learn from the theoretical physicists something of the methods they employ, I advise you to stick to one principle: Don't listen to what they say, pay attention to what they do.'

It should perhaps be mentioned that what is said above in the text regarding the importance of 'the use' for getting back to the presuppositions is taken directly, as is the whole section in which it occurs (Ch. VIII, §2), from my essay on the possibility of scientific philosophy ('Hur är filosofi som vetenskap möjlig?') written in 1928. This is one of the plainest indications that there is a marked trend in recent philosophy towards the position maintained here. It is also evidence of the affinity of contemporary philosophy with the 'logical analysis of presuppositions', to which attention has already been drawn (above, pp. 163ff.). See further pp. 261ff. below, where the formula 'Don't ask for the meaning, ask for the use' is specifically analyzed.

[6] It has rightly been pointed out as a weakness of Kant's 'transcendental deduction' that it starts with Kant's implicit faith in Newtonian physics as representing the last word of science. As modern natural science has to a large extent turned in other directions (quantum mechanics, theory of relativity, etc.), the concept of causality has come to be seen in a new light, and the question has arisen whether this concept can any longer be used as an example of a category or basic presupposition. We have been able to use it as an example, however, because what matters is not the ideas which Kant or anyone else may have formed about it, but the *use* that is made of it in the context of science. Even in the new situation the natural scientist does not refrain from making

Presuppositional analysis differs from conceptual analysis in two respects. It does not start like the latter with an existing concept or given idea in order to test its tenability, but with a *use*, a scientific procedure, from which it seeks to get back to its logical presuppositions. Only by this means can a fundamental concept be discovered. Furthermore, it is characteristic of presuppositional analysis that its starting point must be something generally accepted, something of which the validity is not in doubt. For nothing else can serve as a basis on which to demonstrate the validity of principles.

With this our question how philosophy as a science is possible has been answered. Philosophy is the science of first principles. Its task is to examine critically the ultimate presuppositions or first principles of experience, and for this purpose it has at its disposal two strictly scientific, objective tools: conceptual analysis and the logical analysis of presuppositions. The former makes it possible for philosophy to expose false basic concepts and principles as nothing but contradictory agglomerations of ideas and meaningless verbiage. By means of the logical analysis of presuppositions philosophy works its way from given experience to its logical presuppositions. Only that which can be shown to be such a presupposition is recognized by it as a philosophical principle or category. With this therefore the possibility is given of a scientific investigation of principles. We are no longer at the mercy of metaphysics with its arbitrary, dogmatic proclamation of principles, but we possess a critical standard by which to test them. The principles do not hang in the air above experience, but are anchored in experience, being inherent in every empirical judgment as necessary presuppositions and categories. But this means that they are principles of a quite different sort from those of metaphysics. The position is not that some metaphysical principles pass, while others fail, the test of presuppositional analysis. The whole metaphysical way of thinking about principles is rejected from start to finish, and its place is taken by 'principles' of a quite different kind, namely categories and presuppositions that are conditions of experience.

This means of course also that the relation to experience is other than that of inductive metaphysics. When presuppositional analysis starts with given experience in its quest for first principles, its mode of procedure has nothing to do with induction. Induction is synthetic, the logical analysis of presuppositions analytic—as its name indicates. Inductive metaphysics looks for the principle in a *forward* direction, at the point where in its view

experiments. The philosopher's question is simply: What presuppositions has he made in doing so? What suppositions are implied as necessary presuppositions for the experiment? Here it may be that our traditional conceptions of the meaning of causality must be more or less completely reformulated. But this does not do away with the presuppositions of the experiment, and the need to subject these to a philosophical analysis of presuppositions.

218

the *results* of the special sciences converge; the logical analysis of pre-suppositions seeks the principle in a *backward* direction, as the *presupposition* of experience. If induction requires as extensive a material as possible to work on in order to be sure of its conclusions, presuppositional analysis finds a single empirical judgment in principle sufficient. For that which is a logical presupposition of all experience must clearly be capable of being shown to be inherent in every particular judgment. Indeed we can go further and say that for presuppositional analysis the starting point need not even be a definite datum of experience, but it is quite enough to have 'the possibility of experience', the concept of experience.

3. The Possibility of Objective Argumentation in Philosophy

It is now easy to see how extraordinarily important the logical analysis of presuppositions is for the question of the possibility of philosophy as a science. We can only speak of science where there is a possibility of objective argumentation. As regards the object of philosophy—ultimate presuppositions—there used to be no basis for such argumentation. Every dogmatic metaphysical outlook set up its own principles, and assertion stood against assertion with no possibility of objective argumentation because there was no common approach to the problem. Then in due course the transcendental method came in, and now the logical analysis of presuppositions follows with its thesis that: Nothing can be validly regarded as a philosophical principle or ultimate presupposition unless it can be shown that experience and validity as such are impossible without its being presupposed. With this the different conceptions of the principles are subsumed under a common perspective, and they can press their arguments against one another on a common basis. There is no longer any need for assertion to stand against assertion. Anyone who wishes to affirm something as a principle or ultimate presupposition must demonstrate by means of presuppositional analysis that experience and validity can exist only if this presupposition is acknowledged. The opponent of a principle, on the other hand, must try to show how experience can exist and validity be maintained even without accepting this principle as valid.

What primarily interests us here, however, is the method of proof itself, that is, the possibility of some kind of objective argumentation with regard to ultimate presuppositions, which will put philosophy on the same level as the rest of the argumentative sciences. It used always to be the weakness of philosophy that it lacked the possibility of giving grounds for the principles it proclaimed. In other sciences it is not enough simply to postulate and assert. We demand reasons for the assertion, we seek to test the strength of these reasons, and if they do not pass the test the assertion is rejected as groundless. It may of course be a correct assertion, but as long as no adequate reason for it is produced it cannot be put forward as a scientific judgment. A judgment arrived at by another route than that of science *can* be true, for after all one may have guessed right. On the other hand, a judgment arrived at according to all the rules of science *can* be false—there may for example have been a defect in the scientific apparatus or the scientific conceptualization, which in the present state of science cannot be detected. What determines whether a judgment should be described as scientific are the grounds that support it, the argumentation that leads up to it.

With this the definitive line is drawn between metaphysical and scientific philosophy. Metaphysics cannot produce any argumentation, certainly not any objective argumentation, for the ultimate principles and axioms on which it builds. An axiom neither can nor should be proved. Relying on this, metaphysics relinquishes all claim to objective argumentation. Starting with its arbitrarily chosen axioms it constructs an axiomatic system which may well be logically consistent, but which is in every way vulnerable because it rests on an insecure, untested, arbitrary foundation. Scientific philosophy makes it its business to *test*, not these axioms, for they are essentially untestable, but the ultimate presuppositions of experience; and as presuppositions these are not only essentially testable, but they are actually established by having their relation to experience tested and their necessity to it demonstrated.

4. The Logical Structure of Presuppositional Analysis

In view of the central importance of the subject it will not be out of place to give a little more attention to the logical structure of the philosophical analysis of presuppositions. One statement in particular which we have made about it requires further explanation. When we said that the procedure of presuppositional analysis is 'deductive' but that it moves 'in the opposite direction' to what is usual in deduction,[7] this statement may have seemed vague and imprecise. In order to see more clearly what it means, we should look at the matter in terms of two ideas familiar to us from logic, namely that of 'implication' and that of the distinction between 'necessary and sufficient conditions'. Taken together these two really say all that is needed to clarify the logical structure of the philosophical analysis of presuppositions.

(1) The idea of *implication* is one that immediately comes to mind when one seeks to determine the logical structure of presuppositional analysis. In the preceding discussion it has made a place for itself automatically, so to speak, and that with very good reason. It is simply not possible to speak of presuppositional analysis without speaking of implication, for in both cases we are dealing essentially with one and the same thing. 'Presupposition' and 'implication' are both relational terms. They point to the relation between a proposition and what it logically presupposes, the relation

---

[7] Above, p. 214.

between a proposition and a presupposition, an implying proposition and an implied presupposition.

Now the idea of implication can be used in different senses, and a distinction is commonly made between 'material implication' and 'strict implication'.[8] In the philosophical analysis of presuppositions it is exclusively with 'strict implication' that we are concerned. This is what gives presuppositional analysis its 'deductive' character. Just as deduction can never yield any new content, but only gives us in explicit form what is already implicit in the proposition we analyze, the same is true with regard to logical presuppositions—a fact which also finds expression in the old designation 'transcendental *deduction*'.

In spite of the rather complicated nature of the expressions 'logical analysis of presuppositions' and—still more—'transcendental deduction', the idea behind them is from a logical point of view very simple and elementary. It is simply an attempt to discover what is logically implied in an empirical proposition which no one denies. What do I necessarily have in mind when I form a judgment? Or, if I do not have it consciously in mind, what do I implicitly acknowledge? What is there so inseparably bound up with the judgment that if I denied it I should have to abandon the proposition in which the judgment is expressed? To this we need only add that 'a proposition which no one denies' does not mean here some particular proposition that is accepted by everybody; for that would no doubt be difficult to find. The point is rather that in forming any judgment whatsoever we make certain logical assumptions or employ certain logical presuppositions, and that by constantly expressing judgments everyone constantly bears renewed testimony to the validity of the presuppositions implied in them. 'A proposition which no one denies' is thus to be understood in a completely general sense, with reference to the fact that just as we cannot totally abstain from making any judgments at all, so neither can we avoid accepting the presuppositions implied in the very act of making them. It is therefore on the same lines as the idea of a 'condition of the possibility of experience', and it can serve as an interpretation of that phrase. In neither case is there any question of an ontological-metaphysical attribute, but in both cases it is a matter of logical consequence, logical implication. It has to do with the relation between propositions and their presuppositions, or between 'experience' and its logical conditions.

But if the philosophical analysis of presuppositions has to do exclusively with this matter of implication, and is accordingly of a purely *deductive* character—even though its starting point is empirical propositions—it

---

[8] On this distinction see Lewis and Langford, *Symbolic Logic*, pp, 123f. and *passim*. *Cf.* A. Tarsky, *Introduction to Logic*.—With regard to this subject I have profited from extensive discussion with Dr Urban Forell on the basis of his unpublished dissertation concerning the ambiguity of the term 'presuppositions' and also his work on the twin terms 'analytic—synthetic'.

must at the same time be said that it is a deduction *of a very unusual kind*. Ordinarily when we speak of deduction we are accustomed to think of the way in which axioms imply theorems, so that the latter can be inferred or deduced from the former thanks to the strict implication which here exists. Since by means of this logical operation we acquire no new knowledge, but only a different version of something already predicated, the word 'tautology' has rightly been used in this connection. New and wider knowledge can only be obtained by turning to experience. Deduction however, never goes beyond the bounds of the logical-tautological.

What we have just said about implication and tautology applies also to the logical analysis of presuppositions—with the important qualification that here we have a kind of implication and deduction that moves in a directly opposite direction to the usual one. The question here is not how particular propositions or theorems are implied in general axioms, but instead how general presuppositions are implied in particular empirical propositions. Presuppositional analysis has to do with the relation between our propositions and their presuppositions; and what the analysis or deduction seeks to do is to show that the propositions necessarily include certain presuppositions, and to indicate what these presuppositions are. But this results, or at least seems to result, in a rather awkward situation. In the one case the question is how the universal implies the particular, while in the other it is how the particular implies the universal; so that in both cases it is a question of implication and nothing but implication. Hence it may well be asked, which really is the one that implies the other? Is it the presuppositions that imply the propositions, or the propositions that imply the presuppositions? But the difficulty here is that we cannot without more ado say that it is either one or the other. The only right answer is that it is both, that there is a reciprocal relation between them. This answer, however, only increases the impression that we are faced with a paradox.

(2) A way out of this difficulty is provided, however, by the second of the two logical conceptions mentioned above, namely that of the distinction between *'necessary and sufficient conditions'*. If we reckon with this distinction, then all traces of paradox in the idea that propositions and presuppositions mutually condition one another disappear. For it becomes immediately clear that they presuppose one another in quite different senses, so that no more is claimed than that each points to the other and neither can be maintained without the other. It is impossible to maintain a proposition without at the same time maintaining the presupposition implied in it, and it is equally impossible to maintain a presupposition without recognizing that it is presupposition of something. To speak of a presupposition 'in itself' is meaningless, and it is so because 'presupposition' is a relative term, which loses its meaning if it is made absolute.

The logical relation between proposition and presupposition can be expressed simply thus: the presupposition which is implied in the proposition is the *necessary* condition for the proposition, while the proposition is the *sufficient* condition for the presupposition. Both parts of this statement are clearly illustrated in the foregoing discussion. That the presupposition is a necessary condition for the proposition is evident from the fact that the proposition cannot be maintained apart from recognition of the presupposition (necessarily) implied in it. That the proposition on the other hand is a sufficient condition for the presupposition is evident from the fact already pointed out, that a single proposition, or even the possibility of a proposition, is sufficient to show the necessity of the presupposition. The two are thus in a logical sense inseparably interlocked, though in such a way that while each is certainly a condition of the other, they are so—if the expression may be permitted—in directly opposite ways, as can be plainly seen from the following schema:

The presupposition is the *necessary but not sufficient condition* for the proposition.

The proposition is the *sufficient but not necessary condition* for the presupposition.

It is this two-sidedness of implication that underlies and makes possible the philosophical analysis of presuppositions. In the last resort the logical analysis of presuppositions is nothing else but the working out of what is involved in logical implication. From another point of view also it is of the utmost importance to keep clear the logical relation indicated here between the proposition which implies and the presupposition which is implied. For it has been the prevailing lack of clarity on this point that has given rise to the constantly recurring objection, primarily directed against the transcendental method but naturally affecting also every form of philosophical analysis of presuppositions, that its argument is circular.

5. Presuppositional Analysis, a Logical Circle?

It has long been objected to the transcendental method that it is guilty of logical circularity. The idea is that it first bases the validity of principles on the validity of experience and then proceeds to argue for the validity of experience on the ground that the principles thus shown to be valid are employed in it. A similar view can only too easily be taken of the logical analysis of presuppositions, and it is therefore necessary to take a look, if only very briefly, at this question.

If this criticism were directed against the traditional way of stating the epistemological problem, it would be justified. When it is regarded as the function of epistemology to demonstrate that there is anything valid at all, and when as a basis for this it appeals to certain principles that are 'valid in themselves', its procedure becomes a ceaseless oscillation between these principles and experience, which are held to be mutually supportive. Here it is entirely right to speak, as has been done, of an epistemological *petitio principii*. It should however be observed that the transcendental analysis, and still more the logical analysis of presuppositions, signifies a completely new start in the matter of epistemology. There is here no question whatever of trying to demonstrate that such a thing as validity exists. When the logical analysis of presuppositions, with its starting point in experience, has worked its way back to the presuppositions and principles of experience, its demonstration of these has in no way strengthened the validity of empirical knowledge. Nor is it necessary that it should do so. The special sciences do not need the support of philosophy in order to attain the rank of objective science. The significance of presuppositional analysis lies rather in the fact that it enables *philosophy* to attain—in Kant's phrase—'the sure progress of a science'.

The problem that prompts the methodological work of philosophy and leads to the method of presuppositional analysis, is not due to any lack of objectivity in the special sciences, but rather to the difficulty philosophy itself has had in attaining a similar objectivity in relation to its own subject, the question of presuppositions and principles. The logical analysis of presuppositions points the way by which philosophy too can attain such objectivity. It links philosophical investigation firmly with the special sciences and gives it precisely the same objectivity as belongs to the sciences whose presuppositions it clarifies.

From this it is also clear that presuppositional analysis has nothing to do with the idea of principles that are valid 'in themselves'. It is only in relation to experience that there is any meaning in speaking of presuppositions or principles; and to say that they are valid means simply that they are inherent in experience as its logical presuppositions. There can thus be no thought of any intrinsic validity of the principles '*an sich*'. With regard to the affinity which exists between presuppositional analysis and Kant's transcendentalism, it must be emphasized here that the vestiges of metaphysics which undoubtedly adhere to Kant's basic idea must be completely eradicated. When by means of the transcendental method Kant discovered the synthetic unity of apperception as 'the supreme principle of all understanding', this was and remained for him not merely a transcendental presupposition but also a principle in the old metaphysical sense of a self-validating principle from which all other validity is derived. Only if the logical analysis of presuppositions is consistently carried through, without any deviation in a metaphysical direction, can it in conjunction with the method of conceptual analysis provide philosophy with the possibility of attaining, without any surrender of its universal tendency and its character as a science of principles, 'the sure progress of a science'.

If we now add to all this what was said above about the distinction between 'necessary and sufficient conditions', it at once becomes clear that what possibly—through misunderstanding—underlies the notion of a logical circle here, namely the *reciprocity* that exists between a proposition drawn from experience and the presuppositions implied in it, has not the slightest connection with a logical circle. Such is the simple fact of the matter, and such the unfounded nature of the oft-repeated objection that all epistemological inquiry involves a *petitio principii*. If only we take note of what the logical analysis of presuppositions is intended to do, and if we also understand the significance of the distinction between 'necessary and sufficient conditions', then the charge of logical circularity automatically falls to the ground.[9]

[9] Writing from the standpoint of Friesian metaphysics, Leonard Nelson in a series of books (see Bibliography) delivers an increasingly sharp attack on epistemology in general and transcendental analysis in particular, seeking to show that both of them depend entirely on a logical circle. On this *cf.* my RAP, pp. 212f.: 'When L. Nelson seeks to refute the transcendental method, he proceeds on the false assumption that its purpose is to prove that there is any valid knowledge at all, and from this point of view it is not difficult for him to show that in fact it presupposes what it is meant to prove. But who says it is meant to prove this? Certainly not critical philosophy itself.'—Nelson's position has recently been subjected to critical examination from a somewhat different point of view by H. A. Schmidt in his essay, 'Der Beweisansatz von L. Nelson'. Schmidt seeks to show that Nelson's argument is indefensible, not least because it rests on a presupposition which 'for reasons of logical structure must be rejected'. 'With this . . . the conclusiveness of the argument by which the impossibility of epistemology was to have been demonstrated, disappears' (p. 234), and consequently the allegation that epistemology involves logical circularity also disappears (pp. 246f.).—on the whole subject *cf.* R. Ingarden, 'Uber die Gefahren einer Petitio Principio'.

CHAPTER IX

Meaning and Context

1. Meaning and Method

THE heading of this section, 'meaning and method', is the same as the title of our investigation as a whole. The reason for this is that the inquiry has now reached a turning point, a point both of arrival and departure, and hence a point where it is necessary to orient ourselves by taking a look both backwards and forwards.

The first stage of our investigation was concerned with the question of the function of philosophy. The attempt to answer that question was complicated by the fact that we find such different meanings attached to 'philosophy' that no single definition of its function can possibly cover them all. This difficulty was overcome by making a clear division between metaphysical and scientific philosophy. It was the function of the latter—scientific philosophy—that we had to determine. What then were we to understand by 'science', the concept on which we must base ourselves here? What is it that is characteristic of scientific argumentation in general? How does philosophy fit into this context, and what is its specific function? The answer to this question was that philosophy is analysis of meaning or analysis of validity.

This led to the second stage of the investigation and further questions. What possibility has philosophy of engaging in objective argumentation within its own province, the analysis of meaning? What method has it at its disposal for carrying out this task? In all sciences as in all experience there are certain general presuppositions which we do and must make because apart from them no science and no experience whatever would be possible. Without these presuppositions everything becomes meaningless. Hence we are led from the question of meaning to that of method. In seeking to elicit these universal, inescapable presuppositions, philosophy has to employ, besides the general analysis of concepts, a method particularly suited to its purpose, namely 'the logical analysis of basic presuppositions'. This analysis is just as objective in its argumentation, just as strict in its operation, and just as open to inspection and correction as any other scientific analysis.

With this we have in a certain respect reached a terminal point. The question of 'meaning' and 'method' has found a preliminary answer: philosophy is analysis of meaning and its method is the logical analysis of presuppositions. But this answer is still very preliminary. The relatively terminal point is also a turning point. We now turn back to the question of 'meaning'. For the concept of meaning still awaits further analysis, and what we have said about the method of philosophy opens up new possibilities of probing and defining it. Hence we must draw out the implications of our last chapter, of which the most important is that 'meaning and context' belong inseparably together. Without presuppositions, no meaning; but the presuppositions point to the fundamental importance of the context: *without context no meaning.*

At this point all the lines we have pursued thus far converge, and from this point all the lines we have yet to pursue branch out.

The question of the importance of the context for meaning is much more far-reaching than may at first sight appear. For not only does the meaning of a particular statement depend on the immediate context of which it is part, but this context itself derives its meaning from the total context of which it too is part. Hence the question of 'meaning and context' leads quite logically and by a certain necessity to that of the 'context of meaning', or rather, the various comprehensive 'contexts of meaning' each of which is characterized by its own basic presuppositions. For example, scientific investigation is subject to quite other conditions than ethical decision, and the latter to yet other conditions than aesthetic appreciation, and so forth. It is with regard to such comprehensive 'contexts of meaning' as these that it is of vital importance to take account of the basic presuppositions by which they are governed. If we fail to do this—if, for example, we treat an ethical judgment as if it were a scientific proposition—nothing can be properly understood. The result is that we inevitably either misinterpret the meaning of the particular statement or find it completely meaningless. Thus the question of 'meaning and method' leads on to that of diverse, comprehensive 'contexts of meaning', with regard to which the final and decisive question is how these contexts, each determined by its own basic presuppositions, are related to one another, how they differ from one another, and how possibly in the last resort they are dependent on one another.

This enables us, among other things, to define the problem of the philosophy of religion. It is the business of the philosophy of religion to investigate the religious context of meaning with regard to its basic presuppositions, its distinctive character and meaning in relation to other contexts of meaning, and its connection with these other contexts. It is thus an extremely large and knotty complex of problems that falls to the lot of the philosophy of religion—just as philosophical problems in general are all-encompassing and hence not easily mastered. It is therefore important that these problems should be handled with the greatest possible exactitude. One thing that complicates matters as regards the religious context of meaning is the fact that the meaning of a religious statement is by no means guaranteed simply by referring it to the religious context of meaning and interpreting it accordingly. It is only when in addition to this we take into account what may be called the 'motif context' that it becomes possible to determine the meaning of a religious statement precisely and unambiguously. The context of meaning thus leads us on to a new problem, that of the 'motif context'.

The analysis of meaning has therefore to proceed in two stages: first the analysis that leads to the context of meaning, then that which has in view the 'motif context', which as regards its significance for the meaning of a statement can be described as a secondary or subsidiary context of meaning. Here 'meaning' and 'method' go hand in hand. Just as the method relative to the context of meaning is the logical analysis of basic presuppositions, so a special method of its own is required for the 'motif context', a method which can be described broadly as 'motif research'. With this light is shed also on the connection between philosophy of religion and theology. Each of them has its own task and its own special method, though they are tasks and methods that are not unrelated to one another. The philosophy of religion having thus been clearly defined both with respect to meaning and method, and in relation to both philosophy and theology, the task of our '*Prolegomena*' is completed. The otherwise problematical philosophy of religion can turn with a clear understanding both of its task and its method to the problems with which it is its business to deal.

2. 'Sinn und Bedeutung'

When we seek to define the concept of meaning, an obvious place to start is with the distinction drawn by Gottlob Frege between *Sinn* and *Bedeutung*. For it is undoubtedly in no small measure due to Frege that the question of meaning has come to be so central in contemporary philosophy. In his short but extremely important essay 'Über Sinn und Bedeutung', written in 1892,[1] he gave a penetrating analysis and differentiation of these two ideas, and his way of doing this can still be a useful guide to us even today in our own analysis of meaning.

In taking Frege's distinction between *Sinn* and *Bedeutung*—'meaning' and 'reference'[2]—as our starting point, however, we are not suggesting

---

[1] For particulars of this see Bibliography. That it has been reprinted and several times translated in recent decades indicates the revival of interest in Frege that has taken place. Although in his own lifetime he attracted little or no attention, and afterwards stood for the most part in the shadow of Russell, there is today much to support what G. H. von Wright says of him: 'Thus at length Frege won belated recognition and fame as Russell's predecessor. This fact has tended to give a somewhat distorted impression of Frege's place in the history of logic. Frege's star is still in the ascendant. It would not surprise me if in the future Russell were remembered as Frege's successor in logic and semantics rather than Frege as Russell's predecessor' (*Logik, filosofi och språk*, pp. 6of.).

[2] There is no agreed English equivalent, as can be seen from the different titles under which Frege's essay has been published in translation ('Sense and Reference',

that he was the first to concern himself with the problem of 'meaning', or even the first to demonstrate the importance of maintaining this distinction. We regard ourselves rather as heirs of a long tradition in this matter. To take only one example of an earlier date, we may recall Schleiermacher's treatment of the problem in his work on theological hermeneutics.[3] Here almost everything that has emerged in the discussion of the subject in our time is in one way or another anticipated. We find statements like the following: 'Some call that which the word by itself brings to mind, the *Bedeutung*, and that which it brings to mind in a given context, the *Sinn*. Others say that a word has only a *Bedeutung*, not a *Sinn*, while a sentence by itself has a *Sinn* but not yet a *Verstand* ['sense'], the latter being possessed only by a fully completed discourse. . . . If a discourse is broken down into its individual parts, each of these is something indeterminate. Thus any individual sentence torn out of all context must be an indeterminate thing.'[4] 'In its individual occurrence the word is not isolated, and it does not produce its determinateness out of itself but takes it from its surroundings.'[5] 'The *Sinn* of any word in a given place must be determined by its connection with those that surround it.'[6] 'The individual can only be understood in the light of the whole.'[7]

From these statements it is clear that all the most important ingredients of the present-day discussion are to be found in Schleiermacher: the distinction between *Sinn* and *Bedeutung*, the question of words and their meanings, sentences and their meanings, the matter of isolation and context, the difference between words developed naturally in ordinary speech and the expressions of technical language.[8] When we read Schleiermacher's *Hermeneutik und Kritik* we are often reminded of Frege, and when we read Frege's *Sinn und Bedeutung* we are often reminded of Schleiermacher. They were facing the same kind of problem, though they approached it from different sides, Schleiermacher from the theological-hermeneutic and Frege from the mathematical-semantic. They therefore complement one another and provide a good starting point for dealing with the importance of the context for meaning.

What then is the precise significance of the distinction between *Sinn* and *Bedeutung* for Frege? By way of introduction he illustrates the difference between them by an example thus: 'Let a, b, c, be straight lines

---

'Sense and Nominatum'). In the present work 'meaning' is preferred for *Sinn* and 'reference' for *Bedeutung*. It will be seen later that for Russell the latter equals 'denoting'—and the distinction between it and *Sinn* is obliterated.

[3] Schleiermacher, *Hermeneutik und Kritik, Ges. Schr.* VII.
[4] *Op. cit.*, pp. 41f.
[5] *Op. cit.*, p. 48.
[6] *Op. cit.*, p. 69.
[7] *Op. cit.*, p. 36.
[8] *Op. cit.*, p, 51.

which connect the corners of a triangle with the midpoints of the opposite sides. The point of intersection of a and b is then the same as that of b and c.'[9] The point of intersection is one and the same whether we describe it as the point of intersection between a and b or between b and c. The point of reference, the *Bedeutung*, is the same, but the *Sinn* is different in the two expressions. When I speak of the point of intersection between the lines a and b, I mean the intersection between precisely *these* lines; I am not speaking of all the other lines that happen to intersect at this point.

Better known and perhaps a better illustration of the need for a clear distinction between *Sinn* and *Bedeutung* is Frege's second example, that of the evening and morning star. The two names, 'evening star' and 'morning star', have the same *Bedeutung* (reference) but a different *Sinn* (meaning).[10] There was a time when it was believed that these two names referred to two different heavenly bodies. Much experience and great numbers of astronomical observations were needed before the discovery was made that it was in fact one and the same 'star' to which the two names referred.

What Frege seeks to make clear by these examples and by his whole essay is that *Sinn* and *Bedeutung* are two different things and they ought not to be confused. The discovery that the reference is to one and the same object tells us nothing about the meaning, nor can we draw any conclusions from the meaning with respect to the reference. 'By the fact that one grasps a *Sinn*, one is not yet assured of a *Bedeutung*.'[11] In other words, I can discuss the 'meaning' of a proposition without having first determined how far its subject, or indeed any of the 'parts' of which it is composed, has an object corresponding to it and so a 'reference'. Frege undoubtedly had considerable success in clarifying the concept of 'meaning' and distinguishing it from that of 'reference'—a major achievement in logic and semantics. At the same time there remain a great many problems surrounding these concepts that are still far from clear.

A question which immediately presents itself is that of the relation between word and reference on the one hand, and sentence or proposition and meaning on the other.

Naturally we expect a word to have a *Bedeutung*, a reference, so that there is something it points to, something it signifies. What the word refers to need not necessarily be a particular empirical object, for we can

---

[9] Frege, SuB (= 'Sinn und Bedeutung' 1892), p. 26; ed. Patzig, p. 39; ET*. Feigl-Sellars, p. 86.

[10] The difficulty of finding an adequate rendering of Frege's distinction between *Sinn* and *Bedeutung* in English (*cf.* above, p. 229, n. 2) is further illustrated by the fact that in the ETT of Wittgenstein's *Tractatus* (e.g. 5.4735) 'sense' is used for *Sinn* and 'meaning' for *Bedeutung*.

[11] SuB, p. 28; Patzig, p. 40; Feigl-Sellars, p. 87.

speak of other things than that. But it is of the very nature of a word in its capacity as a *signum* that there should be something which it signifies or refers to, and hence that it should have a *Bedeutung*. There is nothing mysterious or difficult to explain about this, and nothing that requires us to develop any kind of ontology in order to deal with it. The 'problem' that is often supposed to be involved here, as to how a word can represent an object, is really nothing but a pseudo-problem, similar to the old pseudo-problem of how the consciousness can go outside itself and make contact with the objective world in cognition, or how the subject can come over to the object. Just as it is of the nature of consciousness to be conscious of something, so it is of the nature of a word, a linguistic expression, to point or refer to something extra-linguistic. A consciousness that is not conscious *of* anything is not a consciousness at all. A language that has no extra-linguistic reference is no language at all. Just as 'consciousness *of*' is merely an explication of what is involved in the concept of consciousness, so the *Bedeutung*, the signification or reference, of a word is merely an explication of what is involved in the concept of language, what is meant by the word 'word'. It is as simple as that, and as innocent of ontological-metaphysical mysteries.

But just as a word is expected to have a *Bedeutung*, so a sentence or proposition is expected to have a *Sinn*, a sense or meaning. A proposition cannot be a meaningless collocation of words. Words arbitrarily piled upon words yield no proposition. The closeness of the relation between meaning and proposition finds expression in Swedish grammatical usage in that a complete sentence or period is often called a *mening* ('meaning').

Now it might seem the obvious thing simply to partition *Sinn* and *Bedeutung* between propositions and words: the words have *Bedeutung*, the propositions have *Sinn*. For Frege the matter is considerably more complicated, and the reason is that for him there is no sharp demarcation between words and propositions. The line is crossed from both sides, both that of the word and that of the proposition. The example of the evening and the morning star is of course a matter of individual words and names rather than propositions. The names 'evening star' and 'morning star' have different meanings even though they have the same reference. Here then it is the words that have 'meaning'. On the other hand, sentences and propositions can also have a *Bedeutung*. Admittedly Frege raises the question whether it is really right to look for a *Bedeutung* here. He asks: 'Has a sentence as a whole perhaps only a *Sinn* and not a *Bedeutung*?'[12] What compels him to abandon this idea, natural though it might seem from his standpoint, is his reflection on the 'truth-value' of a proposition. For a proposition has a truth-value; it is either true or false. And since the truth-value is connected with the *Bedeutung*, it follows that a proposition must have a *Bedeutung* as well as a *Sinn*.

[12] SuB, p. 32; Patzig, p. 45; Feigl-Sellars, p. 90.

The relation between a word and a proposition is therefore such that *the reference of the word is 'part' of the reference of the proposition*, and the reference of the proposition is then doubtless also the sum of the references of the words it contains. It is true that Frege is extremely hesitant on this point, and he admits that 'this way of putting things is objectionable'.[13] Yet although this train of thought is rather liable to obscure the distinction between *Sinn* and *Bedeutung*, what it is getting at is plain enough. Frege's failure to reach an adequate formulation, however, may in a measure explain the aberrations of his followers, particularly Bertrand Russell, who have completely lost sight of Frege's otherwise very clear distinction between *Sinn* and *Bedeutung*.

Another thing that has helped to obscure the concept of meaning in Frege is his ontological metaphysics. Acute as he is in his analysis of concepts, he has not been able to prevent the underlying platonizing metaphysics from occasionally showing through. This is one of the chief difficulties with Frege's theory of meaning, that it never becomes really clear just what sort of a thing 'meaning' is. A sign has a *Bedeutung*, it has something to which it refers; and this must be something given, an 'object', which we can describe as some kind of 'entity'. But when besides its *Bedeutung* the sign has also a *Sinn*, the question arises, what kind of being this *Sinn* represents. Is it too an 'entity' alongside of the entity to which the sign points in virtue of its *Bedeutung*? If so, the door is thrown wide open for all kinds of platonizing speculation. With Frege this is in the background, but with Bertrand Russell it comes openly into view. Russell is not afraid of constructing entities by the dozen, in spite of the fact that he otherwise accepts Ockham's razor (*entia non sunt multiplicanda praeter necessitatem*), and in spite of his generally empiricist attitude. It is here above all that criticism must be brought to bear, if Frege's significant distinction between *Sinn* and *Bedeutung* is not to be totally lost.

It is the more important to give attention to this point, inasmuch as the influence of Frege from the beginning and all the way from Russell to Quine has suffered from the confusion of logic and ontology, logical meaning and ontological entity.[14] Theory of meaning and metaphysical ontology must be kept absolutely apart. If in analyzing the concept of meaning we link up with Frege, it is essential that we get rid of these metaphysical ingredients. We can fully agree with Christian Thiel when he writes: 'We regard the Fregean inclusion of ontology in the doctrine of *Sinn* and *Bedeutung* as an absolutely impermissible contamination.'[15] And again: 'Only where there is a strict separation of ontics and semantics as two quite separate dimensions is it possible to succeed in preserving

[13] SuB, p. 36; Patzig, p. 48; Feigl-Sellars, p. 92.

[14] W. V. Quine, *From a Logical Point of View*, pp. 22, 130f. On this see also G. Küng, *Ontologie und logistische Analyse*.

[15] C. Thiel, *Sinn und Bedeutung*, p. 158; ET pp. 151f.

Frege's contribution and developing it into a pure, and more particularly a non-ontological semantics.'[16]

Closely related to his ontological train of thought is Frege's tendency to regard all linguistic expressions—not only proper names in the strict sense, but words in general and also sentences and propositions—as *names*. This involves a certain shift of emphasis from *Sinn* to *Bedeutung*, and it can be said to have prepared the way for Russell's aberration in this direction.[17]

The important question for our purpose, however, is not whether Frege succeeded at the points we have mentioned or elsewhere in reaching an adequate definition of his theory of *Sinn* and *Bedeutung*. Here as usual our interest is not primarily in the solution of the problem but in the statement of it, and ultimately in the problem itself.[18] The main question is what contribution Frege has made or can make towards tracking down and getting to grips with the problem of meaning, and hence what significance he holds for the contemporary discussion of the problem. In this respect his significance—in spite of the objections that can be brought against his procedure—is very great indeed. We will confine ourselves here to mentioning only two things, his antipsychologism and his recognition of the importance of the context for 'meaning'.

1) *Antipsychologism.* Frege was extraordinarily clear about the necessity of avoiding anything that could be called psychologism in connection with the analysis of meaning. This is a point where contemporary discussion might learn much from him. When someone inquires about the meaning of an expression, asking 'What do you mean?', it seems very natural to reply by explaining what I had in mind when I used the expression—the 'conception' I associated with it, or the 'intention' I had in using it. It is difficult in defining the 'meaning' of a particular expression to avoid entirely the thought of 'conception' and 'intention'. But this makes it only too easy for the whole question of meaning to be transformed into a psychological question, and hence into a question that is essentially unanswerable. For if we take 'meaning' to refer to what different people find themselves thinking when a particular expression is used, the answer can only be that one person thinks one thing and another another. If we are ever to get a grasp of the question of meaning, every form of psychologism must be banished. It is not what I have psychologically had in mind that is the object of inquiry when someone asks about the 'meaning' of an expression.

The question of meaning is not a psychological but a logical question.

---

[16] *Op. cit.*, p. 165; ET p. 161.

[17] Already in the *Tractatus* Wittgenstein directed critical attention to this; *cf. Tr.* 3.143, 5.02.

[18] *Cf.* above, pp. 175ff.

Frege is therefore concerned to distinguish between *Bedeutung* and *Sinn* on the one hand and *Vorstellung* (conception or image) on the other. 'From the *Bedeutung* and the *Sinn* of a sign the *Vorstellung* associated with it is to be distinguished. . . . It is not always the same *Vorstellung*, even in the same person, that is connected with the same *Sinn*.'[19] Frege gives an instructive example: a painter, a rider, a zoölogist probably connect very different conceptions with the name 'Bucephalus'. Each of these conceptions is the psychical property of a particular subject, and as such a part or mode of the individual person's mind. But it is not such psychologically subjective conceptions that we are referring to when we speak of 'meaning'. It is a question of something that is the 'common property of many', or in other words, something intersubjective and in that sense objective.[20] By clarifying the difference between *Sinn* and *Vorstellung* Frege has removed one of the most insidious obstacles to a correct analysis of meaning. And in his antipsychologism Frege is even clearer and more definite than Husserl and his school.[21]

2) *The importance of the context.* The way in which Frege links together 'meaning' and 'context' can also give us significant guidance in our own analysis of meaning. The question of 'context' had from the beginning a central place in Frege's thinking. Already in his *Grundlagen der Arithmetik* (1884), we find the principle: 'The meaning (*Bedeutung*) of words must be sought in the context of the sentence, not in their isolated selves.' We are also told: 'It is enough if the sentence as a whole has a *Sinn*; from this its parts also acquire content.'[22] Although a good deal remains unclear here, it is at all events plain that in Frege's view it is useless to start with the words in isolation if we wish to get at the meaning. The only possible starting point is the context, and primarily the context of the sentence. It is only as parts of a context that words have meaning. This puts Frege's thinking very much at the heart of the contemporary debate. But more of this in the last section of this chapter.

To get a real idea of how central and far-reaching the distinction between *Sinn* and *Bedeutung* is, one should first observe where Frege's essay on that subject fits into the total pattern of his work. Frege is the strict logician and mathematician, whose aim is to show that arithmetic is nothing else but an extension of logic, a *'weiter entwickelte Logik'*. This is what he is working at in his *Grundlagen der Arithmetik*, and it occupies him also in a number of other writings. But he is not content simply to widen

---

[19] SuB, p. 29; Patzig, pp. 41f.; Feigl-Sellars, pp. 87f.

[20] 'Yet it is objective in that it can serve several observers'—SuB, p. 30; Patzig, p. 42; Feigl-Sellars, p. 88.

[21] It should be pointed out in this connection that Husserl's antipsychologism derives ultimately from Frege.

[22] Frege, *Grundlagen*, pp. X and 71; *Cf.* p. 73: 'Only in the context of a proposition do the words mean anything.'

the scope of logic in this direction; its function must be stretched still further. In his *Begriffsschrift* (1879) he seeks—on lines suggested by Leibniz's *Mathesis Universalis*—to give thinking as a whole the character of a logico-mathematical calculus, every step of which can be inspected and checked and reduced to a formula. By this he became one of the founders of symbolic logic or logicism. It should however be said that Frege is considerably less doctrinaire than some later representatives of logicism. It is the familiar story: the pioneers are notably more open both to the limitations of their own viewpoints and the legitimacy of others than are the epigoni. When a new approach is discovered it is considerably simpler to use it in a technical-mechanical way than to subject it to independent examination and think critically through to its presuppositions and thus to its limits. If in his *Begriffsschrift* Frege very strongly pleads the case for an ideal language, '*eine logisch volkommene Sprache*', yet he does not fall into the very common error of excessive and unqualified admiration for it. Whereas logicists have not infrequently succumbed to the temptation to treat it as a universal scientific method, a key to unlock all doors, Frege guarded himself against this by proposing it as a method meaningful in its own sphere, without trying to impose it on other areas to which it was not suited, or in other words, without expecting from it the solution of all problems.

When Frege's *Sinn und Bedeutung* is viewed against this background, the need to raise the question of *Sinn* as an independent question may well seem to be a disturbing factor. For a historian or hermeneutist the position is different. It is quite inevitable for them to raise the question of meaning—a fact exemplified in the passages from Schleiermacher quoted above. Frege approaches the question from a quite different point of view. Yet as he works at his logico-mathematical problems he discovers that it is impossible to escape from the *Sinnfrage*. He takes it up and handles it with characteristic acumen, and thus becomes one of the founders of semantic philosophy and in some measure also a precursor of ordinary language philosophy.

If Frege's *Begriffsschrift* and his *Sinn und Bedeutung* are viewed side by side, the impression can be gained that they run on two separate lines. Instead, it is a proof of the breadth and comprehensiveness of Frege's statement of the problem, that he has room for both. The common practice is to choose between logicistic formalism and 'meaning' with its fulness of content. Frege was able to hold them together as one, and that is no small reason for regarding him as important. The concept of *Sinn* is not, as has often been supposed, only a historical category, but is of universal significance. This becomes clear when it is pointed out, as it is by Frege, that the distinction between *Sinn* and *Bedeutung*, or meaning and reference, must be maintained no less in the logico-mathematical and natural scientific fields, and that unless it is carefully observed the result is confusion

236

and *Sinnlosigkeit*, meaninglessness, in any field. Hence the concept of *Sinn* is not merely a hermeneutical, but in the strict sense of the word a *philosophical* basic concept. In spite of his platonizing conceptual realism and his ontology, Frege succeeded in maintaining the distinction. But in the development that followed, the difficulties that stood in the way of preserving it proved insuperable. We need only think of what happened to *Sinn und Bedeutung* in the work of his immediate heirs, Bertrand Russell and logical empiricism, in order to see that the rich legacy of Frege was squandered, and that when Wittgenstein and his disciples came along they had hard work in trying to gather it together again.

3. Logical Atomism. Verification as a Criterion of Meaning

The distinction between *Sinn* and *Bedeutung* is fundamental for the question of meaning. Where this distinction is obliterated there is hopeless confusion and 'meaning' is totally lost. That is precisely what happened in the discussion of the question of meaning after Frege. We shall therefore give a brief historical sketch of how this happened and with what results. We shall show how the light which Frege with his distinction between *Sinn* and *Bedeutung* was able to shed on the question of meaning, was extinguished because that distinction was not maintained; how this led to a relapse into metaphysics and made possible the growth of an atomistic metaphysics that smothered all genuine analysis of meaning, and how the way was thus opened for 'the verificationalist fallacy'; and finally, how modern philosophy has been put to great pains in restoring what was thus lost, and how it is still faced with the task of finding its way to an understanding of the problem of 'meaning', although such an understanding was already within reach through the distinction between *Sinn* and *Bedeutung*. In this way a direct connection is made between Frege's work and a living contemporary issue.

There are above all two things that have contributed to the destruction of the question of meaning: 1. logical atomism with its attempt to construct an atomistic theory of meaning, and 2. the verification principle employed as a universal criterion of meaning.

(1) *The atomistic theory of meaning*

Bertrand Russell can be said to be in many ways Frege's disciple and heir. This applies in the first place to his logicistic attitude, displayed above all in his *Principia Mathematica*, which is to a large extent a detailed working out of Frege's logico-mathematical ideas. But also in his theory of meaning he is largely dependent on Frege—though negatively dependent, so that he finds himself eventually in the directly opposite camp. Whereas for Frege the question of meaning depends entirely on the context, Russell finds the answer to it in a pronounced atomism, in what he calls 'logical atomism'. Yet in spite of this diametrically opposed view, there is still an

237

evident connection between him and Frege. It is the latter's thought of *Sinn und Bedeutung*, meaning and reference, that provides both the starting point and the background for Russell's thinking too—only Russell mixes things up which Frege was so anxious to keep separate. He starts with Frege's distinction, but refuses to accept it. He wishes to make a unity of the two, and he does this at the expense of 'meaning'. What happens may be put briefly thus: because the 'meaning', which depends on the context, is completely absorbed by the 'reference', which stresses the isolated point, the whole discussion moves away from the context into atomism.[23]

Russell's essay 'On Denoting' has been described with some justice as his most important contribution to philosophy in the strict sense.[24] That essay is largely taken up with contesting Frege's *Sinn und Bedeutung*, and can in some measure be described as Russell's counter-proposal to it. Russell's position is summed up in his statement 'that the whole distinction of meaning and denotation has been wrongly conceived'.[25] Hence in putting forward his own view he shows no respect for that distinction but uses the terms as completely interchangeable. It need therefore hardly be said that when Russell speaks of 'meaning', this in no way corresponds to what Frege intended by that term, but corresponds rather to his *'Bedeutung'*. 'Denotation' is all that really survives, and to it everything, including 'meaning', is reduced. Whereas Frege makes a clear distinction between the linguistic expression (the sign), its meaning (or significance) and its reference (or signification), Russell mixes them together in an undifferentiated unity in which 'meaning' is swallowed up in 'denotation'. As opposed to Frege's view that a linguistic term expresses a meaning and denotes a reference, Russell insists: 'In the theory, which I advocate, there is no *meaning*, and only sometimes a *denotation*.'[26] It is true that Russell retains the idea 'that denoting phrases have no meaning in isolation',[27] and from this it might look as if the context and not the atomism of isolated words should be the decisive thing. This is neutralized, however, by the fact that 'meaning' has already been dissolved in 'denotation' ('reference'), and there is therefore strictly speaking no occasion to speak of anything but denotation. Thus the entire atomistic theory of meaning comes to hang in the air. ' "Referring to" takes the place of "meaning".'[28]

---

[23] Striking proof of the extent to which Russell's quarrel with Frege is based on 'obvious misunderstandings' is furnished by Christian Thiel, *op. cit.*, pp. 105ff.; ET pp. 103ff.

[24] In *Mind*, 1905; reprinted in Feigl-Sellars, *Readings*, and Russell, *Logic and Knowledge* (= LAK).

[25] Feigl-Sellars, p. 110; LAK, p. 50.

[26] Feigl-Sellars, p. 107; LAK, p. 46.

[27] Feigl-Sellars, p. 114; LAK, p. 55.

[28] Russell, 'On Propositions', LAK, p. 315. This essay is of particular interest to us here, inasmuch as Russell expressly states that he intends to 'define what constitutes meaning' (p. 285, n.).

The catastrophic consequences which this confusion of meaning and reference has had for the question of meaning have become quite clear during the subsequent discussion of Russell's theory. In this connection mention should be made above all of P. F. Strawson's penetrating criticism of Russell,[29] by which the latter's attempt to evade Frege's distinction between *Sinn* and *Bedeutung* can be regarded as having been dismissed from the discussion.[30] Whereas Russell declared 'that the whole distinction of meaning and denotation [= reference] has been wrongly conceived', it is by now very evident that the 'wrongly' is all on Russell's side, that is, it is Russell who is at fault when he 'wrongly assumes that meaning is the same as reference'.[31]

A comparison of the views of Russell and Frege turns out almost wholly to the advantage of Frege. It shows that nearly everything Frege sought to do, and indeed partly accomplished, by his analysis of meaning, has been totally lost in the Russellian revised version. This is plain not only from the fact that the concept of meaning in Russell has been absorbed by that of denotation (reference), but also from the fact that the two leading ideas of Frege which we mentioned above—his antipsychologism and his stressing of the context—have been abandoned by Russell.

As regards the antipsychologism, Russell's whole argument shows that his conception of 'meaning' is thoroughly psychologistic. One wonders why Russell has to speak about 'meaning' at all, seeing that for him it means nothing other than 'denoting' or 'reference'. It does not make for lucidity to begin by explaining a concept away and then go on using it as if nothing had happened. But that is precisely what Russell does. Time and again we find him speaking of 'meaning', and just as often of 'meaning-lessness'. It is, however, plain that when Russell speaks of 'meaning', he has not at all the same thing in mind as Frege. Frege's *logical* concept of meaning has been replaced by a *psychological* concept. Russell flatly declares: 'I think that the notion of meaning is always more or less psychological, and that it is not possible to get a pure logical theory of meaning.'[32] As in another context Russell equates 'meaning' with what Frege called *Bedeutung* or 'reference', so here he equates it with what Frege called *Vorstellung* ('conception'), a term which Frege carefully distinguished from 'meaning'—and that with an antipsychologistic intention and precisely in order to guarantee 'a pure logical theory of meaning'. The contrast between Russell and Frege could not be sharper than it is here.

---

[29] In *Mind*, 1950, pp. 320–44. See also Strawson, *Introduction to Logical Theory*, pp. 184ff.

[30] That the Russellian tradition still survives in some quarters, however, is shown by statements like that of G. Bergmann in his *Logic and Reality*, p. 85: 'The *meaning* of a word is what it refers to. As for words, so for sentences. The word *means* what it refers to. So does the sentence. This is the reference use of "means" and "meaning".'

[31] J. N. Mohanty, 'On Reference', in Delius and Patzig *Argumentationem*, p. 162.

[32] Russell, 'The Philosophy of Logical Atomism' (1918), LAK, p. 186.

The contrast is no less sharp, however, with regard to the other main issue: *context* in Frege, *atomism* in Russell. What is it that gives an expression its meaning? According to Frege it is the context in which the expression occurs that is decisive. It is in the context and only in the context that the expression has its function. 'Only in a proposition do words really have meaning.' 'We must never try to define the meaning of a word in isolation, but only as it is used in the context of a proposition.'[33] According to Russell, on the other hand, it is the atomistic expression or the isolated word that is ultimately the bearer of meaning. If we are to understand a coherent proposition, we must begin with the units, the atoms, out of which it is constructed. Only one who understands the parts understands the whole. The function of the analysis of meaning is therefore to break down every expression into the smallest parts of which it is composed, its 'constituents'. It is in a way analogous to what happens in a chemical analysis, where an object is resolved into its ultimate chemical constituents. 'You can understand a proposition when you understand the words of which it is composed.'[34]

This applies to propositions, but (Russell continues): 'this characteristic, that you can understand a proposition through the understanding of its component words, is absent from the component words when those words express something simple.'[35] When we have reached the absolutely simple, the logical atoms, nothing remains to be broken down. If we are to continue further with the analysis of meaning, the question arises, what possibility we have of understanding these atomic particulars at all,[36] and how we can ascribe any meaning to them. Russell's reply is that this can be done only by 'direct acquaintance with the objects which are the meanings of certain simple symbols'.[37] The analysis must therefore take place in two stages: so long as one is dealing with something complex it consists in resolving the complexity into its simple constituents, then with regard to the latter it consists in referring to direct acquaintance with these particulars, or possibly in giving a paraphrastic description of them. What Russell envisages by these atomic particulars, he himself explains thus: they are 'such things as little patches of colour or sounds.'[38]

As anyone can see, we have here an extremely primitive 'theory of meaning', according to which we first become acquainted with some 'little patches' and then by putting these together we produce a complex meaning. It is here that the idea of sense-data comes to the fore. Russell is anxious to insist that he is concerned with logical atoms and not physical

[33] Frege, *Grundlagen*, pp. 71, 116.
[34] Russell, LAK, p, 193.
[35] *Ibid.*
[36] LAK, p. 179.
[37] LAK, p. 194.
[38] LAK, p. 179.

atoms.[39] But he has done nothing to distinguish them from metaphysical atoms. His logical 'little patches' are nothing else but metaphysical constructions, and 'logical atomism' is less a logical than a metaphysical theory. Only when his reflection has issued in a metaphysical theory has Russell reached the goal he has set himself. If we ask what it is that ultimately motivates his interest in the logical structure of language, there can be no doubt that it is the metaphysical consequences he believes he can draw from it. Interest in the structure of language is prompted in Russell by the view that this structure exactly corresponds to the structure of the world, so that it is possible by the roundabout means of language to find the way to a metaphysical theory of the structure and essential nature of existence.

Although philosophers with an analytical bent have generally been opposed to metaphysics, or at least have treated it with reserve, it is characteristic of Russell that he has always openly confessed to being a metaphysician. A scientific philosophy is quite beyond his purview, and its demand for objective argumentation is quite foreign to him. If the advice that scientific philosophy gives to the philosopher is: Don't indulge in airy, unverifiable speculations and hypotheses about the universe and its nature, for that isn't your business; let the sciences take care of formulating hypotheses, for they see to it that their hypotheses are duly and objectively tested, and with their objective argumentation they set a limit to immature speculations about the universe and its nature; your business is not arbitrarily to *postulate* presuppositions, but to *analyze* them and discover what presuppositions are with a certain necessity made in the different areas of life—if, I say, this expresses the attitude of scientific philosophy then Russell's view runs directly counter to it. What he expects of philosophy is that it should—uninhibited by the restrictions of scientific procedure—boldly proclaim presuppositions and postulate unverifiable and unfalsifiable hypotheses. 'Philosophy should be bold in suggesting hypotheses as to the universe which science is not in a position to confirm or confute.'[40] Where there can be no confirming or confuting it is possible to say very nearly anything; and of that possibility Russell has certainly made use—hence his many metamorphoses in metaphysics!

It has been said of Russell that he 'was often careless about words when not directly concerned with formal logic.'[41] With regard to the concept of

[39] The sort of metaphysics (metaphysical atomism) that springs from Russell's logical atomism can be seen in a condensed form at the conclusion of his essay on 'Logical Atomism' in LAK, pp. 341ff., where he gives 'an outline of the possible structure of the world'.

[40] LAK, p. 431.—That what Russell calls 'philosophy' is really nothing but metaphysics of the most quixotic sort is evident from a statement like this: 'The point of philosophy is to start with something so simple as not to seem worth stating, and to end with something so paradoxical that no one will believe it' (LAK, p. 193).

[41] J. O. Urmson, *Philosophical Analysis*, p. 37.

meaning he has indeed been more than careless. It is a pity that he did not read his Frege more carefully and get a better grasp of the problems which the latter was tracking down and largely succeeded in mastering. If he had done so, philosophy might have been spared the trouble of getting into a blind alley from which it has since had hard work to get out.

(2) *The verification principle*

Having already discussed the verification principle of logical positivism as a criterion of meaning[42] and shown the danger of 'the reductive fallacy',[43] we need do no more here than illustrate a single point which reveals the deepest reason why that principle is useless as a criterion of meaning. The reason for dealing with this point here is that it is very closely related to Frege's distinction between *Sinn* and *Bedeutung*, meaning and reference, and to what subsequently happened to that distinction in the hands of Russell and certain representatives of logical empiricism after him. As long as we maintain with Frege a clear distinction between *Sinn* and *Bedeutung* there is no possibility of making the meaning or meaninglessness of a proposition depend on the possibility of its verification.

Even in its most highly modified form it is impossible to use the verification principle as a criterion of meaning, and that for the simple reason that the question of verification, that is of truth or falsity, is connected with *Bedeutung* and not with *Sinn*.[44] These two are as it were on different levels, and no conclusion can be drawn from one to the other in either direction. We can determine the meaning of a proposition without having either knowledge of its truth-value or the possibility of coming to a decision about it. 'As to whether there is also a *Bedeutung* corresponding to the *Sinn*, nothing is hereby said.'[45] Frege's position is thus clear: 'meaning' is completely independent of 'reference' and therefore any talk of verification as a criterion of meaning is 'meaningless'.

The situation is completely changed, however, if we jumble up meaning and reference in a single, undifferentiated confusion. Then it is of course possible to work the question of verification into that of meaning, because they are no longer two distinct questions. But it is at the expense of meaning that this confusion takes place. For meaning disappears, being absorbed into reference or denotation, so that although the word 'meaning' is retained its purport is nothing but 'reference'. And the inevitable result of this is 'the reductive fallacy'. A great deal that is plainly and in the highest degree meaningful is in this way pronounced 'meaningless', all

[42] Above, pp. 142ff.

[43] Above, pp. 150ff.

[44] SuB, p. 34; Patzig, p. 46; Feigl-Sellars, p. 91: 'Thus we find ourselves persuaded to accept the *truth-value* of a sentence as its *Bedeutung* [= "reference"]. By the truth-value of a sentence I mean the circumstance of its being true or false.'

[45] SuB, p. 28; Patzig, p. 46; Feigl-Sellars, p. 87.

because it is not in accord with the arbitrarily decreed criterion of meaning. The impracticable nature of this limited, reductionist criterion very soon became apparent, and an attempt was made to evade its worst absurdities by successive modifications of the verification principle—though without success. There was a fundamental mistake, which could not be remedied by incidental restrictions.

An initial error cannot be corrected piecemeal and by *ad hoc* measures, as the following illustration may show. If owing to a defect in its manufacture a girder intended to support a whole building is practically broken through from the start, it is useless when a widening crack appears simply to plaster it over time after time; for the whole building is in jeopardy. In a similar way here, there is an initial mistake that lies in the confusion of *Sinn* and *Bedeutung*, meaning and reference, and it is this confusion that needs to be cleared away. If we start with the idea that meaning is the same as reference or—in other words—the same as truth-value, then the verification principle is merely a public exhibition of our own preconceived opinion, our prejudice, our initial error, based on the confusion of *Sinn* and *Bedeutung*, and a confession that we are ensnared in our own 'reductive fallacy'.

Actually the issue was in the main already clear in Frege. But the clarity which he achieved was completely lost in the development that followed. Ludwig Wittgenstein was the first to bring clarity back into this subject.

4. From Atomism to Context of Meaning

If the way from Frege to Russell led from the context to atomism, the way from Russell to the mature Wittgenstein led from atomism to the context, and—we may add—to the 'context of meaning'. At the beginning Wittgenstein stood close to Russell, but in the end he could rather be described as his antipode. An extraordinarily interesting development took place between that beginning and end, a development which is something of a paradigm. It shows how it is possible even from a most unfavourable initial position to reach very favourable results if only *the problem* is kept in view and one refuses to be carried away by fortuitous currents of thought.

I.

The position at the beginning was not quite as unfavourable as might at first sight appear. For although the early Wittgenstein was in many respects a disciple of Russell, yet he was never dependent on him to the extent that has often been supposed. There was from the start a very marked difference in basic tendency between these two. In Wittgenstein it is thoroughly *logical*, in Russell *metaphysical*. The result is that even when they use the same expressions they often mean different things. It is

243

therefore a serious mistake, though one that has often been made, to interpret Wittgenstein's *Tractatus* with the aid of Russell's logical atomism.[46]

It has in general been Wittgenstein's misfortune to be interpreted in the light of differently oriented types of thought. This is in no small measure due to the fact that from the beginning his influence was communicated through personal discussions before he took occasion to set down his views in writing. It could thus easily happen that anyone who had learnt something from him in discussion, might interpret Wittgenstein's views more or less in terms of his own. That is how it was with the *Tractatus*. Already a couple of years before it was published, some of its ideas had been put into circulation in Russell's interpretation. In this connection what Russell says in his preface to 'The Philosophy of Logical Atomism' (1918) is illuminating. He writes that this essay is 'very largely concerned with explaining certain ideas which I learnt from my friend and former pupil Ludwig Wittgenstein. I have had no opportunity of knowing his views since August 1914, and I do not even know whether he is alive or dead. He has therefore no responsibility for what is said in these lectures beyond that of having originally supplied many of the theories contained in them.'[47] When the *Tractatus* subsequently appeared, there was already an expectation that the same ideas would be found in it as in Russell's 'Logical Atomism', and it was naturally read in the light of that. This impression was further strengthened by Russell's Introduction to the *Tractatus*, in which he wrongly reads into Wittgenstein's work an avowal of his own ideas.

Now it is plain that there is a vast difference between Wittgenstein's outlook in the *Tractatus* and in the *Philosophical Investigations*, and that the latter is in many ways a direct confutation of the former. The result of this has been that less attention has been paid to the continuity between them in respect of the problem they are concerned with, and the idea that there is any development in the ordinary sense of the word has hardly been considered. There has consequently been a failure to perceive the dramatic struggle that leads from atomism to the context of meaning, a struggle of

---

[46] See particularly J. Griffin, *Wittgenstein's Logical Atomism*. Griffin says: 'By the "old" interpretation I mean Russell's and the Vienna Circle's: that is the interpretation which makes Wittgenstein's elementary propositions into Russell's atomic propositions or Carnap's protocol sentences. . . . The important thing about this interpretation is that it places the *Tractatus* in a certain philosophical tradition; it presumes that Wittgenstein shares the common philosophical belief that only immediate experiences are really reliable, and that everything else we speak of is reliable only to the extent that it is built up out of immediate experiences' (p. 4); this 'whole presumption about the tradition the *Tractatus* belongs to is mistaken' (p. 5).—Of the abundant literature on the *Tractatus* note further M. Black's *Companion*, G. E. M. Anscombe's *Introduction*, E. Stenius's *Wittgenstein's Tractatus*, and J. O. Urmson's *Philosophical Analysis* (where in his Introduction Urmson dissociates Wittgenstein from Russell). See also D. Favrholdt, *An Interpretation*; and G. Bergmann, *Logic and Reality*, pp. 225–71.

[47] Russell, 'The Philosophy of Logical Atomism', LAK, p. 177.

which we today are able to trace the development, thanks to the posthumous material. Instead, these two writings have been in the main regarded as quite distinct and separate from one another. They have been treated like erratic blocks dropped into the contemporary philosophical landscape, having no very strong relationship to their surroundings nor any close relationship with each other. Each work bears the stamp of a quite new approach, and each of them is the point of departure for its own particular philosophical line, the *Tractatus* for logical positivism or empiricism, the *Philosophical Investigations* for linguistic philosophy. Justus Hartnack writes: 'The *Philosophical Investigations* in many ways represents a break with the *Tractatus*. Wittgenstein has won a unique place in the history of philosophy by writing in his youth a single work which by its genius has had a decisive influence on the philosophical thought of the age, and then in his maturity repudiating this work of his youth and creating in its place a new philosophy, which in point of originality does not lag behind the other. There are in the history of philosophy many philosophers who have enriched their subject with ideas of genius, and for some of them it has been possible to develop from one view to another—to develop in the sense that one can trace a line of development from the earlier to the later view. But for one philosopher on two occasions, and each time, as it were, from scratch, to create something of genius, is unique.'[48]

This is undoubtedly an accurate account of the situation provided that attention is directed to the philosophical standpoints which find expression in the *Tractatus* and the *Philosophical Investigations* respectively, and that the particular results of each work are considered. For the two works do in fact reflect widely different and mutually irreconcilable standpoints, and this has been emphasized not least by Wittgenstein himself, when he quite openly departs in the *Philosophical Investigations* at certain important points from the views he espoused in the *Tractatus*. The difference between the two works is apparent and must not be minimized.

We can, however, look at the matter from another point of view. When we consider not the philosophical standpoint but the problem, the situation is completely changed, and it is quite misleading to maintain that there is no continuity between the earlier and the later Wittgenstein, and that there is in his work no development in the sense that 'one can trace a line of development from the earlier to the later view'. It is the problem that gives continuity to Wittgenstein's thought; the discontinuity lies in the solution, which is sought in directions so diametrically opposed that they can be described by the opposite terms 'atomism' and 'context of meaning'.

[48] J. Hartnack, *Wittgenstein*, pp. 16f.; ET p. 6. *Cf. ibid.*, p. 66; ET p. 49: 'There is no continuity between the *Tractatus* and the *Philosophical Investigations*; the ideas of the *Philosophical Investigations* cannot be regarded as the logical consequence of the ideas of the *Tractatus*. There is a logical gulf between these two works; the ideas of the one are nothing less than a break with the ideas of the other.'

This continuity of problem and discontinuity of outlook are interdependent; if Wittgenstein had not been occupied throughout with a relatively uniform problem, then the contrast in outlook would not have been so decisive. It is his struggle with the problem that takes him from one outlook to the other, and it is because the different outlooks constitute opposing answers to approximately the same question that they stand in such sharp contrast to each other.

There are various circumstances that made it possible for the continuity of the problem to be overlooked. One such circumstance is that after publishing the *Tractatus* Wittgenstein withdrew for a long time into complete silence on philosophical questions, and when he reappeared he had largely abandoned the views he formerly propounded. It was a natural consequence of this long silence that attention should be focused more on the difference of outlook than on the similarity of the problem. Another contributory circumstance was that the *Tractatus* had to a great extent been accepted as the philosophical basis of logical positivism or empiricism, and had therefore become a constituent and even a transforming element in much contemporary philosophical thought. It was thus all the more astonishing when the author of the *Tractatus* himself came out in opposition to many of its basic ideas. The explanation lies in the fact already indicated, that Wittgenstein in his struggle with the problem had realized that the solution attempted in the *Tractatus* was not a true solution, and that the answer must be sought elsewhere. When this is understood we are no longer so astonished: it is simply that the problem remains the same, but the solution changes.

2.

To express briefly what the problem is that governs Wittgenstein's thought in its various stages, one may take up a central statement in the *Tractatus* where he says: 'All philosophy is a "critique of language".'[49] Philosophy is concerned with language and its meaning or lack of meaning, the relation of language to what it expresses, the pseudo-problems which arise when language is used without regard to its logical structure, and the solution of such pseudo-problems (which Wittgenstein often calls 'the problems of philosophy', though it might be better to call them 'the problems of metaphysics' since it is clearly these he has in mind): it is all this that forms the background of Wittgenstein's work from beginning to end. It is in this sense that he can say 'All philosophy is a "critique of language".'

In the discussion of the philosophical problems of language Wittgenstein is at the start essentially under the influence of Bertrand Russell, with regard both to the problem itself and to the way he attempts to solve it. It was the impression made on him by Russell's demonstration that the linguistic form of a proposition often does not correspond to its logical

[49] *Tractatus* 4.0031.

246

form, but rather conceals it, that in general led Wittgenstein to the problem of the logical structure of language. Here too Wittgenstein calls attention to his dependence on Russell. Immediately after the pronouncement 'All philosophy is a "critique of language",' he adds: 'Russell's merit is to have shown that the apparent logical form of the proposition need not be its real form.'[50] Again Wittgenstein is following Russell when he seeks the solution along the lines of 'logical atomism', and this finds verbal expression in the basic concept of 'atomic facts'.[51] Furthermore, in the last resort it is the individual expressions making up a proposition that carry its meaning: 'I conceive the proposition—like Frege and Russell—as a function of the expressions contained in it.'[52]

What is it to understand the meaning or content of a proposition? Wittgenstein's answer is: 'One understands it [a proposition] if one understands its constituent parts.'[53] It could now appear as if logical analysis consisted of breaking the proposition into its constituent parts, and stating clearly and unambiguously the meaning of each part individually, if possible by using one particular word or symbol always for the same thing and for nothing else. Thereby it should be made possible to treat all thought as a calculus. It is undoubtedly possible to cite statements by Wittgenstein which can be interpreted in this way. Nevertheless it is certainly an oversimplification of his thought when Russell in his Introduction to the *Tractatus* maintains that Wittgenstein is primarily attempting to establish an 'ideal language', 'an accurate symbolism', 'a logically perfect language'.[54] Certainly the shadow of Russell lies heavily over the *Tractatus*, and we may believe that Russell quite simply thought he was rediscovering his own ideas in its pages, but it is also very significant that Wittgenstein was not altogether satisfied with Russell's Introduction. Wittgenstein's thought is too many-sided and undoctrinaire to be captured in formulae such as Russell uses in the Introduction—for example: 'The meaning of the series of words which is a proposition is a function of the meanings of the separate words. Accordingly the proposition as a whole does not really enter into what has to be explained in explaining the meaning of a proposition',[55] or 'The essential business of language is to assert or deny facts. Given the syntax of a language, the meaning of a sentence is determinate as soon as the meaning of the component words is known.'[56]

Even if Wittgenstein under the shadow of Russell regards language as consisting of words which get their meaning from the object they refer to or denominate—the view the whole of his later work sets out to combat—

[50] *Ibid.*
[51] *Tractatus* 2, 2.01ff.
[52] *Tractatus* 3.318.
[53] *Tractatus* 4.024.
[54] *Tractatus*, Introduction (1922) p. 8., (1961) p. IX.
[55] *Ibid.*, (1922), p. 20, (1961) p. XX
[56] *Ibid.*, (1922), p. 8, (1961) p. X.

and even if a great deal of the *Tractatus* is obscure, he is nevertheless quite certain that 'the *separate* words' cannot be treated as isolated units of meaning quite apart from the context in which they appear. Even in the *Tractatus* we find this statement: 'Only the proposition has sense: only in the context of a proposition has a name meaning.'[57] In the last resort it is not what a word or name refers to that determines its meaning, but the context in which it appears. This idea points to the future: this is the point of departure for Wittgenstein's later demolition both of his own view in the *Tractatus* and of Russell's view. Nor is the thought that it is the use we make of a word or symbol that is decisive for its meaning, lacking in the *Tractatus*.

3.

This brings us to a question of the greatest importance for the whole of Wittgenstein's thought, the question of his relationship to metaphysics. Is the Wittgenstein of the *Tractatus* a metaphysician or not? It is difficult to give an unambiguous answer. On the one hand he clearly takes a negative attitude to all that is called metaphysics. 'The problems of philosophy [metaphysics] are not real problems, but pseudo-problems arising exclusively from unclear thinking, from inability to perceive the logic of language. 'We cannot, therefore, answer questions of this kind at all, but only state their senselessness. Most questions and propositions of the philosophers result from the fact that we do not understand the logic of our language. . . . And it is not to be wondered at that the deepest problems are really *no* problems.'[58] Therefore, 'all philosophy is a "critique of language" ' with the task of setting aside all such pseudo-problems. On the other hand it is equally clear that the standpoint of the *Tractatus* has itself metaphysical implications. In this respect the very opening words of the *Tractatus* are significant: 'The world is everything that is the case.'[59] It is beyond all doubt that logical atomism, the picture theory, the use of the concept of substance, and much else besides are coloured by metaphysics. This however does not tell us much about Wittgenstein's real attitude to metaphysics, and here a comparison with Russell will be of help.

For Russell metaphysics is a completely natural mode of thought. In his development he has embraced one metaphysics after another, and he can present even his mathematical philosophy against the background of a platonizing metaphysics. The case of Wittgenstein is quite different. In him there is from the beginning a strong anti-metaphysical streak which causes those of Russell's metaphysical ideas that he freely takes over in the *Tractatus* to lose much of their real metaphysical content. The same observation can be made about Wittgenstein's relation to logical positivism. Notwithstanding that the *Tractatus* was accepted to a great extent by the Vienna School as the foundation of their philosophical work, Wittgen-

[57] *Tractatus*, 3.3.   [58] *Tractatus* 4.003.   [59] *Tractatus* 1.

stein for his part refused to be associated with that circle. He had too clear an understanding of the arbitrariness of the metaphysical suppositions on which logical positivism rested. And when the attempt was made to support the verification principle from the *Tractatus* and from his statements in another context, and to make him outright the originator of that principle, Wittgenstein repudiated this, apparently on the grounds that he was not willing to draw from his relatively similar sounding expressions the metaphysical consequences that positivism required.

This point never becomes fully clear, either in the *Tractatus* or in later writings, where the anti-metaphysical tendency is more marked. The reason for this is that Wittgenstein has nowhere fully worked out the antithesis between metaphysical and scientific philosophy. This in turn is connected with a residue of metaphysics which remains even after metaphysics has been in principle exposed and overthrown. Wittgenstein's difficulty in talking of a 'scientific philosophy' is related to the narrow concept of science which is the result of the metaphysical element in the *Tractatus*, particularly the picture theory. Philosophical statements are statements that try to express in words that which *cannot be said*, that is, cannot be represented in language. From this point of view Wittgenstein is perfectly consistent in describing all philosophical propositions as meaningless, and in including among them not only the metaphysical pseudo-problems that he resolves, but also those philosophical statements that he himself uses to resolve them.

In this context should be quoted the closing words of the *Tractatus*, which deal with this very problem of philosophy and metaphysics:[60]

The right method in philosophy would really be this: to say nothing except what can be said, i.e. the propositions of natural science—i.e. something that has nothing to do with philosophy—and then, whenever someone else wished to say something metaphysical, to demonstrate to him that he had given no meaning to certain signs in his propositions. This method would be unsatisfying to the other person—he would not have the feeling that we were teaching him philosophy—but it would be the only strictly correct method.

My propositions are elucidatory in this way: anyone who understands me eventually recognizes them as senseless, when he has climbed out through them, on them, over them. (He must, so to speak, throw away the ladder after he has climbed up on it.)

He must surmount these propositions; then he will see the world rightly.

Whereof one cannot speak, thereof one must be silent.

We note here that 'what can be said' is equivalent to 'propositions of natural science'. Nothing else can be said. Why this limitation? It is a simple consequence of the picture theory. Philosophical propositions do not represent or picture anything, and consequently cannot be said. This

---

[60] *Tractatus* 6.53f., 7.

of course applies not only to the clearly illegitimate metaphysical propositions, but also to such propositions as are used in disposing of illegitimate pseudo-propositions, since they too do not represent anything. Yet on the other hand there is a vast difference between these two sorts of 'philosophical propositions', for the first sort are propositions that perpetrate error and give rise to confusion, while the second are propositions that correct error and result in clarity, 'make propositions clear' and effect 'the logical clarification of thoughts'.[61] Wittgenstein hesitates to call these latter 'philosophical propositions'.[62] That is however of secondary importance: what is significant is that he describes both forms of philosophy as 'senseless' or 'nonsensical'.[63]

When Wittgenstein describes his own propositions as meaningless, he is only making a concession to an arbitrary metaphysical determination of what ought to be considered meaningful and meaningless. His propositions are not at all meaningless or 'nonsensical'; it is only his metaphysical picture theory and the arbitrarily restricted conception of science following from it that compel him quite unnecessarily to abandon the scientific nature and the meaningfulness of philosophy. One can agree with Wittgenstein that the task of philosophy is 'the logical clarification of thoughts', without thereby surrendering the scientific character of philosophy. He is, of course, right when he says: 'Philosophy is not one of the natural sciences. The word "philosophy" must mean something which stands above or below, but not beside the natural sciences',[64] but to say this is not to deprive philosophy, conceived as 'the logical clarification of thoughts', of its status as a scientific discipline. Everything depends on the way science is defined: if it is defined, in accordance with the picture theory, as simply identical with natural science, then of course philosophy is not a science. Once the picture theory is abandoned, as it is by the later Wittgenstein, then we are no longer limited to the narrow concept of science (i.e. that only natural science is science) and there is no obstacle to recognizing every inquiry that is marked by objective argumentation as a scientific inquiry. Metaphysics is not a science, not because it fails to represent anything, but because it shuns objective argumentation. Hence Witt-

[61] *Tractatus* 4.112.

[62] 'Philosophy does not result in "philosophical propositions", but in the clarifying of propositions'—*Tractatus* 4.112.

[63] *Tractatus* 6.54. (Both 'senseless' and 'nonsensical' are used for '*unsinnig*' in ETT.—Tr.) It should be noted that Wittgenstein here speaks of 'my propositions' as 'nonsensical'; thus even his own philosophy is a matter of 'propositions', of 'philosophical propositions', and of their being 'nonsensical'. It is this view of his own philosophy that leads Russell in his Introduction to the *Tractatus* to say half-teasingly of Wittgenstein: 'In accordance with this principle the things that have to be said in leading the reader to understand Mr Wittgenstein's theory are all of them things which that theory itself condemns as meaningless, With this proviso we will endeavour to convey the picture of the world which seems to underlie his system' (p. 11).

[64] *Tractatus* 4.111.

genstein's philosophy, in so far as it is not metaphysical but is limited to 'the logical clarification of thoughts', is a scientific philosophy; and it becomes the more so when in his later thinking Wittgenstein more and more frees himself from the metaphysics that still determines his thought in the *Tractatus*, and when he allows philosophy to assume more decisively the character of a 'critique of language' and 'the logical clarification of thoughts'.

4.

In the *Philosophical Investigations* as in the *Tractatus* the task of philosophy is to be a 'critique of language', though in a rather different sense. In the *Tractatus* Wittgenstein is reckoning with only one language, and language has for him only one function, namely to represent reality; but in the *Philosophical Investigations* he has discovered that there are many 'languages', an unlimited number of 'language games [*Sprachspiele*]', and that language has many different functions. Wittgenstein took up an erroneous position in the *Tractatus* when, following Russell, he postulated an ideal language with the single function of representing 'atomic facts' and combinations of them, and asserted that the basic factor of language was words and the naming of things: 'As if what we did next were given with the mere act of naming. As if there were only one thing called "talking about things". Whereas in fact we do the most various things with our sentences.'[65] His own ideas in the *Tractatus* are also expressly under fire when he says: 'It is interesting to compare the multiplicity of the tools in language and of the ways they are used, the multiplicity of kinds of word and sentence, with what logicians have said about the structure of language.'[66] There is no limit to the number of possible languages or 'language games'.

This however involves also a change with regard to the function of philosophy as a 'critique of language'. The aim is still 'the logical clarification of thoughts', and it is still the use of language with no regard for its logic that is the source of confusion in philosophy and the reason why 'the problems of philosophy' are very largely pseudo-problems; but these things now acquire a somewhat different significance. Even in the *Tractatus* Wittgenstein is aware of the ambiguity of words and linguistic expressions, but this is to be regarded as a defect in ordinary, everyday language, which must be overcome by restoring language to its proper logical form. According to the *Philosophical Investigations* the ambiguity of linguistic expressions is not a defect, but only a consequence of the multiplicity of 'language games'. If in one 'language game' and its context a word or expression has one meaning, and in another 'language game' and its differently constituted context another meaning, it is nevertheless equally correct in

[65] *Philosophical Investigations*, § 27, p. 13.
[66] *Ibid.*, § 23, p. 12.

both cases. The trouble starts when the different 'languages' get mixed and the different meanings of the word in the various contexts are confused. 'The problems of philosophy', or as we should perhaps rather say, 'the problems of metaphysics', arise when diverse 'language games' are mixed.

In these circumstances there can no longer be any question of overcoming the pseudo-problems arising from the ambiguity of language by constructing an ideal language in which every word is given an absolutely unambiguous meaning in all different contexts. This is in any case an unreasonable enterprise, since in order to carry it out words must be defined by means of sentences in which the constituent words must in their turn be absolutely clearly defined and unambiguous, and so on *ad infinitum*. The only way to overcome the pseudo-problems is to examine the context in which a word is used, and never to use it in *that* context with any other meaning than that which the context demands.

In the *Tractatus* Wittgenstein is already aware that ordinary language presents words in a variety of shifting meanings, depending on what is presupposed in the different contexts. 'The tacit assumptions involved in understanding ordinary language are enormously complicated.'[67] In the *Tractatus* he wishes to remedy this by means of the sort of critique of language recommended there. In the *Philosophical Investigations* this has to be replaced by another sort of critique of language, namely one that takes account of the context in which a statement is made and the 'tacit assumptions' by which its meaning is determined, and thus pays attention to the way in which the word or proposition is used.

The standpoint of the *Philosophical Investigations* is far removed from that of the *Tractatus*; between them is the path from atomism to contexts of meaning in philosophy, which Wittgenstein has been constrained to travel. What occurred in the interval between these two works to cause their author to make this complete change of front?[68] When the *Philosophical Investigations* was first published posthumously in 1953, it was the gulf separating the two works that most compelled attention. This gulf was at least partly filled by the publication of *The Blue and Brown Books* in 1958; these were described by the editor as 'Preliminary Studies for the 'Philosophical Investigations'' '. If *The Brown Book* stands nearer to the final view of the *Philosophical Investigations* and in many ways anticipates it, it is *The Blue Book* that is of greater interest for us in this context, since it to some extent represents the missing link between the *Tractatus* and the *Philosophical Investigations*.

[67] *Tractatus* 4.002.

[68] Already in 1931–2 Wittgenstein was moving decidedly away from the *Tractatus*. This is clear from a letter to M. Schlick quoted in *Wittgenstein, Schr.* 3 (ed. McGuinness), p. 24. He says there of the *Tractatus*: 'With very very many of the formulations in the book I am today out of sympathy.'

The difference between the *Tractatus* and *The Blue Book* is most striking when we look at the way each begins. The *Tractatus* starts with a proposition about the 'world' and thus betrays its metaphysical leaning. *The Blue Book* starts with the question 'What is the meaning of a word?' The difference is obvious; Wittgenstein has perceived the fundamental metaphysical error in the *Tractatus*—belief in the one ideal language, which is formed under a certain psychological compulsion with one eye on the language of (natural) science. 'Philosophers constantly see the method of science before their eyes, and are irresistibly tempted to ask and answer questions in the way science does. This tendency is the real source of metaphysics, and leads the philosopher into complete darkness.'[69] Wittgenstein attacks his own former idea 'that the meaning of a word is an image, or a thing correlated to the word'[70] and that the purpose of words is to name things. He directs this criticism against his former position: 'We are looking at words as though they all were proper names, and we confuse the bearer of a name with a meaning of the name.' Here Wittgenstein has already arrived at the insight *that it is the particular use of a word only which gives the word its meaning. . . .* The use of the word *in practice* is its meaning.'[71]

If we add to this that here Wittgenstein has also arrived at the idea of 'language games' and 'family resemblances' which was later central in his thinking, it might appear as if he had already come to his final position. That this nevertheless is not the case is clear, for although the meaning of a word is its 'use', this does not yet exclude its 'reference' as also decisive for its meaning. Thus *The Blue Book* in some respects still takes up the position held in the *Tractatus*, in other respects it has begun to move towards that of the *Philosophical Investigations*.

5.

We cannot here consider in detail the many important things. Wittgenstein says in the *Philosophical Investigations* about meaning and its connection with *use* and *context*. We may say in summary that Wittgenstein's contribution to philosophy is that he has focussed attention in new ways and with a new emphasis on those contexts of meaning—the term is is equivalent to what Wittgenstein calls 'language games'—which determine the meaning of words and propositions. In other words he has shown in his philosophy the error of trying to understand a statement in isolation[72] and the necessity of taking account of its 'surroundings'[73] and thus of understanding it within and from its context. The statement must be seen in its immediate context, in the 'wider context'[74] of which that is part, and

[69] *Blue Book*, p. 18.   [70] *Ibid.*   [71] *Blue Book*, p. 69. Italics ours except '*in practice*'.
[72] *Philosophical Investigations*, § 595, p. 155: 'It is natural for us to say a sentence in such-and-such surroundings, and unnatural to say it in isolation.'
[73] '*ihrer Umgebung*'—op. cit., §584, p. 153.
[74] *Op. cit.*, § 539, p. 145.

finally in the comprehensive context of what Wittgenstein calls a 'language game'—a 'context of meaning' in the widest sense—which shows the 'sort of context' in which a word stands and through which it ultimately receives its meaning.[75] To belong to a language and to belong to a context are one and the same thing.[76]

Wittgenstein has thus brought his investigation to the point at which the deepest philosophical problem occurs. This problem has of course been noticed and treated before in philosophy. It is, to call it by its traditional name, the problem of categories. It has long been realized that the mixing of different categories leads to confusion, and also that this mixing of categories has played a decisive part in the rise of metaphysical thought. Wittgenstein's achievement is that he has started from a quite different angle and has worked with completely concrete material to get at this problem, and thus has opened up new ways of dealing with it. He has shown the possibility of a new approach in philosophy, an approach which at first sight seems to narrow the scope of philosophy in an unprecedented way and to set aside its main problems, but which gradually leads not only to the treatment of these very problems, but also to their treatment at a deeper level.

Let a saying of Bertrand Russell's about Wittgenstein serve as a tail-piece. Russell's judgment will obviously not be particularly favourable. He writes: 'The later Wittgenstein . . . seems to have grown tired of serious thinking and to have invented a doctrine which would make such an activity unnecessary. I do not for one moment believe that the doctrine which has these consequences is true . . .'

'The desire to understand the world is, they think, an outdated folly.'[77]

It is the old atomistic metaphysician's sigh over the frustration of his hopes of a philosophical-metaphysical *Weltanschauung* on the basis of logical atomism; it is his disappointment at seeing his most hopeful 'disciple' abandoning atomistic metaphysics and following the path to the philosophical concept of the great contexts of meaning. Russell's negative judgment on Wittgenstein's later philosophy is therefore the most appropriate illustration of its significance and its influence on the philosophy of the last decades.

5. Importance of the Context for Meaning and Argumentation

In the attempt to deal with the problem of meaning, as the foregoing pages have shown, two directly opposite courses have been pursued: atomism and contextualism.[78] Here the Frege-Russell-Wittgenstein constellation

---

[75] *Op. cit.*, II. ix, p. 188.
[76] *Op. cit.*, II. xi, p. 217; 'They must surely belong to a language and a context.'
[77] From Russell's Introduction to E. Gellner, *Words and Things*.
[78] On these *cf.* my essay 'Atomism eller sammanhang'.

furnishes excellent illustrative material.[79] For all their differences of out-look these three men have enough of a common denominator to make it worth while to compare them and see what contribution they can make towards elucidating the question of meaning. They are all mathematically oriented, preoccupied with mathematical logic or logicism, and all bent on answering the question of meaning. Frege is clear that it is the context that is ultimately decisive for meaning. Russell takes over from Frege, but turns his thought upside down: it is the particular, isolated, atomistically con-ceived word that is ultimately the bearer of meaning. Wittgenstein takes over from Russell, but gradually turns his thought upside down, and we are thus back again with the context as the decisive thing. But the detour via Russell has not been unprofitable. The idea of an artificial language and of meaning as attached to isolated words or sentences has provided a background against which the significance of the context can be all the more plainly seen. Thus the importance of the context for everything that can be called meaning and argumentation is more sharply delineated in Wittgenstein than in Frege. It was Wittgenstein who switched on to the right track again after Russell's deviation. This is one of the most import-ant contributions of Wittgenstein's thought, which emerges particularly in his *Philosophical Investigations*.

To describe Russell's atomistic theory of meaning as a deviation is a way of saying that atomism and contextualism do not represent two equally reputable views, between which one has to choose. Nor is it a case of that familiar historical phenomenon, the swing of the pendulum between different views, as if after pointing in Frege to the context it swung with Russell over to atomism and then with Wittgenstein back again to the context. The fact is rather that Russell's atomistic theory of meaning is not really a theory of meaning at all. It is not a theory of 'meaning' but of 'reference'. Russell happens to have lost track of the problem of meaning, and is speaking of something quite different, though he continues to call it 'meaning' and still thinks he is speaking of that problem. Hence we can properly speak here of a deviation.

What occasioned this deviation, and what made it so natural for logical positivism to follow Russell at this point, is not difficult to discover. The background of it all is the powerful metaphysical tradition by which so much of philosophical thinking down to our own time has been un-consciously governed. It should be noted, moreover, that this involves a *double* line of metaphysical tradition: on the one hand there is the rationalist line of Plato–Leibniz–logicism, and on the other the empiricist line of Berkeley–Hume–positivism. Owing to its empirical tendency it is easy to

[79] As our purpose here is to draw conclusions from the foregoing in preparation for a discussion of 'contexts of meaning', a certain amount of repetition of what has already been said is unavoidable; but this will not be altogether regrettable if it helps, as it may, towards a greater clarification of the issues.

forget the metaphysical cast of the latter, yet in fact it represents just as pronounced a metaphysic as the former. Now when these two lines of tradition meet and unite as they do in logical atomism or logical empiricism, the impression is easily gained that we have arrived at an exact scientific philosophy. For what else is the combination of the logical and the empirical but a gathering up of axiomatic and empirical argumentation into a higher philosophical unity, so that philosophy is a direct extension of the accepted modes of argumentation, which in it attain their perfection. That, however, is only how it appears. What really happens is that two *metaphysical* streams unite to form a single river; and that is certainly not the way to produce a scientific philosophy.

Metaphysics flourishes in different forms. It can assert itself not only in rationalistic outlooks but at least equally well in empiricistic. A glance at the history of thought shows this very clearly. To put it in a rather over-simplified formula we may say: Twice in the history of thought there have occurred momentous revolutions which have strait-jacketed thinking for centuries ahead, because they have produced models for thought to which it became almost self-evident for subsequent thinking to conform.

The *first* great revolution took place when Plato hypostatized the universal concepts and thus laid the foundation of the conceptual realism which thereafter came to serve as a model for metaphysics. The ground was thus prepared for that *objective idealism* which has dominated the thinking of centuries, not to say millennia. Here the pattern was set so effectively that it became determinative not only for those who espoused the Platonic doctrine of Ideas, but also for those who reacted negatively to it.

The *second* great revolution, the second fateful change of direction, took place when Descartes propounded his '*cogito, ergo sum*', or perhaps better, when the idea of '*esse est percipi*' was born. This was responsible for that subjectivizing of being which has been such an outstanding feature of modern philosophy. The result of it has been subjectivism, sometimes called *subjective idealism*, which in turn has led to *phenomenalism*. This pattern of thought too has proved so unyielding and irresistible that even those who have been consciously opposed to anything in the nature of idealism have had to follow it. In doing so, however, they have simply shut their eyes to the fact that this too is a case of metaphysics, though metaphysics of an opposite type to the old.

There is an unbroken line that runs from Berkeley and Hume all the way to Mach, Russell and Carnap, with continual variations on the subjectivist-phenomenalist theme. Even where its representatives believe themselves to be standing most firmly on empirical ground, their metaphysical posture is displayed in their reduction of all knowledge to sense-data, their insistence on protocol-sentences and their demand for a unified 'physicalistic' language, not to mention their perpetually recurring debates for and against the existence of material objects. The form in which meta-physical thinking has chiefly held sway in more recent times is the last-named, the phenomenalist-sensualistic. The concept of 'meaning', which was introduced as a means of attacking and overcoming every form of metaphysics, has in practice proved to be an effective means of perpetuating a particular sort of metaphysics, and that just because it has been set in the context of subjectivistic phenomenalism.

When meaningfulness is equated with reducibility to elementary per-ceptions and sense-data, we have plainly not got beyond the psychologism which we have otherwise seen to be untenable. If the empirical tendency so understood is joined with the logical, then the result is logical atomism. When logical atomism is seen against the background of this double meta-physics it is at once evident that all its ingredients go back to metaphysical influences and it owes strictly speaking nothing to the problem of meaning. Here we find for example in Russell the Platonic-metaphysical habit of regarding universal concepts as entities, together with the atomistic way of thinking that goes back to Hume—the latter unchanged except that Hume's psychological atomism has been transformed into logical atomism, while its metaphysical basis remains unaffected. When psychologists have perceived the unsoundness of the Humean atomistic association-psy-chology,[80] we have still less reason to commit ourselves to logical atomism, and least of all to expect it to be of any use to us in the analysis of meaning. When Russell declares: 'My own *logic* is atomistic', this means only that his own *metaphysics* is atomistic. The metaphysics comes first and the rest follows from it. It was in seeking to overcome a metaphysical monism (Bradley's in particular) that he developed his ontological pluralism—and thus got on to the atomistic track; but even there he is moving on meta-physical lines.[81]

It was necessary to digress as we have done, in order to make it clear that Russell's atomistic theory of meaning is not strictly a theory of mean-ing at all in the analytical sense, but is from start to finish a metaphysical theory. If we begin by adopting an atomistic standpoint, we shall start our alleged analysis of meaning, as Russell does, with individual, isolated words as atomic bricks with which sentences are built up and from which they derive their meaning. The sentences 'are composed of words, and have a meaning derivative from the words that they contain.'[82] If therefore we wish to know the meaning of a statement, we must take account of every individual word and find out what it means. By knowing the signifi-

---

[80] On this *cf.* among others A. Michotte, *The Perception of Causality*, pp. 7ff. and 255–66. 'As a result, nearly two centuries had to pass before it was realized that a wrong course was being followed . . . it had the result of splitting the phenomenal world into pieces and making the most interesting psychological facts disappear' (p. 8).

[81] Russell, LAK, p. 234.

[82] Russell, *An Inquiry*, p. 34.

cation of every word 'in isolation' and quite apart from the context in which it now stands, we know also the meaning of the statement as a whole. Russell is of course aware that there are words which lack any such independent signification or reference. 'Many words only have meaning in a suitable verbal context—such words as "than", "or", "however", cannot stand alone.'[83] But these words form a rather exceptional group; and the rule, which according to Russell applies to the great majority of words— the 'object-words'—is that they have their 'meaning' independently of the context. They 'can be used in isolation'[84] or, as he also puts it: 'object-words have a meaning which does not depend upon their occurring in sentences.'[85] What primarily has meaning is thus the individual, isolated word, and a sentence acquires meaning only secondarily and derivatively as being a collocation of verbal atoms or atoms of meaning, the signification of which is settled in advance.

It is plain that such a *static* conception does justice neither to the nature of language nor to 'meaning'. It is not only the group of words which Russell acknowledges as lacking any independent meaning of their own— the so-called syncategorematic words—that have no meaning 'in isolation'. This can be extended to apply to all words when they are taken 'in isolation' and divorced from their context. A word thus mishandled eludes the attempt to determine its meaning. It possesses meaning—definitive meaning—only in a context, the context of the sentence and the larger context of which it is part. Torn out of all context one and the same word can mean all sorts of different things. In what follows we shall show by a number of examples how important the context is for determining the real meaning of an expression.

It might easily be suspected that there is a certain necessary connection between the idea that a word as such must have a definitive meaning, and the notion of an 'ideal language' or an 'artificial language' in which every word corresponds to one and only one object or thought. Russell's rather odd theory of meaning, in which the context is thrust into the background, would then be a simple consequence of his logicistic outlook. That logicism does not necessarily lead to such a result, however, is very evident from the fact that its two nineteenth century pioneers, Augustus de Morgan and Gottlob Frege, drew no such consequences from it, but took a directly opposite view. For Frege, as we saw above, it is the context that is decisive for meaning; and as for Augustus de Morgan, he will have no truck with any view that neglects the context, but puts it quite simply on his list of 'Fallacies'.[86] There is thus no occasion to make symbolic logic responsible for logical atomism. The latter is entirely Russell's own affair, and it is

[83] *Op. cit.* p. 25.
[84] *Ibid.*
[85] *Op. cit.*, p. 29.
[86] A. de Morgan, *Formal Logic*, p. 285 (where he attacks 'omission of the context').

sufficiently explained, as was shown above, by his atomistic metaphysics. We have here further evidence that in Russell it is the metaphysics that has directed the logic and not, as he himself imagines, the logic that has directed the metaphysics. This is a point of special importance in our context because his treatment of the question of meaning bears throughout the stamp of his metaphysical atomism. If one does not share this metaphysics, there is no longer any reason to speak of an atomistic theory of meaning.

In such circumstances it may seem surprising that a theory which starts with isolated words and seeks to find its way from them to 'meaning', should have been able to survive as long as it has. It must not, however, be overlooked that there are a number of factors which at least superficially seem to favour it.

First and foremost there is the *manageability* of the theory. We need go no further than vocabulary and syntax, both of which are easily mastered in a mechanical way. Words are a sort of 'bricks', furnished with a mysterious something called 'meaning'. These bricks can be put together according to the rules of syntax to form a sentence, which is then also meaningful thanks to the meaning inherent in the bricks. To this, however, there is the obvious objection that language does not after all consist merely of vocables and syntax, but there is also something called 'context'; which raises a question that is considerably more difficult to master. For the context is situationally determined. Instead of the simple putting together of statically given bricks, we have an extremely diversified use of words and functioning of expressions. The context cannot be captured in a single formula. In this it resembles 'meaning', which is not amenable to any universal criterion of meaning. Because of this dynamic diversity it is often suggested that to speak of the context is to introduce an unpredictable element into the discussion. But that is by no means the case. The context is no more unpredictable than the words and syntax. What is really unpredictable, however, is the ascription of 'meaning' to isolated words, which is sheer verbal legerdemain.

The *second* factor that may seem to favour the atomistic idea, is quite simply the *lexicon or dictionary*. This is so because in the dictionary we find words arranged in sequence according to the mechanical principle of alphabetical order, so that they stand 'in isolation' with the meanings assigned to them. Then grammar and syntax seem to furnish instructions as to how sentences and contexts may be constructed out of the units of meaning drawn from the dictionary. This is however only superficially and seemingly so. In fact the dictionary provides unambiguous evidence that the opposite is the case; it testifies to the primacy of the context for meaning. For a dictionary is not merely a list of words, nor does it attach only one meaning to each word, but gives a multiplicity of meanings for one and the same word. Where has the lexicographer obtained all these meanings? He has met the word in different contexts, and has seen that it has one meaning in one context and another in another. Apart from such contexts he would know nothing of these different meanings of words. We may add, moreover, that if the dictionary were larger it would list a still larger number of meanings. Yet however large the dictionary, it sometimes happens that I do not find the right meaning for a word among those it lists. In such a case I must do as the lexicographer does, and infer the meaning of the word from the context in which it occurs. It is useless here to fall back on a meaning arbitrarily assigned to a word 'in isolation'; nothing helps but looking at the word in its context. It is therefore very far from the case that the dictionary or lexicon favours an atomistic theory of meaning; on the contrary, it completely refutes such a theory. Here as always it is the context that determines the meaning.

A *third* factor that has possibly favoured an atomistic view, might be described as *typographical*. This has to do with the fact that we are accustomed to seeing words in writing and print as clearly differentiated units, and as the constituent parts of which a sentence is composed. When, however, we try to construe the 'meaning' by adding together these simple constituents, to which some sort of aboriginal minimum of meaning has been attached for the purpose, the result is more like a caricature, not to say a grotesque. In order to show the absurdity of such a way of doing things, a caricature of the caricature may perhaps be useful. Why should we stop at the words? Are there not here also smaller 'constituents' to be considered? Words are after all from a typographical point of view composed of letters. We see the letters arranged in sequence, and taken together they form words. Sentences consist of words, and words of letters. What happens to the meaning then? It retreats from the sentence to words, from words to letters, from letters to 'little patches' of which they are composed; that is to say, it disappears into complete meaninglessness.

Now that is a caricature, as we have said, yet it is not one that we have merely imagined or contrived, but one that has actually occurred. An investigator conducting a logico-psychological experiment on certain persons, had used exclusively alphabetical material. When objection was raised to this on the ground that the result might have been different if he had used more natural and meaningful material, which the persons concerned could more easily have held in mind, he replied: 'Then surely the same should apply to words, which don't consist of much else but letters.' That is what one can come to if the question of the meaning of a sentence is taken to be identical with that of the words of which it is composed. Russell mixes up these two questions, Wittgenstein keeps them apart. With the view here described logical atomism has run its course, and in doing so has disqualified itself as a theory of meaning. Since the letters 'in isolation' are without meaning, the consequence is that the words composed of them, and also the sentences composed of the words, are meaningless—

derivatively meaningless. That such a conception cannot serve as the starting point for an analysis of meaning could not be more plain.

The only way to deal effectually with the question of meaning is to start from the opposite end, not from the words in isolation, but from the context. It is to Wittgenstein's credit that he has seen this and has shaped the whole of his later philosophy accordingly. The significance of the context was present in his thought from the very first. Although during his earlier period he was to a considerable extent under the influence of Russell, yet as regards the fundamental importance of the context he was decidedly opposed to him. Already in the *Tractatus* we read: 'Only the proposition has sense [*Sinn*]; only in the context of the proposition has a name meaning [*Bedeutung*].'[87] In that statement there is the embryo of a theory of meaning directly opposite to that of Russellian atomism. It was, however, only in Wittgenstein's later period that his new theory of meaning came to be worked out.

The contrast between Russell and Wittgenstein can be seen very clearly if we put them side by side and allow Wittgenstein to speak both from his earlier and his later work.

Russell says.

The sentences are composed of words, and have a meaning derivative from that of the words that they contain.[88]

Wittgenstein says in the *Tractatus*:

Nur der Satz hat Sinn; nur im Zusammenhang des Satzes hat ein Name Bedeutung,[89]

and in the *Philosophical Investigations*:

Wie setzt sich der Sinn des Satzes 'Ich habe ihn noch immer nicht gesehen' aus den Bedeutungen seiner Wörter zusammen? The sentence is composed of the words, and that is enough.[90]

We have here used alternately the German and the English text, since now one and now the other gives clearer expression to Wittgenstein's meaning and to the contrast between him and Russell. The contrast emerges particularly clearly in the last statement cited from the English text, in which Wittgenstein directly employs Russell's words and contradicts them. It looks as if Wittgenstein formulated these propositions in direct opposition to Russell, and in order to set up an antithesis to him. Whether he did this deliberately or not, it is not important for us to know, but it can certainly be said that there *is* a direct antithesis.

[87] *Tractatus* 3.3.
[88] *An Inquiry*, p. 34.
[89] *Tractatus* 3.3.
[90] *Investigations*, II. vi, p. 118.

The nature of Wittgenstein's new theory of meaning can be concisely expressed in terms of the formula which has become so familiar in recent times: 'Don't ask for the meaning, ask for the use.' But then it is important to understand this formula correctly. Otherwise when it is used as a maxim for a contextual theory of meaning, it may at first sight seem rather bewildering. For in it there is no mention of 'context', and as for 'meaning', the question of meaning is just what we are told to avoid. This formula has, as a matter of fact, occasioned a great deal of misunderstanding. It has been taken to imply that the later Wittgenstein abandoned the question of meaning, which was originally so important to him, and turned instead to a general linguistic investigation of the use of words in 'ordinary language'. That, however, is by no means the case. Far from having begun with an interest in the question of meaning which he later abandoned in favour of an inquiry into the 'use' of words, Wittgenstein continued to regard the question of meaning as the crucial issue, and simply discovered a new way of getting at the meaning by paying attention to the 'use' of words.

The formula 'Don't ask for the meaning, ask for the use' involves two things, one negative and the other positive. On the one hand it implies the rejection of a wrong way of approaching the question of meaning, and on the other an indication of the right way. 'What do you mean?' is a good and necessary question. But 'don't ask for the meaning' in the way that became customary in connection with the quest for a universal criterion, of meaning. There is not and cannot be any such universal criterion. 'Don't ask for the meaning' of separate individual words, for words 'in isolation' have no definitive meaning. Don't try to formulate a definition of what *exactly* a word means, for if you do, the thing you are looking for will elude you. If we are to get to grips with the question of meaning, we must ask it in a new way, not focusing our attention on alleged, static verbal atoms, but paying heed to the way in which words are actually used when they are functioning in living language. Only by studying this can we discover their meaning. Therefore 'ask for the use'. The use of an expression, or the way it functions in its context, *is* its meaning.[91]

With this the answer is also given to the question of the significance of the context for argumentation. As we earlier put forward the proposition 'without context, no meaning', so now we can just as truly say: *without context, no argumentation*. Scientific argumentation does not occur at random, but depends on contextual relationships and implications. Only as set in a context does it have meaning and cogency. Thus an experiment is a highly meaningful undertaking, and it is so just because it is not a disconnected and arbitrary activity. Throughout its entire course it is related

[91] That it is the primary task of philosophy to investigate the 'use' is emphasized in my essay 'Hur är filosofi som vetenskap möjlig?' (1928). Wittgenstein's formula, 'Ask for the use', says much the same thing, and his *Philosophical Investigations* is a classic example of work on a closely related task.

to a definite context, and that for a definite purpose. I wish, for example, by means of particular observations to test a general hypothesis. Do the particular observations made during the experiment harmonize with the general context postulated by the hypothesis? Or take another example. When an archaeologist in his digging comes across a fragment of pottery with peculiar ornamentation, he is interested in it not as an isolated bit of matter, but as a pointer to a context, a whole of which it once was a part. Starting with this he attempts to reconstruct the vessel to which it belonged. If he finds more fragments, they may possibly upset his first hypothesis: the vessel must have had a different shape from what he supposed. Or these new finds may possibly give further support to his hypothesis.

How is it that these fragments can be cited as arguments for or against his attempt at reconstruction? Obviously it is because they can be fitted into a context, a whole of which they are parts. Do the parts he actually comes across fit into the whole as he conceives it? Do they harmonize with the context, or must he revise the context in order to fit them in? In either case the essential thing, and the thing that makes the investigation meaningful, is the attention paid to the context. The fragments are like pieces of a jig-saw puzzle that have to find a place in the picture. Such a piece interests us, not as the bit of wood or cardboard that it is, but because it points to a context, fits into a context, and becomes an argument for the context. The parts can be used to test the whole—though only on the supposition that there is a context. If there were not, everything would be chaotic and no argumentation would be possible. What is more, the research occasioned by the 'fragment' has not attained its goal merely by the reconstruction of the 'vessel'. The latter is a cultural object, which derives its significance from the place it occupies in its historical milieu. Then the inquiry proceeds further, to the question of historical influences and the great vistas of civilization they open up—vast contexts which would remain unnoticed if the fragment were merely considered 'in isolation'. It is only when its isolation is broken down that the fragment becomes significant for scientific argumentation.

Once we have realized the importance of the context for meaning and argumentation, the horizon broadens step by step to include ever larger contexts. If we now return to the 'proposition', we cannot be content with the limited context which it provides, nor with its immediate surroundings. The proposition, which has a meaning we wish to understand, is set in a certain contextual relation to preceding and following propositions which determine its import. If my immediate interpretation of the proposition is incompatible with this context of which the proposition is a part, then my interpretation cannot be correct. Furthermore, I naturally cannot stop at the propositions immediately surrounding it, but must also consider what its function is in the total context. Thus the perspective widens from the proposition to the immediate context, from that to the larger context, and from that to the total context, the comprehensive 'context of meaning'. The problem I am dealing with must in the last resort be placed within its appropriate 'frame of reference'. So long as I pay no attention to that, I cannot be sure that I grasp the real meaning of the proposition, or rather, I can be quite sure that I do not correctly grasp its meaning. Thus the question of 'Meaning and Context' necessarily leads to that of 'Contexts of Meaning'[92] and the presuppositions that govern them.

[92] The importance of 'the context' and 'the context of meaning' has gained recognition in the most diverse quarters in the contemporary world. Modern atomic physics, for example, is not nearly as 'atomistic' in outlook as might be expected. It is significant that one of the most distinguished atomic physicists, Werner Heisenberg, has entitled one of his works 'Der Teil und das Ganze. Gespräche im Umkreis der Atomphysik'—with the emphasis on the 'whole', the context, as essential for any understanding of the 'part'. Here we find also the idea of the 'context of meaning'. Heisenberg quotes from a conversation with Niels Bohr the following statement regarding the religious context of meaning: 'This context of meaning (Sinnzusammenhang) too belongs to reality, just as much as does our conditioning by natural science, and it would be a gross oversimplification to attribute it exclusively to the subjective side' (p. 128). In this regard it can be said that natural science in its most recent phase (Planck, Einstein, Heisenberg, von Weizsäcker) has contributed greatly towards widening our intellectual horizon and overcoming an earlier narrowness of outlook.—Cf. also above, p. 123, n. 56, and below, p. 271, n. 6, and pp. 287–92.

CHAPTER X

Contexts of Meaning

1. Terminology

THERE is a general awareness that the things we talk about must be set in their proper contexts if there is to be any *meaning* in discussion of them. Detached utterances can mean very nearly anything. It is only through the context in which it occurs that a statement acquires a clear, unambiguous content. Yet agreed though we may be upon that, closer inspection soon shows that this important subject has been allowed to remain in a far too vague and indefinite state, which is reflected in the ambiguity of the terminology used with regard to it. We lack here the support which a settled, uniform terminology can give. It will therefore be appropriate to begin by spending a little time on the question of terminology.

If in doing this we briefly review some of the terms most commonly used in this connection, our primary purpose will naturally be to clear the way for a serviceable and as far as possible adequate terminology. But the review can also serve an additional purpose. No one term can possibly cover everything, and it may therefore be of importance to associate something of the other terms with it. Although we shall have to settle on one of the various alternatives, our exposition will be richer and less formalistic if overtones from the others are in some measure taken along with it. There is also the further point that the multiplicity of ways of expressing one and the same thing is evidence of the central importance of that thing. They show in how many different ways the attempt has been made to move in a similar direction. The question of terminology is of course always to some extent a matter of convenience; but it should at least be our aim to secure a terminology that is as adequate as possible without depriving ourselves of the enriching insights which other alternatives can provide.

(1) To begin with there is the familiar and latterly much used term *'universe of discourse'*. One can guess of course roughly what this term is intended to signify, and what its function is meant to be. But its weakness lies in its general and rather vague formulation. Why speak of 'universe' here? And what exactly is implied by connecting it with 'discourse'? Light is shed on this if we take a look at the very interesting history of the expression and trace it to its source. It was the sharpsighted mathematician and logician Augustus de Morgan who in order to resolve a quite specific difficulty in traditional logic introduced this term, though not quite in the form that has since become prevalent, but in the form of 'the universe of a proposition'.[1]

[1] A. de Morgan, 'On the Structure of the Syllogism', TCPS VIII, iii, p. 380. *Cf.* de

The difficulty to be overcome is that the mere contrary of X, namely not-X, appears to include everything in the entire universe which is not X, and so to be of a completely indefinite or, in Aristotelian terms, an aorist character. To this de Morgan replies: 'but the universe of a particular assertion or argument may be limited in any matter expressed or understood.' It is only when I understand what we are speaking about, that I understand the limits within which it holds good. We can see at once that this has to do with putting things in their appropriate context, and we also see the reason for the odd use of the word 'universe' in this connection. Whereas traditional logic allows the contraries, X and not-X, to divide 'the whole universe of possible conceptions' between them (for a thing is either X or not-X, since there is no other possibility), de Morgan shows that a proposition itself implies a certain limitation. We are, in other words, not dealing with the whole universe, but with a universe delimited by the proposition, and it is this that de Morgan, 'inventing a new technical name', calls 'the universe of a proposition'. De Morgan's discovery, however, is significant not only for the particular matter that primarily led him to make the distinction, but it is applicable to all meaningful discussion. It is necessary to observe the limitation which the discussion itself presupposes.

This brings us to the 'universe of discourse' and its relevance for our present purpose. It reminds us that in any discussion we must pay attention to 'what it is about', and not import into anything that is said another meaning than it has in the context of that particular discussion. The point is aptly made by Mario Bunge when he says: *'a common universe of discourse . . .* is necessary for establishing logical relationship among the members of a set of formulas'.[2] It is an indispensable requirement of semantics that the different terms in a discussion should 'belong to the same semantical family' or be 'semantically homogeneous'.[3]

The term 'universe of discourse' says very clearly a number of vitally important things. It says, for example, that no subject can be meaningfully discussed in isolation, but must be seen as pointing to a universal context of which it forms a part, and that there must be no slipping over from one context to another. It is necessary always to remain within the context that is prescribed by the nature of the discussion. On the other hand, this terminology has also its weaknesses. Apart from a knowledge of its precursor, 'the universe of a proposition', it is hardly possible to be aware of

---

Morgan, *Formal Logic*, p. 55: 'By the *universe* of a proposition, I mean the whole range of names in which it is expressed or understood that the names in the proposition are found.'

[2] M. Bunge, *Scientific Research*, p. 292.

[3] *Ibid.* On these and related concepts *cf.* M. Bunge, 'Physics and Reality', in *Objectivité et Realité*, pp. 182f., 192f.

the full implications of the oddly formulated phrase 'universe of discourse'. Besides which, the word 'universe' easily evokes associations of a metaphysical nature, which must at all costs be resisted if the formula is to serve its purpose.

(2) Another term which has come to be widely used for a similar purpose is *'frame of reference'*. In order to be rightly understood, an expression must be set in the frame of reference to which it naturally belongs. If it is transferred to another frame of reference, it will no longer have the same meaning as it originally had, and it may have no meaning at all. This terminology is uncomplicated and readily usable, but it too has certain weaknesses. The idea of a 'frame' tends to suggest something rather external and static, as if the main thing were to stay within the frame originally given, and the only danger lay in transferring an expression from one frame to another. In itself this is a sound point, but there is nothing to show why it is important. Why should we not put one and the same picture, one and the same expression, in different frames? It is not made clear how this changes or distorts the whole meaning. Furthermore, the idea of 'reference' can divert attention from the all-important idea of 'meaning'. 'Meaning' and 'reference' have after all to do with two different things (*cf.* Frege's *Sinn und Bedeutung*). Note also that what is said here about 'frame of reference' applies equally to such terms as 'point of reference', 'reference system', 'reference set', which have been used as alternatives to it.

(3) When an expression is referred to a general context, it is not uncommon to speak of the latter in terms of *'standpoint'* or *'perspective'*. The standpoint in question is of course of a universal sort, and a context is implied by the very word 'perspective', for to view things in a certain perspective is to see them in a certain context. The danger in using such expressions is that they can easily be conceived in a subjectivistic way. I can adopt different standpoints as I see fit, and every new point gives me a new perspective. How can arbitrariness be avoided here? And how is justice to be done to the objective content of 'meaning'?

(4) In order to overcome the difficulties indicated here, it is tempting to employ the expression *'areas of experience'*. In our actual 'experience' we have to do with widely different things, of which one cannot forthwith be reduced to another or understood in terms of another. An ethical judgment, for example, is not of the same nature as a scientific judgment, yet both belong indispensably to human experience. They must not be confused with one another, for only as each is allowed to be what it is can it retain its meaning. The simplest way of ensuring this is to distinguish them from one another as belonging to different 'areas of experience'. Each of them is valid in its own area and its own context.

This makes for clarity with regard to the different fundamental contexts, to which statements in the several 'areas' owe their characteristic sense. Yet even this terminology is not without its dangers.

To begin with, the idea of 'experience' is itself equivocal. It is easily interpreted in empirical-sensualistic terms. And when that happens, it leads both to an undue cramping of the whole approach to the problem ('reductionism') and also to psychologism, both of which get us away from the question of 'meaning'. If we are to employ the concept of experience in this connection, it must be made clear that we are using it in a specifically philosophical sense, as equivalent to 'valid experience'. But the term 'experience' itself is so loaded that there is little prospect of making clear to everybody the specific sense in which it is used here. There is also the temptation to try to undergird the discussion of these various forms of experience with psychological considerations. As for the phrase '*areas* of experience', the idea of 'areas' can easily mislead us into thinking of en-closed spaces, areas fenced off from one another, which is not at all what is meant. The ethical and the scientific are not two separate areas in that sense, but two distinct attitudes and points of view, both of which can often have reference to one and the same object. Science is not excluded from any area. It can for example investigate the psychology of the ethical life; but it is not therefore synonymous with ethical evaluation and decision.

What is said here of 'areas of experience' applies equally if we speak in-stead of different 'sectors' of experience—the scientific sector, the ethical sector, and so forth. They do not lie side by side as separate segments or parts of experience, but each of them covers from its own point of view the entire range of experience.

(5) The term most frequently used in contemporary philosophy to denote what we are talking about here is the one introduced by Ludwig Wittgenstein: '*language games.*' Thanks to this concept the question of the importance of the context for meaning has become a central issue in the current debate, and a semantically oriented philosophy has received an extremely valuable corrective. The fundamental question we have to ask with regard to any statement is that of the 'language game' to which it belongs, for a statement has quite different meanings according as it is assigned to one or another 'language'. These ideas have become public property, and this has meant a great step forward as regards clarification of 'the question of meaning'.

It must however be said here as in the previous cases, that even this terminology is not without its risks. These risks are in part connected with what is really the strength of the theory. What has made it so irresis-tible is its simplicity and obviousness. No one can help but see that one and the same expression can have extremely different meanings in differ-ent contexts or 'languages'. But here the danger arises that we make it all too easy for ourselves and imagine we have solved a problem by simply saying that it is a question of a different 'language' or 'language game'. For this is just where the problem begins. The commonest way of evading the issue is to let the two parts of this formula become separated and content oneself with talking simply of different 'languages' or different 'games'.

In Wittgenstein's theory of 'language games' both parts of the formula are equally important, and it is only as they are held together that the formula is properly understood. If we speak only of 'languages'—as it has become very popular to do—it is easy to imagine that we ought to be able to 'translate' what is said in one language into another. But that is just what we cannot do. This is clear as soon as we take the idea of 'games' into account. These 'languages' are in the nature of the case untranslatable, for every 'game' obeys its own rules. How could chess be translated into the language of tennis? Either we play chess, and then we abide by the rules of chess, or we play another game according to other rules. Yet there is no less risk if we speak only of different 'games', for this can easily give the impression of something conventional and arbitrary. There is no limit to the number of different games that can be invented, each with its own special rules. But it is not that aspect of games that is in mind when they are taken as a model in connection with language. The idea that philosophy is concerned with different 'language games' does not mean that every arbitrary system of rules can be made an object of philosophical investigation. Against such a misunderstanding the thought of 'language' is a safe-guard, for language is not a merely arbitrary collocation of words. What the idea of 'games' is intended to illustrate here is the very opposite of arbitrariness. The point is that in playing a game we have to abide by the rules of the game.[4] Similarly in using a language we have to abide by its rules, and where *different* 'languages' are concerned, by the 'rules of the game' that are applicable in each case—which are nothing else but the 'presuppositions' implied in them.

(6) If we wish to have a term capable of expressing all that is intended by those so far discussed, while avoiding as far as possible the risks they entail, it seems best to stick to '*context of meaning*'.[5] This expression in some measure gathers up the results of our entire investigation so far. In particular it takes account of 1. the concern of philosophy with '*meaning*', and its function as 'analysis of meaning'; 2. the decisive importance of *the context* for meaning; and 3. the *presuppositions* which govern and give

---

[4] On the subject of games—rules of the game—meaning of the game, *cf.* E. Husserl, *Logische Untersuchungen*, II, 1, p. 69.

[5] Here a comment on my own terminology may be in place. In my earlier writings I used the term 'areas of experience', but it proved almost impossible with this to guard against misinterpretation. The word 'experience' caused trouble, because in spite of my insisting that what I had in mind was not the empiricistic but the 'critical' concept of experience, it was too easily interpreted in an empiricistic or psychologistic direction. The word 'area' also gave rise to misunderstanding, in as much as it seemed to suggest something like different geographical territories, and so to involve not only a distinction but a separation. Consequently, in the late twenties I abandoned the expression in favour of the term 'contexts of meaning', which is both more adequate and less liable to be misconstrued.

coherence to every such context. For apart from these presuppositions neither the comprehensive contexts of meaning nor the meaning of individual statements contained in them can be rightly understood; they are the 'rules of the game' presupposed by the various contexts, which prevent everything from falling into chaos. In what follows we shall have occasion to illustrate in more detail what all this involves. For the moment it is enough that in drawing attention to the diversity of terminology we have given an idea of the preoccupation of contemporary philosophy in various quarters with the problem to which we have given the name 'context of meaning', or perhaps preferably 'contexts of meaning' in the plural, since there is more than one such context.

2. Philosophy and the Different Contexts of Meaning

Broadly speaking, the difference between the atomistic and the contextual theory of meaning is that the former starts with words as the real bearers of meaning—the original constituents or units that go to make up meaning as a whole—whereas the latter starts with the sentence as the original bearer of meaning, since it is in the sentence that we first find a context and therefore meaning. This account of the difference does not, however, take us very far, and if there were no more to be said the difference between the two theories would not be particularly important. It would merely be a matter of substituting sentence-molecules for verbal atoms, which would be no great gain. For although sentence-molecules are better fitted to be bearers of meaning, and are therefore a more suitable starting point for the analysis of meaning, yet the pattern of thought as a whole would not be changed, and the approach to the question of meaning would remain the same in both theories. Just as atomism first takes note of the 'meaning' of individual words in order to put together the 'meaning' of a sentence, so contextualism would begin by noting the meaning of each individual sentence and then put these partial meanings together into a meaningful whole. But that would obviously be a miserable way of treating the contextual theory, making it little more than a variant of the atomistic view.

This shows that we cannot stop here. The context is far more constitutive of meaning than the above view suggests. If we begin with the meaning documented in the sentence, we set out on a path which of necessity leads us on step by step until we finally arrive at what we have called a 'context of meaning'—call it 'universe of discourse' if you will, or any other name you prefer. In attempting to determine the meaning of a sentence we can never be content with the sentence 'in isolation'. It is not only detached words that lack definitive meaning, but the same is true, though to a lesser degree, of sentences. In detachment from their context, their exact meaning is not fully clear; we need the help of the context in which a sentence belongs in order to see what it really means. For a proof that what we are saying is correct, one has only to think of the immense mischief that can be done with detached quotations. A quotation which is verbally accurate but torn from its proper context is all that is needed to make an author appear to be saying the direct opposite of what he really says. In order to refute such misrepresentations we have to put the words quoted back into the context from which they came; that is the only way to grasp their real meaning.

Just as a word comes into consideration only as part of a meaningful sentence, so the sentence comes into consideration as part of a series of sentences which together with it express a 'meaning'. And where does the series end? For it is not only its immediate neighbours that affect our understanding of a sentence, but it and they together play a definite part in a more comprehensive movement of thought, and it is only as we see what the latter is about that we understand the part these sentences play and what they mean. It is in principle impossible to draw a definite line as to how much of the nearer and remoter context must be taken into account in order to reach a correct understanding of the meaning of a given statement. The position—as we have said earlier—is broadly this: the given sentence refers us for its meaning to its neighbours, and these again to a still wider context, and so forth.[6]

But that is not all there is to be said about the importance of the context for the meaning. The most significant thing from a philosophical point of view is still to come. For there are two ways in which meaning can be lost through neglect of the context. We have already spoken of one of these, where the sentence is taken 'in isolation', detached from both its nearer and its remoter context. But there is a much more insidious way of ruining the meaning, namely by placing the sentence in a wrong 'context of meaning'. Although the sentence is not then 'in isolation', yet it can be said to be 'detached'—detached from its own context and transferred to an alien context. For it is not only what is directly stated in a sentence that shapes and determines its meaning, but still more the necessary presuppositions on which it rests, which are for the most part unexpressed and often overlooked. If we happen to be mistaken with regard to these, so that we put the sentence under the wrong heading, so to speak, and associate it with other presuppositions than its own, then something happens to its meaning, often without our noticing it. Even if in such a case we pay all possible attention both to the nearer and the remoter context, we shall nonetheless get the meaning completely wrong.

This is where the question of context first begins to be of direct philosophical significance. It is not the business of philosophy to keep an eye

---

[6] *Cf*, above, pp. 263f. A similar line of thought is found in W. V. Quine, who sharply attacks 'the impossible term-by-term empiricism' and adds: 'But what I am now urging is that even in taking the statement as a unit we have drawn our grid too finely. The unit of empirical significance is the whole of science' (*From a Logical Point of View*, p. 42).

on the individual sciences, for example, and see how far they have taken account of all the relevant contextual circumstances in settling an issue; that is the responsibility of the particular science itself. When philosophy is described as analysis of meaning, it is to be understood as having to do with those general presuppositions which impart to everything within their province a specific structure and make it a 'context of meaning', a context from which it is impossible to detach an individual statement without perverting its meaning.

Philosophy and context of meaning belong inseparably together. As a rule we understand quite well the meaning of the sentences we meet in ordinary language, without having consciously made clear to ourselves the presuppositions implied in them; and the same is true to an even greater degree as regards the scientific use of experiment and propositions, where the terminology is more precise. As a rule we can rely in these matters on an unerring instinct. But these presuppositions which are more or less unconsciously assumed, philosophy brings to the light of day and makes them conscious, and it does so for a purely theoretical purpose. This does not mean, however, that philosophical analysis is of no practical significance. The so-called 'cultural debate' flourishes largely on vagueness and lack of clarity as to the different contexts of meaning. Here philosophical analysis can be of real cultural service by introducing clarity and thus getting rid of a number of problems that are nothing but pseudo-problems, and 'meanings' that are merely examples of meaninglessness.

Philosophy is *one*, the contexts of meaning are *many*. From one point of view philosophy can be said to have a single, indivisible function, namely the analysis of meaning or the clarification of meaning by philosophical analysis. But the very uniformity of this function forces upon philosophy a diversity of tasks; for not everything that has meaning is subject to the same presuppositions, and serious attention must be paid to these if the meaning is not to be missed. We encountered this problem earlier,[7] in the form of the distinction between 'philosophy' and 'philosophy of . . .', when we were trying to come to terms with the idea of 'philosophy of religion'. At that stage we could get no further than the apparently paradoxical affirmation that there is no other form of philosophy than philosophy pure and simple, or what is sometimes called 'philosophy proper', and yet there is no philosophy that is not at the same time 'philosophy of . . .' When we now return to this subject, however, we find that every trace of paradoxicality has disappeared. The function of philosophy is to clarify 'meaning'; but just for this reason it is obliged to take account of the different 'contexts of meaning', since there is no such thing as 'meaning in itself' but meaning always emerges against the background of certain presuppositions.

[7] Above, p. 26.

As long as philosophy aspired to construct a metaphysical system it was apt to find the idea of different contexts of meaning intolerably disturbing, for it had to be able to reduce everything to a single formula and deal with everything on one and the same level. But it was this passion for undifferentiated unity that reduced metaphysics to confusion and self-contradiction. When, however, philosophy renounces these systematizing aspirations and contents itself with the less pretentious but more practically significant task of analyzing meaning, it at once becomes clear that we cannot establish any uniform system of meaning, but must recognize that meaning can present itself in different forms. Philosophy as it works at the analysis of meaning must not lend itself to the questionable business of setting up a universal 'criterion of meaning' which can be used as a test of whatever may be regarded as meaningful; if it does so it will land itself in 'the reductive fallacy'. There is not only *one* 'meaning of meaning', but there are many different contexts of meaning, and it is the business of philosophy to analyze *these* and show what is the real meaning in the different contexts. The very fact that in each case a genuine context can be established, is proof that there is a meaning present, and whatever bears the marks of meaning has a claim on the attention of philosophy. Hence philosophy as analysis of meaning becomes an analysis of the different contexts of meaning. Its first task is then to clarify the *difference* between these and clearly mark their boundaries, after which it can go on to the question of the *relation* between them.

3. The Autonomy of the Contexts of Meaning

The idea of a context of meaning is inseparable from that of autonomy. To speak of the former without in some way implying the latter is to make quite improper use of the term 'context of meaning'.

It must, however, be observed that 'autonomy' is a highly ambiguous and heavily loaded term. If therefore we are to use it, we must clearly distinguish its different meanings from one another and show which of them we have in mind. Above all, we must draw a sharp distinction between 'the autonomy of the context of meaning' and 'the autonomy of the subject', for these are two vastly different things which must on no account be confused with one another.

The concept of autonomy owes its vogue in philosophy most of all to Kant, who gave it a central place in ethics. But it is easy to see how in his thought this concept oscillates between the two meanings just mentioned. He quite rightly employs the idea of autonomy to safeguard the uniqueness of the ethical as an independent and autonomous context of meaning, which does not derive its meaning and validity 'heteronomously' from something else.[8] Thus he speaks of 'the autonomy of the will as the

[8] On this *cf.* my essay, 'Det etiska omdömets självständighet'.

supreme principle of morality', and contrasts it with 'the heteronomy of the will as the source of all inauthentic principles of morality'.[9] This means that any attempt to establish the legitimacy of the ethical by referring it to something else, no matter what, involves the destruction of the ethical. Now so long as 'autonomy' means only this—so long as it is simply an affirmation that the ethical represents a context of meaning which exists in its own right and obeys its own laws without being dependent on anything else ('hetero-nomy')—all is well. But things go badly wrong when Kant will not be content with the autonomy of ethics, but includes in the idea of autonomy that also of the ethical *subject*.[10] Every human being as a rational being is 'self-legislating', 'autonomous'. As a rational being, a member of the intelligible world, he is himself the maker of the law which as a member of the sensible world it is his duty to obey.[11] Man as an ethical subject is—in Kant's own phrase—*'ein gesetzgebendes Glied im Reiche der Zwecke'*, 'a legislating member in the kingdom of ends'.

Where did these ideas come from? The answer cannot be in doubt. We recognize at once the historical milieu in which they developed. Behind them lies the ideal of the French Revolution. As a 'member of the legislative assembly' man has to exercise his autonomy in the ethico-religious context which Kant characterizes as 'a republic under laws of virtue.'[12] He subjects himself to and obeys the law which he has himself established. Here metaphysics with its distinction between the intelligible and the sensible world makes its entry into Kant's ethics. From this it is clear that the idea of ethical autonomy has undergone a complete transformation. Instead of 'the autonomy of the ethical' we now have 'the autonomy of the subject'. We may recall that there is a certain parallel to this idea of autonomy in Kant's theoretical philosophy, where the knowing subject similarly fulfils a legislative function when by means of his categories he 'prescribes laws for nature'[13] which also is a metaphysical deviation from the critical train of thought.

There is of course a certain artificiality in speaking of a 'deviation' in Kant. For naturally he did not begin by giving a pure account of 'the autonomy of the ethical' and then deviate from it into another conception of autonomy. From the very first his idea of autonomy includes something of both, and the confusion is present from the start. Even where Kant moves most definitely along the line of 'the autonomy of the ethical', his

---

[9] Kant, *Metaphysic of Ethics*, Reclam, pp. 78ff., Abbott, pp. 277f., Manthey-Zorn, pp. 59ff.; *cf. Critique of Practical Reason*, Reclam, pp. 39f.; Abbott, pp. 304f.

[10] For an analysis of the double concept of autonomy see my essay, 'Kant och den kristna etiken'.

[11] Kant, *Metaphysic of Ethics*, Reclam, pp. 94f.; Abbott, pp. 282f.; Manthey-Zorn, pp. 72ff.

[12] Kant, *Religion Within the Limits of Reason Alone*, Reclam, p. 104; Green and Hudson, p. 114.

[13] *Cf.* above, pp. 201ff.

tendency to subjectivism is revealed by the fact that he always speaks of 'the autonomy of the *will*' and 'heteronomy of the *will*'.

It was necessary to take a little time over this ambiguity in the concept of autonomy if we were to make any use of the latter for our purposes. It is no doubt as a rule associated mainly with the second of its two meanings, namely the autonomy of the self; but this is just what we do *not* intend here. We are concerned with it exclusively in its first sense, the autonomy of the context of meaning, and the autonomy of the ethical context discussed above is only an example of something that applies to every such context. This, however, tells us something very essential about the nature of a context of meaning. We can establish by purely analytical means that if there is any such thing as a context of meaning, then it is subject to its *own* laws, which find expression in its 'presuppositions' or 'categories' or whatever else we may choose to call the principles or rules that are constitutive of a context of meaning. To say that it is autonomous is to say that it can be correctly judged only from its own point of view, or in terms of the categories that are relevant to it. If we deal with it in terms of presuppositions other than its own, we lose both meaning and context.

Thus far we have spoken quite generally of different contexts of meaning, and have introduced the ethical simply as an example. We must now face the question, just what contexts these are. In principle we could say with Wittgenstein that there is the possibility of an unlimited number of different 'games'.[14] Every game gets its distinctive character from the rules that apply to it. Change the rules and you have another game. And since there are no set limits to the rules that can be devised, there is the possibility of an unlimited number of games.

But while this may be true of games, it is not equally true of contexts of meaning. The latter is a more definite and limited concept than that of 'language games'. For we are not in actual fact confronted by an endless multiplicity of contexts of meaning, but by a small number of comprehensive viewpoints or ways of looking at things which have gradually crystallized in the course of history. We do not have to construct them for ourselves, they are there already before we begin to do anything about them. In this respect there is a certain analogy between them and 'ordinary language'. The latter also is something we do not invent, but it has grown up and developed certain modes of expression which we have to analyze and see what meaning they have when they are in use. Like language, the contexts of meaning are *given* phenomena, and it is the task of philosophy to analyze what is given. We do not ourselves create these great contexts, but we encounter them as historically given realities, and we find that each of them has created its own social patterns and forms: science, morality, art, religion.

It is this that finds expression in what are traditionally the basic con-

[14] Wittgenstein, *Philosophical Investigations*, p. 11.

cepts of philosophy: the true, the good, the beautiful, the eternal. So they have been called ever since antiquity and the time of Plato. These things are not merely imaginary, but they have a solid foundation in something given. Nor is there, as has often been supposed, anything specifically Platonic about them. Plato did not invent science, morality, art, religion. What was specifically Platonic was his hypostatizing of their basic concepts and his use of these as corner-stones in his world of Ideas. But the phenomena as such were there independently of Plato, and they are there still, being implicit in the contexts of meaning as their presuppositions, the rules that determine their meaning.

This brings us back to the question of autonomy. In its presuppositions each context of meaning possesses the laws that must be observed within its own particular province. Each is autonomous and must be judged according to its own laws. To put it simply:

> *Science* must be *scientifically* judged. Otherwise its propositions lose their scientific meaning.
>
> The *ethical* must be *ethically* judged. Otherwise its propositions lose their ethical meaning.
>
> The *aesthetic* must be aesthetically judged. Otherwise its propositions lose their aesthetic meaning.
>
> The *religious* must be *religiously* judged. Otherwise its propositions lose their religious meaning.

Or, to put the last point in terms drawn from the religious context itself: 'A man who is unspiritual refuses what belongs to the Spirit of God; it is folly to him; he cannot grasp it, because it needs to be judged in the light of the Spirit.'[15]

Now it may be questioned whether we are not making things too easy for ourselves by taking the contexts of meaning as *given*. Ought not philosophy to derive them from a common principle in order to be able to say with certainty that there exist just these contexts of meaning and no others? For if we simply take them as given, there will always be a suggestion of arbitrariness about them. Yet no ultimate principle of selection and justification has been mentioned, and that of set purpose. It is most important that we should not try to produce such a principle. The very idea of a universal 'principle of meaning' from which the different contexts of meaning might be deduced, is fundamentally wrong. It arises from the wishful thinking of metaphysics with its desire for an ultimate self-validating principle from which to derive the validity of all that is valid, or a common 'meaning in itself' or 'meaning as such' from which to derive the meaningfulness of everything that has meaning.

The very idea of an ultimate principle of meaning or 'meaning in itself' is perverse. Scientific philosophy has once for all put an end to such specu-

[15] 1 Cor. 2: 14 (NEB).

lations. It starts, as it should, with something *given*. In this it finds elements that are accepted as valid and elements that are rejected as invalid, elements that are meaningful and elements that are meaningless. It is the business of philosophy to analyze this given material with respect to its presuppositions, and so to clarify and shed light on the whole question of meaning and validity. The reality with which philosophy is confronted, and by which it is challenged to engage in critical analysis, is therefore this: there are as a matter of experience vast contexts, scientific, religious, socio-ethical, aesthetic. What is it that gives them coherence, makes them contexts, and so gives them meaning? What applies to one context does not necessarily apply to another.

That these great contexts of meaning given to us in our tradition call for philosophical investigation is abundantly clear. The fact that they are given in the tradition and are sustained by extensive social organizations, strengthens rather than weakens their claim to attention.[16] They are no merely ephemeral phenomena, but have proved their durability down the ages. There have of course been plenty of attempts to construct something corresponding to these contexts of meaning independently of what has been given, but the results can hardly be other than castles in the air.

If we start with the contexts of meaning as given, however, there is a further question we must face. What guarantee have we that these traditionally given contexts are really exhaustive, or that there cannot be any other autonomous contexts of meaning? The answer is that we have no such guarantee. The contexts of meaning do not constitute a closed system, in which no room can be found for anything else. Yet since the business of philosophy is not to create but to analyze, we must pay heed to what is presented to us in reality. There must be room for all of this in the open system of the contexts of meaning. The only question is whether it should be called a 'system', for that word smacks too much of metaphysics. The main thing is that philosophical analysis is open to the possible emergence of new contexts. The great contexts of meaning we have named have endured through the ages, but this does not rule out the possibility of other autonomous contexts of meaning appearing alongside them. Take only a couple of examples from recent times, namely economics and technology. There has long been talk of the *Eigengesetzlichkeit* of economic life, i.e. its autonomy. And has not technology developed to a point where we can no longer do full justice to it by including it in the scientific context of meaning as 'applied science'? Should it not rather be granted complete autonomy and allowed to represent a context of meaning of its own? If so, philosophy would acquire a new field for its critical analysis. These are not questions into which we can enter here, but we have cited them to

[16] *Cf.* G. H. von Wright, *Logik, filosofi och språk*, which starts from 'the four great powers of civilization, the state, religion, art and science', pp. 9–24 (2nd edn., pp. 11ff.). *Cf.* M. Polanyi, *Science, Faith and Society*, pp. 47, 59.

illustrate the possibility of new contexts of meaning, and to make the point that philosophical inquiry must be open to this possibility.

Yet although we hold open the possibility of new contexts of meaning alongside those traditionally given, the number of phenomena that can be referred to as 'contexts of meaning' in the technical sense in which we are using the term, will always be relatively small. In this connection it is interesting to see how even Wittgenstein, who in principle has to reckon with an unlimited number of 'language games', is obliged to impose a certain limitation. In the same breath as he speaks of 'the multiplicity of language games' ('*countless* different kinds of use'), of which he gives a host of examples, he also defines the term 'language game' as 'a form of life'.[17] This involves a limitation inasmuch as games, although they can be invented in unlimited number, cannot all without more ado be described as 'forms of life'. The distinction lies in the fact that the game can be invented, whereas the form of life is something given. And the task of philosophy is not to be continually inventing new rules for games, but to discover by its analysis of actually given forms of life the rules or presuppositions that give them their coherence and meaning.

4. The Absolutization of the Contexts of Meaning

The autonomy of the contexts of meaning means that they are free and independent of one another. None of them needs to justify itself in another's eyes or to be measured by its standards. Each of them is autonomous in its own province as long as it keeps within its bounds. Each is subject only to the laws that are given in and with its own implicit presuppositions. The idea of autonomy denies the right of any one context of meaning to set itself up as a judge over the others. So long as they all show mutual respect for one another's autonomy, no difficulties arise.

The trouble is, however, that respect for the autonomy of the others is by no means always shown. The idea of autonomy is often conceived as *absolutizing* a particular context—despite the fact that the two notions are diametrically opposed. Autonomy excludes all absolutism. When an autonomous state promulgates its laws, this does not mean that it seeks to impose its laws on other states. It is merely exercising its sovereignty in its own sphere. Similarly with the autonomous contexts of meaning. But just as in politics we continually see the more powerful seeking to demonstrate their 'sovereignty' by forcing their ideas on others and subjecting them to their laws, so history furnishes multitudinous examples of the way in which a particular context of meaning will invade the territory of others and try to bring them under its own jurisdiction.

In different periods different contexts of meaning have held the centre of the stage and been able to dominate the rest. During the Middle Ages and for some time after, it was the religious context of meaning. Every-

[17] Wittgenstein, *Philosophical Investigations*, p. 11.

thing had to find its place in the theological system and draw its legiti-mation from thence. Science and philosophy occupied a subordinate position as an '*ancilla*' ('handmaid')—though it should be noted that the metaphysics inherited from antiquity largely had the decisive voice in theology. The liberation that subsequently took place was therefore as much a liberation from the dominance of the religious context of meaning as from metaphysics. If, however, the liberation from the former was so complete that no one nowadays need fear any claim to supremacy over the rest on the part of religion, the liberation from metaphysics was less successful. We are reminded here of Kant's saying in the Introduction to the *Critique of Pure Reason*: 'There was a time when metaphysics was called the Queen of all the Sciences', to which he adds: 'Now it is the fashion of the time to show it all contempt'. It may be true that the latter statement was and still is in some measure justified, yet metaphysics has managed nonetheless in various disguises to retain a decisive influence. As for the ethical context of meaning, there is no tendency on its part to arrogate to itself any superiority over the rest. It is rather one of the things that in recent times has suffered a massive devaluation.

The context of meaning which in our time has most of all been liable to absolutization is that of science. There has been good reason to speak of '*scientism*' and '*scientific superstition*'. By 'scientism' is meant an outlook that makes 'science' the measure of all things, refusing to grant the validity of anything but what is 'scientifically proved' and insisting that in the last resort nothing is meaningful unless it can be expressed in a scientific formula.[18] As we pointed out earlier, this superstition with regard to science is found not so much among scientists themselves as in popular conceptions of what science is and means.[19] To anyone who has engaged in genuine scientific work in any field it is perfectly clear that science is not the whole of life, and that there are other legitimate activities besides science. Only the ignorant, who do not know what science is, can expect the scientist to provide answers to all of life's questions—as for example the question what ethical or aesthetic ideal one should adopt, or what form of religion one should accept. Science has no answers for such questions, and it has none precisely because it is science and as such can only answer scientific questions.

The genuine scientist is aware of the limits of science, which are limits set by the very nature of scientific argumentation. Admittedly there are no external limitations on science; it has to investigate all the different forms of life, not only the scientific, but also the ethical, aesthetic, religious,

---

[18] A generation or more ago this kind of thinking could crop up among logical empiricists. *Cf.*, e.g., C. G. Hempel, 'The Logical Analysis of Psychology', in Feigl-Sellars, *Readings*, p. 381: 'The logical analyses originating in the Vienna Circle . . . teach us that every meaningful question is, in principle, capable of a scientific answer.'

[19] *Cf.* above, pp. 115ff.

and so forth. But this does not mean that science is transformed into an ethical, aesthetic, or religious activity, any more than it means that the ethical, aesthetic, or religious is transformed into science. These lose nothing of their autonomy in relation to it.

'Scientism' is an absolutization which is foreign to science, and which science rejects as much in its own interest as in that of the other contexts of meaning. How clearly this point is seen among scientists, and how they are on guard against 'scientism' can be illustrated by quotations from two recent sources. M. Born writes: 'We have to be careful that scientific thinking in abstract terms does not extend to other domains where it is not applicable. Human and ethical values cannot be based on scientific thinking. . . . However attractive and satisfactory abstract thinking for the scientist, however valuable his results for the material aspect of our civilisation, it is most dangerous to apply these methods beyond the range of their validity, to religion, ethics, art, literature, and all humanities,' It is, according to Born, most important 'to restrict the scientific methods to that domain where they reasonably belong.'[20] And a similar view is taken by M. Bunge when he writes: 'This is not to say that science is gradually absorbing all of human experience: that we shall end by loving and hating scientifically just as we can cure and kill scientifically. Except scientific research itself, human experiences are not scientific knowledge: what can be and should be scientific is the study of any such experience.'[21]

Scientism is completely foreign to genuine science. By absolutizing 'science' and treating it alone as valuable, and by regarding 'what is scientifically proved' as all that counts, it rides rough-shod not only over the other contexts of meaning, but also and above all over science itself, of which it represents nothing but an overweening travesty.[22]

The temptation to absolutize the scientific context of meaning is understandable when we think of the revolutionary changes in our whole material existence which have been brought about by a scientifically based technology. But it is surprising that a similar absolutization should have taken place also with respect to the aesthetic context of meaning. It is surprising because art cannot by any means be compared with science in its influence. The explanation lies in historical and psychological circum-

[20] M. Born, 'Symbol and Reality', in *Objectivité et Realité*, p. 157.
[21] M. Bunge, *Scientific Research*, p. 33.
[22] An outrageous example of 'scientific superstition' was given by a speaker who, in a discussion of nuclear fission and the danger of a possible chain-reaction, averred that even if there were a 90 per cent probability of our planet being blown to pieces, nuclear testing should nevertheless continue, since—if unexpectedly the catastrophe did not occur—it would give us new scientific insight, and that after all was all that mattered. No better proof could be found that the absolutization of science is foreign to all genuine science, and is nothing else but 'scientific superstition'. Here the old saying, '*fiat justitia, pereat mundus*', has been parodied to mean: 'Let science go on, though the world perish.'

stances. Ever since the time of the Renaissance 'the artist' has been invested with a special aura and credited with a special 'inspiration' that distinguishes him from other men. In consequence of this the general public has become an easy prey to what might be called 'aesthetic superstition'. Here again, just as in the 'superstition of science' discussed above, we have a case of confusion between autonomy and absolutization. The autonomy that properly belongs to the aesthetic context of meaning is wrongly equated with its absolutization. To say that the aesthetic is an autonomous context of meaning, is simply to say that the aesthetic must be aesthetically judged, and this precisely in order that it may retain its meaning. It will not do to say: This work of art does not conform to the canons of science, therefore it is not a work of art at all. Nor can we say: What is portrayed is here sub-standard from an ethical point of view, therefore it is not a work of art. That would be just as false as to say that an outstanding piece of scientific research was not science because it was not presented in the form of belles lettres. Whether anything is a work of art or not is determined solely by its aesthetic quality. That is the meaning of the autonomy of the aesthetic, and it can be derived from the latter by purely analytical means.

Now there are in the life of human society quite a number of contexts of meaning, each of them autonomous, and very little reflection is required to see that it simply will not do to absolutize one of them and demand that the rest by subordinated to it. But that is just what happens in the case of 'aesthetic superstition'; and it is all the more disastrous because we cannot say of it as we did of 'scientific superstition' that it is for the most part those who know least about the subject that are responsible for this absolutization. For not only has the general public fallen victim to the absolutization of art, but so to a large extent have the artists themselves. Sometimes it is held that the artist and his work have a claim to 'immunity' as regards the rules that apply to ordinary citizens. There is no place, it is said, for those rules in his world: he is after all concerned with 'Art'. But then the question arises: why must we tolerate in the realm of art a kind of 'superstition' that we do not tolerate in other areas? In art as much as anywhere else, absolutization can be a real threat to culture. Who says that the aesthetic is the absolute standard by which everything must be judged?

What we have said can be illustrated by a current example. The use of narcotics, particularly among young people, has recently increased to an alarming extent and become one of the major problems of our time. The health and careers of many are in danger of being wrecked. Yet while society fights an uphill battle to rescue the young, an undisguised propaganda for narcotics is made (through films, the mass media and art exhibitions) in the name of 'art'.[23] For 'the freedom of art' is at stake! Art exists

[23] 'Fiat justitia, pereat mundus' has been parodied here to mean: 'Let art flourish, though the young people perish', or more accurately—since it is not really a question of

to 'inform', to reflect reality—and that is what reality is like! There is muddled thinking here, and a primitive confusion of ideas, a failure to distinguish between autonomy and absoluteness. It is this confusion among other things[24] that leads artists in some circles to delight in choosing subjects bordering on the ethically questionable or downright bad—pornography, drug-addiction, 'psychedelic' art, etc. The artist must be free from the inhibitions of the Philistine! 'Art must be in the van of progress!' No doubt; but on the other hand it is by no means clear that the possessor of a talent for aesthetic form is the best reformer. When he nevertheless claims to be a reformer, he betrays his art and turns it into cheap, time-serving propaganda.

In a word, absolutization is a violation of the context of meaning. Science must not be compromised by 'scientific superstition'. Art must not be compromised by 'aesthetic superstition'.

5. Category Mixing and Meaninglessness

Absolutization, by which one context of meaning claims supremacy over the rest, denying their autonomy and demanding their submission to itself, is not the only way of discounting the autonomy of the contexts of meaning. This is much more often done by confusing them with one another and moving about indiscriminately among them instead of keeping them distinct. Nothing is commoner than this, and it results in what have been called 'category mistakes' or 'category mixing'. One passes without noticing it from one context to another, never realizing that in the end we are talking about nothing at all. The terms we use oscillate between different meanings, which conflict with one another, contradict one another, cancel one another out.

(1) It is this that makes the philosophical task of language analysis so extraordinarily important. The analysis has first of all the negative purpose of showing how an incorrect use of language influences thought and deceives it with problems that are no problems, but pseudo-problems, which are fundamentally nothing but misleading concatenations of words

---

'art', but of 'aesthetic superstition'—'Let the sacred cow of art live, even if many human beings have to die for it.'

[24] 'Among other things'—for there are of course also other motives, such as profit-hunger and the attempt to gain by other means the attention one has failed to gain by aesthetic merit. In many cases these motives have been openly acknowledged by artists. When that is so, the confusion of contexts spoken of above is only a means to these other ends—and therefore still an attack on the autonomy of art. (Another aspect of the matter might be that the contemporary cult of art represents a reaction against 'scientism'. To some extent, at least, it springs from a realization that 'man does not live by bread alone', not even the affluent bread of science and technology. Unfortunately it fails to realize that art is only another sort of bread, albeit more highly spiced.—Tr.)

that yield no unified meaning. That they seem to be problems is due to the fact that we are accustomed to the idea that an expression *must* have a meaning. When we come across a linguistic expression which appears to be grammatically correct, we take it for granted that it is also logically and as to its content meaningful, and if it raises a question or poses a problem we endeavour to find a solution for the difficulties it presents. But what if these difficulties arise from the fact that the question itself has no real meaning? Then however long we work at it we shall never find a solution for the problem, because there is no problem. To a meaningless question there can be no real, meaningful answer. The solution lies, not in finding a new answer, but in dissolving the question and letting it return to the nothing out of which it arose only by the fiat of a linguistic formulation. There was in fact nothing thought of, nothing inquired about.

The most important result of this analysis of meaning is that it definitively reveals where the error lies in all metaphysics. When we describe the problem of metaphysics as a pseudo-problem we are by no means saying that everything contained in a metaphysical argument is meaningless talk. With regard to much of it we can follow the reasoning and find a clear meaning in it. It is not the individual propositions in the metaphysical context that are meaningless. They are often based on sound observation, and in this way metaphysics has made many useful contributions to science. The meaninglessness lies elsewhere. It is the metaphysical statement of the problem, the metaphysical approach as such, that is meaningless. We have already had frequent occasion to refer to this fact, and now we are in a position to say what the deepest reason for this meaninglessness is. The analysis of meaning and of presuppositions and the different contexts of meaning makes it possible for us to give a clear and unambiguous answer to this question. *The meaninglessness of metaphysics is due to the fact that metaphysics on principle mixes up different contexts of meaning.* It moves to and fro among the various contexts without belonging to any of them. It mixes up what ought to be kept separate. It is unaware of the presuppositions of the different contexts, and in consequence there is something indefinite and uncertain about its propositions. Metaphysics could be compared to a double exposure on a film, or perhaps rather a multiple exposure. The different pictures are all there, but they run into one another and blur one another's outlines, so that we get no clear idea of what it is all about. Metaphysics is not a science, though it professes to be scientific. It makes scientific claims, but does not submit to the conditions of science. It is this self-contradictory ambiguity that robs it of meaning.

At an earlier stage we asked what it is that makes the question of meaning philosophically relevant. It has no such relevance if it is merely a question of how a word is conventionally used, or what it signifies in everyday use. That is not a philosophical question. What makes the question of meaning philosophically relevant, or rather, what makes it and the question of the different contexts of meaning so extremely important for philosophy, is the fact that a great part of the philosophical tradition owes its character and content precisely to neglect of the need for a clear distinction between the different contexts of meaning. It is typical of metaphysical philosophy that it rests on a confusion of these different contexts. As a general rule it can be stated that meaninglessness arises from the confusion of different 'languages' or contexts of meaning.

We often have difficulty in perceiving the meaninglessness arising from a confusion of the great, comprehensive contexts of meaning. Just because they are so comprehensive and the issues are so extremely general and abstract, the meaninglessness more easily escapes detection. It may therefore be helpful to take a somewhat analogous instance from a very limited context of meaning, in which the meaninglessness involved in a confusion of contexts is too obvious to be missed.

When we wish to measure a spatial distance we do it in units of *length*: metres, kilometres, miles, and so forth.

When we wish to know how heavy an object is, we use another sort of units, those of *weight*: gramme, kilogram, ounce, pound, and so forth.

Where any measurement is concerned, we must in the nature of the case stay within the context to which it belongs, and employ a standard of measurement that is applicable to it. If we measure something in one context by a standard applicable to another, the result will not only be false, but meaningless. If I ask how far it is from New York to Chicago, and am told it is fifty miles, then the answer is empirically false, but it is not meaningless. If on the other hand I am told it is fifty pounds, it is meaningless; and it would be just as meaningless to be told that it is 833 pounds. Whatever the figure, the answer would be equally meaningless. Meaninglessness does not arise from an empirical mistake, but from a category mistake. It comes from the employment of a standard of measurement that is validly applicable in one area, to another area where it has no validity and makes no sense.

This rough example may serve to illustrate where the difficulty lies with the metaphysical approach. Metaphysical questions are impossible to answer, not because they are too difficult or complex, nor yet because the necessary premises are concealed from us, so that no conclusion can be drawn. There are, of course, problems of that kind, but the impossibility of metaphysics is of a quite different sort, for it is due to the fact that the question itself is without meaning.

(2) What has now been said shows what an important tool the analysis of meaning provides for philosophy in its attempt to clarify its own task and get rid of the pseudo-problems that so easily arise in a philosophical context. And in this connection the negative concept of 'meaninglessness' plays perhaps an even greater part than the positive idea of 'meaning'.

But here, as is so often the case, strength and weakness are close companions. At the same time as the concepts of 'meaning' and 'meaninglessness' have made it possible for philosophy to take hold of both old and new problems and 'solve' or 'dissolve' them according to the sort of problems they are, these same concepts have shown themselves to contain a serious danger for philosophy, inasmuch as they may tempt it unduly to limit its horizon. Contemporary philosophy cannot be said to be free from a certain tendency towards a reduction of philosophical problems. With the term 'meaningless' ready to hand, there is only too much temptation to use it in order to deliver oneself from troublesome problems which, properly handled, are by no means meaningless. The concept of meaning is of advantage to philosophy only if it is properly defined; otherwise it can have a very destructive effect. If 'meaning' is too narrowly defined, the result must be that 'meaninglessness' is given all the wider scope. But it cannot be in the interest of philosophy to dismiss as meaningless questions which are by no means so, but which when properly understood have a legitimate place in the philosophical field.

It is important to be on guard against narrowness in the concept of meaning, or in other words, against allowing this concept to be used in the service of reductionism. How careful it is necessary to be, and how easily 'meaning' can become the enemy of the meaningful, may be illustrated by two examples, one taken from Swedish philosophy, the other from logical positivism.

One of the most striking features of the philosophy of the last hundred years has been the tremendous advance made in logic, an advance without parallel in all the two thousand years of its history since Aristotle. Logic had long been thought of as something fully developed, securely established and unchanging through the years; and then came the great renewal. Whereas traditional logic had reckoned only with class concepts, logic was now broadened to include also relational concepts; and this of course brought it into much closer touch with contemporary science than had been possible for traditional logic. Yet the distinguished Swedish philosopher Axel Hägerström, being bound by the traditional logic, insisted that the concept of relations was metaphysical and therefore devoid of meaning and indefensible; hence it must be banished from our scientific vocabulary. What would have happened if his advice had been followed? We should have had to rule out that whole section of logic which deals with relational concepts, logic would have remained a prisoner of its old status, and its renewal would not have taken place—all because of the hasty impression that there is no place for relational concepts among those classed as meaningful. On this point the more recent Uppsala philosophy has not followed the master's lead, but has enthusiastically devoted itself to developing 'the new logic'.

Now for the second example. Early in its career logical positivism propounded its much-disputed theory of the principle of verification as a general criterion of meaning.[25] The purpose of this was to provide a touchstone by which to distinguish between what was meaningful and what was meaningless. The idea was that a proposition is meaningful only if it can be verified or falsified, and it was assumed as self-evident that the vertification or falsification must be done by empirical means, *i.e.* it must be based on the immediate evidence of the senses—that is the legacy of positivism. But it is only too plain that the concept of meaning so defined is extraordinarily narrow, and that the area of the meaningless is correspondingly enlarged. Here too we must ask ourselves, what would happen if this theory were adopted? We should have to rule out by far the greater part of what we find in cultural life, as if it were meaningless nonsense because it is clearly not amenable to that kind of verification.

Now it may well be that this principle of verification was never intended to be such a universal touchstone for everything whatever that is meaningful. But the general nature of the terms in which it has been formulated, undoubtedly gives the impression that that was its purpose. It is devised with regard to a particular kind of scientific investigation, and in that area it has its legitimacy. It is an indispensable requirement of all science that there should be the possibility of objective argumentation. Where that is not the case—where assertion stands against assertion without that possibility—there is no science. But here too there is a question to be raised, namely whether the decision between different assertions must in all circumstances be reached by going back to immediately given sense-data. Even from the point of view of scientific theory the principle of verification as formulated here must be regarded as too narrow. And this is still more the case if it is intended as a universal criterion for everything that is to be recognized as meaningful.

Within the ranks of logical empiricism itself there were those who in various quarters realized the danger of defining the principle of verification so narrowly and rigidly that it could be used as a principle of reduction. C. I. Lewis writes: 'All of us who earlier were inclined to say that unverifiable statements are meaningless—and I include myself—have since learned to be more careful.'[26] And in his essay on 'Logical Empiricism' Herbert Feigl says: 'A word of warning should not be amiss here. The danger of a fallaciously reductive use of the meaning-criterion is great, especially in the hands of young iconoclasts. It is only too tempting to push a very difficult question aside and by stigmatizing it as meaningless to discourage further investigation.'[27]

---

[25] As this question and that of reductionism have been dealt with already (pp. 143ff., 150ff.), we can confine ourselves here to pointing out what is relevant to the present context.

[26] 'Some Logical Considerations' in Feigl-Sellars, *Readings*, p. 391.

[27] Feigl-Sellars, *Readings*, p. 13.

It is important to take seriously the implications of this insight. 'Empirically indemonstrable' is not the same as 'meaningless'. It can appear so only if we insist on a false uniformity, permit one area to encroach on another, and absolutize one context of meaning at the expense of the rest—in this case in the shape of a 'scientism' based on a singularly narrow concept of science. The greatest danger to philosophy is that of uniformitarianism with its accompanying peril of the closed mind. When a method has proved successful in one area, it is natural to try to apply it in others, and develop it into a universal method. We proceed as if we had found a key to unlock all doors. We begin to see everything in terms of the matter we happen to have been dealing with. The method we are familiar with from our own special field sets the pattern for dealing with everything else. What does not happen to fit the pattern is simply dismissed. Or, to return to the idea of a key, when we come to a door which refuses to be opened by the key in our possession, we assume that there can 'therefore' be nothing of importance behind it, and that it would be a waste of time to look for a key to fit its lock.

This ever-present danger is particularly acute for a philosophy which sees its task to be analysis of meaning. Its anaytical work must naturally start in the field of science, where meaning and method have had most work done on them. But if what the analysis of meaning discovers in this area is allowed to become the pattern to which all meaning whatsoever is shaped, it results in a narrow concept of meaning and turns philosophy into a bed of Procrustes on which experience is abbreviated and mutilated instead of being clarified.

Category mixing, no matter of what kind, always leads to meaninglessness, or at any rate to loss of the meaning intended. The meaning of a statement can only be preserved if it is seen in the light of the presuppositions which obtain in its context of meaning. A philosophy that seeks to be analysis of meaning must therefore regard it as its primary task to establish order among the different contexts of meaning, so that they are not arbitrarily jumbled together and confused with one another. Or, to put it in other words, its primary business is to serve as a clearing house for the contexts of meaning.

6. Philosophy as a Clearing House for the Contexts of Meaning

The heading of this section could just as well have been: 'The narrow and the broad perspective' or 'The closed and the open perspective' or 'The limited and the universal perspective'. For what we have to do here is to exhibit the universal task of philosophy in connection with the distinct and separate contexts of meaning. As we have seen already many examples of the narrow perspective and how it leads to meaninglessness, so now we must show how philosophy, just by analyzing these different contexts and clarifying their presuppositions and autonomy, provides for the broad, open, universal perspective, and thus takes due account of the meaningfulness there is in the different areas of human life.

There is a popular notion that the universal perspective is represented by metaphysics, while 'scientific philosophy' as committed to objective argumentation in its scientific task[28] is necessarily confined within rather narrow limits. But this is an extremely misleading idea. It is true that metaphysics has a universal aim: it has no intention of being kept within the narrow limits of a special science, but claims to furnish a philosophical explanation of every aspect of existence and the world as a whole. But it has a rather curious way of doing this. The universality of its intention is plain, yet because it does not reckon with different contexts of meaning it is forced to compress everything into one limited mould, and thus lands itself in the narrow, limited perspective. It has to discount everything that does not fit into its metaphysical system. Metaphysics claims to provide an all-embracing *world*-view: that is its universal intention. But it *views* the world from a particular standpoint and takes what it sees to be all there is to see: that is the narrow perspective.

It is a curious and basically absurd idea that all the rich variety of existence should be comprehensible from a single point of view. In poetry, of course, including metaphysical poetry, the universe can be mirrored in a drop of dew; but no one is likely to suppose it is really the universe that is mirrored, except in a purely emotional sense. Yet it is out of something very like this that metaphysics tries to construct its system. Since, however, it provides no place for any but its own single perspective, it cannot help but produce a closed and limited system. Metaphysics gets caught in its own systematic trap and dies of suffocation.

As is so often the case, however, there is *some* justification for this passion for system. It is not enough to have different perspectives or contexts of meaning standing side by side unrelated to one another. A systematic approach is needed here, though it must be one that envisages an *open* system, open to new possibilities. The question of what is to be regarded as a context of meaning, and how such a context is to be understood, cannot be settled by a preconceived theory. These contexts come to us from without, and philosophy must approach them without prejudice. A scientist does not say that anything which is not science is not worth taking seriously—that would be 'scientism' or 'scientific superstition'. An artist does not say that art is the only thing that deserves respect—that would be 'aesthetic superstition'. And still less may a philosopher indulge in prejudice or 'superstition' of any kind.

The philosopher is interested in everything, and in that sense his outlook is universal. He encounters, for example, a phenomenon that goes by the name of science. He may himself at some point have worked in the scientific field, so that he is able to look at science from the inside, so to

[28] *Cf.* above, p. 219.

speak. If science were not a reality, there would be nothing there for the philosopher to analyze.[29] But it is there and he has encountered it, and now his task is to analyze it with regard to its presuppositions. He encounters, furthermore, in the life both of individuals and of society, something that goes by the name of morality or ethics. He has certainly often been in the kind of situation that enables him to understand this phenomenon from the inside, and now it is his task as a philosopher to analyze it as a context of meaning and clarify the presuppositions which make it and all that goes on in it both a context and meaningful. Again, he encounters a phenomenon which has played a big part in all ages and diverse civilizations, and which goes by the name of art. He also encounters a phenomenon which has had throughout history a still greater and more universal significance, and which goes by the name of religion. He may perhaps not have been directly involved in these areas, and that will make it more difficult for him to understand them from within and on their own terms; but here as elsewhere philosophy has the right to engage in its analysis of meaning and presuppositions.

The attempt has sometimes been made to limit the task of philosophy to the scientific context of meaning, and so to equate philosophy with the philosophy of science. But to do this is to land oneself in the narrow perspective. There are after all other meaningful things besides science. T. E. Hill is right when he says: 'Philosophy has always endeavoured to interpret not one aspect only of the human experience but all aspects, and human experience includes much besides science. . . . It includes ethical, aesthetic, and religious experiences that philosophers have always supposed it their duty to try to elucidate.'[30] To this we will only add that the way in which metaphysics has handled these questions has tended rather to obscure their meaning, and that genuine elucidation is obtained only by scientific philosophy with its analysis of meaning and presuppositions.

Now it might perhaps be objected that what we said above about the 'narrow perspective' implies an attack on the special sciences, each of which has its own clearly delimited range of problems. Is it this, then, that we are criticizing? Naturally not. The distinction between the narrow and broad perspectives is simply not applicable here. A special science adopts the perspective required by its task and its subject matter, and there is no point in asking whether it is broad or narrow. It is as it is and as it must be. At the same time we must remember that the perspective of a particular science is not the only possible perspective and does not include everything. Nor does science make any such claim. If it did, it would no longer be science but metaphysics, and then the criticism of its narrow perspective

---

[29] Here we have to pick up and develop further the train of thought on pp. 276f. above.

[30] T. E. Hill, *Contemporary Theories*, pp. 468ff.

would be in place. For the narrow perspective arises precisely when a partial perspective is selected and treated as if it were the whole. In short, it is not science but 'scientific superstition' that is narrow, and not art but 'aesthetic superstition', and so forth.

Against all such narrowness, of no matter what kind, philosophy stands on guard, and it does so just by means of its analysis of the different contexts of meaning. By clarifying the presuppositions of each of them, and thus the limits within which they legitimately move, philosophy prevents any individual context from overstepping its bounds and subjecting other contexts to itself. In this sense it can be said that philosophy has to serve as a clearing house for the different contexts of meaning, or to use John Dewey's phrase, 'it is a liaison officer'[31]—though not in the sense intended by Dewey. It is not its business to co-ordinate the *results* of the sciences, but to clarify the *presuppositions* of the different areas of experience and meaning. Philosophy thus stands surety for the broad perspective against all cramping limitations. It guarantees that the disparate viewpoints and perspectives, the disparate contexts of meaning, really have justice done to them.

What makes such a clearing house indispensable is first of all the theoretical concern for clarification of the distinctive character of different kinds of statements. But it is secondly also of the greatest practical importance in erecting a barrier against the tendency to treat one's own perspective as all there is. This tendency is encouraged by the simplification and economy of effort which it seems to offer: it does away with the need to adjust one's instruments. It is so easy to imagine that what I cannot see from the viewpoint I have chosen, and with the contingent setting of my instrument, either does not exist or has no meaning. From this arises the one-track mind which is the enemy of all profounder inquiry into the problems, and which at bottom is nothing but a form of stupidity.

An excellent illustration of what we have in mind here can be found in a collection of essays published about a century ago, in which one of the essays has for its theme 'Stupidity'.[32] Its author tells how he was sitting one day in the railway station at Hamburg waiting for a train. A family of three boys and their parents was also sitting waiting near by, and he gathered from their conversation that they were going to a family reunion in the little town of Kyritz. Shortly before the train was due to leave, a largish crowd of intending passengers had assembled, and as they began to board it the smallest of the boys exclaimed: 'But what are all these people going to do at Grandpa's in Kyritz?' To which his older brothers replied: 'Oh, you stupid!' Where was the stupidity? The boy was going to Grandpa's in Kyritz, and since with his limited experience he could not imagine any other reason for taking the train, then all these other people

[31] J. Dewey, *The Quest for Certainty*, p. 311.
[32] J. E. Erdmann, *Filosofiska miniaturer*, pp. 191–217.

must be going to Grandpa's in Kyritz too. He was peeping through his own little key-hole—there was his stupidity. And key-holes like that can be made of religion, science, morality, art, and much besides. That is what happens when we play them off against one another instead of letting each of them be what it is and offer what it has to offer.

There are always people who feel they have to screen things out to prevent the world from being so richly varied that they cannot cope with it. When they have succeeded in mastering a few of the problems it poses, they would like to think they have dealt with them all. And this screening out is naturally done by each of them from his own point of view. What he does not happen at the moment to see, naturally does not exist. What he does not happen to understand, must of course be meaningless.

Language possesses a number of different ways of describing this state of affairs, all of which point in the same direction. When it is said of someone, for example, that he is 'simple', the idea is that he is only capable of seeing one thing, the thing that happens to be directly in front of him or falls within his limited circle of vision. Or we can speak of a person as 'limited' or 'circumscribed'—terms which themselves suggest the idea of being fenced in and screened off.

There is a saying that 'the head corrects the folly of the heart'. But here we must ask, who corrects the folly of the head? Who corrects narrow-mindedness and the limitation of meaning? The answer is that this is precisely the business of philosophy. Philosophy has to ensure that every context of meaning is understood and accepted in its uniqueness and with due attention to its own presuppositions, which alone make the statements found in it meaningful.

This may appear to be a simple and obvious task, but in fact it is the hardest possible. For it is much easier to mix up the contexts of meaning than to keep them distinct. Nothing is commoner or more natural than category mixing. One who falls into this error is unconscious of it, for he imposes his own perspective on everything. He is like a man looking at the world through coloured spectacles and believing implicitly the evidence of his own eyes. In loyalty to truth he cannot say anything else but that the world is of this colour. He says this in good faith, and is bound to believe that anyone who says anything else must be either blind or dishonest. In a simple case like that one could say: Take off your spectacles and you'll see the whole spectrum of colours. But in the case we are dealing with it is not quite so simple.

In every judgment we make, we start of course with certain presuppositions. We therefore need the warning: See to it that you employ the right presuppositions. Don't start attacking an idea on the basis of wrong presuppositions. If you do, you'll be blaming other people for views they don't hold, and may be even further from holding than their critic. For the critic can at least imagine somebody holding such views, although he himself 'knows better' and declares these views meaningless. The meaninglessness and the limitations are in that case entirely on the side of the critic, for it is his own imagination he is fighting against. The *praeterea censeo* of philosophy, on the other hand, runs: See to it that you always operate with the proper presuppositions, the appropriate categories. Only so will the discussion be meaningful. It will be meaningless if you base it on presuppositions which you happen to find handy, but which may not be at all appropriate to the context concerned. What philosophy has to contend against is ordinary one-sidedness, the limited perspective, the key-hole view, which we described above as 'stupidity'. This recalls the saying that 'against stupidity the gods themselves fight in vain'—how much more, then, philosophy? But philosophy must not therefore abandon its struggle for the broad perspective and the diversity of the contexts of meaning.

When contemporary philosophy speaks of different 'languages' and of the need to be aware of the differences in their logical status, it is seeking to do justice to the very thing we are discussing here.[33] But the whole idea of different languages can be rendered illusory if the relation between the different languages of the different contexts of meaning is conceived as analogous to that between languages in the ordinary sense, where what is said in one language can be directly translated into another. No such direct translation from the language of one context of meaning to another is possible; and it is impossible precisely because they start with different presuppositions and therefore have and must have different meanings. It is this that makes the once popular idea of a unified language of the sciences—'physicalism'—meaningless, for the rest of the contexts of meaning could not be translated into such a language without losing their meaning. This essential untranslatability of the different contexts of meaning into one another's languages is a fundamental insight to which contemporary philosophy has come.[34] Just as kilometers cannot be translated into kilograms, or the terms used in tennis into those used in chess, so neither can one context of meaning be translated into the terms of any other. Each of them must be allowed to preserve its own distinctive character and fulfil its own specific function.

7. Integrity and Integration

The heading of this section could just as well have been the same as the last: 'Philosophy as a clearing house for the different contexts of meaning', for that is still the theme with which we are concerned. Our latest con-

[33] *Cf.* above, pp. 153ff., 268f.

[34] For example, C. L. Stevenson, *Facts and Values*, p. 214: 'It is impossible, in my opinion, to "translate" an evaluative sentence into either an imperative or a factual sentence—or even into a gerundive sentence. One can clarify it only by describing or "characterizing" its typical functions'.

clusion, however, concerning the untranslatability of the different contexts of meaning, seems to call in question the whole idea of philosophy as a clearing house. If the currency of one context cannot be exchanged for that of another, what advantage is there in having philosophy as a clearing house? If the language of one context cannot be translated into another, what is the function of philosophy as analysis of language?

(1) This difficulty, however, is more apparent than real. For it is precisely the danger of confusing the contexts and thereby landing in meaninglessness, that makes philosophical clarification so extremely important. If we are not clear with regard to the basic presuppositions, we shall not get any clear meaning out of what is said. If we get the basic categories mixed up, we shall make no proper sense of individual statements. It is therefore a matter of first importance that light should be shed on these basic questions; and no other discipline but philosophy undertakes this task. Just because it does not confine its analysis to a single context of meaning, but takes in a diversity of contexts, it has the possibility of characterizing and distinguishing them in a universal perspective. Naturally its first duty here is to mark the boundaries between them and see to it that they do not get mixed up with one another. This is an entirely legitimate and most necessary task. For while on the one hand the basic presuppositions are of fundamental importance for understanding what anything is about, they are on the other hand often so well hidden that we do not observe that they are there. In consequence we often completely overlook them and imagine there are no presuppositions at all, with the result that we miss the real meaning.

In order to illustrate the consequences of failing to pay attention to presuppositions, whether because one imagines there are none or thinks he can manage without them, a musical analogy may be cited. If on a page of musical notation a melody is inscribed without indication of the clef or signature, it is impossible to get any precise idea of the tune. Certain things will be plain, such as the length of the notes and the approximate intervals between them, but the melody as a whole is beyond our grasp. The value of the different notes can vary exceedingly depending on the key one presupposes. The only way to get a true idea of the tune is to find out the correct key, that is to say, the one that the composer intended. It is this that gives the melody its 'meaning'. Give it a wrong signature and even the most inspired and spirited composition will seem meaningless and spiritless.

Every analogy breaks down somewhere—otherwise it would not be an analogy but an identity. The weakness of the above analogy is that when once the right key has been found, the melody can be transposed into another key without entirely losing its native character. It may of course give an impression of having lost in the transposition something of the lustre of its original tone, but this does not alter the fact that the main impression it makes is that of being the same piece as before. This, however, is just what cannot be said with regard to the contexts of meaning. One context cannot be thus transposed into another, that is, its language cannot be translated into that of another. If we attempt such translation, not only are certain nuances lost, but the entire meaning disappears. Yet so long as we keep in mind the point at which the analogy breaks down, we can carry its application further and describe the work of philosophy by saying: Philosophy seeks to discover the 'signatures' of the various contexts of meaning. This means that it must begin with a proper understanding of the material examined, and must not measure it by a standard that is alien to it. That is what has unfortunately been done to far too great an extent in philosophy, which has consequently become narrow and constricted. What is needed is a widening of perspective so that justice can be done to the different aspects of life, or in other words, so that justice can be done both to the universal nature of philosophy and to the richness and manifoldness of life.

What has now been said demonstrates *one* aspect of the function of philosophy as a clearing house: it has to maintain the *integrity* of the contexts of meaning, so that each of them preserves its distinctive character and is allowed to be just what it is and mean what it means, without being blurred or distorted by confusion with others.

(2) But it must now be just as plainly stated that philosophy as a clearing house has a further task, namely that of ensuring the *integration* of the contexts of meaning and not allowing the connection between them to be broken. Otherwise the affirmation that one context cannot be translated into the language of another might easily be taken to imply that the different contexts are wholly unrelated to one another, and that the theory of contexts of meaning divides life up into a series of parallel lines of meaning which never meet, and between which there is no connection at all—a truly incredible if not self-contradictory idea. For it would be strange if we could insist so stubbornly that what constitutes meaning of any kind is the context, and yet be content to let the several contexts of meaning stand side by side without any contextual relation to one another. But this sort of absurdity is avoided when philosophy as a clearing house makes itself responsible for the context of the contexts, that is, for their inter-relatedness and integration.

At first sight it might seem next to impossible to combine these two tasks. Will not integration infringe upon integrity, and the maintaining of integrity prevent any sort of integration? It only seems to be so. In reality the two tasks belong inseparably together. It is only when we clearly understand how the various contexts of meaning are distinct from and yet inseparably bound up with one another, that we can be said to have grasped the meaning of the term 'context of meaning'. One context differs from another, and therefore they must be kept distinct; but this does not mean that they are to be thought of as in watertight compartments. 'Distinction' is not the same as 'separation'. Unless we distinguish them the meaning is lost; if we separate them the context is lost. In either case the context of meaning is destroyed, which it is the chief business of philosophy to safeguard.

The relation between the contexts of meaning is *complementary*. One context does not exclude another, but points to it—and points to it precisely as a different context of meaning. One makes up for the other, so to speak, by saying things which the other because of its particular way of looking at things is unable to say, but which also must be expressed. This should not surprise us when we recall that even within the special science of physics it has been found necessary to adopt a 'complementary' approach (Niels Bohr) and to work with apparently contradictory and mutually exclusive concepts. The best known example of this is the corpuscle and wave theories of light. These had long been regarded as excluding one another, so that accepting one meant rejecting the other; but both of them are now accepted as necessary in order to do justice to the given facts of the case. This being so, it should admonish us how much more necessary it is to regard the different areas of experience and the diverse contexts of meaning in a similar way, even though they cannot be regularly deduced from one another. Only a false metaphysical conception of unity, a conception which seeks unity in the wrong place, leads us to imagine we have to deny one context of meaning in order to affirm another, and so drives us onto the path of reductionism and the narrowly circumscribed view. Critical, scientific philosophy on the other hand must keep the different possibilities open and clarify their different presuppositions.

Besides the idea of complementarity we can speak also of the element of perspective in all experience. We need to be clear about the perspective or point of view from which a question in a given context is approached. It is this that is clarified when we are shown what presuppositions underlie the case in point. Yet this does not exclude the possibility of adopting another perspective and employing other presuppositions.

The primary issue, however, is that of *meaning*, and for an adequate treatment of this we must always first study the different contexts of meaning in their own light, clarifying the presuppositions proper to them and not allowing any one of them to absolutize itself and invade the autonomous provinces of the rest. This makes no slight demand on philosophy. For although its business is with formal presuppositions, it requires a more than superficial knowledge of the material to which the presuppositions are meant to apply. Without such knowledge the logical analysis of presuppositions can easily become an exercise in formalistic irrelevancy. But it is just as important for an adequate treatment of the *context* that we should study the relation between the different contexts of meaning. In that case we must note that the relationship is never between particular statements in the several areas. These are as such incommensurable with each other. Their methodological starting points are so different that there is no possibility of synthesizing them into one unified view. In that sense no integration is possible. The integration must come about through the presuppositions. For these are not only presupposed by their several contexts of meaning, but they are presupposed also by one another.

When philosophy comes to deal with this final question of integration, it still moves along its usual philosophical lines. It engages in no other form of argumentation than that which is characteristic of it in every area. Here too the role of philosophy is that of the 'logical analysis of presuppositions'. The only difference is that in analyzing a particular context of meaning it starts with the propositions found in that context and tries to get back to the presuppositions implied in them, whereas in examining the relation between the different contexts of meaning it has to start with their several presuppositions and try to get back to the presuppositions implied in these. In the former case it is, in short, a question of the presuppositions of the propositions, and in the latter of the presuppositions of the pre-suppositions. In both cases what is involved is a 'logical analysis of pre-suppositions'.

It should, however, be observed that the idea of 'the presuppositions of the presuppositions' in no way implies an attempt to get back to a self-validating principle from which everything else can be derived. On the contrary, all it is intended to say is that one assumption implies another, and to take one presupposition for granted is implicitly to take the other as well; which means that the ultimate presuppositions of the different contexts of meaning mutually condition one another and stand or fall with one another. That is the way in which philosophy proceeds towards a genuine integration of the contexts of meaning.

If, as has often been supposed, the way to the integration of the contexts lay in taking a synoptic view of their results, it would mean the end of their automony and integrity. But when the integration is connected with their presuppositions, it carries with it respect for their integrity. The position is one that can be described perhaps most clearly in terms of the Chalcedonian formula so well known in the history of Christian thought: 'without confusion or change, without division or separation' (ἀσυγχύτως, ἀτρέπτως, ἀδιαιρέτως, ἀχωρίστως). This formula has often been regarded as paradoxical and absurd; for if one thing is inseparably united with an-other, it must surely by entering into such a union have ceased to be what it previously was, and to have become in fact so fused together with the other as to have been changed. The relation between the contexts of meaning, however, is an illustration of the fact that there is nothing at all contradictory or paradoxical here. The individual context of meaning must preserve its complete distinctiveness and not be confused with other contexts, for such a confusion—such category mixing—inevitably results in a change and distortion of meaning if not in complete meaninglessness. On the other hand the individual context must not be isolated, it must not be detached from its indivisible and inseparable connection through pre-suppositions with the rest of the contexts of meaning, for that would result in disintegration and the annihilation of the context. So 'without confusion or change' stands for *integrity* and 'without division or separa-tion' for *integration.*

CHAPTER XI

The Religious Context of Meaning

1. The Task of the Philosophy of Religion

OUR inquiry has now—strange to say—reached the point where we were already in Chapter II. There we raised the question 'What is philosophy of religion?' We were not then, however, in a position to answer it. We had to be content with pointing out certain circumstances which have made the philosophy of religion a highly problematical science, while at the same time insisting that the problem on which it turns is real and inescapable. Our contention that it is only as a purely philosophical discipline that the philosophy of religion can handle this problem, complicated the issue. There was much that was obscure and must be clarified before we could hope for an answer to the question of the nature and function of the philosophy of religion. A major difficulty was that 'philosophy' is anything but an unambiguous term, and therefore the statement that the philosophy of religion is at all events a philosophical discipline does not tell us very much. In what sense is it philosophical? If the answer is that it must of course be a scientific philosophy, this gives rise to new questions. In what sense scientific? What is it that is characteristic of scientific work, or more precisely of scientific argumentation? And what is the place of philosophical argumentation in this context? We have seen these questions answered step by step.[1] The task of philosophy is the analysis of meaning and validity, and the method by which this task must be carried out is that of the logical analysis of presuppositions. Presupposition, meaning, context, context of meaning—these in brief are the fundamental concepts of philosophy. From all this we found it possible to conclude that the function of philosophy is to serve as a clearing house between the different contexts of meaning, showing equal regard both for their integrity and their integration.

We have made a long detour, which has given us many insights into the structure and mode of argumentation of science and philosophy. Now, however, the circle closes and we are back at the point from which we started. Once more we are faced with the question of the nature of the religio-philosophical problem. What is philosophy of religion? It is the same question with which we began, but now we are in a far different position as regards answering it. The detour was not made for its own sake, simply to see what it might offer by way of different viewpoints on the

[1] See above, pp. 209ff., where the train of thought is summarized which we are here developing further in connection with the philosophy of religion.

general questions of science and philosophy—though it must be admitted that these questions are so important and fascinating that at many points, where the resolution of old problems and pseudo-problems lay immediately to hand, we spent rather more time on them than was strictly necessary for defining the philosophical approach to religion. Yet even where we have given these general scientific problems relatively independent treatment, this has not been altogether unprofitable for the clarification of the religio-philosophical problem. As it turns out, what we have done on our detour has had the additional effect of clearing up the tangled confusion in which to begin with we found the philosophy of religion. For what applies to philosophy applies, and necessarily applies, in all relevant respects to the philosophy of religion as well. Even where the philosophy of religion has not been explicitly named, it has been implicitly present all along, and now all we have to do is to draw the conclusions pertinent to it from what has already been said.

If philosophy has to do with the contexts of meaning, then it is the task of the philosophy of religion to subject the religious context of meaning to philosophical analysis, or in other words to elucidate the ultimate presuppositions that are determinative of meaning in the religious context. The philosophy of religion is the logical analysis of the fundamental presuppositions in the area of religion. On this basis it has to explain the distinctive character and meaning of religious language. In its procedure and method it is philosophy pure and simple, though it is directed to a particular object, namely religion and its problems. It is 'philosophy', and more precisely 'philosophy of religion'. What was suggested initially as a possibility, that the concept of religion might be understood as a 'presuppositional concept',[2] has thus been confirmed and can now be fully and explicitly stated as follows: If the philosophy of religion has to do with the concept of religion, then it is concerned precisely with the logical analysis of presuppositions in the sense in which we have defined that term. Our protracted detour has thus proved highly profitable. If at the outset we had answered the question 'What is philosophy of religion?' by saying that it was a logical analysis of the religious context of meaning with regard to its basic presuppositions, these would at that stage have been merely empty words. But thanks to the investigation we undertook after raising the question, that answer is now thoroughly well founded and in every way meaningful. The initial obscurity has disappeared because every term used here has been carefully defined. The ideas involved, by delimiting one another and exercising mutual surveillance, so to speak, have been given all possible precision.

It might now seem as if we had reached our goal; but instead, this is just where the business of the philosophy of religion seriously begins. In order to carry out its task it needs a mass of factual knowledge from the

2 Above, p. 25.

religious sphere. It is true that for the analysis of religious presuppositions a single indubitably religious judgment is in principle sufficient as a starting point, since the aim is of course to discover what is implied in such a judgment. The difficulty lies in the idea of an 'indubitably religious judgment', for in order to find such a thing extensive knowledge of the material in the field is required. The position here is parallel to that in other areas when their presuppositions are to be analyzed. In the case of science, for example, and its necessary presuppositions, it is sufficient in principle to have a single indubitably scientific judgment as the starting point for the analysis. Indeed in the last resort no more is needed than the *possibility* of scientific judgments. On the other hand, it is clear that we cannot get very far with such a narrow base for the analysis. It is science as a *given* phenomenon that philosophy analyzes with regard to its indispensable actual presuppositions. And so it is in all areas, all contexts of meaning.

Philosophy starts with something given. It does not create its subject matter, but analyzes something it finds already there. It is therefore clearly of the utmost importance for it to have an intimate knowledge of the subject matter it is analyzing, so that it really knows what it is talking about, and knows it quite concretely and in a way that is possible only for one who is himself active or at least quite at home in the field. One who does not have from his own experience a knowledge of science and how it works in different areas is not equipped for making a contribution to the philosophy of science. One who is unfamiliar with the concrete realities of ethical life can soon go wrong in attempting a philosophical analysis of the ethical. One who is unsympathetic towards the manifestations of the religious life, yet wishes to make a philosophical analysis of religion, can easily speak of it in a way that shows he does not really know what it is all about. He understands the religious words and phrases in a quite other way than they are meant. To require that the philosophy of religion should be based on a knowledge of the facts, is to make no more than a perfectly obvious and quite minimal demand. But in this matter we are still suffering from the effects of an old tradition which saw in the philosophy of religion a metaphysically creative discipline, so that everyone could develop from his own arbitrary starting point a conception of religion which he regarded as normative. It is perhaps more necessary to insist on the importance of an objective knowledge of the facts in connection with the philosophy of religion than in any other area, since the need for this has been more often disregarded here than elsewhere.

If the point we have now reached is only the starting point for the philosophy of religion, the point where its real work has to begin, the position is different as far as our present investigation is concerned. This is not intended to be a fully fledged philosophy of religion, but only 'prolegomena' to a scientific philosophy of religion—and this aim has now been achieved. The ground has been cleared of all the traditional clutter, and the ground-plan of the new building broadly outlined. We have thus reached the point where the prolegomena are complete and the construction of a scientific philosophy of religion can begin. We need therefore do no more here than illustrate by a few actual examples the importance of observing the principles here laid down for such construction. In spite of its philosophically formal character the philosophy of religion occupies, as these examples will show, a key position also with regard to theology, so that a mistake made in the philosophy of religion can have serious theological consequences.

When we turn to contemporary theology we find that many of the difficulties with which it has to contend are ultimately due to ambiguous religio-philosophical premisses. It would be easier to reach conclusions with regard to particular matters of detail were it not for an underlying philosophical outlook, sometimes unconscious, sometimes frankly acknowledged, which colours the whole, and therefore of course the parts, so that they acquire a meaning other than that originally intended. It is here that the philosophy of religion is of decisive importance for theology, since if the false presuppositions illegitimately smuggled in are of a kind that belong to a world-view or philosophy of life, they can be removed only by means of a philosophical critique. The otherwise obvious alternative of putting things right by an appeal to the plain facts of the case is unfeasible, because these very facts have been re-interpreted in accordance with the presuppositions in question and have thus acquired a character and significance corresponding to the light in which they have been viewed.

Before giving our examples, however, we must forestall a possible misunderstanding. Our statement that the philosophy of religion occupies a key position with regard to theology, for which its work has far-reaching consequences, might possibly be taken as implying that it has a certain supervisory function in relation to theology. For particularly in recent years the idea has not been uncommon that it is the business of philosophy as concerned with semantics to examine the language used by the different sciences in their several fields in order to see how far it is acceptable, and if it is not, to correct it. The responsibility of philosophy for clarification and language analysis seems to favour this view, and yet it cannot be too strongly emphasized that it is completely wrong. A philosophy that meddles in that sort of way with the different sciences and areas of life is a monstrosity. Philosophy has no primacy over the rest of the sciences, and it is not for philosophy to decide what is right or wrong in these other areas.

The statement that philosophical or religio-philosophical analysis has far-reaching consequences for theology means almost the opposite of that. There can be no question of any interference with theology on the part of philosophy, for that would involve an encroachment on the religious context of meaning, a denial of its autonomy, and thus an indirect attack on philosophy itself. The position is rather this, that until the question of the religious context of meaning has been philosophically clarified by the philosophy of religion, all kinds of foreign notions of a more or less metaphysical nature can have free scope in theology. This becomes impossible once the philosophy of religion has demonstrated the autonomy of the religious context of meaning: for if it is autonomous, then it must be judged from its own point of view. Alien and extraneous ways of looking at it are disqualified. That is the theological consequence of religio-philosophical clarification, and it means that theology must respect the uniqueness of the religious context of meaning and not allow it to be obscured by confusion with other contexts. In this way philosophy fulfils its function as a clearing house *between* the different contexts of meaning. It does not interfere in the internal affairs of any of them, but sees to it that none of them gets mixed up with any other and that each retains its own distinctive character.

It is as important in the religious sphere as any other to avoid category mixing. Admittedly there are considerable difficulties here, inasmuch as religion and metaphysics are quite generally held to belong closely together—though that is not at all the case, except with regard to a particular sort of religion. Theology above all needs to be reminded of this, because it has to do with two contexts of meaning and can easily overlook the difference between them. Its subject matter belongs to the religious context of meaning, while it itself as a science belongs in the theoretical-scientific context. All too often this has led to a blurring of distinctions, so that theology has been conceived as a scientific form of religion instead of being allowed to be—'without confusion or change'—a scientific study of religion. But whether it appears as 'scientific religion' or 'religious science' the mixing and confusion of categories is equally disastrous. What a soundly constructed philosophy of religion has to say to theology, therefore, is this: Don't confuse your contexts of meaning, but let the religious context be what it is!

This brings us to our two examples of category mixing and its effects, both of them taken from current theological discussion. The first has to do with the *demythologizing theology* so much debated in recent years, and the second with Paul Tillich's understanding of the relation between philosophy and theology or philosophy and religion in terms of his *theory of correlation*.

2. Demythologization

(1) *A pseudo-problem*

The problem of demythologization, as it is called, is a remarkable illustration of the way in which the theological scene can be dominated by a pseudo-problem. Its main thesis is very simple and can be stated as follows. The New Testament, like the ancient world in general, is characterized by a 'mythological' world-view. This world-view long ago became a thing of the past, and no one now accepts it or thinks in its terms. It has been replaced for modern man by another world-view, which is 'scientific'. Even if we never give a thought to it, all of us in everything we do operate with this new world-view, and we cannot help doing so. If therefore modern man is to grasp what the New Testament is about and to benefit from its message, it must be 'demythologized'. To the extent that the New Testament is mythological it does not and cannot any longer have any meaning for us, because it cannot be fitted into our scheme of reality. It is incompatible with our modern world-view, and has therefore nothing to say to us.

In this situation what are we to do? An obvious answer would be to put the New Testament aside and say that while for men in the past it may have been meaningful, times have changed and it is not so now. But that is not the answer given by the demythologizing theologian. He is convinced that the New Testament is extremely important even for modern man, and that rightly understood it has a great deal to say to him. The idea therefore is not to dismiss or reject it, but to give it its proper meaning. This involves on the one hand the negative task of ridding the New Testament of the mythological features which make it inaccessible to modern man, and on the other hand the positive task of drawing out the elements that are acceptable to the modern mind. Both tasks are performed with the help of an 'existential interpretation', which includes both an *Entmythologisierung des Neuen Testaments* that purges away all mythological elements, and a positive interpretation that enables the true significance of the New Testament message to be seen. Whereas the latter in its mythological form represents God and divine things as objectively given realities, it must now be re-interpreted 'existentially' so that the theological becomes an anthropological question, a question concerning man himself and his *Selbstverständnis* or 'self-understanding'.

The term 'existential interpretation' itself furnishes a clue to the source from which its inspiration is drawn—the philosophy of existence. Bultmann and the rest of the demythologizing theologians are convinced that this philosophy, especially in its Heideggerian form, has satisfactorily answered the question of human nature and human existence. It was not unnatural that theologians should be drawn to this type of thought, inasmuch as it largely goes back to Christian influences and is particularly indebted, for example, to Augustine, Pascal and Kierkegaard. Moreover its vocabulary, with words like '*Sorge*', '*Angst*', 'alienation', seemed to provide a very appropriate anthropological background for the interpretation of the Christian message.[3] This philosophy, which has often been taken by theologians to be a strictly objective and scientific philosophical interpretation of human nature and the conditions of human existence,

[3] On this *cf.* above, pp. 131–8.

seemed therefore specially suited to serve as the *Vorverständnis* or pre-understanding which opens the way to a correct understanding of the New Testament message and of religion in general. In this way the 'existential interpretation' actually becomes the key to the proper interpretation of the Christian *kerygma* ('message'). Although it cannot itself supply the Christian answer, it can at least point to the question to which it is an answer. By means of its analysis of existence it can exhibit the state of need which is inseparable from man's existence, and to which the answer is given in the Christian *kerygma*.

Now it is not our purpose here to add yet another to the interminable arguments for and against the theology of demythologization.[4] That is ruled out by the fact that we have already described the problem of demythologization as a pseudo-problem. A pseudo-problem is not solved by giving new answers to the question it poses, but only by showing that the question is wrongly put. The only way of 'solving' a pseudo-problem is to 'dissolve' the question itself. Our purpose therefore is in that sense to 'dissolve' the demythologizer's way of putting the question, and to show that it is only wrong treatment of it that gives rise to the impression that the problem is real.

(2) *The basic error: category mixing*

Where then does the πρῶτον ψεῦδος in the theory of demythologization lie? After what has been said it is not difficult to identify the basic error. It is a matter of category mixing, the confusion of contexts of meaning. From this fundamental error all the rest naturally follow. We shall illustrate this with regard to the three concepts of 1. theology, 2. mythology, and 3. 'existential interpretation'.

---

[4] The course of this debate can be traced through works of the following authors and editors as listed in the Bibliography: Bartsch, Bornkamm, Bultmann, Ebeling, Fuchs, Funk, Jaspers, Kegley, Lorenzmeier, Niebuhr, Ogden, Schumann, Schnübbe, Schmithals, van Buren, Zahrnt.—For a well-informed, sharp and in many ways effective attack on the demythologizing theology and its 'existential interpretation' see P. H. Jørgensen, *Die Bedeutung des Subjekt-Objektverhältnisses für die Theologie.*

Dietrich Bonnhoeffer's ideas about a 'non-religious' or 'worldly' interpretation of biblical concepts (particularly in his posthumous *Widerstand und Ergebung*) are often taken as belonging to the demythologizing school. That this is wrong should have been obvious from his attitude to existentialism, of which he says, 'that is the attitude that I am contending against' (op. cit., 1951, p. 170; 1966, p. 231; ET p. 189); for in other cases the demythologizing theology always has a background of existentialist metaphysics. This misinterpretation of Bonnhoeffer has put his ideas at the service of forces he was unwilling to serve. It is part of his tragedy that it is not enough for him to have been personally martyred, but the martyr must be harnessed now to one, now to another triumphal chariot. It has been Bonnhoeffer's fate to have his often only half-formed ideas exploited for purposes which in reality are quite alien to him. His literary remains have been to a large extent treated as a quarry out of which everyone takes what suits him and uses it for his own ends. On Bonnhoeffer see Benkt-Erik Benktsson, *Christus und die Religion.*

1) One consequence of the confusion of categories is an extremely un-critical *concept of theology*. Theology is held on the one hand to be a purely scientific discipline, which puts it in the scientific context of meaning, while on the other hand it is credited with a religiously creative function, which puts it in the religious context of meaning. It is scientific, but at the same time religious; it is religious, but at the same time scientific. The ambiguity arising from this mixing of categories and motifs finds concentrated expression in such formulas as these: 'Theology is the scientific utterance (*Zur-Sprache-Kommen*) of the Word of God'[5] and 'The subject of theology is God'.[6] The 'utterance of the Word of God' clearly belongs in the context of faith, and is not accessible to any science. 'God' and 'the Word of God' are not 'scientific' concepts. No science can as such demonstrate 'God' or prove that certain words are to be regarded as 'the Word of God'. Nor has theology the right to claim that kind of hegemony in the realm of faith. If theology is a science, as indeed it is, then it must beware of such encroachments on the province of faith, as it must of any attempt to place the religious context of meaning under the jurisdiction of science. But once the idea is accepted that science has the last word in matters of faith (which is a species of scientism), it is quite logical to expect science—in this case theology—to be able to effect an adjustment of faith that will bring it into line with 'the scientific world-view' or, as it has also been put, that will make possible 'a proclamation suitable for modern man'. And that of course is precisely the aim of demythologization.

2) Another consequence of the confusion of categories is the uncritical use of the *concept of myth and mythology*. What is meant by mythology? If we are to speak of demythologizing, it is obviously of the utmost importance to have the term 'mythology' clearly defined. The fact is, however, that the words 'myth' and 'mythology' are far from representing a univocal concept. 'Myth' covers such diverse phenomena as the mythology of primitive society, of antiquity, of gnosticism; and we may also recall Plato's use of the *mythos* in philosophy when *logos* no longer suffices.[7] Beyond these we can trace the wanderings of myth through the centuries down to Alfred Rosenberg's *Mythus des XX. Jahrhunderts*—and why not to Bultmann's favourite nineteenth century myth, the conception of natural science which scientists long since discarded and relegated to the realm of myth?

When Bultmann tries to explain the meaning of the word 'mythical' he takes as his starting point a particular 'world-view' which he supposes to be the modern, scientific world-view.[8] In consequence, anything in the

[5] G. Ebeling, *Wort und Glaube*, p. 456; ET, p. 433.

[6] R. Bultmann, *Glauben und Verstehen*, I, p. 25; ET*, p. 52.

[7] *Cf.* my *Agape and Eros* (1953), pp. 166ff. Eros in Plato is a mythologically coloured symbol, Agape as exhibited in the self-sacrifice of Christ is a historical reality.

[8] *Cf.* above, pp. 44ff.

New Testament that does not harmonize with this world-view, shaped as it is by science and technology, is described as mythology. But this really includes everything, for it is not only certain isolated features of the New Testament that are of a mythical character. 'The world-view of the New Testament is a mythical world-view', Bultmann tells us. It must therefore be completely demythologized and translated into the non-mythological language of our time. The only usable language for this purpose is that of existentialist philosophy, which is both the scientific language of today and a language capable through its profound analysis of human existence of doing justice to that which the old mythology sought in its imperfect way to express.

But what if all this turns out to be a construction which is inapplicable to the New Testament? What if the New Testament has nothing whatever to do with mythology? A heavy price is paid for the category mixing involved in demythologization, and for the failure to make clear which context of meaning we are dealing with. We may start with our 'scientific' world-view, and if world-view is not what religion (and the New Testament) is about, then we are approaching the subject from a wrong point of view, with a foreign criterion, and our procedure is 'heteronomous'. Since we do not reckon with an autonomous religious context of meaning, we see no alternative but to have recourse to a supposedly 'scientific' criterion. Then when we come across something that belongs to the religious as distinct from the scientific context of meaning, we regard it forthwith as 'mythical'. We set an arbitrary rubric over expressions of religious meaning and reduce them to meaninglessness, and then we are free to 'interpret' them in such a way that they acquire a meaning agreeable to our own way of thinking. First we mythologize the New Testament in flat contradiction of its own meaning, then we demythologize it in harmony with our own idea of meaning, and in both cases we entirely miss its real meaning. The gospel is not mythology, nor is it existentialist metaphysics. It is something quite different, though this escapes the notice of those who lack the appropriate category for understanding it. Its living water runs to waste, so to speak, because they have no receptacle in which to collect it.

There is always a risk in approaching a subject with a key-word picked up elsewhere, as the word 'mythology' has been. The idea is that we must have a 'Demythologization of the New Testament'. Yet the New Testament does not present us with mythology or myth, but these concepts are imported from without, from the surrounding heathen world and from confrontation with our modern world-view. Such references to mythology as there are in the New Testament, are couched in terms of absolute negation.[9] It is indisputable that 'the decisive rejection of myth belongs to those distinctions which are peculiar to the NT. Myth is a heathen

[9] 'They will stop their ears to the truth and turn to mythology' (2 Tim. 4: 14, NEB). *Cf.* also 2 Pet. 1: 16.

category.'[10] Hence it follows that 'myth as such has no place on biblical ground, whether 1. as a direct communication of religious "truths", or 2. as a parable, or 3. as a symbol.'[11] We are therefore rightly warned that 'the use of expressions like "Christ-myth", popular though it may have become in form-critical research, should be firmly rejected as a μετάβασις εἰς ἄλλο γένος.'[12]

This last quotation has not been chosen at random, but because it puts its finger on the weak spot of the demythologization theory. It does so particularly with the phrase '*metabasis eis allo genos*', for it is this that is the cardinal error. There are two respects in which the demythologizing theology is guilty of a *metabasis*. First there is what we may call—anticipating our discussion in the next chapter—a *metabasis* from one motif-context to another, and this may well be what is primarily intended by the word in the above quotation. Mythology belongs to a quite different circle of motifs than that of the New Testament. It is remarkable that scholars who are otherwise thoroughly at home in the field of historical research, do not notice this fundamental difference of motifs, which is really just as striking as that between a major and minor key. The explanation lies in an atomistic habit of thought, which allows itself to be content with an outward similarity of words, without paying attention to the often directly opposite meaning which comes from their belonging to different motif-contexts. Secondly, there is the form of *metabasis* which chiefly interests us in our present discussion, namely the transition from one context of meaning to another. The demythologizing theology furnishes an instructive example of both these forms of *metabasis*, illustrating not only the resulting confusion of contexts but also the effect this has on the handling of the historical material. It is impossible to indulge either in category mixing or the mixing of motifs without serious consequences both for the method and the particular material. Meaning and method belong inseparably together, and where there is no clarity about the contexts of meaning there can be no clarity about the meaning of the concrete material. The demythologizing theology is thus culpable on three counts: 1. category mixing, 2. motif mixing, and 3. doing violence to the texts.

The root of the trouble with the demythologizing program lies in the mixing of categories. It is this that opens the way for 'existential interpretation' and the arbitrary re-interpretation of the contents of the New Testament. Once started on this way, the only question is how far we should go in demythologizing. Bultmann stops where God and Christ are concerned. For although in his view there is a good deal of mythology in New Testament thinking about God and Christ, so that we can rightly speak of 'the Christ-myth', there is nevertheless something theologically

[10] G. Stählin in TWNT, IV, p. 800; ET p. 793.
[11] *Ibid.*
[12] *Op. cit.*, p. 801, n. 180; ET p. 794, n. 180.

indispensable about the thought of God and Christ. Without it, the new *Selbstverständnis* or 'self-understanding' which is of the essence of Christian faith could not arise. It is true that philosophy (existentialism) by means of its anthropological analysis of existence can put us on the right road and give us that *Vorverständnis* or 'preunderstanding' without which the Christian *kerygma* is not understood, but the answer to the question of existence and the solution of its problems, which is the new, Christian 'self-understanding', can only be given by the *kerygma* itself, and this is bound up with Christ.

3) This brings us to the third point: the *concept of 'existential interpretation'*. As was said above, it is not Bultmann's intention totally to eliminate mythology, but to interpret it, that is, to expound it in accordance with its deepest intention and so to give more adequate expression to what in its own inadequate way it has been trying to say. Or to put it more precisely we might say that the interpretation aims at saying to modern man in modern terms what the mythology said to ancient man in his mythological language. For a concrete illustration of this we may turn to the 'Christ-myth'. If we had no more than a purely historical interpretation of the person of Jesus, he would be a figure belonging wholly to the past and without any significance for us. But when Jesus is called Christ and thus connected with the Christ-myth, we are being told that he possesses a significance for all ages and therefore also for us. This is the legitimate intention of the Christ-myth. The only difficulty is that just as the historical Jesus belongs to the past, so does the Christ-myth, and it cannot in its mythological form have anything to say to us. It must be told to modern man in the language of modern man. It is this that according to Bultmann compels us to turn to philosophy for help.

Is there any philosophy that can provide us with an adequate means of expressing what mythology can no longer say to us? Bultmann's answer is to point us to the earlier philosophy of Heidegger, particularly his work on *Being and Time*. Theology is in the dilemma of being no longer able to use the language of myth and yet having to recognize that in what myth is seeking to say there is something right which must in one way or another be preserved. This is where the 'existential interpretation' comes in. With unbounded confidence in the existentialist understanding of man, Bultmann and most of the demythologizing theologians attach themselves to Heidegger's metaphysics as the only true philosophy. The situation is very like that in the Middle Ages, when theologians could speak of Aristotle as 'the Philosopher', except that for the demythologizers 'philosophy' means existentialism and 'the Philosopher' par excellence is Heidegger. It is assumed that modern man thinks in Heideggerian categories, and that the language of existentialist philosophy is the language of modern man.[13]

[13] It should be remembered in this connection that Bultmann turns to philosophy for the solution of certain theological problems. He has not developed a philosophy of

What Heideggerian existentialism does for Bultmann is to provide the conceptual framework for his theology. Such a philosophical framework is necessary, according to Bultmann, because without it we could not understand the *kerygma*. When we seek to understand anything, no matter what it may be, there is a general rule that we can only approach it on the assumption that we already have some understanding of what it is about. 'In order to understand anything, we must already have some preunderstanding (*Vorverständnis*) of the subject matter.'[14] Here we have the concept which is so fundamental to Bultmann's theology, that of 'preunderstanding'. He himself defines it thus: 'Basically, preunderstanding is the understanding of one's own existence which can be clarified conceptually through philosophy. To this end, I use the concept of authentic and inauthentic existence and of history and historicity developed by Heidegger in his *Being and Time*.'[15] This explains why Bultmann has committed himself to the existentialist philosophy. He is, however, anxious to insist that this in no way determines the content of the *kerygma*. He writes: 'The philosophical analysis of existence has for me only propaedeutic significance, and prejudges nothing concerning the existential life of the individual.'[16] Philosophy only provides us with the concepts of authentic and inauthentic existence, only furnishes the formal scheme into which the *kerygma* must be introduced if its specific character is to be understood. Philosophy 'offers the possibility of speaking of Christian existence in a language which is comprehensible today.'[17]

Now the question immediately arises: is it really impossible to understand the Christian message without having first grasped Heideggerian metaphysics? It would probably be hard to persuade anyone of the necessity of that for a 'preunderstanding', and still more to show that the obscurity and difficulty of existentialist philosophy is specially adapted to

---

his own, but has taken over one that was already there, which he has selected with an eye to its suitability for his purpose. His one-sided use of philosophy has been sharply criticized also from the existentialist side. K. Jaspers writes: 'The limiting of philosophy to one book of Heidegger's and, I rather think, the misunderstanding of that book through concentrating on its "scientific", objective, doctrinal aspects, means that Bultmann is in fact cut off from all philosophy' (*Die Frage der Entmythologisierung*, p. 13, ET, p. 9). *Cf.* O. Schnübbe's conclusion in his *Der Existenzbegriff*, p. 140: 'Bultmann is a theologian and not a philosopher.'

14 J. Macquarrie in Kegley, *Bultmann*, p. 139.
15 Bultmann in Kegley, *op. cit.*, p. 274.
16 *Ibid.*
17 *Ibid.* In his *Eksistensialfilosofien*, A. Valen-Senstad has shown by painstaking analysis how the leading ideas of Christianity are derived by Bultmann down to the last detail from the basic Heideggerian ontology, and that they therefore also remain within the formal ontological sphere. Even as regards content—in so far as we can speak of any 'content' here—the gospel is determined in the last resort by the formal ontology of Heidegger. Note particularly the last chapter of V.-Senstad's work. *Cf.* also Lögstrup and Hygen, 'Eksistential-filosofi og åpenbaringsteologi' (in NTT, 1970, pp. 1–29).

shed light on the gospel for modern man and make it easier for him to accept. We can take the question further, however, and ask: is there any need for a 'preunderstanding' at all? And is there not a danger that such a preunderstanding may be simply a 'prejudice' which prevents a genuine understanding? Although Bultmann himself is convinced that the acceptance of existentialist philosophy as a preunderstanding 'prejudges nothing', and although he conceives his dependence on Heidegger to be purely formal, so that he can say, 'I learned from him not *what* theology has to say, but *how* to say it, in order to speak to the thinking man of today in a way that he can understand,'[18] yet we have every reason to be sceptical of this position. What we have already seen, together with the fact that Bultmann is unaware that existentialism not only furnishes a formal scheme but is also a metaphysic with substantive implications, makes it impossible to accept his self-appraisal at face value. He fails to realize that the metaphysical background of his *Vorverständnis* or 'preunderstanding' results in a shifting of the centre of gravity, so that the Christian message acquires a content other than it originally had. If '*how* to say it' means that instead of speaking about God and Christ I speak about myself and my own *Selbstverständnis* or 'self-understanding', then it means also an encroachment on '*what* to say'. No one, unless he is firmly committed to existentialism, can maintain that when the Christian message says 'God' it *means* my 'self-understanding'.

The inability of the existential interpretation to preserve the Christian *meaning* of the word 'God' is due to the fact that it has torn the word out of the religious context of meaning and given us the alternative of either taking it as mythology or giving it an existential interpretation, an alternative to which the Christian response must be a 'neither—nor'. The preunderstanding has closed the door to an understanding of the Christian meaning of 'God'. When the Christian gospel comes with its message of God's love shown to me in Christ, it is quite in order to point out that this includes a '*pro me*' ('for me'); and we can speak if we will of the 'existential character' of the gospel, though we should do better to call it a personal message, which loses its point if it is conceived merely as objective information of no vital personal interest to the one to whom it is addressed. If I, as the one to whom the 'word' or message is directed, am taken out of the picture, then there is no longer any question of an actual message or of Christian faith. But what happens 'for me' (*pro me*) is grounded in the fact that 'God is love' and that he has shown me his love in the self-sacrifice of Christ. This, which is the real import of the gospel, gets lost if I shift the centre of gravity from God and Christ to myself, orienting everything from myself and my own authentic or inauthentic existence.

The defect in existential theology of which we are speaking here, is not

[18] Bultmann in Kegley, *op. cit.*, p. 276.

only a matter of a single item, however important, but it affects the entire structure and range of thought. The properly religious point of view has been set aside in favour of a metaphysical *Selbstverständnis*, and this in turn is motivated by the idea that there is in the mythology an element of 'self-understanding' which ought to be preserved, but which can be preserved only with the aid of this metaphysic. There is an obvious question as to which is primary and which is derivative: is it the mythology that calls for an 'existential interpretation', or is it the existentialist philosophy that has first been accepted and then found to be a suitable instrument for the detection and recovery of something valuable in the myth? What makes the latter the more probable is that it seems rather far-fetched to ask what kind of 'self-understanding' or what special understanding of man lies behind the myth, unless one has started with the existentialist key-word, *Selbstverständnis*. We can, however, leave this question open. The main point is that both of these two poles, the mythology and the existential interpretation, are necessary to one another in order to give meaning to the problem of demythologization, but neither of them has any room for the religious content of the New Testament message concerning God and what God has done in Christ. That message does not fit into either of these categories; it belongs neither to mythology nor to the metaphysics of *Selbstverständnis*, but is quite independent of both. For lack of an adequate religious category the notion arises that 'God' is primarily to be understood as a myth, but a myth which by means of demythologization can be made more or less meaningful as an expression of man's *Selbstverständnis*. The mythical or metaphysical understanding of human existence thus replaces the religious message of the *kerygma*. Anthropology takes the place of theology.

With regard to God and Christ Bultmann is relatively restrained in his demand for demythologization. He does not hesitate, for example, to speak of God's action in Christ. It is true that man's *Selbstverständnis* always remains his point of orientation, so that the shift of emphasis we mentioned above determines his view; it is also true that there is in his thought a comparable shift from the *Christus-Ereignis* or 'Christ-event' to the *Predigt-Ereignis* or 'Preaching-event', which obscures the significance of the former and puts all the stress on the latter; yet it never becomes quite clear what is the relation between them. It is not what once happened through Christ that is of decisive importance, but rather the fact that I am permitted here and now through the preaching to hear a word addressed directly and personally to me, a word that faces me with a *decision*, a choice between inauthentic and authentic existence, or between remaining in my *Uneigentlichkeit* and accepting my *Eigentlichkeit*. This is the demythologized meaning of the idea of the Word made flesh and the mythological language concerning the incarnation of Jesus Christ (Phil. 2:6ff.).[19]

[19] 'That there is such a word addressed to me, in which God . . . appears as *my* God,

(3) *The 'secular meaning' of the gospel*

If it is only with reserve that Bultmann applies his demythologizing procedure to God and Christ, his reserve is not shared by all the demythologizing theologians. Some demand a more thoroughgoing application of the principle, so that both God and Christ are far more radically and completely demythologized. In this connection we need only mention such names as Herbert Braun, Schubert M. Ogden and Paul M. van Buren. But no matter what changes of position or phraseology are made, there is no escaping the πρῶτον ψεῦδος of the theological starting point. When 'God' is conceived as a '*Sprach-Ereignis*' ('language-event'), we have reached a point where we are bound to ask whether it is also a '*Sinn-Ereignis*' ('meaning-event'), or whether language and words are mere 'sound and fury signifying nothing'? Yet meaninglessness was precisely what the demythologizers hoped to avoid by means of their 'theological' and 'philosophical' considerations. Again, to mention another rephrasing of what is meant by 'God', we often find the currently fashionable word '*Mitmenschlichkeit*' ('fellow-man-ness', 'human togetherness', 'common humanity'). God is said to be the same as 'common humanity'. Here the speaker has seized on a term whose meaning he thinks he understands, and says this is the meaning of the otherwise incomprehensible word 'God'. The term '*Mitmenschlichkeit*' is sufficiently vague and ill-defined to be able to mean all sorts of things and to be used for the most diverse purposes. Compare, for example, the following two sentences:

'God is a particular kind of *Mitmenschlichkeit*' (H. Braun).[20]

'The State is nothing else but a form of *Mitmenschlichkeit*' (H. W. Bartsch).[21]

---

who here and now speaks to *me*, and speaks through the lips of men—this is the "demythologized" meaning of ὁ λόγος σὰρξ ἐγένετο, the Church's doctrine of the Incarnation. And the Christian proclamation is tied to a tradition and looks back to a historical Figure and his history only so far as it sees in this Figure and his history the legitimation of the word thus addressed' (Jaspers-Bultmann, *op. cit.*, pp. 71f.; ET p. 70). The only 'criterion' for the truth of the revelation is that the preached word, *die Predigt*, faces man with a decision, 'namely the decision as to how he will understand himself. . . . For man can understand what the word of revelation says, because it offers him the two possibilities for his own self-understanding' (*op. cit.*, p. 71; ET, pp. 69f.).

[20] H. Braun, *Ges. Studien*, p. 431: 'God is the Whence of my "I ought" and "I may",' or the Whence 'of my being constrained and my acting'. Braun also puts it thus: 'I can speak of God only when my "I ought" is accompanied by "I may".' Now I know, of course, very well where my 'I may' and 'I ought' come from. 'Privilege and obligation do not come to me out of the universe, but from the other, my fellow-man.' Hence it follows that 'God is a particular kind of human togetherness (*Mitmenschlichkeit*)'. 'God' demythologized = Human togetherness. What the latter is, we know more or less, and with this we have a concrete meaning for the mythological word 'God'.—*Cf.* also the discussion between Braun and Gollwitzer in *Post Bultmann Locutum* (ed. Bartsch).

[21] H. W. Bartsch, *Entmythologisierende Auslegung*, p. 57.

The latter statement is immediately clear, for human beings do after all live together in the State—though their 'human togetherness' can take very different forms, their 'common humanity' can express itself in very diverse ways. But that 'common humanity' can signify the same as is meant by 'God' seems to be a thoroughly mythological idea, in spite of all attempts to explain it. At all events it is plain that 'the word "God" ' causes the demythologizers a great deal of trouble.

To sum up, we may say that the intention of all the various forms of demythologizing theology has found terse and pregnant expression in van Buren's formula, 'The Secular Meaning of the Gospel'.[22] The assumption is that modern man is thoroughly secularized and has therefore quite lost the capacity to understand the meaning of the gospel. It is therefore necessary to translate the gospel into his secularized language, or as it has been put, to 'translate the language of Christian faith into the language of unbelief'.[23] The impossibility of doing this is only too obvious. What is being demanded of us here is that we should fall into the trap of category mixing and try to translate from one context of meaning to another and perhaps from one motif context to another. But it has been shown clearly enough in our earlier discussion that such a procedure can only lead to meaninglessness, since the different contexts of meaning will cancel one another out. In reply to such attempts at 'translation' it is enough to recall something we have already said: 'Just as kilometers cannot be translated into kilograms, or the terms used in tennis into those used in chess, so neither can one context of meaning be translated into the terms of any other. Each of them must be allowed to preserve its own distinctive character and fulfil its own specific function.'[24]

As we have shown, what is wrong with the demythologizing theology is not simply a matter of sundry points of detail, but something that affects the entire structure of thought. The whole composition has been given a false signature, set in a false key,[25] which makes it wrong both in general and particular. If we change the key of a melody we change the melody, making it strange and unfamiliar even though the details of the notation remain the same. The theory of demythologization is an extraordinary example of the danger of muddled thinking with regard to fundamental presuppositions, and of the need for philosophical (religio-philosophical) clarification. When the religious context of meaning has been lost, we are bound to try to express what belongs to that context but has now become homeless, in terms of other categories. It is in this situation that the mythology-metaphysics schema is introduced. In a way it is a correct observation that these two belong closely together and can to a certain

[22] P. M. van Buren, *The Secular Meaning of the Gospel*.
[23] E. Fuchs, *Zum hermeneutischen Problem*, p. 10.
[24] Above, p. 292.
[25] On the subject of the 'signature' *cf.* above, pp. 293f.

extent be substituted for one another. To put it in a formula: metaphysics is a form of mythology[26]—modernized mythology—while mythology is a form of metaphysics—primitive metaphysics. On the other hand, we cannot use the categories of mythology and metaphysics as a substitute for religious faith, for that is something essentially different.

It is not surprising that there is no firm grasp of the Christian faith when men try to comprehend it in such inadequate categories. If we begin at that end we never escape from mythology; we merely juggle around with primitive mythology and modernized, metaphysical mythology. That is the inner contradiction in the idea of 'demythologization'. The only way to avoid mythology is to recognize from the start the independence and distinctiveness of the religious context of meaning. If we try to force upon religious phenomena the alternative of 'mythology or existential interpretation' the result in either case will be to turn religion into mythology. The idea that the Christian faith must first be understood as mythology and then demythologized, has nothing to do with the nature of the faith itself, but arises from the demythologizer's own commitment to a false scheme of thought, an unviable alternative, a false 'preunderstanding'. It depends, in other words, ultimately on a personal prejudice. What has in fact been mythologized away is the religious meaning and message of the gospel as such.

When the whole structure of thought is wrong, not even the most extensive knowledge of the historical material is of any help. No one can deny that Bultmann and the rest of the demythologizing theologians have a wide knowledge in the historical field. In that respect their researches have made valuable contributions to scholarship. But as far as their total view is concerned, it has been rendered valueless by their category mistakes. They have at their disposal a mass of particular details, but when it comes to putting these together to make a complete picture, they subsume them under inappropriate categories. In this way the parts also are distorted and the whole loses its meaning. We cannot but recall here the words of Mephistopheles in *Faust*:

> He who would know and treat of aught alive,
> Seeks first the living spirit thence to drive;
> Then are the lifeless fragments in his hand,
> There only fails, alas, the spirit-band.[27]

When the difficulties in the way of giving 'the word "God"' a clear meaning have proved so great, it is only a short step further to the position which the so-called 'death of God theology' has taken. We have no occasion here to go into this 'theology', which attracted attention for a time but now

[26] *Cf.* above, pp. 29f.
[27] Goethe, Ernst Ausgabe VI, pp. 187f.; ETT* ed. Bohn, p. 58, ed. Hedge, p. 80.

seems itself to be on its deathbed.[28] It will be enough to make one or two brief comments.

When Nietzsche coined the phrase 'God is dead', there was something of an *Ereignis*, an 'event', about it. He was at least in some measure aware of its implications. He put it on the lips of a madman, who cried:

Where has God gone? . . . I will tell you! *We have killed him*—you and I. We are all his murderers! . . . What did we do when we loosened this earth from its sun? Where is it going now? Where are we going? Away from all suns? Aren't we plunging perpetually on? . . . God is dead! God remains dead! And we have killed him! How shall we console ourselves, we most murderous of all murderers? The Holiest and Mightiest that the world ever yet possessed has bled to death under our knife—and who will wipe this blood from us?[29]

How different these words of Nietzsche sound from those of his modern imitators in the 'death of God theology', which so largely bears the marks of a theological conversation piece.[30] And there is another difference: Nietzsche was far too clear-headed to pretend that what he was saying was 'theology'. Our contemporary 'death of God theologians' could profit from reflecting on the opening words of Nietzsche's *Die Fröhliche Wissenschaft*, where he speaks of 'the intellectual conscience'.[31]

In reply to the main thesis of the 'death of God theology' it is sufficient to quote Dag Hammarskjöld's remark in his *Vägmärken*: 'God does not die on the day we no longer believe in a personal deity, but we die on the day that life is no longer irradiated for us by the ever renewed light of wonder from sources beyond all reason.'[32]

3. The Method of Correlation

Our first example of the disturbing consequences of category mixing in more recent theology has been taken from the work of the demythologizing theologians, and in order to bring out the essential points we have found it necessary to go into the matter at some length. We can deal with our second example, the method of correlation, in considerably less space, but this must not be taken to imply that this theory is of less importance than the demythologizing theology. On the contrary, Tillich is of far greater stature both as a philosopher and a theologian than Bultmann. The strength of the latter lies in the historical field, but he is weak in philosophy and the general area of theology, and this as we have shown has had a detrimental effect on his interpretation of the historical particulars as well.

[28] *Cf.* P. M. van Buren, *Theological Explorations*, p. 6: 'Now that the hot air has leaked out of the recent "death of God" balloon.'

[29] Nietzsche, *Die fröhliche Wissenschaft* 18, pp. 255f.; ET, pp. 167f.

[30] We can also describe it in van Buren's words (*op. cit.*, p. 6) as 'journalistic nonsense'.

[31] Nietzsche, *op. cit.*, p. 245; ET, p. 133.

[32] D. Hammarskjöld, *Vägmärken*, p. 48; ET, p. 56.

It is for a quite different reason that we are able to deal with Tillich's correlation theory more briefly. As we are introducing this theory simply to give a further example of category mixing, much of what we have already said on that subject applies also to it and need not be repeated here. We can therefore confine ourselves to showing how the method of correlation depends on category mixing from beginning to end.

(1) *A philosophical question and a theological answer*

What is the relation between philosophy and theology?—That is the question which above all has dominated Tillich's thought and is reflected throughout his writings. In his own words: 'the boundary line between philosophy and theology is the center of my thought and work'.[33] His tendency is to view them as closely together as possible without allowing them to merge. It is the task of philosophy, as he sees it, to answer the question, 'What is the meaning of being?' Or to put it in Heideggerian terms, which he is also willing to use, 'Why is there being and not notbeing?'[34] Tillich is aware that by putting the question in this way philosophy comes close to the mythological thinking out of which metaphysics originally developed; but he takes the risk because he believes that this way of putting the question is inseparable from man's whole way of existing. Still echoing Heidegger, he says: 'Man is that being which asks what being is.' But it is just this that, according to Tillich, makes it so difficult to draw a clear distinction between philosophy and theology. The task of philosophy is 'to understand being itself'. But what else is the task of theology? When theology speaks about God, it means nothing other than this 'being itself'. The two seem therefore simply to coincide: 'This makes the division between philosophy and theology impossible'.[35] On the other hand, they cannot be completely identical.

That is the dilemma in Tillich's theory of the relation between philosophy and theology: they are the same yet they must be different. How does Tillich handle this problem? It is clear that he finds it easier to let philosophy and theology, or in other words, metaphysics and religion, intermingle than to keep them apart. When we examine the subject matter of philosophy and the question it raises about it, we discover according to Tillich that what gives rise to philosophy is something of a theological nature; while if we examine the subject matter and question of theology, we find that there is something of a philosophical nature implied in it.[36] What then distinguishes them? Since Tillich affirms that 'philosophy and theology are divergent as well as convergent', he has to face the question in what respects they diverge and converge, and his answer is: 'They are

---

[33] P. Tillich, *The Protestant Era*, p. 83.
[34] *Op. cit.*, p. 85; *cf.* above, p. 36.
[35] *Op. cit.*, p. 86.
[36] *Op. cit.*, p. 88.

317

convergent as far as both are existential and theoretical at the same time. They are *divergent* as far as philosophy is basically theoretical and theology is basically existential'.[37] In other words, the difference is ultimately a matter of emphasis. They have the same subject matter and at bottom the same task, but they put the stress on different points. Philosophy is more theoretical, theology more existential. The difference is even further reduced, however, when we recall that the philosophy here in question is that of existentialism. The question therefore still remains, what really is the difference? The answer is given in the theory of 'correlation'. Characteristic of this is its use of the scheme of 'question and answer': philosophy puts the question, theology provides the answer; man asks, God answers. Or to state the old problem of 'reason and revelation' in these terms, we may say: reason raises the question, revelation furnishes the answer.

If in theology we are to speak meaningfully of God, we must according to Tillich know to what question talk about God is the answer. It is no use talking about God in a vacuum or at random, but what is said must correspond to the human situation. Now it is this situation that philosophy clarifies by its analysis of existence. As a finite being man participates in being, but his being is such as to be constantly under the threat of annihilation—hence the existential *Angst* that is characteristic of humanity. It is owing to this situation that man asks, and cannot but ask, about being— real, permanent being. And what he is then asking about is in reality God. Thus far philosophical analysis can take us, to the question about God, but the answer to this question is beyond the reach of philosophy. Only theology or religion can furnish the answer. It points man to God as 'being itself', and in this answer man recognizes what he was really seeking and asking about.

The word 'God' and talk about God are meaningful, Tillich holds, inasmuch as they provide an answer to man's inescapable existential question. God is the ground and source of being, the real being in all that is. God is 'being itself', 'the abyss of being', 'the structure of being'. Here we see the fundamental difference between essence and existence. God is essence, man is existence. Man has not his being in himself, but from God; and when as existence he breaks away from God, he lands in the anxiety which is the basic characteristic of existence. He is alienated from his source and ground, 'being itself', and therefore also from himself, his fellow men, and the world around him. His entire existence is marked by this alienation. Just as the 'Fall' meant a transition from essence to existence, and therefore alienation, salvation means that man who has become separated from God, finds the way back to the ground of his being, 'being itself' which is God. The saving work of Christ consists in his having overcome the alienation, won the 'victory over existence' and restored essence,

37 *Ibid.*

bringing man back to his source, to God, who is 'being itself'. Salvation consists in the fact that Christ has thus established 'the new being' and makes us participant in it.

It is an old song, which has been sung many times in the course of history and is easily recognizable even in this slightly disguised form. It is reminiscent in particular of Augustine's idea of God as the *summum et incommutabile bonum*; man as created by God and therefore possessing a relative being, yet at the same time created 'out of nothing' and therefore always in danger of falling back into nothing; the fall as occurring when man breaks his relationship with the One in whom he lives; and man as *inquietum* (anxiety) till he finds his *bonum* and his *quies* in God.[38] These traditional ideas need not detain us, though we ought to take note of the powerful ontological thrust characteristically given to them by Tillich. At every point everything centres on the ontological concepts of 'being', 'essence', 'existence': God = 'being itself', man = 'a being', but of a relative sort and threatened by 'non-being', Christ = 'the new being', sin = the separation of 'existence' from 'essence', and salvation = the reunion of 'existence' with 'essence'. These ontological-metaphysical ideas act for Tillich as a dowsing rod with which he tries to locate the pure springs of our faith which can still supply living water even for modern man, and to identify those elements in the religious and Christian tradition that are no longer alive because they do not answer the ontological-metaphysical questions of modern man.

But this ontology, which is the very nerve of the correlation theory, is at the same time its weakest point.[39] For what sense is there in saying that an 'ontological' doctrine is the proper starting point for an understanding of the gospel? What sense does it make to say that it is philosophy's business to put the question and theology's to answer it? If we keep our distinctions clear and avoid category mixing, it is obvious that a philosophical question can only be philosophically answered, and a theological answer implies that the question has been theologically put.

The very way in which Tillich links question and answer shows how his method depends on category mixing and the confusion of different contexts of meaning. He himself is aware that his combination of philosophy and theology is liable to be criticized from a philosophical point of view as resulting in 'an impure mixture of two incompatible methods of thought',[40] but he fails to give a convincing reply to this objection. He

---

[38] For the Augustinian background of Tillich's thought, see above, pp. 131ff.

[39] Tillich's ontology has been severely, and rightly, criticized in many quarters; e.g. W. F. Zuurdeeg, *An Analytical Philosophy of Religion*, pp. 150–65; P. Holmer, *Theology and the Scientific Study of Religion*, pp. 126ff.; K. Hamilton, *The System and the Gospel*; W. A. Christian, *Meaning and Truth in Religion*, pp. 181ff.; A. Valen-Senstad, 'Ontologiske implicationer'; P. Holmer, 'Metaphysics and Theology'; J. H. Randall, 'The Ontology of Paul Tillich'.

[40] Tillich, *The Protestant Era*, p. 83.

holds on the one hand that there is a constant 'mutual immanence of theology and philosophy', and on the other that it is necessary to establish 'a qualitative difference between philosophy and theology—a difference which must be stated sharply and clearly',[41] yet how all this can be so he never really explains. It is and remains an '*impure mixture*', a hopeless confusion of categories, and that not merely by accident, but on principle, since the entire outlook is based on this mixture of religion and philosophy, both of which are merged in an apparently unified metaphysical system. In such circumstances it is meaningless to ask which of the two, philosophy or theology, is the injured party, for category mixing as a rule injures both parties alike. A philosophy which puts the question in a way designed to suit the theological answer, is at all events not a 'scientific philosophy' but at best an arbitrarily chosen metaphysic. The 'apologetic' advantage (the word is Tillich's) which he and other theologians have expected from the method of correlation, does not materialize, for scientific philosophy cannot be expected to agree with it, and the only metaphysical philosophy that can accept it is one of their own existentialist kind. Nor are the consequences for theology any less devastating, since what is put forward as a theological answer is completely robbed of its religious meaning.

(2) *Category mixing and the destruction of religious meaning.*
Taken together, the two examples just given of category mixing and its consequences in contemporary theology—Bultmann's demythologizing theology and Tillich's correlation theory—give a very adequate picture of the situation. If we compare Tillich's and Bultmann's views, we find not only agreements, such as the dependence of both men on Heidegger's existentialist metaphysics, but also important differences. This has to do in the first instance with Tillich's use of the term 'symbol'. Owing to his view of the significance of symbolism in religion, he is obliged to reject all forms of demythologizing theology. Myth and symbol belong closely together, and religion according to Tillich cannot dispense with either of them. To do away with them is to do away with religion itself. Symbols and myths are 'the language of faith'. Certainly it is important to recognize that they are not meant literally, but to rule them out would be to condemn faith to silence.

There can be no doubt that Tillich has the deeper insight here, and that he shows a finer sensitivity to the distinctive nature of religion than Bultmann does; but this does not mean that Tillich's theory of myth and symbol is adequate. He is right in insisting that symbolism is the peculiar and irreplaceable language of religion. We have, however, already seen that myth has no rightful place in the Christian faith; and now we find that for Tillich even the concept of symbol ultimately falls victim to 'ontology'. It is ironic that the very Tillich who has so zealously championed the cause of

[41] Tillich's 'Reply' in Kegley, *Tillich*, pp. 336f.

symbols and pressed for a deeper understanding of them,[42] the Tillich who sees in every non-symbolic statement about God a threat to the purity of faith, nevertheless in the last resort succumbs to the desire to find a completely adequate, non-symbolic, metaphysical definition of God.[43] He writes: 'In order to speak of symbolic knowledge one must delimit the symbolic realm by an unsymbolic statement. . . . The unsymbolic statement which implies the necessity of religious symbolism is that God is being itself.'[44] A symbolic statement points beyond itself to that which it symbolizes, but the statement that God is 'being itself' is a non-symbolic statement, which does not point beyond itself, does not symbolize, but means just what it says, and is thus an adequate expression of what God is, of his essence. With this, Tillich plunges straight into ontological metaphysics. We can, according to him, give a completely adequate metaphysical definition of God, and while this is a concept belonging to philosophical metaphysics, what makes it religious is the fact that this 'being itself' becomes a matter of 'ultimate concern', 'unconditional concern'. In this way the religious and the metaphysical are merged—and the category mixing is a *fait accompli*.

What is it that has lured Tillich along this path? Obviously his 'apologetic' interest. He needs a firm 'ontological' foundation for his theology. The language of religious faith is symbolical and therefore necessarily inadequate. Therefore it must be 'translated' into the language of science, that is, of metaphysics, which says the same thing in an adequate, non-symbolic way. This is where the category mixing comes in. What in its own sphere is meaningful is 'translated' into another language which makes it more or less meaningless. The translation of religious into scientific language is intended to give adequate expression to it, but the result is instead that it loses its real meaning and may become quite meaningless. Talk about God in a religious context is highly meaningful, although this does not mean that we have or can have an exact, scientifically defined 'concept of God'. There can in the nature of the case be no 'definition' of God in the strict sense of that term, for such a 'definition' would not be what religious faith *means* by 'God' but merely an intellectualistic caricature. '*Le Dieu défini est le Dieu fini!*'

[42] 'He who says "only a symbol" has completely misunderstood the meaning of symbol; he confuses symbol with sign, and ignores that a genuine symbol participates in the reality of that which it symbolizes' (*op. cit.*, pp. 334f.), We must not say 'only a symbol', Tillich insists, but 'nothing less than a symbol'.

[43] In a similar way with regard to Bultmann it could be said to be an irony of fate that the very man who has so vigorously sought to promote the 'kerygma' should be the one who himself in the last resort transforms the message into a metaphysical doctrine and theology into 'anthropology'.

[44] Tillich, *op. cit.*, p. 334. The term 'being itself' is for Tillich the only adequate description of God, 'the statement which I call the only non-symbolic one, that God is being itself' (p. 335). It is the *only* adequate one, all other descriptions are inadequate symbols.

When a metaphysician asks what intellectual content he is to give to the word 'God', it is understandable that he should try to see what he can do with the answer that 'God' is synonymous with 'being itself'. There are after all many things of which we say that they 'are', and with a bit of metaphysical substantivizing and substantializing we can credit them with some sort of 'being'. Starting with this the metaphysician should be able to work his way to the concept of 'being itself' as an ultimate abstraction, and as signifying something which 'is' in an entirely general sense but not in any particular way. Although this of course is a pseudo-concept that conveys no real meaning, at least its purpose is understandable. And when the metaphysician goes on to say that this ultimate abstraction has religious significance inasmuch as it becomes a matter of 'ultimate concern', here too we can in a measure understand what he is driving at. At the same time it seems pretty clear that this does not give expression to what religious faith really *means*. To argue in the way just indicated is to read into religious affirmations a metaphysical idea that is foreign to them, and it is this substitute idea that comes to be of final and decisive importance.

This situation can be studied in Tillich. His programme calls for philosophy merely to put the question, leaving the answer to religion and theology. Philosophy is to have a purely formal role, and content must be sought elsewhere. That is the programme; but now does it work out? What actually happens is that philosophy furnishes the content. Admittedly it is laid down as a general principle that 'God is the answer to the question implied in human finitude. This answer cannot be derived from the analysis of existence.' But then the argument proceeds with statements that completely contradict this principle. To the extent that God is viewed in correlation with the existential question, which arises from the threat posed by non-being to being, it is inevitable that he should be regarded as 'the infinite power of being' which can overcome the threat posed by non-being.[45]

The position is therefore this: the word 'God' is first heard as an empty sound, and in order to get it filled with content we are directed to philosophy. The existential analysis reveals man's finitude and shows how his being is constantly threatened by non-being. Against this background, and correlative to it, God must be defined as 'being itself' and 'the infinite power of being'. Then, and only then, have we a definite content to ascribe to the word 'God'. With this we know what we are talking about when we use the word 'God': we are talking about 'being itself'. But it is *philosophy*, we should note, that has given us this definition of the *content*. What religion contributes is not the content of the idea of God, but the 'ultimate concern' which lends religious dignity to a philosophical concept. Beyond this, religion has nothing to offer by way of content but inadequate sym-

[45] Tillich, *Systematic Theology*, I, p. 64.

bols, for which philosophy provides the adequate, non-symbolic formula: God is 'being itself'.

But now we must ask again whether this is really what religion *means* when it speaks about God? If we go with this question to religion itself, which is after all the only competent witness in this case, it at once becomes clear that this is by no means an adequate account of what religion means. When a Christian, or indeed any religious person, confesses his faith in God, he certainly does not mean to say that he believes in such a hazy, indefinite abstraction as 'being itself'. That is not a correct rendering of the religious meaning of 'God'. God is no pale abstraction. But the identification of God with 'being itself' reduces the rich vitality of religion to a dry metaphysical abstraction, of which it can be questioned whether it has any meaning at all, and which cannot in any case become a matter of 'ultimate concern'. If a Christian were to be catechized about 'being itself' he would most certainly reply: I believe in God, and just therefore I don't in any sense believe in 'being itself'. What has happened as a result of introducing this formula is quite simply that the meaningful religious way of speaking about God has been replaced by meaningless metaphysical talk about 'being itself'.

With this the verdict is given on the method of correlation. When religion is made to furnish the answer to an extraneous, metaphysical question, the answer itself is changed. To discover what the religious answer is, we must go to religion itself and find out what the religious question is. If we compel religion to answer a question that is foreign to it, the answer will likewise be foreign. The way in which the method of correlation employs the idea of 'question and answer' reveals that it is involved in category mixing and the meaninglessness that that entails.

In fairness to Tillich—and in a measure this may apply also to Bultmann—it should be pointed out finally that there are some indications that when these men speak of a 'philosophical question' or a 'preunderstanding' they are essentially fumbling after something like what we have called 'presuppositions'. What above all seems to support this view is that both of them are concerned to insist that the 'philosophical question' or 'preunderstanding' is of a purely *formal* nature. Our preceding discussion, however, has shown this to be an illusion. Both the 'philosophical question' and the existential 'preunderstanding' force upon religion a question which is *foreign* to it, and which prevents it from expressing what it itself wants to say. By contrast, our inquiry into the presuppositions of the religious context of meaning has to do with the presuppositions of that context itself, to the exclusion of all foreign philosophical questions and all preunderstandings arrived at in advance. Here we see the importance of drawing a clear distinction between 'presupposition' and 'preunderstanding', the latter being in fact nothing else but a 'prejudice'.[46]

[46] On the contrast between presupposition and prejudice, and on the relation

Bultmann derives his philosophical 'preunderstanding' from just one philosopher, Heidegger. It is in the last resort Heidegger's views that are decisive of what may be regarded as religious and Christian. Tillich's philosophical repertoire is far more extensive. He stands in a great philosophical tradition that reaches back to the pre-Socratics and comes down to the Existentialists of our time, who are heirs to the great succession that begins with Parmenides and Plato (essence and existence). Tillich, like the Existentialists generally, represents a late flowering of that tree which has in the past borne such fruit as Philo—Plotinus—Gnosis—Alexandrian theology—Augustine (in part)—Proclus—Pseudo-Dionysius—Mediaeval Mysticism (Eckhart)—Jacob Boehme—German Idealism (Schelling-Hegel).[47] There is as a rule not much awareness of this long line of tradition, and it is easy for existentialism to be regarded as a novelty only recently arrived on the scene. It is therefore well to take note of its preceding history, and see how it represents a very ancient way of thinking which still has compelling power and captivates those who come under its spell. This also explains Tillich's statement that what he is seeking is not 'God' but 'God beyond God', his idea of God as the 'Abyss' and other such mythological notions, which are familiar in this line of tradition. It is, for example, the old principle of '*gnothi seauton*' ('know thyself') that still lives on in the existentialist's 'self-understanding'. For *self*-understanding is the key to the understanding of *being* and ultimately also to the understanding of *God*. That is why anthropology is the key to theology. Enter into yourself—so we are admonished—and take a good look at your own existence; you will then discover your finitude, and along with it, correlative to it, you will also discover God, infinite being, 'being itself'. In this way the broad stream of religious metaphysics comes pouring in to theology.

Behind this whole way of looking at things there lies the Aristotelian-Neoplatonic idea of a vast, cosmic process originating in the divine One (τὸ ὄν), the primal ground from which all being issues forth and to which in cosmic eros (ἔρως) it returns—this idea also is to be found in Tillich. When one contemplates the strange excrescences to which this metaphysical way of thinking has given rise in theology, and the bewildering confusion of categories and motifs which it has brought in its train, one

---

between presupposition and preunderstanding, *cf.* above, Chap. VII, §§1 and 4, pp. 187ff. and 199ff. As for the idea of 'question and answer', this can be quite correctly employed, as the next chapter will show, for distinguishing questions with a determinate content from categorical questions. The 'question' is then, however, simply a way of saying (in categorical terms) 'what it is a question of' or 'what it is about', and not, as with Tillich, a metaphysical question with a positive content which already includes part of the answer.

[47] A more detailed account of this long line of metaphysical tradition is to be found in my *Agape and Eros*.

cannot help asking whether it is not high time to let the Christian faith speak for itself in its own language instead of being reinterpreted in Aristotelian-Neoplatonic terms. It is in general such reinterpretation that causes complications in the contemporary theological discussion.[48]

4. The Problem of Hermeneutics

Hermeneutics is an extremely old discipline, which in recent years has experienced an unexpected rejuvenation both in theology and philosophy. It has long been conceived—to use Schleiermacher's definition of it—as the '*Kunst des Verstehens*', the 'art of understanding'. It thus has to do with the scientific methods and rules which it is necessary to apply in order to reach a correct understanding of a given text. It is a matter of the correct reproduction, translation, exposition, explanation and interpretation of the text, so that the latter comes to be understood as far as possible in the way it is intended. This is both a scientific task and an art. What we are concerned with here, however, is not hermeneutics itself as a science and an art, but the problem it sets us to solve—'the hermeneutical problem'.

The liveliness of the hermeneutical debate today is very largely due to the change that has taken place in the meaning of the term, which is now often used in a sense other than it formerly had. And this change of meaning is due in turn to the influence of existentialist philosophy on Continental theology. Nevertheless, there is a clear continuity as regards the hermeneutical problem, in a line clearly traceable from Schleiermacher's hermeneutics via Dilthey and Husserl to Heidegger, Bultmann, Fuchs and Ebeling. At the end, however, the idea of 'hermeneutics' has become quite different, and in some ways the direct opposite of what it was to begin with.

(1) *Two kinds of 'hermeneutics'*
Hermeneutics is 'interpretation' and has to do with 'understanding' and

[48] *Cf.* the fuller treatment of these questions in my article, 'Religion och metafysik' (in *Kristen Humanism*, 1967, pp. 34ff.). I say there (pp. 44f.): 'What would happen if we could rid ourselves of the Aristotelian conception of God? We should at once have done with a number of the most ill-considered and pointless discussions of our time, such as "demythologization" and the "death of God" theology—not to mention Robinson. Underlying all these is the confusion between religion and metaphysics, and a concept of God that is foreign to Christianity.' In the same article I quote (pp. 42f.) a statement by R. Kroner which is of importance for this subject: 'After rejecting Hegel's dialectical metaphysics of "being and nothing" as "completely unbiblical", Kroner states briefly and to the point: "The biblical revelation categorically rejects all metaphysical interpretation". And he goes even further. With reference to all the confusion and contradiction in which metaphysical thinking entangles us, and in answer to the question how we are to get out of it, Kroner adds: "only religion, not concepts, can deliver us from the contradictions of thought and the fragmentation of our human existence. Contemporary 'existentialism' is just as incapable as, or even less capable than, German Idealism with its imposing systems, of doing this".' For Kroner's statement see his 'Philosophie und Christentum', pp. 18f.; and for Robinson see his *Honest to God*.

'meaning'. In the case of a New Testament text, for example, the interpreter finds himself in the middle between the scripture and the one for whom it is to be interpreted. The meaning of something written nearly two thousand years ago is to be interpreted for the man who is alive today, modern man. That is to say, its content is to be brought near to him, so that it becomes intelligible to him. Nor is it only the foreign language and the great distance in time that makes an interpretation necessary, but the gulf between the scripture and its latter day reader which is due to his different circumstances has also to be interpretatively bridged.

The words 'interpretation' and 'understanding' can, however, be used in two widely different senses. On the one hand they may mean that we must seek to interpret the texts in such a way that we get as close as possible to their original meaning. This is the aim of Schleiermacher's hermeneutics, and it is this that leads him not only to the lexicographical and grammatical interpretation, but also to what he calls the 'psychological'. For what he seeks is not only to understand the individual words and their associations, but the meaning of the whole, or what the scripture in question is trying as a whole to say. Only when this has been done has the text been really understood, and it is this comprehensive understanding . that it is the business of hermeneutics to provide. But for this we need more than grammatical comprehension: we must be able to enter into the mind of the author and grasp empathetically what he is after and what he means. Only so do we really understand him. Such an understanding is possible, according to Schleiermacher, only through an act of 'divination'. Real understanding thus always includes, as he sees it, a subjective element. The presupposition of a correct understanding is that the interpreter has become so absorbed in his material that he identifies himself with the author ('*sich dem Urheber gleichstellt*'). In other words, it involves a kind of subjectivity that is wholly absorbed in the object. It is not Schleiermacher's intention to introduce a subjectivistic element into the interpretation. The point of orientation is always the meaning intended by the author, not my personal, subjective meaning.

On the other hand, the words 'interpretation', 'understanding' and 'hermeneutics' can be used in a way which requires that the text be re-written, or its content re-stated, in terms applicable to the situation of the modern reader, so that it has something to say to him in the sense of being found meaningful by him and in that sense understood by him. Both the starting point and the goal here are the opposite of Schleiermacher's. On his view the subject must seek to become wholly absorbed in what is objectively given, but here the subject is the fixed starting point. That which is to be interpreted has meaning only in so far as it answers to the subject's needs. In recent years the name of 'hermeneutics' has been very widely given to a kind of interpretation which is conditioned by the demands of the present situation. It has not least been the theology influenced by existentialist philosophy that has made this the normative view of hermeneutics. According to that theology, we must take as our starting point an anthropological investigation of modern man and his existential situation; for it is only as an answer to man's existential needs that the Christian message can be of any significance. But it is only too evident that this is no genuine interpretation, for the result is not that we gain insight into the original and proper meaning of the message, but only into what an accommodating re-interpretation, an adaptation of it to the present situation, might possibly mean for us. As an 'interpretation' this can hardly be regarded as anything but an anachronism. A 'hermeneutic' of this sort is certainly not scientific. For in the first place, there cannot be any science of 'man's existential situation and needs', and in the second place, this alleged science has usurped the role of the preacher, whose business it is to mediate the message to real human beings, not to some supposedly typical 'modern man'.

When theologians of the latter sort none the less speak of 'interpretation', their use of the word is analogous to its use in law or art. Just as a judge 'interprets' an old statute so as to make it applicable to circumstances which had not arisen or even been contemplated when the legislation was enacted, so that by means of his 'interpretation' he in a measure creates law; or just as a musical composition can be performed with a new 'interpretation' which may in certain respects depart from the original or traditional form, but which just because of its novelty may make the music more accessible to a modern audience; just so it is supposed to be the task of theology or of hermeneutics to 'interpret' the content of the gospel so as to make it accessible to modern man and enable him to get something out of it on his own account. That we have a right to undertake such an 'interpretation', which is bound to be in some measure a 're-interpretation', is held to follow from the nature of the gospel as a message. That is to say, the gospel itself by virtue of its own specific character demands such an interpretation. Just as it was a message for those to whom it was first addressed, so it claims to be a message for every succeeding generation of men. But as historical circumstances change, and men with them, men cease to be able to grasp it as a message addressed to them, and it becomes more or less irrelevant for them. In this situation, merely to repeat the message in its original form, regardless of whether men grasp its meaning or not, is to rob the gospel of something essential to it. This is what makes a new interpretation necessary, an interpretation which has an eye to what men today can regard as meaningful. Only when it is thus re-interpreted does it speak to modern man as a living word; and then it has recovered its character as a message.

The existentialist hermeneutic has undoubtedly put its finger on an extremely important point. The gospel can preserve its proper character only by being a gospel for somebody. Man as the recipient of the message must be there if the message is to remain a message. Without him it is no message but merely an objective word. This fact, however, which is supposed to furnish the justification for a re-interpretation of the message, is the very thing that most strikingly exposes the fallaciousness of the theory. If we take seriously the fact that the gospel is a *message*, we quickly discover that it rules out the kind of analogies on which this theory depends.

To 'interpret' a message is an entirely different thing from 'interpreting' a legal statute or a musical composition. Even in a matter of law the interpreter is of course bound to a certain extent by the intention of the legislator, and respect for the composer requires that the interpretation of a musical composition shall not depart too far from his original idea. But in these areas there is a wide margin for free interpretation in the light of a later situation. The position is different, however, with regard to a 'message' in the proper sense of that word. There we are bound in a quite different way by the intention of the sender of the message. Certainly the recipient plays an essential part, since it is on his account that the message exists. If it does not reach him, or if he does not understand it, or at important points misunderstands it, it has not fulfilled its purpose as a message. It is therefore often both possible and necessary to speak of 'interpretation', but this must be confined within narrow limits. If on the way from the sender to the recipient a message acquires through interpretation a different sense from what the sender intended, the message is in effect annulled.

The interpretation has no right to say anything but what the message says. For example, if two nations are at war with one another and one of them sends the other a message containing an offer of peace, the recipient will naturally make this the subject of intensive study and detailed interpretation, in the course of which it may often be necessary to 'interpret' (in the sense of explicate and elucidate) both the language and the terms of the offer. The purpose of such interpretation is to make completely clear what is actually contained in the message. This is all that matters. No analysis of the recipient's own situation, and nothing of what he himself needs or desires, must be allowed to influence the interpretation, for that would only lead to wishful thinking and self-deception. The offer can be accepted or rejected, and in that regard the recipient's own situation comes into the picture, but as long as it is a question of interpreting the meaning of the message, the latter must be taken as it stands. Here, as always where a message is concerned, the 'interpreter' must make it his primary aim to represent the meaning intended by the sender as accurately as possible. The interpretation must not in any circumstances become a 're-interpretation'. Here the limit is set for 'hermeneutics'. It is not its business either to create or to re-create. Any attempt on its part to do so leads to distortion of the message.

In this matter the new 'theological hermeneutics' has often gone astray, and 'philosophical hermeneutics' could help to get the discussion on sounder lines. We have good reason to listen to what a representative of philosophical hermeneutics like Hans-Georg Gadamer has to say on the subject. Speaking of *theological* hermeneutics and its common practice of drawing a parallel between the interpretation of law and the interpretation of Scripture, he writes: 'But there is a still greater difference. The sermon is not, like a legal judgment, a productive expansion of the text which it expounds. From the preaching of the sermon therefore, nothing accrues to the message of salvation by way of content that is comparable to the effect of a judicial decision in supplementing the law. It is simply not the case that the message of salvation first acquires clarity and definiteness from what the preacher thinks. The preacher does not speak in the congregation with dogmatic authority as the judge does in court. . . . The Holy Scriptures are God's Word, and this means that Scripture takes absolute precedence over the doctrine of those who expound it.'[49] It could be wished that theologians were generally as clear as this philosopher about the nature and conditions of 'theological hermeneutics'. Despite his dependence at many points on Heidegger's thought, he can offer a penetrating criticism of Bultmann's 'preunderstanding'.[50]

The positive contribution of the new theological hermeneutics lies in its insistence that the aim of the gospel is to evoke a decision affecting the whole of life. It is possible to speak about the gospel in such an 'objective' way that this vital element of decision is missing; but then the *content* of the gospel is misrepresented, for its ceases to be what it is meant to be if it is bereft of the character of a message. This defect is not remedied, however, by shifting the centre of gravity to the anthropological side, so that our understanding of the gospel is made to depend on an existentialist 'pre-understanding' and 'self-understanding'. It is odd that the very theology which stresses the 'kerygmatic' nature of the gospel should deprive it of its character as a message. Instead of being a genuine communication, the message is transformed into a monologue in which I ruminate on my 'self-understanding' and am chiefly preoccupied with my own decisions. That the gospel addresses itself to the concrete human being with a message of decisive importance for his entire existence has always been known, although it has been overshadowed at times by a concern for the correct formulation of doctrine. The new hermeneutics has brought this sometimes forgotten fact to the fore, yet by taking the discussion of the conditions of human existence as a 'preunderstanding' for the interpretation of the gospel it has determined what the gospel may be allowed to contain, and has thus constricted it and robbed it of its character as a message and caused essential aspects of it to be lost. This is re-interpretation but not hermeneutics: the actual content of the message is lost, at

[49] H-G. Gadamer, *Wahrheit und Methode*, p. 313.
[50] *Op. cit.*, p. 314.

least in part, at the very time when its character as a message is being discussed.

One of the reasons why the content of the message has been treated as variable in relation to different historical circumstances and patterns of human thought, and why theology has been assigned the task of re-interpretation—one of the reasons for this besides the above-mentioned misleading analogy between the 'interpretation' of a message and 'interpretation' in law and art—is almost certainly the lack of a clear conception of theology and the nature of scientific work. There has been a failure to grasp the essential difference between a scientific problem and a religious message. I can work at a problem so that something new emerges from it;[51] indeed it can be said of problems that they continually call for new attempts at solution, and if a particular solution or even statement of a problem is taken as final, the result can only be stagnation. It is of the nature of a problem to be continually transformed. But a message has to be delivered, not transformed into something else. The content of a message is determined by the one who sends it, and the one who transmits it (the 'interpreter') has no business to remodel it to suit either his own or the recipient's ideas. Here again we see the consequences of the category mixing about which we have said so much already—the confusion between the religious and the scientific context of meaning.

'Hermeneutics' is supposed to be a science. Now the most elementary reflection will tell us that it can never be the business of science to prove that something is the word of God.[52] Should any science try to do this, it would mean that science was trespassing on the province of faith and seeking to deputize for faith. There are things that are certain for religious faith, but they do not depend on scientific proof. That Jesus is the Christ, the Messiah sent by God, is a matter of immediate certainty for Christian faith, although faith neither possesses nor desires any scientific proof of it. It is not because science says so, that the Christian believes in God and Christ. His faith rests on its own ground, its religious ground. To attempt to support it by scientific means would be to compromise both faith and science. When Judaism denies that Jesus was the promised Messiah, no science can decide between it and the Christian faith. That would involve an overstepping of the boundary between different contexts of meaning, or in other words a confusion of categories, and what that entails we know very well from what we have seen above. A religious question is not settled by a scientific argument, any more than a scientific question is settled by a judicial decree.

There is a further point worth noticing here. To speak of 'interpreting' anything is to imply that there is something obscure about it, something

[51] *Cf.* above, pp. 175ff., on 'Problems, Statements of Problems, Solutions of Problems'.

[52] *Cf.* above, p. 306.

not yet clearly enough understood, which needs to be clarified. This means, in other words, that 'interpretation' is a kind of clarification. In that case there must be something wrong with an interpretation when the text that is being interpreted is actually clearer and more intelligible than the 'interpretation'. Yet that is all too often the case with existentialist hermeneutics. This is connected, of course, with the fact that the interpreters have chosen for the 'preunderstanding' which is their starting point, such an obscure and in many respects vague metaphysical outlook as existentialist philosophy.[53] For in its laudable desire to show that human life has other aspects than the purely scientific, existentialism has proceeded to cultivate certain indefinable ideas which transform it into a sort of obscure 'conceptual poetry'. Undoubtedly it can be of assistance in making us aware of certain possibilities of interpretation, particularly in those areas where a 're-interpretation' or 'new interpretation' may be in place, as for example in lyric poetry or in art generally. In theology, however, where the interpretation must move within narrower limits, an imprecise method of that kind is often quite disastrous for any genuine understanding. As a general rule it can be said that while hermeneutics must not pretend that the text is clearer than it is, neither must it indulge in unnecessary ambiguity and make the text obscure when it is in fact clear.[54]

[53] For more on this see above, pp. 131–8.

[54] To illustrate this we may cite Ernst Fuchs, who goes in for hermeneutics in a big way as the chief theological discipline, yet frequently succeeds in producing, not clarification, but sheer obfuscation and confusion. In fact, we should often be completely at a loss if we did not already know and understand the texts that are being interpreted, so that with their help we can in a measure divine the meaning of the 'interpretation'. Take for example his *Marburger Hermeneutik*, pp. 47f., 50, with its exposition of '*Die Zeitverbrach der Liebe*', 'Love's expenditure of time':

Love [says Fuchs] has its own time. . . . We can thus read off the phenomenon of time in it. Yet more! Love is innocent. That would be possible with Eros only in a very transitory way. Now because the time of love is of such a nature *that it becomes all the stronger the more unambiguously it is expended*, love is indeed something intermediate between poverty and riches inasmuch as its time simply *must* be expended. But that is how the matter looks from the outside. Because its time seeks to assert itself through the *lovers*, it would be better to say that precisely the poverty of love constitutes its riches. The lover remains dependent throughout on the time of love as a time *for* love. But: because he *rejoices* in it, he is in love as himself free for the future, and is able to do all that can be expected of him. The lover expends the *time* of love because he lives towards its repetition (Jas. 3:18): love is the *source* of time! Love *fulfils* itself temporally through itself incessantly, if not in me, then in you (Jn. 4:36–38). This fulness in an existence which is free because wholly dependent on love is spoken of in 1 Cor. 13. . . . How is the duration of love compatible with love's expenditure of time? We said love is the source of its time. And of this renewal of time we said it grants rest. So it may be supposed that duration itself acquires *in love* a liberating, but *without love* a threatening significance, because love is the source of its time (which cannot be said of nature). The restfulness of authentic existence is accompanied in fact, through the *inner* certainty that

(2) *Hermeneutics and contexts of meaning*

The reason why we have taken up the problem of hermeneutics here is plain. Hermeneutics and interpretation have to do with 'understanding'; to understand something is to grasp its meaning; and with this we are back at the question of the context of meaning. Not only is it a fact, however, that contexts of meaning and hermeneutics are very intimately related to one another, but we can go further and say that to a large extent they quite simply coincide. It has indeed been the problem of hermeneutics in the widest sense of the term, with which we have been occupied all along. For 'contexts of meaning' do not exist for their own sake, just as their ultimate 'logical presuppositions' do not, but in order to make possible a proper understanding of the concrete material in whatever 'area' it may be. We must know 'what it is about' in order to be able to give a correct interpretation. We must see a particular problem in relation to its wider, general context if we are to get any grasp of it at all. And exactly the same is true with regard to the 'motif contexts' with which we shall be dealing in the next chapter. There too we shall be concerned with nothing else but 'hermeneutics' and 'interpretation'. To be ignorant of the 'motif context' is to lack the presupposition necessary for a correct interpretation of the concrete material.

We can now see quite concretely the implications of what we demonstrated earlier on the abstract level. It is only when placed in its *own* context of meaning and its *own* motif context that the concrete material bears its *own* meaning. Otherwise it can mean very nearly anything and be 'interpreted' almost anyhow. It is at this point that 'existential interpretation' makes its fundamental mistake. The problem of 'understanding' is not: How can I, while maintaining my own previously adopted standpoint, fit this unintelligible or scarcely intelligible material into *my* context, so as

---

duration is inherent in love, by a peace (Rom. 5:1–5). This peace corresponds to true love, because it passes all understanding (Phil. 4–7). [Italics original.]

No one could say that this passage from Fuchs is marked by any high degree of clarity such as one would normally expect in a 'hermeneutical' exposition. It has been quoted as an illustration of how the text is often clearer than the 'interpretation'. If one did not know of Plato's *eros* as something intermediate ($\mu\epsilon\tau\alpha\xi\acute{u}$) between poverty and riches (Penia and Poros), and if one did not know the content of the Bible passages alluded to, and of course above all if one did not know the Heideggerian vocabulary, one would simply not understand what Fuchs is saying at all. And even with the help of Platonic and Biblical ideas as a background, it is only dimly that we can see what he is getting at. What is, however, very clear, is that this cannot be regarded as any sort of interpretation. At best it is a misinterpretation and distortion. One can only ask why this existentialistic smog should be called 'hermeneutics'. The result in brief is this: Plato is clear, Fuchs is obscure; Heidegger, who is supposed to help with the 'interpretation' is obscure, therefore Fuchs also is obscure. '*Sprachlichkeit*' has got the better of '*Sachlichkeit*', loquacity has prevailed over objectivity. 'Language "speaks", as Heidegger has recently insisted. . . . Is language *divine*? That is in all seriousness the question!' (Fuchs, *Zum hermeneutischen Problem*, p. 114). [See Additional Note IV].

to get something out of it for myself? The problem of 'understanding' is rather this: What has this material to say in its own context? What does it mean if it is taken straightforwardly as it stands 'without confusion or change'—'without confusion' with anything else and 'without change' by any re-interpretation of its content?

In light of this the absurdity of the 'preunderstanding' theory is obvious. It is of course very common for something to appear at first sight unintelligible. I do not rightly understand something I have had no reason to be familiar with. What to the initiated is perfectly clear and intelligible, appears to the uninitiated mystifying. If I wish to discover the meaning of words that are spoken, the proper thing to do would surely be to acquaint myself with the subject they are about. But there is an alternative procedure, a well-trodden short cut to a certain kind of understanding. I set up a 'preunderstanding' and interpret the material accordingly. If it does not fit in with my 'preunderstanding', I 're-interpret' it so that it does—and as thus re-interpreted I 'understand' the subject. I understand it in my own way, and believe I have at least some grasp of it. But this is in fact the worst imaginable hermeneutical procedure. A simple mistake, which should have been avoided, has here become irremediable by being transformed into a fundamental defect. Simple category mixing has been turned into a fundamental principle—here is 'confusion'—and simple obscurity is supposed to be overcome by re-interpretation in accordance with one's own 'preunderstanding'—here is 'change'.

The 'preunderstanding' theory is essentially an attempt to place the material that is to be interpreted in a context and so to get a uniform understanding of it. This goal can be said to have been reached in so far as I am able to incorporate the material in the wider context which is furnished by my 'preunderstanding'. For then I obtain at least some grasp of the subject and understand it 'in my own way' according to my 'preunderstanding.' But whether I have understood it rightly, that is, in accordance with its own intention, is quite another question, and one that should not be strange to any 'hermeneutics'.

The whole theory of a 'philosophical preunderstanding' rests doubtless on a simple confusion of ideas—the confusion of 'philosophical preunderstanding' with 'logical presupposition'. The former is after all as much a 'pre-supposition' as the latter. If it is impossible to engage in any discussion or scientific argumentation except on the basis of those logical presuppositions which it is the business of philosophy to demonstrate, why should we not just as readily take from philosophy certain general presuppositions that can serve as a 'preunderstanding'?—Here the questioner has allowed himself to be misled by the similarity of the words '*pre*supposition' and '*pre*understanding'. In both cases there appears to be something *a priori*, something established 'in advance' as a base for further operations. But this similarity is only apparent and quite deceptive. Philosophy never settles anything 'in advance'. Instead, it is characteristic of philosophy to conduct its analysis *a posteriori*, 'in retrospect'. It postulates nothing that we must first accept before we can proceed with scientific investigations, but it starts with scientific judgments as existing data, and analyzes them so as to show what presuppositions are in fact implied in them. Nor does philosophy postulate anything in any other area in which it operates—ethical, religious, aesthetic, or whatever—but conducts its analyses in an exactly similar way, 'in retrospect'. It can therefore be said that philosophy knows essentially nothing of any '*pre*-understanding' (*Vorverständnis*), but only of a '*post*-understanding' (*Nachverständnis*). Philosophy analyzes ('in retrospect') presuppositions that have already been made, but postulates nothing 'in advance'.

It is therefore literally preposterous to speak of a 'philosophical pre-understanding', and hence the ground is cut away from under existentialist hermeneutics. At the same time the ground is prepared for a hermeneutic that takes for its chief methodological tool the 'context of meaning'. Only that 'interpretation' of a religious text, or of any other religious phenomenon, which sees these things in terms of their own religious context of meaning, can give a correct account of their meaning, their own meaning. This and nothing else must be the aim of philosophical and theological hermeneutics.

5. Metaphor, Symbol and Paradox as Expressions of Religious Meaning

Anyone who inquires into the distinctive nature of 'religious language' must soon be struck by the decisive part played in it by metaphors, symbols and paradoxes. Metaphors and similes or parables are constantly used in religion, and indeed they seem indispensable to it. As for symbols, it has been aptly said that 'symbolic language is the mother-tongue of faith'.[55] And so far from being disturbed by contradictions and paradoxes, religion seems to have a predilection for them, as if they were specially suitable for the expression of religious meaning.

The outstanding example of the religious use of metaphor and simile is in the parables of Jesus. When Jesus speaks of God and the kingdom of God he nearly always does it in parabolic form. 'He taught them many things by parables (ἐν παραβολαῖς)', indeed 'He never spoke to them except in parables', we are told in the gospel of Mark.[56] In short, the parable, the symbol, and even to some extent the paradox are evidently normal forms of expression for religious faith.

Now from this the conclusion has not uncommonly been drawn that

[55] G. Aulén, *Dramat och symbolerna*, p. 151; ET*, p. 119.

[56] Mk. 4: 2, 4: 34. In the same chapter (4: 30) Jesus asks: 'How shall we picture the kingdom of God, or by what parable shall we describe it?' (NEB). It is this question that lies behind the whole series of parables in the gospels.

religion is a vague and obscure affair which cannot be expressed in clear and simple language. But that, we must insist, is in the last analysis a completely false conclusion. Superficially the matter may appear simple, but in reality it is extremely complicated. We are actually told very little by the statement that religious language can be distinguished from other sorts of language by the fact that it characteristically uses metaphors, parables and symbols. Religion certainly employs symbols and metaphors, and it could not function without them. But what language does not employ symbols and metaphors? What language can do without them? Religious language is not alone in using metaphors and symbols, but these are characteristic of language as such. What else are *words* but symbols for the reality we talk about and describe by means of them? If it is objected that at least in the exact sciences we deal with reality without having to resort to symbols, this objection is refuted by the sciences themselves. Otherwise, why do we speak of 'symbolic logic', why use the symbolic language of mathematical formulae, which is taken for granted by the exact sciences? Algebraic signs are, to a far greater degree than our ordinary words, *symbols* of something other than themselves which they signify.

In saying this our purpose is not to discuss the concept of 'symbol', but simply to show how little we are in fact told when religious language is distinguished from other kinds by referring to its symbolic character. This is a feature of all language, and therefore cannot be taken as specially distinctive of religious language. Nor is the concept of 'metaphor' any more precise. When we speak of a metaphor we tend to assume, as the word itself implies, that there is an original, literal and 'proper' meaning of words, and that their metaphorical use is therefore strictly speaking 'improper' or inexact. But very often the fact of the matter is that we use words in different senses, and which is the 'proper' one is often difficult or impossible to decide, especially at an advanced level of culture. We ought to be clear from the start that discussion of this question can be quite meaningless as far as making a point in an argument is concerned. The study of the etymological roots of a word has its own importance, but for the purpose of argumentation it is generally irrelevant. For a good many of our commonest words were probably once 'metaphorical' but are no longer so, and therefore we may reasonably ask whether their present meaning is not the 'proper' one—if indeed, when a word is used in a variety of senses, there is any point in trying to decide which is 'proper' or even which is primary and which derivative.

An example of this, which will also serve as an introduction to the question of religious language, may be taken from psychology. With our tendency to think in terms of spatial analogies, it can naturally be said that many psychical realities are described in language drawn from the spatial realm.[57] Yet when we speak psychologically of an 'inward' experience,

[57] *Cf.* A. Nyman, *Rumsanalogierna.*

who any longer imagines that this refers to something spatially 'inside'? What it refers to is well known and is connected with this linguistic sign, and it is therefore pointless to discuss whether it is used here 'properly' or 'improperly', literally or symbolically. Only a simpleton would be likely to misunderstand it.

The same is true with regard to religious language. When for example God is spoken of as 'the Most High', it takes a lot of simple-mindedness to understand this as a spatial definition, as if God existed at a great distance from us, away 'up there'.[58]

Many instances could be given of the extreme fluidity of the distinction between the literal and the metaphorical use of terms, and of the way in which they can change places, but one illustration will suffice. When in 1 Peter 2: 4f. Christ is spoken of as a 'living Stone' and Christians are said to be 'living stones' built into his spiritual temple, the metaphorical nature of these expressions is obvious. But the spiritual reality to which they refer has become so far dominant that we can often be uncertain as to which is primary and which secondary for us. When in the restoration of a cathedral the plaster of a later period is stripped from the walls, so that instead of dead, flat surfaces we see the original stonework in its manifold variety, the entire building 'comes alive', begins to 'live' in a quite new way. If we should express our experience of this by speaking of a 'temple built of living stones', it would be quite pointless to ask whether these words were meant 'literally' or not, and whether this was their original or a derivative meaning. Without the literal, physical meaning of the expression 'a temple built of stones' we should not have had 1 Peter 2; yet is equally true that without the spiritual reality described in 1 Peter 2 as a 'temple built of living stones' we should never have had our vision of the 'living stones' in the cathedral. Which is here primary, 1 Peter 2 or the newly restored cathedral? Which is literal and which is metaphorical, the spiritual reality or the architectural? Unprofitable questions! Both are realities and both are metaphors—each for the other.

The idea of parables, metaphors, symbols and paradoxes as expressive of religious meaning can easily be misleading. Too often these terms are taken to imply something negative: 'only a parable', 'no more than a metaphor', 'merely a symbol', 'a paradox, i.e. sheer contradiction, i.e. plain nonsense'. But this negative attitude is completely uncalled for. Rightly understood every one of these expressions—parable, metaphor,

[58] When the Russian astronauts on returning from their first voyage in space reported that in spite of eagerly looking for him they had not been able to find any trace of God above the clouds, this was of course exploited as an argument against religion in a variety of popular publications, though otherwise it only excited the ridicule of half the world. Yet astonishingly enough, the thought of God as the Most High has given rise even in 'theological' circles to questions as to whether we ought not to stop talking about God as 'up there' and talk of him instead as 'down here' in the depths of our most intimate relationships.

symbol, paradox—has a clearly positive significance. This becomes evident when we observe how the question here under discussion is intimately bound up with that of the different contexts of meaning. If we wish to express something belonging to one context of meaning in the language of another, we cannot do this (as we have already seen above) by direct translation, but only by symbolic or metaphorical periphrasis, or by means of a parable. On this subject, however, there is a great lack of clarity.

Even those who are aware of the nature and importance of symbols easily slip into the old, wrong ways of thinking. Paul Tillich, for example, is very conscious of the inadequacy of the traditional idea of a symbol as 'only a symbol', and he insists that we should say instead 'nothing less than a symbol'. Nevertheless, he himself in effect does the opposite when he sets out to find an *adequate* formulation of the idea of God, and thinks he has found it in the concept of 'being itself'. All other religious ways of speaking about God are inadequate symbols—'only symbols' in fact! But in reply to Tillich it must be asserted that the 'being itself' which he proclaims to be the only adequate concept of God, is in fact the least adequate. There can never be an adequate concept of God in Tillich's sense, for what he is trying to do is to replace the imperfect, merely symbolic expressions of religion with a supposedly adequate metaphysical concept of God—which is a typical bit of category mixing. If we are to speak of an *adequate* expression of religious belief in God, we must rather say that it is precisely the parable or symbol that is adequate. We have no need to improve on it or get beyond it, since it is the correct and in that sense adequate way of expressing religious faith.

A similar comment to that on Tillich can be made with regard to Emil Brunner's treatment of 'the doctrine of God'. Although in general Brunner is anxious to maintain the autonomy of religion, he none the less seeks to develop a doctrine of God that is more 'scientific' than the biblical one. From the metaphorical and symbolic, and in a measure anthropomorphic, ideas of the Bible—or as he puts it, from their poetic and childlike, unreflective form—Brunner holds that theology, and particularly dogmatics, must work its way to what is from a scientific point of view a more adequate concept of God. Not that Brunner is unaware of the risks involved in this procedure. For he says: 'The more that reflection, exact definition, strictly logical argument, reasonable classification, method and system predominate in Christian doctrine, the more "scientific" it becomes, and the further it moves from the original truth of faith from which it proceeds, and to which it must continually refer.'[59] The only solution Brunner has for this problem is a kind of balancing-feat between the biblical revelation and rational thought, or 'faith' and 'rationality', in which rational discussion goes far beyond the affirmations of 'faith', though it must always be prepared to be held in check by these. Underlying these ideas,

[59] E. Brunner, *The Christian Doctrine of God*, p. 64.

337

however, there is always the thought that the rather inexact, pictorial conceptions of faith can and should be given more adequate expression by theology.

What in these and similar cases prevents a genuine understanding of religious statements is the mistaken notion that *one* context of meaning, *e.g.* the scientific ('scientism'), takes priority over the rest, and that only what can be expressed in *its* language is 'adequate'. The fact is, on the contrary, that no context of meaning has priority over the rest, since each is autonomous in its own province; and from this it at once follows that the only 'adequate' form of expression is one that puts things correctly in the language proper to the context in question. A religious statement does not become more 'adequate' by being 'translated' into scientific language, but rather the reverse. Its real intention cannot be expressed in that language. It is true that science has a task to perform in every area, including that of religion; but its task is simply and solely to clarify what a thing means in its own context, and not in any way to 'tidy up' the religious by making it more 'scientific'. Once this is realized, so that we insist on the autonomy of the different contexts of meaning to the exclusion of all category mixing, the question of the distinctive nature of religious language becomes quite clear. Metaphors, symbols and parables are not inferior forms of expression, which ought if possible to be replaced with better ones, but they are the very things that are adequate for the expression of religious meaning, and best suited to the distinctive character of religious life.

With this, light is shed also on the religious use of 'paradox'. It is not at all a question of paradoxes in the sense in which paradoxes have been discussed by thinkers throughout history, from Zeno to Russell. That kind of paradox, occurring time and again in the theoretical context of meaning, is due as a rule to logical carelessness. It is a sign that something has gone wrong with the definition of terms and the argumentation, and it can therefore not be tolerated. Paradoxes in that sense exist in order to be resolved and removed. The religious paradox, on the other hand, is there to stay. It is more apparent than real. The reason why it appears as a paradox or a contradiction is that it represents an attempt to express what is given religiously in terms borrowed from the theoretical sphere. When religious faith speaks of God in a diversity of parables and with a variety of words, its different statements may sometimes appear to cancel one another out. But that is often only because attention has not been paid to the function of the words in the religious context, and they have been misunderstood as if they were intended to provide a theoretical definition or proof. This, however, is not at all the purpose of these expressions. To try to give a definition of God is a meaningless undertaking, for a God who can be 'defined' is no real God. Any attempt in that direction would be the real contradiction.

In this connection, the religious paradox has the important function of making it quite clear that what is being said belongs in a quite different context from the theoretical-scientific. To try to get rid of the paradox would be to tear what is said out of its own context and treat it as if it belonged to the theoretical context. It is analogous to the attempt to remove all traces of anthropomorphism from religious language. The only result of this is that we are left with a number of empty, unmeaning words, and—what is worse—we imagine that with them we have achieved an 'adequate' knowledge. Religious faith knows that there cannot be any adequate knowledge of that sort. The more that religious faith employs paradoxical and anthropomorphic expressions, the more obvious it should be to any intelligent person that they are not intended as theoretical-scientific statements, and that it is unintelligent to discuss them as if they were.

Parables, metaphors and paradoxes have both a positive and a negative function. *Positively* they are from a religious point of view the means of expression appropriate to the religious context of meaning, and in that sense 'adequate' vehicles for conveying the religious content to us, while *negatively* they cannot be bettered as a caution against meaningless category mixing. Their positive aspect is primarily the concern of theology, while the negative is chiefly important for the philosophy of religion, which it supports in its attempt to keep the various contexts of meaning distinct and to maintain the specific character of the religious context. The paradoxical element is a kind of warning sign and call to be alert, so that we do not read into what is said a meaning alien to it; for if we do that, then the meaning of the whole is destroyed. That is why we said above that the religious paradox is there to stay. What at first sight and from an alien point of view looks like a sheer contradiction, although when understood in its own context it is not, has the twofold function to fulfil which we have indicated here. When we encounter the striking and perhaps challenging paradox, it both points to the fact that there is something unusual about religion, and provides access to the religious meaning which it is designed to express. The function of paradox has been aptly described by Jaakko Hintikka thus: 'It constitutes an invitation to interpret the statement in some unusual way.'[60] It would be a pity to get rid of this warning sign and this invitation to a right understanding of the religious context of meaning. The misunderstandings are so numerous and so widespread that every call to alertness and every invitation is very much needed.

[60] J. Hintikka, *Knowledge and Belief*, p. 102. Hintikka himself relates the matter to the question of correct 'presuppositions' and thus indirectly to that of contexts of meaning. He speaks of 'presuppositions which must be fulfilled in order that the utterance is to serve any normal purpose which utterances may be calculated to serve' (p. 99); and he goes on to say: 'The purposes of religious discourse [context of meaning] are not normally defeated by the speaker's failure to know what he is saying, in the way that the purposes of scientific (factual) discourse are thereby defeated' (p. 100).

To sum up. No context of meaning has any essential advantage over the rest. None of them can claim to be the standard to which the others must conform. When something that finds expression in one of them is viewed from the perspective of another, it has the appearance of paradox. But in its own context it need not be at all paradoxical, still less contradictory, but can be a consistent expression of the reality to which it refers. An apparent contradiction can often be an entirely legitimate way of calling attention to different factors which from an external and inappropriate point of view appear, because they are misunderstood, to be mutually exclusive. Whether this really involves a contradiction can only be determined by reference to the function the expression has in the context to which it actually belongs. It must be measured by its own standards. In this way the idea of contexts of meaning furnishes the solution also for these intricate problems.[61] Once we have become aware of the significance of this idea, we find it of decisive importance in dealing with concrete issues as well.

At this point it may be useful to refer to one of the alternative descriptions of contexts of meaning which we discussed above, namely that in which they are compared to different 'languages'. When we meet someone who speaks a language we do not know, we do not understand the meaning of what he says. To this there are various ways in which we might react. One would be to maintain that whatever is not spoken in our own language and immediately understood by us is completely without meaning— though only a linguistic ignoramus could say that. Another way would be simply not to bother about what the man was saying, but to treat it as quite unimportant, since in any case it could not be understood. A third way would be to learn the foreign language—and so to understand what was

[61] There is an abundance of relevant literature. Note particularly works by the following authors as listed in the Bibliography: (i) on *symbolism*, titles containing that term by Cassirer, Whitehead, Langer, Tillich, Aulén; (ii) on *metaphors*, Zuurdeeg (pp. 197ff.), Cohen (pp. 95ff.—where there is reference also to New Testament metaphors, p. 99); (iii) on *parables*, Funk, Dodd, Jeremias, Hof; (iv) on *paradox*, Ryle (*Dilemmas*), Regnell (pp. 82ff.).

We have considered 'paradox' here exclusively from a point of view relevant to the philosophy of religion. It has, however, also a theological aspect, which has attracted wide attention in contemporary theology, particularly owing to the influence of Kierkegaard. Yet quite apart from Kierkegaard there is an important problem for Christian theology in the idea of paradox. On this see G. Ljunggren, 'Paradoxen', and R. Bring 'Paradoxtanken'.

It may be of interest here to recall H. Rickert's steadfast refusal to speak of Christianity as 'paradoxical'. To do so is in his view to apply to Christianity an intellectualistic-rationalistic criterion derived from Greek philosophy, although Christianity is of a wholly different nature. 'The paradoxical is the intellectual, only with a negative signature.' It is therefore best, according to Rickert, completely to avoid using the term 'paradox' in a Christian context. 'The Christian religion is in fact completely incompatible with an intellectualistic philosophy like that of the Greeks.' No doubt, but why must the Christian conception of 'paradox' be the same as the Greek? (See Rickert, *Kant*, pp. 86–93.)

being said in it. It often turns out that what is being said is of very considerable importance. Perhaps that is precisely the case with 'religious language'.

The 'paradoxes' are in their way a sign that we have here a 'foreign' language. If we take the words as they stand and try to interpret them according to supposedly 'scientific' principles, starting with the meaning they have in the language we commonly speak, we shall go completely astray. What then must we do? Precisely the same as when we learn a new language. The more we familiarize ourselves with it, the better we come to grasp the meaning of the various sentences. There was recently on the Swedish radio an interesting testing program, in which a number of elementary school pupils were asked how far they were able to follow and understand the educational programs presented on the radio. Most of them confessed that a particular musical presentation had been almost impossible to understand. But then a girl, who was clearly rather better versed in the subject, made the comment: 'If you play yourself it's not so difficult to understand.' One can of course dismiss the matter by saying: I've no desire to spend my time and energy on a language in which I find it difficult to see any meaning. But here as in many other cases we have reason to affirm the truth of M. R. Cohen's remark: 'Obviously they have no meaning for those who prefer not to see their meaning. None are so blind as those who do not wish to see.'[62]

6. The Category Problem

In earlier chapters we showed the function of philosophy in general to be analysis of those logical presuppositions which as basic categories 'govern' the various contexts of meaning and determine the structural differences between them. When we then began in the present chapter to apply this in particular to 'the religious context of meaning', it might have seemed the natural thing to do if we had turned directly to the problem of the presuppositions and categories which are the concern of the philosophy of religion, and tried to discover what categories, or what basic category, can be seen to obtain in that context. We chose, however, to approach the subject in a more indirect way by discussing first some examples of what happens when the category problem is overlooked. Our reason for doing this was the obvious one, that it is far easier to discuss negatively the disastrous consequences of failure to employ the appropriate categories than to demonstrate positively what those categories are. That is why we started with a discussion of contemporary trends in which category mixing is specially evident, as it is in the demythologizing theology, the correlation theory and very much of modern hermeneutics. This led us also to discuss a number of the modes of expression which are characteristic of religious language—metaphors, parables, symbols, paradoxes. All this may

[62] M. R. Cohen, *A Preface to Logic*, p. 197.

be regarded as a preparation for dealing with the ultimately decisive issue, the category problem.

Even after this preparatory work, however, there are still considerable difficulties in the way of a positive elucidation of the religio-philosophical category. The categories are the ultimate presuppositions on which the possibility of understanding what is given in a context of meaning essentially depends. As presuppositions they are implicitly assumed, though as a rule we live in ignorance of having assumed them. People are unaware of many of the things they in fact presuppose or take for granted, and this is particularly so with regard to the 'ultimate' presuppositions or categories. We are reminded here of Wittgenstein's remark: 'It is senseless to want to define that on which the possibility of all communication and understanding depends.'[63] Yet this seems to be precisely the task that faces us here, namely to clarify that upon which the possibility of all religious communication and understanding depends. If the operative word is 'define', then of course Wittgenstein's statement is undoubtedly correct. A regular definition of the content of the most general presuppositions or categories is not possible. All we can do is to show that certain things are in fact presupposed, and necessarily presupposed, since without them the entire context of meaning in question, and everything that falls within its sphere, would have no meaning and be no context. It is, for example, quite obvious that all theoretical discussion would be meaningless if one did not start with the presupposition that there is a distinction between true and false. But that is not to say that one is in possession of a 'definition' of the term 'true'. To be unwilling to presuppose the idea of truth before one has succeeded in giving a clear definition of it is obviously 'senseless', for without this presupposition all discussion, and consequently any 'definition', is impossible.

What we are concerned with here, however, is a different question. It is neither 'senseless' nor impossible to show what in fact is presupposed when I express a judgment or state a proposition of whatever kind. An ethical judgment presupposes certain categories as necessary in that area, and a religious statement likewise implies certain necessary presuppositions in the religious area. There is nothing unreasonable in seeking to draw out by means of analysis what is thus actually and necessarily presupposed. We have already studied the method—the logical analysis of presuppositions—which must be employed for that purpose. This task is not meaningless, though it is extremely difficult and we shall be wise not to underestimate the difficulties. For if it is difficult in general, it is for various reasons still more so in the area of religion. To begin with, we find here a multitude of contradictory and mutually exclusive religions—where then are we to find a common denominator? Furthermore, religion is the most intimately personal of realities—how then are we to make it objec-

[63] Wittgenstein, *Schriften* 3, p. 224.

342

tively comprehensible? At least it is clear that we cannot define it in the sense of including everything that is called religion in one common, universal concept.[64] The only possibility is that of looking for the 'pre-suppositional concept' of religion, and it is this that can be said to be the fundamental problem of the philosophy of religion.[65]

Enough has been said to show how extensive and complex a problem the philosophy of religion has to handle. As our present study is simply concerned with prolegomena, it is not incumbent on us here to carry out the material research necessary for solving it. Prolegomena are not meant to solve problems, but only to point them out and show where they are located. It is sufficient to bring the problem to light, even if we are not yet in a position to solve it. In order to indicate more clearly how the land lies, however, it may be desirable to anticipate at least sketchily the direction in which the solution is to be sought.

In an earlier work, *Religiöst Apriori* (1921), in which I outlined the problem of the philosophy of religion, I concluded that 'the category of the eternal' was the fundamental category of religion. Although my exposition of it there was of a rather brief and preliminary sort, I still think 'the category of the eternal' is the most suitable term for describing the basic presupposition of the religious context of meaning. What particularly commends it for this purpose is the fact that, more than any other pre-suppositional concept we might think of, it meets the requirements that must be fulfilled by a basic presupposition. On the one hand it draws a clear distinction between the religious context of meaning and other contexts of meaning, while on the other hand it gives expression to the way in which the various contexts of meaning in the last resort belong together. In other words, it takes care of both the integrity and the integration of the religious context of meaning.[66] What is more, as a purely formal category, the category of the eternal leaves room for the differences between the various religions as regards their content.

The question of the eternal is a completely open question, which involves no preconceptions whatever as regards content. It allows every religion to give its own characteristic answer. The category itself prescribes nothing as to what the answer must be. Knowledge of the answer can be obtained only by going to the actual religions. Here there is room for such diverse answers as the Greek-Platonic concept of eternity with its timeless World of Ideas, and the quite differently oriented Christian idea of eternity, in which time and eternity interact and meet in God's 'good time' (*kairos*) when the new 'age' (*aeon*) is inaugurated through Christ to be consummated in eternal life—to mention only two of the most outstanding examples. Wherever we turn in the world of religion we find

[64] *Cf.* above, pp. 24f.
[65] *Cf.* my *Det religionsfilosofiska grundproblemet.*
[66] *Cf.* above, pp. 292ff.

confirmation of the thesis: Take away the perspective of eternity and religion disappears, and then every religious statement loses its meaning, and conversely: Take account of the perspective of eternity, and you have a vast context of meaning which can do justice to the actually given religions and provide the key to a meaningful religious language.[67]

As the category of the eternal can thus do justice to the multiplicity of religions, serving so to speak as their common denominator, and making it possible to speak of the religious context of meaning as a unity, so it also proves capable of overcoming the second difficulty we noted, namely that of giving expression to the thoroughly personal nature of religion.

It is true that the concept of eternity quite often occurs in connection with metaphysics, and then as a rule it is of an extremely abstract and impersonal character. But this only shows that we are not then within the realm of religion, even though religious expressions are used. Real religion is never merely abstract, it is not simply a matter of an *idea* of the eternal. Real religion is always concrete, and in it the eternal is found as the content of actual experience.[68] Religiousness is not peculiar to any of the familiar psychological categories; it has to do with everything in our life, it engages our whole being. It is this personal involvement, this thoroughly 'existential' aspect of religion (in Kierkegaard's sense of 'existential'), that clearly distinguishes religion from metaphysics.[69] The confusion of religion with metaphysics is as indefensible as it is common. The two represent essentially different interests, and have nothing in common beyond a number of words and phrases. It is therefore a matter of first importance for the philosophy of religion to keep them distinct and not allow them to intermingle.[70]

In contrast to the pallid and abstract metaphysical idea of eternity, the eternal in the context of religion always has definite significance for concrete life, a vital bearing on the actual here and now. Religion is, so to speak, the point of intersection between time and eternity, where neither of them can be left out of account. The eternal means at once revelation, judgment, reconciliation and communion with God—all of which is completely foreign to metaphysics.[71] In Christianity all this is concentrated in one single figure, Jesus Christ. He is the revelation of God in the world, in him the Eternal has come to dwell among us, he is the effulgence of the

[67] On this subject note, in addition to my above-mentioned *Religiöst Apriori*, also my essays, 'Är evighetskategorien en religiös kategori?' and 'Till frågan om den transcendentala metodens användning'.

[68] *Cf.* my *Essence of Christianity*, pp. 39ff.

[69] Paul Tillich rightly sees religion as characterized by 'ultimate concern', but this does not prevent him from mixing up religion and metaphysics.

[70] *Cf.* J. Hemberg, *Religion och metafysik*, and my essay with the same title in *Kristen Humanism*.

[71] See my *Det bestående* (ET in *Essence of Christianity*), in which the content of religion is analyzed with reference to these four elements.

Divine glory manifested in time, at a particular point in our world. And just for that reason he is the judgment on a world estranged from God, the judgment on our entire life when it sets itself against the will of God. But in him is also the reconciliation, and he is the one who leads us to communion with God and gives us eternal life.[72] For Christian faith, time and eternity are not mutually exclusive. At one point in human history, at a particular time and in a particular place, the two have become one. In Jesus Christ, in the concreteness of his actual life, is the point where—to use Chaim Wardi's striking phrase—'eternity irrupted into time'.[73] That expresses better than anything else what it is all about: not simply a human life lived once long ago, nor yet simply an eternal principle, but precisely the concrete life in which 'eternity irrupted into time'. How could anyone who has been seriously confronted by this be personally unaffected by it?

From what has been said it is clear that religion encompasses the whole of life and is concerned with the deepest issues of our existence. 'Eternity' in a religious sense is anything but an abstract notion or idea. It is something interfused with the concrete stuff of life, something of momentous import for life in its entirety, which therefore summons man to complete surrender and utter devotion. In order to make this clear there is no need for recourse to any existentialist 'preunderstanding'. Religious reality itself bears sufficient witness to it.

A more detailed investigation might no doubt result in the discovery of other religious categories besides that of the eternal. But the latter, as enabling us to deal with the problem both of the integrity and the integration of the religious context of meaning, is assured in any event of its place as the *fundamental* category of religion. With this, however, we have already gone beyond the bounds of prolegomena and raised questions that belong to the province of the philosophy of religion itself.

7. Religion, Philosophy of Religion, and Theology

Philosophy of religion and theology have to do, each in its own way, with the problem of religion. If there were no religion as a *given* phenomenon, there would be no philosophy of religion and no theology. Both of these sciences, however, have often felt called upon to try to take the place of religion.

Owing to the multiplicity of religions, the philosophy of religion has

[72] See e.g., for revelation, Jn. 1:14, Heb. 1:3; for judgment, Jn. 3:19, 9:39; for reconciliation, 1 Jn. 2:2, Rom. 5:11; for communion with God and eternal life, Rom. 6:23, Jn. 14:6, 17:3. See further my *Essence of Christianity*, pp. 38–62.

[73] Chaim Wardi, 'The Christian Perspective' in *Ariel*, 1969, p. 22. *Cf.* M. Muggeridge, *Jesus Rediscovered*, p. 36: 'the intersection of time and eternity', and p. 72: 'in him [Christ] time and eternity . . . came together'.—It need hardly be pointed out that this does not answer the question of the *content* of the Christian faith. It simply touches on that aspect of Christianity which shows the relevance of the category of eternity to it.

long been subject to the temptation of claiming to represent a universal religion, a 'natural religion', a 'rational religion', or whatever else it may be called. We have already seen that this mistake rests upon an unwarrantable conceptual realism. When we subsume the various species of trees—birch, oak, lime, fir, and so forth—under the concept of 'tree', this does not mean that we eliminate these species and replace them with a universal tree which is both all and none of them. Nor can the philosophy of religion, when it uses the concept of religion to cover Christianity, Buddhism, Shinto, Mohammedanism, and so forth, eliminate these concrete religions and replace them with a universal religion which is both all and none of them. The impossibility of doing this is all the greater inasmuch as the concept of religion is a 'presuppositional concept', to which there is no corresponding entity. This fact should put an end once for all to any attempt at interpretation that involves conceptual realism.

Theology too, however, both in the past and down to our own time, has come forward with the claim to be able to do for us what only real religion can do. Time and again attempts have been made to produce a theologically refined and improved version of existing religion. During the Enlightenment the aim was to adapt religion to the 'truths' of the rationalistic credo, in Idealism it was to adapt it to one's own metaphysics, and in '*Kulturprotestantismus*' it was to rid it of whatever was uncongenial to the educated modern mind. More recently, the 'demythologizing theology', for which everything that disagrees with what is supposed to be the 'modern worldview' must be labelled 'mythology', has seen it as the theologian's task to interpret or re-interpret the gospel in harmony with a contemporary philosophical trend which the theologian in question happens to consider identical with 'philosophy'.

We are here in the peculiar position of having to defend religion as it actually exists against the sciences whose business it is to investigate the problem of religion, that is, against philosophy of religion and theology. The American theologian Thor Hall recently published an essay under the title 'Let Religion be Religious'.[74] That phrase could very well have been used as the heading of the present section and indeed of this whole chapter. For our continually recurring theme has been: Let religion be what it is, let it preserve its distinctiveness and autonomy. Don't start re-interpreting it, for such secondary versions of it are always devaluations; they deprive it of something essential to it. Don't try to justify religion on non-religious grounds. Don't ask about its 'secular meaning' but about its own meaning, its religious meaning. Let religion be religious![75]

[74] *Interpretation*, 1969, pp. 158–89.
[75] It is of course in general a sound principle to let things be what they are—to let each be what it is and mean what it means. We may recall here P. S. Watson's well-known interpretation of Luther, *Let God be God*, or the ecumenical slogan, 'Let the Church be the Church'.

There has been during recent decades a campaign by certain theologians against the concept of religion. Behind this one can often detect a certain apologetic concern, the Christian faith being contrasted as something that is true, with religion as something that is false. Nevertheless, it has had consequences which were certainly not envisaged from the start: Christianity has been emptied of its religious content. And with the loss of the orientation point ('what is it about?') the way has lain open for all the varieties of arbitrary re-interpretation from the 'secular meaning' to the ' "death of God" theology'. When people lose their religious bearings, they cast about in all directions asking if anyone anywhere has any use for 'God'. Is God needed as a scientific hypothesis? No! Is he needed as a guarantor of morality? No! Is he needed as an archetype for art? No! Then we don't need God! So God is dead! The idea that God might have a religious significance is never even considered. To which we can only reply: 'Let God be God! Let religion be religious!'

There is an instructive story about Laplace and Napoleon. It is said that Napoleon once asked Laplace where in his theory there was still a place for God; to which Laplace is supposed to have replied: 'Sire, I have no need of that hypothesis.' In other words, the hypothesis of God is not needed to fill up the gaps in science. If this reply comes as a shock, that can only be because we are not letting religion be what it is. God as a scientific hypothesis—what a blasphemous idea! In our time something like Laplace's thought has become quite widespread. On which we will only comment that it is all to the good if this perfectly obvious fact has at last dawned even on those outside religious circles, so that it is no longer thought remarkable.

What is needed above all is a complete re-thinking of the function of both the philosophy of religion and theology. As a counterpart to the call to 'Let religion be religious' we might issue another: 'Let philosophy of religion and theology be scientific.' These two disciplines must for a start take seriously the nature of scientific procedure, characterized as it is by 'the possibility of objective argumentation'. Where this possibility does not exist, there must be no specious contrivance of results, which could not be anything but pseudo-science. If only one can free oneself from the traditions of centuries as to what philosophy and theology are, the position proves to be quite simple. One sees what questions can be put and where the boundaries of objective argumentation lie, and one is thereby also freed from the otherwise inevitable peril of category mixing. Religion is allowed to be religion, and science to be science.

What we have just said applies equally to philosophy of religion and theology. These represent two different scientific ways of dealing with religion, and their scientific orientation ought to prevent them from tampering with the given reality of religion or attempting in any way to remodel it. Here we must let science be science, and not surrender the

347

principle of objective argumentation either for apologetic purposes or in order to produce a religion with scientific credentials. Not to respect the autonomy of religion is to abandon the scientific attitude, whether in philosophy of religion or theology. It is thus evident that the two demands, 'Let religion be religious' and 'Let science be scientific', are complementary.

Philosophy of religion and theology belong as regards their function and their mode of argumentation to the scientific, not the religious, context of meaning, though their subject matter, religion, belongs to the religious context of meaning, not to the scientific. Yet while from this point of view philosophy of religion and theology are on the same level, there is nonetheless a very definite difference between them as regards both their aim and their method. They have two quite different questions as the object of their inquiry. The philosophy of religion is an 'analysis of presuppositions'. By means of a logico-philosophical analysis of the religious as such, it seeks to get back to the ultimate presuppositions or categories that obtain in that area. Or to put it another way, it asks about the 'rules' that govern religious language. By its very nature as presuppositional analysis it undoubtedly possesses scientific status, for that which is actually or necessarily presupposed is accessible to objective argumentation. There is, however, another question, which concerns the actual content of religion, and this is the question of theology. But the religions are many, and consequently the answers they give to the question of content are many. It is the clarification of the Christian answer, or of the content of the Christian faith, that is the task of Christian theology. This is a purely scientific task, for here arguments can be put forward for and against a proposed hypothesis. As long as theology sticks to this task, its scientific status is clear. But theology is constantly tempted to set itself up as a religious authority and try to establish a normative doctrine—tailored very likely to meet contingent historical requirements. Against all such tendencies it must be emphatically stated that the theologian is an investigator engaged in research, and his sole task is to give an objective account of the content of the Christian faith.[76]

[76] Putting it in other words, we could say that the theologian's business is to answer scientifically the question 'What is Christianity?' It is not, however, his business as a theologian to deal with the question 'Is Christianity true?' These are two quite distinct questions, which ought never to be confused. The first can be answered scientifically, the second cannot. Unfortunately they usually are confused, with the result that the theologian becomes primarily an apologist, whose account of what Christianity is, comes to be shaped by what he supposes his audience will accept as true. (See next note.) It should perhaps also be observed that there is no reason why we should not have a scientifically systematic theology of other religions than Christianity if we wish. The theological methodology advocated in this book is not applicable only to Christianity, as Nygren himself has shown by his use of it in *Agape and Eros*, where it has enabled him to give a clear and objectively verifiable account of, e.g., the Neoplatonic outlook.

It is important to insist that the work of the philosophy of religion and the work of theology represent two quite different kinds of research. They are both sciences of religion, but they have widely differing goals. Neither can do duty for the other. The common idea that philosophy of religion is a more scientific form of theology is thus ruled out of court.[77] We are now in a position to state exactly what the fundamental difference between them is. It consists above all in the fact that they are situated on different levels, the philosophy of religion on that of the category, theology on that of the motif. Both of them are concerned with contexts—otherwise they could not engage in argumentation—but each with a different kind of context. The philosophy of religion has to do with a context of meaning, theology with a motif context. As in the preceding chapters we have sufficiently defined the term 'context of meaning', all we now need in order to make the distinction between the two disciplines finally clear is a corresponding definition of the term 'motif context', and this will be the theme of our concluding chapter.

We may add here, however, that contemporary philosophy has very recently given us a new means of making this distinction and preventing confusion, by its own distinction between *object-language* and *meta-language*. Using this terminology we can say that theology is concerned with the object-language of religion, and the philosophy of religion with its meta-language. If we do so, we must of course always bear in mind that 'meta-language' has nothing to do with metaphysics, but simply discusses the question 'What is it about?' This distinction will then help us to avoid the confusion that arises from using meta-language and object-language

---

Indeed, this methodology is applicable also in other than theological fields, and has been so used (see Additional Note V).—Translator's note.

[77] It has long been customary to regard both the philosophy of religion and theology as serving an *apologetic* purpose. This has been possible, however, only because their scientific character has been renounced; for there is in the very idea of apologetics a motive which is alien to science. It is true that from one point of view science can often be said to have an apologetic *effect*, inasmuch as it clears away common misunderstandings. In many instances the best apologetic for anything is simply to give an objectively factual account of it. By this means many groundless objections are removed. But this is precisely an argument against apologetics in the ordinary sense, which seeks to give a 'persuasive' rather than objectively factual account. At all events, when apologetics is given a decisive place in the philosophy of religion and theology, it has a disastrous effect on their scientific status. The outstanding example of this in recent times is Paul Tillich's theologico-philosophical system. In the Introduction to his *Systematic Theology* he says explicitly that it is 'written from an apologetic point of view', and he insists into the bargain that apologetics must be 'an omnipresent element of systematic theology'. That is the ultimate reason why his theology takes the form of a 'metaphysics of being' and is thus no genuine theology (*cf.* above, pp. 316ff.). It should be added that the whole method of 'correlation' rests on an apologetic basis.

indiscriminately and treating philosophy of religion and theology as essentially the same.[78]

[78] Just as recent philosophy has been largely preoccupied with linguistic questions, so the philosophy of religion and philosophically oriented theology have often turned to the analysis of 'religious language'. *Cf.*, e,g., I. T. Ramsey, *Religious Language*; Flew and MacIntyre, *New Essays in Philosophical Theology*: F. Ferré, *Language, Logic and God*, and *Basic Modern Philosophy of Religion*; Ferré and Bendall, *Exploring the Logic of Faith*; R. W. Funk, *Language, Hermeneutics and the Word of God*; J. Barr, *The Semantics of Biblical Language*; H. Lyttkens, 'Metoder att klassificera religiösa påståendesatser'; G. Friedrich, 'Zum Problem der Semantik'.

CHAPTER XII

Motif Contexts

1. Necessary and Self-Evident Presuppositions

IN the preceding chapters we have had a great deal to say about 'presuppositions'. This has all been about 'necessary' presuppositions—necessary in so far as it is only with their help that anything whatever can have meaning and context for us. In order to show what is characteristic of these necessary presuppositions, we distinguished them in Chapter VII from a number of other concepts with which they are very commonly confused. For 'presupposition' is often used simply as a synonym for 'prejudice', 'preunderstanding', 'prescription', which are all examples of *illegitimate* presuppositions. If I let a 'prejudice' affect my attitude to a question, then I do not genuinely ask the question, for I already have the answer. My mind is made up in advance, my judgment on the matter is formed before I have considered the relevant facts. In other words, it is a case of *prae-judicium*, a 'pre-judgment' in the literal sense of the word. Similarly, if I start with a particular *Vorverständnis* or 'preunderstanding', then again I have anticipated the answer. By choosing this starting point I have arbitrarily limited the possible answers, since the answer can only be one that is congenial to my already determined preunderstanding. Or again, I may start with the idea that my presuppositions are 'prescriptions' which 'prescribe laws for nature', instead of letting nature reveal its own laws, as it does under proper experimental conditions. Here too it is a case of coming with my own preconceived ideas and seeking to force a given material into their mould. It is illegitimate thus to presuppose what ought to be proved, and in this way to determine the result before the investigation takes place.

In contrast to all such illegitimate presuppositions, we have been concerned hitherto exclusively with the kind of presuppositions which alone make a meaningful investigation possible, and which are proved by that very fact to be logically necessary. Unless I acknowledge a distinction between true and false, it is meaningless to make any attempt at scientific research. Unless I acknowledge a distinction between good and evil, it is meaningless to make any ethical judgment. These are the kind of necessary and inevitable presuppositions or categories that govern the different contexts of meaning.

More than once, however, during our preceding discussion there have been hints of another sort of context, which in contradistinction to the context of meaning we have called a 'motif context'. We must now take a closer look at this. In both cases we have to do with a context that is held together and governed by its own 'presuppositions', and although they are of very different kinds and subject to very different conditions, yet both of them are necessary for the understanding of a given material, that is, of expressions used and statements actually made. We have thus two kinds of *legitimate* presuppositions, which on the one hand belong closely together, yet on the other must be kept clearly distinct because they are on two different levels, one on that of the context of meaning and the other on that of the motif context. In order to bring out the fact that both of them are inevitable, but with a different sort of inevitability in each case, we distinguish between 'necessary' and 'self-evident' presuppositions.[1] The former have the force of logical necessity, the latter of something historically self-evident. Both are equally necessary for an understanding of the statements we find actually made. Neither of them can be ignored without imperilling the meaning of what is said.

From one point of view these two terms could be used as synonyms. For the ultimate logical presuppositions are obviously 'self-evident'—so much so that we do not as a rule reflect on the fact that we have pre-supposed them. And the self-evident presuppositions of history are 'necessary' in the sense that men cannot emancipate themselves from them at will, but carry them with them wherever they go, so that it is impossible to understand the meaning of things said without taking them into account. Nevertheless the distinction is plain. For while the ultimate category-presuppositions are logically necessary, and can be shown to be so by means of logical analysis, the ultimate motif-presuppositions are not logically demonstrable. As long as they are conceived as self-evident, it is impossible to get away from them, but if anyone questions them, no one can prove that any of them is the only possible presupposition. Another person can start with a different self-evident motif-presupposition, and there is no possibility of refuting him.

It might seem appropriate to speak here on the one hand of a logical, and on the other of a psychological necessity; but it would not in fact be quite accurate. There is nothing psychologically compulsive about the self-evident presuppositions that characterize a particular historical period, although it is necessary to take them into account as being actually present if we are to have any understanding whatever of the period and its outlook. Enough has been said above on the subject of 'necessary presuppositions', and we must now give attention to that of 'self-evident presuppositions'. It should be noted, however, that this takes us out of the philosophical into the historical field.

(1) *The role of the self-evident in history*
The question of 'the role of the self-evident in history' is a subject to which

[1] *Cf.* above, p. 207.

little attention has been paid in theories of historical knowledge and method, but it is nonetheless of extraordinary importance if we are to have a clear grasp of the nature and conditions of historical understanding.[2]

What is meant by understanding 'historically' a period of the past? It has been aptly said that the sole task of a historian is to describe things 'exactly as they were' ('*wie es eigentlich gewesen ist*'). That in fact says all there is to be said. If the historian has succeeded in giving an accurate and faithful picture of the period he has undertaken to describe, nothing more can be required of him. At first sight, therefore, the historian's task may seem very simple and easy. For it should surely not be very difficult to tell the story of past events, at least if the sources are at all adequate. Yet on closer examination the difficulties soon appear. This is not due primarily to the fact that the sources often contradict one another. For it is plain that the historian must not accept any and every piece of information without question, but must sift his material critically—that point does not need to be argued. The profoundest difficulties are of another kind and on a deeper level, for they are bound up with the underlying conditions of historical interpretation.

Here we are immediately faced with the question of the role of the self-evident in history. Every age has that which it accepts as self-evident, and it is this that sets the profoundest mark on an age. No doubt it is most natural that in seeking to characterize a particular period one should point to the ideas and concepts which in that period clashed with one another and contended for mastery; for it is these that have left the clearest traces in the annals of the day, as having led to the formation of parties, sects and movements of various sorts. It is therefore not surprising that history tends to focus attention on these controversial issues: they were after all the focus of attention in their own time. Men were preoccupied with them, they argued and fought about them. But there is also something else in every age which we can easily overlook, something that gives deeper expression to the character of the age than do its conscious issues. This consists of the self-evident presuppositions on which the entire age builds, and which are held in common by all, friend and foe alike. Precisely because these presuppositions are accepted as self-evident, they do not become a subject of discussion. If they were subjected to discussion, they could be accepted by some and rejected by others; but they are not. Self-evident presuppositions are not discussed, they are merely assumed and made use of as something self-evidently valid. They are taken for granted, like the air we breathe, the atmosphere in which we live.

Against this background we at once see the historian's dilemma. He himself lives in one age and shares its self-evident presuppositions, which he cannot help using; but the area of his investigation belongs to another

[2] On this see my 'Det självklaras roll i historien', from which much of what follows is taken, and also my 'Atomism eller sammanhang i historiesynen'.

353

age, which was dominated by different assumptions. How then can he give a faithful picture of that age? Its real character is only to be seen against the background of its own self-evident presuppositions, which are different from those of the historian and his contemporaries.

The answer to the historian's difficulty, then, would seem to be that he should enter so fully into the spirit of the past that its presuppositions become his own. Only thus will he be able to view events as the past itself saw them, and only thus can he see them as they really were. But the situation is not so simple. For *if* the historian could so immerse himself in a past era as to identify completely his own thought with it, then all historical understanding would be made impossible. There is such a thing as standing so close to a matter that perspective is lost. That is the primary reason why we cannot very well see our own age in historical perspective. We are still too close to it. We live in the midst of it and operate willy nilly with its self-evident assumptions, without being able to discern what these actually are. Only when the present has slipped into the past and its presuppositions have given way to others is it possible to view it in historical perspective.

We thus find ourselves in the peculiar position that the very thing that constitutes the historian's chief difficulty is the very thing that is prerequisite to a historical perspective. He needs to have both distance and congeniality of outlook. An understanding of history is possible only when these two are balanced against one another and made to work together.

If distance is lacking, that is, if the historian so immerses himself in the period he seeks to describe that its assumptions become also his, then he loses historical perspective and ceases to be a historian. He sees only what anyone living at the time might have seen, and has forfeited the chief advantage of a historian, namely the ability to see what the self-evident presuppositions of the period were, of which those who then lived were unaware.

This difficulty, however, can safely be said to be less common than its opposite. The trouble is not usually that the distance is too small, but that it is too great, or what amounts to the same thing, that there is too little congeniality of outlook. Sometimes the historian—and this is particularly true with regard to the history of ideas—moves quite cavalierly into the period he intends to study, as if nothing more were necessary for understanding it than to consider it in the light of his own self-evident presuppositions. In so doing he makes himself guilty of the worst of all historical errors, anachronism. Every science has its own particular perils, mistakes into which it is very easy to fall. The special mistake of the historian is the anachronism. For χρόνος, time, is the principle of history. This does not of course mean clock time, in which every segment of time is like every other. Time in that sense is our own construction, a quantitative concept of time. In what we are saying here we are concerned rather with historical time as we described it above, in which every period has its own special quality, its distinctive character, as resting on its own self-evident presuppositions.

There are two different kinds of anachronism. One is the common, simple and relatively harmless anachronism which places things or persons in a milieu to which they do not belong. Such errors are generally soon detected and corrected. The other kind may be called the anachronism of method or principle. It arises when one who attempts to interpret a period of the past does not seek out its peculiar presuppositions, but misreads it in the light of the self-evident presuppositions which he himself happens to hold.

But how can we be sure that we have rightly understood what the self-evident presuppositions of a particular period are? Seeing that these are for the most part unexpressed and often unconsciously held, how can we guard against arbitrariness in our view of them? The answer, strange though it may seem, is that we are guaranteed against this by the subject matter itself. If the historian turns to his subject matter with presuppositions that are false and foreign to the period, he soon discovers that the facts are against him. They become unmanageable for him, they resist him and refuse to fit into his alien pattern. There is something that can be called the stubbornness of the facts. When this becomes apparent, it is a sure sign that one has come to the subject matter with the wrong presuppositions. In consequence, one is compelled to subordinate the facts to all sorts of artificial interpretation and do violence to them in order to get any kind of meaning out of them. When on the other hand one has found the right presuppositions, their rightness is corroborated by the facts, which need no forcing to fit them. The simple and clear meaning that then emerges, testifies that a correct understanding has been reached.

From this it is possible to draw a very important conclusion as to method. Anyone who is familiar with the way in which histories of thought are written, knows how again and again we find in them a methodological approach which almost threatens to become the patent, standard procedure in this area. In seeking to give an account of a system of thought, it is a common practice to start by pointing out inconsistencies and contradictions of which the thinker is alleged to have been guilty, and to explain them in terms of the effect of various influences upon him. His outlook is analyzed into dissimilar lines of thought which cancel each other out, and with this it is supposed that everything necessary has been done for the interpretation of the outlook in question.

But we have good reason to be sceptical of such a methodology. Is it really credible that the greatest thinkers of the past were guilty of such elementary mistakes and incessant contradictions? Is there any reason to think that they were so much poorer than we at logic? Is it not methodologically sounder and more profitable to assume at least the possibility that

355

there seem to be contradictions only because we have not gone deep enough in our interpretation, but have come to it with presuppositions foreign to the view under study, which has consequently and inevitably been torn apart? The apparent contradictions should therefore send us back to dig deeper and check our presuppositions. An interpreter has not fulfilled his task when he has merely dismembered a thinker's system into an array of contradictory ideas. His most important business is to try to get back to the original presuppositions that gave unity to views which now appear contradictory. Not until that is done is a system really understood. At all events, an interpretation which makes unified sense of an outlook is more likely to be right than one which can do no more than represent it as an array of contradictions.

(2) *Three self-evident presuppositions*

We have now delayed rather long over general, abstract, methodological issues, and it is time that we turned to the question of content. Naturally we cannot attempt here to expound the whole gamut of self-evident presuppositions which have succeeded one another in the course of history and set their mark on different periods—though that would be an extremely fascinating thing to do. It will have to suffice to characterize briefly three great examples of such presuppositions, which have exerted their influence over vast periods of time and together have dominated almost the whole history of Western culture. The ideas involved were originally anything but self-evident. They owe their existence to acts of great creativity. Yet when once they had been produced, they came to play the part of self-evident presuppositions for succeeding generations.

1) The first that should be named is the Greek-Hellenistic total view of existence, which found its highest expression in the Platonic doctrine of the two worlds, the dualism between the world of ideas and the world of the senses, or the world of eternal types and the world of their transient shadow-images. This is the background of those ascetic views and tendencies which have affected even Christian history. For the important thing here is to turn away from this world, the world of appearance, and mount up to the world of eternal being and true reality. It should be noted that this doctrine of the two worlds is not simply one among others. It is the underlying assumption of everything else, the bond of unity, the self-evident presupposition which sets its mark on the thought and life of more than a millennium.

2) Alongside this we find another total view, the Christian view. This also has its doctrine of two worlds and its concept of eternity; but both of these are essentially different from the Greek. To oversimplify a little, it could be said that the Greek concept of eternity is spatial and static: the eternal world lies in eternal repose above the sense world, wholly apart from the world of appearance. The Christian concept of eternity, on the

other hand, is temporal and dynamic—which to the Greek mind is a contradiction, since time and eternity are mutually exclusive. When Christianity speaks of two 'ages' or 'aeons'—*aion* being of course the Greek
word for eternity—it is speaking of something going on here in our
human world. This world is not wholly separate from God and the eternal;
from the beginning it is God's own world. Yet at the same time it is a
world in which evil powers, hostile to God, carry on their work. God has
never forsaken his world, and at one point in its history he has manifested
his *dynamis*, his power, in a quite special way. This happened when he sent
Christ into the world as the head of a new humanity. Then the new aeon
dawned: 'If anyone is in Christ, he is a new creation; the old has passed
away, behold, the new has come'.[3] The thought of the two aeons is reflected in our division of history into the time before and after the birth of
Christ. History is the arena for the struggle between good and evil, truth
and falsehood, God and the forces of destruction. When Christianity talks
about the two aeons and about Christ as the turning point between them—
and the turning point in the human drama—it must be said here too that
this is not one doctrine among others, but the basic Christian presupposition.

It was, however, neither the Greek-Hellenistic nor the Christian presupposition that alone and in its pure form came to set its mark on the
next millennium and a half. The general outlook was determined rather
by a compromise between these two, found in the so-called Alexandrian
world-scheme. Here the whole of existence—God, the world, and man—
is gathered up into a simple, all-inclusive view. From God, who is conceived as the undifferentiated One, τὸ ἕν, existence flows forth in all its
manifoldness; and to God it will finally return and be re-absorbed into the
divine One. The principle for the whole course of the world is the Divine
self-love, eternally bent upon itself, ever going forth from itself and returning to itself in a vast 'cycle'. In harmony with this, the world process
is conceived as moving through two stages: a *descent*, from God to the
world, and an *ascent*, from the world back to God, an emanation and a
remanation, a procession and a return, πρόοδος and ἐπιστροφή, as the
Neoplatonist Proclus called it. This became the self-evident pattern on
which almost the whole of mediaeval thinking was based. We find it
wherever we turn. It underlies the *Summa Theologica* of a schoolman like
Thomas Aquinas; it appears in the teaching of a mystic like Henry Suso
concerning the 'outflow and return of the Spirit'; and on it a poet like
Dante builds his *Divine Comedy*—to name but a few examples.

3) In the meantime, however, a vast transformation of the general outlook was in preparation. A new self-evident presupposition was developing.
It broke through in the Renaissance, reached its fulness in the Enlightenment, and plainly shows its effects still today. The Renaissance discovered

[3] 1 Cor. 15:17 (RSV).

357

Man—so it is commonly said. It would be better to say that it put Man at the centre of existence; it discovered the divinity of Man. If we wish to study this new mood—and we can do so best where it appears in its most unvarnished form—there is an excellent example of it in Marsilio Ficino, the founder of the 'Platonic Academy' in Florence. Ficino's whole work is a kind of apotheosis of Man, a hymn in praise of Man. And on what does Man's exalted position rest? It rests on the idea that he is a microcosm who comprehends in himself all the rest of existence, the macrocosm. His nature gives him his place as the centre of existence. Beneath him he has the world of material things; above him is God and the spiritual world. Each of these represents only a part or aspect of existence—God the spiritual aspect, material things the sensible aspect—whereas Man comprises it all in his own person. He is sovereign lord over the four elements, earth, air, water and fire. He treads upon the earth; he ploughs the sea with his vessels; he mounts into the air on his high towers—not to mention the wings of Daedalus and Icarus; he kindles fire and enjoys it on his hearth. Man is God upon earth, *Deus in terris*. By the power of his thought he can fathom and trace out the construction of the world; indeed—says Ficino—he could doubtless make the heavens if only he had the necessary tools and access to the proper material. It is therefore not surprising that Man appears as the rival of God and worships himself as God.

In true Renaissance manner, Ficino is intoxicated with the power and glory of Man. And in man's conviction of his own divinity and his worship of himself, Ficino finds the real meaning both of Christianity and of Platonism. He aimed at nothing other than a renewal of Platonism, and his chief work bore significantly enough the title of 'Platonic Theology'. Yet he was thoroughly mistaken in thinking of himself in that way. His outlook is actually quite different from Platonism. In Platonism it is not man, empirical man, that stands at the centre of the stage, but that place is occupied by the world of ideas. In Ficino there is a complete shift from the objective to the subjective, from the transcendent to the immanent. In fact the Renaissance with its emphatic placing of man at the centre is less akin to Plato than to his opponents, the Sophists, with their principle of *homo mensura*, 'man the measure of all things'.

Something of this exaltation of man, operating as a self-evident presupposition, has to a very large extent dominated recent centuries and imparted to them a subjectivistic character. This is discernible in the most diverse places, not only in the philosophical subjectivism that has prevailed ever since Descartes, but—to mention only a few examples—in political Machiavellianism, in the 'social contract' theory, in the uninhibited self-assertion of national states, in the optimism of the Enlightenment as to development and progress, and in the positivism of the last century.

Men have not as a rule been aware that they were operating with a self-evident presupposition. They have believed that while earlier times were naturally under the sway of certain prejudices, they themselves had at last reached a purely scientific, presuppositionless view of the universe. But this is only another illustration of the fact that men do not perceive the self-evident presuppositions by which their own age lives. In this connection it may be apropos to recall Auguste Comte's three stages of cultural development, the theological, the metaphysical and the positive. Only when man comes to the third stage has he finally freed himself from all arbitrary assumptions and prejudices. Here man builds only on what is positively given and scientifically demonstrable. But that is of course an illusion; for no age lives without inarticulate, self-evident presuppositions. Nevertheless there is a hint of truth in what Comte says about the theological and metaphysical stages. The self-evident presuppositions on which a culture rests have often originally sprung from the soil of religious faith. Plato, for instance, got the impulse for his doctrine of the two worlds from the Greek mystery religions, and in Neoplatonism the idea turns back to its religious origin. When the self-evident presuppositions are torn loose from their religious basis, they become metaphysical. When man ceases to believe in God, he starts trying to prove the existence of God. There have been many attempts to define metaphysics, none of them wholly satisfactory; but at least we hit upon one essential aspect of it if we say that metaphysics is secularized religion. We can moreover go a step further and say that Comte's positivist stage is nothing but a disguised metaphysics which has convinced itself that it has dispensed with all self-evident presuppositions. We need not therefore be surprised that Comte finally lets his positivism culminate in a 'religion of humanity' in which he makes man, as *le Grand-être*, 'the Great Being', the object of religious worship. Here his hidden presupposition breaks out into broad daylight.

2. The Fundamental Motif as a Historical Problem

As we seek to show what is involved in the idea of a 'motif context' it should be borne in mind from the start that we have stepped outside the province of the philosophy of religion, and that what follows is therefore not strictly within the bounds of our present inquiry. Why then have we included this discussion of 'motif contexts' at all? The answer is simple. The sole purpose of this final chapter is to draw a clear distinction between the task of the philosophy of religion and that of theology. As long as we are not concretely aware of what lies on the other side of the boundary, we are always in danger of mixing up things which ought to be kept separate. To put it very briefly: the philosophy of religion has to do with the religious context of meaning, and theology with the religious motif context.

It is not the business of the philosophy of religion to provide any content for an answer to the religious question, but only to determine the meaning of the question. It has to clarify what we *mean* when we ask the religious question, or in other words, to show by means of analysis 'what

359

it is about' when religion is the subject of discussion. But it does not have to discuss possible answers and decide which of them is the right one. Just as the philosophy of science analyzes the distinctively scientific mode of argumentation, or the scientific way of putting questions, but does not presume to take sides and decide between different scientific theories and competing answers—it leaves that to the individual sciences—so it is the task of the philosophy of religion to analyze the structure and distinctive character of the religious context of meaning in order to see what it is about, but not to take sides and make decisions as between the answers given by the different religions—it leaves that to the individual religions. The religious answer falls entirely outside the province of philosophy. It is something that cannot be philosophically constructed, but only historically ascertained.

(1) *Categorical questions and historical answers*

Here we are faced once more with the problematical business of 'question and answer'. It is problematical because 'question' and 'answer' belong on the one hand most intimately together and deeply affect one another, while on the other they are subject to quite different conditions and must be kept clearly distinct if the result is not to be hopeless confusion. How little even on a less complicated level the problematical nature of this situation is recognized, and how often it is supposed that merely by asking the question we can handle the subject and more or less settle it in advance, is shown by the very prevalent idea that 'to a straightforward question we can expect a straightforward answer, a simple yes or no'. But if the question—no matter how straightforward it is intended to be—rests on a confusion of thought and is thus strictly speaking meaningless, the questioner will not really be enlightened by any answer, even though the primary facts on which it is based may be impeccably accurate. For even so the answer will be meaningless. Accurate information does not help in the least to overcome a basic error, for this is transmitted automatically from the question to the answer. The only real help is to correct the question, to free it from its meaninglessness by getting it properly stated.

The problem becomes still more complicated when we consider it in terms of the relation between a philosophical question and an empirical answer, or a categorical question and a historically given answer. We have already come across this issue several times, but generally with reference to an illegitimate case.[4] It is always illegitimate when the question in any way dictates the answer. A genuine question always leaves open the possibility of different answers, and which answer is the right one cannot be decided simply by analyzing the question. If the answer is already determined by the way in which the question is put, then both the question and the answer are specious. In a scientific investigation the result must not

---

[4] *Cf.* above, pp. 200, 317ff., 322f.

be determined in advance and smuggled into the question; otherwise the arguments that are produced will be nothing but a sham. That is why both the theory of preunderstanding and the theory of correlation are pure sophistries. In this matter the greatest caution is necessary, for far too often a question is 'slanted'. The question as such possesses already the power of suggestion—something of which abundant use has been made both in education and propaganda. The very way in which the question is put determines the direction of the answer. Formally there are different possible answers, but rationally only one of them seems possible. There is only one intelligent answer to the question—as it is now put. With this the purpose of the questioner is achieved. It was this he was after when he put the question in the way he did, and left no alternative that anyone could reasonably propose.

It is just in order to prevent such an illegitimate 'slanting' of the question, that we have here introduced the contrast between a categorical question and a historical answer. Here if anywhere it is clear that the answer can *not* be derived from the question, or the fundamental motif from the category, but must be sought in what is historically given. At the same time it is clear how inseparably the question and the answer belong together. The answer is after all an answer to a question, although it is subject to quite other conditions than the question and can never be analytically derived from it.

What we are saying can be illustrated by the following example. When anyone makes an ethical judgment, we can tell at once by analysis that it is the ethical category that is being applied. But in order rightly to understand the meaning of the judgment, there is another thing we must know. We must know what ethical criterion is being employed in that judgment, what fundamental ethical motif underlies it, what ethical ideal is favoured by the one who makes it. And this ethical ideal cannot be derived from the category, for the latter is essentially 'empty' and makes room for quite a diversity of content, that is, for different ideals and bases of judgment. The same can be said also of a religious statement. Even when we know that as regards its form it is an answer to a question that belongs to the religious category, we can give no clear account of its content, nor indeed any account at all, unless we know also the fundamental motif which gives it its distinctive character and determines its meaning.

Using the idea of 'question and answer' and taking the precautions mentioned above, we can now define the term 'fundamental motif' and its relation to the 'category' as follows. By the fundamental motif of a particular outlook we mean the fundamental answer which it gives to a question of a categorical nature, and by which its individual judgments, valuations and decisions are held together in a meaningful unity. We could indeed speak here of the fundamental motif as the presupposition of a 'secondary context of meaning', for it is only from the fundamental motif that the individual statement or proposition gets its definitive character and its meaning. It is true that by describing something as 'religious' I assign it to the religious context of meaning and thereby give a general indication of the level on which its meaning is to be sought, yet this says nothing about its more particular character. There are after all so many religions—Christianity, Buddhism, Taoism, etc.—each characterized by its own fundamental motif, which sets its mark on everything in the religion concerned. Here too we must see to it that we do not mix up the different fundamental motifs. The fundamental motif is constitutive of a context, a 'secondary context of meaning', which alone gives meaning to the individual statement.

An investigation which seeks to penetrate to the fundamental motif that governs a particular outlook, we call motif research. That such an investigation is subject to a twofold condition is immediately clear; for while the question is philosophically defined, the answer must be sought from historically given reality. Both of these points are of vital importance. The fact that the question is philosophically defined means that motif research does not come with any question it pleases to the historical material, and therefore it cannot seize on anything it pleases in that material and give it out as the fundamental motif. It is to quite definite questions, categorical questions, that motif research seeks answers. Hence only what is appropriate as an answer to a categorical question can be regarded as a fundamental motif.

Yet while motif research thus begins with a philosophically defined question—that of the category—it is just as important to insist that the answer cannot be obtained by any philosophical device, but must be derived from history, that is, from historically given reality as we actually encounter it. What the fundamental motif of a particular religion is, can only be determined by direct observation of that religion as it presents itself in historical form, and the investigation of it is therefore subject to the same conditions as any other historical investigation. Motif research has no right at any point to exempt itself from the general conditions of historical research. We are thus faced with the question of the fundamental motif as a historical problem. How can we by purely historical means arrive at the fundamental motif?

Here, however, the question at once arises, whether the fact that we start with a philosophically defined categorical question and seek an answer to it in historically given material does not mean that we do violence to the latter and in fact 'slant' the answer by means of the question? Who has said that the historical material must necessarily respond to a question put in this way? And if we assume that it must, shall we not be in immediate danger of unhistorical construction? Is it not wisest simply to be content with the historical material as it stands, and not approach it with questions raised from outside? These doubts and hesitations, however, overlook two things.

First of all, the categories are not arbitrary questions raised from outside, but are necessary and inescapable presuppositions. The very idea that an ethical outlook, for example, should not respond to the ethical category and the question implied in it, is too absurd to need refutation. Even if an ethical outlook is not theoretically clear as to the fact that it operates with that kind of presupposition, yet the latter is actually and in practice included in every ethical judgment and decision. Where, on the other hand, a given outlook bears no relation to the ethical category, this only indicates that it is ethically irrelevant and must be looked at from some other categorical viewpoint, from which its real meaning and purport can be seen. We need not fear therefore that the categorical question will put a strait jacket on the factual material.

Secondly, the idea that without adopting any viewpoint at all we can stick exclusively to the immediately given material is a complete fiction. There is no historical material that is immediately given in this way, wholly unaffected by any viewpoint. Historical reflection consists precisely in ordering the material under certain major viewpoints, and it is first through such ordering that the material is given historical significance. Actually the viewpoint which motif research adopts is more objectively inescapable and anchored in 'the historical material' itself, than any of the other viewpoints which might be adopted in the study of history. Of this one can best be persuaded by noticing how the immediately given material is appropriated.

(2) *The way to historical understanding*

Here the starting point is the fact indicated above, that to speak of something immediately given in history is to speak of something that does not exist. As soon as material can be termed 'historical', it has already undergone a certain selection, ordering, and interpretative reworking. Only a chaotic variety of impressions (persons, things, happenings) is 'immediately given'. How is it then that a historical picture develops from this? In acquiring and gaining mastery over this chaotic material, there are two opposite ways that can be taken. One way is to seek to recount as completely as possible the elements that enter into a given manifold: this is the method of the *chronicle*. But no matter how inclusive and complete the chronicle may become, it never corresponds to the immediately given manifold. Everything cannot be recounted. Already in the fact that as a chronicler one begins to list various things and events, there has been a selection—even if a quite arbitrary and barely conscious selection.

But it is possible also to move in the opposite direction. Instead of trying to give a complete account of the immediately given manifold, one can lift out certain more striking individual features of it. One can be content to note what appears to be more unique, without reflecting that this may perhaps be only a relatively insignificant detail: this is the method of

363

caricature. It fastens upon that which strikes one as peculiar, the unusual. This it takes out of its context, emphasizes and enlarges. That this also does not mean a direct reproduction of the reality at hand, but its transformation, is quite apparent. As opposed, however, to the very tempting idea that the chronicle is related to reality as a photograph, and the caricature as its distortion, it should be emphasized that a caricature takes us no further away from reality than does a chronicling account of it. Both give expression to something found in reality, and both present it reworked and transformed, though in doing so they move out along different lines, the one more in the direction of the general and the average, the other more in the direction of the unique. It can therefore often happen that the caricature, which one-sidedly emphasizes certain features, is able to bring us closer to the reality thus represented than the presentation which faithfully registers all the different features.

It is important to pay attention to this in order to escape the not uncommon misconception that the chronicling treatment, which without added ingredients seeks to reproduce reality, should stand in a more immediate relation to it than history, and that the latter to the extent that it applies more inclusive viewpoints more and more moves away from reality. The actual situation is just the opposite. Each step further in the historical direction means a closer approximation to the immediately given reality. It is an attempt to neutralize the error that was committed in the first reworking and transformation.

Basically it is one and the same weakness that besets both of the ways indicated, namely, the arbitrariness in their treatment of the historical material. The error of the chronicle is not that it makes a selection, for this must be done if one is at all to assimilate the given manifold, but its error consists in the fact that this selection occurs arbitrarily. And the error of the caricature does not consist in the fact that it emphasizes the unique, for this must be done if one is at all to grasp the contours of the reality which is to be represented, so that one's conception of it does not remain at the level of the chaotic manifold; the error is rather that the caricature seeks the unique at arbitrary points. In both cases it is necessary to replace the arbitrary viewpoints with essential ones. This is what happens when on one line we raise ourselves from the level of the chronicle to that of historical reflection, and on the other line from the level of caricature to that of characterization. For *history*, historical reflection, sets out to place the material under viewpoints essential to the material, while *characterization* sets out to grasp what is central and essentially unique in an event and in this sense characteristic.

The actual victory over arbitrariness, however, is gained on both lines only through placing the events in their larger context, that is, only through rising from particular observations to a more inclusive perspective. This, which superficially can appear to be a withdrawal from the immediately given reality, is actually instead a way of coming closer to it. It is the presupposition for an objective apprehension of the immediately given and an aid in coming to clarity about its concrete meaning. As long as we consider the individual historical figure or period in isolation, we are always in danger of unhistorically reading into it ideas from our own time and sphere of thought. Not until we see the individual event in its place in the context of its own period, not until we see the individual outlook in its proper place in the more inclusive context of the history of ideas, have we understood it in a manner which genuinely comes close to reality. And the same is true of characterization. This attempt to reach that which is centrally and essentially unique in an event can only to a very limited extent be achieved as long as the event is considered in isolation. Not until it is included in a larger systematic context can its central uniqueness quite clearly appear. Thus characterization leads directly to systematization.

Step by step the two lines, the historical and that of the distinctive and unique, have come closer together. In motif research they become one. A fundamental motif provides an answer to the highest systematic question in the widest perspective of the history of ideas. The categorical question about the context of meaning receives here its historically conditioned answer. Only on this basis and after the individual judgment is placed in its own (secondary) context of meaning, is its meaning fully and unequivocally understood.

The way that has here been sketched from the immediately given chaotic manifold—through chronicle, history and the history of ideas on the one hand, and caricature, characterization and systematization on the other—to the completely unequivocal determination of the concrete judgment through its inclusion in the context of meaning discovered by motif research, can be simply illustrated by the following diagram:

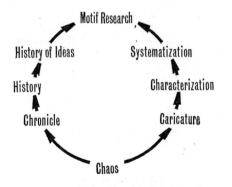

3. The Hermeneutical Significance of the Fundamental Motif

The main thesis in the preceding discussion has been that the individual statements and propositions that we find in history do not receive a completely unambiguous meaning until one knows not only the context of

365

meaning, but also the motif context, to which they belong. Two judgments which are verbally similar can have totally different meanings if they are governed by different fundamental motifs. In order that the discussion may not remain merely on an abstract level, what has been said can be concretely illustrated by an example drawn from the religious context of meaning. In my work *Agape and Eros* it has been shown how within the history of Christian thought two religious fundamental motifs have struggled with one another for supremacy, namely the Hellenistic Eros motif and the Agape motif of primitive Christianity. Originally arising out of totally different sources and representing two different spiritual worlds, these two basic motifs have during the course of history entered into relation with each other, and in varying degrees have put their mark upon the different points of view which have confronted one another within Christianity. If we neglect to pay attention to the extent to which one or the other of these basic motifs is predominant within a certain outlook, we deprive ourselves of the possibility of understanding it and run the risk, even in purely concrete matters of interpretation, of making the most fatal historical mistakes.

Now for the example—which is also an example of an analysis in motif research. It is based on two statements, one by Thomas Aquinas, the other by Martin Luther. In external form these two statements are almost identical. But motif-analysis shows that despite their outward similarity they have different and indeed quite opposite meanings.

When Thomas Aquinas in his *Summa Theologica* wishes to explain in what sense one can speak about love in God, he maintains that love has an essentially different meaning according as it is a question of God's love or ours. Human love, he says, is called forth and comes into existence through the goodness of its object, whereas God's love infuses and creates goodness in things.[5] The contrast here indicated can also be expressed in such a way that the relationship between the love and its object in the two cases is completely reversed. When God loves an object, his love is primary: the love is the cause of the *bonitas* ('goodness') of the object; that God loves is the reason why the object has any *bonitas* at all. When man loves an object, the condition of the object is primary: here the *bonitas* of the object is the cause of the love; that the object possesses a certain *bonitas* is the reason why it is loved at all.

In the 28th thesis of the Heidelberg Disputation, Martin Luther contrasts God's love and human love in a manner which may seem very close

---

[5] ST I, q. 20, a. 2: 'Deus omnia quae sunt amat. Non tamen eo modo sicut nos. Quia enim voluntas nostra non est causa bonitatis rerum, sed ab ea movetur sicut ab objecto, amor noster, quo bonum alicui volumus, non est causa bonitatis ipsius: sed e converso *bonitas ejus, vel vera vel aestimata, provocat amorem,* quo ei velimus et bonum conservari quod habet, et addi quod non habet: et ad hoc operemur. *Sed amor Dei est profundens et creans bonitatem in rebus.*'

to Aquinas' distinction cited above. God's love, Luther says, does not discover its object but creates it. Man's love, on the other hand, is created by its object.[6]

From the point of view of anyone who considers faithfulness to history and closeness to its actual reality to be guaranteed by sticking as much as possible to the individual expressions, and who regards every attempt to view them in the light of the larger context in which they occur as a departure from historical reality, the matter seems simple enough. Both St. Thomas and Luther are understood to be saying in the same sense that God's love is a creative love, while human love is a love evoked by the quality of its object. Even if this common basic idea is subsequently expressed by both of them in various modified forms, this in no way rescinds their fundamental agreement. In any event it seems obvious that the two men are here speaking of the same thing. The difference between them can at most be one of emphasis.

In a work on the history of doctrine, which has made it its aim to keep strictly to the historically given, these statements of St. Thomas and Luther have been compared in the manner suggested.[7] The difference between them according to this account, boils down to this: 'the catholic conception limits the divine love's *creation* of the object of its love to a momentary event. That which is once created possesses at least a relative goodness, is to some extent a *worthy* object of God's love'. For Luther, on the other hand, it is not only a question of 'the creative act, through which man comes into existence', nor only of 'the moment in which the spiritual new creation takes place. In his view it is a principle applying to the whole of man's earthly existence that man is lovely in God's sight only because he is loved by God without worthiness or merit.' That this difference is still to be regarded mainly as a difference of emphasis is plain from the summarizing statement with which the discussion concludes: 'In the statement that God creates the object of his love, it is implied both that God really creates something new, and that his judgment in the activity of love is not determined by the actual situation. The two elements cannot

---

[6] WA 1, 365, 1ff.: '*Amor Dei non invenit sed creat suum diligibile, Amor hominis fit a suo diligibili.* Secunda pars patet et est omnium Philosophorum et Theologorum, Quia obiectum est causa amoris ponendo iuxta Aristotelem, omnem potentiam animae esse passivam et materiam et recipiendo agere, ut sic etiam suam philosophiam testetur contrariam esse Theologiae, dum in omnibus querit quae sua sunt et accipit potius bonum quam tribuit. Prima pars patet, quia amor Dei in homine vivens diligit peccatores, malos, stultos, infirmos, ut faciat iustos, bonos, sapientes, robustos et sic effluit potius et bonum tribuit. Ideo enim peccatores sunt pulchri, quia diliguntur, non ideo diliguntur, quia sunt pulchri. Ideo amor hominis fugit peccatores, malos. Sic Christus: Non veni vocare iustos, sed peccatores. Et iste est amor crucis ex cruce natus, qui illuc sese transfert, non ubi invenit bonum quo fruatur, sed ubi bonum conferat malo et egeno. Beatius est enim dare quam accipere, ait Apostolus. Unde Psal. 41: Beatus qui intelligit super egenum et pauperem.'

[7] S. von Engeström, *Förlåtelsetanken*, pp. 164ff.

be wholly separated. In the two main Christian confessions these two elements have nonetheless been emphasized in wholly different ways. Even *within* the geographical boundaries of the confessions, the emphasis has in fact fallen in quite different ways upon the two elements.'

It must, however, be said about this account of the matter that in spite of all verbal links with St Thomas and Luther it is still erroneous. Its main error consists in the fact that it starts by taking it as entirely self-evident that relatively like-sounding formulations are unequivocal in their meaning and thus reveal a factual correspondence, or that at least they can be regarded as having a common denominator and as located on the same level. There is no recognition that they are found in different motif contexts and thus have totally different meanings. When this is perceived, it becomes immediately clear that St Thomas and Luther are speaking of completely different things, and that their formally similar expressions are therefore incommensurable.

The statements of St Thomas discussed here belong wholly within the sphere of the Eros motif. When he speaks of the love of God he finds himself in the great Eros-tradition from Proclus and Pseudo-Dionysius. From them he has learned that God is absolute causality (*aitia*) and therefore also love (*eros*). God's love is here equivalent to Divine causality. It is something of the same idea that appears in Pseudo-Dionysius under the name of 'ecstatic love'. That God loves means quite simply that he lets something of his own fullness of reality flow out—in varying degree—into his creatures. Thus the whole world process is an expression of God's love and in the last analysis of his self-love, which 'ecstatically' proceeds from him but also causes everything to return at last to him again.

In order further to clarify St Thomas' position, we may consider a parallel train of thought from his commentary on the Epistle to the Romans. In discussing Divine election he points out that there is a difference in the order of events as between *electio* and *dilectio* ('choosing' and 'loving') in God and in man; for man's will is moved to love by the *bonum* ('good') which it perceives and beholds in the beloved object, and which is the reason why it prefers this object to another and directs its love to that which it thus prefers. The will of God, on the other hand, is the cause of all *bonum*, everything good, which is to be found in the creatures. Therefore the *bonum* in virtue of which one created thing is preferred to another, is a result of God's will.[8]

[8] Ad Rom. cap. IX, lectio 2, fol. 38a: 'Electio autem et dilectio aliter ordinantur in deo et in homine. In homine enim electio praecedit dilectionem, voluntas enim hominis movetur ad amandum ex bono quod in re amata considerat, ratione cuius ipsam praeelegit alteri et praeelectae suum amorem impendit. Sed voluntas dei est causa omnis boni quod est in creatura, et ideo bonum per quod una creatura praefertur alteri per modum electionis, consequitur voluntatem dei quae est de bono illius quae pertinent (?) ad rationem dilectionis. Unde non propter aliquod bonum quod in homine eligat deus eum diligit, sed potius eo quod ipsum diligit, praefert eum aliis eligendo.'

With this the background is given for an understanding of the meaning of the first passage we quoted from St Thomas. The question he has to answer is whether it can be said that God loves all things. This, however, at once puts him in a difficulty. For even to speak of any love at all in God can seem strange, since we are ordinarily in the habit of associating the idea of desire and need with the concept of love. This gives St Thomas the occasion to indicate the different meanings of the term 'love' when it is used with respect to God and with respect to us. When *we* love, this means that we direct our desire and longing towards an object which we consider a *bonum* worth striving for. In this sense one can of course not speak of love in God. God is himself the *summum bonum*, the Highest Good, the quintessence of all the advantages towards which desire can be directed. When we nonetheless speak of love in God, then obviously the word receives a wholly different significance. Here love becomes equivalent to the Divine causality. But if in God there is such an identity between causality and love, then we have here also the answer to the question whether God loves all things. He does so in the sense that all that exists is traceable to his causality. All that is has its existence or, what amounts to the same thing, its *bonitas* from God. That God loves all things means basically the same as that he has created and brought forth all things, that he is the ultimate cause of everything.

This then is the meaning of St Thomas' saying that God's love in contrast to man's is creative. It means quite simply that God's love is the same as his causality. In order to be entirely clear about this, however, attention must also be directed to the meaning of the term *bonitas*, which in this context has nothing whatever to do with 'moral goodness'. *Bonitas* and *existentia* are for St Thomas interchangeable terms: 'For all existing things, in so far as they exist, are good.'[9] In the usual manner of metaphysics and the Eros tradition, being and good are regarded as identical with one another. Both express the same reality, though being represents it simply as existent, while good represents it as an object of desire. 'Goodness and being are really the same, and differ only in idea; which is clear from the following argument. The essence of goodness consists in this, that it is in some way desirable.'[10] Every existing thing has thus a certain *bonitas*, a certain degree of reality, and the higher the degree of reality, the greater the *bonitas*. That God loves an object means therefore that by virtue of his causality he imparts to it a certain degree of reality or *bonitas*.

Now that we have come to understand the meaning of what St Thomas says about the love of God which infuses and creates *bonitas* in things, it is immediately clear that his words have been subjected to a thoroughgoing

[9] ST I, q. 20, a. 2: 'Nam omnia existentia, inquantum sunt, bona sunt.'
[10] ST I, q. 5, a. 2: 'Bonum et ens sunt idem secundum rem: sed differunt secundum rationem tantum. Quod sic patet. Ratio enim boni in hoc consistit, quod aliquid sit appetibile.'

reinterpretation in the work cited above. When his term '*bonitas*' is rendered as 'noble attributes', this must be quite simply described as a wrong translation, occasioned by the fact that attention has not been paid to the special meaning which *bonitas* acquires when it appears in the context of the Eros motif. And it is equally wrong on the basis of St Thomas' words about God's creating love to say: 'That which is once created possesses at least a relative goodness, is to some extent a *worthy* object of God's love.' This is again to confuse divine and human love, which St Thomas sought to avoid. For God's love consists precisely in his causality.

If we now turn to what Luther says about divine and human love, we move into a wholly new world. If in St Thomas the Eros motif is predominant, it is equally clear that in Luther the Agape motif prevails, and this sets its mark on his distinction between divine and human love. Human love 'seeks its own' in everything. It goes where it can find something good, something to its own advantage, which it can egocentrically enjoy. It is more eager to receive good than to give. From which it follows that human love is a derived love, a love that is first called forth by the desirable attributes of its object. For testimony that this is the nature of human love, Luther can appeal to the ancient philosophers, who meant by love acquisitive desire. In sharpest opposition to this he now sets God's love. When he seeks to describe the nature and significance of God's love, he cannot borrow features to characterize it from the area of human life or the thoughts of the philosophers. He takes his description from God's revelation in Christ. And here he turns significantly enough to the classic expression of the Agape motif in Mark 2: 17. When Christ says, 'I came not to call the righteous, but sinners', he shows us an entirely new kind of love, which does not seek its own, which does not turn to what is valuable in order to participate in it, but to the worthless and the lost in order to help and to save. This is the divine, creative love which turns to that which is nothing in order to make something of it. It is the love that comes to meet us most clearly of all in the cross of Christ: '*Iste est amor crucis ex cruce natus*'—the love of the Cross, born of the Cross.

Finally the question arises, what connection there is between what St Thomas says about the divine love as equivalent to the causality which gives reality (*bonitas*) to things, and what Luther says about the divine love which in mercy seeks out the lost and reveals itself at its deepest in the cross of Christ? The answer can only be that there is no connection at all. Despite the formal similarity in their modes of expression, St Thomas and Luther are speaking of completely different things. Neither by love nor its object nor the *bonitas* called forth by love do they mean the same thing or even something similar. In that case there is no longer any sense in speaking of 'the statement that God creates the object of his love' as a unified statement that includes in itself two elements which receive different emphasis in the two confessions.

We have illustrated with a concrete example how necessary it is in interpreting individual judgments to pay attention to the motif context to which they belong. Many other similar examples could be offered. The one chosen was particularly suitable and illuminating in that the statements compared were verbally so deceptively similar, yet were found in their real meaning to belong to completely different worlds.

From this example we now return to our main train of thought. When a statement is to be interpreted, it is undeniably plain that we cannot be content with the statement in isolation, but must pay due attention also to the context. Otherwise a statement detached from its context can acquire a completely different meaning from the one intended. But more than this must be said. It is not enough to look only at the immediate context; we must have regard also to the wider context (both of meaning and motif) of which this is part and from which it ultimately derives its character. In this way we are led in the direction of motif research, the philosophical and historical ramifications of which we have sought in the foregoing pages in some measure to explain.

4. Systematic Theology and Motif Research

What is the task of systematic theology? If it is true that the task of any science is to seek to understand and explain or clarify its subject matter, then the task of systematic theology cannot be other than to seek to understand and elucidate the Christian faith in its uniqueness, its distinctively Christian character. Its business is to clarify the nature of that faith, its precise meaning and content, showing what is specifically Christian about it that makes it different from everything else. It has to exhibit—and this is what makes it 'systematic'—the various affirmations of the Christian faith in their own context and in relation to their own centre. In other words, it is not called upon to produce any external systematization, but rather to allow the Christian faith to be seen in its own inner organic coherence.

As long as we take this definition of the task of systematic theology simply in the abstract, everything seems simple and clear. If we look at it rather more closely, however, we soon discover that it is extremely complicated. What above all makes it difficult is the problem of getting an unambiguous definition of the subject matter of systematic theology, the Christian faith. When we say that systematic theology has to analyze 'the Christian faith', and insist that it must show how that faith itself looks at things, we seem to be operating with 'the Christian faith' as a completely unified, factually given and objectively definable phenomenon. But where is this Christian faith to be found? Is it not rather the case that the Christian faith appears in a variety of individual forms, each of which claims to express the Christian faith? Which of these is systematic theology to take as the subject matter for its analysis? As long as we are dealing only with a single expression of the Christian faith, there is no difficulty at all in determining its meaning. What does 'the Christian faith' mean, for example, in Tertullian, or in Augustine, or Aquinas, or Luther? To these questions it is possible to give an unambiguous, objectively discussable answer. And this possibility can be extended to include even the more comprehensive manifestations of the Christian faith, such as the Roman Catholic, the Evangelical and so forth.

But what sense is there in speaking of 'the Christian faith' in all generality and ignoring every concrete expression of it? Will not this open the door to all kinds of subjectivity and arbitrariness? Must not the result simply be that the individual theologian will present his own personal view of the Christian faith, while claiming at the same time that this is *the* Christian faith? And if in order to escape such arbitrariness we attempt to present something which can be said in a more objective sense to be 'the Christian faith', the question immediately arises: Is this quest for something other than the given, individual forms of Christianity, something that can be called '*the* Christian faith', really anything else but ordinary conceptual realism? Are we not here doing something very like what used to be done when it was thought that we could get at what was essential to all religion—'the essence of religion'—by eliminating everything that was specific for the different religions?

The difficulties here indicated are of fundamental importance for our whole conception of systematic theology. If we are to avoid the speculative and churchly-positivistic notions of it which we have seen to be impossible, it appears that the only possibility is to define the task of systematic theology as being to clarify the uniqueness or distinctive character of the Christian faith. But now this definition also seems to run into difficulties. The rocks on which it threatens to make shipwreck are on the one side subjective arbitrariness and on the other the metaphysics of conceptual realism. Is there any way of escaping these difficulties? Is there any possibility of determining the uniqueness of the Christian faith in a purely objective manner? The answer to this question will in the last resort be decisive for the possibility of systematic theology.

At this point motif research comes in, and its significance for systematic theology consists precisely in the fact that it provides an objective way of determining the uniqueness of the Christian faith.

Instead of motif research we could in this connection speak just as well of typological research or structural research. The task for which these terms stand is one of the most immediately urgent for contemporary theology and the scientific study of religion. For far too long these have been preoccupied with the tracing of parallels from the history of religions and derivations from the history of doctrine. Admittedly those are highly important and indispensable scientific tasks, but in comparison with motif or structural research they are none the less of secondary significance. One does not understand a religion by understanding its different elements and their genetic derivation; we cannot speak of real understanding until we understand its fundamental motif and its structure.[11] The limitation of a study that deals only with the history of religion or only with the history of doctrine is that its orientation is too peripheral. By merely observing that a certain idea or conception is to be found in different religious environments, we do not obtain any decisive information as to the real meaning of the idea. In spite of external and formal similarity, it can have a quite different meaning in one setting from what it has in another. The only thing that can be decisive here is insight into the context to which it belongs in the different settings, and the relation it bears to its different environments. It is therefore obvious that theology and the scientific study of religion in general cannot be content simply with the outward appearance of ideas, but must penetrate to the underlying motif.[12] Genuine understanding—it should hardly be necessary to say—is concerned not only with what is said, but with the meaning of what is said.

In calling now for motif or structural research, however, our interest is not limited simply to the points we have so far made. It is not enough that theology should refuse to be content simply with dogmatic formulations or creeds, and should seek to penetrate to their underlying meaning. What more, then, can be required of theology? The answer at its simplest is this: theology cannot be content merely to discover certain particular 'Christian motifs', but must penetrate further to the *fundamental* motif of Christianity. What is the motif that sets its mark on every aspect of the Christian relationship to God and determines the structure of that relationship? That is the ultimate question for motif research when it is employed for the purpose of elucidating the nature of Christianity.

All real religion has to do with man's relationship to God; it seeks to bring man into fellowship or communion with God. It is true that from the point of view of the philosophy of religion or the history of religions a question can be raised as to whether it is not possible to speak of religion even where the idea of a relationship to God is absent, as in classical Buddhism. For our present purpose, however, we can ignore this question and simply think of religion as fellowship with God, since no other form of religion than this can be of any significance when we are seeking to distinguish the Christian fundamental motif from other basic religious motifs. This conception of religion makes it impossible for us to be content to

---

[11] In the Introduction to my *Agape and Eros* I have dealt more fully with the nature of motif research, giving special attention to the problems of 'Fundamental Motifs and Motif-research', 'Motif-research and Historical-genetic Research', and 'Motif-Research and Value-judgments'. On the problem of 'the history of dogma and the history of motifs' see my *Urkristendom och reformation*, pp. 7ff.

[12] *Cf.* G. Aulén, 'Motiv och föreställning inom teologien'.

have a variety of Christian motifs, and compels us to press on to the fundamental motif. If Christianity were only a system of religious doctrine, it would be possible to point out a number of ideas and conceptions that could be said to be its characteristic motifs. But it would always then seem more or less arbitrary if one of these were picked out and elevated to the rank and dignity of a fundamental motif. The position is quite different, however, when we think of Christianity as fellowship with God. The question is then: What is the nature of the fellowship which Christianity establishes between God and man? What kind of a relationship is it and what is its general structure? The answer to this question will be the fundamental Christian motif. We do not select an idea or conception at random from among those found in Christianity, and arbitrarily claim it to be the fundamental motif, but we reserve the title of fundamental Christian motif for that which specifically characterizes Christian fellowship with God and marks it as distinctively Christian.

If we now turn with this question of the fundamental motif to Christianity itself as a historically given phenomenon, there cannot be any doubt as to what the answer must be. From the very beginning Christianity appears as a gospel, as good news about the divine love which in Christ has come down to us, and which gives and sacrifices itself to save the lost. Christian fellowship with God is characterized by the fact that it is God himself who establishes it in his love and grace. Nothing in man himself can be regarded as a motivation for God's entering into fellowship with him. The divine love is in this sense 'unmotivated'. God loves because he himself is love. God seeks fellowship with man, not because man has this or that value—this idea is contradicted by the fact that man always stands before God as a sinner—but because it is of the nature of love to institute fellowship. God is *agape*. Here is the starting point for the whole of the Christian life, and here is the reason why the entire Christian ethos can be summed up in the one word 'love', or in the double commandment of love for God and one's neighbour. The fundamental Christian motif is *the Agape motif*. Without this, Christian fellowship with God loses its coherence and its distinctively Christian character.

The Christian fundamental motif, the Agape motif, is seen most clearly when we observe how it has found itself throughout history in conflict with and struggling against other fundamental motifs, which have also claimed to determine the nature and conditions of fellowship with God. Looking at the matter purely in the abstract, we might suppose there were a very great many different fundamental motifs, each setting its characteristic mark on its own type of religion. If, however, we go to the actually given religions, we find that there are really only a few great fundamental motifs, which can be traced throughout the history of religions. Besides the Agape motif we find here principally two others: the Nomos motif and the Eros motif. With both of these Christianity from the

374

beginning and all through its history has had a great deal to do. Against both of them it has had to defend itself and assert its own fundamental motif in a hard struggle.

The Nomos motif is encountered by Christianity in its own pre-history, in Judaism. For no matter how much the Old Testament may speak of the grace and mercy and love of God, and no matter how many points of contact there are therefore in it for the New Testament concept of Agape, the fact remains nonetheless that in later Judaism fellowship with God is in principle bound to the presupposition of the law. The law is the norm and form for fellowship with God. Fellowship with God is normally reserved for the righteous. It is against this nomistic background that we must understand the saying of Jesus: 'I came not to call the righteous, but sinners.' He did not come to establish fellowship with God on a nomistic foundation. And it was the Nomos motif rising up in self-defence when Jesus' opponents branded him as 'a friend of tax-collectors and sinners' (Matt. 11: 19). They felt instinctively that there was here something new and very different from the conception of fellowship with God which they had inherited from their forefathers.

The Eros motif was the fundamental religious motif of the Hellenistic world which was the environment of early Christianity. Through the medium of Hellenistic Judaism Christianity had also from the beginning been acquainted with this fundamental motif. If the Agape motif signifies the condescension and self-giving of divine love and the fellowship between God and man established by this, the meaning of the Eros motif is its direct opposite. Eros is man's longing for the divine life with its fulness of riches; it is man's attempt to mount up to the level of the divine. Fellowship with God in terms of the Eros motif is therefore conceived as the meeting of man's desire and his *summum bonum*.

The history of Christianity is a history of the struggle of the Agape motif with these alien fundamental motifs. It unfolds in a constant alternation between synthesis and reformation, that is, between attempts to assimilate the alien motifs and attempts to separate and exclude them.[13] Here the difference between traditional history of doctrine and the study of historical motifs is clearly evident. The traditional history of doctrine concentrates on developed and sanctioned dogma, seeking to show how it arose, where its various ingredients came from, and so forth. Research in the area of historical motifs, on the other hand, is not so much interested in the genetic question as in that of type. When it comes across a dogmatic formula, its primary question is not where this has come from, but what basic motif finds expression in it. And in this way dogma acquires another and deeper significance, inasmuch as the fundamental Christian motif is often seen to have been at work in its formation. The 'finished' dogma is of interest to motif research primarily to the extent that there can be

[13] *Cf.* in this connection my essay, 'Syntes eller reformation?'

discerned in it the results of a struggle between the different fundamental motifs.

5. Objective Argumentation in Theology

We have given a very brief sketch of the significance of motif research as applied to the Christian faith. Our intention in this has been to show that there is an objective way of determining the uniqueness or distinctive character of Christianity. When a theologian speaks of what is essentially and distinctively Christian, this does not need to mean that he has arbitrarily picked out of Christianity certain ideas which are of personal importance for him, and is claiming these as 'the essence of Christianity'. What is uniquely distinctive about Christianity is discovered by going to Christianity itself and observing its history. There, in the struggle of the Christian fundamental motif, the distinctive character of Christianity is revealed. In this way systematic theology obtains the firm, objective starting point that it needs.

Now, however, two difficulties present themselves, which may seem to render the results so far reached illusory.

First of all, it is a question whether subjective arbitrariness does not return, though transferred to another point, in the matter of determining the 'fundamental motif' of Christianity. Is it really possible to learn from history itself what this motif is, or is it not rather the case that the individual theologian's personal point of view will determine what he is prepared to recognize as the fundamental Christian motif? How can one be so sure that in the Agape motif one has found that which is ultimately decisive for Christianity? The Christian faith includes, after all, a great deal more than just the idea of love. It is of course most unlikely that it would occur to anyone to assert that the Eros motif is the fundamental motif of Christianity. But it is more difficult to draw a clear boundary between the Agape motif and the Nomos motif. The motif of judgment (and therefore law, *nomos*) does after all seem to occupy just as central a place in Christianity as that of love. Is it not therefore arbitrary, in the light of the facts, if in seeking to describe the essential nature of Christianity we take either one or the other of these motifs as our starting point? Is not the decision made here according to the preference of the individual theologian? For one man, because of his religious orientation, the thought of God as Judge is the obvious starting point, while for another, with a different religious orientation, the thought of God as love is just as obviously the place to begin.

The second difficulty is this. Even if it were possible in a scientifically objective way to determine the fundamental Christian motif, could we by this means do anything more than determine it *hypothetically*? If not, does not this rule out the idea that the fundamental Christian motif might serve as the starting point for systematic theology? Must not systematic theology build on something that is absolutely certain? Is it not of the essence of an essay in dogmatics that it should make unconditioned claims, so that it is poorly served by a starting point which at most can claim only hypothetical validity?

On closer examination, however, these difficulties prove to be more apparent than real.

With regard to the first of them, it appears to be a real difficulty only so long as we are moving on the level of general and abstract reasoning. Then it may certainly seem as if a scholar could quite arbitrarily put the emphasis wherever he pleased, and then, starting with this as a fundamental motif, give his interpretation of Christianity in the light of it, without there being any possibility either of corroborating or refuting it in an objective way. Such an idea is not, however, indicative of any great familiarity with the actual history of Christianity. That history does not permit itself to be interpreted without resistance in any manner the interpreter pleases. There is, as we have already had occasion to observe, something that can be called 'the stubborness of the facts'. This gives us a criterion by which different theories can be tested. That theory is to be preferred which does least violence to the facts. When a scholar proposes something as the fundamental Christian motif, this means no more than that he is presenting a hypothesis, which must be verified by reference to the historical material. But not all hypotheses are equally appropriate, equally capable of explaining or clarifying the material. Hence if another scholar maintains that something else must be regarded as the fundamental motif of Christianity, we can only say to him: Try to apply this motif to the factually given material in the history of Christianity. Such an attempt will show whether that history can in fact be accommodated easily and without any forcing to the pattern of this motif. If it cannot, then the proposed fundamental motif is refuted by the history of Christianity itself.

Anyone who is familiar with the inner development of Christianity, can hardly be blind to the struggle described above between the Agape motif and the Nomos and Eros motifs. Naturally there may be differing nuances in the description of this struggle, but in essentials the matter seems very clear. Hence if someone were now to argue—not merely as an intellectual exercise, but as a serious hypothesis—that the Nomos motif rather than the Agape motif is fundamental to Christianity, then he would have to demonstrate concretely how from this starting point he could do justice to the history of Chrisianity from its very beginning. He would—to give only one or two concrete examples—have to show what it is that makes Christianity something new in relation to Jewish nomism; he would have to explain how Jesus' own understanding of his mission and message (expressed in such sayings as 'I came not to call the righteous, but sinners', and 'I did not come to judge the world but to save the world')[14] derives from the Nomos motif, and how that motif is the basic motif underlying

14 Mk. 2:17; Jn. 12:47.

Paul's idea of justification and his struggle against the law. In the greater tractability or resistance of the material in relation to the various theories about the fundamental Christian motif, there is the possibility of deciding objectively between them. The situation is misrepresented when it is held that we can get no further in this matter than purely subjective assertions. On the contrary, there is here clearly the possibility of objective argumentation. At the same time it is also clear that we can never by this means get beyond the kind of relative certainty that is typical of all scientific investigation which is concerned with historical material.

This brings us, however, to the second difficulty. Can an exposition of 'Christian doctrine' be satisfied with such a shaky foundation? Must it not maintain a claim to absolute validity? The answer is simple. The desire to claim absolute validity for systematic theology is due to a failure to distinguish between faith itself and the scientific study of that faith, with the result that what properly applies to the former is applied also without qualification to the latter. Of faith it is certainly true that it involves an absolute commitment and absolute certainty; but from this it does not follow that scientific reflection about faith should have the right to claim for itself the same character of absoluteness. On the contrary, as a part of the general scientific enterprise, it is subject to the same conditions as other scientific research.

The foregoing presentation has made it evident that systematic theology, thanks to motif research, can secure an objectively definable starting point for its investigation. From this, however, it might appear as if the most important question of systematic theology—that of its objective starting point in the fundamental Christian motif—lay outside its own domain. It might look as if systematic theology could not itself solve its own most important problem, but must live on charity, as it were, by borrowing the solution from a purely historical investigation. In order therefore completely to clarify the relation between systematic theology and motif research, it must finally be very briefly emphasized that 'motif research' is by no means of a purely historical nature. It is rather a method specifically belonging to systematic theology, although it has to be applied to historically given material. It is in fact itself a part of systematic theology. What is more, motif research is actually the fundamental and hence the most important part of systematic theology. It is fundamental in the sense that it lays the foundation on which everything else rests. If motif research succeeds in clarifying the fundamental Christian motif, then the problems of systematic theology are in principle solved. For the answer is thereby given to the question of the essential character of the Christian faith, which is the chief and all-controlling question of systematic theology. What systematic theology has to do beyond this is simply to draw out in different directions the implications already present in the fundamental Christian motif.

378

ADDITIONAL NOTE I

The Concept of Experience (*Translator's Note*)

'Experience' is a word that can be used in a variety of senses. In Chap. X, n. 5, the author indicates that he uses it in the 'critical' sense, i.e., the sense it bears in the 'critical philosophy' inaugurated by Kant. In RGP p. 55 he quotes Kant (*Prolegomena*, Reclam, pp. 77, 80; ET pp. 45, 48) and explains: 'only that is recognized as experience, which can claim a validity going beyond the individual occasion and individual subject in virtue of an apriori necessity inherent in the experience itself.' Hence in RAP p. 143 he gives the following definition: 'Experience (*erfarenhet, Erfahrung*) in the critical sense is an experience (*upplevelse, Erlebnis*) which is of a necessary and universally valid nature.' What this means is stated in other terms in 'Den metafysiska filosofiens betydelse', p. 57, n. 1: 'The concept of experience is here understood in a quite other sense than . . . [it has] in the contrast between experience and reason, or in that between the apriori and the empirical (=based on experience). It is connected rather with the contrast between experience and illusion. What we call "experience" (*erfarenhet*) in this sense includes all those "experiences" (*upplevleser*) which can furnish evidence of being authentic and valid, whether they are practical, theoretical, aesthetic, or religious.'

In other words, we can distinguish among the various senses of the word 'experience' two in particular, which we may call Experience-1 and Experience-2. Experience-1 stands for anything anyone may have lived through, whether individually or collectively. (*Cf.* such expressions as 'my experience', 'the Black experience', 'the experience of mankind'.) It has to do with what persons have done, suffered, perceived, felt, thought, imagined, dreamed, etc. It includes things both rational and empirical, and things we call subjective and illusory as well as things we call objective. Experience-2, on the other hand, includes only such elements of Experience-1 as exhibit a certain distinguishing characteristic. These are elements which, when we are confronted with them, impress us with an immediate sense of their unconditional validity and meaningfulness. (*Cf.* RGP pp. 56f.; and for the equation of 'meaning' and 'validity' see Chap. VI of the present work.) For example: try as I will I *cannot* think the logical law of contradiction invalid; I cannot conceive of anything as ever being at the same time and in the same respect both A and not-A. It would be easier to emancipate myself from the moral law. Yet that would be true only with regard to particular prescriptions and their particular applications, which are never unconditionally valid. It would not apply to moral obligation as such, or the validity of looking at things from an ethical

379

point of view. I cannot think *that* to be invalid or meaningless. Nor can I think of it as valid only for myself, i.e. only individually and subjectively valid. On the contrary, it is (or claims to be) universally valid—always, everywhere and for everybody.

Now the fact that anyone has this (psychological) feeling and conviction about certain things, does not of course prove anything as to their meaning and validity. It does not in itself justify us in distinguishing (as we commonly do) between elements in Experience-1 which are purely subjective and perhaps illusory, and elements which are objective. But the fact that it attaches to some things and not others, at least invites an inquiry as to what *logical* ground there is for it. Is there anything in the nature of the different experiences, which justifies us in attributing at most subjective validity to some, while asserting the objective validity of others? This is precisely the inquiry with which critical philosophy is concerned. It approaches the various forms of Experience-2 (of which the scientific, ethical, aesthetic and religious are the classical examples) with one and the same essential question: With what justification does this form of experience claim to be neither illusory nor of merely subjective validity, but objectively valid?

Note that critical philosophy does not seek to prove that there is such a thing as valid experience, but presupposes it and seeks to understand its nature and grounds. Nor does it investigate the validity of particular scientific, ethical, aesthetic, or religious judgments (which are the business of the special disciplines in those fields), but rather the validity of the scientific, etc., ways of looking at things. Finally, it does not seek to reduce the validity of any one of these forms of experience to another, nor to deduce them all from some preconceived norm of validity, but to discover the validity characteristic of each and to exhibit both the distinction and the relation between them.

ADDITIONAL NOTE II

On the Use of the Terms 'Metaphysics' and 'Truth' (*Translator's Note*)

1. *Metaphysics.* That the word 'metaphysics' is often used as vaguely and ambiguously as the author suggests in Ch. III (pp. 33f.) is undeniable. It is therefore highly important to pay attention to his explanation of what he himself means by it (pp. 34-9) if his own 'anti-metaphysical' position is not to be misunderstood. It should be particularly noted that he will not allow us to speak of *religious* realities as 'metaphysical', although to many this might seem a very natural thing to do. Religion is, after all, concerned with things *meta ta physica*, 'beyond the physical'—and beyond the psychological as well. Nevertheless, the ambiguity of the term makes it risky to call them metaphysical, and if it carries with it the sort of connotations indicated in Nygren's characterization of metaphysics, it is

wrong. For him, metaphysics is 'secularized religion' (p. 359), which even when it speaks of God, does not speak of him in a religious sense. In religion God is a reality man encounters and worships (whether out of fear or love); in metaphysics 'God' is a concept man borrows from religion and adapts to his own uses.

Metaphysical concepts do not, of course, necessarily exclude the possibility of religious encounter. They may indeed have much to do with the shaping of it, at least as regards man's response. They demonstrably did so in, e.g., St Augustine's neoplatonized version of Christianity, and they have done so throughout most of Christian history. For it has been commonly assumed that religious faith needs a metaphysical basis and metaphysical buttressing, and that some form of idealistic metaphysics is the most suitable for this purpose. (Hence, no doubt, such notions as 'religious philosophy', 'philosophical theology', etc., to which Nygren takes exception in Ch. II, pp. 15ff.) Today, however, it is increasingly realized that this has been a very mixed blessing for Christian faith and life. Yet although much of contemporary theology, like contemporary philosophy, has declared itself anti-metaphysical, it oftener succeeds in ridding itself of idealism than of all metaphysics. It is also often far from clear about the difference between metaphysics and religion, so that in extremer cases it becomes 'non-religious' (not to say 'anti-religious') and even 'atheistic'.

What Nygren is after with his 'anti-metaphysics' is to disentangle both theology and the philosophy of religion completely from metaphysics, and to let each have its own distinct function in a co-operative enterprise of understanding, in which both religion and Christianity are allowed, so to say, to stand on their own feet and speak for themselves.

2. *Truth.* On pp. 82f. above, the author describes a process by which 'truth' becomes a metaphysical entity. It starts (he says) 'with substantivization' and 'goes on through the addition of the definite article and the use of the plural form to substantialization'. The mention of the definite article here may seem rather wide of the mark in English, where it is less common than in some other languages to use the article with an abstract noun. It might be more to the point to recall the not unfamiliar practice of spelling the substantive with an initial capital—'Truth', 'Truths'—which (except at the beginning of a sentence) clearly marks its metaphysical status. Yet with or without the article, the capital, or the plural form, a substantive very easily suggests a substance. *Cf.* the theological use of the word 'grace', which began as a description of the redemptive activity of God, but very early in its career came to designate a supernatural power imparted to man. *Cf.* on this, P. S. Watson, *The Concept of Grace*, pp. 16f., 76.

It is largely in order to avoid such metaphysical errors that Nygren rather severely restricts his use of the words 'true' and 'truth'. In ordinary speech, at least in English, it is not uncommon to employ these terms in a variety of contexts—without as a rule any serious confusion as to their meaning. It can be said, e.g., that 'there is a truth of poetry as well as of prose, of art as well as of science—and a truth of morality and religion besides'. Nygren would here insist that for clarity's sake we should not say 'truth' but 'meaning' or 'validity'. Admittedly science is concerned with truth (though not with a capital T), but in the other contexts other categories obtain. Admittedly also there are disciplines that deal with these other contexts and categories from a scientific point of view—ethics, aesthetics, philosophy of religion, theology. But to be genuinely scientific, such disciplines must recognize and respect the differences between the several contexts and categories. They must let each be what it is, and seek to understand it on its own terms. There must be no 'category mixing'. And in that regard there is everything to be said for calling different things by different names—cf. p. 101 above.

ADDITIONAL NOTE III

Subjectivity and Objectivity (*Translator's Note*)

Few terms are as slippery as 'subjective' and 'objective', and much misunderstanding arises from their being used equivocally. In FOM pp. 178ff., where he is examining the possibility of scientific objectivity in the study of religion and theology, Nygren distinguishes four senses in which they can be used, thus: Subjective: objective: 1. content of consciousness: thing in itself, 2. psychical: physical, 3. evaluative: non-evaluative, 4. arbitrary: necessary. On these distinctions the following observations may be made.

1. All experience is both subjective and objective, inasmuch as it involves the experiencing by a subject of an object, real or imaginary. The real and the imaginary can also be described as objective and subjective respectively, inasmuch as the real shows signs which the imaginary does not, of existing in its own right, independently of any subject. Nevertheless, as part of the content of a subject's consciousness, anything experienced can be said to be subjective, in contradistinction to the objective 'thing in itself' which supposedly underlies and gives rise to it—and of which we have of course no knowledge because no experience. This inescapable subjectivity of experience is, however, not only no obstacle to scientific objectivity, but a precondition of any kind of scientific investigation; for what enters into no one's experience cannot be investigated. Furthermore, although we may never have complete and perfect knowledge of any object, there is no sufficient ground for doubting that scientific investigation of objects yields genuine knowledge of them.

2. Psychical (or psychologically inward) experience is obviously subjective in a way that the physical is not, although both are included in the content of consciousness. Yet it is as much experience 'of' something

as any other kind of experience, and in that sense objective. What is more, it is itself the object of psychological investigation, which, although it is concerned with what goes on solely within the experiencing subject, need not be any less scientifically objective than the natural sciences, whose methodologies it largely parallels. Hence the fact that religious experience belongs essentially within the psychical sphere, constitutes no insuperable obstacle to the scientific investigation of it.

3. All experience in the realm of values—ethical, aesthetic, religious—is subjective, not only as belonging to an evaluating subject, and as occurring essentially within his psyche, but also as depending on the sort of person he is. Here 'tastes differ', the sense of values differs in different persons, and no scientifically objective standard can be established by which to judge between them. No science can show us, e.g., that a particular religious outlook is the 'right' one, by which all others can be judged. From this it is often assumed that there can be no objective discussion of religious issues. Nevertheless, although one's personal religious attitude is something which everyone must decide for himself, it is also true that different religious outlooks exist, for or against which people in fact decide, and these can very well be made objects of scientific investigation. All of them claim in their own way to be valid, and it makes good sense to inquire (as the philosophy of religion does) into the nature and grounds of this claim, and (as theology does) into the distinctive character and structure of any religion that makes it—for although by theology we usually mean Christian theology, we could equally well have a theological investigation of any other religion. Such investigation can, moreover, be thoroughly objective.

4. When from a scientific point of view an idea is said to be 'subjective', this means simply that it is an arbitrary idea, for which there is no logical necessity. It is an expression of preference or prejudice on the part of the subject, not the fruit of unbiased examination of the subject matter (or object) under investigation. The aim of any scientific investigation is to understand a given subject matter as fully and clearly as possible, and this can only be done by approaching it with questions that are logically necessary for that purpose, i.e., questions to which answers can be elicited from it, not imported into it. To be 'objective' here means, therefore, resolutely to set aside all personal predilections as arbitrary factors which must not be allowed to influence the investigation. This may be psychologically difficult to do when dealing with a subject matter to which one attaches either a positive or a negative value—for both the believer and the unbeliever are liable to be prejudiced—but there is no logical reason why it cannot be done. Unless it is done, moreover, we cannot hope for any clear understanding of what precisely it is that the believer and the unbeliever are in disagreement about.

ADDITIONAL NOTE IV

Marburg Hermeneutics (*Translator's Note*)

Lest it be thought that the English rendering of the passage from Professor Ernst Fuchs's *Marburger Hermeneutik* quoted in note 54, p. 331 above may not have done justice to it, the original German text is appended here:

Die Liebe hat ihre eigene Zeit. . . . Wir können also das Zeitphänomen an ihr ablesen. Weiter! Liebe ist unschuldig. Das wäre beim Eros wohl nur sehr vorübergehend möglich. Weil nun die Zeit der Leibe so beschaffen ist, *dass sie um so stärker wird, je eindeutiger man sie verbraucht*, so ist die Liebe zwar insoweit ein Mittelding zwischen Armut und Reichtum, als ihre Zeit eben verbraucht werden *muss*. Aber so sieht sich die Sache nur von aussen her an. Weil sich ihre Zeit bei den *Liebenden* durchsetzen will, sollte man besser sagen, dass gerade die Armut der Liebe ihren Reichtum ausmacht. Der Liebende bleibt von der Zeit der Liebe durchaus als von einer Zeit *zur* Liebe abhängig. Aber: weil er sich dessen *freut*, ist er in der Liebe als er selbst für die Zukunft frei und vermag alles zu tun, was von ihm erwartet werden kann. Der Liebende verbraucht die *Zeit* der Liebe, weil er auf ihre Wiederholung hin lebt (Jak. 3, 18): Liebe ist *Quelle* von Zeit! Liebe *erfüllt* sich zeitlich durch sich selbst fort und fort, wenn nicht an mir, so an dir (Joh. 4, 36–38). Von dieser Fülle in einer freien weil ganz von der Liebe abhängigen Existenz redet 1 Cor. 13. . . . Wie verträgt sich der Dauer der Liebe mit dem Zeitverbrauch der Liebe? Wir sagten, die Liebe sei die Quelle ihrer zeit. Und von dieser Zeiterneuerung sagten wir, sie gewähre Ruhe. So lässt sich vermuten, dass gerade der Dauer *in der Liebe* eine befreiende, aber *ohne die Liebe* eine drohende Bedeutung zukommt, weil diese Quelle ihrer Zeit ist (was man von der Natur nicht sagen kann). Zur Ruhe eigentlicher Existenz gesellt sich tatsächlich aus der *inneren* Gewissheit, dass der Liebe Dauer innewohnt, ein Freide (Rom. 5, 1–5). Dieser Friede entspricht wahrer Liebe, weil er höher ist denn alle Vernunft (Phil. 4, 7).

ADDITIONAL NOTE V

Motif Research in a Variety of Fields (*Author's Note*)

During the past several decades there has been some lively debate about motif research as a theological method, and some interesting developments in its application and use even outside the theological sphere. These matters would merit more detailed discussion, but they do not fall within the scope and purview of the present work, which is concerned with the essential relation and distinction between motif research and philosophical inquiry, but not with the further exposition and refinement of the former—which would in any case require far more space than we can allow. It will, however, be appropriate to draw attention to a number of important contributions that have been made to the subject.

First among these is that of Ragnar Bring, who in his *Till frågan om den systematiska teologiens uppgift* and numerous subsequent publications has dealt with crucial issues relating both to contexts of meaning and motif contexts. A review and evaluation of Bring's work, with suggestions for its further development, has recently been presented by Thor Hall in his *A Framework for Faith*.

Valuable clarification of the meaning of motif research has been given by P. S. Watson, particularly in his Translator's Preface to my *Agape and Eros* and his essay on 'Systematic Theology and Motif Research'; and his book, *Let God be God*, is an example of its application. Another very significant example is R. Johannesson's *Person och gemenskap*, which shows how fresh light can be shed on familiar material by developing and refining this method of research.

Finnish scholarship has also made notable contributions in this area, among which O. Castrén's *Bernhard von Clairvaux* should be mentioned, as well as numerous works by L. Haikola and L. Pinomaa. The latter's Introduction to my volume of essays entitled *Tro och vetande* is of particular interest.

The wider possibilities of motif research are illustrated in Bernhard Erling's *Nature and History*, where a strong case is made for its use as a general method of research in the historical field; and they are exemplified also elsewhere.

Although motif research was first developed in the area of theology in order to deal with problems arising there, there is nothing to prevent its being used in many other areas, as indeed it has been—e.g. in exegesis, the history of religions, history, literary history, and so on. As regards the last-named, E. M. Christensen has shown in his *Ex auditorio* and several more recent works, how the literary historian can make fruitful use of it. And in the field of New Testament interpretation the Roman Catholic scholar, Victor Warnach, has done a monumental piece of motif research in his work on *Agape*.

Another significant figure is Nels Ferré, who in his *Swedish Contributions to Modern Theology* gave considerable space to the question of method, and has since devoted the greater part of his scholarly work to drawing out the implications of the Agape motif in a variety of directions. See, e.g. his *The Christian Understanding of God*.

Note further Ulrich Mack, 'Motivforschung als theologische Methode' —an article based on his unpublished dissertation (Heidelberg University) with the same title and with the subtitle 'Eine Untersuchung zur Methodologie Anders Nygrens'. Note also E. M. Lindahl's dissertation, 'On Relating Philosophical Inquiry to Religious Convictions', in which some account is given of the philosophical background of motif research.

For an adequate discussion of the above-named works and not a few others which have contributed to the development of motif research, we should need a separate volume, since as we have said, both limitations of space and the purpose of the present work make it impossible here.

As it happens, however, there is a volume that deals quite largely with the idea of motif research, its relation to the philosophy of religion and its theological significance, viz. the symposium entitled *The Philosophy and Theology of Anders Nygren* (ed. C. W. Kegley). As the contributors to this are scholars representing different disciplines and different points of view, who in their own work have had to deal with similar or related problems, they have been able to give a critical appraisal of motif research with respect both to its procedure and its results.

There is also a general survey of the subject in V. Lindström's article on 'Motivforschung' in RGG, 3rd edn.

Nels Ferré has rightly pointed out that motif research is still in its infancy. He says: 'Generations of scholars are needed to carry through these beginnings of exploring the implications of agape for a fuller Christian theology' (Kegley, *Nygren*, p. 254). It is a beginning 'and the end is not yet'.

Bibliography

Abbott, T. K. (tr.), Kant, *The Critique of Practical Reason*, London and New York, 1898, and *Fundamental Principles of the Metaphysic of Morals*, London and New York, 1900—both reprinted in BGBW (see Hutchins)

Agassi, J., 'The Nature of Scientific Problems and their Roots in Metaphysics' (in Bunge, *The Critical Approach*)

Ahlberg, A. (ed.), *Filosofiskt lexikon*, 3rd. edn., Stockholm, 1951

Allport, G. W., *The Nature of Prejudice*, Cambridge, Mass., 1954

Anscombe, G. E. M., *An Introduction to Wittgenstein's Tractatus*, London, 1959

Aquinas, T., *The Summa Theologica of St. Thomas Aquinas* (ET) London, 1912, *Summa Theologiae* (Latin text and ET), New York, 1964

Aulén, G., 'Motiv och föreställning inom teologien', STK 1930, pp. 249ff. *Dramat och symbolerna*, Stockholm, 1965; ET *The Drama and the Symbols*, Philadelphia, 1970

Austeda, F., *Axiomatische Philosophie. Ein Beitrag zur Selbstkritik der Philosophie* (Erfahren und Denken, 10), Berlin, 1962

Austin, J. L., *Philosophical Papers*, Oxford, 1961
How To Do Things With Words, Oxford, 1962
'A Plea for Excuses' (in Chappell, *Ordinary Language*)

Ayer, A. J., *Language, Truth and Logic*, 2nd. edn., London, 1946, Dover Publications, New York, n.d.

Baker, S. F., 'Must Every Inference be Either Deductive or Inductive?' (in Black, *Philosophy in America*)

Barr, J., *The Semantics of Biblical Language*, Oxford, 1961

Bartsch, H. W. (ed.), *Kerygma und Mythos*, I–IV, Hamburg-Bergstadt, 1948–55; ET *Kerygma and Myth*, 2 vols., Naperville, Ill., 1962–64
Entmythologisierende Auslegung (Theologische Forschung, 16), Hamburg-Bergstadt, 1962
Post Bultmann Locutum (Theologische Forschung, 37), Hamburg-Bergstadt, 1965

Beck, L. W. (tr.), Kant, *Prolegomena to Any Future Metaphysics*, New York, 1951

Bejerholm, L., and Hornig, G., *Wort und Handlung. Untersuchungen zur analytischen Religionsphilosophie*, Gütersloh, 1966

Benktson, B-E., *Christus und die Religion. Der Religionsbegriff bei Barth, Bonhoeffer und Tillich*, Stuttgart, 1967

Bergmann, G., *The Metaphysics of Logical Positivism*, New York, 1954, 2nd. edn., Madison, Wisc., 1967

Meaning and Existence, Madison, Wisc., 1960
Logic and Reality, Madison, Wisc., 1964
Black, M., *Problems of Analysis*, London and Ithaca, N.Y., 1954
Models and Metaphors, London and Ithaca, N.Y., 1962
A Companion to Wittgenstein's 'Tractatus', Cambridge, 1964
(ed.) *Philosophy in America. Essays*, London and Ithaca, N.Y., 1965
Blake, R. M., Ducasse, C. J., Madden, E. H., *Theories of Scientific Method: the Renaissance through theNineteenth Century* (ed. Madden), Seattle, 1960
Blegvad, M., 'Mill, Moore and the Naturalistic Fallacy' (PEGA pp. 9–19)
Bonhoeffer, D., *Widerstand und Ergebung*, Munich, 1951, 13th. edn., 1966; ET *Letters and Papers from Prison*, London and New York, 1967
Born, M., 'Symbol and Reality' (in *Objectivité et Réalité dans les différentes Sciences*—Archives de l'Institut Internationale des Sciences Theorétiques, 14, Brussels, 1966)
Bornkamm, G., Bultmann, R., Schumann, F. K., *Die Christliche Hoffnung und das Problem der Entmythologisierung*, Stuttgart, 1954
Braun, H., *Gesammelte Studien zum Neuen Testament und seiner Umwelt*, 2nd. edn., Tübingen, 1967
Bretschneider, W., *Sein und Wahrheit. Über die Zusammengehörigkeit von Sein und Wahrheit im Denken Martin Heideggers*, Meissenheim am Glan, 1965
Bring, R., *Till frågan om den systematiska teologiens uppgift med särskild hänsyn till inom svensk teologi föreliggande problemställningar*, I, Lund, 1933
'Paradoxtanken i teologien', STK 1934, pp. 3ff.
Brown, T. K. (ed.), *Socratic Method and Critical Philosophy*, New York, 1949
Brunner, E., *The Christian Doctrine of God*, London, 1949, Philadelphia, 1950
Bultmann, R., *Glauben und Verstehen*, I, 2nd. edn., Tübingen, 1954; ET *Faith and Understanding*, New York, 1969
Jesus Christ and Mythology, New York, 1958
Existence and Faith, New York, 1960
'Reply' in Kegley, *Bultmann*
— and others. See Bornkamm, Jaspers.
Bunge, M., *The Myth of Simplicity. Problems of Scientific Philosophy*, Englewood Cliffs. N.J., 1963
(ed.) *The Critical Approach to Science and Philosophy. In honor of Karl R. Popper*, London and New York, 1964
Scientific Research, I (Studies in the Foundations, Methodology and Philosophy of Science, Vol. 3/1), Berlin, Heidelberg, New York, 1967
'Physics and Reality' (in *Objectivité et Réalité*—see under Born)

Carnap, R., *Der logische Aufbau der Welt*, Berlin, 1928; ET *The Logical Structure of the World*, Berkeley and Los Angeles, 1967
   The Unity of Science, London, 1934
Cassirer, E., *Die Philosophie der symbolischen Formen*, I–III, Berlin, 1923–29; ET *The Philosophy of Symbolic Forms*, I–III, New Haven, Conn., 1953–7
   Axel Hägerström, Gothenburg, 1939
Castrén, O., *Bernhard von Clairvaux. Zur Typologie des mittelalterlichen Menschen*, Lund, 1938
Chappell, V. C. (ed.), *Ordinary Language. Essays in Philosophical Method*, Englewood Cliffs, N.J., 1964
Christensen, E. M., *Ex auditorio. Kunst og Idéer hos Martin A. Hansen*, Fredensborg, 1965
Christian, W. A., *Meaning and Truth in Religion*, Princeton, N.J., 1964
Cohen, M. R., *A Preface to Logic*, New York, 1944, Meridian Books, 1956
Collingwood, R. G., *An Essay on Philosophical Method*, Oxford, 1933
   Philosophical Essays, II, *An Essay on Metaphysics*, Oxford, 1940
Courcelle, P., *Les Confessions de Saint Augustin dans la tradition littéraire. Antécédents et Posterité*, Paris, 1963

De Burgh, W. G., *Towards a Religious Philosophy*, London, 1938
Delekat, F., *Immanuel Kant. Historisch-kritische Interpretation der Hauptschriften*, Heidelberg, 1963
Delius, H., *Untersuchungen zur Problematik der sogenannten Sätze a priori*, Göttingen, 1963
— and Patzig, G. (eds.), *Argumentationen. Festschrift für Joseph König*, Göttingen, 1964
De Morgan, A., *On the Structure of the Syllogism and on the Application of the Theory of Probabilities* (1846)—in *Transactions of the Cambridge Philosophical Society* VIII, iii, Cambridge, 1847
   Formal Logical or the Calculus of Inference, Necessary and Probable, London, 1847
Dewey, J., *The Quest for Certainty*, Gifford Lectures, 1929, Capricorn Books, New York, 1960
Dijksterhuis, E. J., *The Mechanisation of the World-picture*, Oxford, 1961
Dodd, C. H., *The Parables of the Kingdom*, London, 1935, reprinted 1960
Donagan, A., *The Later Philosophy of R. G. Collingwood*, Oxford, 1962
Ducasse, C. J., 'William Whewell's Philosophy of Scientific Discovery' (in Blake, Ducasse, Madden, *Theories*—see Blake)

Ebeling, G., *Wort und Glaube*, Tübingen, 1960; ET *Word and Faith*, London and Philadelphia, 1963
   Theologie und Verkündigung. Ein Gespräch mit Rudolf Bultmann,

Tübingen, 1962; ET *Theology and Proclamation*, London and Philadelphia, 1966

Engeström, S. von, *Förlåtelsetanken hos Luther och i nyare evangelisk
teologi*, Stockholm, 1938

Erdmann, J. E., *Ernste Spiele*, Berlin, 1855; Sw.T *Filosofiska miniaturer*,
Stockholm, 1873

Erling, B., *Nature and History. A Study in Theological Methodology with
Special Attention to the Method of Motif Research*, Lund, 1960

Eucken, R., *Der Wahrheitsgehalt der Religion*, 3rd. edn., Leipzig, 1912;
ET (of 2nd. edn.) *The Truth of Religion*, London and New York, 1911

Favrholdt, D., *An Interpretation and Critique of Wittgenstein's Tractatus*,
Copenhagen, 1964

Feierls, K., *Die Umprägung der natürlichen Theologie in Religionsphilosophie. Ein Beitrag zur deutschen Geistesgeschichte des 18 Jahrhunderts*
(Erfurter Theologische Studien, Bd. 18), 1965

Feigl, H., 'On the Vindication of Induction' (*Philosophy of Science*, vol. 28,
1961, pp. 212–16)
'Logical Empiricism' (in Feigl-Sellars, *Readings*)

— and Sellars, W. (eds.), *Readings in Philosophical Analysis*, New York,
1949

Ferré, F., *Language, Logic and God*, New York, 1961
Basic Modern Philosophy of Religion, New York, 1967

— and Bendall, K., *Exploring the Logic of Faith*, New York, 1962

Ferré, N. F. S., *Swedish Contributions to Modern Theology*, New York,
1939, rev. edn., 1967
The Christian Understanding of God, New York, 1951
'Nygren's theology of Agape' (in Kegley, *Nygren*)

Flew, A., and MacIntyre, A. (eds.), *New Essays in Philosophical Theology*,
London and New York, 1955

Frege, G., *Begriffschrift*, Halle, 1879; ET in Geach and Black, *Translations
Grundlagen der Arithmetik. Eine logisch-mathematische Untersuchung
über den Begriff der Zahl*, Breslau, 1884, Berlin, 1934; ET *The
Foundations of Arithmetic*, Oxford, 1950
'Über Sinn und Bedeutung' (*Zeitschrift für Philosophie und philoso-
phische Kritik*, N.F. 100, 1892, pp. 25–50; reprinted in Patzig,
Gottlob Frege, 1962); ETT 'Sense and Reference' (in *The Philo-
sophical Review*, vol. LVII, 1948, pp. 209–30, and Geach and Black,
Translations), 'On Sense and Nominatum' (in Feigl-Sellars,
Readings)

Friedrich, G., 'Zum Problem der Semantik' (*Kerygma and Dogma*, 1970,
pp. 41–57)

Fries, M., *Verklighetsbegreppet enligt Hägerström*, Uppsala and Leipzig,
1944

Fritz, K. von, 'Die ΑΡΧΑΙ in der griechischen Mathematik' (*Archiv für Begriffsgeschichte*, hrsg. von E. Rothacker, Bd. I) Bonn, 1955

Fuchs, E., *Zum hermeneutischen Problem in der Theologie. Die Existentiale Interpretation. Gesammelte Aufsätze*, I, Tübingen, 1959

Marburger Hermeneutik, Tübingen, 1968

Funk, R. W., *Language, Hermeneutic and the Word of God*, New York, 1966

Funke, G., *Phänomenologie—Metaphysik oder Methode?* Bonn, 1966

Gadamer, H-G., *Wahrheit und Methode. Grundzüge einer philosophischen Hermeneutik*, Tübingen, 1960

Geach, P. T., and Black, M., *Translations from the Philosophical Writings of Gottlob Frege*, Oxford, 1952, 2nd edn., 1960

Gellner, E., *Words and Things*, London, 1959, Boston, 1960

Goethe, J. W. von, *Faust, Erster Teil (Studierzimmer)*, Grossherzog Wilhelm Ernst Ausgabe, Bd. 6; ET by Anna Swanwick in *Dramatic Works of Goethe* (ed. H. G. Bohn), London, 1875, and *Faust, A Tragedy* (ed. F. H. Hedge), New York, n.d.

Griffin, J., *Wittgenstein's Logical Atomism*, Oxford, 1964

Greene, T. M., and Hudson, H. H. (trs. and eds.), Kant, *Religion within the Limits of Reason Alone*, Chicago, 1934, Harper Torchbooks, 1960

Hägerström, A., *Die Philosophie der Gegenwart in Selbstdarstellungen*, Bd. VII, Leipzig, 1929

Philosophy and Religion (tr. R. Sandin), New York, 1964

Hall, T., 'Let Religion be Religious' (*Interpretation*, vol. XXIII, 1969, pp. 158ff.)

A Framework For Faith. Lundensian theological methodology in the thought of Ragnar Bring. Leiden, 1970

Hamilton, K., *The System and the Gospel. A Critique of Paul Tillich*, London and New York, 1963

Hammarskjöld, D., *Vägmärkn*, Stockholm, 1963; ET *Markings*, New York, 1964

Hanson, N. R., 'The Very Idea of a Synthetic Apriori' (*Mind*, vol. 71, 1962)

Hartnack, J., *Wittgenstein og den moderne Filosofi*, Copenhagen, 1960; ET *Wittgenstein and Modern Philosophy*, London and New York, 1965

Heidegger, M., *Was ist Metaphysik?* Bonn, 1929; ET in *Existence and Being*, London and Chicago, 1949

Sein und Zeit, Tübingen, 1927; ET *Being and Time*, London and New York, 1962

Heinemann, F. H., 'Truths of Reason and Truths of Fact' (*The Philosophical Review*, vol. LVII, 1948, pp. 458–80)

Heinz, P., *Soziale Vorurteile. Ein Problem der Persönlichkeit, der Kultur und der Gesellschaft*, Köln, 1957

Heisenberg, W., *Der Teil und das Ganze. Gespräche im Umkreis der Atomphysik*, Munich, 1969

Hemberg, J., *Religion och metafysik* (with English summary: 'Religion and Metaphysics. The Religious Theories of Axel Hägerström and Anders Nygren and their Influence on Religious Discussion in Sweden'), Stockholm, 1966

Hempel, C. G., 'Geometry and Empirical Science' and 'The Logical Analysis of Psychology' (in Feigl-Sellars, *Readings*)
'Problems and Changes in the Empiricist Criterion of Meaning' (in Linsky, *Semantics*)

Hill, T. E., *Contemporary Theories of Knowledge*, New York, 1961

Hintikka, J., *Knowledge and Belief. An Introduction to the Logic of the Two Notions*, Ithaca, N.Y., 1962

— and Suppes, P. (eds.), *Aspects of Inductive Logic*, New York, 1966

Hobbes, T., *The English Works of Thomas Hobbes, Vol. III: Leviathan*, London, 1889, reprinted 1962

Hof, H., 'Reference and Meaning in Religious Statement' (PEGA, pp. 46–63)

Holm, S., *Ontologi*, Copenhagen, 1964

Holmer, P., *Theology and the Scientific Study of Religion*, Minneapolis, 1961
'Metaphysics and Theology' (*The Lutheran Quarterly*, vol. 18, 1965, pp. 291–315)

Holton, G., 'Über die Hypothesen, welche der Naturwissenschaft zugrunde liegen' (in *Gibt es Grenzen der Naturforschung?* Eranos-Reden, Zürich, 1966, pp. 37–111)

Hornig, G.—see Bejerholm

Hudson, H. H.—see Greene

Hume, D., *A Treatise of Human Nature* (ed. L. A. Selby-Bigge), Oxford, 1888, reprinted 1951
Enquiries Concerning the Human Understanding (ed. L. A. Selby-Bigge), 2nd edn., Oxford, 1902, reprinted 1966

Husserl, E., *Logische Untersuchungen*, Bd. II, 1 Teil, 2 Aufl., Halle a.d.S., 1913; ET *Logical Investigations*, 2 vols., New York, 1970

Hygen, J. B., and Løgstrup, K. E., 'Eksistensialfilosofi og åpenbaringsteologi' (*Oppositionsinlegg*, NTT, 1970, pp. 1–29)

Ingarden, R., 'Über die Gefahren einer Petitio Principii in der Erkenntnistheorie' (*Jahrbuch für Philosophie und phenomenologische Forschung*, IV, 1921)

Jackson, R., *An Examination of the Deductive Logic of John Stuart Mill*, London, 1941

Jaeger, W., *Aristoteles. Grundlegung einer Geschichte seiner Entwicklung*, 2 Aufl., Berlin, 1955; ET *Aristotle: Fundamentals of the History of His Development*, 2nd edn., Oxford, 1948

Jaspers, K., and Bultmann, R., *Die Frage der Entmythologisierung*, Munich, 1954; ET *Myth and Christianity*, New York, 1958

Jeremias, J., *The Parables of Jesus*, New York, 1963

Johannesson, R. H., *Person och gemenskap enligt romersk-katolsk och luthersk grundåskådning*, Stockholm, 1947

Jørgensen, P. H., *Die Bedeutung des Subjekt-Objekt Verhältnisses für die Theologie. Der theo-ontologische Konflikt mit der Existenzphilosophie*, Hamburg-Bergstadt, 1967

Kant, I., *Kritik der reinen Vernunft*. Text der Ausgabe 1781 mit Beifügung sämtliche Abweichungen der Ausgabe 1787, hrsg. von K. Kehrbach, Reclam, Leipzig, n.d.; ETT—see Meiklejohn, Müller, Kemp Smith
Kritik der praktischen Vernunft (1788), hrsg. von K. Kehrbach, Reclam, Leipzig, n.d.; ET—see Abbott
Grundlegung zur Metaphysik der Sitten (Kants Gesammelte Schriften, hrsg. von der Königlichen Preussischen Akademie der Wissenschaften, Berlin, 1902ff., Bd. IV); ETT—see Abbott, Manthey-Zorn
Die Religion innerhalb der Grenzen der blossen Vernunft (1793), hrsg. von K. Kehrbach, Reclam, Leipzig, n.d.; ET—see Greene and Hudson
Prolegomena zu einer jeder künftigen Metaphysik, die als Wissenschaft wird auftreten können. Hrsg. von K. Schulz, Reclam, Leipzig, n.d.; ET—see Beck

Katz, J. J., *The Problem of Induction and Its Solution*, Chicago, 1962

Kegley, C. W. (ed.), *The Theology of Paul Tillich*, New York, 1959
(ed.), *The Theology of Rudolf Bultmann*, New York, 1966
(ed.), *The Philosophy and Theology of Anders Nygren*, Carbondale, Ill., 1970

Kemp Smith, N. (tr.), *Immanuel Kant's Critique of Pure Reason*, 2nd edn., London, 1933, New York, 1965, London, 1968

Kittel, G. (ed.), *Theologisches Wörterbuch zum Neuen Testament*, Bd. IV, Stuttgart, 1942; ET *Theological Dictionary of the New Testament*, Vol. IV, Grand Rapids, Mich., 1967

Kneale, W., *Probability and Induction*, Oxford, 1949

Kroner, R., 'Philosophie und Christentum' (*Philosophy and Christianity. Philosophical Essays dedicated to Professor Herman Dooyeweerd*, Kampen, 1965, pp. 11–19.)

Küng, G., *Ontologie und logistische Analyse der Sprache: Eine Untersuchung der zeitgenössischen Universaliendiskussion*, Wien, 1963; ET *Ontology and the Logistic Analysis of Language*, New York, 1968

Langford, C. H., 'A Proof that Synthetic *A Priori* propositions Exist' (in *The Journal of Philosophy*, vol. 46, 1949)

Langer, S. K., *Philosophy in a New Key. A Study in the Symbolism of Reason, Rite and Art*, Cambridge, Mass., 1942, Mentor Books, 1961

Leibniz, G. W., *Philosophische Werke* III. (Der Philosophische Bibliothek, Bd. 69, ed. E. Cassirer, Leipzig, 1915)
Neue Abhandlungen über den menschlichen Verstand, ed. E. Cassirer, Leipzig, 1915; ET *New Essays Concerning Human Understanding*, 3rd edn., Lasalle, Ill., 1949

Lewis, C. I., *Mind and the World Order*, Chicago, 1929, New York, 1956
'Some Logical Considerations Concerning the Mental' (in Feigl-Sellars, *Readings*)
— and Langford, C. H., *Symbolic Logic*, 1932, 2nd edn., New York and London, 1959

Liebert, A., *Das Problem der Geltung*, 1914, 2nd edn., Berlin, 1921

Lindahl, E. M., 'On Relating Philosophical Inquiry to Religious Convictions, with Special Reference to the Early Writings of Anders Nygren' (Dissertation, Northwestern University, Evanston, Ill., 1966)

Lindroth, H. A., *Schleiermachers religionsbegrepp. Förutsättningar och konsekvenser* (Uppsala Universitäts Årsskrift, 1926, Teologi: I)
'Anders Nygrens kriticism i förhållande till Kant och Schleiermacher' (*Nordisk Teologi. Till Ragnar Bring den 10 juli 1955*, Lund, 1955, pp. 169–86)
'Anders Nygren und der Kritizismus. Eine Untersuchung der philosophischen Voraussetzungen seiner Theologie' (*Studia Theologica*, Vol. X, Fasc. II, 1957, pp. 89–188)
Verkligheten och vetenskapen. En inblick i Axel Hägerströms filosofi, Uppsala, 1929

Lindström, V., 'Motivforschung' (in *Die Religion in Geschichte und Gegenwart*, 3rd edn.), Tübingen, 1957

Linnér, S., *Litteraturhistoriska argument*, Stockholm, 1964

Linsky, L. (ed.), *Semantics and the Philosophy of Language*, Urbana, 1952

Ljunggren, G., 'Paradoxen som teologisk uttrycksmedel' (STK 1928, pp. 333ff.)

Logren, E., *Huvuddragen av Hägerströms filosofi*, Uppsala, 1944

Lögstrup, K. E.,—see Hygen

Lorenzmeier, Th., *Exegese und Hermeneutik. Eine vergleichende Darstellung der Theologie Rudolf Bultmanns, Herbert Brauns und Gerhard Ebelings*, Hamburg, 1968

Lotz, J. B., *Sein und Existenz*, Freiburg, 1965

Ludwig, G., *Das naturwissenschaftliche Weltbild*, Osnabrück, 1962

Lumpe, A., 'Der Terminus *APXH* von den Vorsokratikern bis auf Aristoteles' (*Archiv für Begriffsgeschichte*, hrsg. v. E. Rothacker, Bd. I., Bonn, 1955)

Lyttkens, H., 'Metoder att klassificera religiösa påståendesatser' (STK 1967, pp. 1–20)

Mace, C. A. (ed.), *British Philosophy in the Mid-Century*, New York, 1957

MacGregor, G., *Introduction to Religious Philosophy*, Boston, 1959

Mack, U., 'Motivforschung als theologische Methode' (*Neue Zeitschrift für systematische Theologie und Religionsphilosophie*, 1965, pp. 274–96)

Macquarrie, J., 'Philosophy and Theology in Bultmann's Thought' (in Kegley, *Bultmann*)

Madden, E. H.—see Blake

Malcolm, N., 'Moore and Ordinary Language' (in Chappell, *Ordinary Language*)

Manthey-Zorn, O. (tr.), Kant, *The Fundamental Principles of the Metaphysic of Ethics*, New York, 1938

Marc-Wogau, K., *Att studera filosofi*, Stockholm, 1961

Marhenke, P., 'The Criterion of Significance' (in Linsky, *Semantics*)

Martin, G., *Leibniz' Logic and Metaphysics*, Manchester, 1964

McGuinness, B. F.—see Pears

Meiklejohn, J. M. D. (tr.), Kant, *The Critique of Pure Reason*, New York, 1902, reprinted in Hutchins, BGBW

Meredith, J. C. (tr.), Kant, *The Critique of Judgement*, Oxford, 1952, reprinted in Hutchins, BGBW

Michotte, A., *The Perception of Causality*, London, 1963

Mill, J. S., *System of Logic Ratiocinative and Inductive, Being a Connected View of the Principles of Evidence and the Methods of Scientific Investigation*, I and II, 10th edn., London, 1897

Mohanty, J. N., 'On Reference' (in Delius and Patzig *Argumentationen*)

Moore, G. E., 'Refutation of Idealism' (*Mind*, 1903)
'A Defence of Common Sense' (in Muirhead, *Contemporary British Philosophy*)
'Autobiography' (in Schilpp, *G. E. Moore*)

Mostowski, A., *Thirty Years of Foundational Studies*. (Acta Philosophica Fennica, Fasc. XVII, 1965)

Muggeridge, M., *Jesus Rediscovered*, London, 1969

Muirhead, J. H., (ed.) *Contemporary British Philosophy*, London and New York, 1925

Müller, M. (tr.), Kant, *The Critique of Pure Reason*, New York, 1896

Naess, A., *Interpretations and Preciseness*, Oslo, 1953
Empirisk semantik, Stockholm, 1966

Nelson, L., *Die kritische Methode und das Verhältnis der Psychologie zur Philosophie*, Göttingen, 1904; ET in Brown, *Socratic Method*
Über das sogennante Erkenntnisproblem, Leipzig, 1908
Die Unmöglichkeit der Erkenntnistheorie, Leipzig, 1911; ET in Brown, *Socratic Method*

Neurath, O. (ed.), *International Encyclopaedia of Unified Science*, Chicago, 1938–

Niebuhr, R. R., *Resurrection and Historical Reason. A Study in Theological Method*, New York, 1957

Nietzsche, F., *Menschliches, Allzumenschliches* (*Werke*, II–III, Leipzig, 1899ff.); ETT *Human, All Too Human*, Chicago, 1908, and *The Complete Works of Nietzsche*, vols. 6 and 7, London and New York, 1909f.

Die Fröhliche Wissenschaft (Kroner Ausgabe, Bd.; I) ET *The Joyful Wisdom* (in *The Complete Works of Nietzsche*, vol. 10, London and New York, 1910)

Northrop, F. S. C., *The Logic of the Sciences and the Humanities*, New York, 1947, reprinted 1953

Nygren, A., *Det religionsfilosofiska grundproblemet* (=RGP), Lund, 1921 (based on article with same title in *Bibelforskaren* XXXVI, 1919, pp. 290–313, and XXXVIII, 1921, pp. 11–39, 86–103)

Religiöst Apriori, dess filosofiska förutsättningar och religiösa konsekvenser (=RAP), Lund 1921

Det bestående i kristendomen, Stockholm, 1922; ET in *Essence of Christianity*—see below

Die Gültigkeit der religiösen Erfahrung (=GRE) Gütersloh, 1922

Dogmatikens vetenskapliga grundläggning med särskild hänsyn till den Kant-Schleiermacherska problemställning (=DVG), Stockholm, 1922, Lund and Leipzig, 1935

Filosofisk och kristen etik (=FKE), Stockholm, 1923, Lund and Leipzig, 1932

Etiska grundfrågor, Stockholm, 1926

Urkristendom och reformation, Lund, 1933

Agape and Eros, 1st edn., I (tr. A. G. Hebert), London, 1932, II–III (tr. P. S. Watson), London, 1938–9; 2nd rev. edn., 1 vol., (ed. P. S. Watson), London and Philadelphia, 1953

Filosofi och motivforskning (=FOM), Stockholm, 1940

Die Konfessionen Augustins, ihr Sinn und ihr literarischer Aufbau, Berlin, 1958

Essence of Christianity, London, 1960

Tro och vetande. Religionsfilosofiska och teologiska essayer, Helsingfors, 1970

'Den metafysiska filosofiens betydelse för religionsvetenskapen' (*Bibelforskaren* XXXV, 1918, pp. 131–57; ET in E.M. Lindahl, 'On Relating Philosophical Inquiry', pp. 266–89)

'Är evighetskategorien en religiös kategori?' (*Kristendom och vår tid*, 1922, pp. 220–41)

'Till frågan om den transcendentala metodens användbarhet inom religionsfilosofien' (*Bibelforskaren* XL, 1923, pp. 273–93)

'Kant och den kristna etiken' (in *Kristendom och vår tid*, 1924, reprinted in *Etiska grundfrågor*; GT in *Zeitschrift für systematische Theologie*, 1924, pp. 679ff.)

'Det etiska omdömets självständighet' (STK, 1925, reprinted in *Etiska grundfrågor*; GT in *Zeitschrift für systematische Theologie*, 1926, pp. 211ff.)

'Söka och finna. Några reflexioner till Kanttolkningen' (in FHL, 1927, reprinted in FOM, 1940)

'Syntes eller reformation?' (in *Urkristendom och reformation*)

'Hur är filosofi som vetenskap möjlig' (in FAH, 1928, reprinted in FOM, 1940)

'Atomism eller sammanhang i historiesynen. Något om det självklaras roll i historien' (Lund, 1939, reprinted in FOM, 1940)

'Det självklaras roll i historien' (Presidential Address on the 25th anniversary of Kungliga Humanistiska Vetenskapssamfundet, Lund, 29th September, 1943; ET 'The Role of the Self-Evident in History' in *Journal of Religion*, Vol. XXVIII, 4, 1948)

'Filosofiens centrum och periferi' (in *Festskrift till Anders Karitz. Skrifter utgivna för Förening för filosofi och specialvetenskap*, I, Uppsala and Stockholm, 1946)

'From Atomism to Contexts of Meaning in Philosophy' (PEGA, 1963, pp. 121-36)

'Religion och metafysik' (in *Kristen Humanism*, Årsbok, 1967)

Nygren, G., *Religion och sanning. Studier i Axel Hägerströms religionsfilosofi med särskild hånsyn till hans kritik av dogmatiken*, I, (Acta Academiae Åboensis), Åbo, 1968.

Nyman, A., *Rumsanalogierna inom logiken. En undersökning av den logiska evidensens natur och hjälpkållor*, Lund and Leipzig, 1926

Ogden, S. M. (ed.), Bultmann, *Existence and Faith*, New York, 1960
Christ without Myth, New York, 1961

Ohlsson, E., 'Människan i den moderna naturvetenskapens världsbild' (*Svensk Farmaceutisk Tidsskrift*, LXII, 1968, pp. 617ff.)

Ott, H., 'Martin Heidegger' (in Schultz, *Tendenzen*)

Owens, J., *The Doctrine of Being in the Aristotelian Metaphysics*, Toronto, 1951

Parkinson, G. H. R., *Logic and Reality in Leibniz' Metaphysics*, Oxford, 1965

Patzig, G., *Gottlob Frege: Funktion, Begriff, Bedeutung*, Göttingen, 1962

Pears, D. F., 'Wittgenstein and Austin' (in Williams and Montefiore, *British Analytical Philosophy*)

— and McGuinness, B. F., *Wittgenstein, Tractatus Logico-philosophicus. The German text with a new translation*, New York, 1961

Phalén, A., 'Kritik av subjektivismen i olika former' (in *Festskrift tillägnad E. O. Burman*, Uppsala, 1910)

Das Erkenntnisproblem in Hegels Philosophie. Die Erkenntniskritik als Metaphysik, Uppsala, 1912
'Om omdömet' (in FHL, 1927)
Polanyi, M. *Science, Faith and Society*, London, 1946
Popper, K. R., *Die Logik der Forschung*, Vienna, 1935; ET *The Logic of Scientific Discovery*, New York, 1959
Conjectures and Refutations, London and New York, 1963
'Philosophy of Science' (in Mace, *British Philosophy*)

Quine, W. V., *From a Logical Point of View*, Cambridge, Mass., 1953

Ramsey, I. T., *Religious Language*, London, 1957
Randall, J. H., 'The Ontology of Paul Tillich' (in Kegley, *Tillich*)
Regnell, H., *Semantik*, Stockholm, 1958
Reichenbach, H., 'Die philosophische Bedeutung der neueren Physik' (*Erkenntnis* I, 1930/31, pp. 49–71)
The Theory of Probability, Berkeley, 1949
Rickert, H., *Die Grenzen der naturwissenschaftlichen Begriffsbildung*, 1902, 2nd edn., Tübingen, 1913, 5th edn., 1929
Kulturwissenschaft und Naturwissenschaft, 2nd edn., Tübingen, 1910, 7th edn., 1926; ET *Science and History: A Critique of Positivist Epistemology*, Princeton, N.J., 1962
Kant als Philosoph der modernen Kultur, Tübingen, 1924
Robinson, J. A. T., *Honest to God*, London and Philadelphia, 1963
Rodhe, S. E., 'Correspondence and Coherence' (*Theoria*, vol. V, 1939, pp. 3–40)
Roubiczek, P., *Existentialism, For and Against*, Cambridge, 1964
Russell, B., *A Critical Exposition of the Philosophy of Leibniz*, 1900, 2nd edn., London and New York, 1937
An Inquiry into Meaning and Truth, New York, 1940
Logic and Knowledge. Essays, 1901–1950 (=LAK) ed. R. C. Marsh, London, 1956
'On Denoting' (*Mind*, 1905; reprinted in Feigl-Sellars, *Readings*, and in LAK)
'The Philosophy of Logical Atomism' (*The Monist*, 1918; reprinted in LAK)
'Logical Atomism' (in Muirhead, *Contemporary British Philosophy*; reprinted in LAK)
'On Propositions: what they are and how they mean' (in *Proceedings of the Aristotelian Society*, Supplementary Volume, 1919; reprinted in LAK)
— and Whitehead, A. N.—see Whitehead
Ruytinx, J., *La Problematique Philosophique de l'Unité de la Science.*

Seconde Partie: un mouvement unitaire contemporaine: l'empirisme logique, Paris, 1962

Ryle, G., *Philosophical Arguments*, London, 1945
The Concept of Mind, New York, 1949
Dilemmas, Cambridge, 1954
'Ordinary Language' (in Chappell, *Ordinary Language*)
'The Theory of Meaning' (in Mace, *British Philosophy*)
(ed.) *The Revolution in Philosophy*, London, 1956

Saenger, G., *The Social Psychology of Prejudice*, New York, 1953
Sandin, R., 'Axel Hägerström's Philosophy of Religion with special reference to his theory of knowledge and his concept of reality' (Dissertation, University of Minnesota, 1959)
(Tr.) Hägerström, A., *Philosophy and Religion*
Sartre, J-P., *L'être et le néant*, Paris, 1943; ET *Being and Nothingness*, New York, 1956
Schilpp, P. A. (ed.), *The Philosophy of G. E. Moore* (Library of Living Philosophers), Chicago, 1942
Schleiermacher, Fr., *Sämmtliche Werke, Bd. VII: Hermeneutik und Kritik*, Berlin, 1838
Schlick, M., *Gesammelte Aufsätze 1926–36*, ed. Fr. Waismann, Vienna, 1938
Schmidt, H. A., 'Der Beweisansatz von L. Nelson für die "Unmöglichkeit der Erkenntnistheorie" als Beispiel eines retroflexiven Schlusses' (Delius-Patzig, *Argumentationen*, pp. 216–48)
Schmithals, W., *Die Theologie Rudolph Bultmanns*, Tübingen, 1966
Schnübbe, O, *Der Existenzbegriff in der Theologie Rudolph Bultmanns*, Göttingen, 1959
Scholz, H., *Religionsphilosophie*, Berlin, 1921
Metaphysik als strenge Wissenschaft, Köln, 1941
Mathesis Universalis, Basel and Stuttgart, 1961
Schultz, H. J. (ed.), *Tendenzen der Theologie im 20 Jahrhundert*, Stuttgart und Otten, 1966
Schumann, F. K.—see Bornkamm
Segerstedt, T. T., 'Science, Humanities and Social Science' (in PEGA, 1963)
Simonsson, T., *Kyrkomötet argumenterar*, Lund, 1963
Snow, C. P., *The Two Cultures and the Scientific Revolution*, Cambridge, 1959
Specht, E. K., *Die Sprachphilosophischen und ontologischen Grundlagen im Spätwerk Ludwig Wittgensteins* (Kantstudien. Ergänzungshefte 84), Köln, 1963; ET *Foundations of Wittgenstein's Late Philosophy*, New York, 1969
Stählin, G., 'Mythos' in Kittel, *Theologisches Wörterbuch IV*

Stenius, E., *Wittgenstein's Tractatus. A Critical Exposition of the Main Lines of Thought*, Helsingfors and Ithaca, N.Y., 1960

Stenström, T., *Existentialismen. Studier i dess idétradition och litterära yttringar*, Stockholm, 1966

Stevenson, C. L., *Facts and Values. Studies in Ethical Analysis*, New Haven and London, 1963

Strawson, P. F., 'On Referring' (*Mind*, 1950, pp. 320–44)
Introduction to Logical Theory, London and New York, 1952, reprinted, 1960

Tarsky, A., *Introduction to Logic and to the Methodology of Deductive Sciences*, 2nd edn., New York, 1946

Thiel, C., *Sinn und Bedeutung in der Logik Gottlob Freges*, Meisenheim am Glan, 1965; ET *Sense and Reference in Frege's Logic*, Dordrecht, 1968, New York, 1969

Thomson, A., 'Fakta eller frihandsteckning? Ett bidrag till den officiella historieskrivnings historia' (in *Kyrka, Stat, Folk. Till Sven Kjöllerström*, Lund, 1967)

Tillich, P., *The Protestant Era*, Chicago, 1948, Phoenix Books, 1957
Systematic Theology I–III, Chicago, 1951–63
Symbol und Wirklichkeit, Göttingen, 1962
'Reply' (in Kegley, *Tillich*)

Torstendahl, R., *Historia som vetenskap*, Stockholm, 1966

Toulmin, S., *The Uses of Argument*, Cambridge, 1958

Troeltsch, E., *Psychologie und Erkenntnistheorie in der Religionswissenschaft*, Tübingen, 1905

Urmson, J. O., *Philosophical Analysis*, Oxford, 1956

Valen-Senstad, A., *Eksistensialfilosofien som fundamentalontologi för apenbaringsteologien. En analyse av grundleggende eksistensialfilosofiske motiver i Rudolph Bultmanns tenkning*, Oslo, 1969
'Ontologiske implicationer i Paul Tillichs korrelationsmetode' (in NTT 1970)

Van Buren, P. M., *The Secular Meaning of the Gospel*, London and New York, 1963
Theological Explorations, New York, 1968

Wardi, C., 'The Christian Perspective' (in *Ariel, A Quarterly Review of Art and Science in Israel*, 23, Jerusalem, 1969)

Warnach, V., *Agape. Die Liebe als Grundmotiv der neutestamentlichen Theologie*, Düsseldorf, 1951

Watson, P. S., *Let God Be God! An Interpretation of the Theology of Martin*

Luther, London and Philadelphia, 1947, 2nd edn., Philadelphia, 1970; GT *Um Gottes Gottheit*, Berlin, 1952
The Concept of Grace, London and Philadelphia, 1960
'Systematic Theology and Motif Research' (in Kegley, *Nygren*)
Wedberg, A., *Filosofiens historia från Bolzano till Wittgenstein*, Stockholm, 1966
Wein, H., *Philosophie als Erfahrungswissenschaft. Aufsätze zur philosophischer Anthropologie und Sprachphilosophie*, Den Haag, 1965
Weinberg, J. R., *An Examination of Logical Positivism*, London, 1936, 1950, New York, 1960
Weizsäcker, F. C. von, *The Relevance of Science* (Gifford Lectures, 1959–60) London and New York, 1964; GT *Die Tragweite der Wissenschaft*, Stuttgart, 1964
Whitehead, A. N., *Symbolism, Its Meaning and Effects*, New York, 1927
— and Russell, B., *Principia Mathematica* I–III, Cambridge, 1910–13, 2nd edn., 1925–7
Williams, B., and Montefiore, A. (eds.), *British Analytical Philosophy*, London, 1966
Wisdom, J. O., *Foundations of Inference in Natural Science*, London, 1952
Wittgenstein, L., *Tractatus Logico-philosophicus*, New York and London, 1922, 8th impr. 1960; see also Pears and McGuiness
Philosophical Investigations, Blackwell, Oxford, 1958, 3rd edn., New York, 1968
The Blue and Brown Books, Blackwell, Oxford, 1958, 2nd edn., 1960, Harper Torch Books, 1965
Schriften 2: Philosophische Bemerkungen. Aus dem Nachlass hrsg.v. R. Rhees, Blackwell, Oxford, 1964
Schriften 3: Wittgenstein und der Wienerkreis, von Fr. Waismann. Aus dem nachlass hrsg. v. B. F. McGuinnes, Blackwell, Oxford, 1967
Wright, G. H. von, *The Logical Problem of Induction*, Oxford, 1941, 2nd edn., New York, 1957, 1965
Logik, filosofi och språk, Stockholm, 1957, 2nd edn., 1965

Zahrnt, H., *Die Sache mit Gott. Die Protestantische Theologie im 20 Jahrhundert*, Munich, 1966; ET *The Queston of God: Protestant Theology in the Twentieth Century*, London and New York, 1969
Zimmermann, A., *Ontologie oder Metaphysik? Die Diskussion über den Gegenstand der Metaphysik im 13. und. 14. Jahrhundert. Texte und Untersuchungen* (Studien und Texte zur Geistesgeschichte des Mittelalters, hrsg. v. J. Koch, Bd.VIII) Leiden, 1965
Zuurdeeg, W. F., *An Analytical Philosophy of Religion*, Nashville, 1958, London, 1959

INDEX

(1) *Proper Names*

Agassi, J., 57
Ahlberg, A., 147
Allport, G. W., 188
Anaximenes, 29
Anselm, 195f.
Aquinas, 366–70, 372
Aristotle, 16, 31ff. 36, 80, 105, 109, 194, 196, 285, 309, 324
Anscombe, G. E. M., 244
Augustine, 36f., 131–3, 304, 319, 324, 372
Aulén, G., 334, 340, 373
Austeda, F., 121f.
Austin, J. L., 154, 157f.
Ayer, A. J., 143

Bacon, F., 109
Baker, S. F., 109
Barr, J., 350
Bartsch, H. W., 305, 313
Bejerholm, L., 155
Benktson, B-E., 305
Bergmann, G., 36, 145, 239, 244
Berkeley, G., 129, 139f., 255, 256
Black, M., 89, 109, 244
Blake, R. M., 109
Blegvad, M., 109
Bohr, N., 123, 264, 295, 297
Bonhoeffer, D., 305
Born, M., 280
Bornkamm, G., 305
Boström, C. J., 139
Boehme, J., 324
Bradley, F., 257
Braun, H., 313
Bretschneider, W., 133
Bring, R., 340, 385
Broad, C. D., 109
Brunner, E., 337
Bultmann, R., 200f., 303–16, 320, 323, 325, 329
Bunge, M., 57, 99, 120, 144, 145, 198, 266, 280

Carnap, R., 76, 129, 145, 154, 244, 256

Cassirer, E., 141, 340
Castrén, O., 385
Chappell, V. C., 154
Christensen, E. M., 385
Christian, W. A., 319
Cohen, M. R., 340, 341
Collingwood, R. G., 194–9
Comte, A., 76, 142, 151, 359
Courcelle, P., 132

Dante, 357
De Burgh, W. G., 16
Delekat, F., 84, 120
Delius, H., 185
de Morgan, A., 258, 265f.
Descartes, 80, 86, 90, 139, 256, 358
Dewey, J., 90, 290
Dijksterhuis, E. J., 45
Dilthey, W., 43, 129, 325
Dionysius the Areopagite, 17, 324
Dodd, C. H., 340
Donagan, A., 196
Ducasse, C. J., 109

Ebeling, G., 305, 306
Eckhart, 324
Einstein, A., 217, 264
Engeström, S. von, 367ff.
Erdmann, J. E., 290
Erling, B., XI, 385
Eucken, R., 21
Euclid, 105, 106

Favrholdt, D., 244
Feierls, K., 16, 20
Feigl, H., 89, 144, 151, 231ff., 235, 238, 242, 279, 286
Ferré, F., 350
Ferré, N. F. S., 385, 386
Ficino, M., 358
Flew, A., 16, 350
Forell, U., 221
Frege, G., 9, 79, 129, 141, 142, 155, 229–37, 242, 243, 247, 255, 258, 267

Friedrich, G., 350
Fries, M., 141
Fries, J. F., 225
Fritz, K. von, 35
Fuchs, E., 305, 314, 325, 331f., 384
Funk, R. W., 305, 340
Funke, G., 166

Gadamer, H-G., 329
Galileo, 109
Gellner, E., 254
Gödel, K., 177
Goethe, 315
Gollwitzer, H., 313
Griffin, J., 244

Hägerström, A., 34, 46, 139, 141, 146, 285
Haikola, L., 385
Hall, T., 346f.
Hamann, J. G., 20
Hamilton, K., 319
Hammarskjöld, D., 316
Hanson, N. R., 185
Hartnack, J., 245
Hegel, G. W. F., 17, 36, 131, 139f., 324
Heidegger, M., 36, 131, 133, 135f., 165, 200, 304, 309, 310f., 317, 324, 325, 329
Heinemann, F. H., 80
Heintz, P., 188
Heisenberg, W., 123, 264
Hemberg, J., 34, 141, 147, 344
Hempel, C. G., 115, 143, 279
Herder, J. G., 20
Hilbert, D., 177
Hill, T. E., 289
Hintikka, J., 113
Hobbes, T., 93, 98
Hof, H., 340
Holm, S., 36
Holmer, P., 319
Holton, G., 118
Horace, 51
Hornig, G., 155
Hume, D., 52f., 58, 81f., 87f., 92, 129, 151, 174, 177, 178, 255, 256, 257
Husserl, E., 129, 135, 165f., 235, 269, 325
Hygen, J. B., 310

Ingarden, R., 225

Jackson, R., 109
Jaeger, W., 31, 33
Jaspers, K., 131, 305, 310, 313

Jeremias, J., 340
Johannesson, R., 385
Jørgensen, P. H., 305

Kant, I., 3, 33, 51, 58, 81, 84, 129, 139, 174, 176, 178, 180, 185, 201–5, 210–15, 224, 273, 279, 379
Katz, J. J., 89
Kegley, C. W., 305, 310, 311, 320, 386
Kemp Smith, N., 139, 202, 204, 214
Kierkegaard, S., 131, 133, 304, 344
Kneal, W., 89
Kroner, R., 325
Küng, G., 159, 233

Lange, F. A., 53
Langer, S. K., 340
Langford, C. H., 80, 141, 185, 221
Laplace, P. S., 347
Leibniz, G. W., 7, 42, 58, 79–101, 129, 141, 142, 149, 153, 174, 236, 255
Leibrecht, W., X
Lewis, C. I., 80, 102, 141, 221, 286
Liebert, A., 167
Lindahl, E., 385
Lindroth, H. A., 141, 174f.
Lindström, V., 386
Linnér, S., 67
Linsky, L., 144
Ljunggren, G., 340
Locke, J., 129
Logren, E., 141
Lögstrup, K. E., 310
Lorenzmeier, Th., 305
Lotz, J. B., 133
Ludwig, G., 45
Lumpe, A., 35
Luther, M., 366–70, 372
Lyttkens, H., 350

Mace, C. A., 178
MacIntyre, A., 16, 350
MacGregor, G., 16
Mach, E., 142
Machiavelli, 358
Mack, U., 385
Macquarrie, J., 310
Madden, E. H., 109
Malcolm, N., 154
Marcel, G., 131
Marc-Wogau, K., 136
Marhenke, P., 144
Martin, G., 80

McGuinness, B. F., 252
Michotte, A., 257
Mill, J. S., 88f., 108
Mohanty, J. S., 239
Moore, G. E., 109, 139f., 141, 154, 173
Mostowski, A., 105
Muggeridge, M., 345

Naess, A., 67
Napoleon, 347
Nelson, L., 225
Neurath, O., 76
Newton, I., 109, 113
Niebuhr, R. R., 305
Nietzsche, F., 190, 316
Northrop, F. S. C., 71
Nygren, A., 174, 306, 324, 325, 344f., 386
Nygren, G., 141
Nyman, A., 335

Ockham, 43, 151, 233
Ogden, S. M., 305, 313
Ohlsson, E., 123
Ott, H., 135f.
Owens, J., 33

Parkinson, G. H. R., 80
Parmenides, 324
Pascal, B., 131, 304
Patzig, G., 231ff., 235, 242
Pears, D. F., 154
Phalén, A., 139, 141, 147, 164
Philo, 324
Pinomaa, L., 385
Planck, M., 264
Plato, 17, 31, 43, 55, 58, 80, 196, 255, 256, 257, 276, 306, 324, 358, 359
Plotinus, 324
Polanyi, M., 277
Popper, K. R., 57, 89, 113, 144
Proclus, 324

Quine, W. V., 151, 233, 271

Ramsey, I. T., 350
Randall, J. H., 319, 350
Regnell, H., 340
Reichenbach, H., 89
Reimarus, H. S., 19
Rickert, H., 46, 73, 340
Robinson, J., 325
Rodhe, S. E., 119

Rosenberg, A., 306
Roubiczeck, P., 133
Russell, B., 9f., 42, 79f., 139f., 141, 142, 147, 149, 154f., 177, 229f., 233f., 237–42, 243–8, 250, 251, 254–61, 338
Russell, P. W., XI
Ruytinx, J., 145
Ryle, G., 127, 155, 157–9, 165, 178, 340

Saenger, G., 188
Sandin, R., 141, 147
Sartre, J. P., 133, 135, 137
Scheler, M., 135
Schelling, F. W., 324
Schilpp, P. A., 173
Schleiermacher, F., 20, 21, 129, 174f., 230, 236, 325, 326
Schlick, M., 129, 142, 144, 252
Schmidt, H. A., 225
Schmithals, W., 305
Schnübbe, O., 305
Scholz, H., 40ff., 67, 79f.
Schultz, H. J., 136
Schumann, F. K., 305
Segerstedt, T. T., 120
Simonsson, T., 67
Snow, C. P., 71
Specht, E. K., 159
Spranger, E., 73
Stählin, G., 308
Stenius, E., 244
Stenström, T., 133
Stevenson, C. L., 151, 292
Strawson, P. F., 239
Suso, H., 357
Suppes, P., 113

Tarsky, A., 106, 221
Thales, 29
Tertullian, 372
Thiel, C., 233, 238
Thomson, A., 117
Tillich, P., 16, 22, 33, 131, 133, 200f., 303, 316–25, 337, 344, 349
Torstendahl, R., 117
Toulmin, S., 67
Troeltsch, E., 21

Urmson, J. O., 241, 244

Valen-Senstad, A., 310
Van Buren, P. M., 305, 313f., 316
Voltaire, 34

Waismann, F., 144
Wardi, C., 345
Warnach, V., 385
Watkins, J. W. N., 145
Watson, P. S., X, XI, 346, 385
Wedberg, A., 148, 154
Wein, H. H., 153
Weinberg, J. R., 144
Weizsäcker, F. C. von, 108, 264
Whewell, W., 113
Whitehead, A., 141, 177
Windelband, R., 73

Wisdom, J. O., 113
Wittgenstein, L., XI, 4, 10, 91, 129, 139, 141, 142, 154f., 157–9, 164f., 170, 184, 217, 231, 234, 243–55, 260–2, 268, 275, 278, 342
Wolff, Chr., 33
Wright, G. H. von, 89, 229, 277

Zarnt, H., 305
Zeno, 338
Zimmermann, A., 33
Zuurdeeg, W. F., 319, 340

(2) *Subjects*

Absolute Being and Absolute Value (God), 36
Absolute commitment, 378
Absolutization of Contexts of Meaning, 11, 278–82, 287, 295
'Abyss of being', 318, 324
'Activity', 61
Adequate (inadequate) expression, 337ff.
'Aeons', 357
Aesthetic, 280
'Aesthetic superstition', 280ff., 288ff.
Agape motif, 366, 374, 376
Alexandrian theology, 17, 324
Alexandrian world-scheme, 357
Alienation, 132, 134, 304, 318
Amor crucis ex cruce natus, 367, 370
Anachronism (of method), 327, 354f.
Analysis
— in motif research, 366–71
— of concept (see Conceptual analysis)
— of meaning, 7, 62, 207
— of presuppositions, 7, 62, 104, 164ff., 169f., 182f., 205f., 222, 289, 301, 348
Ancilla, 279
Angst, 318
Answer (see Question)
Anthropology, 200, 309, 312, 324, 327
Anthropomorphism, 339
Anti-metaphysics, 249
Anti-psychologism, 234f., 239
'Anxiety', 318
Applicable measurement, 280, 284
Appropriate categories (contexts, presuppositions), 266, 291f., 295, 335ff.
Apologetics, 22, 347, 348f.

Apotheosis of man, 358
A priori—analytical, 212f., (see Synthetic judgements *a priori*)
Areas of experience, 267f., 269
Argumentation (objective, scientific), 7, 9, 12, 161, 170, 177f., 182, 250, 254f., 286, 347f.
— different forms of argumentation: 61, 63–125, 180
— axiomatic, 7, 102–7, 163, 179, 192, 256
— empirical, 7, 102ff., 107–17, 163, 179, 192, 256
— philosophical, 7, 63, 179, 182f., 209ff.
Art, 275, 281f., 289, 347
ἀρχή, 35
Assumptions, 189, 191
'Atomic facts', 247
Atomistic metaphysics, 255–61
Atomistic theory of meaning, 255, 259, 270
'Authentic and inauthentic existence', 133, 310f.
Autonomy, 11, 203, 295, 346
— of the contexts of meaning, 273–8, 303, 307, 337
Axiom, 48, 163, 191ff.
Axiomatic (see Argumentation)

Basic presupposition, 216, 290
Begriffsdichtung, 53
Being, 38, 42
— and value, 36f., 43f., 53
'Being as such', 'Being itself', 35, 42, 317ff., 321ff.
— meaning of being, 317

— 'the new being', 319
Bonum, 37, 132, 368f.
Broad perspective, 287ff., 296

Calculation, 59, 84, 161, 236, 247
Calculus ratiocinator, 80
Caricature, 363f.
Categories, 10, 207, 218, 341ff., 348f., 351
Categories of religion (see Eternity), 11
Category mistakes, 165, 282, 315
— category-mixing, 23, 165, 254, 287, 303, 305f., 316ff., 319, 330, 347
Category-mixing and meaninglessness, 10f., 52, 282–7, 323
Causality, 87f., 216f., 257
— Absolute causality (God), 368ff.
Cause-effect, 171
Certainty, 90, 98ff., 378
Chalcedonian formula, 296
Characteristica universalis, 41
Characterization, 364
Christ-event, 312
'Christ-myth', 308f.
Christian faith (in its organic coherence) 347, 371ff.
— fundamental motif, 372f., 374, 378
Christianity versus religion, 21f.
Chronicle, 363
Circle, logical (circulus in demonstrando), 9, 50, 223–5
Clarification, 177, 183, 250f., 272, 290, 295, 302f., 378
'Clearing house', 11, 287–92,
Coherence and correspondence, 119
Commitment, 378
Common sense, 140, 141, 154
Complementarity, 295
Concept of religion, 25, 347
— statistical, universal, 24f.
— structural, normative, 25
Concept of presupposition, 187–207
Conceptual analysis, 164, 215f.
'Conceptual poetry', 47, 51, 53–6, 331
Conceptual realism, 24, 38, 46f., 256, 346, 372
Conditions of experience, 213ff.
Confusion, 11f., 22, 23, 26, 45, 46, 47, 51, 52, 75, 101, 179f., 181, 187, 243, 252, 284, 287, 303, 330, 348, 360
— of religion with metaphysics, 344
Consequence, 93f., 105, 194
Consistency, 107, 191, 194, 213
Constituents, 240, 247, 270

Contingent, 80, 85
Content of the christian faith, 24, 348
Context, 70, 161, 228, 230, 235ff., 238f., 248, 252, 254, 259f.
— appropriate context, 271
— different contexts, 284, 314
Contexts of meaning, 10, 12, 228, 243, 265–97, 314
— from atomism to context of meaning, 243–54
Contextualism, 261–4, 270
Contradiction, 141, 339f., 355f.
Correlation, method of, 11, 22, 303, 316–25, 349, 361
Correspondence (see Coherence)
Cosmogonies, 29
'Creative', 207, 301
Criterion of meaning, 184, 237, 242f., 262, 286
Critique of language, 165, 246–51, 252
Critical method, 209–15
Critical philosophy, 178, 202ff., 210ff.

'Death of God' theology, 315f., 325, 347
Decision, 313, 329
Deduction, 38f., 84, 89ff., 104, 108ff., 191, 221f.
Deductive metaphysics, 47–50
Definition of God, 321, 338
Demythologization, 11, 303–16, 320, 325, 346
Denoting, 230, 238f.
Desire, 369, 375
Destruction of the concept of truth, 100f.
Determinative of meaning, 207
Deus in terris, 358
Dialectical theology, 21f.
Diagram, 365
Dieu défini, 321
Different contexts of meaning, 270–3, 293, 330, 352
— motif contexts, 308, 352, 362
— presuppositions, 295, 314
Dilemma of scepticism, 211f.
Ding an sich, 204
Distinction between religion and philosophy, 23
'Divination', 326
Dogmatism, 210ff.

'Ecstatic love', 368
Eigentlichkeit, 312
Eleatics, 29

Elements ('the four elements'), 358

Empiricism, 59, 81, 87f., 94ff., 97ff., 255, 256

Enlightenment, 16–20, 21, 22, 33, 346, 357f.

Ens qua ens, 35

Entity, 43, 83, 233, 257

Epistemological subjectivism, 139f., 202

Eros motif, 366, 374f.

Esse est percipi, 256

Essence-Existence, 318f.

Essence of Christianity, 25

— of Religion, 19, 24, 372

Estrangement, 134

'Eternal and contingent truths', 78–102

Eternal life, 343

Eternity, category of, 12, 343ff.

— Christian concept of, 343, 356f.

— Greek concept of, 343, 356f.

— 'Eternity irrupted into time', 345

Ethics, 289

Evaluation, 37, 292

Evening star and morning star, 231

Existence (see Essence-Existence)

Existence of God (see Ontological proof), 19

Existential interpretation, 304f., 309, 324, 326ff.

Existentialism, 7, 131–8, 304f., 309ff., 320, 325, 331

Experience, 8, 49, 53, 193, 213ff., 221, 267, 289

Explicit, 106, 205, 221

External world (reality of), 181

'Faculties' (psychological), 202

Faith in God, 306, 330

Fallacy, 258

Falsification, 163

'Family resemblances', 253

Fellowship with God, 373ff.

Finitude, 324

Foreign criterion, 307

— language, 341

— presuppositions, 323

Formalize, formalism, 80, 236

Form-critical research, 308

Frame of reference, 264, 267

French revolution, 274

Fundamental concept, 216

— motif, 12, 198, 207

Fundamental motif as a historical problem, 359–65

Fusion of philosophy and religion, 17f.

Geisteswissenschaften, 73

Generalization, 88f., 109ff., 191

Geometry, 105

'Given' (in experience, historically, religiously), 192, 218, 275, 277f., 301, 326, 345, 361, 363, 371, 374

— Contexts of meaning as *given* phenomena, 275, 277f., 301

— Religious motiv contexts (Christian faith) as *given* phenomena, 345, 371, 374

Gnosticism, 17, 324

Gnothi seauton, 324

God, 36, 311ff.

— 'God beyond God', 324

— God is Agape, 311, 374

— God's love—man's love, 366ff.

— God's love = God's causality, 366

— God's love = selfgiving, 375

God's revelation in Christ, 312

Gospel, 200, 307, 314, 327

Grand -être ('Great Being'), 359

Hermeneutics, 199, 230, 325–34

— and Contexts of meaning, 332–4

— philosophical, 237

— theological, 11, 230, 328ff.

Hermeneutical significance of the Fundamental motif, 365–71

Heteronomy, 273ff., 307

Highest being and highest value, 36

Historical material, 363, 377

Historical religions, 18

— perspective, 354

— research, 362, 373

— understanding, 353f., 363ff.

History

— of Christianity, 376ff.

— of Philosophy (and Problems of Philosophy), 172, 173–5

— the role of the self-evident in, 352

Homo mensura, 358

'Human existence', 304f., 307

Humanities, Science and the, 71–7

Hypostatized, 256

Hypothesis, 8, 49, 50, 74, 163, 191ff., 347, 377

Hypothetical, 93, 105f., 376f.

Idealism, 37, 44, 346

— German, 17, 324f.

— objective and subjective, 256

Idea of God, 85
Ideal language, 247, 251, 252, 253, 258
Images, 54
Immortality, 19
Implication, 9, 105, 194, 205, 220ff., 228, 262, 269, 311, 378
— strict implication, 221f.
Implicit, 69, 106, 201, 205
Inappropriate categories, 315
Incarnation, 312f.
Incommensurable, 296
Incompleteness theorem, 177
Inconsistency, 181
Indefinability of science, 66f.
Indemonstrable, 198, 287
Independence of philosophical argumentation, 209
Induction, 38f., 88ff., 108ff., 218
— 'problem of induction', 49, 89, 108ff.
Inductive metaphysics, 47–50, 192, 218
Inference, 109, 191
Infinite being, 324
Integration, Integrity, 11, 292–7, 343–5
'Intellectual conscience', 316
Intelligible world, 274
Interchangeable (meaning and validity), 167–70
Interpretation, 74, 199, 326ff., 356
Intersubjectivity, 107, 182, 235
Inquietum, 131, 319
Intrinsic validity, 224
Introspection, 58
Intuition, 105
Intuitionism, 177
Isolation ('in isolation'), 235, 238, 247, 253, 255, 257ff., 261ff., 266, 271, 365

Juncture, 79
Justification, 179–85

Key position (of philosophy of religion), 302
Kerygma, 305, 309f., 321, 329
Kulturprotestantism, 346
Kulturwissenschaft, 73

Language (Meta-language, Object-language), 183, 349
— analysis, 165, 282
— artificial language, 171, 236, 255, 258
— 'language games', 165, 251–4, 268f., 275, 278
— ordinary, 59, 171f., 236, 251, 262, 275

— rules of, 348
Laws of nature, 46, 108, 177, 193
'Let God be God', 346
'Let religion be religious', 346ff.
'Let science be science', 347
Limits of science (of scientific argumentation), 279
Linguistic philosophy, 7, 60, 165, 234, 245, 350
Literal meaning, 335ff.,
Logic, 60
— Class logic, relational logic, 285
Logical analysis of presuppositions, 9, 161f., 209–26
— atomism, 10, 237–43, 255–8
— empiricism, 7, 184, 237, 242, 246, 256, 286
— implication, 105, 194
— positivism, 40, 52, 76, 246, 248, 255
— structure of presuppositional analysis, 220–3
Logically necessary fundamental presuppositions, 9, 205ff., 351ff.
Logicism, 40, 59, 177, 236, 255, 258
Love (see God)

Machiavellianism, 358
Man, the centre of existence, 358
Marxism, 43f.
Mathematical, 46, 53, 58, 60, 75, 84, 105ff., 177, 183, 192, 230, 235
Mathesis universalis, 41, 59, 236
Material and method, 3ff.
Materialism, 37, 38, 44
Matters of fact, 81
Meaning and Context, 227–64
— and method, 227–9
— and validity, 8, 165, 167–85
Meaninglessness, 54, 91, 168f., 171, 211, 242, 249, 260, 272, 277, 293, 321, 360
— through category mixing, 314
Mening (Swedish), 232
Message, christian, 327, 329f.
Meta-language (see Language)
— logic, 183
— mathematics, 183
Metaphor, Symbol and Paradox as expressions of religious meaning, 54, 334–41
Method
— of scientific philosophy, 209ff., 215
— expansion of, 74
Metaphysics, metaphysical, 2, 5ff., 27,

33–57, 163, 165, 177, 183, 194ff., 201ff., 215, 224, 233, 241, 243, 248ff., 253, 255ff., 279, 288, 295, 303, 309, 311f., 319f., 325, 359 (See also use of the term 'Metaphysics')
'Metaphysical analysis', 197
Metaphysical and scientific philosophy, 29–63, 249
Mitmenschlichkeit (= God 'demytholo-gized'), 313f.
Models, 46
'Modern man', 304, 309, 326ff., 346
'Modern world-view', 346
Monism, 76, 257
Morality, 190, 275, 289, 347
'*More geometrico*', 59, 191f.
Motif contexts, 12, 229, 314, 332, 349 351–78
— mixing, 308, 314, 362
— research, 229, 362, 371–6, 384–6
Multiplicity of meanings, 259
— of religions, 345f., 362
Musical composition, 327ff.
Mysteries, 17
Mystery religions, 17, 359
Mysticism, 17f., 34, 324
Mythological cosmogonies, 17, 30
Mythos, mythological, 31, 304, 306–9, 314, 324, 346

Narrow mindedness, 291
— horizon, perspective, 201, 285, 286ff., 289f., 294f.
Narcotics, 281
Natural disposition, 51f.
— science, 192, 249f.
— theology, 16, 19, 20
'Nature of existence', 55
Necessary and self-evident presupposi-tions, 351–9
Necessary and sufficient conditions, 222–6
Necessity (logical, psychological), 205
Neoplatonism, 17, 324f.
New Testament, 303–13, 326
Nomos motif, 374f., 376
Nomothetisch-Ideographisch, 73
Non-religious interpretation, 305
Nonsense, 54f.
'Nonsensical', 250
Non-symbolic, 321
Nothing, nothingness, 36f., 131ff., 134, 319, 325

Objective argumentation, 67, 209
— in philosophy, 209ff.
— in the sciences, 67–78
— in theology, 376–8
Objectivity, 55
Ockham's razor, 43, 151, 233
One (The divine One), 324, 357
Ontological, 32, 42, 50, 51, 213, 319ff.
— proof, 195
Ontology, 35f., 195, 200, 204, 232f., 310
Open (perspective, system), 287f.
Optimism, 358
Orphism, 17

Parables, paradoxes (see Metaphor)
Persuasive, 55, 349
Petitio principii, 223ff.
Phenomenalism, 256
Phänomenologie, 75, 165
'Philosophical faith', 16
'Philosophical theology', 16, 22, 26
Philosophy, 17, 205ff.
— applied, 26
— philosophy proper and philosophy of . . ., 10, 26, 272
— and theology, 317, 359
Philosophy of religion, 11, 15–27, 228, 299, 347, 359
Physicalism, 76f., 256, 292
Physicalistic language, 76, 256, 292
'Picture theory', 248ff.
Platonic Academy in Florence, 358
Platonic doctrine of the two worlds, 356
Platonism, 17, 43, 358
Platonizing, 248
Poetry, 288, 331
Possibility of objective argumentation, 67–71, 119ff., 219ff.
Positivism, 358f.
Post-understanding (philosophical), 334
'Preaching event', 312
Prejudice, 8, 49, 187–91, 311, 315, 323, 351, 359
Prescription, 9, 201–5, 213, 274
Presuppositions, philosophical, 8, 62, 106, 164, 296
— absolute, 8, 194–9
— axioms, hypotheses, 191–4
— metaphysical, 56
Presuppositional concepts, 164, 346
Presuppositionless, 106f., 187f., 359
Preunderstanding, 9, 199–201, 310f., 315, 323, 329, 333ff., 351

Principium, 35
Probability, 95f.
Problem, Statement of problem and solution of problem, 175–9, 203, 246
Prolegomena, 6, 302, 343
Proof, 91, 181f.
Protocol sentence, 244, 256
Pseudo-problem, 48, 59, 176, 232, 246, 249f., 252, 272, 282, 303, 305
Psychology, psychological, 58, 60, 202ff., 213, 235, 352
— association psychology, 58
Psychologism, 178, 234, 268
Pythagoreans, 29, 58, 75

Quantification, 75
Quantum mechanics, 217
Quaestio facti–quaestio juris, 178
Question and answer, 11, 196, 200, 283, 305, 309, 319
— categorical question and historical answer, 360–3
— philosophical question and theological answer, 317–20, 322ff.
Quies, 319

Ratio, 85
Rationalism, 59, 81, 87f., 92–4, 97ff., 256
Reality, 42, 46, 52, 146f., 171, 369
Reason, 318
Reciprocity (between proposition and presupposition), 225
Reducibility, 76
Reduction, 76, 83–9, 90, 104, 151, 256, 273, 285
Reductionism, 268, 285f., 295
Reductive fallacy, 151, 202, 243, 273, 286
Reference, 238, 239, 253
Reformation, 375
Refutation, 56, 139
Reinterpretation, 327
Relations of ideas, 43, 81
Religion, 6, 275, 279, 289
— 'Natural religion', 19, 21, 346
— positive, rational, 18f.
— of humanity, 359
— as a *given* phenomenon (see 'Given')
Religion, Philosophy of Religion and Theology, 345–50
Religious categories, 343ff.
— context of meaning, 11, 228, 276, 299–359
— context of motif (see motif contexts)

— language, 11, 334–41, 348, 350
'Religious philosophy', 16
'Religious science', 303
Renaissance, 72f., 357f.
Resistance of the material, 377
Revelation in Christ, 370
Rules, 165, 275, 278, 348

Salvation, 318
Same words—different meaning, 366ff.
Scepticism, 92, 94f., 97, 210ff.
Scholasticism, 17, 20, 33, 80
Science, 30, 57, 275, 277, 307
— Concept of science (narrower, wider), 65–78
— empirical sciences, 32, 48
— special sciences, 35, 37, 49, 58, 59, 61, 289
Scientific
— philosophy, 1f., 7, 57–63, 65–77f., 163, 184, 256, 289
— 'scientific religion', 5ff., 303
— status, 1f., 5ff., 15, 27
— status of metaphysics, 39–57
— 'scientific superstition', 279f., 282, 288ff.
— tendency, 33
— theology, 1f., 72, 337f.
Scientism, 6, 44, 164, 279f., 287f., 306, 338
Secondary context of meaning, 362, 365
Secularized religion, 314, 359
'Secular meaning of the gospel', 11, 314, 346f.
'Selbstverständnis', 304f., 324
Self-evident (logically, historically), 3, 191, 198, 207, 352
— presuppositions (categories, fundamental motifs), 351ff.
Self-giving love (divine), 375
Self-love, 357
Self-understanding, 304, 309–13, 324, 329
Self-validating, 224, 276, 296
Semantics, 5, 7, 172, 230f., 234, 236, 266, 268, 302
'Sense and Nominatum', 53, 240, 257
Sense-data, 230
Sense-world, 43
Sensualism, 257
Separate words (see Isolation)
Signature (key), 293f., 314
Sinn und Bedeutung (Frege) 9, 229–37, 267, (Schleiermacher) 230
Slave-morality, 190

Social patterns, 275
— prejudices, 188
Sociology, 60
Solipsism (idealistic, sensualistic), 100
Sophists, 358
Sorge, 304
Spatio-temporal reality, 151
Starting point, 301
Stoicism, 17
Structural research, 372f.
Structure of language, structure of the world, 241
Struggle between different fundamental motifs, 374f., 377
Stubborness of facts, 377
Stupidity, 290ff.
Subjectivism, 139f., 358
Subjectivity and Objectivity, 382f.
Substance, substantialize, 42, 83
Summum bonum, 132, 319, 375
Summum ens and *Summum bonum*, 36
Super-man, 190
Syllogism, 105
Symbol, 11, 320f., 334-41
Symbolic language, 335ff.
— logic, 236, 335
Synthesis, 375
'Synthetic judgments *a priori*', 184f.,210ff.
System, metaphysical, 39, 50, 288
Systematic theology and motif research, 371-6
Systematization, 365

'Tacit presuppositions', 197
Tautology, 53, 101, 184
Technology, 45, 280, 307
Terminology, 180, 195, 265-70
Testing, 49, 56, 69, 74, 77f., 193-219f.
Theology (see Philosophy, and Scientific), 305f., 348
Theory of relativity, 217
Time (quantitative, historical), 354f.,
Thought, act of (see Unconscious)
Transcendental deduction, 202, 213ff., 217, 321
Translate, 199, 269, 291, 314, 321, 337
Trans-scientific, 75, 77
Trivial, 3f.
'True by virtue of definition', 101
True-false, 171, 232
'Truth', (empirical, eternal, logical, necessary, rational), 7, 69, 78-102 (see also, Use of the term 'Truth')

Truth value, 232, 242f.
Typological research, 372
Typographical, 260

'Ultimate concern', 321f.
Unconscious presuppositions, 355
— thought, 197ff.
Understanding, 326
Uneigentlichkeit, 312
'Unified science', 76, 256, 292
Uniqueness of the contexts of meaning, 291
— of the Christian faith, 372ff.
'Universal religion', 18, 21, 346
Universal perspective, 287f., 293
— science, 38, 39, 60-3, 78, 162
Universalizing tendency, 29, 33
'Universe of a proposition', 265
'Universe of discourse', 265, 270
Unprejudiced, 188f.
Untranslatability, 269, 292f.
Uppsala philosophy, 164, 285
'Use' (meaning and use), 217, 248, 252f., 261-4
— On the use of the terms 'Metaphysics' and 'Truth', 380-2

Valid, 166, 175
— 'valid in themselves', 224
Validation, 179-85, 215
Validity, 8, 165, 175f., 178f., 182, 224
— 'Validity itself', 47
Value, 38
Verification, 74, 91, 179-85
— as criterion of meaning, 142f. (See Criterion of meaning)
Verification principle, 237, 242f., 286
Verités de raison et verités de fait, 80ff.
Vienna Circle, 130, 140, 145, 244, 248
Violation of the context of meaning, 282
Violence to the texts, 308
Vorentscheidung, 201
Vorurteil (see prejudice)
Vorverständnis, 9, 199, 310, 351

Weltbild (see World-view and World-picture)
Wesensschau, 135
'What is it about?' 266, 332, 347, 349
Word of God, 330
World-picture, 45
World-view, 37f., 44ff., 55, 201, 288, 304ff.
'Worldly' interpretation of the gospel, 305